The Adobe® Illustrator® CS4
WOW!
Book

Tips, tricks, and techniques
from 100 top Illustrator artists

SHARON STEUER
and the Illustrator Wow! team

Peachpit
Press

The Adobe Illustrator CS4 Wow! Book

Sharon Steuer

Peachpit Press

1249 Eighth Street

Berkeley, CA 94710

510/524-2178

Find us on the Web at: www.peachpit.com

To report errors, please send a note to errata@peachpit.com

Peachpit Press is a division of Pearson Education

Real World Adobe Illustrator CS4 excerpted content is ©2009 Mordy Golding

Used with permission of Pearson Education, Inc. and Peachpit Press.

Copyright © 2009 by Sharon Steuer

Contributing Writers & Consultants to this Edition: *Cristen Gillespie, Steven H. Gordon, Lisa Jackmore, Aaron McGarry, Conrad Chavez, Ryan Putnam, Dave Awl, Randy Livingston, Andrew Dashwood, Mordy Golding*
Technical Editor: *Jean-Claude Tremblay*
Line Editor: *Elizabeth Rogalin*
Cover Designer: *Mimi Heft*
Cover Illustrator: *Michel Zappy*
Indexer: *Rebecca Plunkett*
First edition *Illustrator Wow! Book* designer: *Barbara Sudick*
***Wow!* Series Editor:** *Linnea Dayton*

Notice of Rights

Notice of Liability

Trademarks

ISBN 13: 978-0-321-60558-0

ISBN 10: 0-321-60558-6

9 8 7 6 5 4 3 2 1

Printed and bound in the United States of America.

The Adobe® Illustrator® CS4
WOW!
Book

Wow!
Contents
at a
Glance...

Contents

Blends, Gradients & Mesh

8

The Adobe Illustrator CS4 Wow! Book
Team of Contributing Writers and Editors

Sharon Steuer is the originator of *The Illustrator Wow! Book,* and author of *Creative Thinking in Photoshop: A New Approach to Digital Art.* Sharon has been teaching, exhibiting, and writing in the digital art world since 1983. In between *Wow!* books, Sharon is a full-time artist working in traditional and digital media (www.ssteuer.com). She lives with her cats and her professor husband, Jeff Jacoby (jeffjacoby.net). As always, she is extremely grateful to her *Wow!* team members (past and present), Peachpit, Adobe, and of course the *Wow!* artists for making this book possible.

Jean-Claude Tremblay is the owner of Proficiografik, a consulting and training service for the graphic and print community, designed to help clients work efficiently. He has over 20 years of experience using Illustrator. After serving as a magnificent *Wow!* tester, Jean-Claude returns for his third mandate as the *Wow!* technical editor, chief advisor, software collector, and resident magician. He lives in the greater Montreal area with his wife Suzanne and his wonderful daughter Judith.

Cristen Gillespie has contributed to other *Wow!* books, including co-authoring the current edition of *The Photoshop Wow! Book.* She has also co-authored articles for *Photoshop User* magazine. Newly armed with a broadband connection, Cristen creatively tackles lessons, galleries, and introductions with equal strength and committment. She is a wonderful writer and a fabulous collaborator, and we hope she'll stay with *Illustrator Wow!* for many years to come.

Steven H. Gordon is a returning co-author for Step-by-Steps and Galleries. Steven has been an ace member of the team since *The Illustrator 9 Wow! Book.* He has too many boys to stay sane. If only they wouldn't fall off cliffs in Bryce—the national park, not the software. Steven runs Cartagram (www.cartagram.com), a custom mapmaking company located in Madison, Alabama. He thanks Monette and his mom for their encouragement, and the boys for their cessation of hostilities.

Lisa Jackmore is a contributing writer for Galleries, as well as for Step-by-Steps. She is an artist both on and off the computer, creating miniatures to murals. Lisa continues to share her talent, evident throughout this book, as a writer and a digital fine artist. She would like to thank the sources of distraction—her family and friends—as they are so often the inspiration for her artwork.

Aaron McGarry is a San Diego-based writer and illustrator who spends time in Ireland, where he is from. While writing provides his bread, commercial illustration supplements the bread with butter. He paints and draws to escape and relax, but finds his greatest source of joy with his wife Shannon, a glass artist, and their resplendent 4-year-old daughter Fiona. Please visit: www.amcgarry.com.

Conrad Chavez began his relationship with the Pen tool as the support lead for Aldus (later Macromedia) FreeHand 1.0–4.0, continuing in the 1990s as a technical writer for print, Web, and video products at Adobe Systems Inc. Now a Seattle-based writer and trainer, Conrad also works the bitmap side as a fine-art photographer (www.conradchavez.com), and is co-author of *Real World Adobe Photoshop CS4 for Photographers* (Adobe Press).

Ryan Putnam (rypearts.com), a designer, illustrator, and blogger, makes his contributor debut to *Illustrator Wow!*. Also know as Rype, Putnam runs Vectips (vectips.com), a blog dedicated to Illustrator tips, tricks, and tutorials. In addition to Vectips, Putnam does client-based projects, and creates stock vector illustrations, but he couldn't do it all without the support of his wife Carmen.

Dave Awl is a Chicago-based writer and editor, and the author of *Facebook Me! A Guide to Having Fun With Your Friends and Promoting Your Projects on Facebook* (Peachpit Press). Dave is also a poet, performer, and alumnus of Chicago's Neo-Futurists theater company. Find out more about his various projects at his website: Ocelot Factory (www.ocelotfactory.com).

Randy Livingston has contributed to *Illustrator Wow!* books since the mid-1990s. For this edition, he wordsmithed several chapter introductions. Randy is Assistant Professor of Media Design at Middle Tennessee State University. When he's not teaching and writing, he's racing motocross.

Andrew Dashwood (www.adashwood.com) is a Swiss illustrator and returning writer to the *Wow!* book. Andrew has been working with Illustrator and Adobe's other products throughout Europe since the release of the original *Illustrator Wow!*. He is currently working in the Netherlands illustrating for Nike. He thanks his brother and dad for their lifetimes of help and support.

Mordy Golding has been a contributor to the *Illustrator Wow!* books from the beginning, and was author of the web chapter in the second edition. Since then, Mordy has been busy writing his own books and working for a while as product manager for Adobe Illustrator. Mordy is author of *Real World Illustrator CS4* and a collection of Illustrator training video titles at www.lynda.com.

Additional contributing writers and editors: **Elizabeth Rogalin** is the returning editor of the *Illustrator Wow!* books and the rest of the team is grateful that she continues as line editor. She is a writer and freelance editor living in New Jersey with her two sons. **Laurie Grace** is an artist, illustrator and university professor who teaches Illustrator, as well as all things digital. Laurie is one of the original artists featured in the book, and returns periodically to help us update screenshots. **Peg Maskell Korn** is a woman of many hats. After rescuing Sharon in the last hours of the first edition, she has transformed into the master proofer of the visuals and text in the entire book. Please see the Acknowledgments for a thorough listing of the *Wow!* team contributors.

Important: Read me first!

Are you a beginner?

If you're a beginner computer user, you are of course most welcome to look for inspiration in this book. However, please be aware that the assumed user level for this book is intermediate to professional. A good place to start before diving in here might be a basic computer literacy class. If you're comfortable with basic computer navigation and consider yourself a beginning Illustrator user, you might find some of the simpler information in the introduction sections and in the *Zen of Illustrator* chapter helpful. (Also see the Tip "Additional Illustrator Training" on the next page.)

Plug-ins & software on the CD

Wow! technical editor Jean-Claude Tremblay and Jay Nelson, editor of *Design Tools Monthly*, teamed up to collect and summarize for you their favorite Illustrator-related plug-ins and software on the *Wow! CD*. Find this listing, along with bonus Illustrator tips compiled from *Design Tools Monthly* by Jay Nelson, in a *Wow! Appendix*. You can also find this appendix in PDF (with clickable links to the products' websites) on the *Wow! CD*, along with back issues of *Design Tools Monthly*.

Back in 1994 when I embarked on the creation of the original *Illustrator Wow! Book* (with no version number!), Adobe Illustrator was still a fairly simple program. Even though the first edition was only 224 pages, it was packed with almost every detail found in the longer "bible" type books at the time.

First of all, I want readers to know that this tenth edition, now the *The Adobe Illustrator CS4 Wow! Book*, is a truly collaborative project. In order to provide you with the most thoroughly updated information as possible, in a timely manner (as close as possible to the shipping of the new version of the program!), this book now requires a large team of experts working simultaneously. Rest assured that our technical editor, Jean-Claude Tremblay, and I are involved with every page of the book, all along the way. Each of our cowriters works with us on sections based on their expertise in Illustrator, and then the rest of the writers (and our stellar team of *Wow!* testers) test and critique that section. This book is the result of this amazing group of experts scattered around the globe, coming together by email, iChat, and PDF to deliver the best book possible to you, the reader. I'm immensely proud of and grateful to everyone who works with me on this project.

With the skyrocketing price of printing in full-color, we can no longer increase the page count without considerably raising the price of the book. As a result of trying to keep the book to a minimal page count, we can no longer address all aspects of Illustrator. Instead, this book should be thought of as a reference by and for artists that focuses on creating art and design with Adobe Illustrator. We'll leave the most technical aspects of the program to more comprehensive books, such as *Real World Adobe Illustrator CS4*, by Mordy Golding. Mordy continues to consult on this book (especially the web chapter in this edition, and by allowing us to include the kuler section from his book as an appendix), and both of us feel strongly that our books should be considered companion books, as there is very little overlap in content.

I am always sad to delete wonderful artworks from previous editions, but it's also exciting to add dozens of new gorgeous examples of art, essential production techniques, and time-saving tips—all generously shared by *Illustrator Wow!* artists worldwide. In addition to the wonderful contributing artists and co-authors, our amazing team of *Wow! testers* sets this book apart from all others. This team thoroughly tests every lesson and gallery to make sure everything actually works. We deliberately keep all lessons short to allow you to squeeze in a lesson or two between clients, and to encourage the use of this book within the confines of supervised classrooms.

The user level for this book is "intermediate through professional," so in order to keep the content in this book relevant to everyone, I've assumed the reader has a reasonable level of competence with basic Mac and Windows (Win) concepts such as opening and saving files, launching applications, copying objects to the Clipboard, and performing mouse operations. I've also assumed that you understand the basic functionality of most of the tools.

Unfortunately, you can't learn Adobe Illustrator simply by flipping through the pages of this book; there really is no substitute for practice. The good news is that the more you work with Illustrator, the more techniques you'll be able to integrate into your creative process.

Use this book as a reference, a guide for specific techniques, or simply as a source of inspiration. After you've read this book, I encourage you to read it again— you'll undoubtedly learn something you missed the first time. The more experienced you become with Adobe Illustrator, the easier it will be to assimilate all the new information and inspiration you'll find in this book. Happy Illustrating!

Sharon Steuer

How to use this book...

With the All Swatches icon selected, choose "Sort by Name" and then "List View" from the Swatches pop-up menu

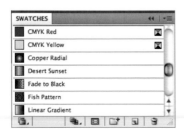

The Swatches panel viewed with "Sort by Name" and "List View" selected

Before you do anything else, read the *Wow! Glossary* on the pull-out quick reference card at the back of the book. The Glossary provides definitions for the terms used throughout *The Adobe Illustrator CS4 Wow! Book* (for example, ⌘ is the Command, or Apple, key for Mac).

WELCOME TO WOW! FOR WINDOWS AND MAC

If you already use Adobe Photoshop or InDesign you'll see many interface similarities to Illustrator. The similarities should make the time you spend learning each program much shorter. Your productivity should also increase across the board once you adjust to the new shortcuts and methodologies (see "Shortcuts and keystrokes," following, and the *Illustrator Basics* chapter).

Shortcuts and keystrokes

Because you can now customize keyboard shortcuts, we're restricting the keystrokes references in the book to those instances when it's so standard that we assume you'll keep the default, or when there is no other way to achieve that function (such as Lock All Unselected Objects). We'll always give you Macintosh shortcuts first, then the Windows equivalent (⌘-Z/Ctrl-Z). For help with customization of keyboard shortcuts, and tool and menu navigation (such as single key tool access and Tab to hide panels), see the *Illustrator Basics* chapter.

Setting up your panels. In terms of following along with the lessons in this book, you might want to enable the "Type Object Selection by Path Only" option (see Tip "Selecting type by accident" in the *Type* chapter). Next, if you want your panels to look like most of our panels, you'll want to sort swatches by name. Choose "Sort by Name" and "List View" from the Swatches pop-up menu. (Hold Option/Alt when you choose a view to set this as the default for all swatch kinds in the Swatches panel.)

Illustrator sets an application default that could inhibit the way Illustrator experts work. In order for your currently selected object to set all the styling attributes for the next object you draw (including brush strokes, live effects, transparency, etc.), you must open the Appearance panel (Window menu) and disable New Art Has Basic Appearance by choosing New Art Has Basic Appearance from the Appearance panel pop-up menu (✔ shows it's enabled). Your new setting sticks even after you've quit.

HOW THIS BOOK IS ORGANIZED...

You'll find six kinds of information woven throughout this book—all of it up-to-date for Illustrator CS4: **Basics, Tips, Exercises, Techniques, Galleries,** and **References.** The book progresses in difficulty from chapter to chapter.

1 Basics. *Illustrator Basics* and *The Zen of Illustrator* qualify as full-blown chapters on basics and are packed with information that distills and supplements your Adobe Illustrator manual and disk. Every chapter starts with a general overview of the basics. These sections are designed so advanced Illustrator users can move quickly through them, but I strongly suggest that novices and intermediate users read them very carefully.

2 Tips. When you see this icon ⊙, you'll find related artwork on the *Adobe Illustrator CS4 Wow! CD* (referred to hereafter as the *Wow! CD*) within that chapter's folder. Look to the information in the gray and red boxes for hands-on Tips that can help you work more efficiently. Usually you can find tips alongside related text, but if you're in an impatient mood, you might just want to flip through, looking for interesting or relevant tips. The red arrows ──▶, red outlines and **red text** found in tips (and sometimes with artwork) have been added to emphasize or further explain a concept or technique.

3 Exercises. (Not for the faint of heart.) We have included step-by-step exercises to help you make the transition to

If you want your currently selected object to set all styling attributes for the next object, disable New Art Has Basic Appearance by choosing it from the pop-up menu in the Appearance panel

1

2 ⊙ *The CD icon indicates that related artwork is on the* Adobe Illustrator CS3 Wow! CD

Tip boxes
Look for these gray boxes to find Tips about Adobe Illustrator.

Red Tip boxes
Red Tip boxes contain warnings or other essential information.

3

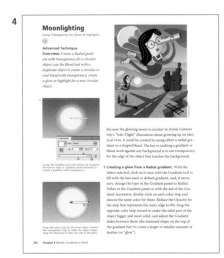

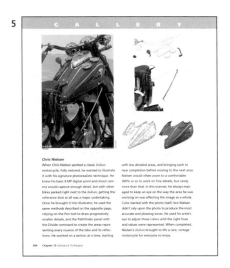

Illustrator technician extraordinaire. *The Zen of Illustrator* chapter and the *Zen Lessons* on the *Wow! CD* are dedicated to helping you master the mechanics (and the soul) of Illustrator. Take these lessons in small doses, in order, and at a relaxed pace. All of the Finger Dances are customized for Mac and Windows.

4 Techniques. In these sections, you'll find step-by-step techniques gathered from more than 100 *Illustrator Wow!* artists. Most *Wow!* techniques focus on one aspect of how an image was created, though we'll often refer you to different *Wow!* chapters (or to a specific step-by-step technique, Tip, or Gallery where a technique is introduced) to give you the opportunity to explore a briefly covered feature more thoroughly. Feel free to start with almost any chapter, but each technique builds on those previously explained, so you should try to follow the techniques within each chapter sequentially. Some chapters include **Advanced Technique** lessons, which assume that you have assimilated all of the techniques found throughout the chapter. *Advanced Techniques* is an entire chapter dedicated to advanced tips, tricks, and techniques.

5 Galleries. The Gallery pages consist of images related to techniques demonstrated nearby. Each Gallery piece is accompanied by a description of how the artist created that image, and may include steps showing the progression of a technique detailed elsewhere. *Illustrator & Other Programs* consists almost entirely of Gallery pages to give you a sense of Illustrator's flexibility.

6 References. Throughout the book, we'll sometimes refer you to the various appendixes at the back of the book. Also at the back of the book, find the extensive *General Index* and the pull-out *Glossary* card, and. In addition, we will occasionally direct you to *Illustrator Help* when referring to specific information that's well-documented in the Adobe Help Viewer. To access this, choose Help > Illustrator Help.

Acknowledgments

As always, my most heartfelt gratitude goes to the more than 100 artists and Illustrator experts who generously allowed us to include their work and divulge their techniques.

Special thanks must also go Jean-Claude Tremblay, our amazing technical editor; we are so lucky to have JC advising us on every technical detail of this project, collecting all the software demos, and even producing our press-ready PDFs! Thanks to Mordy Golding, who, as author of *Real World Adobe Illustrator CS4,* continues to champion this book and to share his expertise with the *Wow!* team. And thanks to the folks at Adobe, especially David Macy, Terry Hemphill, Brenda Sutherland, Ian Giblin, Teri Pettit, Michael Ninness, and John Nack.

This revision is the result of a major team effort by an amazing group of friends and collaborators. Thankfully Cristen Gillespie somehow just had enough time (again) between *Photoshop Wow!* revisions to contribute the vast majority of new lessons and Galleries, a number of critical introductions, and even update our style guide. Also blessedly returning were veteran *Wow!* artist/writer Lisa Jackmore (who did a great job with Galleries, lessons, *Wow! CD* file collection, and the *Illustrator CS4 Wow! Course Outline*), and cartographer/writer Steven Gordon (who returned to create and update important lessons and Galleries, join me on curatorial duties, and contribute dry wit when needed). Also returning are Conrad Chavez (who thankfully finished *Real World Photoshop CS4 for Photographers* in time to update lessons and introductions), Dave Awl (who finished his wonderful new book *Facebook Me!* in time to update a couple of chapter introductions), Andrew Dashwood (on loan from Nike Amsterdam), and Randy Livingston (who contributed between teaching and surgery). We are thrilled to have two new authors joining the team: veteran Illustrator blogger and artist Ryan Putnam (who created new lessons), and artist/ writer Aaron McGarry (who updated chapter introductions and created new lessons and a Gallery). Thank you Elizabeth Rogalin for returning to masterfully juggle so many edits from so many of us, with humor and kindness. A special thanks goes to our stellar team of testers: Nini Tjäder, Federico Platón, Bob Geib, Nicholas van der Walle, Scott Weichert, Laurie Wigham, Chris Nielsen, Chris Leavens, and Adam Z Lein (who also helped set up and back up the fabulous Sharepoint database that tracks who's doing what). Thanks to Sandee Cohen who acts as our official kibbitzer. And thanks to Rebecca Plunkett for being so flexible and creative with the index, and to Joanne Gosnell and Liz Welch for proofing. Thank you to Jay Nelson for the partnership between *Wow!* and *Design Tools Monthly.* And heartfelt thanks to Peg Maskell Korn, for being involved since the beginning, and putting up with me on a moment-to-moment basis.

Thank you to CDS for the fabulous printing job. And thanks to everyone at Peachpit Press for all the things you do to make sure this book happens, *especially* Nancy Peterson, Tracey Croom, Lupe Edgar, Nancy Davis, Nancy Ruenzel, Gary-Paul Prince, Sara Jane Todd, Karyn Johnson, Mimi Heft (for the gorgeous cover design), Glenn Bisignani, and Eric Geoffroy (our patient and thorough media producer). Thank you Linnea Dayton for being *Wow!* series editor, and for sharing Cristen. And last, but not at all least, heartfelt thanks to all my wonderful family and friends.

1

Illustrator Basics

This chapter contains a multitude of tips and techniques carefully chosen to help you use Adobe Illustrator with optimal ease and efficiency. Whether you're a veteran user of Illustrator or a relative newcomer, you'll find information here that will greatly increase your speed and efficiency using the latest features. Make sure you read the "Start here!" Tip at left.

Start here!

Make sure to read both "How to Use This Book" earlier in the book, and the pullout *Glossary*.

Minimum system requirements

Macintosh:

- PowerPC® G4 or G5 or Intel® processor
- Mac OS X v.10.4.8-10.5

Windows:

- 2GHz or faster processor
- Microsoft® Windows® XP with Service Pack 2 (Service Pack 3 recommended) or Windows Vista® Home Premium, Business, Ultimate, or Enterprise with Service Pack 1 (certified for 32-bit Windows XP and Windows Vista)

Both systems:

- 512MB of RAM (1GB is recommended)
- 2GB of available hard-disk space with additional free space required during installation (you cannot install it on Flash-based storage devices)
- 1,024 x 768 pixel monitor resolution with 16-bit video card
- DVD-ROM drive for installation
- QuickTime 7 software required for multimedia features
- Broadband Internet connection required for online services.

COMPUTER & SYSTEM REQUIREMENTS

The software world has seen significant improvement in the past few years, and Adobe Illustrator is no exception. Minimum system requirements have drastically risen to accommodate the demands of faster and more powerful applications. It is very likely that Adobe Illustrator CS4 will not run well (if at all) on older computer systems. For example, Illustrator CS4's minimum RAM requirement is 512MB (1GB recommended). You'll also need more hard disk space than ever before—at least 2GB. Another consideration: the Adobe Illustrator CS4 DVDs contain bonus content that you may wish to store on your hard disk. Your monitor should accommodate a resolution of at least 1024 x 768 pixels so your work area won't be cramped. Even so, major improvements have been made that help minimize panels while maximizing your document working area. It's now possible to customize your workspace better than ever before.

SETTING UP YOUR PAGE
New Document Profiles

When you first launch Illustrator, and whenever all document windows are closed, you'll see a Welcome screen that offers two primary routes for getting started with your new session: Open a Recent Item and Create New. Just as you'd expect, Open a Recent Item lists the nine most recent documents you've had open in Illustrator. The list is chronological, with the most recent document at the top. At the bottom of the list, there's a folder icon labeled "Open," which will bring up the Open dialog. From the Open dialog you can navigate to and open any pre-existing file.

In the Create New list you will see six default document profiles; Print, Web, Mobile and Devices, Video and Film, Basic CMYK, and Basic RGB. These each have pre-configured settings on which to base your new document. Of course, you can override or change all the settings in the New Document dialog that comes up when you click any document profile in the list. Keep in mind that you can create and save your own document profiles (see the Tip "Create document profiles" to the right).

New, New from Template, Open, and Open Recent Files are accessible from the File menu. In the New Document dialog, you can name your new file and confirm the New Document Profile type, as well as confirm the Size, Color Mode (CMYK or RGB), Artboard options, and other parameters you want for a particular project.

If you don't see it, the Welcome screen is always available from the Help menu.

Using Templates

Under Create New on the Welcome screen is the From Template folder icon. Clicking this icon opens the New from Template dialog, which takes you to Illustrator's collection of stock templates. You can also open template files by selecting File > New from Template. To save any of your own work as a template, choose File > Save as Template. Template files make it easy for you to create a new document based on finished designs. This comes in handy when you need to create a number of documents or pages with common design elements or transposable content.

Illustrator's templates are actually a special file format (ending in .ait). When you choose New from Template (from the File menu or from Template on the Welcome screen), a new Illustrator document (name ending in .ai) is created based on the template. The original .ait template file remains unchanged and ready to use again. No matter

The Welcome screen offers a number of useful options for starting your session, as well as convenient access to online training and resources

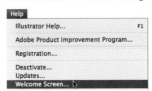

Create document profiles

Create a new document in Illustrator using one of the default Profiles, customize it (change Artboard size, Paragraph Style, etc.), and save it with a descriptive name to:

For Mac: (User)\Application Data\Adobe\Adobe Illustrator CS4 Settings\(localization folder)\New Document Profiles\

For Windows: Documents and Settings\(User)\Application Data\Adobe\Adobe Illustrator CS4 Settings\(localization folder)\New Document Profiles\

By basing your new document on one that fits your intended output space (web, print, etc.), you'll maintain the metadata encoding Illustrator uses to identify the document profile type, and your customized document will appear in the Welcome Screen menu.

what changes you make to your new document, the original template file will not be affected.

When you create a new file from a template, Illustrator automatically loads the various settings from the template file such as dimensions, swatches, type styles, symbols, or guides, as well as any content the template contains.

You can create as many original templates as you need or want. You can also take advantage of the more than 200 professionally designed templates included with Illustrator—everything from business cards to Web pages to restaurant menus.

Viewing Artboards

In the Document window, with any tool but the Artboard tool selected, the box with a solid black outline defines the artboard dimensions, i.e., the final document size. Double-click the Hand tool to fit the active artboard in the window, (or use ⌘-0/Ctrl-0). ⌘-Opt-0/Ctrl-Alt-0 fits all the artboards in the window. With the Artboard tool selected, the dashed outline with crop marks indicates the active artboard's bounds. Outer red lines indicate you have established a document-wide bleed setting, and you can choose in the Artboard Options dialog to display guides for web and video. View > Show Print Tiling displays the dotted lines that represent the printable area according to the paper size chosen in the Print dialog. (Currently this is useful for a document with only one artboard, and hasn't been updated for use with multiple artboards. Print tiling with multiple artboards is controlled entirely through the Print dialog.)

With Illustrator's sophisticated print controls (File > Print), you can make very precise choices about what to print. From Print > Range, you can choose which artboards to print, whether All or a Range, to ignore artboards (and use tiling and/or scaling to print all the artboards as one image), or to include or skip blank artboards. In the Media pop-up, you can choose the document size to print or display the artboard(s) on, ranging from Custom (the current size of the artboard) through several preset sizes, and the Options section lets you scale or tile your artboard(s) to accommodate the Media you chose. See the *Artboards & Type* chapter for a full discussion on using multiple artboards in Illustrator.

The One-Stop Print Dialog

Illustrator's full-service Print dialog lets you control all print functions from one interface. It's not necessary to use a Page Setup dialog to change things like page size and orientation. (In fact, it's recommended that you set all options from within Illustrator's Print dialog.)

The preview area in the Print dialog shows you the current artboard on the media's printable area. Any choice you make in the Print dialog applies to all artboards in your document, but even if you have multiple artboards of different sizes, you can choose to fit them to the media or scale them by a custom amount. Using the Placement icon or input fields, you can anchor the artboard to an area on the page, or you can drag in the print preview image to manually position the artwork relative to the media. But be careful if you choose to position your artwork manually when your document contains artboards of different sizes. It is easy to accidentally position an artboard that isn't currently being previewed beyond the page itself, which then won't print. You must choose Ignore Artboards to print any artwork that is not on an artboard, or to tile your artwork, rather than printing individual artboards to separate pages.

Illustrator lets you save your Print settings as time-saving presets. For example, if you frequently work with very large media sizes, you can set the appropriate printing scale and then save it as a Print preset for easy access. Using a Print preset eliminates having to check and set all the various parameters each time before you print.

MAKING YOUR MOVES EASIER

Take time to study this section in order to learn about the many ways to select tools and access Illustrator features. These simple navigation techniques will free you from

Illustrator's one-stop Print dialog—note the preview area in the lower-left corner, which shows you the printable area of the page, and the selected artboard—the lower-right offers options for scaling or tiling your artwork

By default, artwork that extends beyond an artboard won't print, making it important to watch not only for artwork left off the artboard, but for artwork that has been manually positioned on the page in the Print dialog

Custom keyboard shortcuts

To assign a shortcut to a menu item or tool, select Edit > Keyboard Shortcuts. Making any changes will rename the set "Custom." If you choose a shortcut already in use, you'll get a warning that it's currently being used and that reassigning it will remove it from the item to which it is currently assigned. When you exit the dialog you will be asked to save your custom set. You can't overwrite a *preset*.

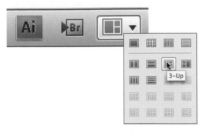

Open documents may be tabbed together or float individually

The Arrange Documents icon on the Application Bar gives you access to several automatic document views, often referred to as N-up view

With the Application Bar in the Window menu enabled, quickly arrange your documents by choosing a layout icon in the drop-down list; you can still drag documents into different docked positions with each other, resize each document's window, and change your zoom view for each window

Manually resizing panels

You can resize most panels by hovering your cursor over an edge, which switches it to a double-headed arrow. When you see this icon, drag to change the width or height of a panel.

having to mouse to the Tools panel, or to rely solely on pull-down menus.

Keyboard shortcuts for tools and navigation

Save time and use a key instead of going to the Tools panel. Press "T" to choose the Type tool, "P" for the Pen tool, and so on. Choose any tool in the Tools panel by pressing its keyboard shortcut. To learn the default keyboard shortcuts for your tools, hold the cursor over any tool in the Tools panel (the default Show Tool Tips option in General Preferences must be enabled), and its keyboard shortcut will appear in parentheses next to the tool name. **Note:** *Keyboard shortcuts won't work while you're in text editing mode. Press the Esc key to leave text editing mode and use a keyboard shortcut. Your text will remain unchanged, with edits preserved.*

Changing keyboard shortcuts

To change a shortcut for a tool or menu item, open the Keyboard Shortcut dialog (Edit > Keyboard Shortcuts). Making a change to a shortcut will change the set name to "Custom." When you're finished making changes and want to exit the dialog, you will be asked to save your shortcuts to a new file. This custom file will be saved in Preferences > Adobe Illustrator CS4 Settings and will end in ".kys." In addition, every time you make any changes to a saved set (not a default preset), you'll be asked if you want to overwrite that set. You can also use the Save button to create a new keyboard shortcut file. Click the Export Text button if you need a text file as a reference for a specific set of shortcuts, or if you need to print them.

MANIPULATING WINDOWS AND PANELS
Tabbed documents and the Application Frame

Under Preferences > User Interface, one of your choices is to open each document window tabbed with others, instead of free-floating. With tabbed documents you don't have to hunt through the pile to find the one you want, or remember the filename and locate it in the Window menu to bring it to the front. You click on a tab to activate the document and, if you have too many open to be able to read each tab, a double arrow appears on the right side of the tabbed bar that opens a list of filenames from which to select—quicker to get to than the Window menu. You're not stuck with having to change your Preferences in order to change from a tabbed document to a floating one, and vice versa. You can drag any document away from the tab setting just as you would a panel that was nested with others, and you can drag a free-floating document back to nest with other documents. Look for a blue bar to appear as you drag, to show that you're successfully docking the image again with the other tabs.

If you're on a Mac, you also have the option of an additional Application Frame, disabled by default on installation. The Application Frame creates a solid window-wide background for your documents, almost identical to the standard Windows interface. Any accidental clicking outside of a document window won't bring to the front whatever you clicked on that's outside of Illustrator. You enable/disable the Application Frame in the Window menu. If you have enabled the Application Frame, you automatically enable the Application Bar, as well. The Application Bar contains icons for Illustrator, for launching Bridge, and for choosing to arrange documents in a variety of patterns (N-up view).

Tabbed documents and panels are "spring-loaded." If you drag a document from one window onto the tab of another, that document window will be activated to let you drop your copy into it. When you reduce panels to icons, they, too, become spring-loaded. If you create a graphic style in the Appearance panel, for example, you can drag that onto the icon for Graphic Styles and the panel will pop open to receive it.

The Control panel

The Control panel is one of Illustrator's handiest features and, by default, it's docked at the top of the working area. It is a contextual panel in that it displays different tools

Flotation device

You can "float" any panel, including the Control panel, and position it anywhere you like just by dragging its gripper bar (the double row of dots). To redock the panel, just drag it back to the edge of the screen or another panel. When you see the blue bar, let go and it will snap back into place.

Magic peekaboo panels

Use Tab to toggle hide/show panels (Shift-Tab to hide panels but keep Tool and Control panels visible). With panels hidden, mouse over the area where panels were and they'll magically appear!

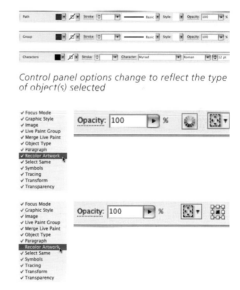

Control panel options change to reflect the type of object(s) selected

The Control panel menu at the far right lets you customize what controls appear on the bar; click to enable/disable a control—here, Recolor Artwork

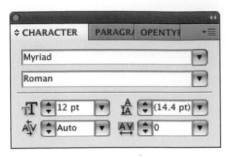

Nested panels grouped together by similar function—floating in this view, as indicated by the close button in the top upper left (Mac is shown)

A double-headed arrow in the upper left (next to the panel name), indicating that you can display more, or fewer, options in the panel

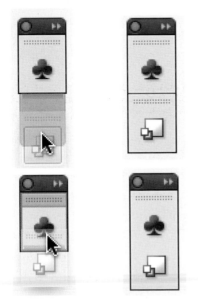

Drag to dock without nesting (top), and drag to dock with nesting (bottom)

and controls depending on the type of object currently selected. For example, if you select a text object, the panel will display text-formatting controls; on the other hand, selecting an art object will display options such as Stroke, Brush, Style, or perhaps Expand and Release buttons, depending on the kind of object. If you have multiple kinds of objects selected, the Control panel displays alignment controls in addition to other options for all the selected objects.

You can customize the Control panel by clicking on its menu button. From that menu, you can choose to dock the Control panel to the bottom of your working area rather than the top, and select or deselect various types of controls for display in the panel. The Control panel can also be repositioned as a floating panel by simply grabbing the panel's handle and dragging it where you want it. When you drag the Control panel to the top or bottom of the work area, at a certain point you'll see a blue bar indicator appear. When you see this, simply stop dragging and let go to re-dock the panel.

When you see underlined words in the Control panel, you can click them to display relevant options. For instance, clicking on the word Stroke will display Stroke options as a kind of pop-up panel. Clicking on the word Opacity opens a pop-up Transparency panel. Clicking on the arrows will reveal mini pop-ups, such as the arrow to the right of Opacity, which reveals a handy pop-up Opacity slider!

Dockable icon panels

You can dock all the other panels in Illustrator to either side of your screen, to each other stacked in a column, or to the side of a panel, forming another column. You can also nest panels together in tabbed "bundles" by dragging on the tab of one panel to the top bar of another; let go when you see a blue bounding box in the receiving panel. To dock a panel to the top, or bottom, or side of another, drag the panel until you see a thin blue line where you want them to dock together, and then let go.

Panels can be reduced to icons, dragged wider to show part or all of their names, or fully expanded to reveal the entire panel. Many panels also have a resize icon (a triangle of dots) in the lower-right corner. You can drag on the icon to increase/decrease both the width and height of a panel. Panels often open by default without displaying all their options. If a panel has a double arrow to the left of the panel name, click on the arrow to further expand the panel. Continuing to click on that arrow will cycle through the range of display options, from only the tab showing, to having all of the options on display.

If you click on the Expand Dock arrow at the upper right of a column of docked panels, all the icons in that column will expand or collapse together. However, if you click on an individual icon, the panel opens and closes individually. Enable Auto Collapse Icons Automatically in Preferences >User Interface, and any icon you open as a panel will close as soon as you click anywhere *except* on another panel or icon in a different column. If you want a panel to remain open while you work, disable this preference or place it in a column you keep expanded; one panel per column will now stay open until you click to close it, or until you click on another icon in the same column.

If you want a panel to stay open until you manually close it, tear it away from a dock and let it float over your document area. You can still reduce it to an icon; simply click once on the dark bar at the top of the panel. If you prefer to keep the tab showing, click once in the medium-gray area to the right of the tab. Double-click on the tab itself, or click on the Expand Panel arrow to re-expand the panel. Note, however, that with floating panels the Expand Panel arrow only expands the panel widthwise. If you have previously reduced your display options with the double arrow on the tab, it won't display more options than you already chose to show.

Should you prefer to work without any of the clutter of panels or icons, but still want to be able to easily access these panels, you can use the Tab key to hide all the panels (Shift-tab to hide all but the Control panel), and the

An example of a clickable underlined word in the Control panel; if you click on the word Stroke, a drop-down version of the Stroke panel will open

Expand or contract panel width by a fixed amount with the double arrow in the upper right; customize the width manually when the cursor turns into a double-headed arrow, allowing you to click-drag to resize the panel

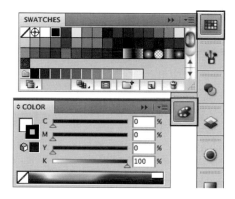

With Enable Auto Collapse Icons Automatically not checked in Preferences, one panel per column stays open until you either minimize it to an icon again (click the double arrow), or you click on another icon in that same column

Changing measurement units

Set units of measurement for rulers, panels, and some dialogs, as well as units for measuring strokes and text, in the Units & Display Performance area in Preferences. **Note:** *Control-click (on Mac) or right-click (with a two-button mouse) on a ruler to select different units, or cycle through ruler units with ⌘-Option-Shift-U/Ctrl-Alt-Shift-U.*

Tear-off panels

Staying with the artwork using context-sensitive menus

Trading spaces

On a Mac, Workspaces are stored in (User)\Library\Preferences\ Adobe Illustrator CS4 Settings\ (localization)\Workspaces. You can share a Workspace with other Macs by placing the Workspace file in that same location on any other Mac. On Windows the file will go in: C:\Documents and Settings\<username>\Application Data\Adobe\Adobe Illustrator CS4 Settings\Workspaces. Replace <username> with your log-in name.

Workspace menu showing saved workspaces at the top and Adobe-created workspaces below

icons will reappear while you hover your cursor over the edge of your screen. This also works in Full Screen mode.

Tear-off panels

The Illustrator Toolbox lets you *tear off* subsets of tools so you can move the entire set to another location. Click on a tool with a pop-up menu, drag the cursor to the arrow end of the pop-up, and release the mouse.

Context-sensitive menus

If you're not already familiar with Context-sensitive menus, you might find them to be a great time saver. Windows users merely click the right mouse button. If you're on a Mac with a single-button mouse, press the Control key while you click and hold the mouse button. In both cases a menu will pop up (specific to the tool or item you are working with), providing you with an alternative method to choose options.

WORKSPACES: MANAGING YOUR WORKING AREA

Once you've arranged your panels and the other features of your working area to your liking, the Workspaces feature allows you to save that arrangement as a custom workspace. If you like to have different arrangements of panels for different kinds of tasks, you can save multiple workspaces and then easily switch back and forth between them as you're working. Multiple users who share a computer setup can each create their own saved workspaces.

To save a custom workspace, once you've got everything arranged on your screen, just choose Workspace > Save Workspace from the Window menu. Enter a name for your custom workspace in the Name field, and click OK. Once you've created and saved a custom workspace, its name will show up in the Window > Workspace submenu, so you can easily switch between different workspaces just by clicking on their names. And you can always click on [Essentials] in the Workspace submenu to restore the basic Illustrator workspace.

The Manage Workspaces dialog allows you to delete, duplicate, or rename your custom workspaces at any time. Choose Window > Workspace > Manage Workspaces, and select the name of an existing custom workspace in the dialog. Rename it by changing the text in the Name field, click the New icon to create a duplicate of the current one, or click the Trash icon to delete.

WORKING WITH OBJECTS

Anchor points, lines, and Bézier curves

Instead of using pixels to draw shapes, Illustrator creates objects made up of points, called "anchor points." They are connected by curved or straight outlines called "paths" and are visible if you work in Outline mode. (Choose View > Outline to enter Outline mode, and View > Preview to change back.) Illustrator describes information about the location and size of each path, as well as its dozen or so attributes, such as its fill color and stroke weight and color. Because you are creating objects, you'll be able to change the order in which they stack. You'll also be able to group objects together so you can select them as if they were one object. You can even ungroup them later, if you wish.

If you took geometry in your school days, you probably remember that the shortest distance between two points is a straight line. In Illustrator, this rule translates into each line being defined by two anchor points that you create by either clicking with the Pen tool or drawing with the Line Segment tool.

In mathematically describing rectangles and ellipses, Illustrator computes the center, the length of the sides, or the radius, based on the total width and height that you specify.

For more complex shapes involving free-form curves, Adobe Illustrator allows you to use the Pen tool to create Bézier curves, defined by non-printing anchor points (which literally anchor the path at those points), and direction points (which define the angle and depth of the curve). To make these direction points easier to see and

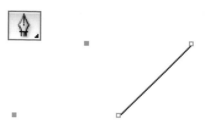

Clicking with the Pen tool to create anchor points for straight lines

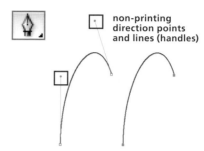

non-printing direction points and lines (handles)

Click-dragging with the Pen tool to create anchor points and pulling out direction lines for curves

When direction handles are short, curves are shallow; when handles are long, curves are deep

The length and angle of the handles determine the "gesture" of the curves

Quick selection tool switch

You can switch from the Selection tool to the Direct Selection tool on the fly by holding down the ⌘/Ctrl key. ⌘-Option/Ctrl-Alt will get you the Group selection tool.

Ways to "hinge" Bézier curves

A Bézier curve is "hinged" when it's attached to a line, or to another curve by a corner.

- **To hinge a curve as you draw #1:** While you are click-dragging to draw a curve, press Option/Alt to hinge the curve—pulling the handle in a new direction.
- **To hinge a curve as you draw #2:** With the Pen tool, hold Option/Alt and click-drag over the last drawn anchor point to hinge the curve—pulling the handle in a new direction.
- **To add a curve to a line:** Place the Pen tool on a line's anchor point and click-drag to pull out a direction handle for your next curve.
- **Drag with the Convert Anchor Point Tool** to smooth hinged anchor points and hinge curves.

Closing paths—Pencil & Brush

If you hold down the Option/Alt key when you are ready to close a path drawn with the Pencil or Brush tool, a straight line segment will be drawn between the first and last anchor points. If you hold down the Option/Alt key and extend slightly past the first anchor point, the path will close automatically. Set the tool preferences to low numbers to make closing easier. — *Sandee Cohen*

manipulate, each one is connected to its anchor point with a non-printing direction line, also called a "handle." The direction points and handles are visible when you're creating a path with the Pen tool or editing the path with either the Direct Selection tool, or one of the path editing tools accessed from the Pen tool (see figures opposite). While all of this might sound complicated, manipulating Bézier curves can become intuitive. Mastering these curves, though initially awkward, is the heart and soul of using Illustrator. And being comfortable with Illustrator's Pen tool can help you immensely when you're working in Photoshop and InDesign as well.

More about Bézier curves

If you're new to using Bézier curves, take some time to go through the Adobe training materials. Also, the "Ch02-zen_lessons" folder on the *Wow! CD* includes several "Zen" practice lessons that will help you fine-tune your Bézier capabilities (such as the "Zen of the Pen" Bézier lessons, which include QuickTime demonstrations on drawing and editing paths and curves).

Many graphics programs include Béziers, so mastering the Pen tool, though challenging at first, is very important. Friskets in Corel Painter, paths in Photoshop and InDesign, and the outline and extrusion curves of many 3D programs all use the Bézier curve.

The key to learning Béziers is to take your initial lessons in short doses and to stop if you get frustrated. Designer Kathleen Tinkel describes Bézier direction lines as "following the gesture of the curve." This artistic view should help you to create fluid Bézier curves.

Some final rules about Bézier curves

- The length and angle of the handles "anticipate" the curves that will follow.
- To ensure that the curve is smooth, place anchor points on either side of an arc, not in between.
- The fewer the anchor points, the smoother the curve will look and the faster it will print.

- Adjust a curve's height and angle by dragging the direction points, or grab the curve itself to adjust its height.

WATCH YOUR CURSOR!

Illustrator's cursors change to indicate not only what tool you have selected, but also which function you are about to perform. If you watch your cursor, you will avoid the most common Illustrator mistakes.

If you choose the Pen tool:

- **Before you start**, your cursor displays as the Pen tool with "×," indicating that you're starting a new object.

- **Once you've begun your object,** your cursor changes to a regular Pen. This indicates that you're about to add to an existing object.

- **If your cursor gets close to an existing anchor point,** it will change to a Pen with "–" indicating that you're about to delete the anchor point! If you click-drag on top of that anchor point, you'll redraw that curve. If you hold the Option (Mac)/Alt (Win) key while you click-drag on top of the point, you'll pull out a new direction line, creating a corner (as in the petals of a flower). If you click on top of the point, you'll collapse the outgoing direction line, allowing you to attach a straight line to the curve.

- **If your cursor gets close to an end anchor point of an object**, it will change to a Pen with "o" to indicate that you're about to "close" the path. If you do close the path, then your cursor will change back to a Pen with "×" to indicate that you're beginning a new object.

- **If you use the Direct Selection tool to adjust the object as you go,** be sure to look at your cursor when you're ready to continue your object. If it's still a regular Pen, then continue to place the next point, adding to your object. If the Pen tool has "×" (indicating that you are about to start a new object), then you must redraw your

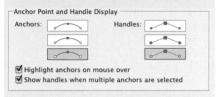

 Starting an object

 Adding a point

 Removing a point

 Creating a corner (when over an existing point)

 Continuing from an anchor point

 Joining two line segments

 Closing an object

Basic cursor feedback for the Pen tool

last point. As you approach this last anchor point, your cursor will change to a Pen with "/"; click and drag over this last point to redraw the last curve.

To form a hinged corner on a point *as you draw*, hold down Option (Mac)/Alt (Win) as you click-drag out a new direction line.

BÉZIER-EDITING TOOLS

Bézier-editing tools are the group of tools you can use to edit Illustrator paths. To access them, click and hold the Pen, Pencil, or Scissors tool and drag to select one of the other tools. You can also tear off this panel. You can also make your anchor points easier to see in Preferences (see Tip "Get to the point" on the previous page). (To learn how to combine paths into new objects, read about the Pathfinder panel in the *Beyond the Basics* chapter.)

- **The Pen tool** and **Auto Add/Delete** can perform a variety of functions. Auto Add/Delete (which is on by default, but can be disabled in General Preferences) allows the Pen tool to change automatically to the Add Anchor Point tool when the tool is over a selected path segment, or to the Delete Anchor Point tool when over an anchor point. To temporarily disable the Auto Add/Delete function of the Pen tool, hold down the Shift key. If you don't want the path to constrain to an angle, release the Shift key prior to releasing the mouse.

- **The Convert Anchor Point tool,** hidden within the Pen tool (Shift-C), converts an anchor point from a smooth curve to a corner point when you click on it. To convert a corner point to a smooth curve, click-drag on the anchor point counterclockwise to pull out a new direction handle (or twirl the point until it straightens out the curve). To convert a smooth curve to a hinged curve (two curves hinged at a point), grab the direction point and hold Option/Alt as you drag out to the new position. With the Pen tool selected, you can temporarily access the Convert Anchor Point tool by pressing Option/Alt. You can also convert selected anchor points and make corner points into curves, or smooth curves, by clicking on the corresponding Convert icon in the Control panel.

- **The Add Anchor Point tool,** accessible from the Pen pop-up menu or by pressing the plus key (+), adds an anchor point to a path at the location where you click.

- **The Delete Anchor Point tool,** accessible from the Pen pop-up menu or by pressing the minus key (–), deletes an anchor point when you click directly on the point. You can also delete a selected anchor point by clicking the button that will appear in the Control panel.
  Note: *If you select the Add/Delete Anchor Point tools by pressing + or –, press P to get back to the Pen tool.*

- **The Pencil tool** reshapes a selected path when Edit selected paths is enabled in Pencil Tool Options. Select a path and draw on or near the path to reshape it.

- **The Smooth tool** smooths the points on already-drawn paths by smoothing corners and deleting points. As you move the Smooth tool over your path, it attempts to keep the original shape of the path as intact as possible.

- **The Path Eraser tool** will remove parts of a selected path (use any Selection tool to select the path). See the *Beyond the Basics* chapter for more about the Path Eraser tool.

- **The Blob Brush tool** creates filled, unstroked objects and automatically merges overlapping shapes that use the same Fill color. The Blob Brush tool uses the same brush options as the calligraphic brushes, but behaves more like an expanded Pathfinder tool. For more on using the Blob Brush, see the *Beyond the Basics* chapter.

- **The Eraser tool** removes a swath from vector objects as you "slice through" them. If a vector object is selected, the Eraser tool will affect only that selected object. If

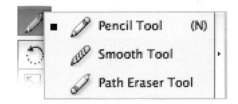

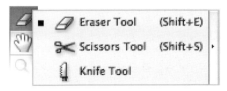

Basic tools for editing paths

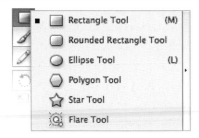
there is nothing selected, all vector objects that are touched by the Eraser tool will be affected (through all unlocked and visible layers). The Eraser tool makes it easy to reshape objects created with the Blob Brush. See the *Beyond the Basics* chapter for more about working with, and controlling the effects of, the Eraser tool.

- **The Scissors tool** cuts a path where you click by adding two disconnected, selected anchor points exactly on top of each other. To select just one of the points, deselect the object, then click with the Direct Selection tool on the spot where you cut. This will allow you to select the upper anchor point and drag it to the side in order to see the two points better.

- **The Knife tool** slices through all unlocked visible objects and closed paths. Simply drag the Knife tool across the object you want to slice, then select the object(s) you want to move or delete. Hold down the Option (Mac)/Alt (Win) key to constrain the cut to a straight line. The Knife tool creates closed paths in the objects it divides.

GEOMETRIC OBJECTS

The Ellipse, Rounded Rectangle, Polygon, and Star tools create objects called "geometric primitives." These objects are mathematically described symmetrical paths grouped with a non-printing anchor point, which indicates the center. (In order for the center of a star or polygon to be visible, you'll need to choose Window > Attributes and then click the Show Center icon.) Use the centers of the geometric objects to snap-align them with each other, or with other objects and guides. You can create these geometric objects numerically or manually (see the section following for directions on how to do this). Access the hidden tools in the pop-up panel from the Rectangle tool in the Toolbox. (See the *Zen of Illustrator* chapter for exercises in creating and manipulating geometric objects, and the tips "Tool tolerance options" and "Serious fun with shapes" in this chapter.)

- **To create a geometric object manually,** select the desired geometric tool, and click-drag to form the object from one corner to the other. To create the object from the center, hold down the Option (Mac)/Alt (Win) key and drag from the center outward (keep the Option/Alt key down until you release the mouse button to ensure that it draws from the center). Once you have drawn the geometric objects, you can edit them exactly as you do other paths.

- **To create a geometric object with numeric input,** select a geometric tool and click on the Artboard to establish the upper-left corner of your object. Enter the desired dimensions in the dialog and click OK. To create the object numerically from the object's center, Option-click (Mac)/Alt-click (Win) on the Artboard.

  To draw an arc, select the Arc tool and then click and drag to start drawing the arc. Press the "F" key to flip the arc from convex to concave, and use the up and down arrow keys to adjust the radius of the arc. Pressing the "C" key will "close" the arc by drawing the perpendicular lines that form the axes, and pressing the "X" key will flip the arc without moving these axes ("F" flips both the arc and the axes). Release the mouse to finish the arc.

  To draw a grid, select either the Rectangular Grid tool or the Polar Grid tool and click-drag to start drawing the grid. You can control the shape of the grid by pressing various keys as you draw (see *Illustrator Help* for details). Release the mouse to finish the grid.

SELECTING & GROUPING OBJECTS
Selecting

The Select menu gives you easy access to basic selection commands, including the ability to select specific types of objects and attributes. You can choose to select all objects in the document (⌘-A/Ctrl-A), or all only in the active artboard (⌘-Opt-A/Ctrl-Alt-A). You can use the Selection tools to select individual or multiple objects. You can use the target indicators in the Layers panel to

Variations on lines in geometric objects

Making a Rectangular Grid

For a lesson using the Rectangular Grid tool, see "Of Grids & Lines" in the *Zen of Illustrator* chapter.

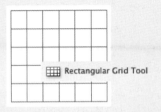

Resizing and stroke weight

Double-click the Scale tool to resize your selection with or without altering line weights:

- To scale a selection while also scaling line weights, enable Scale Strokes & Effects.
- To scale a selection while maintaining your line weights, disable Scale Strokes & Effects.
- To decrease line weights (50%) without scaling objects, first scale the selection (200%) with Scale Strokes & Effects disabled. Then scale (50%) with it enabled. Reverse these steps to increase line weights.

Selection tool   Direct Selection tool   Group Selection tool

select and target objects, groups, and layers. Targeting a group or layer selects everything contained within it, and makes the group or layer the focus of the Appearance and Graphic Styles panels. (For detailed instructions explaining targeting and selecting via the Layers panel, see the *Layers & Appearances* chapter.)

Use the Lasso tool to select an entire path or multiple paths by encircling them. Combining Option/Alt with the Lasso tool subtracts entire paths from a selection (though this may require a certain amount of finesse). Combining Shift with the Lasso tool adds entire paths to a selection.

You can also use the Direct Selection tool or the Lasso tool to select individual anchor points or path segments. Click with the Direct Selection tool to select points, or click-drag to draw a marquee around the area you wish to select. With the Lasso tool encircle the points or path segments that you wish to select. Combining Option/Alt with the Direct Selection or Lasso tool subtracts anchor points from a selection; Shift with the Lasso tool adds anchor points to a selection.

Grouping and selecting

Many programs provide you with a grouping function so you can treat multiple objects as one unit. In Illustrator, grouping objects places all the objects on the same layer and creates a "<Group>" container in the Layers panel; remember, don't choose Group if you want your objects on different layers. (For more on layers and objects, see the *Layers & Appearances* chapter.) So, when *do* you want to group objects? Group objects when you need to select them *repeatedly* as a unit or when you want to apply an appearance to the entire group. Take an illustration of a bicycle as an example. Use the Group function to group the spokes of a wheel. Next, group the two wheels of the bicycle, then group the wheels with the frame. We will continue to refer to this hypothetical bicycle below.

- **With the Direct Selection tool.** Click on a point or path with the Direct Selection tool to select that point or portion of the path. If you click on a spoke of a wheel, you'll select the portion of the spoke's path you clicked.

- **With the Selection tool.** Click on an object with the Selection tool to select the largest group containing that object. In our example, this would be the entire bicycle.

- **With the Group Selection tool.** Use the Group Selection tool to select sub-groupings progressively. The first click with the Group Selection tool selects a single spoke. The next click selects all of the spokes. The third click selects the entire wheel; the fourth selects both wheels, and the fifth, the entire bicycle. (Or, marquee part of the objects to select all of them.) To move objects selected with the Group Selection tool, drag without releasing the mouse. If you continually click with the Group Selection tool, you're always selecting additional groups.

- **You must select your object(s) before you can make changes.** With your objects selected, you can click on the label or inside any edit box in the panel containing text and begin typing. If you're typing something that has limited choices (such as a font or type style), Illustrator will attempt to complete your word; just keep typing until your choice is visible. If you're typing into a text field, use the Tab key to move to other text fields within the panel. Certain panels (including the Character, Paragraph, and OpenType panels) contain a Reset Panel command that allows you to easily restore the panel's default settings. **IMPORTANT:** *When you've finished typing into panel text fields, you must press Return/Enter. This action tells the application that you are ready to enter text somewhere else or to resume manipulating your artwork.*

- **There are many ways to fill or stroke an object.** Focus on a selected object's fill or stroke by clicking on the Fill or Stroke icon near the bottom of the Toolbox, or toggle between them with the "X" key. To set the stroke or fill to None, use the "/" key (forward slash). Set your

Don't forget about your edges!

Once you hide your edges in Illustrator (View > Hide Edges or ⌘-H/Ctrl-H), they stay hidden for all subsequent paths and selections. If you are trying to select a path or draw a new object, but the anchor points and path are not visible, try toggling to Show Edges.
Note: *If you have the Bounding Box visible (View menu), Hide Edges won't "hide edges" entirely.*

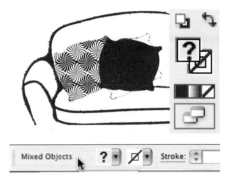

Selecting multiple objects with different properties displays in the toolbar (top right) and Control panel (bottom) with a question mark, to indicate mixed objects have been selected

Copying stroke and fill

It's easy to copy your stroke and fill settings from one object to the next. Select an object with the stroke and fill you want for your next object. Illustrator automatically picks up those attributes, so the next drawn object will have the same stroke and fill as the last one selected.
Note: *This doesn't work for type.*

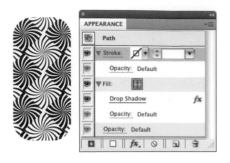

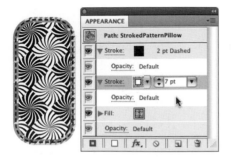

The top panel shows the object alongside has no stroke, and the bottom panel shows multiple strokes added using the Appearance panel; the Appearance panel also displays properties such as Fills, Opacity, and Effects

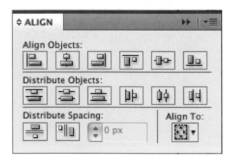

The Align panel with all of its options displayed; the Distribute Spacing controls are found only in the Align panel (not in the Control panel)

Align and Distribute buttons in the Control panel, and the "Align to" pop-up menu

color by: 1) adjusting the sliders or sampling a color from the color ramp in the Color panel, 2) clicking on a swatch in the Swatches panel, 3) sampling colors from the color picker, or 4) using the Eyedropper to sample from other objects in your file. Or you can change the Stroke or Fill directly within the Appearance panel (see the *Layers & Appearances* chapter). In addition, you can drag color swatches from panels to selected objects or to the Fill/Stroke icon in the Toolbox.

- **You can associate appearances with objects, groups of objects, or layers.** *Appearance attributes* are properties that affect the way an object appears, without actually altering the path itself. This book uses the term *appearance* to refer to an object's collective attributes, such as strokes, fills, transparencies, and effects. All objects have an appearance, even if that appearance is "no stroke and no fill." (See the *Layers & Appearances* and *Live Effects & Graphic Styles* chapters for working with appearances.)

- **Take time with the "Finger Dance" lessons in the *Zen of Illustrator* chapter.** These exercises are designed to help you navigate the subtleties of making selections.

USING THE ALIGN PANEL

The Align panel (Window > Align) contains a highly useful set of tools that allow you to control how selected objects, or selected anchor points, are aligned or distributed in relation to other objects, selections, or artboards. If you select objects with the Selection or Group Selection tool, then these functions will align and distribute the selected objects. However, if your selection includes any anchor points selected with the Direct Selection or Lasso tools, then these functions will align *all of the points in the selected objects*, as if you used the Average function (see the section below on Joining & Averaging). Even though most Align and Distribute controls also appear in the Control panel, Distribute Spacing controls are found only in the Align panel.

To make sure all of the Align panel's options are showing, click the double triangle on the Align panel tab or choose Show Options from the panel's menu.

The Align panel lets you align objects along a specified axis, according to either the edges or the anchor points of objects. Begin by selecting the objects that you want to align or distribute. If you want to align or distribute relative to the bounding box of all the objects you have selected, just click whichever button on the Align panel reflects the arrangement you want.

If you want to align or distribute relative to a specific object, select all the objects, then click again on the "key" object you want the Align commands to respond to. A heavy outline in the layer's color indicates that all the other objects will now align relative to this object. You can change the key object any time simply by clicking on another selected object.

You can use the icon in the Control panel or the expanded Align panel to access all your aligning options, which include aligning to a selection or the artboard. You can also use this icon if you want to maintain your selection, but don't want to use Align to Key Object anymore.

Note that by default, Illustrator uses the paths of objects to determine how the objects will be aligned and distributed. But you can also use the edge of the stroke to determine alignment and distribution, by choosing Use Preview Bounds from the panel menu. (This is useful for objects with differing stroke weights.) But keep in mind that "the edge of the stroke" includes any effects applied to that object, including things that extend well beyond the visible edge of the stroke, such as drop shadows.

The Align panel even lets you specify exact distances by which objects should be distributed. First, select the objects you want to distribute; then, in the Distribute Spacing field of the Align panel, enter the amount of space by which the objects should be separated. (Remember, you may need to choose Show Options in order for the Distribute Spacing field to be visible in the Align panel; these controls don't appear in the Control panel.)

After Shift-selecting objects, clicking again on one object sets it as the key object, shown here (center) with a solid teal boundary

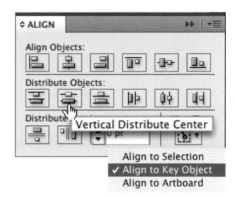

Using the Align panel to orient and align objects

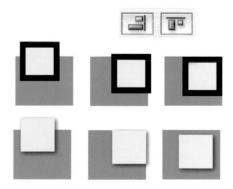

Use Preview Bounds helps visually align stroked objects, but yields mysterious results with live graphic effects such as drop shadows: The left rectangles are unaligned; at center are the same rectangles, each pair having been aligned top and right; at right the pairs are aligned top/right with "Use Preview Bounds" enabled

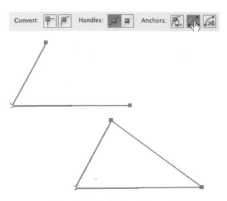

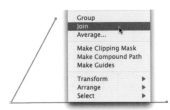

Joining selected endpoints with a straight line using the Control panel icon

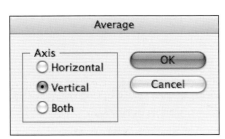

Choosing the Context-sensitive menu (Ctrl-click/ right-click) to join or average selected endpoints

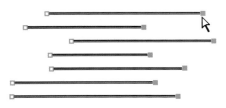

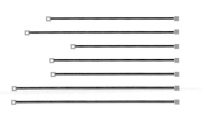

Averaging anchor points on one axis

Using the Selection tool, click on the path of the object you want to remain fixed, while the other objects distribute themselves relative to it. Then click either the Vertical or Horizontal Distribute Space button. (Choose Auto from the pop-up menu to cancel this option.)

JOINING & AVERAGING

Two of Illustrator's most useful functions are Average and Join. (Both are found within the Object > Path menu or in the Context-sensitive menu. Or to simply join selected endpoints, you can click the "Connect selected end points" button in the Control panel.)

To average, use the Direct Selection tool or Lasso tool to marquee-select or Shift-select any number of points belonging to any number of objects. Then use the Context-sensitive menu (Control-click (for Mac), or right-click on a two-button mouse) to Average, aligning the selected points horizontally, vertically, or along both axes.

You can also use the Average function (or the Align buttons) to stack two selected endpoints on top of each other. The Join function will connect two endpoints; Join operates differently depending on the objects.

- **If the two open endpoints are exactly on top of each other,** then Join opens a dialog asking if the join should be a smooth point or a corner. A smooth point is a curved Bézier anchor that smoothly joins two curves, with direction handles that always move together; a corner point is any other point connecting two paths. Once you've clicked OK, both points will fuse into a single point. However, keep in mind that a true smooth point will only result if the proper conditions exist: namely, that the two curves that you are trying to join have the potential to join together into a smooth curve. Otherwise, you'll get a corner point, even if you chose Smooth in the dialog.

- **If the two open endpoints are not exactly on top of each other,** then Join will connect the two points with a line. If you try to Join two points to fuse as one but don't get a dialog, then you've merely connected your points with a line! Undo (⌘-Z for Mac/Ctrl-Z for Windows) and see "To Average & Join in one step" below.

- **If you select an open path** (in this case, you don't need to select the endpoints), then Join closes the path.

- **If the two open endpoints are on different objects,** then Join connects the two paths into one.

- **To Average & Join in one step,** use the following keyboard command: ⌘-Option-Shift-J (Mac)/Ctrl-Alt-Shift-J (Win); there is no menu equivalent! This command forms a corner when joining two lines, or a hinged corner when joining a line or curve to a curve.

TRANSFORMATIONS

Moving, scaling, rotating, reflecting, and shearing are all operations that transform selected objects. Since this chapter is devoted to Illustrator basics, this section will concentrate on the tools and panels that help you to perform transformations. (For live effects that perform transformations, see the *Live Effects & Graphic Styles* chapter.) Begin by selecting what you wish to transform. If you don't like a transformation you've just applied, use Undo before applying a new transformation—or you'll end up applying the new transformation on top of the previous one. In Illustrator, you can perform most transformations interactively by using a transformation tool directly on the selected object in the document, or manually, using a dialog for numeric accuracy. Illustrator remembers the last transformation you performed, storing those numbers in the appropriate dialog until you enter a new transform value or restart the program. For example, if you previously scaled an image and disabled Scale Strokes & Effects, the next time you scale (manually or numerically), your strokes and effects won't scale. (Also see the Tip "Transform again" later in this section, and see the *Zen of Illustrator* chapter for exercises using transformations.)

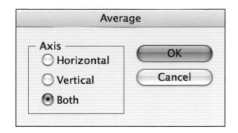

Using the Average command to align selected endpoints vertically, then choosing Both

Joining warning

If you get an error message that you can't join points, do the following—in addition to the conditions in the warning:

- Make sure you've selected only two points (and no third stray point selected by mistake).
- Make sure you've selected *endpoints*, not midpoints.

Panel modifiers

To modify your transformations when you press Return/Enter, hold down Option/Alt to transform and make a copy. Click a point in the Control or Transform panel to select a reference point.

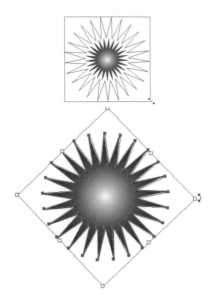

Showing the Bounding Box with the double arrow of the Selection tool cursor indicating the box can be transformed either by scaling (top), or rotation (bottom)

Units and math in panels

To use the current unit of measurement, type the number, then Tab to the next text field or press Return/Enter. To use another unit of measurement, *follow* the number with "in" or " (for inch), "pt" (point), "p" (pica), or "mm" (millimeter) and press Return/Enter. To resume typing into an image text block, press Shift-Return. You can also enter *calculations* in panels. For example, if you were specifying the size of a rectangle, you could type 72 pt + 2 mm for the height. Illustrator would then perform the calculation and apply the result. Partial calculations work as well; if you type + 2, Illustrator will add two of whatever unit you're currently using. Try it!

The bounding box

The bounding box should not be confused with the Free Transform tool (which allows you to perform additional functions; see discussion of the Free Transform tool below). The bounding box appears around selected objects when you are using the Selection tool (solid arrow), and can be useful for quickly moving, scaling, rotating, or duplicating objects. With the bounding box, you can easily scale several objects at once. Select the objects, click on a corner of the bounding box, and drag. To constrain proportionally while scaling, hold down the Shift key and drag a corner.

By default, the bounding box is on. Toggle it off and on via the View > Hide/Show Bounding Box, or switch to the Direct Selection tool to temporarily hide it. To reset the bounding box after performing a transformation so it's once again square to the page, choose Object > Transform > Reset Bounding Box.

Note: *As long as one of the bounding box handles is selected, holding down the Option/Alt key when you transform with the bounding box will not create a duplicate, but will instead transform from the center.*

Moving

In addition to grabbing and dragging objects manually, you can specify a new location numerically: Double-click the Selection arrow in the Toolbox or use the Context-sensitive menu to bring up the Move dialog (select the Preview option). For help determining the distance you wish to move, click-drag with the Measure tool the distance you wish to calculate. Then *immediately* open the Move dialog to see the measured distance loaded automatically, and click OK (or press Return/Enter).

The Free Transform tool

The Free Transform tool can be an easy way to transform objects once you learn numerous keyboard combinations to take advantage of its functions. In addition to performing simple transformations that can be performed with the bounding box (such as rotate and scale), you can also shear, and create perspective and distortions (see the Tip "Free Transform variations" on this page, and the "Distorting Views" lesson in the *Drawing & Coloring* chapter). Bear in mind that the Free Transform tool bases its transformations on a fixed center point that cannot be relocated. If you need to transform from a different location, use the individual transformation tools, Transformation panel, or the Transform Each command.

The Transform panel

From this panel, you can determine numeric transformations that specify an object's width, height, and location on the document, as well as how much to rotate or shear it. You can also access a panel pop-up menu that offers options to Flip Horizontal and Vertical; Transform Object, Pattern, or Both; and to enable Scale Strokes & Effects. The current Transform panel is a bit odd: You can Transform Again once you've applied a transformation, but the information in the text fields is not always retained. To maintain your numeric input, apply transformations through the transformation tool's dialog, discussed in the next section.

Individual transformation tools

For the scaling, rotation, reflection, and shearing of objects with adjustable center points, you can click (to manually specify the center about which the transformation will occur), then grab your object to transform it. For practice with manual transformations using these individual tools, see the *Zen of Illustrator* chapter. Each transformation tool has a dialog where you can specify the parameters for the tool, whether to transform the object or make a copy with the specified transform applied, and whether to transform just the objects and/or any patterns they may be filled with. (For more on transforming patterns see the *Drawing & Coloring* chapter.)

Here are three additional methods you can use to apply the individual transformation tools to objects:

Free Transform variations

With the Free Transform tool, you can apply the following transformations to selected objects:

- **Rotate**—Click outside the bounding box and drag.
- **Scale**—Click on a corner of the bounding box and drag. Option-drag/Alt-drag to scale from the center, and Shift-drag to scale proportionally.
- **Distort**—Click on a corner handle of the bounding box and ⌘-drag/Ctrl-drag.
- **Shear**—Click on a side handle of the bounding box and ⌘-drag/Ctrl-drag the handle.
- **Perspective**—Click on a corner handle of the bounding box and ⌘-Option-Shift-drag/Ctrl-Alt-Shift-drag.

Transform again

Illustrator remembers your last transformation—from simple moves to rotating a *copy* of an object. Use the Context-sensitive menu to repeat the effect (Transform Again), or ⌘-D/Ctrl-D.

Scaling complex files...

If you want to scale a file that contains Live Effects, brushes, patterns, gradients, and gradient meshes, it's probably best to scale the final image once it's placed it into a page layout program (such as InDesign or QuarkXPress).

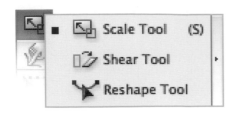

- **Double-click on a transformation tool** to access the dialog. (Or press Return/Enter with a transformation tool already selected.) This allows you to transform objects numerically, originating from an object's center.

- **Option-click/Alt-click on your image with a transformation tool** to access the dialog that allows you to transform your objects numerically, originating from where you clicked.

- **Click-drag on your image with a transformation tool** to transform the selected objects, originating from the center of the group of selected objects.

Reshape & Shear

The Reshape tool is different from the other transformation tools. Start by selecting all the points in the paths you wish to reshape (use the Group Selection or Selection tool). Next, choose the Reshape tool (hidden under the Scale tool) and marquee or Shift-select all points you wish to affect, then drag the points to reshape the path. The selected points move as a unit, but rather than move the same distance, as they would if you dragged with the Direct Selection tool, the points nearer to the cursor move more, and the ones farther away move less.

ATTEBERRY

Drawing one squiggle of hair; using the Reshape tool to reshape it; holding Option/Alt while dragging to make copies; reshaping all three strands, then with the Reshape tool selecting only the top anchor on each strand to reshape all three together; reshape again to form the surprised witch's hair and hat

You will also find the Shear tool hidden under the Scale tool. Use the Shear tool to slant objects. Click once on an anchor point to set it as the point around which the shear occurs; then drag on other anchor points. Shear is useful for creating the illusion of perspective.

Scaling objects to an exact size

Using either the Control or Transform panel, type the new width or height in the panel and press ⌘-Return/Ctrl-Return. (Or click the Lock icon in that panel to scale proportionately.)

Note: *When scaling objects, be sure to enable Scale Strokes & Effects, either within a transformation dialog, or in Preferences >General.*

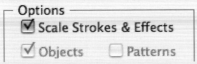

Transform Each

To perform multiple transformations at once, open the Transform Each dialog (Object > Transform > Transform Each). You can perform the transformations on one or more objects. Additions to this dialog include the ability to reflect objects over the X and Y axes, and to change the point of origin. If you want to apply a transformation, but you think you might want to change it later, try a Transformation Effect (see the *Live Effects & Graphic Styles* chapter for more about live effects).

WORKING SMART

Saving strategies

Probably the most important advice you'll ever get is to save every few minutes. Whenever you make a substantial change to your document, use File > Save As and give your document a new name. It's much more time-efficient to save incremental versions of your image than it is to reconstruct an earlier version.

Back up, back up, back up!

Back up your work at least once a day before you shut down. Just think to yourself, "If this computer never starts up again, what will I need?" Develop a backup system using CDs, DVDs, or external storage drives, so you can archive all of your work. Use a program such as Dantz's Retrospect or Apple's Time Machine to automatically add new and changed files to your archives.

Get in the habit of archiving virtually everything, and develop a file-naming system that actually helps you keep track of your work in progress—simplifying your recovery of a working version if necessary. Also, make sure you keep all files in a named and dated folder that distinguishes them from other projects. Use Bridge, discussed later in this introduction, to add metadata, making future searches easier. (For more information about saving in other formats see "Image Formats" later in this chapter.)

Multiple Undos

Some programs give you only one chance to undo your last move. Illustrator allows "unlimited undos," which, practically speaking, means that the number of undos you can perform is limited only by how much memory you have available.

Even *after* you save a file, your Undos (and Redos) will still be available (as long as you haven't closed and reopened the file), making it possible for you to save the

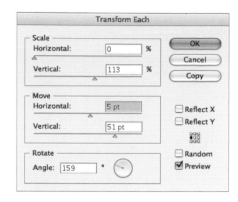

The Transform Each dialog (Object > Transform > Transform Each)

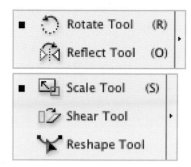

Tear-off panels for basic transformations

Adding metadata (keywords, file description, contact info, client, etc.) to make it easier to find a file later on through Bridge

Save As (and Save a Copy) allows you to keep versions of a project by using different file names. This strategy can be very useful if you need to backtrack for any reason.

current version, undo it to a previous stage and save it again, or as a different name, or continue working from an earlier state. But once you close your file, your undos are cleared from memory, so they won't be available the next time you open the file.

You can also revert the file to the most recently saved version by choosing File > Revert, but you can't undo a revert, so you'll want to be careful.
Note: *Not all operations are undoable. For example, changes to Preferences aren't affected by Undo, and neither are screen zooms.*

CHANGING YOUR VIEWS

From the View menu, you can show and hide several items, such as grids, guides, smart guides, transparency grids, edges, Artboards, and page tilings.

Preview and Outline

To control the speed of your screen redraw, learn to make use of the Preview mode and the Outline mode, which can be toggled in the View menu. In Preview mode, you view the document in full color; in Outline mode, you see only the wire frames of the objects.

Illustrator also offers a great way to control the speed and quality of your screen redraws when using the Hand Tool. In the Units & Display Performance area of Preferences, there's a Display Performance slider for the Hand Tool that lets you set your own preferred balance between the speed and quality of redraws.

New View

In truth, this feature hasn't worked reliably since Illustrator layer structures included sublayers and objects. Theoretically, using View > New View allows you to save your current window viewpoint, remembering also your zoom level and which layers are hidden, locked, or in Preview mode. Custom views are added to the bottom of the View menu to let you recall a saved view. You can rename a view, but the views themselves are not editable. (For detailed help with layers and sublayers, see the *Layers & Appearances* chapter.)

New Window

Illustrator gives you the ability to display different aspects of your current image simultaneously. This allows you to separately view different Proof Setups, Overprint or Pixel Previews, and zoom levels. You can resize each window separately, and for each window you can make edges hidden or visible, or hide or lock different *layers* in Preview or Outline (see the *Layers & Appearances* chapter and "Hide/Show Edges" later in this chapter). For instance, using multiple windows of the same file, you can view the full image in Preview and simultaneously work on close detail in Outline mode. This can be useful if you are using a large monitor or multiple monitors. Most window configurations are saved with your file when you save.

Window controls

There are four choices to Change Screen Mode at the very bottom of the Tools panel. The default is Standard Screen mode (desktop showing around the edges of your file), Full Screen mode with menu bar (file window visible, but confined to the center of the screen with no desktop showing; you can access your menu bar), Full Screen mode (same as above, but you cannot access your menu bar), and Maximized Screen mode (desktop hidden around the edges of your file). You can toggle among the views by pressing the "F" key.

Zooming in & out

Illustrator provides many ways to zoom in and out:

- **From the View menu** Choose Zoom In/Out, Fit Artboard in Window (⌘-0/Ctrl-0), Fit All in Window (⌘-Option-0/Ctrl-Alt-0), or Actual Size (⌘-1/Ctrl-1).

- **With the Zoom tool.** Click to zoom in one level of magnification; hold down the Option/Alt key and click to zoom out one level. You can also click-drag to define

Make it colorblind-proof

Choose View > Proof Setup > Color Blindness to see how those afflicted with the most common forms of color blindness will see your work—vital for knowing if your signs and other informational graphics will work.

The proof is in the preview

Want the best on-screen preview for your art? Illustrator allows you to preview precise anti-aliasing by choosing View > Pixel Preview mode. Choose View > Overprint Preview for the best way to view, on your screen, how overprinted inks and traps will look when professionally printed.

Zoom shortcuts while typing

Press ⌘/Ctrl with the spacebar to zoom in or ⌘-Option/Ctrl-Alt with the spacebar to zoom out. As long as you press ⌘/Ctrl first, this works even while you're typing in text-entry mode with the Type tool. (If you then let go of the spacebar, you'll have the Hand tool.)

Zippy zooming

Current magnification is displayed in the bottom-left corner of your document. Access a list of percentages (3.13% to 6400%) or Fit on Screen from the pop-up, or simply select the text and enter any percentage within the limit.

If you avoided Smart Guides in the past, try leaving them on now. Smart Guides have been greatly refined and enhanced and can be really useful. Here's what each preference setting does:

- Color sets the display color for the guides. If the guides are getting lost against your artwork, change the color here.
- Alignment Guides help you align objects and/or artboards to each other when you create or move them.
- Anchor/Path Labels let you know what part of an object you're manipulating, and its position relative to other anchors and paths.
- Measurement Labels provide a readout of changes based on the tool you're using—e.g., with the Move tool the label shows the x,y distance, while using the Rotate tool displays angle.
- Object Highlighting shows the original shape of the object below the cursor as it was before a Live Effect was applied.
- Transform Tools displays established angle lines, even if all other guides are disabled.
- Construction Guides help you establish angles as you draw to match either Preset settings or your own custom angles.

Note: *You can't align using Smart Guides if View > Snap to Grid is enabled.*

an area, and Illustrator will attempt to fill the current window with the area that you defined.

- **Use the ⌘/Ctrl keys for Zoom.** With any tool selected, use ⌘-hyphen/Ctrl-hyphen (minus sign)—think "minus to zoom out"—and ⌘+/Ctrl+ (plus sign)—think "plus to zoom in." Or, you can hold ⌘-spacebar/Ctrl-spacebar and click-drag to zoom in; add Option/Alt to zoom out.

- **Use Context-sensitive menus.** With nothing selected, Control-click (Mac) or right-mouse button (on a two-button mouse) to quickly access zoom in/out, change views, undo, and show/hide toggles for guides, rulers, and grids.

- **Navigator panel.** With the Navigator panel, you can quickly zoom in or out and change the viewing area with the help of the panel thumbnail (see Tip "The Navigator panel & views" earlier in this chapter).

Rulers, Guides, Smart Guides, and Grids

Toggle Illustrator's Show/Hide Rulers (one per document no matter how many artboards you have), or use the ⌘-R/Ctrl-R shortcut. With Rulers showing, use its Context-sensitive menu to change units of measurement. The per-document ruler units can be set in Document Setup. If you want all new documents to use a specific unit of measurement, change your preferences for Units (Preferences > Units & Display Performance).

Even though the rulers meet in the upper-left corner of the page, the location of the ruler *origin* (0,0) is in the lower-left corner of the page. To change the ruler origin, grab the upper-left corner where the rulers meet, and drag the crosshair to the desired location. The zeros of the rulers will reset to the point where you release your mouse (to reset the rulers to the default location, double-click the upper-left corner). But beware—resetting your ruler origin will realign all patterns and affect alignment of Paste in Front/Back between documents (see the *Layers & Appearances* chapter for more on Paste in Front/Back).

Multiple Artboards also have their own rulers (View > Show Artboard Rulers). Currently, artboard rulers are useful primarily to artists who need to measure device-specific pixels for output to video. You can't use them for measuring in units of your choosing or for dragging guides onto your artboard, nor can you change your units of measurement here using a Context-sensitive menu.

To create simple vertical or horizontal ruler guides, click-drag from one of the rulers into your image. A guide appears where you release your mouse. You can define guide color and style in General Preferences. Guides automatically lock after you create them. To release a guide quickly, ⌘-Shift-double-click (Mac)/Ctrl-Shift-double-click (Win) on the guide. You can lock and unlock guides with the Context-sensitive menu in Preview mode. You should note that locking or unlocking guides affects *every* open document. If you have too many guides visible in your document, simply choose View > Guides > Hide Guides. To make them visible again choose View > Guides > Show Guides. If you want to delete them all permanently, choose View > Guides > Clear Guides. This only works on guides that are on visible, unlocked layers. Hiding or locking layers retains any guides you have created. To learn how to create custom guides from objects or paths, see the "Establishing Perspective" lesson in the *Layers & Appearances* chapter.

Illustrator also has automatic grids. To view grids, select View > Show Grid, or use the Context-sensitive menu. You can adjust the color, style of line (dots or solid), and size of the grid's subdivisions from Preferences > Guides & Grid. You can also enable a snap-to grid function. Toggle Snap to Grid on and off by choosing View > Snap to Grid (see Tip "Glorious grids" at right).

IMPORTANT: *If you adjust the X and Y axes in Preferences > General > Constrain Angle, it will affect the drawn objects and transformations of your grid, as they will follow the adjusted angle when you create a new object. This works out well if you happen to be doing a complicated layout requiring alignment of objects at an angle.*

Glorious grids

Customize your grids in Illustrator. Select a grid style and color.

• View > Show Grid, use the Context-sensitive menu or ⌘-'(Mac)/ Ctrl-'(Win) (apostrophe).

• Toggle Snap to Grid on and off from the View menu or use the shortcut ⌘-Shift-'(Mac)/ Ctrl-Shift-'(Win) (apostrophe).

• Set the division and subdivision for your grid in Preferences > Guides & Grid and choose either dotted divisions or lines and the color of those lines.

• To toggle the grid display in front or in back of your artwork, check or uncheck the Grids In Back checkbox (Preferences > Guides & Grid).

• Tilt the grid on an angle by choosing Preferences > General and then changing the Constrain Angle value.

Note: *The Constrain Angle affects the angle at which objects are drawn and moved. (See the* Drawing & Coloring *chapter on how to adjust it for creating isometrics.)*

Images & files cropped!

When you place or open an image in another application or a previous version of AI, art extending beyond the artboard(s) will be cropped, unless it's a bleed set inside Illustrator. To avoid this, use the Artboard tool to expand artboard(s) to fit your artwork.

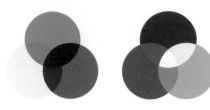

CMY Color Model   RGB Color Model

CMY (Cyan, Magenta, Yellow) **subtractive** *colors get darker when mixed; RGB (Red, Green, Blue)* **additive** *colors combine to make white.*

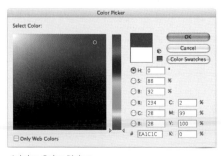

Adobe Color Picker

View Transparency Grid & Simulate Colored Paper

You can view a transparency grid in the background of your Artboard (to help you see transparency), and/or change the white of your Artboard to a color; neither the transparency grid nor simulated paper color will print.

To view the transparency grid, select View >Show Transparency Grid. You can customize the grid colors in the Transparency section of Document Setup. To change the white background of your Artboard document to a non-printing color, enable the Simulate Colored Paper option and change the top grid swatch to a color.

Hide/Show Edges

If looking at all those anchor points and colored paths distracts you from figuring out what to do with selected objects in your current window, choose View >Hide/Show Edges to toggle them on or off (or use the shortcut: ⌘-H/ Ctrl-H). Once you hide the edges, all subsequent path edges will be hidden until you show them again. Hide/ Show Edges is saved with your file.

COLOR IN ILLUSTRATOR

Consumer-level monitors, which display color in red, green, and blue lights (RGB), cannot yet match four-color CMYK (cyan, magenta, yellow, black) inks printed onto paper. Therefore, you must retrofit the current technology with partial solutions, such as calibrating your monitor.

Working in RGB or CMYK

Illustrator offers you the flexibility of working and printing in either RGB or CMYK color. This is a mixed blessing, because the printing environment cannot accurately capture vibrant RGB colors. As a result, the RGB colors are usually muddy or muted when printed. If your final artwork is going to be printed, work in CMYK!

Work in an RGB color space when creating artwork that will be displayed on-screen, or to simulate a spot color (such as a day-glo color) on your printer. (For more on working in RGB, see the *Web & Animation* chapter.)

Single color space

When you open a new document, you select a color model (or color space). Illustrator no longer allows you to work in multiple color spaces at the same time. If you work in print, always check your files to make certain they are in the appropriate color model before you output. The document's color model is always displayed next to the file name, on the title bar. You can change the document's color mode at any time by choosing File > Document Color Mode > CMYK Color or RGB Color.

Opening legacy documents (documents created with older versions of Illustrator) with objects containing mixed color spaces will invoke a warning asking you to choose a color space (RGB or CMYK). Currently, linked images are not converted to the document's color space. If you open the Document Info panel and select Linked Images, the "Type" info is misleading. For example, if you have a CMYK document with a linked RGB image, the linked image type is Transparent CMYK. The linked image has not been converted, but the image preview has been converted to CMYK. See the *Drawing & Coloring* chapter for more about working with color.

SAVING AS PDF

Although you may be used to thinking of PDFs and Illustrator files as two different animals, underneath their hides they have a lot in common. In fact, as long as you save your Illustrator file (.ai) with "Create PDF Compatible File" enabled in the Illustrator Options dialog, for all intents and purposes it *is* a PDF, and can be viewed in Adobe Reader and other PDF viewers.

However, if you want more control over the final PDF product you create, Illustrator makes it easy, letting you choose what version of PDF you'd like to save as, while providing handy PDF presets that let you quickly save PDFs with different settings for different circumstances.

To save a document as a PDF, choose File > Save or File > Save As, and choose Illustrator PDF from the Format menu. After you click Save, you'll be presented with

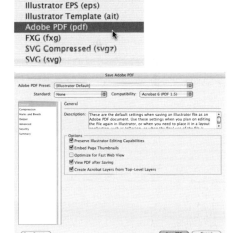

Choosing Illustrator PDF in the Format menu of the File > Save or File > Save As dialog opens the dialog with PDF options

Acrobat 4 (PDF 1.3)
Acrobat 5 (PDF 1.4)
✓ Acrobat 6 (PDF 1.5)
Acrobat 7 (PDF 1.6)
Acrobat 8 (PDF 1.7)

The Compatibility menu in the Save Adobe PDF dialog

Custom

✓ [Illustrator Default]

[High Quality Print]
[PDF/X-1a:2001]
[PDF/X-3:2002]
[PDF/X-4:2008]
[Press Quality]
[Smallest File Size]

The Preset menu in the Save Adobe PDF dialog

Verify PDF settings

When preparing a PDF file for a commercial printer or service provider, remember to check with the provider to find out what the final output resolution and other settings should be. It may be necessary to customize the settings for a particular provider, in which case you may find it helpful to create a custom preset.

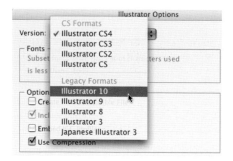

To access legacy formats, you must first choose the standard Illustrator format (.ai) from the Save or Save As dialog; in the resulting Illustrator Options dialog, then choose the desired legacy format from the Version pop-up menu

the Save Adobe PDF dialog, where you can choose from a variety of options and settings, including compatibility (PDF version), compression, printer's marks and bleeds, security settings, and more.

Always be sure that you ask your printer which format they want you to send your files in, and/or which version of PDF, if applicable, the printer prefers.

You can quickly access frequently used preset PDF settings from the Preset menu. You can create your own custom presets by choosing Custom from the menu, adjusting your settings, and then clicking the Save Preset button at the bottom of the dialog. Additionally, Illustrator ships with a number of predefined presets for experimenting. PDF settings can also be shared among different applications within the Creative Suite.

IMAGE FORMATS

You might need to open a document created in an earlier version of Illustrator (CorelDraw, and some 3D programs allow you to save images in older Illustrator formats). To open any file saved in an earlier version (known as a *legacy file*), drag it onto an Illustrator alias, or open the older formatted file from within Illustrator by choosing File > Open and selecting the document you want to open. Your document will be converted to Illustrator's current format, and [Converted] will be added to the file name if enabled in Preferences. If you want to save it in an Illustrator legacy format, you can do so by choosing File > Save As and then choosing Adobe Illustrator Document from the Format menu in the dialog. After you name your file and click Save, you'll be presented with the Illustrator Options dialog, which lets you choose from among earlier versions, as well as providing options for handling multiple artboards.

If you open legacy files containing type, you will get a dialog asking you how to handle the conversion. Since text reflow can happen should you convert, you may want to work on a copy of the file. See the *Artboards & Type* chapter for more information about working with type.

Other image formats

Illustrator supports many file formats (such as SWF, SVG, GIF, JPEG, TIFF, PICT, PCX, Pixar, and Photoshop). You can also open and edit PDF documents, and even "raw" PostScript files, directly from within Illustrator. If you place images into a document, you can choose whether these files will remain *linked* (see Tip "Links are manageable" at right) or will become *embedded* image objects (see the *Illustrator & Other Programs* chapter for specifics on embedding, and the *Web & Animation* chapter for details on Web-related formats). If you use File>Open, then images become embedded, which increases your file size. Check Adobe's Web site (www.adobe.com) for the latest information on supported formats, as well as other file format plug-ins. (For more on file format issues, see the *Illustrator & Other Programs* chapter.)

Saving in AI format and file sizes

If your file is going to be placed in another application, saving it in .ai format with PDF compatibility enabled is the most assurance you can have that other applications (and earlier versions of Illustrator) will be able to correctly interpret it, and that it will be fully editable later on. But if you know you're going to be working with the file within this version of Illustrator itself, you can significantly reduce file size, and the time it takes to save, by disabling PDF compatibility. PDF compatibility forces Illustrator to embed the PDF that, with multiple artboards, can run to a great many megabytes of data. With PDF compatibility enabled, Illustrator files sizes can easily begin to approach the typical size of other image files.

ACTIONS

Actions are a set of commands or a series of events that you can record and save as a set in the Actions panel. Once an action is recorded, you can play it back in order to automate complex or repetitive tasks (such as a placing registration marks, copying and transforming objects multiple times in an array, or deleting all unused styles).

Links are manageable

The Links panel keeps a running (and updatable) list of all images in your document, whether they are linked or embedded. The key features of this panel are:

- You can quickly find out if you are missing a link (stop sign icon on the link layer) or need to update a link (exclamation icon).
- You can replace a link, update a link, go to a link, or edit a link with the click of an icon.
- You can change a linked image into an embedded image through the pop-up menu.
- You can find out information about the link (file name, location, size, kind, date modified, and transformations made) by double-clicking on a link layer to open the Link information dialog (not all information is available for all formats).

Note: *Until the Links panel includes info on the color mode (RGB, CMYK, Grayscale, or raster images)—make sure to check your links manually!*

Smaller Illustrator files...

To keep file size small and make saving faster, PDF Compatibility can be turned off. However, if you need to place or open an Illustrator file in another application, or an earlier version of Illustrator, then you probably need PDF compatibility enabled.

Select the action in the Actions panel and activate it by clicking the Play icon at the bottom of the panel, by choosing Play from the pop-up menu, or by assigning the action to a keyboard "F key" (function key) so you can play the action with a keystroke. You can select actions that include other actions, or play a single command within an action. To exclude a command from playing within an action, disable the checkbox to the left of the command. Load action sets using the pop-up menu.

Begin a new action by clicking the Create New Set icon, or by targeting a set in the Actions panel. Name the action set and click OK. With the new set selected, click the Create New Action icon, name the action, and click Record. Use the panel menu to start and stop while recording. When you've finished recording, you'll need to save the action file by selecting the action set and choosing Save Actions from the pop-up menu.

Keep in mind that not all commands or tools are recordable. However, you may be able to insert a menu item or select an object using the Actions menu.

Although many of the practical aspects of working with Scripting is technically beyond the scope of this book, you can find samples scripts and documentations in the Adobe Illustrator CS4 > Scripting folder. For even more information, visit http://www.adobe.com/devnet/illustrator/scripting/.

THE NEW HELP
A connected community

Beginning with CS4, Adobe is no longer placing more than a bare bones Help file on your hard drive. Instead, with a live internet connection, clicking on Help or pressing F1 while in Illustrator will take you to Adobe's Community Support site. You can also type a Search term into the Search field on the Application bar. In this case, instead of arriving at the Community Support Home page first, you will be taken directly to the Search Community Support page with a long list of responses to your query, drawn from all over the web.

The Community Support site is also the location to find the complete Help manual in PDF format, available for download. Having the manual on your hard drive to search from within Acrobat can save time when you only need to refresh your memory about how a tool or command works. But if you want a more comprehensive understanding of a feature or technique, the Community Support site will link you to videos, articles, and designer interviews both on Adobe's own web site, and throughout the internet. You can choose to search for responses only on the Adobe site itself, if you prefer, and you can reach Adobe support through the Community Support site.

Users are also encouraged to add their own knowledge to the Community, turning the Help feature into a wiki-style, growing knowledge base.

ADOBE BRIDGE

Adobe's Creative Suite includes a file management application called Adobe Bridge. Bridge can thumbnail or "play" many files, including multi-page PDFs, movies, 3D, and audio files. The Preview panel lets you view every artboard in a document. It's a bridge both in the sense of a command center *and* a link between different places on any of your mounted drives or disks. You can view, search, add metadata to, sort, manage, process, and share files from within Bridge, interfacing between the various Creative Suite applications. You can also run Live Trace from the Tools menu on images selected in Bridge, or open libraries from the Context-sensitive menu with the item "Open As AI Library."

Select an Illustrator file in Bridge with the Metadata tab active, and you can view color plates and spot color, fonts, and all the swatches saved with the file, as well as view or add important contact and copyright information, and even a file description.

Bridge has its own link icon on the Application Bar. You can choose File > Browse in Bridge, or use the shortcut ⌘-Option-O/Ctrl-Alt-O. Illustrator also supports drag-and-drop from Bridge into Illustrator.

The Adobe Community Support site offers to install their own search engine in your browser's Search Engine list, along with Google, Yahoo, and other popular search engines

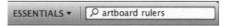

The Search field on the far right of the Application Bar sends your query straight to Adobe's Community Support site

A variety of workspaces (here, Filmstrip) makes it easy to view files the way you want to, even viewing multiple artboards a page at a time

A wealth of metadata is available for a selected Illustrator file, including fonts, color plates, document swatches, copyright, and more

2 The Zen of Illustrator

Zen: *"Seeking enlightenment through introspection and intuition rather than scripture."* *

You're comfortable with the basic operations of your computer. You've gone through some of the video tutorials on adobe.com/support/illustrator/. You've logged enough hours using Illustrator to be familiar with how each tool (theoretically) functions. You might even understand how to make Bézier curves. Now what? How do you take all this knowledge and turn it into a mastery of the medium?

As with learning any new artistic medium (such as engraving, watercolor, or airbrush), learning to manipulate the tools is just the beginning. Thinking and seeing in that medium is what really makes those tools part of your creative arsenal. Before you can determine the best way to construct an image, you have to be able to envision at least some of the possibilities. The first key to mastering Illustrator is to understand that Illustrator's greatest strength comes not from its many tools and functions but from its extreme flexibility in terms of how you construct images. The first part of this chapter, therefore, introduces you to a variety of approaches and techniques for creating and transforming objects.

Once you've got yourself "thinking in Illustrator," you can begin to *visualize* how to achieve the final results. What is the simplest and most elegant way to construct an image? Which tools will you use? Then, once you've begun, allow yourself the flexibility to change course and try something else. Be willing to say to yourself: How else can I get the results that I want?

The second key to mastering Illustrator (or any new medium) is perfecting your hand/eye coordination. In Illustrator, this translates into being proficient enough with the "power-keys" to gain instant access to tools and functions by using the keyboard. With both eyes on the monitor, one hand on the mouse, and the other hand on the keyboard, an experienced Illustrator user can create and manipulate objects in a fraction of the time required otherwise. You'll be able to change tools without frequent trips back to the Toolbox. The second part of this chapter helps you to learn the "finger dance" necessary to become a truly adept power-user.

The ability to harness the full power of Illustrator's basic tools and functions will ultimately make you a true master of Adobe Illustrator. Treat this chapter like meditation. Take it in small doses if necessary. Be mindful that the purpose of these exercises is to open your mind to possibilities, not to force memorization. When you can conceptualize a number of different ways to create an image, then the hundreds of hints, tips, tricks, and techniques found elsewhere in this book can serve as a jumping-off point for further exploration. If you take the time to explore and absorb this chapter, you should begin to experience what I call the "Zen of Illustrator." This magical program, at first cryptic and counterintuitive, can help you achieve creative results not possible in any other medium.

*Adapted from *Webster's New World Dictionary of the English Language*

Building Houses

Sequential Object Construction Exercises

Overview: *Explore different approaches to constructing the same object with Illustrator's basic construction tools.*

1

2

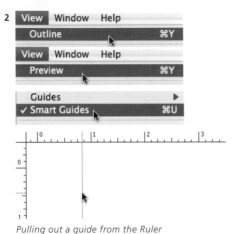

Pulling out a guide from the Ruler

3

4

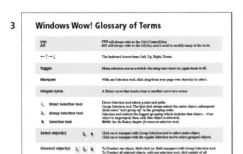

Hold down the Shift key to constrain movement to horizontal/vertical direction. For more modifier key help, see the end of this chapter for the "Finger Dance" lesson.

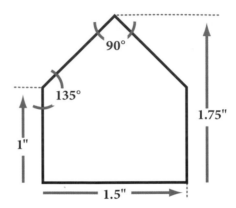

This sequence of exercises explores different ways to construct the same simple object—a house. The purpose of these exercises is to introduce you to the flexibility of Illustrator's object construction, so don't worry if some exercises seem less efficient than others.

So you can more easily follow along, set Units > General to Inches (from Preferences > Units & Display Performance). Also, please read through all of the recommendations below.

1 Use the zenhouse.ai file as a guide. Start with the file zenhouse.ai (copy it to your hard drive from the *Wow! CD* in the Chapter 2 folder) as a guide when needed.

2 Work in Outline mode, with Smart Guides and Show Rulers (View menu). Outline mode eliminates distractions like fills and strokes while it displays centers of geometric objects (marked by "×"). Smart Guides will help you align, and Rulers allow you to "pull out" guides.

3 Read through the *Wow! Glossary.* Please make sure to read *How to use this book* and the *Glossary* pull-out card.

4 Use "modifier" keys. These exercises use Shift and Option (Opt) or Alt keys, which you must hold down until *after* you release your mouse button. If you make a mistake, choose Undo and try again. Some functions are also accessible from the Context-sensitive menu. Try keyboard shortcuts for frequently-used menu commands.

Exercise #1:

Use Add Anchor Point tool

1

1 Open zenhouse.ai and create a rectangle and a vertical guide. Open zenhouse.ai. On the left corner where the side meets the peak, click to create a rectangle 1.5" x 1". Drag out a vertical guide and snap it to the center.

2

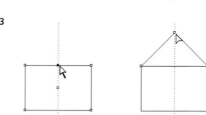

2 Add an anchor point on the top. With the Add Anchor Point tool, click on the top segment over the center guide.

3

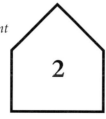

3 Drag the new point up. Use the Direct Selection tool to grab the new point and drag it up into position using the zenhouse as a guide.

Exercise #2:

Make an extra point

2

1

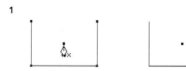

1 Create a rectangle, delete the top path, and place a center point. Create a wide rectangle (1.5" x 1"). With the Direct Selection tool, drag to marquee-select part of the top path, and press Delete/Backspace. With the Pen tool, place a point on top of the rectangle center point.

2

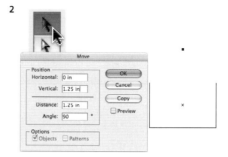

2 Move the point up. Double-click on a selection tool in the Toolbox to open the Move dialog, and enter a 1.25" vertical distance to move the point up.

3

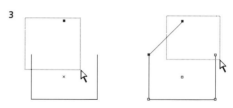

3 Select and join the point to each side. Use the Direct Selection tool to select the left two points and Join (Object > Path > Join, or ⌘-J/Ctrl-J) them to the top point. Repeat with the right two points.

1

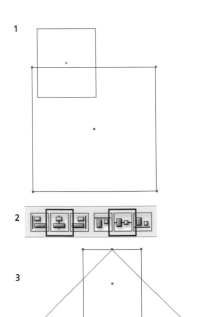

2

3

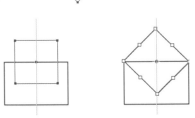

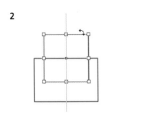

Exercise #3:
*Make two rectangles,
Rotate one, Align,
apply Intersect*

1 Make two rectangles and rotate the second. Click with the Rectangle tool to create a rectangle 1.5" x 1.75". Then click anywhere with the Rectangle tool to create a second rectangle, 3.1795" x 3.1795", and while it's selected, double-click the Rotate tool and specify 45°.

2 Align the rectangles. Select the two rectangles and, in the Control panel, click the vertical center and top Align icons. Then set the fill to white and the stroke to black.

3 Apply the Intersect Pathfinder. Open the Pathfinder panel (Window menu) and, in the Shape Mode section, click Intersect to leave only the intersected house shape.

Exercise #4:
*Using custom
guides, Rotate
and Add*

1

2

3

1 Make two rectangles. Create a rectangle (1.5" x 1"), then drag out a vertical guide, snapping it to the center. Hold Option/Alt, and where the center guide intersects the top segment, click with the Rectangle tool. Enter 1.05" x 1.05".

2 Rotate the square. With the Selection tool, move your cursor along the square until you see a Rotate icon. Hold the Shift key and drag until the square pops into position.

3 Select and Unite. Choose Select > Select All (⌘-A/ Ctrl-A). Then in the Pathfinder panel (Window menu), click Unite to combine both rectangles into one object.

Exercise #5:

Use Add Anchor Points in a three-sided polygon

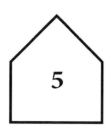

1 Create a three-sided polygon. With the Polygon tool selected (hidden under the Rectangle), click once, then enter 3 Sides and a 1.299" Radius.

2 Use the Add Anchor Points command. With the polygon object still selected, choose Object > Path > Add Anchor Points.

3 Average the two left points, then Average the two right points. Direct-Select the two left points and Average them along the vertical axis (Context-sensitive: Average, or Object > Path > Average), then repeat for the two right points.

4 Delete the bottom point. With the Delete Anchor Point tool, click on the bottom point to delete it.

5 Move the top point down. Use the Direct Selection tool to select the top point, then double-click on the Direct Selection tool (in the Toolbox) to open the Move dialog and enter –.186" vertical distance, 90° for angle.

6 Slide in the sides toward the center. Use the Direct Selection tool to click on the right side of the house and drag it toward the center until the roofline looks smooth (hold down your Shift key to constrain the drag horizontally). Repeat for the left side of the house. Alternatively, select the right side and use the ← key on your keyboard to nudge the right side toward the center until the roofline looks smooth. Then, click on the left side to select it, and use the → key to nudge it toward the center. (If necessary, change your Keyboard Increment setting in the Preferences > General dialog.)

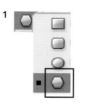
1

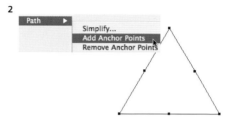

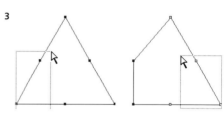

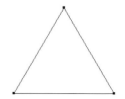

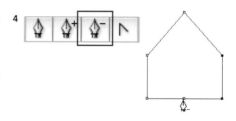

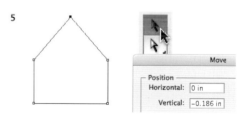

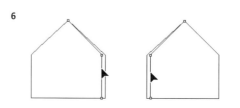

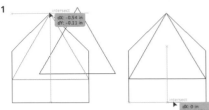

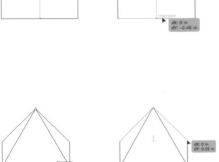

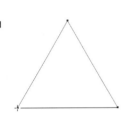

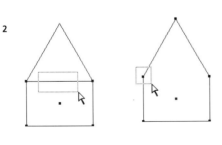

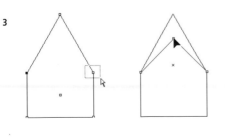

Exercise #6:
*Cut a path and
Paste in Front*

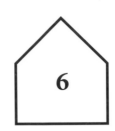

1 Move the bottom of a triangle. In the zenhouse.ai file, click with the Polygon tool and enter 3 Sides and a .866" Radius. With the Direct Selection tool, align the top point with the house peak. Next, select and Cut the bottom path, choose Edit > Paste in Front (⌘-F/Ctrl-F), then grab this path and Shift-drag it into position.

2 Create the sides and move middle points into place. Direct-Select the two right points and join, then repeat for the two left points. Select the two middle points, and grab one to drag *both* up into position.

Exercise #7:
Join two objects

1 Make two objects. Click once with the Polygon tool, enter 3 Sides and a .866" Radius. Zoom in on the lower left corner and, with the Rectangle tool, click exactly on the lower left anchor point. Set the rectangle to 1.5" x 1".

2 Delete the middle lines and join the corners. Direct-Select marquee the middle bisecting lines and delete. Select the upper-left corner points and Average-Join by either Averaging, and then Joining the points (both from the Object > Path menu) or by pressing ⌘-Shift-Option-J/ Ctrl-Shift-Alt-J to average and join simultaneously. Direct-Select, then Average-Join the upper right points.

3 Drag the top point down. Grab the top point, hold the Shift key, and drag it into position.

Exercise #8:

Use Add Anchor Points, then Average-Join

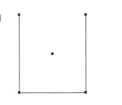

1 **Using zenhouse.ai, make a rectangle, delete the top path, add anchor points, remove the bottom point.** Create a tall rectangle (1.5" x 1.75") and delete the top path. Choose Add Anchor Points (Object > Path), and use the Delete Anchor Point tool to remove the bottom point.

2 **Select and Average-Join the top points and move middles into position.** Direct-Select the top two points and Average-Join (see Exercise #7, step 2). Then Direct-Select the middle points, grab one, and Shift-drag them both into position on the zenhouse.

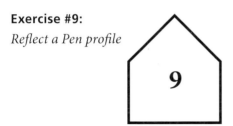

Exercise #9:

Reflect a Pen profile

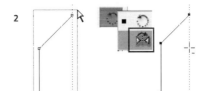

1 **Create a house profile.** Drag out a vertical guide, then reset the ruler origin on the guide. To draw the profile, use the Pen tool to click on the guide at the ruler zero point, hold down Shift (to constrain your lines to 45° angles) and click to place the corner (.75" down and .75" to the left) and the bottom (1" down).

2 **Reflect a copy of the profile.** Select all three points of the house profile. With the Reflect tool, Option/Alt-click on the guide line. Enter an angle of 90° and click Copy.

3 **Join the two profiles.** Direct-Select and Join the bottom two points. Then Direct-Select the top two points and Average-Join (using ⌘-Shift-Option-J/Ctrl-Shift-Alt-J, or Average and then Join from the Object > Path menu).

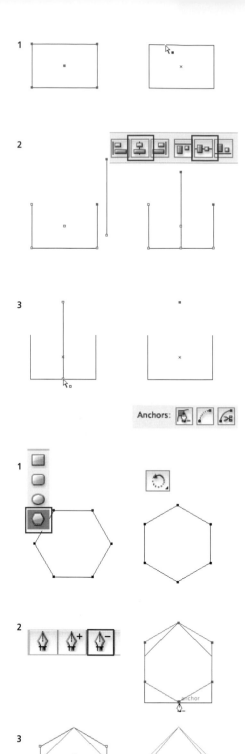

Exercise #10:

*Use the Line tool
and Align*

1 Create a Rectangle. With the Rectangle tool, click on your Artboard and specify 1.5" x 1". Choose Select >Deselect, then click the top edge of the rectangle and Delete.

2 Create and align the peak. With the Line tool, click anywhere and specify a 1.75" Length and 90° Angle. Select both objects and, in the Control panel, click the vertical center and bottom Align icons, then Deselect.

3 Delete the bottom point and form the peak. Using Direct Selection, select the bottom line point and Delete. Then marquee the top point and one of the sides. In the Control panel, click the middle Anchors button to Connect the points. Repeat to form the other peak.

Exercise #11

*Make a six-sided
polygon*

1 Create a six-sided polygon using zenhouse.ai. Open zenhouse.ai. Click with the Polygon tool and enter 6 Sides and a .866" Radius. Then double-click the Rotate tool and enter 30°. Align the peak of this object with the zenhouse.

2 Delete the bottom point. With the Delete Anchor Point tool, click on the bottom point to delete it.

3 Move pairs of points. Use the Direct Selection tool to select the bottom two points. Grab one of the points and Shift-drag in a vertical line into position. Direct-Select, grab and Shift-drag the middle two points into position.

Exercise #12:

With Smart Guides, Rotate and make a Live Paint object

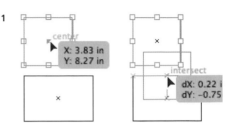

1 Make two rectangles. Enable View >Smart Guides. Create one rectangle 1.5" x 1", and one 1.05" x 1.05". Grab the center point of the square and drag it toward the top center of the wide rectangle until you see the word "intersect" and a vertical line drawn from the rectangle's center to the top line.

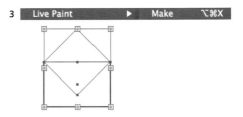

2 Rotate the square. With the square selected, double-click the Rotate tool and specify 45°.

3 Make a Live Paint object. Select both objects and choose Object >Live Paint >Make.

4 Use the Live Paint Bucket to "paint out" the interior lines. Switch to Preview mode (View menu) and set the fill to White, stroke to None. Double-click the Live Paint Bucket and, in Options, disable Paint Fills and enable Paint Strokes, and click OK. Choose None for stroke, then "paint" the interior triangular lines with None.

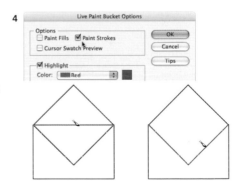

5 If you want to be able to easily paint the interior of the house as one object, delete the interior lines. Return to Outline mode (View menu). Notice that when you make a Live Paint object, it still maintains the separate shapes that made the original objects—even if you color the strokes separately. However, you *can* blend objects of the same style, like the white-filled house objects, into one object by eliminating the dividing lines.

So that the entire interior of the house operates as if it is one fill, you need to delete the triangular lines that divide the interior. Using the Direct Selection tool, marquee the interior lines and Delete. Switch back to Preview mode to see that the house is still intact.

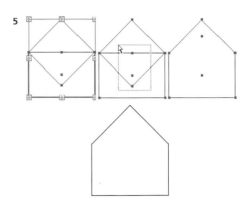

Of Grids & Lines

Four Ways to Create a Grid of Squares

Overview: *Find different ways to construct the same simple grid.*

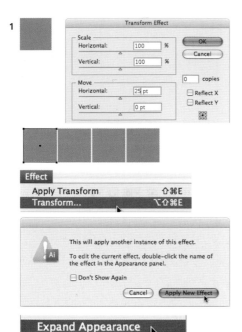

Make one square, apply Effect > Distort & Transform > Transform and specify a Move of 25 pt for Horizontal and 3 Copies, then Effect > Transform to specify a move of 25 pt for Vertical and 3 Copies; for editable squares, choose Object > Expand Appearance

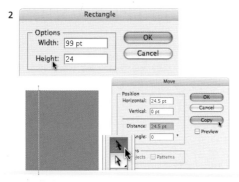

Clicking on the word Height or Width in a dialog will copy the other value; after making a vertical line and using Move to make a copy of it

There's rarely only one right way to create anything. Give different Illustrator experts a problem to solve, and they'll come up with different solutions. This clean logo designed by Jack Tom for Craik Consulting, Inc. provides a great opportunity to explore different ways to create a simple grid of blue squares separated by white lines.

Everybody's mind works differently, and the most obvious solutions to you might seem innovative to someone else. If design changes require you to rethink your initial approach (for instance, if the client wants white areas of a logo to be holes), try to construct it another way.

1 Making separate small squares. With the Rectangle tool, click on your page and specify a 24 pt by 24 pt square. While it's still selected, choose a blue color fill from the Swatches panel and set the Stroke to None. To create the horizontal row choose Effects > Distort & Transform > Transform. Specify a Move of 25 pt for Horizontal, and 3 for Copies and click OK. To fill out the grid vertically, again choose the Transform near the top of the Effects menu and click "Apply New Effect" when you see the warning. This time specify a Move of –25 pt for Vertical and 3 for Copies. If later you want to edit the rectangles separately, you can expand the live effect with Object > Expand Appearance.

2 Making one large rectangle with white lines on top.
This method is a bit longer than the others, but it also allows for more design flexibility. In constructing his actual logo, Jack Tom included white lines over one large blue square, so he could control exactly how and where each line interacted with the logo "figure." He deleted part of a line below the large, white oval, and he nudged other lines slightly, horizontally or vertically.

To make a large square, choose a blue fill, click with the Rectangle tool and specify 99 pt for Width and click the word Height to automatically fill in the same number as Width (99 pt). Hold the Shift key and draw a vertical line that starts above and extends below your rectangle, and set the Fill to None and the Stroke to White. To make a second line, double-click a selection tool in the Toolbox, and, in the Move dialog, enter 25 pt for Horizontal, 0 for Vertical, and click Copy. Make the third line by pressing ⌘-D/Ctrl-D (which is Transform Again). For the cross lines, select your three lines, Group (⌘-G/Ctrl-G), double-click the Rotate tool, enter 90° and click Copy. To align the lines to the square, Select All (⌘-A/Ctrl-A), click the square (to designate the square as the object others align to) and, in the Control panel, click both the horizontal and vertical center Align icons.

3 Splitting the square using a grid. Another way to create this particular grid is to choose a blue fill and click with the Rectangle tool and specify 99 pt Width and Height. Now choose Object >Path >Split Into Grid and specify 4 rows, 4 columns; ignore the height and width but enter 1 pt for each Gutter.

4 Using the Rectangular Grid tool. For this last simple version, set your Stroke to 1 pt White and select a blue Fill. Choose the Rectangular Grid tool (from the Line tool pop-up), click on the Artboard and specify 100 pt for both Width and Height. Enter 3 for each of the divider fields, and be sure to enable both "Use Outside Rectangle As Frame" and "Fill Grid," and click OK.

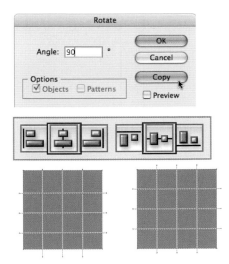

After creating the three vertical lines, using Rotate to make the horizontal copies, and aligning lines with the rectangle

Choosing Split Into Grid and specifying the parameters in the dialog

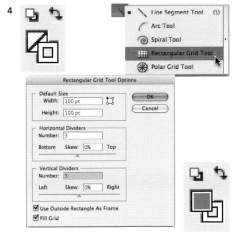

Using the Rectangular Grid tool

Zen Scaling *(with the Scale tool)*

Note: Use the Shift key to constrain proportions. **Zen Scaling** *practice is also on the* **Wow! CD**.

1 Scaling proportionally toward the top Click at the top, grab lower-right (LR), drag up

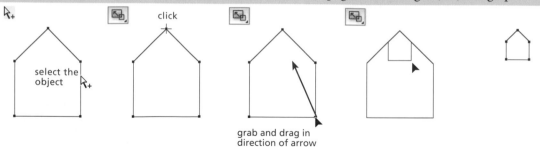

select the object

click

grab and drag in direction of arrow

2 Scaling horizontally toward the center Click at the top, grab LR, drag inward

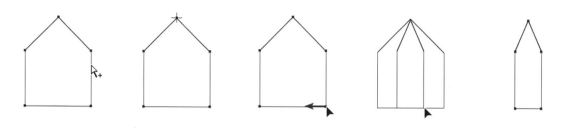

3 Scaling vertically toward the top Click at the top, grab LR, drag straight up

4 Scaling vertically and flipping the object Click at the top, grab LR, drag straight up

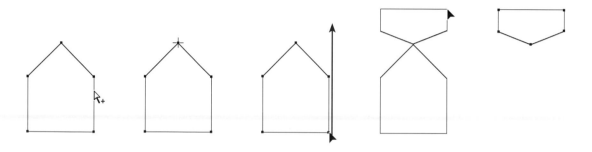

Zen Scaling *(with the Scale tool, continued)*

Note: *Use the Shift key to constrain proportions.* ***Zen Scaling*** *practice is also on the* ***Wow! CD.***

5 Scaling proportionally toward lower-left (LL) Click LL, grab upper-right (UR), drag to LL

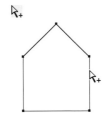 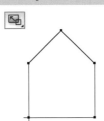  

6 Scaling horizontally to the left side Click LL, grab lower-right (LR), drag to left

   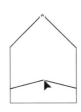

7 Scaling vertically toward the bottom Click center bottom, grab top, drag down

   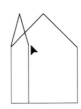 

8 Scaling proportionally toward the center Click the center, grab corner, drag to center

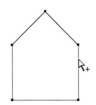  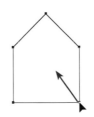 

Or, to scale about the center, use the Scale tool to click-drag outside the object toward the center

Zen Rotation *(with the Rotate tool)* ↻

Note: *Use the Shift key to constrain movement.* ***Zen Rotation*** *practice is also on the* ***Wow! CD***.

1 Rotating around the center Click in the center, then grab lower-right (LR) and drag

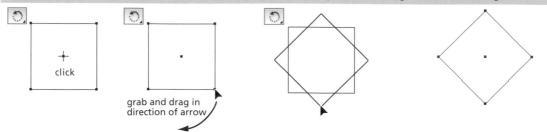

click

grab and drag in
direction of arrow

Or, to rotate about the center, use the Rotate tool to click-drag outside the object toward the center

2 Rotating from a corner Click in the upper left corner, then grab LR and drag

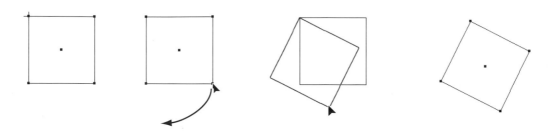

3 Rotating from outside Click above the left corner, then grab LR and drag

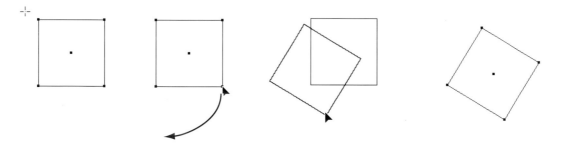

4 Rotating part of a path Marquee points with the Direct Selection tool, then use Rotate tool

Marquee the forearm with Direct Selection tool   With the Rotate tool, click on the elbow, grab the hand and drag it around

Creating a Simple Object Using the Basic Tools

Key: *Click where you see a RED cross, grab with the* GRAY *arrow and drag toward* BLACK *arrow.*

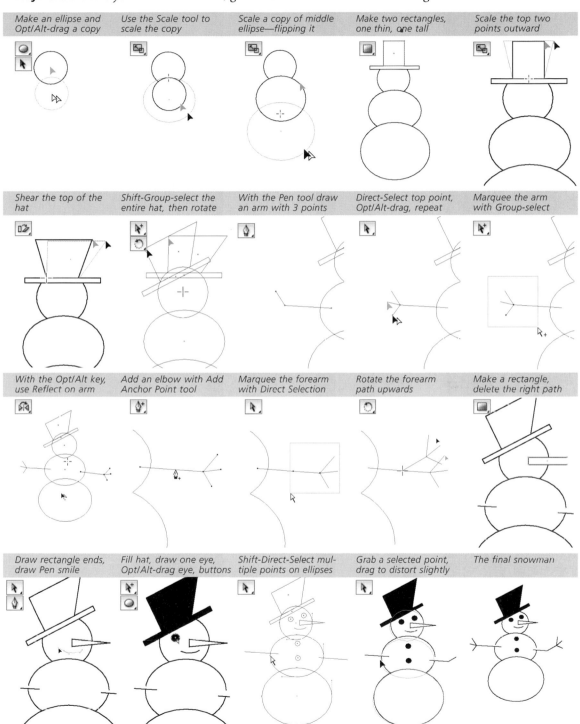

Make an ellipse and Opt/Alt-drag a copy	Use the Scale tool to scale the copy	Scale a copy of middle ellipse—flipping it	Make two rectangles, one thin, one tall	Scale the top two points outward
Shear the top of the hat	Shift-Group-select the entire hat, then rotate	With the Pen tool draw an arm with 3 points	Direct-Select top point, Opt/Alt-drag, repeat	Marquee the arm with Group-select
With the Opt/Alt key, use Reflect on arm	Add an elbow with Add Anchor Point tool	Marquee the forearm with Direct Selection	Rotate the forearm path upwards	Make a rectangle, delete the right path
Draw rectangle ends, draw Pen smile	Fill hat, draw one eye, Opt/Alt-drag eye, buttons	Shift-Direct-Select multiple points on ellipses	Grab a selected point, drag to distort slightly	The final snowman

A Finger Dance

Turbo-charge with Illustrator's Power-keys

Overview: *Save hours of production time by mastering the finger dance of Illustrator's power-keys.*

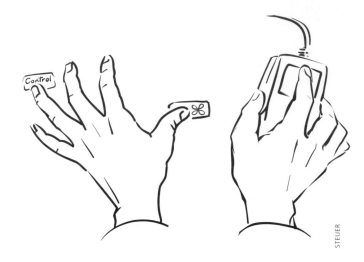

STEUER

Find a summary of Finger Dance power-keys on the pull-out quick reference card

If you are using the mouse to choose your selection tools from the Toolbox, you need this lesson. With some time and patience, you'll be able to free up your mouse so that practically the only thing you do with it is draw. Your other hand will learn to dance around the keyboard accessing all of your selection tools, modifying your creation and transformation tools, using your Zoom and Hand tools and, last but not least, providing instant Undo and Redo.

This "Finger Dance" is probably the most difficult aspect of Illustrator to master. Go through these lessons in order, but don't expect to get through them in one or even two sittings. When you make a mistake, use Undo (⌘-Z/Ctrl-Z). Try a couple of exercises, then go back to your own work, incorporating what you've just learned. When you begin to get frustrated, take a break. Later—hours, days, or weeks later—try another lesson. And don't forget to breathe.

Rule #1: Always keep one finger on the ⌘/Ctrl key.
Even when you're using a new tablet with keyboard characters, in most cases, the hand you are not drawing with should be resting on the actual keyboard, with a finger (or thumb) on the ⌘/Ctrl key. This position will make that all-important Undo (⌘-Z/Ctrl-Z) instantly accessible.

Rule #2: Undo if you make a mistake. This is so crucial an aspect of working in the computer environment that I am willing to be redundant. If there is only one key combination that you memorize, make it Undo (⌘-Z/Ctrl-Z).

Rule #3: The ⌘/Ctrl key turns your cursor into the last-used selection tool. In Illustrator, the ⌘/Ctrl key does a lot more than merely provide you with easy access to Undo. The ⌘/Ctrl key will convert any tool into the selection arrow that you last used. In the exercises that follow, you'll soon discover that the most flexible selection arrow is the Direct Selection tool.

Rule #4: Watch your cursor. If you learn to watch your cursor, you'll be able to prevent most errors before they happen. And if you don't (for instance, if you drag a copy of an object by mistake), use Undo and try again.

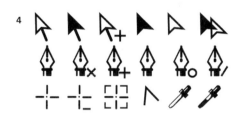

Rule #5: Pay careful attention to *when* you hold down each key. Most of the modifier keys operate differently depending on *when* you hold each key down. If you obey Rule #4 and watch your cursor, you'll notice what the key you are holding does.

Rule #6: Hold down the key(s) until after you let go of your mouse button. In order for your modifier key to actually modify your action, you *must* keep your key down until *after* you let go of your mouse button.

Rule #7: Work in Outline mode. When you are constructing or manipulating objects, get into the habit of working in Outline mode. Of course, if you are designing the colors in your image, you'll need to work in Preview, but while you're learning how to use the power-keys, you'll generally find it much quicker and easier if you are in Outline mode. Use the View menu, or ⌘-Y/Ctrl-Y to toggle between Preview (the default) and Outline modes.

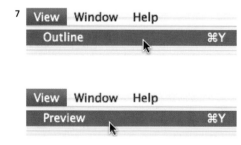

Before you begin this sequence of exercises, choose the Direct Selection tool,
then select the Rectangle tool and drag to create a rectangle.

1 Finger Dance Grabbing a selected object and moving it

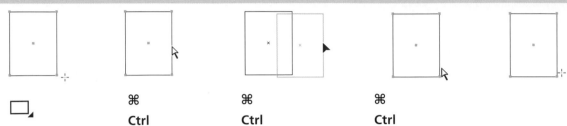

	⌘	⌘	⌘	
	Ctrl	Ctrl	Ctrl	

2 Finger Dance Deselecting an object, selecting a path and moving it

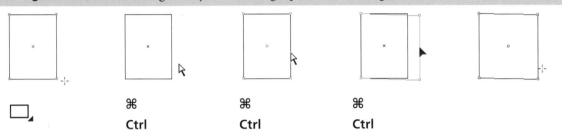

	⌘	⌘	⌘	
	Ctrl	Ctrl	Ctrl	

3 Finger Dance Moving a selected object horizontally

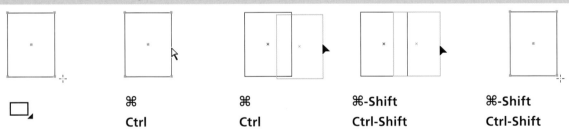

	⌘	⌘	⌘-Shift	⌘-Shift
	Ctrl	Ctrl	Ctrl-Shift	Ctrl-Shift

4 Finger Dance Deselecting an object, selecting a path, and moving it horizontally

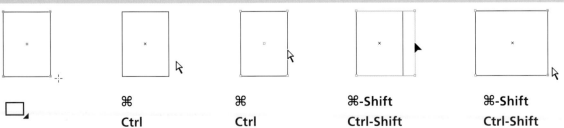

	⌘	⌘	⌘-Shift	⌘-Shift
	Ctrl	Ctrl	Ctrl-Shift	Ctrl-Shift

Before you begin this sequence of exercises, choose the Direct Selection tool, then select the Rectangle tool and drag to create a rectangle.

5 Finger Dance Moving a copy of a selected object

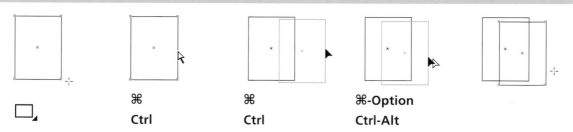

⌘	⌘	⌘-Option
Ctrl	Ctrl	Ctrl-Alt

6 Finger Dance Deselecting an object, moving a copy of a path

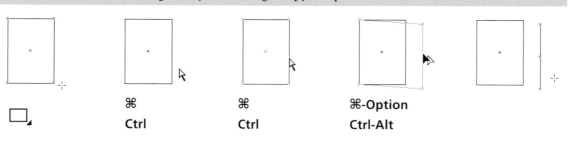

⌘	⌘	⌘-Option
Ctrl	Ctrl	Ctrl-Alt

7 Finger Dance Moving a copy of a selected object horizontally

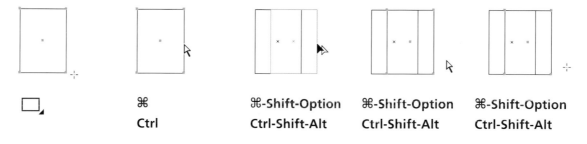

⌘	⌘-Shift-Option	⌘-Shift-Option	⌘-Shift-Option
Ctrl	Ctrl-Shift-Alt	Ctrl-Shift-Alt	Ctrl-Shift-Alt

8 Finger Dance Deselecting, moving a copy of a path horizontally

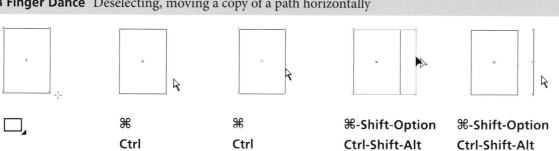

⌘	⌘	⌘-Shift-Option	⌘-Shift-Option
Ctrl	Ctrl	Ctrl-Shift-Alt	Ctrl-Shift-Alt

Before you begin this sequence of exercises, choose the Direct Selection tool,
then select the Rectangle tool and drag to create a rectangle.

9 Finger Dance Deselecting, Group-selecting, moving a copy

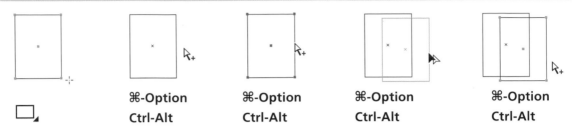

	⌘-Option	⌘-Option	⌘-Option	⌘-Option
	Ctrl-Alt	Ctrl-Alt	Ctrl-Alt	Ctrl-Alt

10 Finger Dance Group-selecting, moving an object horizontally

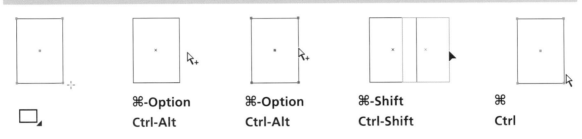

	⌘-Option	⌘-Option	⌘-Shift	⌘
	Ctrl-Alt	Ctrl-Alt	Ctrl-Shift	Ctrl

11 Finger Dance Moving copies horizontally, adding selections

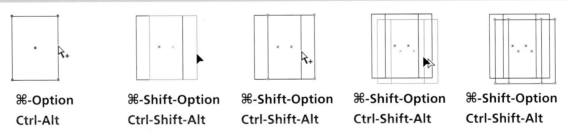

⌘-Option	⌘-Shift-Option	⌘-Shift-Option	⌘-Shift-Option	⌘-Shift-Option
Ctrl-Alt	Ctrl-Shift-Alt	Ctrl-Shift-Alt	Ctrl-Shift-Alt	Ctrl-Shift-Alt

12 Finger Dance Moving a copy, adding a selection, moving

⌘-Option	⌘-Option	⌘-Shift-Option	⌘
Ctrl-Alt	Ctrl-Alt	Ctrl-Shift-Alt	Ctrl

ZEN OF THE PEN LESSONS

*To help you learn to use the Pen tool, see these lessons in the Zen folder on the **WOW! CD***

---

1 **click:** with the **Pen** tool for no handles (straight lines)

IMPORTANT: **click** the **Pen** tool in the toolbox to end object

2 **Shift-click:** with the **Pen** tool for vertical, horizontal or 45° straight lines

IMPORTANT: **click** the **Pen** tool in the toolbox to end object

3

4 Remember to reselect the **Pen** tool to start a new object

IMPORTANT: **click** the **Pen** tool in the toolbox to end object

5 With the **Pen** tool, **click-drag** to place an anchor point and pull out direction handles.

click to place an **Anchor point** and **drag** in the direction of the arrow

IMPORTANT: **click** the **Pen** tool in the toolbox to end object

6 As Kathleen Tinkel says "Watch how the Bézier lines follow the gesture of the curve."

7 IMPORTANT: **Click** the **Pen** tool in the toolbox to end object

8

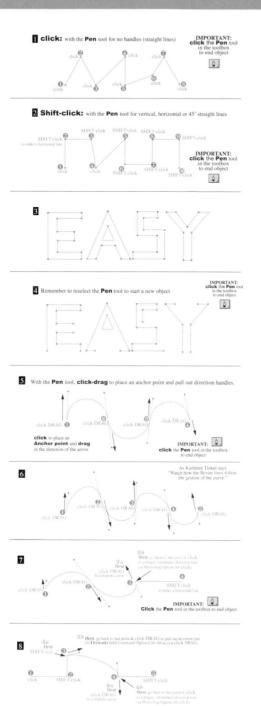

9 Use the **Direct-selection** tool to click on the curve so you can adjust the direction handles until the curves fit the template.

10 **click-drag:** To place anchor points and pull out direction handles.

HINT: Remember to make the general shape FIRST, then go back and adjust the curves.

IMPORTANT: When curves don't fit as you go, you'll have to adjust your curves with the **Direct-selection** tool after you are done with the **Pen** tool (remember to deselect first, then click to see handles).

11 **Click-DRAG** to draw curves. **Click** the **Pen** tool to end object. Use the Direct-selection tool to edit the curves.

Observe how the length and angle of each direction line echoes the gestures of the curves.

not easy

Note: If you're having trouble, use the Layers panel to view Bézier Lines

12 To create Hinged Curves use the **Pen** tool to **click-DRAG** the first curve, then without releasing the mouse button hold the **Option** key (Mac) or **Alt** key (Win) to pull the curve handle in the new direction. Release the mouse button and **click-DRAG** the next curve point.

IMPORTANT: To close an object with a hinged curve, hold down the **Option** (Mac) or **Alt** (Win) key while you **click-DRAG** on the first point

13 Using the Pen tool, trace the maze. Zoom in when necessary.

Start →

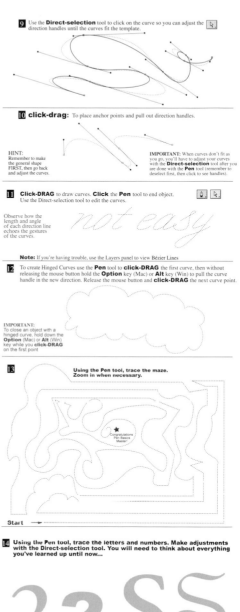

14 Using the Pen tool, trace the letters and numbers. Make adjustments with the Direct-selection tool. You will need to think about everything you've learned up until now...

22 SS

There are many options for placing anchor points, just try to place as few as possible for the most fluid curves. Zoom in to work more accurately. If you work at zoom levels of 800% or higher, you'll have to learn how to add points, work in Outline mode (also called Keyline or Artwork), and learn to edit as you draw.

Note: If you want to see two hand-traced versions, use the Layers palette to view the Bézier tracings layers.

3

An open path shown stroked (left), filled and stroked (center), and filled only (right); note that the fill is applied as if a straight line connected the two endpoints

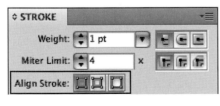

Swapping fill and stroke

When you press the X key by itself, it toggles the Stroke or Fill box to *active* (in front of the other) on the Tools and Color panels. If you press Shift-X it swaps the actual *attributes* or contents of the Stroke and Fill boxes. For example, if you start with a white fill and a black stroke, you will have a black fill and a white stroke after you press Shift-X. **Note:** *Because gradients are not allowed on strokes, Shift-X will not work when the current fill is a gradient.*

The Align Stroke buttons in the Stroke panel (Center, Inside, Outside)

Drawing & Coloring

Illustrator's drawing and coloring tools and panels are robust and rich, yet straightforward and easy to learn. Once you've got these fundamentals under your belt, you'll be ready to move on to the more advanced techniques in later chapters.

STROKE AND FILL

Every object you draw in Illustrator has two components that can be styled—*stroke* and *fill*. *Fill* is what goes inside of a path. A fill can be a color, a gradient, or a pattern, or even a fill of None (which means no fill of any kind). When you fill an open path (where the endpoints aren't connected), the fill is applied as if the two endpoints were connected by a straight line (even though they're not).

Stroke refers to the "outline" of your drawn object. So the fill is the space enclosed by a path, and that path can be stroked to make it look any way you want. You do this by assigning attributes to the path, including weight (how thick or thin it looks), line style (whether the line is solid or dashed), and the styles of line joins and line caps. You can also assign your path a stroke of None, in which case it won't have a visible stroke at all. (Dashed lines, joins, and caps are covered later in this chapter introduction.)

Control whether a stroke on a closed path aligns with the center, inside, or outside of a path by clicking the appropriate Align Stroke button in the Stroke panel. The Align Stroke to Center, Inside, and Outside buttons are only available with a selected, closed, stroked-path.

The many ways to fill or stroke an object

Of the numerous ways to set the fill or stroke for your object, perhaps the most obvious is to use the bottom of the Tools panel. However, you can also use the Control panel, the Appearance panel, the Swatches panel, and the Color and Color Guide panels. You can even use the keyboard: the D key resets to the default Black stroke/ White fill, the X key toggles the focus between stroke and fill, and the "/" key sets the stroke, or fill, to None.

The Appearance panel is a good place to choose fill and stroke, especially if you also need to adjust opacity or add effects. Click on Stroke or Fill to reveal a downward-pointing arrow, then click again to pop up a mini version of the Swatches panel, or Shift-click to pop up a mini version of the Color panel. Select or mix the color you want and then press Return/Enter, or click anywhere else in the panel to hide the pop-up (see the *Layers & Appearances* chapter for more about the Appearance panel).

Take some time to familiarize yourself with all of these ways to set fill or stroke color: 1) adjusting the sliders or sampling a color from the color bar in the Color panel; 2) clicking on a swatch in the Swatches panel; 3) using the Eyedropper tool to sample color from other objects in your file; 4) sampling colors from the Color Picker; 5) clicking on a swatch from the Color Guide panel, 6) clicking the Fill or Stroke icons in the Control panel; or 7) clicking the Fill or Stroke thumbnails in the Appearance panel. (To open the Adobe Color Picker, double-click the Fill or Stroke icon in the Tool panel or the Color panel.) In addition, experiment with dragging color swatches from panels to objects (selected or not), including to and from the Fill/Stroke icon in the Tools panel.

WORKING WITH THE COLOR PANELS

There are now five different panels for working with color: Color, Swatches, Color Guide, Appearance, and Kuler (see the Kuler appendix for more on this). Although you can do much of your color work in the Appearance panel, there may be times that you'll want to have a few different color-related panels open at the same time. For help customizing your workspace, see the "Manipulating windows and panels" section of the *Illustrator Basics* chapter.

Color panel

The Color panel allows you to mix and apply color to your artwork. In addition to the sliders and edit fields for

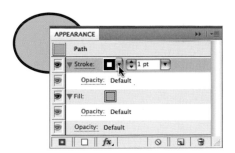

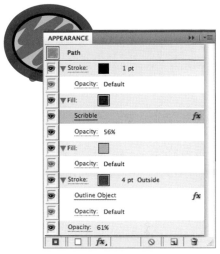

The Appearance panel allows you to set Fill and Stroke (top), (bottom) the Appearance panel also allows you to adjust Opacity, add Effects, as well as add multiple strokes and fills (see the Layers & Appearances chapter for more on working with the Appearance panel)

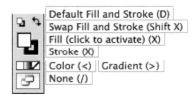

Fill and Stroke section of the Tools panel

The Color panel sliders display the settings for the Fill or Stroke (whichever is in front) and the Web Color Warning (in red at left); when it appears, click the Last Color proxy (in red at right) to return to the last-used color before having chosen a pattern or gradient, or None

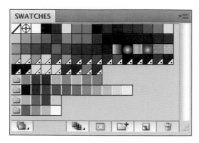

Swatches panel showing all swatches

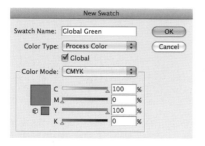

Swatch Options for a global process color

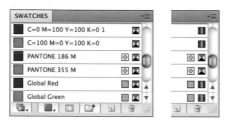

The Swatches panel, shown in list view for color swatches only; the top two swatches are process colors; the middle two are spot colors; and the last two are global colors (at left with the document in CMYK mode, at right the same colors with the document in RGB mode)

The same swatches as in the previous caption, this time shown in large thumbnail view; the left two are process; the middle two are spot (includes a white triangle with a "spot"); the right two are global (includes a simple white triangle)

locating precise colors, this panel includes a None icon (lower left) so you can set your Fill or Stroke to no color at all. You can also click to select a color from the color spectrum bar or the black/white proxy.

The little 3D cube icon that sometimes appears is the Out of Web Color Warning. The color box to the right of the cube icon shows the In Web Color, i.e., how the color will appear as a Web-safe color. Clicking this area of the Color panel allows you to quickly convert a color to the closest match of Web-safe color. If you're creating artwork for the Web, you may also wish to choose Web Safe RGB from the Color panel menu. Adobe maintains these simple features, even though most people agree that Web-safe color is largely a non-issue at this point (all new monitors are capable of displaying millions of colors).

The Color panel's menu options also include Invert and Complement. Search for Invert or Complement in Illustrator Help for Adobe's explanation of these terms.

When you're creating artwork for print, if you choose or mix a color out of the CMYK gamut, an exclamation point appears on the Color panel. Illustrator will suggest to you an "In Gamut Color" that it thinks is a close match; click on the mini swatch to accept the suggestion.

Swatches panel

To save a color from the Color or Color Guide panels to the Swatches panel, drag a square to the Swatches panel, or, to name it as you create it, click the New Swatch icon at the bottom of the Swatches panel. You can also choose New Swatch from the Swatches panel menu, or Create New Swatch from the Color panel pop-up menu.

Whenever you copy and paste objects that contain custom swatches or styles from one document to another, Illustrator will automatically paste those elements into the new document's panels.

The Swatch Options dialog (which you open by double-clicking any swatch or by clicking the Swatch Options icon at the bottom of the Swatch panel) lets you change the individual attributes of a swatch—including its name, color mode, color definition, and whether it's a process, global process, or spot color (see the section following). For pattern and gradient swatches, the only attribute in the Swatch Options dialog is the name.

Process, global process, and spot colors

You can create three kinds of solid fills in Illustrator: process colors, global process colors, and spot colors. These three kinds of colors each appear differently in the Swatches panel, so they're easy to distinguish visually.

- **Process colors** are colors that are printed using a mixture of the four CMYK color values: Cyan, Magenta, Yellow, and Black. (If you're doing non-print work in RGB, your color mixture would use Red, Green, and Blue.)

- **Global process colors** are process colors that have an added convenience: If you update the swatch for a global process color, Illustrator will update that color for all objects that use it in the document. You can identify a global process color in the Swatches panel by the small triangle in the lower-right corner of the swatch (when the panel is in Thumbnail view) or by the Global Color icon (when the panel is in List view). You can create a global process color by enabling the Global option in either the New Swatch dialog or the Swatch Options dialog. (The Global check box is disabled by default.)

- **Spot colors** are custom colors used in print jobs that require a premixed ink rather than a percentage of the four process colors. Specifying a spot color allows you to use colors that are outside of the CMYK gamut, or to achieve a more precise color match than CMYK allows. You can specify a color as a spot color in the New Swatch dialog (by choosing Spot Color from the Color Type menu), or you can choose a spot color from a Swatch library, such as the various Pantone libraries (from the Swatch panel's Swatch Libraries Menu button choose Color Books). All spot colors are global, so they

Accessing the libraries

The Swatch Libraries menu button (lower left in the Swatch panel) opens Swatch libraries for specific color systems (such as Pantone). Or, choose Other Library to access saved colors from any document.

Swatch panel shortcuts

Hold ⌘/Ctrl when you click the New Swatch Button to make it a new Spot color. Hold ⌘-Shift/Ctrl-Shift when you click to create a new Global color. Hold Option/Alt when you click to bypass the New Swatch dialog (it will be named by its color values).

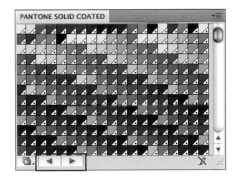

Swatch library panels have left/right arrow buttons at the bottom; click an arrow to go to the next Swatch library (in the same panel)

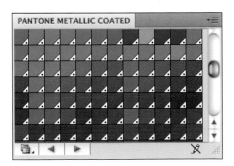

The swatches in this Pantone library all have white triangles with dots to show that they're both global and spot colors

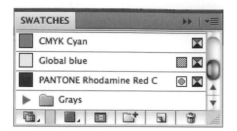

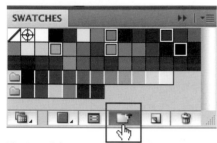

Shown in List view, the Swatches panel includes mini icons that indicate the type of color swatch; from top to bottom the list shows process color (CMYK Cyan), global color (Global blue), spot color (PANTONE), and color group (Grays)

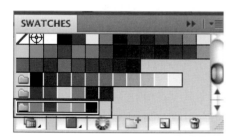

The New Color Group button makes it possible to organize your Swatches panel by grouping colors that you choose; you also specify the name for the group

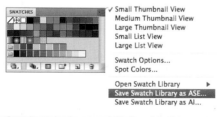

After selecting swatches and clicking the New Color Group button, the new group is added to the Swatches panel

Save Swatch Library as ASE, found in the Swatches panel menu, makes it easy to save custom swatch libraries to use in other Adobe applications

update automatically; and, when the Swatches panel is in Thumbnail view, they have a small triangle in the lower right corner, as well as a small dot or "spot." In List view, they're marked by the Spot Color icon.

Creating Color Groups

You can create and save your own groups of colors with the New Color Group button located at the bottom center of the Swatches panel. To create a new color group, simply select multiple colors from the Swatches panel by Shift-clicking to select contiguous swatches, or by holding ⌘/Ctrl and clicking for non-contiguous selections. Then click the New Color Group button. Alternatively, select objects in your artwork that contain the colors you desire and then click the New Color Group button.

Custom swatch libraries

There are several ways to access the many different swatch libraries included with Illustrator, but probably the simplest method is to click the Swatch Libraries menu button, in the lower-left corner of the Swatches panel (also see the Tip "Accessing the libraries" earlier in this section).

Once you've set up your Swatches panel to your satisfaction, you can save it as a custom swatch library for use with other documents. This can help you avoid having to duplicate your efforts later on. Saving a swatch library is easy—click the Swatch Libraries menu button in the lower-left corner of the Swatches panel and choose Save Swatches. This will, by default, save your swatch library to the Adobe Illustrator CS4 Swatches folder (inside your computer user folder).

Exchanging swatches

Adobe's Creative Suite allows you to easily share swatches among the different Adobe applications. So, you can save your Illustrator swatches for use in InDesign, or save your Photoshop swatches for use in Illustrator, and so on.

To save your current Illustrator swatches for use in other Adobe applications, remove any extraneous swatches, choose "Save Swatch Library as ASE" from the Swatches panel pop-up menu, and then save the swatch library to a convenient location. Now you can load the swatch library you've saved (file name ending in .ase) into most other Adobe applications. Likewise, you can save swatch libraries from other applications to use in Illustrator (in .ase format). To load a swatch library in Illustrator, choose Other Library from the Swatch Libraries menu in the Swatches panel. You'll be presented with a dialog that lets you locate the swatch library you've saved from another application.

Color Guide

There are three distinct tasks you can accomplish using the Color Guide panel: 1) after setting your "base color" (the upper-left mini-square), you can apply "Harmony Rules" (based on scientific color theory) to that color, 2) you can visualize variations of colors generated by the harmony rules, or of a color group from the Swatches panel, and 3) you can select and save swatches, and groups of swatches, to the Swatches panel.

Next to the base color is a horizontal strip of colors with a pop-up menu to access the Harmony Rules. This horizontal color strip contains either a color group (selected from the Swatches panel), or a harmony rule (chosen by the pop-up) as applied to the base color.

Below the color strip is a grid of colors (if you don't see the grid, choose Show Options from the panel pop-up menu). The grid displays a vertical column down the center containing your current colors. On either side of this column are variations of each of the colors based on one of three color models: Tints/Shades, Warm/Cool, or Vivid/Muted (choose which variation from the panel pop-up menu). Adjust the number of steps (vertical columns), and the degree of variation (between the steps) from Color Guide Options in the panel pop-up menu (this opens the Variation Options dialog).

In the examples at right, red is the base color, and the "Brights" color group is loaded into both the horizontal

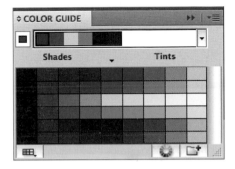

The Color Guide panel showing Tints/Shades of a red (source color), and with the "Brights" color group (in the default 4 steps)

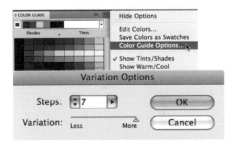

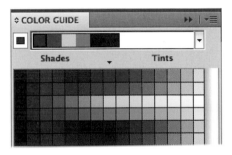

The Color Guide panel after changing the number of Steps to 7 via Color Guide Options

More about the Color Guide...

In addition to the "save color group to Swatches" panel button, the Color Guide contains two additional buttons. The button in the lower left of the Color Guide allows you to limit the colors that the Color Guide is generating to a chosen swatch library. The middle button will be called "Edit Colors" (if you don't have objects selected) or "Edit or Apply Colors" (if you have objects selected); clicking this button opens the main Live Color dialog. Find out more about limiting colors to specific palettes, and working with the Edit Colors/Edit or Apply Colors dialogs in the *Live Color* chapter.

Pantone Goe™

The Pantone Goe™ Color System is an improved version of the Pantone Matching System. It adopts a logical naming scheme and nearly doubles the number of unique colors. Download the free Pantone Goe™ libraries from: http://www.pantone.com/goefree
—*Randy Livingston*

Four-color-process jobs

For documents containing spot colors, you can print four-color-process separations from the Print dialog by enabling the "Convert All Spot Colors to Process" Output option (though there might be color shifts).

color strip, and the center vertical column. To the left of each hue are shades (darker values) of that hue and to the right are tints (lighter values).

To save a highlighted color from the grid, either drag it to the Swatches panel, or, to name the color as you save it, click the New Swatch button in the Swatches panel. To save multiple colors from the grid as a Color Group, first ⌘-click/Ctrl-click to highlight multiple non-contiguous colors, and/or Shift-click to select contiguous colors, and then click the "save color group to Swatches panel" button, in the lower-right corner of the Color Guide panel. Also see Tip at left, and lessons at the end of this chapter, for more about working with the Color Guide panel.

THE TWO-IN-ONE EYEDROPPER

The Eyedropper tool allows you to copy appearance attributes from one object to another, including stroke, fill, color, and text attributes. The Eyedropper tool actually has two modes: the *sampling* Eyedropper picks up formatting and attributes, and the *applying* Eyedropper applies the sampled attributes.

To copy attributes from one object to another using the Eyedropper, first select the Eyedropper from the Toolbox, and position it over an unselected object. You'll see that the Eyedropper tool is in sampling mode (it angles downward to the left). Click the object to pick up its attributes. Now position the Eyedropper tool over the unselected object to which you want to apply the attributes you just sampled, and hold down the Option/Alt key. The Eyedropper will switch to applying mode: It angles downward to the right, and looks full. Click the object to apply the attributes sampled from the first object.

Alternatively, you can use the single-step method: First select the object with the appearance attributes you want to change, and then move the Eyedropper over the unselected object from which you want to copy attributes. Click to sample the unselected object's attributes and apply them to the previously selected object all at once. (With this method, you won't see the Eyedropper change from sampling to applying, since the whole process happens in one step.)

In addition to sampling color from objects, the Eyedropper tool can sample colors from raster and mesh images if you hold down the Shift key as you click. The Shift key can also modify the Eyedropper in other ways. By default, a regular click with the Eyedropper tool picks up all fill and stroke attributes (it picks up the complete appearance of an object, including Live Effects). Using the single-step method described above, adding the Shift key allows you to sample the *color only* (as opposed to sampling the other appearance attributes as well); this will apply the color you sample to the stroke or the fill, whichever is active in the Toolbox at the time you click. If you hold Shift-Option/Shift-Alt when you click, you'll *add* the appearance attributes of an object to the selected object's appearance—instead of just replacing it.

You can control which attributes the Eyedropper picks up and applies by using the Eyedropper Options dialog (accessed by double-clicking the Eyedropper tool). You can also control the size of an area the Eyedropper samples from raster images by using the Raster Sample Size menu at the bottom of the dialog. Choosing Single Point will sample from a single pixel; 3 x 3 will pick up a sample averaged from a 3-pixel grid surrounding the point you click on; and 5 x 5 will do so for a 5-pixel grid. (Averaging helps you to get a more accurate sample of the actual color than the human eye can perceive.)

END OF LINES

Sometimes stroked lines seem to match up perfectly when viewed in Outline mode but they visibly overlap in Preview mode. You can solve this problem by changing the end caps in the Stroke panel. Just select one of the three end cap styles described below to determine how the endpoints of your selected paths will look when previewed.

The first (and default) choice is a Butt cap; it causes your path to stop at the end anchor point. Butt caps are essential for creating exact placement of one path against

From left to right: the Eyedropper tool, the cursor in normal sampling mode, in applying mode (Option/Alt), with Shift then Option/Alt key to add (not replace) appearances, and from type

Sampling from the desktop

Use the Eyedropper tool to sample attributes from any object on your computer's desktop, but keep in mind that the Eyedropper tool will only pick up RGB color when sampling from outside the current Illustrator document. To sample attributes from the desktop, first select the object whose attributes you want to change. Then select the Eyedropper tool, click anywhere on your document and continue to hold the mouse button down while you move your cursor over the desktop object you want to sample. Once your cursor is over the object, just release the mouse button and you'll see the sampled attributes applied to the selected object.

Eyedropper options give control over what to pick up and/or deposit. In addition to stroke, fill, color, and text formatting, you can use the Eyedropper to copy styles and type attributes (which are discussed later in the book).

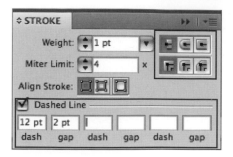

The Stroke panel with the cap/join Dashed Line sections emphasized

At left, three lines shown top to bottom in Outline, Preview with Butt cap, Round cap and Projecting cap; at right, a 5-pt dashed line with a 2-pt dash and 6-pt gap shown top to bottom in Outline, then Preview with a Butt cap, Round cap, and Projecting cap

A dashed line with Butt caps (top) and the same dashed line with Round caps (bottom)

A dashed line (top) is converted into outlines (bottom) with Object>Path>Outline Stroke

A path shown first in Outline, then in Preview with a Miter join, Round join, and Bevel join

Objects with 6-pt strokes and various Miter limits, demonstrating that the angles of lines affect Miter limits

The Free Transform tool

another. The middle choice is the Round cap, which rounds the endpoint in a more natural manner. Round caps are especially good for softening the effect of single line segments. The Projecting cap extends lines and dashes at half the stroke weight beyond the end anchor point. Cap styles also affect the shape of dashed lines.

Corner strokes

The Join style in the Stroke panel determines the shape of a stroke line at its corner points. Each of the three styles determines the shape of the outside of the corner; the inside of the corner is always angled.

The default Miter join creates a pointy corner. The length of the point is determined by the width of the stroke, the angle of the corner (narrow angles create longer points; see illustration at left), and the Miter limit setting on the Stroke panel. Miter limits can range from 1x (which is always blunt) to 500x. Generally, the default Miter join with a miter limit of 4x looks just fine.

The Round join creates a rounded outside corner for which the radius is half the stroke width. The Bevel join creates a squared-off outside corner, equivalent to a Miter join with the miter limit set to 1x.

FREE TRANSFORM & LIQUIFY TOOLS

You can use Illustrator's Free Transform tool to distort the size and shape of an object by dragging the corner points of the object's bounding box. You must first start dragging a bounding box corner point and then also hold down ⌘/Ctrl while continuing to drag. The shape of the object distorts progressively as you drag the bounding box corner points.

Adobe calls the suite of tools grouped with the Warp tool the "Liquify" Distortion tools. These tools allow you to distort objects manually by dragging the mouse over them. The Warp, Twirl, Pucker, Bloat, Scallop, Crystallize, and Wrinkle tools work not only on vector objects, but on embedded raster images as well. Use the Option/Alt key to resize the Liquify brush as you drag.

Similar Distort features are found under the Effect menu (choose Effect > Distort & Transform; and see the *Live Effects & Graphic Styles* chapter for more on Effects).

PATH SIMPLIFY COMMAND

More is not better when it comes to the number of anchor points you use to define a path. The more anchor points, the more complicated the path—which makes the file size larger and harder to process when printing. The Simplify command (Object > Path > Simplify) removes excess anchor points from selected paths. Cartographers, and those importing GIS data, find Simplify a lifesaver.

Two sliders control the amount and type of simplification. Enable Show Original as well as the Preview option to preview the effect of the sliders as you adjust them. The Preview option also displays the original number of points in the curve and the number that will be left if the current settings are applied.

Adjust the Curve Precision slider to determine how accurately the new path should match the original path. The higher the percentage, the more anchor points will remain, and the closer the new path will be to the original. The endpoints of an open path are never altered. The Angle Threshold determines when corner points should become smooth. The higher the threshold, the more likely a corner point will remain sharp.

ADD ANCHOR POINTS & REMOVE ANCHOR POINTS

Use Object > Path > Add Anchor Points to neatly place one point between each existing pair of points on your path. Each time you do this, anchor points are added precisely between pre-existing points. If you use this frequently, choose Edit > Keyboard Shortcuts to assign a shortcut; try ⌘-Shift +/Ctrl-Shift + (plus). (See the "Zen House" lesson in the *Zen of Illustrator* chapter for practical use of this feature.) To remove points while keeping closed paths intact, select points using the Direct Selection or Lasso tool and choose Object > Path > Remove Anchor Points (using the Delete key would also delete the connecting paths).

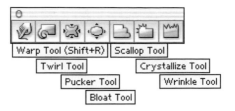

The Liquify Distortion tools' tear off panel can be accessed from the Warp tool: see "Tear off panels" in the Illustrator Basics *chapter*

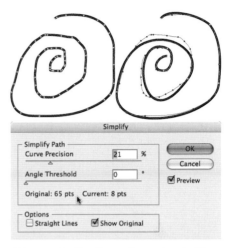

Object > Path > Simplify can be used to significantly reduce the number of points on a path, resulting in smoother curves though less detail

Stubborn snapping to point

If an object annoyingly "snaps" to the wrong place, move it away from the area, release the mouse button, and then try again (grabbing from another point).

Removing stray points...

Use Object > Path > Clean Up to remove stray points, unpainted objects, or empty text paths. To see the stray points before deleting them, use Select > Object > Stray Points to select them; press the Delete key. (Beware, scatter brush points might be deleted too!)

Easy Construction

Character Building with Geometry

Overview: *Draw an object using the Rectangle, Ellipse, and Rounded Rectangle tools; use tints to fill the paths and add highlights and shadows to simulate depth. Use the Appearance panel to alter attributes of the objects.*

JACKMORE

1

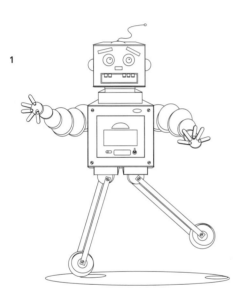

The robot shown in default white fill and black stroke, drawn using only the Ellipse, Rectangle and Rounded Rectangle tools

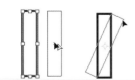

Option-Shift/Alt-Shift dragging a selection to duplicate and constrain it to align with the original; using the Rotate tool to make a variation

Creating artwork in Illustrator can sometimes be achieved with just a few simple tools. Lisa Jackmore created this toy robot using geometric tools and easily colored the objects with the help of the Appearance panel.

1 Creating geometric objects using the Appearance panel, and copying objects. Using the Ellipse, Rectangle, or Rounded Rectangle tools, draw a robot and most of its parts. Jackmore used keyboard shortcuts to toggle between the Ellipse (L) and Rectangle (M) tools.

To make duplicates of objects that are mostly symmetrical, such as the eyes, eyebrows, and arms, Jackmore selected an object, and dragged it while holding Option-Shift/Alt-Shift (Shift constrains the drag; Option/Alt makes the copy). To make changes to an object, click on an object with the Selection tool, and use the bounding box to drag to scale (from the corners) or rotate (move your cursor off the corner to access the Rotate cursor).

2 Filling with colors and tints of colors using the Appearance and Color panels. Up until now, you've probably been drawing your robot using the default black stroke and white fill. To vary the fills in your robot, select some of your objects, and open the Appearance panel (Window > Appearance). Now click on the Fill icon, and choose a color from the Swatches pop-up panel. To adjust the stroke weight, click the word "Stroke" in the Appearance panel. To adjust the stroke color, click the Stroke swatch. Jackmore set her strokes to None by pressing the-When you draw additional objects they will share the same attributes as your last selected objects.

After setting strokes to None, Jackmore filled her robot with tints of custom orange swatches. In order to do this, she first mixed a new color with the Global attribute enabled, and then she filled objects with tints of this color using the Color panel. To create tints of custom colors, click the Fill icon in the Appearance panel, and then click the New Swatch icon at the bottom right of the panel. In the New Swatch panel, adjust the CMYK sliders to mix a color, enable the Global color option, and click OK. The new Global color swatch will appear in the pop-up Swatches panel with a white triangle in the corner (indicating that it's a Global color). Fill objects with this color, and then create a tint by opening the Color panel (Window menu) and adjusting the Tint slider. *Hint: You can also mix tints from Spot colors, such as Pantone and Trumatch Color Books.*

3 Adding finishing touches. Using tools and techniques described in later chapters, Jackmore added more details using the Pen tool (to draw lines and curves, and to add detail, highlight, and shadow), Type on a curve (the lines in the dial), and blends (on the neck and body). For help with the Pen tool see "Digitizing a Logo" in the *Layers and Appearances* chapter and the *Zen lessons* on the *Wow! CD*; see the *Artboards & Type* chapter for working with type and the *Blends, Gradients & Mesh* chapter for details on blends.

2

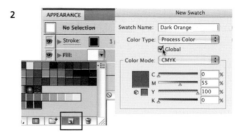

Making a new Global color by clicking Fill in the Appearance panel, clicking the New button in the Swatches panel pop-up, mixing a New Swatch color, enabling Global and clicking OK

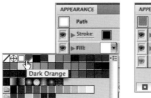

Selecting the new Global swatch from the Swatches pop-up of the Appearance panel,

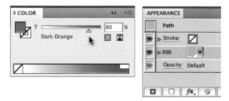

Creating a tint of the new Global swatch by adjusting the slider that appears in the Color panel, and a tint shown in the Appearance panel

A group of objects shown before and after changing solid fills to tints

3

Object shown before finishing touches (left) and after (right)

Custom Coloring

Creating Custom Colors and Color Groups

Overview: *Create an illustration; create custom swatches; create a custom color group from custom swatches; save a swatch library.*

1

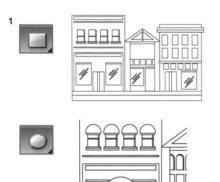

Creating an icon with the Rectangle tool, Ellipse tool, and Pencil tool.

Filling icon paths with default swatches from the Swatches panel

2

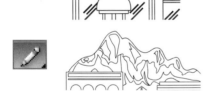

Selecting the correct color mode from the Color panel's pop-up menu

PUTNAM

Ryan Putnam designs many illustrations he uses as icons in stock art and client projects. Creating custom swatches is an integral step in creating compelling and consistent icon illustrations. Illustrator comes with some great default color swatches, but they are not suited for most of Putnam's icon illustrations. Moreover, by creating a custom color group, Putnam can easily apply his custom swatches to other related illustrations.

1 **Creating an icon illustration.** To create the "Destination" icon, Putnam used the Rectangle tool, Ellipse tool, and Pencil tool. Putnam first created the buildings of the icon with varying sizes of rectangles with the Rectangle tool. He then used the Ellipse tool to create windows and awnings for the buildings. Next, he used the Pencil tool to draw the mountains. To distinguish the objects from each other, Putnam filled the building and mountain paths with default swatches from the Swatches panel by selecting each object and clicking the desired swatch.

2 **Creating custom swatches.** After Putnam roughed out the basic color schemes for his illustration, he then began to customize a more natural set of colors. First, he made sure the Color panel was set to the same color mode as

his Document Color Mode. Since Putnam is creating his icon for a website and his Document Color Mode is RGB, from the Color panel pop-up menu he selected RGB. Putnam then selected an object and mixed the desired color with the sliders in the Color panel. Next, he opened the Swatches panel and clicked the New Swatch button in the bottom of the panel. In the Swatch Options dialog he then named the swatch and clicked OK. Alternatively, you can choose Create New Swatch from the Color panel pop-up menu. Yet another option is to drag the mixed color directly to the Swatches panel, though by doing so, you won't get Swatch Options and the opportunity to name the swatch. Putnam then repeated these steps for every custom color he wanted to create.

3 **Creating a new color group.** After creating his custom swatches, Putnam wanted to organize his custom swatches so he could easily apply them to other related illustrations and icons. To do this, he created a custom color group. He selected the desired swatches in the Swatches panel by Shift-clicking to select contiguous swatches, or by holding ⌘/Ctrl and clicking for non-contiguous selections. Then he clicked the New Color Group button, where he was given the option to name his color group. The new color group was then saved for Putnam and ready for use.

To use his custom color group in other documents, Putnam needed to save the color group as a custom swatch library. First, he selected all the swatches he wanted to delete from his custom color group and pressed the Delete Swatch icon in the Swatches panel. Putnam then clicked the Swatch Libraries menu button at the lower left of the Swatches panel and chose Save Swatches. This saved Putnam's swatch library in the User Defined folder in the Adobe Illustrator CS4 Swatches folder (inside the computer user folder). Now whenever he needs the swatch library in other documents, Putnam clicks the Swatch Libraries menu button, chooses User Defined, and selects his defined library.

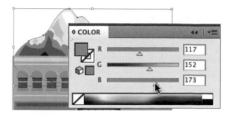

Mixing colors with the color sliders from the Color panel

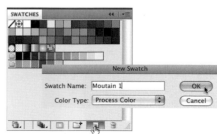

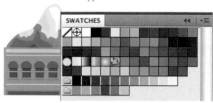

Saving custom swatches in the Swatches panel by pressing the New Swatch button

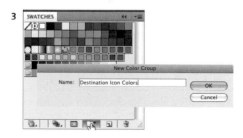

Saving custom swatches as a new color group in the Swatches panel

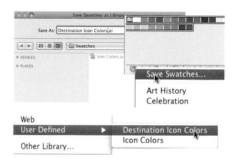

Opening custom color group in the Swatches panel

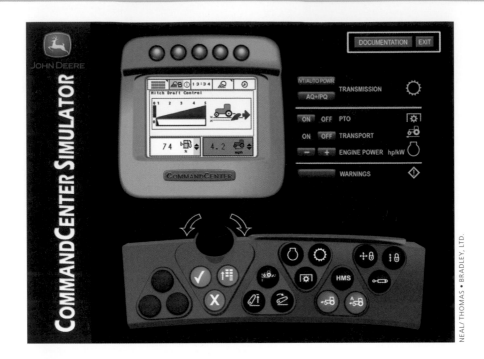

Brad Neal / Thomas • Bradley, Ltd.

Brad Neal created this realistic rendering of a control panel for a John Deere monitoring system with simple geometric tools. Using the same techniques as Lisa Jackmore in the "Easy Construction" lesson in this chapter, Neal drew the geometric objects (left detail). He then applied techniques described in later chapters of this book (such as gradients, transparency, effects, and blends) to create realistic shadows and highlights (right detail). He brought the simply constructed image into Photoshop and made further enhancements to create the final image, above.

ROSTOMIAN

Zosia Rostomian / The Sharper Image®

Using a clever mixture of custom gradients and patterns from the Swatches library, Zosia Rostomian created a sophisticated illustration. Rostomian often has to create many product illustrations within a limited time, and the pattern library speeds the process along. First Rostomian added patterns to the Swatches panel. She clicked on the Swatch Libraries Menu button at the bottom left corner of the Swatches panel and selected Patterns > Basic Graphics > Basic Graphics_Dots. She selected the object and filled it with a dotted pattern from the Swatches panel. She experimented until she found a pattern close to what she needed. With the filled object selected, she

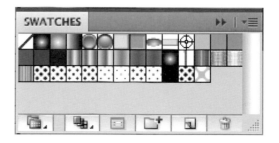

chose Object > Transform > Scale. Rostomian chose Uniform, entered a percentage, and then under Options, she enabled only Patterns. She clicked the Preview button and experimented with various percentages until the pattern was perfectly scaled. For more about Rostomian's drawing techniques, see her galleries in the *Blends, Gradients & Mesh* chapter.

Guides for Arcs

Designing with Guides, Arc, and Pen Tools

Overview: *Create guides on one side of the artboard; reflect and copy guides to the other side; create an arc with the Arc tool; cut and extend the arc with the Pen tool; reflect and copy the arc and join with the two arcs using the Pen tool; print templates using the Tile option.*

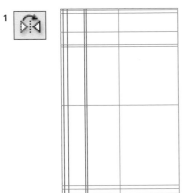

Reflect tool icon on the left; on the right, selected guides (colored magenta) that will be reflected and copied to the other side of the artboard

Tasked with building a garden gate as a functional sculpture for an outdoor exhibition on the grounds of the Norman Rockwell Museum, artist Stephen Klema sat down with Illustrator to create life-sized drawings that would serve as templates for cutting the sculpture's wood pieces.

1 Creating the document and positioning guides.

To start, Klema made a new document with the same dimensions as those of the constructed gate (80" tall by 44" wide). Next, he turned on rulers (⌘-R/Ctrl-R) and dragged guides from the rulers. To position a guide more precisely, first make sure that guides are unlocked (go to View > Guides and choose Lock Guides if it has a check mark before its name), select the guide and use the Control Panel's Transform fields to enter values for the X or Y position of the guide on the artboard.

If your artwork will be symmetrical, like Klema's, you can create guides on one side of the document and then select and copy them to the other side. Start by creating a guide in the exact middle of the document. An easy way to do this is to drag a new guide from the ruler and, making sure that Guides are still unlocked, click the Horizontal Align Center icon in the Control panel to center it horizontally on the artboard (be sure that you've chosen Align to Artboard in the Control panel). Next, activate

Smart Guides from the View menu (this will help position the cursor over the exact middle of the document). Finally, select all of the guides you've created, choose the Reflect tool (it's hidden under the Rotate tool icon) and Opt-click/Alt-click on the guide you created in the middle of the document. From the Reflect dialog, choose Vertical as the Axis and click on the Copy button.

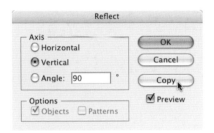

The Reflect tool dialog

2 **Drawing an arch.** Klema turned to the Rectangle, Arc, Ellipse, and Pen tools to draw the different objects in his illustration. For the inner arch, Klema selected the Arc tool (hidden under the Line Segment tool) and double-clicked its icon to bring up the Arc Segment Tool Options dialog. Because he planned on drawing from the center guide outward to the left, Klema clicked on the dialog's Base Along menu and selected the Y Axis option. Next, he clicked on the center guide and dragged down and to the left until the arc was shaped the way he wanted. Depending on the shape of the arc you need, you may have to draw it wider or longer. If that's the case, you'll need to cut the arc with the Scissors tool as Klema did so that it fits the width of the arch shape you want. Next, extend the arc downward as a straight line by selecting the Pen tool, clicking the bottom endpoint of the arc, and then Shift-clicking below to complete the straight line. Duplicate the extended arc using the Reflect tool and the center guide, just as you did in the previous step with the guides. Klema connected the bottom endpoints of the two extended arcs with the Pen tool, creating a single object.

On the left, the Arc tool icon; on the right, the Arc Segment Tool Options dialog

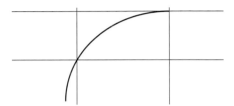

The arc and the guides

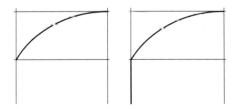

The arc after being cut with the Scissors tool on the left; on the right, the arc extended after drawing a vertical path with the Pen tool

3 **Printing templates for construction.** After drawing all the objects in his design, Klema printed the full illustration and separate illustrations of each of the gate parts (he used the Tile option in the Print dialog because the pieces were bigger than his printer paper). The prints served as templates that he traced on the wood so that he could precisely cut out the individual pieces of the gate. He used the full-sized illustration as a guide for assembling the gate parts into the finished sculpture.

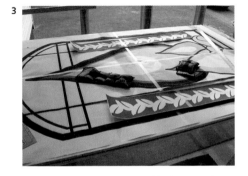

Printed template pages assembled on wood

Isometric Systems

Tools & Formulas for Isometric Projection

Overview: *Create detailed, to-scale drawings of three sides of an object; use an isometric formula to transform the objects; assemble with the Selection tool and Snap to Point; create objects that aren't boxes.*

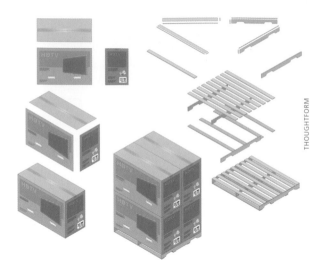

THOUGHTFORM

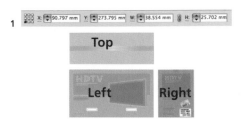

1

Top, left, and right faces that have more than one component are first grouped individually, and always positioned with the side on the left and the front on the right

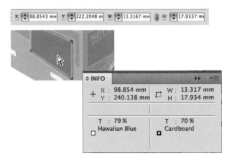

Using the Control or Info panels for drawing to scale

Ellipses are contained by boxes

To construct an elliptical object in isometric view, make a rectangle to fit one side of the "box." Next draw an ellipse inside the rectangle, touching at all edges. Select both objects and scale, shear, rotate, and join them to the rest of the object. Delete the rectangle.

Technical illustrations and diagrams are often depicted in isometric view. Adobe Illustrator has several features that can help you assemble and transform objects in isometrics. Kurt Hess created and transformed the diagrams on these pages using a three-step ISO formula.

1 Creating detailed renderings of the front, side, and top views of your object to scale. When you're ready to begin a technical drawing, you'll want to decide upon your "General" Units in Preferences, setting it to a type that represents the larger units the actual item is measured in. For example, 4 mm on paper might represent one inch of the object's actual size. If you then set the "Keyboard Increment" in General Preferences to 1 mm, you can use the arrow keys to move a line or object to match .25 inches of the item's physical measurement. Use the Control panel or the Info panel (Window >Info) to read width and height between selected points on items already drawn, and to enter measurements directly. Enable View >Snap to Point for assistance in joining edges, and View >Smart Guides to help you locate angles and intersecting nodes. Draw the component parts of the item that will be visible (usually front, top, and one side) face on, in flat, 2D perspective, then Select and Group (⌘-G/Ctrl-G) the elements of each side in preparation for transforming them into an isometric projection.

2 Using an isometric formula to transform your objects, then assembling the elements. To assemble your elements into an isometric view, you can use the transform tools (Scale, Shear, Rotate) in the Toolbox, Object > Transform, or the Transform panel. To assemble the box, select all three views and double-click on the Scale tool to scale them 100% horizontally and 86.6% vertically. Next select the left face, and shear it at a –30° angle. If you've drawn the top to align with the left (figure A), shear it and the right face at 30°. Now rotate the right 30° and the top and left –30°. If you've drawn the top to align with the right (figure B), then shear the top with the left instead (–30º), the right still at 30°. Then rotate the top and right 30º. The left still rotates at –30º. The chart at right shows angles of direction.

To assemble the top, right, and left, use the Selection tool to grab a specific anchor-point from the right view that will contact the left view, and drag it until it snaps into the correct position (the arrow turns hollow). Next, select and drag to snap the top into position. Finally, select and group the entire object for easy reselection.

3 Drawing elements beyond the basic box. To create this wooden pallet, create one top slat and one end. The right face will always wind up aligned with the 30° axis (see illustration, right), although it will not always represent the "front" of the object in the real world. Scale as before. If you've drawn the top to align with the left (figure A), shear it and the right face at 30°, and the left at –30°. Rotate the right 30° and the top and left –30°. If you've drawn the top to align with the right (figure B), then shear the top with the left (–30º), and the right at 30°. Rotate the top and right 30º. The left rotates at –30º. Duplicate and drag each element into position for the opposite side. Join as if they were the top and right side of a box. Create the in-between slats by selecting the end pieces, then double-click the Blend tool to choose Specified Steps (for Spacing) and enter the number of slats (for help, see the *Blends, Gradients & Mesh* chapter).

2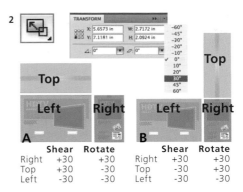

	Shear	Rotate		Shear	Rotate
Right	+30	+30	Right	+30	+30
Top	+30	-30	Top	-30	+30
Left	-30	-30	Left	-30	-30

Using the Scale tool and the Transform panel, applying the formula according to whether the top is aligned with the Left (A) or the Right (B)

Shear and Rotate, then join sides along angle axes, using the Selection tool and dragging an anchor point until the arrow becomes hollow and the edges snap together (View > Snap to Point)

3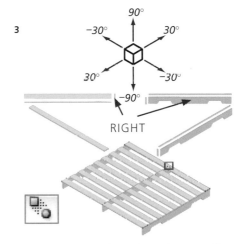

Assembling parts, determining what part will be viewed on the (positive) 30° axis; duplicating pieces, sliding into position and using the Blend tool with Specified Steps to complete a pallet

Automated Isometric Actions!
Rick Henkel of ThoughtForm created *WOW Actions* that automate formulas for isometrics (on the *Wow! CD*).

Distorting Views

Using Free Transform for Productivity

Overview: *Draw basic parts in a "normal" front view, then Free Transform copies for specific illustrations or frames; use Free Transform for creating perspective depth.*

ATTEBERRY

Assembling parts into separate groups, avoiding the need to redraw for every view of the subject

1

Assembled character before using Free Transform to pose the mask

Creating characters that will adopt varying poses throughout a story or animation requires some special preplanning. To avoid drawing the complex elements over and over, Kevan Atteberry creates modular parts for his characters, placing any complex parts in a "neutral" position, then uses the Free Transform tool to position the character parts as needed for each illustration. He also draws elements flat that would be time-consuming to draw in perspective, using Free Transform to adjust them.

1 Drawing the bugs' masks facing front, then transforming them into expressive positions. Because the bugs' masks need to convey the emotion of the story, they are the most complex parts. Atteberry constructed them in a head-on position, using a combination of the Brush tool or Pencil tool for the loose drawing, and compound paths and blends to shape and color them (to learn more about blends, see the *Blends, Gradients & Mesh* chapter). He finally Grouped (⌘-G/Ctrl-G) all the elements for a mask in order to transform the mask as a single unit.

2 Transforming the masks into expressive positions. Atteberry preserved the original masks and worked on duplicates. He next transformed the masks to appear in their final position for the illustration. With a mask copy selected, he chose the Free Transform tool (E). This would allow him to scale, rotate, and distort the mask into place without his having to call upon separate Transform commands. The key to using the Free Transform tool is knowing how to use the modifier keys with it. Atteberry hovered the cursor just outside the bounding box until he saw the curved, double-headed arrow letting him know a click-drag would rotate the object. To distort it, he clicked on a corner of the bounding box, then added the ⌘/Ctrl key. (It is important that you click before adding the modifier key—otherwise you are turning your Free Transform tool into the Selection tool temporarily.) When he saw the arrow turn into a single arrowhead, he dragged on the corner to distort that area of the mask. By clicking on a middle bounding box handle and then ⌘/Ctrl-dragging, he could skew the mask along one side. Adding the Option/Alt key would allow the object to be skewed in two directions at once. He scaled the mask by clicking on any handle on the bounding box to get the double-arrow cursor and dragging without using a modifier key, or he constrained the proportions as he was scaling it by adding the Shift key. Adding the Option/Alt key scaled the object around its center point. In this fashion, Atteberry positioned the masks to fit each body for the illustration (or frame). He also used the Free Transform tool on some of the bug bodies and limbs to depict movement.

3 **Using Free Transform to add perspective.** For this illustration in the bugs' series, Atteberry created the tiles for the floor by drawing them individually on a flat surface. He gave the tiles depth by placing a solid rectangle at the bottom, with black-filled tile objects on a layer above. He grouped and copied the tiles, offsetting the copy just enough that the black tiles, to which he applied a Gaussian Blur, became the shadows of the tiles. Selecting both groups of tiles, he again chose the Free Transform tool. This time he clicked on a top corner point and then used the ⌘-Option-Shift (Mac)/Ctrl-Alt-Shift (Win) keys, dragging horizontally, to transform in perspective.

2

Using the Free Transform tool, with and without modifier keys, to rotate, skew, scale, and distort

The character's basic, reusable parts transformed to fit the needs of this illustration or frame for an animation

3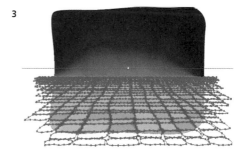

Tile flooring transformed in single-point perspective with the Free Transform tool

Intricate Patterns

Designing Complex Repeating Patterns

Advanced Technique

Overview: *Design a rough composition; define a confining pattern boundary and place it behind all layers; use the box to generate crop marks; copy and position elements using crop marks for alignment; define and use the pattern.*

WEIMER

1

Top, arranging pattern elements into a basic design; bottom, adding the pattern tile rectangle behind the pattern elements

Creating crop marks based on selection of the pattern tile rectangle

Included with Illustrator are many wonderful patterns for you to use and customize, and *Illustrator Help* does a good job of explaining pattern-making basics. But what if you want to create a more complex pattern?

A simple trick with crop marks can help to simplify a tedious process of trial and error. With some help from author and consultant Sandee Cohen, Alan James Weimer used the following technique to design an intricate tile that prints seamlessly as a repeating pattern.

1 Designing your basic pattern, drawing a confining rectangle, then creating crop marks for registration. Create a design that will allow for some rearrangement of artwork elements. ***Hint:*** *Pattern tiles cannot contain* linked *images—to include a linked image in a pattern, select it and click Embed Image in the Control panel.*

Use the Rectangle tool to draw a box around the part of the image you would like to repeat. This rectangle defines the boundary of the pattern tile. Send the rectangle to the bottom of the Layers panel or to the bottom of your drawing layer (Object > Arrange > Send to Back). This boundary rectangle, which controls how your pattern repeats, must be an unstroked, unfilled, nonrotated, nonsheared object. With this rectangle selected, Copy, then Edit > Paste in Front. Next choose Effect > Create > Crop Marks, then Object > Expand Appearance, and finally Ungroup (in step 2, you'll need these crop marks).

2 **Developing the repeating elements.** If your pattern has an element that extends beyond the edge of the pattern tile, you must copy that element and place it on the opposite side of the tile. For example, if a flower blossom extends below the tile, you must place a copy of the remainder of the blossom at the top of the tile, ensuring that the whole flower is visible when the pattern repeats. To do this, select an element that overlaps above or below the tile and then Shift-select the nearest horizontal crop mark (position the cursor on an endpoint of the crop mark). While pressing the Shift-Option or Shift-Alt keys (the Option/Alt key copies the selections and the Shift key constrains dragging to vertical and horizontal directions), drag the element and crop mark upward until the cursor snaps to the endpoint of the upper horizontal crop mark. Enabling Smart Guides (from the View menu) can help you find the correct horizontal and vertical alignment when you are dragging objects. (For any element that overlaps the left or right side of the tile, select the element and the vertical crop mark and hold down Shift-Option/Shift-Alt as you drag them into position.)

3 **Testing and optimizing your pattern.** To test your pattern, select your pattern elements (including the bounding rectangle), and either choose Edit > Define Pattern to name your pattern, or drag your selection to the Swatches panel (then double-click the swatch to customize its name). Create a new rectangle and select the pattern as your fill from the Swatches panel. Illustrator will fill the rectangle with your repeating pattern. If you redesign the pattern tile and then wish to update the pattern swatch, select your pattern elements again, but this time Option-drag/Alt-drag the elements onto the pattern swatch you made before.

2

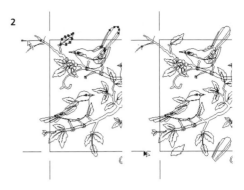

Left, selecting the flower blossom and horizontal crop mark; right, after dragging a copy of the flower blossom and crop mark into position at the top of the pattern tile artwork

Finished artwork for the pattern tile, before turning into a pattern swatch in the Swatches panel

3

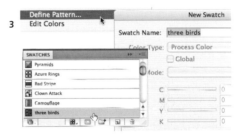

Making a new swatch using Edit > Define Pattern

Speeding redraw with patterns

Speed redraw for an object filled with a complex pattern by setting the object to Outline mode using the Layers panel, or hide it using the Appearance panel (see the *Layers & Appearances* chapter).

Color Guidance

Inspiration from the Color Guide Panel

WHYTE

Advanced Technique

Overview: *Set up the Color Guide panel to generate color groups; create and save color groups based on harmonies in the Color Guide panel; apply, modify, and save color groups from within Live Color.*

In this "Day at the Circus" poster (created for a children's fundraising event), illustrator Hugh Whyte used a very specific palette of colors. Using Illustrator's Color Guide panel, it's simple to generate and save color groups of new palettes based on existing colors. Live Color allows you to apply your new color groups to an existing design, and then continue to experiment with how colors are applied.

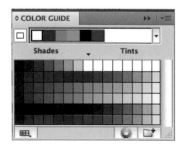

Saving original artwork colors as a color group in the Swatches panel, which automatically places a selected color group with variations into the Color Guide panel

1 **Setting up the Color Guide panel to base new color versions on the original.** For your first attempt, use the Circus image on the *Wow! CD*, or one that has a limited number of colors, to avoid having too many swatches in your original artwork to handle easily. Since you'll be working with both your Swatches and Color Guide panels, drag them away from the dock to float free for easy viewing. Select the artwork and, in the Swatches panel, click on the New Color Group button in order to have the colors that are currently in your artwork saved as a group to work with in the Color Guide panel. When the New Color Group dialog opens, keep the default settings and rename this color group "Original Color." Deselect your artwork. In order to base your color group creations on your original color relationships, click on the small folder icon beside your color group swatches to select the entire group so that it shows up in the Color Guide panel.

2 Creating color groups in the Color Guide panel and saving them to the Swatches panel. Next, you're going to create a variety of color groups in the Color Guide panel. Notice that your original artwork colors run down the middle of the Color Guide's panel of swatches (under the small black triangle). To the right are lighter versions of these colors (tints), and to the left are darker versions (shades). Select the top color in the third row from the right, then Shift-click to select the entire row vertically (⌘-click/Ctrl-click for non-contiguous colors). Click on the Save to Swatches panel button. Now change the relationship between the colors by clicking on the Color Guide's pop-up menu and choosing Show Warm/Cool. Again select the third vertical row from the right and save this new cooler color group to the Swatches panel. Select the group by clicking on its folder icon, select Color Group Options from the Swatches panel pop-up menu, and rename it something like "Cooler Original" by typing a new name in the dialog. Select this group to place it in the Color Guide panel as the new base group for the Harmony Rules. (For the rest of this lesson, you'll create color groups based on this base group. However, you can click on any swatch, then click on the "Set base color to the current color button" on the Color Guide panel to change the current color group; changing the base color will affect all of the Harmony Rules that are based on it.)

Click on the Color Guide arrow to the right of your current colors to make another color group, choosing one of the Harmony Rules, such as the Left Complement shown here. Save and rename that group "Left Complement from Cooler." Be aware that if you create new color groups with fewer swatches than your original artwork, you will be reducing the color variation in your artwork. A Harmony Rule contains no more than five swatches, but the panel contains variations based on those five swatches. You can drag any swatch from either the Color Guide panel or Swatches panel into any saved color group in the Swatches panel. You can also drag colors out of a color group in the Swatches panel.

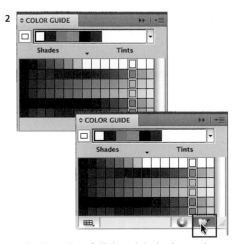

Selecting a tint of all the original colors and saving the new color group to the Swatches panel

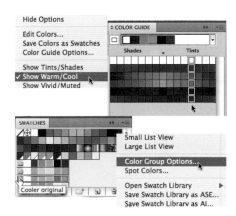

Changing the view of swatches in the Color Guide panel from the menu, selecting, saving and renaming a new color group

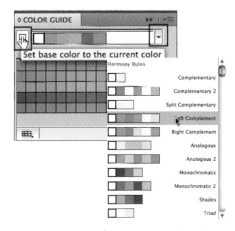

Setting a base color for a Harmony Rule and selecting a new Harmony Rule from the Color Guide list box

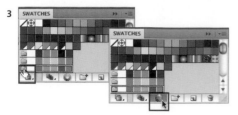

Selecting a color group with its folder icon so no color is actually selected or applied, and entering Live Color using the Edit or Apply Color Group button

Using Randomly change color order button on the Assign tab

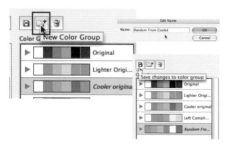

Saving a new color group OR saving changes to an existing color group

Random assignment of saturation and brightness to the pastel color group

3 Applying color groups and creating new ones using Live Color. To protect your original work, choose File > Save As and give your file a new name. (Whenever you create a version you like, repeat saving the file with another file name to protect what you've already created.) Select your artwork and then select the Cooler Original color group by clicking on the folder icon next to it. If you accidentally click on a swatch instead of the color group folder icon, and that color is applied to your artwork, choose Undo. You want to click only on the folder icon so a border shows up around your swatch group, but no color is selected.

Click on the Edit or Apply Color Group icon to enter Live Color. By default, Black and White are protected from being changed by any of the colors in your selected color group. The Cooler Original swatches replace the remaining colors with a random selection of the group's swatches. If you want to try a new version, click on the Assign tab and then on the "Randomly change color order" button. This command assigns any of the swatches from the Color Group to any of the color bars. You can keep clicking until you see a combination you like, but be sure to do this carefully, because there is no Undo in Live Color, so there's no way to return to a combination you liked. Therefore, every time you find a combination that appeals to you, click on the Save New Color Group button and save that combination as a new color group. Double-click on the name to rename it. Be careful not to click on the "Save changes to color group" button (the floppy disk), unless you want to overwrite the color group you had selected and that now has its name in italics. If you don't like the direction your changes are headed, click back on a saved color group you liked for a fresh start at generating different color versions. Whenever you find a version you want to apply, click OK and save it as a new file name. If you want to save your new color groups without changing the art, disable Recolor Art or click on "Get colors from selected art," and then click OK.

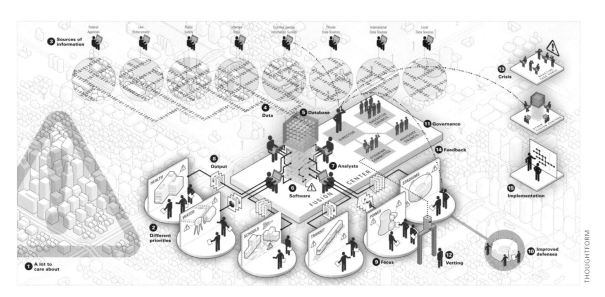

THOUGHTFORM

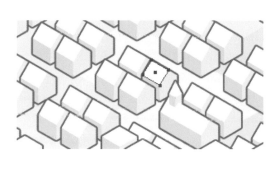

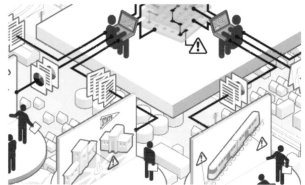

Rick Henkel / ThoughtForm Design

When Rick Henkel created this illustration of a system for information sharing, he chose an isometric view, which is commonly used in technical drawings. He first created a background "grid" of colored squares in isometric view, then overlaid basic objects of varying shapes to represent the city. He next built up the platforms for areas the system connects to, with lines and dots to form the connection. Henkel and other illustrators at ThoughtForm Design store "libraries" of objects such as these for the city, the platforms, and the figures, ready to be reused when different projects require them. They save files according to the object's category, allowing Henkel to concentrate on creating an illustration that provides an unobstructed view of the flow of information, a view isometrics is especially suited to. Adding effects such as transparency and glows not only creates a pleasing design, but also highlights important information for the viewer.

Beyond the Basics

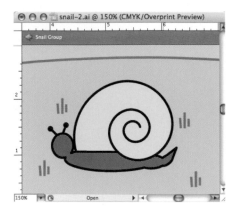

The snail in this image is a group that's currently in isolation mode. The gray isolation mode bar at the top of the window displays the name of the group and layer. Other elements of the image—green background, blades of grass, and skyline—are all dimmed, indicating that they're locked and only the snail group can be edited.

Controlling isolation mode

When you select an object that can be isolated, the Control panel displays the Isolate Selected Object button that lets you enter or exit isolation mode.—*Mordy Golding*

Layers panel and isolation

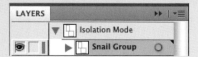

When you enter isolation mode, only the artwork in the group or layer that's isolated will be visible in the Layers panel. Once you exit isolation mode, the other layers and groups will once again appear in the Layers panel.

In the preceding chapters you've learned the basics of drawing and coloring in Illustrator. This chapter will take you beyond the basics into the world of compound paths and compound shapes (including the Pathfinder panel), the Blob Brush tool, Live Trace, and Live Paint. Live Trace lets you transform a raster image into a detailed set of vector paths that remain live and editable. Live Paint allows you to paint areas of a vector graphic more intuitively, as if you were painting by hand on paper or canvas.

This chapter begins with a look at a feature called Isolation Mode, which can be confusing (or even scary) if you encounter it without knowing what it is and how it works, but which is a helpful part of working with groups in general, and Live Paint in particular.

USING ISOLATION MODE

There are times when the object you want to edit overlaps or is contained within other objects, and your challenge is to edit the object without accidentally selecting or altering any other nearby objects. In Illustrator, isolation mode lets you easily edit a specific subset of the illustration while protecting the rest of the illustration from accidental edits. Recent enhancements to isolation mode make it so much clearer and easier to use that you should consider taking advantage of it whenever editing a particular object is difficult because of surrounding objects.

Let's look at how isolation mode works. Suppose you have some grouped artwork. To enter isolation mode, double-click any of the objects in the group with the Selection tool. You can also click the Isolate Selected Object button in the Control panel (see sidebar); or choose Enter isolation mode from the Layers panel menu or from the contextual menu (Control-click (Mac) or right-click on a two-button mouse. At the top of your document window a gray bar appears, indicating that you're now in isolation mode. The gray bar displays the hierarchy that contains the isolated object. In isolation mode, any edits that you make, such as drawing new paths, occur only inside the isolated object. Meanwhile, everything on your Artboard *except* the group you've just isolated will be dimmed, indicating that all other objects are temporarily locked. As long as isolation mode is active, anything you add to your Artboard will automatically become part of the isolated group. If you want to disable the double-clicking method of entering isolation mode, disable "Double-click to Isolate" in Preferences > General.

When you're ready to leave isolation mode, there are several ways to exit: Press the Esc key; click the gray Isolation Mode bar; double-click the Artboard outside of the Isolated artwork; click the Exit Isolation Mode button in the Control panel; or choose Exit Isolation Mode from the Layers panel menu or from the contextual menu you get by Control-clicking (Mac) or right-clicking with a two button mouse on the isolated object. The gray bar will disappear, and you'll be working normally again.

Isolation mode isn't limited to objects you've grouped yourself. Remember that other types of objects exist as groups and isolation mode works for them too, such as blends, compound shapes, or Live Paint objects. In addition to groups, you can also use isolation mode on almost anything, such as layers, symbols, clipping masks, compound paths, opacity masks, images, gradient meshes, and even a single path. For more on working with symbols in isolation mode, see the introduction to the *Brushes & Symbols* chapter.

To isolate a layer, select it in the Layers panel, and choose Enter Isolation Mode from the Layers panel menu. Exiting Isolation Mode for a layer works the same way as it does for other objects.

COMPOUND PATHS & COMPOUND SHAPES

It's often easier to create an object by combining two or more simple shapes than to draw the more complex result directly. Fortunately, Illustrator has tools that let you easily combine objects to get the results you want.

Left to right: two ovals (the inner oval has no fill, but appears black because of the black fill of the larger oval behind it); as part of a compound path the inner oval knocks a hole into the outer one where they overlap; the same compound path with inner oval, which was Direct-Selected and moved to the right to show that the hole is only where the objects overlap

Isolating a single object

You can enter isolation mode for one selected object. This can make it easier to add objects to a complex illustration. For example, you can isolate one path and easily create more paths that are directly in front of or behind it in the stacking order, even if many other nearby objects partially obscure the path of interest.

Expand compound shapes?

- If a compound shape is so complex that interacting with it is noticeably slow, expand it.
- Anything that relies on bounding boxes will behave differently on the expanded shape if that shape has a smaller bounding box than the editable compound shape. This affects all the Align commands and certain transformations.
- You must expand a compound shape before using it as an envelope. See the *Live Effects & Graphic Styles* chapter for more.

—*Pierre Louveaux*

This artwork by Gary Newman is an example of separate outlined letters made into a compound path so they operate as a unit; he then used the compound path as a mask.

The "Making a Typeface" lesson in the Artboards & Type chapter demonstrates how Caryl Gorska created her own letterforms, including letter counters (holes cut into your letter forms for the center of letters) using Pathfinder Shape modes, then expanded into compound paths.

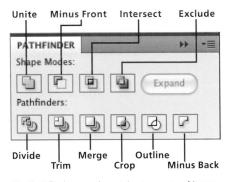

The Pathfinder panel contains two sets of icons that you can apply: Shape Modes (which combine shapes), and Pathfinders (which divide paths). See the figures on the next few pages for visual examples of what these commands do, and see the "Pathfinder panel" section later in this chapter for more explanation about using the Pathfinder panel.

There are three main ways to create new objects by combining and subtracting objects with and from each other: compound paths, compound shapes, and the Pathfinder panel. Compound paths and compound shapes are live and can easily be released to recover the original paths. Compound Paths are used primarily to create holes in objects, whereas compound shapes provide more complex ways of combining objects. The Pathfinder panel icons, perform operations very much like compound shapes except that these operations are applied permanently—the only way to reverse the effects of a pathfinder operation is to immediately Undo.

Compound paths

A compound path consists of one or more paths that have been combined so they behave as a single unit, in even more ways than if grouped. One very useful aspect of compound paths is that a hole can be created where the original objects overlapped. These holes are areas cut out from others (think of the center of a donut, or the letter **O**), through which you can see objects.

To create a compound path, e.g., a donut, or the letter **O**, draw an oval, then draw a smaller oval that will form the center hole of the **O**. Select the two paths, and then choose Object > Compound Path > Make. Select the completed letter and apply the fill color of your choice—the hole will be left empty. To adjust one of the paths within a compound path, use the Direct Selection tool; or select the compound path and enter isolation mode. To adjust the compound path as a unit, use the Group Selection or Selection tool when you aren't in Isolation Mode.

An advanced application of compound paths is to create a mask made up of multiple separate objects. For an example of this using separate "outlined" type elements, see the figure "Careers" by Gary Newman.

Holes and fills with compound paths

For simple holes, the Compound Path > Make command will generally give the result you need. If your compound path has multiple overlapping areas, or you're not getting the desired holes in the spaces, take a look at Fill Rules.pdf on the *Wow! CD*. Or, try using compound shapes (described in the next section), which give you complete control, and many more options.

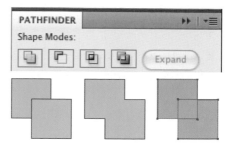

Pathfinder panel

The Pathfinder panel includes the top row of Shape Modes icons and the lower row of Pathfinder commands. The Expand icon in the Pathfinder panel isn't active by default; it's available when you've selected a compound shape, which is discussed in the next section.

The first Pathfinder icon, Unite, combines objects. The remaining Pathfinder icons separate objects; think of these as cookie cutters. The Trim and Merge commands can be applied only to filled objects.

The Pathfinder icons alter the selected objects permanently, slicing them up if needed to achieve the icon's effect. These permanent alterations to the objects may be intended; for example, you might decide to apply the Intersect icon to selected objects so that you can pull apart and further edit the resulting pieces. If you want to preserve the original objects, create a compound shape (see the "Compound shapes" section following).

Compound shapes

A *compound shape* is a combination of shapes where the original objects are preserved and can be restored at any time. You can make compound shapes from two or more paths, other compound shapes, text, envelopes, blends, groups, or artwork with vector effects applied.

You can create compound shapes using the top row of icons in the Pathfinder panel, although it isn't obvious how; you must hold down Option/Alt as you click a Shape mode icon. You can also choose Make Compound Shape from the Pathfinder panel menu, which applies Unite in shape mode.

As long as you keep compound shapes live, you can continue to apply (or remove) Shape modes, or a wide

Unite (For this example as well as the ones below, the first column shows the original shapes; the second column shows the results of the operation shown in Preview mode; and the third column shows the resulting objects selected, so you can see the effects of the operation more clearly)

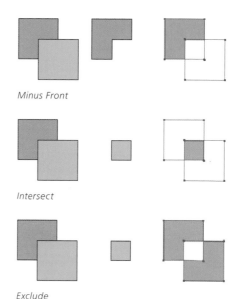

Minus Front

Intersect

Exclude

Shape modes in Illustrator CS4

Contrary to the label, the Shape Mode icons now create expanded shapes by default; Option-click/Alt-click to create compound shapes. This is the opposite of how Shape Mode icons worked previously, where simply clicking the icons produced compound shapes, and you had to hold down Option/Alt while clicking to produce expanded results.

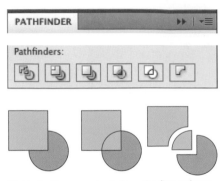

PATHFINDER

Pathfinders:

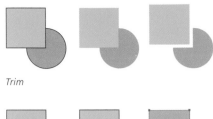

Divide (In the examples below, the first column shows the original shapes; the second column shows the results; and the third column shows the results broken apart or selected, for clarity)

Trim

Merge (Note that Merge only functions correctly if both objects are the same color; otherwise it works the same as Trim)

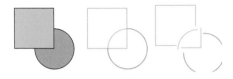

Crop

Outline (Note that after performing the Outline operation, Illustrator applies a stroke of 0 by default—here, a 2-pt stroke has been manually applied)

Minus Back

variety of effects, to the compound shape as a unit. In later chapters, as you work with live effects such as envelopes, warps, and drop shadows, remember that you can integrate effects into your compound shapes while retaining the ability to edit your objects—even if they are editable type. Compound shapes can also be pasted or exported into Photoshop as editable shape layers, although they won't retain their Illustrator appearance.

If you want to restore the original objects that comprise a compound shape, select it and choose Release Compound Shape from the Pathfinder panel menu. To flatten a compound shape while preserving its current appearance, select it and then click the Expand icon on the Pathfinder panel, or choose Expand Compound Shape from the Pathfinder panel menu.

There actually is yet another way to apply a compound shape version of a Pathfinder command. If you wish to apply a Pathfinder command to a layer, type object, or a group, you can apply a live Pathfinder Effect to it from either the Effects menu, or the *fx* icon from the Appearance panel (see the *Live Effects & Graphic Styles* chapter for more about working with live effects).

The price of using compound shapes

The power of compound shapes does come at a cost. As with other live objects, compound shapes require Illustrator to perform many calculations to keep appearances up to date as you edit the illustration. Too many compound shapes or too many operations or effects applied to compound shapes can slow down the screen redraw of your image. Although compound paths are much less powerful or flexible, they won't slow down screen redraw. So if you're working with simple objects, it may be better to use compound paths instead.

USING THE BLOB BRUSH TOOL

The ability to combine or divide paths gives you ways to create a complex object that can be easier than drawing it from scratch. However, it takes a bit of planning to determine and draw the initial paths, position them, and click the correct Pathfinder icon. Wouldn't it be great if paths automatically combined as you drew them? You can do that using the Blob Brush tool.

If you paint the same brushstroke using the Blob Brush tool and the Calligraphic Paintbrush, it may be hard to tell the difference between each tool, at first. If you switch to Outline mode, the difference becomes clear: An Illustrator path runs down the middle of a Paintbrush brushstroke and the application of the Paint-brush remains live, which means the brushstroke can be restyled or edited like any other path in Illustrator (see the *Brushes and Symbols* chapter for more about work-ing with brushes). In contrast, the appearance of the brushstroke painted with the Blob Brush tool is expanded as soon as you complete a stroke. Where a Paintbrush brushstroke is defined by the single path down its middle, a Blob Brush brushstroke is defined by a path around its outer edge. Having the simpler, expanded paths of the Blob Brush tool can save you time if you plan to use Live Paint, which we cover later in this chapter.

Painting with the Blob Brush tool

Using the Blob Brush tool can resemble using ink in that as you apply more brushstrokes on top of existing ones, they can automatically merge into a single stroke.

To paint with the Blob Brush tool, select it, set a stroke color, drag a brushstroke, and then paint more brush-strokes that overlap an existing brushstroke. The Blob Brush merges your new brushstrokes into the existing brushstrokes (depending on conditions discussed later in this section). This makes the Blob Brush tool a quick and easy way to add onto a filled path, or to connect existing paths that use the same fill. You can also carve the con-tour of a Blob Brush brushstroke by using the Blob Brush and Eraser tools together (see Blob Brush lessons later in this chapter, and the Eraser section later in this introduc-tion). Note that editing an open path with the Blob Brush tool will close the path.

Select the Blob Brush tool (left) in the Tools panel, set the stroke color, and drag to create a brushstroke that appears as a filled shape (right)

CHAVEZ

Conrad Chavez drew blades of grass using the Paintbrush tool (left) and using the Blob Brush tool (right)

Same illustrations as above, viewed in Outline view: blades of grass drawn using the Paintbrush tool (left) and using the Blob Brush tool (right)

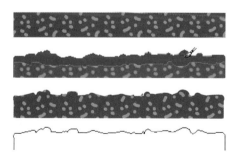

Chavez also used the Blob Brush tool to give the soil a rough top edge. He drew a rectangle (top), set the Blob Brush tool to the same stroke pattern as the rectangle's fill, and painted along the top edge to add to it (second from top). The resulting shape is a single path (bottom two).

If the Blob Brush tool is set to a different fill color than the unselected path (left), the Blob Brush can't edit the path. When you set the current stroke color to match the fill color of the original path (and the Keep Selected option is off), dragging the Blob Brush tool over the original path can edit it (right)

If the Blob Brush tool is set to a different fill color than two unselected paths (left), you can't join them with the Blob Brush tool. You can join them if you set the Blob Brush tool stroke color to match the fill colors of the paths (right)

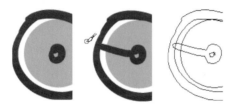

Here the hub and rim do have the same fill and stroke attributes, but dragging the Blob brush to draw a connecting spoke (center) still does not connect them, as Outline view reveals (right). This is because there's a path between the hub and rim in the layer stacking order (below)

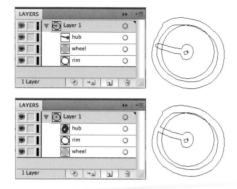

By making the hub and rim adjacent in the Layers panel (left), the Blob brush can connect them, as shown in Outline view (right)

When drawing with the Blob Brush tool, you can temporarily access the Smooth tool by holding Option/Alt as you drag along the outline of a path.

There's an aspect of the Blob Brush tool that seems counterintuitive at first: You establish the color of brushstrokes by setting the current stroke color, but after you complete a brushstroke the path's fill takes the stroke color, and the stroke is removed. This is because the Blob Brush automatically expands brushstrokes into filled paths while maintaining their appearance. The rules are slightly different if you turn on the Keep Selected option in the Blob Brush Tool Options dialog (discussed below). Your last brushstroke's fill color is active because that brushstroke remains selected, so your next brushstroke can merge with the selected one.

Having trouble getting the Blob Brush tool to edit existing paths? Pay attention to color, selection, and stacking order. The Blob Brush tool gives priority to paths filled with the same fill color as the tool's stroke color (or paths filled with the tool's fill color if no stroke color is set). It won't edit stroked paths. Selecting a path is a quick way to allow the Blob Brush tool to edit it, as long as it has a solid color or pattern fill. The Blob Brush tool won't edit multiple selected paths if their fill colors are different.

Note that there isn't anything special about paths created by the Blob Brush tool; you can edit them using any path-editing tool such as the Pen tool. This also means that you can use the Blob Brush tool to modify a path that was drawn using another tool. For example, you can draw a star and then use the Blob Brush tool to add to the star. But the Blob Brush tool can't add to or connect to a live compound shape; expand the compound shape first.

If you can't connect two separate objects with the Blob Brush, rearrange them so they're within the same layer, and adjacent in the stacking order, in the Layers panel. In order to connect multiple paths with the same fill color, avoid dragging over other paths with other fill colors.

You can customize the Blob Brush tool by double-clicking the Blob Brush icon in the Tools panel. The

Selection Limits Merge option is unique to the Blob Brush Tool Options dialog and makes it easier to add to an existing path in a crowded illustration. When Selection Limits Merge is on, the Blob Brush tool will only affect a path if it's selected and you drag over it. Unchecking Selection Limits Merge allows the Blob Brush tool to edit paths regardless of whether or not the paths are selected.

The Blob Brush Tool Options dialog also includes calligraphic brush options, so if you use a pressure-sensitive stylus and tablet (such as a Wacom) you can be as expressive with the Blob Brush tool as you can with the Paintbrush tool, using stylus pressure to change options such as Angle, Roundness, and Diameter.

To prevent certain paths from being affected by the Blob Brush tool, you can select the paths and then lock them, hide them, or enter isolation mode. If the paths are on a separate layer, you can lock or hide their layer.

ERASING PATHS

When you want to delete parts of a path, your first instinct might be to reach for the Scissors tool or other features associated with the Pen tool. That'll work, but you'll find it easier to use the more direct and interactive Eraser tool and Path Eraser tools.

Using the Eraser tool

Think of the Eraser tool as almost the opposite of the Blob Brush tool: It wipes out anything you drag it over, regardless of whether the paths are selected. The Eraser tool also has the calligraphic attributes of the Blob Brush tool and Paintbrush, so you can double-click the Eraser tool in the Tools panel to customize it.

If you're using a Wacom tablet stylus, you don't even have to select the Eraser tool in the Tools panel; just flip over the stylus and drag using the eraser end of the stylus.

As with the Blob Brush tool, you can restrict the effect of the Eraser tool to selected paths only, and you don't have to change any tool options to do this. Select the paths you want to edit, and then drag the Eraser tool

CHAVEZ

The fastest way to put holes into this slice of cheese is with the Eraser tool. Conrad Chavez double-clicked the Eraser tool to set the brush shape and options, selected the cheese path, and dragged the Eraser tool to create a hole that reveals the plate underneath.

Chavez then used the Eraser tool to put more holes in the cheese. When you create a hole by erasing in the middle of a path, the Eraser tool automatically creates a compound path.

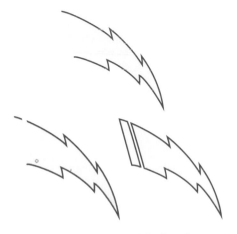

If you start with an open path (top), and you erase all the way through the path (left), the resulting paths will always be closed (right)

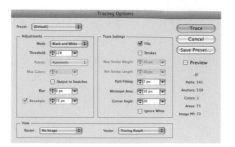

The Tracing Options dialog is an essential stop if you want to have any control over the results of your tracing

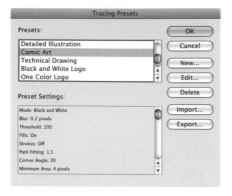

You can manage your tracing presets from within the Tracing Presets dialog.

The Raster View (left) and Vector View (right) buttons in the Control panel

GIBLIN

You don't have to be a rocket scientist to use Live Trace in combination with Live Paint (discussed in the next section)—the two features were designed to work hand in hand. To create the colored rocket above, Ian Giblin began with the scanned drawing on the left, then used Live Trace to create the tracing in the middle. After he converted the tracing to a Live Paint group, it was easy to color the rocket using the Live Paint Bucket.

through them. And, as with the Blob Brush Tool, if you want certain paths to be protected from the Eraser tool when nothing is selected, lock or hide those paths or their layer. You can constrain the direction of the Eraser tool by Shift-dragging, or Option-dragging/Alt-dragging a marquee to erase a rectangular area.

If you drag the Eraser tool all the way across a path to cut it in half, the Eraser tool automatically heals the cuts, resulting in closed paths. Editing a filled open path with the Eraser tool always results in a closed path, but this might not result in a visual difference unless a stroke was applied to the original path.

Carving with the Eraser tool and the Blob Brush tool

You can use the Eraser and Blob Brush tools together to sculpt artwork in a fluid, intuitive way, without tedious point-by-point editing. First double-click each tool in the Tools panel to set their attributes. Use the Blob Brush tool to lay down the positive areas, and then use the Eraser tool to carve out negative areas. You'll find that the Eraser tool is useful for chiseling details out of existing paths. And unlike a Calligraphic Brush mark, with a Blob Brush tool mark you can use the Eraser tool to refine the shape of a stroke edge.

When you use the Blob Brush tool and Eraser tool together, it helps to remember their conveniently similar shortcuts so that you can switch instantly between them: Press Shift-B for the Blob Brush tool, and press Shift-E for the Eraser tool. If you're using a Wacom stylus with a built-in eraser, just flip the stylus over; the Eraser tool will be used when you drag the stylus's eraser.

Using the Path Eraser tool

Drag the Path Eraser tool along (not perpendicular to) a selected path to remove the portion of the path that you drag over; you can even erase a mid-section of a path. This tool is usually more work than the Eraser tool because you have to drag it close to the path, and it leaves the path open. If you want the path to be closed, you have to switch to the Pen tool and manually click on each end-point to close the path yourself.

USING LIVE TRACE

Have you ever wished you could automatically transform a raster image—such as a photo or a scanned drawing—into a detailed, accurate set of vector paths? Illustrator's Live Trace feature grants your wish. In a matter of minutes (and in some cases, seconds) Live Trace renders your original image into vector graphics that can then be edited, resized, and otherwise manipulated without distortion or loss of quality.

Live Trace gives you complete control over the level of detail that is traced. Live Trace options include the ability to specify a color mode and a palette of colors for the tracing object, fill and stroke settings, the sharpness of corner angles, blurring and resampling controls, and more. Tracing Presets allow you to store a set of tracing options for quick access the next time you need them.

Best of all, the tracing object you create with Live Trace remains live (that's of course why they call it Live Trace), so you can adjust the parameters and results of your tracing at any time, as long as you keep it live. Once you're happy with your Live Trace object, you can work with it as vector paths or you can choose to convert it to a Live Paint object and take advantage of the new Live Paint Bucket's intuitive painting capabilities.

The basics of Live Trace

To trace an image using Live Trace, start by opening or placing the file that you'll be using as your source image. Once it's selected, you can trace the object using the default settings by clicking Live Trace in the Control panel, or choosing Object > Live Trace > Make. To set Live Trace options before you trace the image, click the Tracing Presets and Options button in the Control panel (it's a small black triangle to the right of the Live Trace button) and select Tracing Options. (You can also access the Tracing Options by choosing Object > Live Trace > Tracing

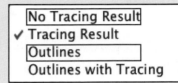

Click the Live Trace button in the Control panel to trace using the default settings

The Tracing Presets and Options button in the Control panel lets you open the Tracing Options dialog or choose a tracing preset

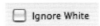

The Ignore White checkbox in the Tracing Options dialog lets you automatically remove a white background from your tracing object

Zoom before tracing

You can't change magnification or view from within Live Trace Options, so make sure to zoom in to see the area that you want to use as a reference before opening Live Trace Options.

Testing a trace

Save a small, representative, cropped version of your image and test your Live Trace settings with that small file. Save your settings, and then apply them to your large file! —*Kevan Atteberry*

Tracing object names

All tracing objects appear in the Layers panel with the default name "Tracing"—until you rename them, expand them, or convert them to Live Paint objects.

Tracing paper

Adobe has published a technical white paper on Live Trace entitled *Creating Vector Content: Using Live Trace.* You can find it as creating_vector_content.pdf on the *Wow! CD.*

Releasing a tracing object

If you want to get rid of a tracing object—but keep the original placed image where it is—all you have to do is release the tracing object by selecting it, and choosing Object > Live Trace > Release.

Options.) Search "live trace" in Help > Illustrator Help for a rundown of the various options in the Tracing Options dialog. You can enable the Preview checkbox to see what your tracing will look like before you actually execute it, but be aware that this can slow you down considerably.

Before you execute your tracing, you can choose a tracing preset in the Tracing Options dialog (from the Preset menu), or click on the Tracing Presets and Options button in the Control panel. If you create a Live Trace setting that you think you'll want to apply to other images in the future, you can save time by saving your current settings as a custom tracing preset.

To create a custom tracing preset, set your options in the Tracing Options dialog and then click the Save Preset button. Illustrator prompts you to type a name for your new preset. Once you do that and click OK, your new preset will be available from the Preset pop-up menu in the Control panel when you have either a raster object or a Live Trace object selected. (Your preset will also be available from the Preset pop-up menu in Tracing Options.) To manage your tracing presets, choose Edit > Tracing Presets to access the Tracing Presets dialog, where you can edit or delete existing presets, create new ones, or click Export to save your presets to a file that can be shared with other users. (To load presets from an exported file, just click the Import button and locate your saved preset.)

When you've set the tracing options the way you want them, click Trace, and then sit back and watch the Live Trace feature go to work. Once Live Trace has traced your image, you can change the way the tracing object is displayed, or adjust the results of the tracing.

Changing the display of a Live Trace object

Because Live Trace is live by definition, your original source image remains untouched. So there are really two parts to a Live Trace object: the original source image, and the tracing that results from Live Trace. Though only the tracing result is visible by default, you can change how both parts of the Live Trace object are displayed.

Start by selecting the Live Trace object. Once you've done that, you can change whether (and how) the original source image is displayed by choosing Object > Live Trace or clicking the Raster View button in the Control panel. Select one of the four options: No Image to completely hide the source image; Original Image to display the source image underneath the tracing result; Adjusted Image to display the image with any adjustments applied during the tracing process; or Transparent Image to see a "ghost" of the source image.

With the Live Trace object selected, you can also change how the tracing result is displayed by choosing Object > Live Trace or clicking the Vector View button in the Control panel. Select one of the four options: No Tracing Result to completely hide the result of the tracing; Tracing Result to display the full tracing result; Outlines to display only the outlines of the tracing object; or Outlines with Tracing to see the tracing result with outlines visible.

Adjusting the results of a Live Trace

Of course, because your Live Trace object is live, you can adjust the results of the tracing whenever you want. Simply select your Live Trace object and choose a new preset from the Control panel preset pop-up menu; or, click the Tracing Options button in the Control panel; or choose Object > Live Trace > Tracing Options. If you choose Tracing Options, you'll get the same Tracing Options dialog you saw before you traced the object, and you can continue to adjust and change any of the options at will. Then, just click Trace to reapply. Also note that you can adjust basic tracing result options, such as Threshold and Min Area (for Minimum Area), right in the Control panel, without even entering the Tracing Options dialog.

Using swatch libraries with Live Trace

You can create a special swatch library with only the colors you want in your tracing, and then specify it in the Tracing Options dialog by choosing its name from the Palette pop-up. You can also specify any open swatch library. In either

✓ No Image
Original Image
Adjusted Image
Transparent Image

The options in the Raster View menu

No Tracing Result
✓ Tracing Result
Outlines
Outlines with Tracing

The options in the Vector View menu

Tracing   Preset: [Default]

Threshold: 128   Min Area: 10 px

With Live Trace objects you can choose Presets, access Options, and adjust Threshold and Min area (for Minimum), directly in the Control panel

When tracing an EPS...

Illustrator has a difficult time tracing EPS images, because it can't access the full image data. So if your source image is an EPS, it's a good idea to make sure it's embedded before you do your trace.

—Jean-Claude Tremblay

Swatch and learn

See the "Trace Techniques" lesson, later in this chapter, for an example of working with swatches while using Live Trace.

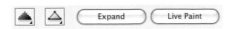

Expand   Live Paint

The Expand and Live Paint buttons in the Control panel

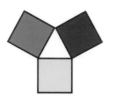

Three squares arranged to form a triangular space in the middle

Clicking a selected group with the Live Paint Bucket turns it into a Live Paint Group. Note the helpful tool tip that appears next to the cursor

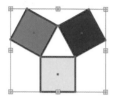

When you select a Live Paint Group with the Selection tool, you'll see this special bounding box

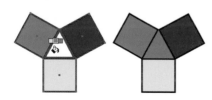

Left: When you position the Live Paint Bucket over an area that can be painted, a highlight appears around the area. Right: After clicking with the Bucket, the area fills with color

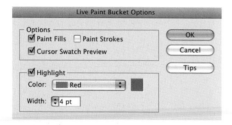

Double-click on the Live Paint Bucket in the Tools panel to access its options

case, make sure you have the swatch library open *before* you open the Tracing Options dialog, or else its name won't appear in the Palette pop-up.

Converting to a Live Paint object or set of paths

Live Trace is designed to work hand in hand with the Live Paint feature (see the "Working with Live Paint" section following this one). Once you're happy with your tracing object, you can easily convert it to a Live Paint object so that you can color it using the Live Paint Bucket. You can also convert the tracing object to paths if you want to work with the elements of the traced artwork as separate objects.

Whether you're converting to Live Paint or to paths, keep in mind that your tracing will no longer be live and editable after you perform this step, so don't convert your tracing until you're satisfied with it. To convert the tracing to a Live Paint object, just select the object and click the Live Paint button in the Control panel (or use Object > Live Trace > Convert to Live Paint). To convert the tracing to a set of grouped paths, click the Expand button in the Control panel or choose Object > Live Trace > Expand.

When you expand your tracing, you can choose to preserve your current display options by choosing Object > Live Trace > Expand as Viewed. In that case, your Raster and Vector View settings will determine what's visible after you expand. So, for example, if your Vector View is set to Outlines, and you set the Raster View to No Image, after you choose Expand as Viewed you'll get a set of paths with no stroke and no fill, and no visible source image either. On the other hand, if you want to preserve the source image to be used as a guide for the paths after you've expanded them, you could set your Raster View to Original Image. At that point, when you choose Expand as Viewed, your source image will also be preserved and grouped together with the new paths.

WORKING WITH LIVE PAINT

With Illustrator's Live Paint function, you can instantly apply color, gradients, and other fills to any enclosed space in your artwork, without having to make sure it's defined as a separate vector object first. That lets you paint shapes and spaces the way your eye sees them—just as you would if you were coloring a drawing by hand.

Painting the intuitive way

Suppose you draw three squares, arranged so that the space between them forms a triangle, as in the example at right. Under normal Illustrator rules, you wouldn't be able to color that triangle because it doesn't exist as a separate vector object. It's just the empty space between the squares. That's where Live Paint comes in. Live Paint says, in effect, "If you don't like the rules, change them!" Just designate the objects you want to paint as a Live Paint Group. Suddenly, you can paint any enclosed area you want, whether or not it's a discrete vector object.

So here's how to paint the empty triangular space. First, select the three squares with the Selection tool. Then choose the Live Paint Bucket tool (it lives just below the Eyedropper tool in the Tools panel) and click on the selected squares to turn them into a Live Paint Group. (You can also turn selected objects into a Live Paint Group by choosing Object > Live Paint Make, or via the keyboard command ⌘-Option-X/Ctrl-Alt-X.) You'll notice a special bounding box around the squares, with little star-shapes in its handles. This bounding box distinguishes a Live Paint Group from an ordinary Group.

Next, choose a bright green color as a fill, and then move the Live Paint Bucket over the triangular space. The triangle becomes highlighted, showing that the area is available for painting. Click on the triangle, and presto— the triangle fills with the chosen color.

By the way, you can change the way the Live Paint Bucket behaves by double-clicking on its icon in the Tools panel. This opens the Live Paint Bucket Options dialog, where you can set options such as whether the Bucket paints fills, strokes, or both, and you can set the color and size of the highlight you see when you position the Bucket over a paintable area. Also, keep in mind that you can

Left: The Live Paint Bucket is positioned to paint the fill. Middle: When the cursor is positioned to paint the stroke, note that the cursor changes from a bucket to a little paintbrush, in addition to highlighting the stroke. Right: After painting the strokes on all three sides of the triangle

Left: the original butterfly outline. Middle: Live Paint lets you select and paint the area of the wing around the two spots. Right: the fully painted butterfly

Cursor swatch preview

The Live Paint Bucket's "cursor swatch preview" feature lets you quickly cycle through color choices in the Swatches panel—both within and between color groups. The preview is visible anytime you choose a color from the Swatches panel to paint with. The middle square is the selected color, and the squares on either side are its neighbors in the Swatches panel— use the left and right arrow keys to move to the previous or next swatch, and the up and down arrow keys to move between color groups and the general group of swatches. You can hide the swatch preview by double-clicking the Live Paint Bucket and disabling the Cursor Swatch Preview checkbox in the Live Paint Options dialog (it's turned on by default).

Left: positioning the Bucket over the intersection of the circles. Right: after clicking on the intersection to fill it with a rainbow gradient

Left: the original circles. Middle: moving the red circle below the green one. Right: changing the size and shape of both circles. The intersection keeps its gradient fill even as it moves around

Fixing a hole

With Live Paint objects, you can create a transparent "hole" in an object simply by choosing the None swatch and using the Live Paint Bucket to fill an area (such as a background, or the center of this donut) with None!
—*Sandee Cohen*

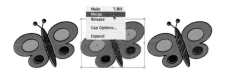

Left: adding six lines to the butterfly's body. Middle: adding the new paths to the butterfly's Live Paint Group. Right: painting the spaces between the lines orange to create three stripes

Deleting can make holes too!

There's another way to make a donut hole: use the Live Paint Selection tool to select the "hole" and delete!

always edit the paths in Live Paint Groups using the Pen tool or other tools.

Painting strokes with Live Paint

As mentioned in the previous section, you can use the Live Paint Bucket to paint strokes as well as fills. Just make sure the Paint Strokes checkbox is enabled in the Live Paint Options dialog, and the Live Paint Bucket will apply whatever Stroke attributes you've defined before you click with the Bucket. When painting the stroke, make sure to position the bucket so that the stroke is highlighted rather than the fill.

Also, even if you haven't enabled the Paint Strokes checkbox in Live Paint Options, you can always paint strokes at will by holding down the Shift key as you click with the Bucket.

Keep in mind that the stroke attributes currently specified in the Stroke panel (or Control panel) will determine the look of the stroke the Bucket paints, so be sure to set them where you want them before you click.

The flat world of Live Paint

One of the rules that falls by the wayside when you're working with a Live Paint Group is the idea of stacking order. Within a Live Paint Group, everything is treated as if it's at the same level.

Here's an example. The simple butterfly figure at left is ready to be colored using Live Paint. Notice that when the Live Paint Bucket is moved over the left wing, Illustrator highlights the area of the wing surrounding the two spots, allowing you to paint the main part of the wing without also coloring in the spots. (You can color the spots separately by moving the Bucket directly over them.) Under the normal rules of Illustrator, you'd have to make sure that the two spots were stacked above the wing shape so you didn't paint over them when you colored the wing. But in the flat world of Live Paint, Illustrator understands that the spots are separate entities, and allows you to simply color around them.

Choose your fill (or go with no fill)

We've seen how Live Paint can apply color to enclosed spaces—but the Live Paint Bucket can paint all kinds of fills, not just solid colors. That means you can choose to paint with a gradient, a pattern, or even no fill at all.

Create two overlapping solid-filled circles, and make them into a Live Paint Group. Now you can fill the intersection between the two circles with a gradient (by choosing a gradient swatch from the Swatches panel, and clicking on the intersection with the Live Paint Bucket). You can even fill the intersection with None, and the intersection will become a hole that lets you see objects or fills below. For an example of what you can do by painting with no fill, see Sandee Cohen's "Fixing a hole" tip.

Putting the "Live" in Live Paint

The "Live" part of Live Paint means that your painting remains editable and changes along with your objects when you resize them, transform them, or move them around. When you move or resize your two overlapping circles, the intersection maintains its fill even as it changes size, shape, and position along with the circles.

Adding paths to a Live Paint Group

After you've created a Live Paint Group, you may decide that you'd like to add some paths to it. Fortunately, it's easy to add new members to a Live Paint Group.

Suppose you want to add stripes to the body of the butterfly example. One way to add them is to draw stroked lines using the Pen or Line tools. Next, select the lines along with the butterfly Live Paint Group, and click the Merge Live Paint button in the Control panel (or choose Object > Live Paint > Merge). The six lines are added to the Live Paint Group, where they serve as three stripes that you can easily paint.

However, there's an even easier way to add new paths to a Live Paint Group—by working in isolation mode, as discussed at the beginning of this chapter.

Using the Selection tool, double-click on any object

Left: The bananas before coloring. Right: The circle indicates the gap that's causing color to flood outside the bananas

The Gap Options dialog

Once the gap was no longer a problem, it was easy to paint the bananas yellow

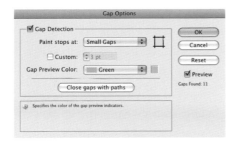

In the Gap Options dialog, enable Preview and Gap Detection, then choose green for the highlight color

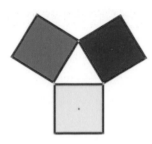

The little green dots at the corners of the triangle reveal where the gaps are

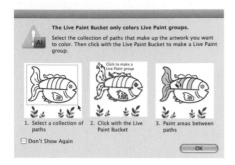

If you click with the Live Paint Bucket and you haven't selected any paths, you'll see the (very informative) dialog shown above

Coloring multiple areas

You can use the Live Paint Bucket tool to color multiple areas with a single color in one step by clicking in one area and dragging across additional contiguous areas.

Easy as 1-2-3

There are three ways to click with the Live Paint Bucket and Live Paint Selection tools:

- Single-click an area to fill it or select it.
- Double-click an area to "flood fill" into, or select across, adjacent areas of the same color.
- Triple-click to fill or select all areas that have the same fill.

in an existing group (or in this case a Live Paint Group). You'll see the gray bar with the current name of your group (as shown in the Layers panel) appear at the top of your window, which tells you you've just entered isolation mode. Once you see the gray bar, your group has been isolated and anything you add to your Artboard will automatically be considered part of the group.

So in the case of the butterfly, double-clicking part of the butterfly with the Selection tool will put you in isolation mode. You can now draw your stripes and they will automatically become part of the Live Paint Group for the butterfly. To exit isolation mode, just press the Esc key.

Live Paint's Gap Options

As you've seen, Live Paint lets you apply color to any enclosed area. But the key word there is *enclosed*. What happens when the area you're trying to paint isn't completely sealed off? What if there are one or more small openings between the paths surrounding the area, causing it to spring a leak? That's where Illustrator's handy Gap Options dialog comes in.

On the previous page is an example developed by author and trainer Sandee Cohen. Sandee created this pair of bananas by tracing a raster image with Live Trace. Sandee then converted the tracing to a Live Paint group and attempted to paint the bananas yellow. But as you can see in the image on the right, when she clicked on the bottom banana with the Live Paint Bucket, color flooded outside the banana because of a small gap toward the end of the banana. (It's indicated with a red circle.) To fix this problem, Sandee selected the bananas and then opened the Gap Options dialog by choosing Object > Live Paint > Gap Options.

Using the drop-down menu labeled "Paint Stops at" located at the top of the dialog, Sandee changed the setting from Small Gaps to Large Gaps. This caused Live Paint to ignore the relatively small gap at the end of the banana, and let her paint the banana yellow, just as if the gap weren't there. If Sandee had wanted to be even more precise, she could have specified an exact size for how large a gap would have to be before Live Paint would recognize it as an opening. To do so, she'd enable the Custom checkbox and enter a number in the field.

If you don't have any Live Paint Groups selected when you open the Gap Options dialog, whatever settings you choose will become the defaults for any new Live Paint Groups you create before you change the settings again.

You can also use the Gap Options dialog to detect gaps in your artwork. Let's look at the example of the three squares again. Suppose that when you try to paint the triangle you can't get the triangle to highlight when you move the Live Paint Bucket over it. That's a good sign that maybe the squares weren't exactly flush. In that case, you can use the Gap Detection feature to see where the problem is, as shown at left. Select the squares, open the Gap Options dialog, enable the Preview checkbox and choose Green as the highlight color from the "Gap Preview Color" drop-down menu. The figure shows the troublemaking gaps highlighted in green at the corners of the triangle. At this point, it's easy enough to move the squares a little closer together to eliminate those gaps.

When you convert a Live Trace object to Live Paint, Gap Detection will be turned off, even if you turned it on before converting. Just re-enable it if you need it.

How to expand (or release) Live Paint Groups

Once you've finished coloring a Live Paint Group, you may find that you're ready to move on and do other things to the objects in the group—some of which will require taking them out of the realm of Live Paint. For example, you may want to be able to work with the objects in the group as separate elements once you've colored them. That's where expanding comes in.

When you select your Live Paint Group and choose Object > Live Paint > Expand (or click the Expand button in the Control panel), the selected objects will be converted to ordinary vector paths. Their appearance will stay the same as before, but they will no longer be Live

Splitting Live Paint groups

With Live Paint groups that are made up of many complex paths, gap detection will impede performance. You will experience better performance by splitting very large Live Paint groups into several smaller Live Paint groups. —*Mordy Golding*

Reapplying fills

Unfortunately, if you move a path so that an enclosed painted area becomes unpainted, Illustrator doesn't remember that the region was filled with a color prior to the edit. Moving the path back to its original position will not bring the fill back and you'll need to reapply the fill color.—*Mordy Golding*

Closing gaps automatically

Illustrator will close gaps for you if you click the "Close gaps with paths" icon at the bottom of the Gap Options dialog. Be aware that Illustrator always uses straight paths to close gaps, and that may not always produce the results you want.

About this section

This section is partially adapted from the article "Live Paint Is a Bucket of Fun," previously published on CreativePro.com. For more of CreativePro's great Illustrator How-To articles, visit www.creativepro.com.

Using the Live Paint Selection tool to select one piece of a line

Selecting and deleting the four line segments around the middle square

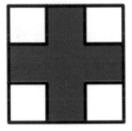

After deleting the four segments, painting the four corner squares white to make the red cross stand out

ATTEBERRY

See Kevan Atteberry's Galleries using Live Trace later in this chapter

Paint objects, and they'll be rendered into separate filled and stroked paths that behave according to the "normal" rules Live Paint allowed you to break.

On the other hand, you may find that you'd like to revert the objects in your Live Paint Group back to their pre–Live Paint state. Maybe you'd like to rework them a little before you paint them, or you decide you'd like to color them the old-school way, without using Live Paint. No problem—just choose Object > Live Paint > Release (or click the Release button in the Control panel) and your objects will be converted back to ordinary paths.

Editing paths the intuitive way

You've seen how Live Paint lets you color spaces the way the eye sees them. You can also edit paths the same way. Use the Live Paint Selection tool (which lives next to the Live Paint Bucket in the Tools panel) to select and alter specific parts of paths based on the way they look (instead of how they were constructed).

You can set options for the Live Paint Selection tool by double-clicking, just like the Live Paint Bucket. Before moving on to the next step, you'll want to open the Live Paint Selection Options dialog to make sure you're able to select strokes as well as fills. You'll be working with a red object in the next step, so change the highlight color to something you can see against a red fill, such as green.

First, create a grid of nine squares by drawing a large red square with a black stroke, and then overlaying this big square with four intersecting black-stroked lines on top. Then convert the whole grid into a Live Paint Group.

Now, by choosing the Live Paint Selection tool and moving it over the divider lines, you can select the smaller segments of the lines that were formed as they crossed each other. At this point, you only have to select and delete four of those small segments to end up with the cross-shaped object in the center of the large square. Then you can use the Live Paint Bucket to paint the four corner squares white, and presto—the result is a red cross on a white background.

GRAHAM

Cheryl Graham

Live Trace is an ideal complement to Cheryl Graham's high contrast drawing style. Graham added her photo to the page (File > Place) then clicked the Live Trace button in the Control panel. She used this Default preset knowing that the Mode setting of Black and White would produce the desired effect (middle detail). Graham then retraced the photo using the Control panel buttons, this time lowering the Threshold. To create a larger area of white, she clicked the Tracing options button, and in the dialog she lowered the Threshold to 90. To bring out greater detail around the eyes and hair, she set Path Fitting to 1px with a Minimum Area of 4px (bottom detail). Satisfied with the results, she clicked Trace. Graham did not save these settings because every photo usually requires a different combination of Tracing Options and plenty of experimentation. Graham clicked the Expand button in the Control panel to convert the Live Trace object to editable paths. She refined the paths with the Smooth tool. Using the Pen tool and variations of the default Art Brush Calligraphy 1, she drew in the remaining details of the portrait. (See her gallery in the *Brushes & Symbols* chapter for more about her drawing technique.)

Combining Paths

Basic Path Construction with Pathfinders

Overview: *Create an illustration by joining and intersecting objects using the Pathfinder panel's Unite, Minus Front, and Intersect.*

1

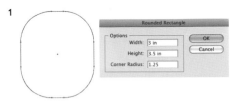

Creating a rounded rectangle by clicking on the Artboard with the Rounded Rectangle tool, setting dimensions, and increasing Corner Radius

Creating a rounded rectangle by clicking on the Artboard with the Rounded Rectangle tool, setting dimensions, and decreasing Corner Radius

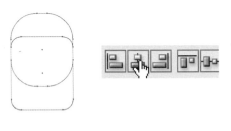

Selecting both rounded rectangles, using Horizontal Align Center, using the Unite Pathfinder command, and changing fill to cyan

To create many eye-catching stock illustrations like the one above, which are used for advertisements, websites, and more, Ryan Putnam frequently uses the Pathfinder panel. Using the Pathfinder's Unite, Minus Front, and Intersect, you too can easily create compelling character illustrations.

1 Constructing the body with the Unite Pathfinder command. Ryan Putnam created the body from two rounded rectangles. To create the first object, he clicked on the Artboard with the Rounded Rectangle tool to open the Rounded Rectangle dialog. In the dialog, he set the dimensions of the rectangle to 3 in for Width, 3.5 in for Height and increased the Corner Radius to 1.25. Putnam wanted the bottom corners of the body to be smaller, so he then created a second rectangle with the same dimensions, used .5 for the Corner Radius, and placed the top a third of the way down from the first rectangle.

Putnam selected both rectangles, clicked the Horizontal Align Center icon from the Control panel, used the Unite command from the Pathfinder panel, and chose a Cyan swatch from the Swatches panel.

2 **Constructing the mouth with the Minus Front Pathfinder command.** With the Ellipse tool, Putnam drew a circle within the body object for the mouth. He then drew an encompassing rectangle halfway up from the center of the circle. He selected both, clicked the Minus Front command from the Pathfinder panel, and chose a brown swatch from the Swatches panel.

3 **Constructing the teeth and tongue with Pathfinder commands.** To create the tongue, Putnam created two overlapping circles within the mouth shape, selected both, and used the Unite Pathfinder command. To fit the tongue into the mouth, he first copied the mouth shape, and then chose Edit > Paste in Front. Selecting both the mouth copy and the tongue, he applied the Intersect Pathfinder command, and then chose a magenta swatch from the Swatches panel for the fill color.

To create the teeth, Putnam drew four objects with the Rounded Rectangle tool. He rotated one tooth with the Selection tool by moving the cursor along the rectangle until he saw the Rotate icon and then dragged the tooth slightly to the right. He then selected all four teeth and combined them into a single compound path using Object > Compound Path > Make (for more about compound paths, see this chapter's intro). To trim off the portions of the teeth that extend above the mouth, Putnam chose Edit > Paste in Front, selected the copied mouth and teeth, and used the Intersect Pathfinder command.

4 **Creating other character features.** Putnam could then add character features as he needed, for instance, a 15-pt stroke for the lips, a circle for the back of the mouth, another pair of circles for eyes, and a rounded rectangle for the stick.

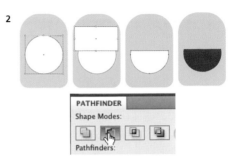

Drawing a circle, drawing a rectangle over the circle, selecting both, using the Minus Front Pathfinder command, and changing fill to brown

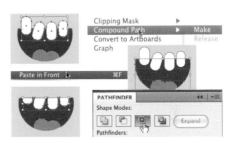

Drawing two ellipses, using the Unite Pathfinder command, Copying the mouth and Pasting in Front, selecting the mouth and tongue, and using the Intersect Pathfinder command

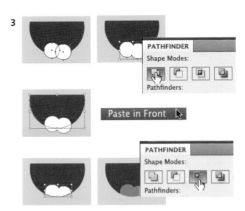

Drawing four rounded rectangles, making a compound shape, Copying the mouth and Pasting in Front, selecting the mouth and teeth, and using the Intersect Pathfinder command

Adding additional features with circles and rounded rectangles

Blob to Live Paint

From Sketch to Blob Brush and Live Paint

PUTNAM

Overview: *Place sketch as a template; trace sketch with the Blob Brush tool; color with the Live Paint Bucket tool.*

1

The original tattoo sketch

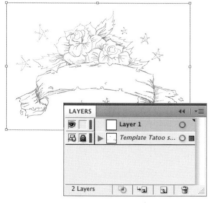

Placing sketch as a template layer

2

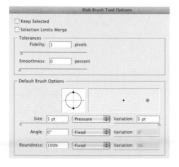

Setting up default Blob Brush tool options

Ryan Putnam has a stock illustration portfolio full of hand-drawn illustrations. Putnam found that using the new Blob Brush tool and his Wacom pen tablet, he could now easily create a hand-drawn look using Illustrator. Moreover, by using Live Paint, he could quickly fill his illustration with color.

1 Creating a sketch and placing it as a template. Putnam first created a tattoo sketch in Photoshop and placed it into Illustrator as a template. Create your own sketch, scan it, or sketch directly into a painting program (such as Painter or Photoshop). Save your sketch as PSD, JPEG, or TIF format. Next, create a new Illustrator document and choose File > Place. Locate your sketch, then enable the Template option and click Place (see the *Layers & Appearances* chapter for more on templates).

2 Setting Blob Brush tool options and tracing sketch. Putnam wanted to create marks that were very true to his stylus gestures and had minimal smoothness. To create this effect with the Blob Brush tool, he first had to modify the default options. To do this, he double-clicked on the Blob Brush tool in the Tools panel. In the Blob Brush Tool Options, he set the Fidelity to 1, Smoothness to 0, and set Size to 5 pt. From the Size drop-down menu he selected Pressure, changed the Size Variation to 5 pt, and clicked OK. If you don't have a pen tablet, change all the same settings except the Pressure and Size Variation.

Using these custom Blob Brush settings, Putnam began to trace the scanned sketch template into the layer above, varying his stylus pressure to re-create the hand-drawn style.

While drawing with the Blob Brush tool, Putnam used the Eraser tool, set up to work with pressure-sensitivity, to modify brush marks and correct mistakes. To do this, Putnam double-clicked the Eraser tool from the Tools panel and changed the Diameter to 5 pt. He then selected Pressure from the Diameter drop-down menu, changed the Diameter Variation to 5 pt, and clicked OK. By setting up the Eraser tool with pressure-sensitive settings, he could move easily between the two tools by simply flipping the stylus around.

3 **Filling areas with Live Paint.** If Putnam used the regular Brush tool to trace his sketch, he would have had to create additional paths defining fill areas to color the drawing. But Blob Brush objects can easily be converted into Live Paint Groups for quick and simple coloring. To convert the illustration to a Live Paint Group, Putnam selected the illustration with the selection tool, chose the Live Paint Bucket tool from the Tools panel, and on first click, the object became a Live Paint Group. With the Live Paint Bucket tool, he hovered over the selected illustration to highlight areas to fill. With the left and right arrow keys, Putnam cycled through the swatches from the Swatch Panel until he found his desired color (see the *Drawing & Coloring* chapter for details on creating colors). Once he found the color, he clicked in the area to fill. He repeated cycling through the swatches and filled in the other enclosed areas of the illustration.

4 **Applying finishing touches.** Putnam added additional features as needed. For instance, he warped the type and added gradients to the Live Paint fills (see the "Arcing Type" lesson in the *Artboards & Type* chapter, and see the *Blends, Gradients & Mesh* chapter for gradients details).

Tracing sketch with the Blob Brush tool

Setting up default Eraser tool preferences and erasing with the Eraser tool

3

Filling areas with the Live Paint Bucket tool

Cycling through swatches with the Live Paint Bucket tool

4

Adding a warped type treatment and gradients

JACKSON

Lance Jackson

Sitting on a commuter train, Lance Jackson took advantage of the moment to follow inspiration with a little pencil-and-paper sketching for an animation he was working on, but ideas on paper take extra steps to get into the computer. He'd already started the project in Illustrator using the Blob Brush tool. With the sketch he drew on the train in mind, Jackson found he had no need to tediously construct paths, or create objects that the Pathfinder commands can use; he could adapt his inspiration to Illustrator as freely as he could with a pencil. But unlike using pencil on paper, Jackson could cleanly erase unwanted marks with the Eraser tool, and his drawings didn't need to be scanned and traced afterwards. When he was pleased with the character development in his Blob Brush sketches, he

continued to use the Blob Brush to draw them in their finished form, this time filling in the silhouettes using the brush's unique ability to merge paths whenever the brush strokes cross over the same color. These silhouetted characters would be used next in a Flash animation.

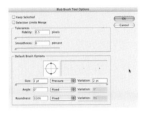

David Turton

For a powerful, yet highly detailed drawing of a tiger's head, David Turton relied upon the natural combination of the Blob Brush tool and the Wacom® Cintiq21UX tablet computer. Because Turton could draw directly on the tablet itself, and his paths would join automatically as they overlapped, he felt he had greater control over this kind of meticulous, but still freehand, pen-and-ink drawing, without having to interrupt the flow to create a new brush or adjust his stroke width. He began a rough sketch with brush settings that most closely emulated natural pen strokes. He kept Fidelity and Smoothness at their lowest settings to be as true to his hand as possible, and used a very fine, 2-pixel point. Gradually Turton refined the tiger's features, filling in more detail, and keeping the brush tip fine and allowing his strokes to merge naturally as he drew over them, thickening the detail in some areas for greater definition. As the file size grew, he began to lock layers he was happy with and to add more detail as the drawing progressed. This prevented strokes from merging and forcing constant re-renders of the drawing. Such extensive detail is very demanding of a computer's resources. When he had completed most of the tiger, he unlocked the layers and merged them all. Lastly, he used the Eraser tool to "draw out" the whiskers by erasing next to their lines, creating an interruption in the strokes in order to enhance the illusion of whiskers overlapping the fur.

TURTON

Live Tracing Logos

Using a Rasterized Logo for Live Trace

Overview: *Rasterizing a vector logo to start fresh, thereby creating cleaner, more economical paths; using Live Trace to acquire clean vector paths and reconstruct the logo.*

ONE WAVE YOGA

ROORDA

1

The first version of the logo, long-since replaced by later versions

Imprecise paths required simplifying for easier future modifications

Selecting the One Color Logo preset from the Live Trace functions on the Control panel

Black paths selected for recoloring after clicking on the Expand button in the Control panel

Illustrator's Live Trace preset "One Color Logo" can be very successful in reconstructing vector logos from rasterized images. Although Jolynne Roorda actually had the vector version of this logo, it had been through several revisions and she wanted to produce a version that was more cleanly constructed. She decided it would be quickest to rasterize the current version of the logo and use Live Trace to retrace the logo with more precise paths.

1 Rasterize the logo and use Live Trace to vectorize it again. Roorda opened the file containing the logo and duplicated the artwork layer. She selected the logo and rasterized it at a high enough resolution for smooth curves. She then used the drop-down list box on the Control panel to select the One Color Logo preset. This preset closely traces the original, but ignores White so the background becomes transparent. The Black and White Logo preset leaves White as part of the tracing, and the "[Default]" preset uses a lower Threshold and traces more loosely. If Roorda hadn't been happy with the default settings for the One Color Logo preset, she could click on the Tracing Options dialog button, enable Preview, and adjust the settings until she was happy with the results.

After tracing the logo, Roorda clicked on the Expand button in the Control panel to turn the tracing back into basic paths. She knew the logo would be used and edited by others and wanted to ensure that no one would have difficulties opening, printing, or editing the file using older software. She then selected the black-filled area and recolored it with the company's turquoise.

empress-3

bountiful
nurturing
sensuality

The seat of
the Empress
honors the
the loving
parent, the
nurturing
mentor, the
artistic MUSE
and is the
civilizing force
of the Arts on
society.

This prolific, fertile energy imparts a lush
SENSUALITY and intense creative fire to surroundings,
projects and personal relationships.

VALENZUELA

Judy Valenzuela

As one of a deck of Tarot cards, Judy Valenzuela began the chair with a hand-drawn and scanned sketch. She wanted the look of spontaneity, and knew Live Trace would maintain this look and be modifiable as a vector object. She chose Inked Drawing as the Preset. Its looser tracing would keep the sketch flowing. She adjusted the Threshold from the default 180 to 245 to fill the lines that were being missed, and checked Ignore White. Before converting the chair to a Live Paint object, Valenzuela clicked on Expand. Because Live Paint on a loose tracing may not create the desired closed shapes, Valenzuela clicked Expand so she could manually close those gaps that would have caused Live Paint to overfill her Empress chair. In keeping with the spontaneous feeling of the subject, she then added calligraphic brush strokes, lesser shapes she hand-drew or transformed, and drop shadows to float the objects in space. Lastly, she added text to complete the card.

Coloring Sketches

From Sketch to Live Trace and Live Paint

Overview: *Import a sketch into Illustrator; apply Live Trace; convert to a Live Paint Group; color with Live Paint Bucket.*

JOLY

The first rough draft of the robot sketch

The refined version of the sketch

Dave Joly drew this robot character as a visualization exercise for an animation project. Joly started by creating a rough sketch by hand. In Illustrator, Joly found that the new Live Trace and Live Paint features were like an express route between his sketch and a polished Illustrator drawing. Live Trace and Live Paint are well integrated for the task of filling sketches with color.

1 Drawing the initial robot concept. Joly sketched the robot using the Natural Media tools in Corel Painter. He then removed stray details and solidified the linework to make the image easier to trace later. When he finished, he saved the image as a Photoshop file.

Although Joly chose to start and edit his original drawing in Painter, you can also sketch an idea on paper and scan it into your computer. If necessary, you can clean up the sketch of your scan in an image editor such as Adobe Photoshop before moving it to Illustrator.

2 Tracing with Live Trace. In Illustrator, you can open a Photoshop image as a new document by choosing File > Open, or add it to an existing Illustrator document by choosing File > Place. Select the image on the Artboard and click the Live Trace button in the Control panel.

Applying Live Trace doesn't just trace the image; it also creates a Live Trace object consisting of both the original image and the tracing. Unlike a hand-tracing, you can change the tracing options to alter the results at any time without starting over. On the Control panel, choose a tracing preset from the Presets pop-up menu, or click the Options button to open the Tracing Options dialog where more Live Trace options are available. The default tracing preset creates high-contrast black-and-white line art that is well-suited for Live Paint. As a result, Joly did not need to change any Live Trace options for this project.

3 Filling areas with Live Paint. With the tracing selected, Joly clicked the Live Paint button in the Control panel to convert it from a Live Trace object to a Live Paint Group. The object no longer contained the original image or allowed easy retracing, but it gained Live Paint attributes: Joly could fill and stroke any naturally enclosed areas in the Live Paint Group without having to draw a path to hold each fill. Joly selected the Live Paint Bucket and chose a Fill swatch from the Control panel. Whenever Joly positioned the Live Paint Bucket over an area that could be painted using Live Paint, a red outline appeared to indicate a Live Paint region. If he wanted to paint the area outlined in red, he clicked the region or dragged across multiple regions.

Initially, gaps between the hand-drawn black lines let color spill into surrounding areas. Joly chose Edit > Undo to remove the spilled paint, and then clicked the Options button in the Control panel to open the Gap Options dialog. Here, you can specify the size of gap to automatically close by using the "Paint stops at" pop-up menu or the Custom field. If you enable the Preview checkbox,

2

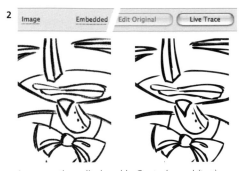

Image options displayed in Control panel (top) for selected image (bottom left); the image after clicking the Live Trace button (bottom right)

Control panel for selected Live Trace object; Options button (for Tracing Options) highlighted

3

Control panel for selected Live Paint Group; Options button (for gap options) highlighted

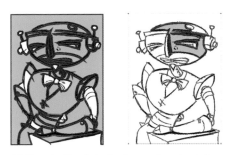

Clicking the Live Paint Bucket on the robot's face with no gap detection (left) and after applying gap detection for large gaps (right)

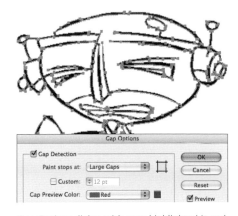

Gap Options dialog with gaps highlighted in red on Artboard because Preview is checked

4

Additional details that Joly drew as paths in front of the Live Paint object; the Live Paint object's fills have been removed here for clarity

Very wide gap in lower left corner (top) and the blue filled path Joly drew (bottom)

You can enter the Live Paint Group Isolation mode by clicking the Group Isolation button in the Control panel (highlighted above at right), or by double-clicking with a Selection tool on the group; to exit the isolation mode, you have three choices: click again on the Group Isolation button, double-click with a Selection tool outside of the group (on the Artboard), or click in the gray strip at the top of the document

red dots on the Artboard mark the gaps detected by your Gap Options settings. For this project, Joly found that the Large Gaps setting worked well.

4 **Completing the drawing.** Joly rapidly colored the rest of the sketch using the Live Paint Bucket, changing the fill swatch as needed and clicking or dragging across Live Paint areas he wanted to fill. Joly also drew additional paths to add new details, highlights, and shading.

Some regions, like the hip at the bottom left of the illustration, had gaps too large for the automatic gap detection settings. Joly drew new paths for those areas.

Joly drew his additional paths separately from the Live Paint object, filling them using the traditional method of selecting each path with the Selection tool and then clicking a swatch. If you wish to add paths to an existing Live Paint Group, you can enter Group Isolation Mode. To enter Group Isolation Mode, either select the Live Paint Group and click the Isolate Group button in the Control panel, or double-click the group with a Selection tool (the top strip of your document becomes gray). When you're in Group Isolation Mode, drawing a new path adds it to the selected Group; you can then paint the new path using the Live Paint Bucket. To exit Group Isolation Mode, click the Group Isolation Mode button, or double-click outside the group (on the Artboard) with a Selection tool.

Filling and Stroking with the Live Paint Bucket

You can control whether the Live Paint Bucket paints fills or strokes. In the toolbox, double-click the Live Paint Bucket to open the Live Paint Bucket Options dialog, and enable or disable the Paint Fills and Paint Strokes checkboxes. If only one checkbox is enabled, pressing Shift temporarily reverses what happens when you click with the bucket. For example, by default, clicking paints fills and Shift-clicking paints strokes. With both checkboxes enabled, clicking the Live Paint Bucket automatically paints a stroke or a fill, depending on how close the bucket is to an edge.

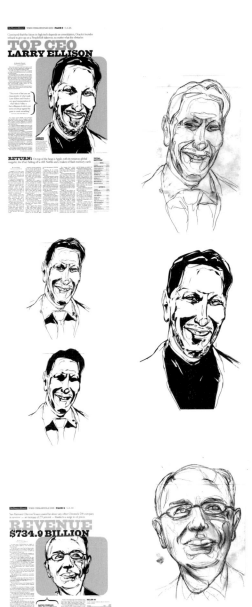

Lance Jackson / *San Francisco Chronicle*

Lance Jackson created these portraits for a *San Francisco Chronicle* special section on high-profile CEOs. Jackson first drew pencil sketches of the CEOs on paper. He scanned his sketches, saved them as JPEG files, and applied Live Trace to the JPEG images in Illustrator. He adjusted Live Trace settings such as Threshold to trace the precise tonal range he wanted from each sketch. Jackson expanded the Live Trace results in order to edit paths and apply additional fills as needed.

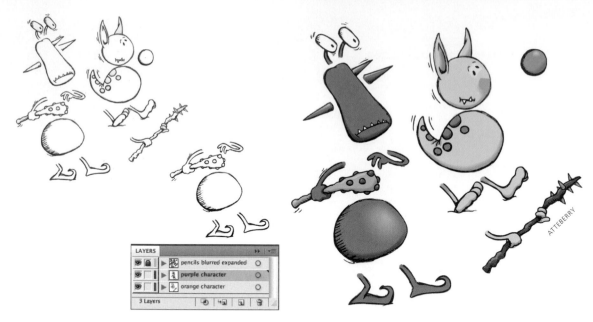

Kevan Atteberry

Illustrator Kevan Atteberry drew a sketch with a traditional paper and pencil sketch of "Lurd pieces" (top left). Atteberry creates characters in pieces so he has the flexibility to place part of a character behind another, to tweak positioning of a posture, and so forth. In the past he would just lay his scanned line drawing in layers above the colored objects (created with shaped blends), but he now applies Live Trace to his drawings first. Because each image requires slightly different settings, and because it can take a while for Live Trace to preview the changes of settings, Atteberry devised an ingenious workflow. When scanning an illustration, he also saves a small representative detail of the image. He began by placing and selecting the small Lurd detail in Illustrator, then he chose Object > Live Trace > Tracing Options. In Tracing Options he enabled Ignore White (in Trace Settings) and Preview, set the mode to Grayscale with the Max colors of 3, and then experimented with the blur settings so the extraneous marks for the Lurds were minimized, while the line shape of the pencil drawing remained preserved. Saving these settings (Save Preset), he then clicked Trace. Placing the main drawing, he chose his preset from the Control panel Preset pop-up, and clicked Trace. Atteberry applied Object > Expand, turning the traced object into separate vector objects filled with black, white, and two grays (a detail shown above the Layers panel). Because he wanted the grays to darken the colors he would be adding (not just laying gray over the colors), he used Select > Same > Fill Color to select both of the grays. In the Control panel he changed the blending mode from Normal to Multiply and reduced the Opacity to 58% (click and hold the triangle to the right of Opacity). Creating layers underneath, Atteberry used the Pen and Pencil tools with blends (see his lesson in *Blends, Gradients & Mesh*) to color the parts.

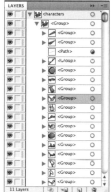

ATTEEERRY

Kevan Atteberry

Using his compositional sketch as a guide (right) and his "Lurd parts" from the Gallery opposite, Illustrator Kevan Atteberry assembled his composition. Before assembling the parts, however, Atteberry selected each "part" made up of the expanded Live Trace line work along with the inner solid shapes and shaped blends (see his lesson in the *Blends, Gradients & Mesh* chapter) and grouped (⌘-G/Ctrl-G). This allows Atteberry to click on each part with the Selection tool to select all of it. He can then move parts easily, reorder them in the Layers panel, and form the characters. Once the characters are formed, he places them within the scene created from shaped blends.

Interlock Objects

Using the Pathfinder Panel & Live Paint

TREMBLAY

Advanced Technique

Overview: *Create a logo from basic geometric objects using Pathfinder commands; create the illusion of interlocking objects and dimension with Live Paint.*

1

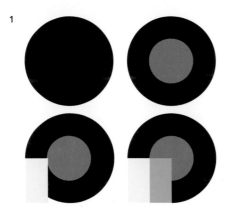

Creating the basic letter form from circles and rectangles

2

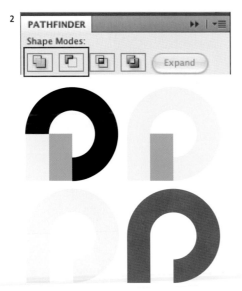

Using Unite and Minus Front in the Pathfinder panel to carve the P form

When Jean-Claude Tremblay decided to design a new logo for his graphics company, Proficiografik, he wanted to emphasize partnership with his clients. Interlocking the shapes in the business name echoed that intention. He not only saw the close relationship in form between an uppercase **P** and a **G,** he recognized that the Pathfinder panel would make it easy to create his new logo using only circles and rectangles. Add in Live Paint's unique ability to recolor overlapping objects, and Tremblay had the basis for his new logo. See his gallery in the *Artboards & Type* chapter for the completed result.

1 Starting the P with only circles and rectangles. To easily distinguish the objects at this phase in the project, assign each object its own Fill color and no Stroke. Tremblay used the Ellipse tool and Option-clicked/Alt-clicked to create a perfect circle (70 x 70 pt). With the circle selected, he double-clicked the Scale tool, chose Uniform and 50%, and clicked Copy. Next, Tremblay selected the Rectangle tool and clicked on the artboard to open the dialog. He entered 17.5 x 35 pt (one quarter the width and half the height of the circle), and clicked OK. He then aligned the rectangle to the bottom left of the larger circle using Smart Guides. He duplicated this rectangle by double-clicking on the Selection tool and entering 17.5 pt Horizontal for Position, 0 for Vertical, and clicked Copy.

2 Using Pathfinder commands to punch out the P, and using transform to create the G. Tremblay selected the two circles and, in the Pathfinder panel, he clicked on Minus Front to make a hole in the large circle (creating a compound path). He then selected the compound path and the left rectangle and clicked on the Unite icon in the Pathfinder panel. To separate the stem of the **P** from the bowl, Tremblay selected the compound path and the remaining rectangle and again clicked Minus Front.

Before constructing the **G**, Tremblay created four custom swatches: one gray for the **P**, one red for the **G**, plus a second darker red and darker gray he would later use for the shadows. He filled the **P** with the lighter gray.

To create the **G**, Tremblay selected the **P**, double-clicked on the Reflect tool, enabled Vertical for Axis, and clicked Copy. He filled the new **G** with the lighter red, and rotated it 90 degrees. To move it, he double-clicked the Selection tool, entered half the size of the circle (35 pt) for Horizontal move, and clicked OK. He subtracted 2 pt from the X field in the Control panel to create space between the letters.

3 Creating the illusion of interlocked letters and shadows. With the letter forms in place, Tremblay used parts of the original paths of the objects to create the paths for the shadows. With the Direct Selection tool, he selected the lower segment of the **G** where it crossed the **P**. He copied the segment (⌘-C/Ctrl-C) and used Paste in Front (⌘-F/Ctrl-F). So that Tremblay could better see these paths, he temporarily invoked the Swap Fill and Stroke command (Shift-X), then moved the path down and to the right (in the Control panel, he added 2 pt to the X field, and subtracted 2 pt from the Y). He repeated these steps after selecting the lower segment of **P**, where it would later cross over the **G**. Once the paths were in place, he prepared them to be used as part of a Live Paint object by setting them both to no Fill and no Stroke. He selected all four objects and chose the Live Paint Bucket tool. To create the illusion that the bottom of the **P** was crossing over the **G**, he selected the lighter gray swatch and clicked on the lower section of the **P**. Then he filled the shadow on the **P** with the darker gray. To complete the illusion that the letters were dimensional and interlocking (arm-in-arm), he filled the shadow area on the **G** with the darker red.

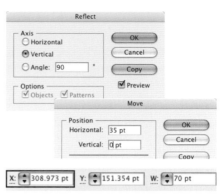

Transforming the **P** into a **G** using the Reflect, Rotate, and Move tools; then moving the **G** by subtracting points in the Control panel's X field

3

Maintaining the perfect geometric form by creating paths from segments of the objects themselves

Selecting the paths and letter objects, and using the Live Paint Bucket tool to divide the objects into sections for coloring

Using the Live Paint tool to fill the shadow objects with custom colors

Trace Techniques

Using Live Trace for Auto & Hand-Tracing

Advanced Technique

Overview: *Use the same image as a foundation for both a background created using Live Trace and a hand-traced foreground.*

Mr. George
Our founder
1907–1996

Swatches panel before and after removing unused swatches

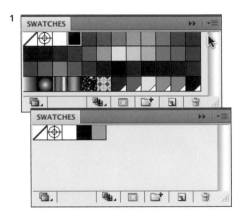

The original photograph Crouse used as the starting point for both the Live Trace background and hand-traced foreground

Scott Crouse drew this portrait of George Jenkins, the founder of Publix Markets, as part of a series of exterior murals for the Publix grocery store chain. To communicate the warm, friendly personality of "Mr. George," Crouse applied his personal illustration style as he hand-traced the portrait from a photograph. The background image did not need to be as distinctive, so Crouse saved time by using the Live Trace feature to create it from the same photograph. For easier hand-tracing, Crouse simplifies images by limiting tonal levels and removing distracting stray bits; in many cases Live Trace can replace Photoshop for this preparatory task.

1 Preparing the document. Crouse chose Select All Unused from the Swatches panel menu, and then he clicked the trash can icon in the Swatches panel to delete the selected swatches. Removing all unused swatches from the document made it easier to see the swatches that will be created later by Live Trace.

Crouse chose File > Place to select the original photograph of Mr. George and add the photo to the page.

2 Copying the image layer. To separate the foreground and background images, you can duplicate them while keeping them aligned. Drag the original layer (not just the image) to the New Layer icon in the Layers panel, then double-click the name to rename it.

To prevent changes to layers other than the one you're editing, click the lock column to lock any layers not in use. The background is edited in the next step, so lock the foreground layer at this time.

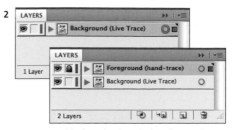

Layers panel before (top) and after (bottom) duplicating the image layer and locking the foreground layer

3 Tracing the background. Crouse selected the photo and chose Object > Live Trace > Tracing Options. You can produce results similar to Crouse's by applying settings like these: For Mode, choose Grayscale; for Max Colors, enter 3 (some images need more levels); and enable Output to Swatches. Leave other options at their default settings. Click Trace to commit the settings. The tracing is live, so you can change the settings at any time by choosing Object > Live Trace > Tracing Options.

Tracing Options dialog

4 Adjusting the background graphic's colors. To keep the viewer's focus on the subject, Crouse gave the background a light, low-contrast appearance. Selecting Output to Swatches in Step 3 added colors to the Swatches panel as global swatches applied to the Live Trace object. This is valuable because editing a global swatch updates all of its applied instances. To edit any of the new global swatches created by Live Trace, double-click them. In this case, the gray tones were changed to colors and lightened overall.

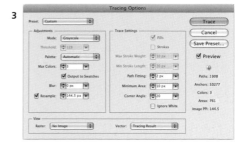

Before (left) and after (right) editing swatches output by Live Trace; white corners signify global swatches

Tracing Options button in the Control panel, located to the right of the Preset pop-up menu

5 Simplifying the foreground copy for hand-tracing. In the Layers panel, lock the background layer and unlock the foreground. Select the foreground image and click the Tracing Options button in the Control panel to edit the Live Trace settings for the selected image. Here, Max Colors was changed to 7, Blur to 1 px, Resample to 150 dpi, Path Fitting to 1 px, and Minimum Area to 10 px. The optimal values depend on the resolution of the image, so try different settings until you see what you want.

Detail of original image (left) and after adjusting for hand-tracing using Live Trace (right)

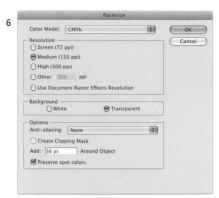

The Rasterize dialog

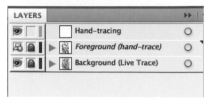

The Layers panel with the foreground tracing image layer set up as a template, and a new layer added to contain the hand-tracing

Completed tracing over the dimmed template (top), and with the template hidden to reveal the actual background (bottom)

6 Rasterizing the hand-tracing template. The Live Trace object contains many vector objects which could slow redraw. Converting it to a raster object simplifies the object and speeds screen redraw during hand-tracing. To rasterize the Live Trace object, select it and choose Object > Rasterize. Medium Resolution is a good compromise between a decent display speed and the ability to trace at high magnifications.

In the Layers panel, double-click the layer containing the foreground tracing image, select Template, and click OK. This locks and dims the layer, putting it in an ideal state for hand-tracing. Click the New Layer icon to provide a layer to contain the paths that will be hand-traced.

7 Hand-tracing the foreground. Crouse used the Pen tool to hand-trace the template image, resulting in the foreground portrait. The goal of hand-tracing is to produce a personal interpretation of the original image, so Crouse didn't follow the template exactly; he added, edited, or removed paths as needed. Through his linework, Crouse enhanced and advanced the desired mood and feeling of the illustration and the physical and facial expressions of the subject.

When he was satisfied with his hand-tracing, Crouse used Save As to save a copy of his working file. With the original version saved, in this final copy of the file he deleted the hand-tracing template layer, leaving his hand-traced foreground over the Live Trace background.

Pre-processing a tracing image in Photoshop

Live Trace works by creating paths along significant changes in contrast. In some photos, the areas you want Live Trace to trace may not contain enough contrast. To address this, open the image in Photoshop and apply a Curves adjustment layer to increase or decrease image contrast or make other changes as needed. After you edit a placed image outside of Illustrator, use the Links panel in Illustrator to update the image link and the Live Trace object will also update.

CROUSE

Scott Crouse

Using many of the same techniques as in Trace Techniques, Scott Crouse created this Illustrator rendering of a Miami Dolphins cheerleader. Crouse used Live Trace to trace a major foreground element—the pom-poms. The pom-poms are so complex that hand-tracing them would take too much time. Crouse realized that using Live Trace to trace the pom-poms would be much faster, and because of the random nature of the pom-poms, the Live Trace results would not be that different from hand-tracing them. Crouse first hand-traced the cheerleader with the Pen tool, but not the pom-poms. He then isolated the pom-poms from the rest of the original photo so that Live Trace would provide a clean outline of just the pom-poms. He did this by opening the original photo in Photoshop, tracing the outline of the pom-poms,

and then applying a single green fill color to everything but the pom-poms. For more control over the final colors, Crouse also used Photoshop to apply a Posterize adjustment layer and the Median filter. He also converted the image to Indexed Color using a 14-color Adaptive palette. He opened the edited Photoshop file in Illustrator and applied Live Trace. He used default Live Trace options with the following exceptions: He set the Mode to Color, the number of colors to 14, and enabled the Output to Swatches checkbox. Crouse then edited the swatches created by Live Trace to brighten them. Finally, he deleted the green area and positioned the traced pom-poms over the rest of the drawing he hand-traced earlier.

HANSEN

Scott Hansen

For this cover of *Game Developer*, a magazine targeted at people in the video gaming industry, Scott Hansen used Live Trace to trace his sketch of a graduate (above right). Hansen wanted to portray a recent graduate considering his options in video gaming: to be a programmer, designer, or artist. Using the version he made with Live Trace as a starting point, Hansen created additional enclosed portions within the original traced objects to define areas that he intended to be filled with different colors or tones. Hansen also "cleaned up" the traced objects that contained a lot of extra "burrs" and points. He used the Delete Anchor Point and Smooth tools to smooth the ragged sections (the final cleaned up version in Outline mode shown directly above). As with most of his projects, Hansen created the finishing details in Photoshop (see the *Illustrator & Other Programs* chapter for more on bringing Illustrator objects into Photoshop).

Scott Hansen

Before departing on a national tour, electronic music duo Dusty Brown commissioned artist Scott Hansen to create a promotional tour poster. To distress graphic pattern elements in the composition, Hansen wanted to create a vector paint stroke. He painted a real media paint stroke, scanned it, and placed it into Illustrator. Selecting the stroke, he used Live Trace to turn the paint mark into a black vector object (top black mark). So that the mark better fit the objects to which he would apply it, he used the Free Distort tool, and rotated and stretched the mark. Then, using the Direct Selection tool, he deleted some of the detailed portions of the mark, and repositioned other parts. When the stroke better matched what he had in mind, he clicked the Merge icon in the Pathfinder panel to form the final stroke (bottom mark). He brought the stroke into Photoshop as a Shape and filled it with the same cream color as the background. He duplicated the shapes on layers above the pattern elements so that they hid portions of the blue and red patterns underneath (see *Illustrator & Other Programs* for more on shapes and Photoshop).

"B" Paintbrush tool; a brush in the Control panel

Brushes & Symbols

Using Brushes and Symbols, you can create the equivalents of many traditional illustration tools, such as pens and brushes that drip and splatter, colored pencils and charcoals, calligraphy pens and brushes, and spray cans that can spray anything—from single color spots to complex artwork. You can use these tools with a pen and tablet, or with a mouse or trackball.

In addition to the Brushes examples in this chapter, you'll find numerous step-by-step lessons and Galleries involving Brushes throughout the book.

BRUSHES

There are four basic types of Brushes: Calligraphic, Art, Scatter, and Pattern. You can use Brushes for everything from mimicking traditional art tools to painting with complex patterns and textures. You can either create brush strokes with the Brush tool, or you can apply a brush stroke to a previously drawn path.

Use Calligraphic Brushes to create strokes that look like they're from a real-world calligraphy pen or brush, or to mimic felt pens. You can define a degree of variation for the size, roundness, and angle of each "nib." You can also set each of the above characteristics to be Fixed, Pressure, or Random.

Art Brushes consist of one or more pieces of artwork that get stretched evenly along the path you create with them. You can use Art Brushes to imitate drippy, splattery ink pens, charcoal, spatter brushes, dry brushes, watercolors, and more.

The artwork you use to create an Art Brush can represent virtually anything: the leaves of a tree, stars, blades of grass, naturalistic brushes (like the Charcoal brush), and so on. Use Scatter Brushes to scatter copies of artwork along the path you create with them: flowers in a field, bees in the air, stars in the sky. The size, spacing, scatter, and rotation of the artwork can all vary along the path.

Pattern Brushes are related to the Patterns feature in Illustrator. You can use Pattern Brushes to paint patterns along a path. To use a Pattern Brush, you first define the tiles that will make up your pattern. For example, you can create railroad symbols on a map, multicolored dashed lines, chain links, or grass. These patterns are defined by up to five types of tiles—side, outer corner, inner corner, start, and end—that you create, and one of three methods of fitting them together (Stretch to Fit, Add Space to Fit, and Approximate Path).

Artwork for Creating Brushes

You can make Art, Scatter, and Pattern Brushes from simple lines and fills, and groups of objects created from them, as well as blends and some live effects. Some complex artwork cannot be used for making brushes; artwork that can't be used in brushes include gradients, mesh objects, raster art, and advanced live effects such as 3D.

Working with Brushes

Double-click the Paintbrush tool to set application-level preferences for all brushes. (The new preferences will apply to work you do with the brushes going forward, but won't change existing work retroactively.) When using Fidelity and Smoothness, lower numbers are more accurate, and higher numbers are smoother. Enable the "Fill new brush strokes" option if you want the brush path to take on the fill color in addition to the stroke color. When Keep Selected and Edit Selected Paths are both enabled, the last drawn path stays selected; drawing a new path close to the selected path will redraw that path. Disabling either of these options will allow you to draw multiple brush strokes near each other, instead of redrawing the last drawn path. Disabling Keep Selected deselects paths as they are drawn, while disabling Edit Selected Paths turns off the adjusting behavior of the Brush tool even when it is near selected paths. If left enabled, the Edit Selected Paths slider determines how close you have to be in order to redraw the selected path, as opposed to

Closing a brush path

To close a path using the Brush tool, hold down the Option/Alt key *after* you begin creating the path, then let go of the mouse button just before you're ready to close the path.

Reversing brush strokes

To change the direction of a brush stroke on an open path, select the path and then click on the opposite endpoint with the Pen tool to establish the new direction toward that point. —*David Nelson*

Changing only selected objects

Adjust options on selected objects with the same applied brush by choosing "Options of Selected Object" from the Layers panel menu, or by double-clicking the brush name in the Appearance panel.

Scaling brushes

To scale artwork that contains paths with applied brushes, enable Scale Strokes & Effects in Preferences > General, or in the Scale dialog.

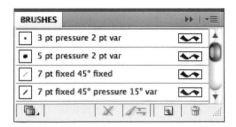

Including brush characteristics in brush name; using List View to make brushes easier to find

Brushes to layers

Scatter Brush artwork can be easily separated onto individual layers for use in animation. For details about distributing artwork to layers, see the "Release to Layers" section in the *Web & Animation* chapter introduction.

But it says I have pressure...

In previous versions of Illustrator, if you didn't have a pressure-sensitive tablet connected to your computer, you wouldn't see possible pressure settings in Calligraphic and Scatter Brush Options. Now you can actually see (and might be able to select) these pop-up options even if you're not connected to a tablet. However, unless you're connected to a tablet supporting the various pressure and tilt options, these settings will not affect your brush marks.

More about brushes

- Pasting a path that contains a brush will add the brush to the Brushes panel.
- Convert an applied brush into editable artwork by selecting the path and choosing Object > Expand Appearance.
- Drag a brush out of the Brushes panel to edit the brush art.
- To create a brush from an applied gradient or gradient mesh, expand it first (Object > Expand).

drawing a new path. The lower the number, the closer you must be to the selected path to redraw it.

To edit a brush, double-click it in the Brushes panel to change its Brush options. Or to modify the art that makes up the brush, drag it out of the Brushes panel, edit the brush object, and then drag the new art back into the Brushes panel. To replace the original brush, press Option/Alt as you drag the new brush art over the original in the Brushes panel.

If there are existing brush strokes in your artwork that were created using the brush you're replacing when you Option-drag/Alt-drag, you'll see a dialog that offers you three options: clicking Apply to Strokes will update the existing strokes to match the edited brush; clicking Leave Strokes will create a new copy of the brush in the panel that reflects your edits, leaving the original brush and its existing strokes unchanged; or, you can click Cancel to do neither.

There are four colorization methods (None, Tints, Tints and Shades, and Hue Shift) you can use with Brushes. "None" uses the colors of the brush as they were defined and how they appear in the Brushes panel. The Tints method causes the brush to use the current stroke color, allowing you to create any color brush you like, regardless of the color of the brush depicted in the Brushes panel. Click on the Tips button in the Art Brush Options dialog for detailed explanations and examples of how all four color modes work.

When drawing with a pressure-sensitive stylus (pen) and tablet, using the Calligraphic Brush tool and a pressure setting in the options dialog, you'll be able to draw with varying stroke thickness and brush shape, according to the pressure you apply to the tablet. If your tablet supports Tilt, in the Calligraphic Brush Options dialog, choose Tilt from one of the parameter pop-ups and increase the variation. For particularly dramatic results, set the Angle for tilt with a flattened shape brush with a large variation. Then the angle at which you hold your pen will affect the brush stroke, producing a dramatic variation in brush-mark thickness (and/or shape) as you draw. For Scatter brush pressure settings, you can vary the size, spacing, and scatter of the brush art. If you don't have a tablet, try choosing Random settings in Calligraphic and Scatter Brush Options.

SYMBOLS

Symbols are special pieces of artwork that you create and store in the Symbols panel. From this panel, you can then add one or more copies (called *instances*) of the symbols into your artwork. When you make changes to a symbol, those changes are automatically applied to all the instances of that symbol.

Symbols can be made from almost any art you create in Illustrator. The only exceptions are a few kinds of complex groups (such as groups of graphs) and placed art, which must be embedded (not linked).

Illustrator offers a variety of convenient controls, in both the Control panel and the Symbols panel itself, to make working with symbols easy and intuitive.

The Symbols panel

The Symbols panel, like the Brushes panel and the Swatches panel, has a handy Libraries Menu icon in the lower-left corner of the panel, which lets you easily load other libraries of Symbols or save the symbols currently in the panel as a new library.

The Place Symbol Instance icon places a new instance of the currently selected Symbol onto the page. The Break Link to Symbol icon makes the selected instance independent. It is now an ordinary piece of artwork and no longer an instance of a symbol. You can then drag this piece of artwork back into the Symbols panel to create a new symbol, or you can replace the original parent symbol with this new version by Option/Alt-dragging the new symbol on top of the old one. The Symbol Options, New Symbol, and Delete Symbol icons round out the panel. (See the Tip "Options trading" at right for a change in how the New Symbol icon functions.)

Create symbols on the fly

You can create a new symbol quickly and easily just by selecting some art and then hitting the F8 key. The new symbol is added to the Symbols panel, and the selected art is automatically replaced by an instance of the newly created symbol. —*Jean-Claude Tremblay*

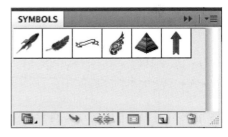

The icons at the bottom of the Symbols panel, from left to right: Symbol Libraries Menu, Place Symbol Instance, Break Link to Symbol, Symbol Options, New Symbol, and Delete Symbol

Options trading

When you click on the New Symbol icon in the Symbols panel, the Symbol Options dialog opens by default. If you want to skip the Symbol Options dialog, you need to Option/Alt-click the icon. (It worked the other way around in some earlier versions of Illustrator, so don't get confused!)

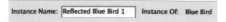

The Instance Name field in the Control panel

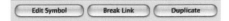

The Edit Symbol, Break Link, and Duplicate buttons in the Control panel

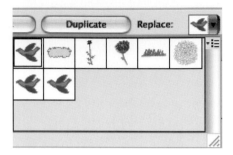

The Replace control in the Control panel, and the drop-down version of the Symbols panel that displays when you click it

The other controls visible in the Control panel when a symbol is selected, from left to right: Opacity, Recolor Artwork, Align, and Transform

The icon next to the Instance Name field reflects whether the Symbol is specified as a Graphic or a Movie Clip in the Symbol Options dialog (see the Tip "Symbol type: graphic or movie?" at the end of this introduction)

Symbols and Flash

Symbols represent the best way of using Illustrator for Flash animation. To learn more about working with symbols and Flash, see the *Web & Animation* chapter.

Another handy control is the Select All Instances command in the Symbols panel menu, which instantly selects all instances in your document of whichever Symbol is currently chosen.

Symbols and the Control panel

When you select an instance of a symbol, you'll see the Control panel change to offer you several useful controls, including a field where you can assign that specific instance its own name. There's also an Edit Symbol button that takes you into Isolation mode (which is discussed in the following section), a Break Link button that severs the link between the selected instance and the parent symbol it's associated with, and a Duplicate button that creates a quick copy in the Symbols panel of the parent Symbol for the selected instance.

The Replace control in the Control panel offers you a handy drop-down version of the Symbols panel, where you can choose another symbol to replace the selected one. (This might save you the step of opening the Symbols panel itself, and help reduce clutter on your screen.)

Editing Symbols (Working with Isolation Mode)

Editing symbols is now much easier than it was in the past. You can edit a symbol by doing any of the following things: double-clicking a symbol in the Symbols panel; double-clicking an instance of a symbol on the Artboard; clicking the Edit Symbol button in the Control panel; or choosing the Edit Symbol command in the panel menu.

Once you perform any of those actions, Illustrator will open the symbol in Isolation mode for easier editing. If Isolation mode is a new concept for you, see the *Beyond the Basics* chapter for a primer on what it is and how it works. Remember that there are several easy ways to exit Isolation mode when you're done editing, or if you find yourself there by accident: Click anywhere in the gray Isolation mode bar, at the top of the screen; double-click anywhere on the Artboard outside of the Isolated symbol; click the Exit Isolated Group mode button in the Control panel; choose Exit Isolated Group from the contextual menu by Control-clicking (Mac) or right-clicking on a two-button mouse; or simply press the Escape key.

After you exit Isolation mode, any changes you made to the Symbol will immediately be reflected in the parent symbol in the panel as well as any and all instances of the symbol in your document.

Working with the Symbolism Tools

There are eight different Symbolism tools. Use the Symbol Sprayer tool to spray selected symbols onto your document. A group of symbols sprayed onto your document is called a *symbol instance set* and is surrounded by a bounding box (you can't select individual instances inside a set with any of the selection tools). Then use any of the other Symbol tools—the Symbol Shifter, Scruncher, Sizer, Spinner, Stainer, Screener, or Styler—to modify symbols in the symbol instance set.

To add symbols to an existing instance set, select the instance set. Then, from the Symbols panel, select the symbol to be added—which can be the same as or different from the symbols already present in the instance set—and spray. If you're using the default Average mode, your new symbol instances can inherit attributes (size, rotation, transparency, style) from nearby symbols in the same instance set. See *Illustrator Help* for details about Average versus User Defined modes.

When you add or modify a symbol instance set, it's important to make sure you have selected both the symbol instance set and the corresponding symbol(s) in the Symbols panel. If you don't, the Symbolism tools can easily appear not to be working.

To remove symbols from an existing instance set, use the Symbol Sprayer tool with the Option/Alt key, and click on an instance to delete it, or click-drag your cursor over multiple instances (they're deleted when you release). See the "Symbolism Basics" lesson later in this chapter for specific instructions on creating and modifying symbols, working with symbol sets, and using the symbolism tools.

Symbols sprayed, sized, and stained

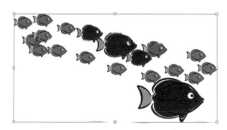

Symbols added using User Defined mode; new symbols are all same color and size

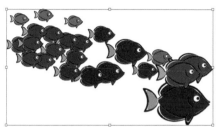

Symbols added using Average mode; new symbols inherit average color and size from symbols nearby (as defined by the brush radius)

Changing tool diameter

To interactively change a tool's diameter, use the square brackets on your keyboard to resize the diameter of the symbolism tool as you work. Use [(left bracket) to decrease and] (right bracket) to increase size. —*Vicki Loader*

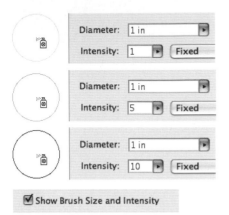

☑ Show Brush Size and Intensity

When Show Brush Size and Intensity is enabled, the intensity of the Symbolism tool is indicated by the shade of gray of the brush size circle

Changing symbol intensity

Press Shift-[to decrease (or press Shift-] to increase) a Symbolism tool's intensity.

Symbol intensity vs. density

The Symbolism Intensity option controls how fast symbol instances get sprayed onto the page. The Density option controls how closely they are spaced. You can also change the Density later. Simply select the Symbol instance set, then adjust the Density slider.

SYMBOLS VS. SCATTER BRUSHES

Symbols are more flexible than Scatter Brushes in terms of the types of changes you can make to them after they are applied; they can represent a greater variety of artwork (such as raster images or gradient-filled objects). One major advantage to using Scatter Brushes, however, is that if you're using a pressure-sensitive tablet, you have more control over varying the Scatter Brush marks you draw initially than you do when first drawing with the Symbol Sprayer tool.

Using the Symbolism tools, you can change many attributes (such as size, rotation, and spacing) to individual symbols in an instance set. Using Scatter Brushes, attributes will be applied to the whole set—you can't change attributes for single objects in a set. With both Symbols and Scatter Brushes, you can redefine the original artwork stored in the panel and have all the instances on the Artboard reflect those changes. But whereas you can remove individual instances from a symbolism instance set, the only way to delete Scatter Brush objects within a stroke is to first expand the artwork, and then select and delete that former brush element.

Unlike other types of vector artwork, the art objects inside Symbols are not affected by the Scale Strokes & Effects preference. Scatter Brush artwork responds in its own unique way. For more details about this, see the file "ScalingScatterBrushes.ai" on the *Wow! CD*.

Symbol type: graphic or movie?

In the Symbol Options dialog, within the section labeled "Type," you'll see the buttons Graphic and Movie Clip. Surprisingly, the default is Movie Clip. But don't worry: This setting only matters if you're bringing objects into Flash, and can be changed from within Flash itself. If you're not going to be working with your objects in Flash, you can safely disregard it. See the *Web & Animation* chapter for more information about working with Flash and Symbols.

Cheryl Graham

Cheryl Graham created this vibrant paint-erly portrait with a custom Art Brush designed to mimic a smudged stroke made with a charcoal stick. To make the "Dreadlock" Art Brush, Graham drew ellipses in different sizes with the Ellipse tool (left detail). She selected the ellipses and applied Pathfinder > Add (middle detail). She then selected the Warp tool and smudged the edges of the ellipse grouping (right detail). She often resized the Warp tool by holding down the Option/Alt key while dragging on the Artboard with the tool to change its diameter. Graham selected the artwork and dragged it to the Brushes panel to make an Art Brush and chose Hue Shift to enable quick color changes. She first drew the individual strands of hair with the Dreadlock brush. To make a basic face shape, she drew additional paths with the Pen and Pencil tools. She further defined the face using the Dreadlock and default Calligraphy 1 brushes modified in a variety of ways. As Graham painted, she increased or decreased the stroke width of the brushes to dramatically vary the shape and size of the brushes. Occasionally she applied a Live Effect to a brush stroke (Effect > Distort & Trans-form > Tweak) or used the Rotate, Shear, and Scale tools. Graham applied Trans-parency and Blending modes such as Overlay, Multiply, and Screen to many of the brushes and shapes. She alternated

GRAHAM

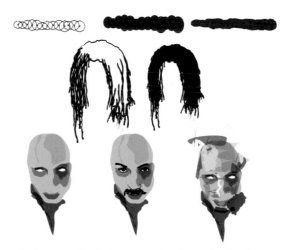

between all of these methods as she built this dynamic portrait. (See the *Live Effects & Graphic Styles* and *Transparency* chapters to learn more about using these features.)

Brushes & Washes

Drawing with Naturalistic Pen, Ink, & Wash

Overview: *Adjust the Paintbrush tool settings; customize a Calligraphic brush; start from an existing image; experiment by using other brushes to stroke the paths and add washes.*

The default Layer 1 renamed Ink, and the original fountain photo placed as an Illustrator template layer below the drawing

The original photo (left), brush strokes drawn over the dimmed template photo (center), and the template hidden (right)

Maintaining your pressure

Only brush strokes *initially* drawn with pressure-sensitive settings can take advantage of pressure-sensitivity. Also be aware that you may alter the stroke shape if you reapply a brush after you experiment with another.

It's easy to create spontaneous painterly and calligraphic marks in Illustrator—and perhaps with more flexibility than in any other digital medium. Sharon Steuer drew this sketch of Place des Vosges in Paris, France, using a pressure-sensitive Wacom tablet and two different Illustrator brushes. She customized a brush for the thin, dark strokes and used a built-in brush for the underlying gray washes. When you use a pressure-sensitive, pen-like stylus and tablet to create highly variable, responsive strokes, you can edit those strokes as *paths*, You can also experiment by applying different brushes to the existing paths.

1 If you're using existing artwork as a reference, import it as a template layer. You can start drawing on a blank Illustrator Artboard, but if you want to use a sketch, scanned photo, or digital camera photo as a reference, set it up as a non-printing template layer. For her template image, Steuer used a scanned TIFF photo of Place des Vosges. To place an image as a template layer, choose File > Place, locate your file, enable the Link and Template checkboxes, and click the Place button. If the image imports at too large a size, unlock the template layer, enter a more reasonable Width value in the Transform panel, and press ⌘-Return/Ctrl-Enter to resize it proportionally.

Toggle between hiding and showing the template layer using ⌘-Shift-W/Ctrl-Shift-W, or by clicking in the visibility column in the Layers panel (the icon for a template layer is a tiny triangle/circle/square, instead of the Eye icon). Illustrator automatically dims the image to make your drawing easier to see.

You can customize the template layer by double-clicking its layer and changing options in the Layer Options dialog. When you import an image as a template, Illustrator automatically enables the Template, Lock, and Dim checkboxes for you. You can't disable the Lock checkbox if the Template checkbox is enabled, but you can still unlock it in the Layers panel.

2 Setting your Paintbrush tool Preferences and customizing a Calligraphic brush. In order to sketch freely and with accurate detail, you'll need to adjust the default Paintbrush tool settings. Double-click the Paintbrush tool in the Tools panel to open Paintbrush Tool Preferences. Drag the Fidelity and Smoothness sliders all the way to the left so that Illustrator records your strokes precisely. Make sure "Fill new brush strokes" is disabled; you don't need to change the other settings.

To create a custom brush, click the New Brush icon at the bottom of the panel and click OK for a New Calligraphic Brush. Experiment with various settings, name your brush, and click OK. For this piece, Steuer chose the following settings: Angle=90°/Fixed; Roundness=10%/Fixed; Diameter=4 pt/Pressure/Variation=4 pt. If you don't have a pressure-sensitive tablet, try Random as a setting for any of the three Brush Options, since Pressure won't have any effect. The Paintbrush uses your current stroke color (if there isn't a stroke color, it will use the previous stroke color or the fill color). Now draw. If you don't like a mark: 1) choose Undo to delete it, 2) use the Direct Selection tool to edit the path, or 3) select the path and try redrawing it using the Paintbrush (to hide or show selection outlines, choose View > Hide/Show Edges). To edit a brush, deselect everything (Edit > Select All),

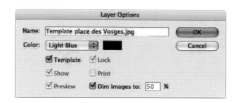

Customizing the template layer options

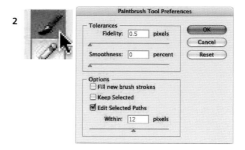

Customizing the Paintbrush Tool Preferences

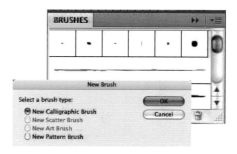

Creating a new Calligraphic brush

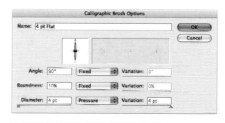

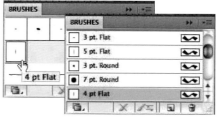

Angle, Roundness, and Diameter can be set to respond to pressure, to vary randomly, or to remain fixed; the new brush in the Brushes panel viewed with tool tips and in List View

3

Strokes made with Steuer's customized 4-pt flat brush (left); applying Adobe's default 3-pt Round brush (center), then a 1-pt Oval brush

4

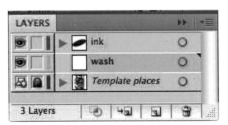

The original drawing before adding a wash

A new layer (wash) created for wider wash strokes to appear under existing darker strokes on the Template placeholder layer

The gray wash strokes underneath the wider dark strokes, and the brush used to draw them

double-click the brush in the Brushes panel, and make changes. Illustrator will ask you if you want to apply the new settings to strokes you've already drawn with this brush; click Apply to Strokes if you want to do this or click Leave Strokes to apply the new settings only to new strokes that you'll create from this point forward, divorcing the original strokes from the edited brush. It's safer to edit a copy of a brush; to do this, drag it to the New Brush icon to duplicate it, and then edit the copy.

3 Experimenting with your artwork. Save any versions of your artwork that you like. Now try applying different brushes to specific strokes and to the entire piece. Access additional brushes from the Brush Libraries Menu icon in the Brushes panel. In this step, two default brushes are applied to the same strokes as the custom brush.

4 Adding a wash. For this piece, Steuer added depth by introducing gray washes underneath the dark brush strokes. To easily edit the wash strokes without affecting the dark ink strokes, create a new layer, and draw your wash strokes into this layer between the ink and template layers. To avoid altering other layers while you brush in the washes, you may want to lock all layers except the one on which you're drawing. To do this, Option-click or Alt-click the wash layer's Lock icon.

Select or create a brush suitable for washes, and select a light wash color. Steuer used the Dry Ink 2 brush from the Artistic_Ink brush library included with Illustrator. In the Layers panel, click the wash layer to make it the current drawing layer, and paint away.

Drawing transparent brush strokes

By default, brush strokes are opaque. You can also draw with semi-transparent brush strokes, which you can use to simulate some types of inks or watercolors; where marks overlap, they become richer or darker. See the lesson "Transparent Color" in the *Transparency* chapter.

Sharon Steuer

This sketch is an extended version of the pen and ink drawing in the previous lesson. In this version, Steuer wanted to add young Noah riding a bicycle past the fountain. A photo of Noah on a carousel motorcycle was a perfect reference for the sketch, but the photo wasn't facing the right direction. To flip the photo, Steuer selected the image, chose Object > Transform > Reflect, and selected the Vertical Axis option. However, the fountain drawing's existing strokes occupied the area where she wanted to add Noah. Steuer solved this using a technique that isn't available with conventional ink: She used the Pencil tool to draw a path over the existing drawing, and filled the path with white to bring back the color of the paper. This restored an empty area where she could

add the drawing of Noah, so it looked like it was there from the beginning. Steuer drew Noah on a separate layer, allowing easy editing independent of the rest of the drawing.

Chapter 5 *Brushes & Symbols* 141

JACKMORE

Lisa Jackmore

Inspired by a crumpled page from an antique garden notebook, Lisa Jackmore created a faded, textured appearance in this illustration as though pencil marks were still visible after they had been erased. Jackmore first made a panel of custom Art Brushes consisting of original and altered default Art Brushes. She created textures for the background by drawing scribble marks with the Pencil tool (using different stroke widths). For each scribble, she selected it and then dragged it into the Brushes panel to create a new Art Brush, and chose the Hue Shift colorization method so that she could vary the brush color as she drew with the art brush. Jackmore drew the vine and bird bath with a pressure-sensitive drawing tablet using varying widths of the Chalk Scribble and Thick Pencil Art Brushes. Jackmore double-clicked on the brush copy icon and in the Art Brush Options dialog, changed the percentage to vary the width. Before drawing with these brushes, she disabled "Fill New Brush Strokes" and "Keep Selected" in the Paintbrush tool Preferences. This allowed her to draw multiple paths close to each other so she didn't accidentally redraw the previous line. Jackmore then deleted any extra points within the brush strokes by tracing over a selected brush stroke with the Smooth tool.

JACKMORE

Lisa Jackmore

To create the brush details in this image, Lisa Jackmore modified custom Art Brushes that she named scribble brushes (used in the drawing opposite). She selected some of the scribble brushes and reduced the opacity by clicking Opacity in the Control panel. Jackmore made an Art Brush to build the frame by drawing a path with the Pen tool. She altered the path with a combination of the Reflect and Shear tools. Jackmore Direct-selected points along the path and reapplied the Reflect and Shear tools to achieve an ink pen look. Then

she selected the path and dragged it to the Brushes panel to make an Art Brush. Jackmore created the texture in the brown oval using a brush made of multiple strokes with the Thick Pencil Art Brush. She grouped the strokes and dragged the group to the Brushes panel to make the Art Brush. She made a clipping mask to contain the large brush stroke within the oval (middle detail). To reduce the size of the brush, she double-clicked on the brush in the Brushes panel and decreased its width.

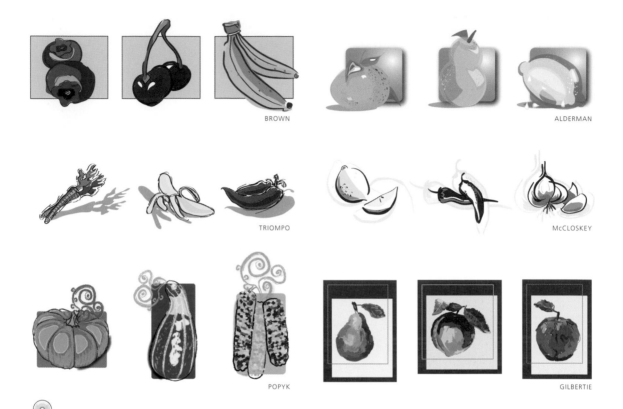

BROWN

ALDERMAN

TRIOMPO

McCLOSKEY

POPYK

GILBERTIE

Stephen Klema's Students:
Dan Brown, Susan E. Alderman,
Matthew Triompo, Laura McCloskey,
Shana Popyk, Nicole Gilbertie

As a class assignment, Professor Stephen Klema challenged his students to create expressive graphic illustrations of organic forms. The students of Tunxis Community College used a variety of default brushes from the Brushes panel. They included both Calligraphy and Art Brushes. Before drawing, the students double-clicked the Paintbrush tool and adjusted the Paintbrush tool preferences. They dragged the Fidelity and Smoothness sliders to the desired positions. The sliders moved farther to the

left had more accurate brush strokes, while those moved to the right were smoother. The "Fill New Brush Strokes" and "Keep Selected" options were disabled to allow multiple brush strokes to be drawn near each other without redrawing the last path. Using a pressure-sensitive tablet, the students drew varying widths and angles of brush strokes, many either on top of or close to one another, for a spontaneous, expressive look. Extra points within the brush strokes were deleted using the Smooth tool or the Delete Anchor Point tool.

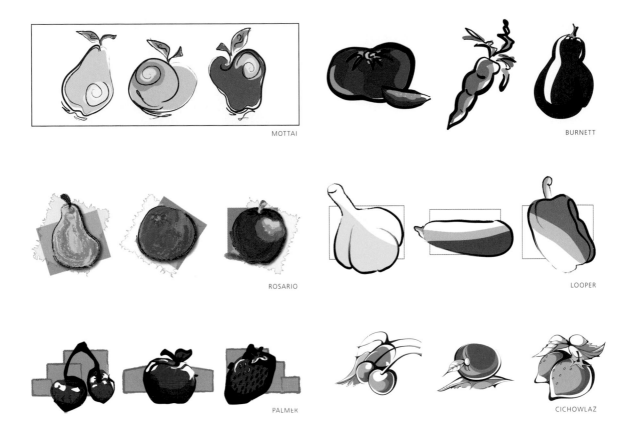

MOTTAI

BURNETT

ROSARIO

LOOPER

PALMER

CICHOWLAZ

Stephen Klema's Students:
Laura Mottai, Cinthia A. Burnett,
Jessica Rosario, Emily Looper,
Theresa Palmer, Kazimiera Cichowla

Using the same techniques described on the previous page, additional student creations are shown above. In some of these illustrations, an Art Brush was applied to paths drawn with the Pencil and Pen tools. The Pen or Pencil path was selected with the Selection tool, then a brush was chosen from the Brushes panel. The Pen or Pencil path then changed to that chosen Brush style. Many types of brushes can be found in the Brushes library. To open the Brushes library, click on the Brush Library Menu icon found in the upper right corner of the Brushes panel. Select Open Brush Library > Artistic, then select the brushes you want to add to the Brushes panel. Find more artwork from Professor Klema's students on his website, StephenKlema.com.

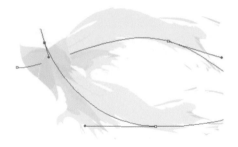

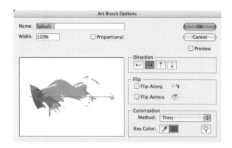

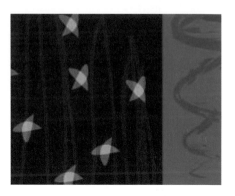

Michael Cronan

To capture the color, ethnic influence, and spirit of San Francisco's popular landmarks, Michael Cronan not only relies on Art Brushes collected over the years, but creates his own. To represent the Japanese Tea Garden, Cronan focused attention on the koi pond, creating the grasses with the Pencil brush and the multi-tones of the shrubbery with the Charcoal brush (both from: Open Brush Library > Artistic > Artistic_ChalkCharcoalPencil). He created a

custom Splash brush that included transparency to represent the koi breaking the surface of the pond. Dry Ink and Chalk brushes added to the strong texture in this poster. Cronan also drew individual filled objects that he duplicated repeatedly in order to create pattern texture. By drawing loosely with the Pencil tool and using Pathfinder commands to break objects into abstract patterns, Cronan created informality and freshness in traditional vector drawing that enchanced the Art Brushes' strokes.

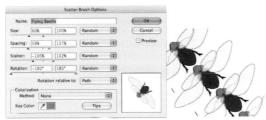

Michael Cronan

Continuing with his series of posters for San Francisco parks, Michael Cronan created Marina Green with his collection of Art Brushes, Scatter Brushes, and Pattern Brushes. He made extensive use of brushes that mimic traditional media. Adobe Illustrator has provided many of these with the program over the years, such as Dry Ink, Charcoal, and Pencil. With Scroll Pen 5 he could draw a variety of elements, from dragon hair to the Golden Gate Bridge and the grassy texture of the Marina Green. He renamed "Scroll Pen 5" to a more descriptive

"Scroll Pen Variable Length" in order to find it easily in his Brushes panel. He created a Scatter Brush for the background stars on the Marina Green strip, and modified a Scatter Brush made from a flying beetle image that he used for one of the kites. A Polynesian design made a Pattern Brush that Cronan used to construct the dragonfly kite's tail, which he drew with the Pencil tool. He also drew vector objects and basic shapes for some of the elements, and colored them with solid or gradient fills.

Pattern Brushes

Creating Details with the Pattern Brush

Overview: *Create the parts that will make up a Pattern Brush separately; place the parts in the Swatches panel and give them distinctive names; use the Pattern Brush Options dialog to create the brushes.*

Adjusting Pattern Brush fit

After you've applied a Pattern Brush to a path, you can still scale, flip, and modify its fit along the path. To do so, select the brushed path and double-click that brush in the Brushes panel. Then modify the settings in the Pattern Brush Options dialog.

1

Creating one zipper tooth, using the Blend tool for the highlight, then positioning a duplicate to mimic the teeth

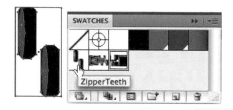

Selecting bounding rectangle and objects, dragging objects for Pattern brushes into the Swatches panel, and naming them

MAXSON

While many Illustrator Brushes mimic traditional art strokes, Greg Maxson often concentrates his efforts on creating Pattern brushes that eliminate the tedious creation of the practical objects he often illustrates. For this product illustration, Maxson saved many hours by creating two zipper brushes, one for just the basic teeth of a zipper, and one that included the zipper pull and stop. Because he would be able to use these brushes over and over again, Maxson knew a little time creating a Pattern brush would save him a lot of time in the future.

1 Creating the parts of the zipper separately.

Maxson first created the zipper teeth. He drew a simple rounded rectangle for the base, and then drew a small, light oval on top of a larger black oval that would become the highlight. Maxson selected both objects and double-clicked on the Blend tool to choose Specified Steps, thus controlling the brush's complexity. He used the keyboard shortcut ⌘-Option-B/Ctrl-Alt-B to blend the highlight, which he placed on the base (you can also blend via the menu by choosing Object > Blend > Make). (See the *Blends, Gradients & Mesh* chapter for more about working with blends.) Maxson duplicated the zipper "tooth" and positioned the copy as it would be in a real zipper. He then drew a no-stroke, no-fill bounding rectangle behind the teeth to add space around each pair of teeth equal to the space between each tooth, thus keeping the teeth spaced evenly. He selected all the objects and chose Edit > Define Pattern. He gave the swatch a name he would recognize when he built the Pattern brush. Pattern swatches are the "tiles" that make up a Pattern brush.

Maxson then created the pull and stop for the zipper. To create the illusion of the pull and stop overlapping the teeth, he layered them on top of copies of the teeth he had already made. He made sure that the stop and pull were facing in the correct direction relative to the zipper pattern tiles (which run perpendicular to the path), and individually placed them in the Swatches panel.

2 Making and using the Pattern brushes. To make the first Pattern brush for the zipper teeth, Maxson opened the Brushes panel's pop-up menu and selected New Brush. He then chose New Pattern Brush, which opened the Pattern Brush Options dialog. He gave his Pattern brush a descriptive name, chose the first box in the diagram (the Side Tile), and then selected the Pattern swatch that represented the teeth alone. When a thumbnail of the Pattern swatch he had chosen (the teeth) showed in the first box, and the other boxes were left empty, he clicked OK to place the brush in the Brushes panel.

To create the version with the stop and pull, he again selected New Brush from the Brushes panel, and chose the same teeth pattern for the Side Tile. Skipping over the corner tiles, he chose the Zipper Pull swatch as the Start Tile, and the End Tile for the Zipper Stop swatch. He named his new Pattern brush so he would know it was built from all three swatches and clicked OK.

To use his new brushes, Maxson drew a path for each zipper. The long, vertical zipper used the brush with the pull and stop, while the short zipper used the brush with only teeth, since the pull required a unique illustration.

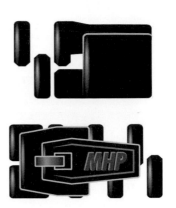

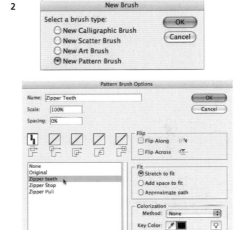

Creating zipper pull and stop, oriented in the outward-facing position Pattern brushes use for their tiles

2

Creating a new Pattern brush with only a Side Tile repeated along the length of the path to make the zipper with just teeth

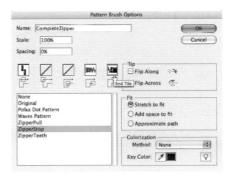

Creating a Pattern brush with Start and End tiles for the zipper with the pull and stop

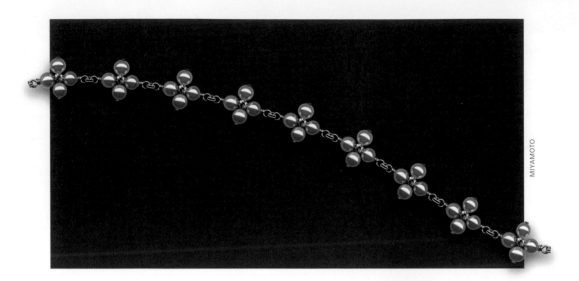

MIYAMOTO

Nobuko Miyamoto / Yukio Miyamoto

Making this intricate beaded necklace at first glance would seem impossibly difficult, but with the use of a Pattern brush, the necklace virtually draws itself. Nobuko Miyamoto designed the necklace and created the bead element (detail above) with a mixture of blended and solid filled objects. Careful attention was paid to the ends of the bead to ensure that when each bead lined up with the next one there would be a seamless connection between them. To make the chained ends, she selected the chain object and dragged a copy (Shift-Option/ Shift-Alt) to the other side of the bead. With the chain selected, she chose the Reflect tool and clicked above and below

the chain to reflect the chain vertically. Yukio Miyamoto then created the Pattern brush with the bead element. He selected and grouped the bead. Yukio clicked the New Brush icon at the bottom of the Brushes panel, selected New Pattern Brush, and clicked OK. In the Pattern Brush Options dialog, he kept the Colorization method as None, and then under Fit he chose Stretch to Fit. To make the necklace, Nobuko drew a path with the Brush tool and selected the bead Pattern brush in the Brushes panel to apply the brush. Now with the bead as a Pattern brush, the necklace can be easily adjusted to any length or path.

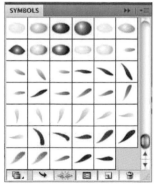

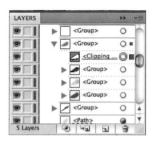

RLSimonson © 2005

SIMONSON

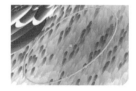

Rick Simonson

When Rick Simonson wanted to create a high level of verisimilitude in his Chipping Sparrow illustration, he turned to Illustrator's symbols as the obvious way to create the hundreds of feathers and seeds he would need. He drew closed paths for single feathers in the different colors and positions necessary to fill the bird's body. He added dimension to the feathers with gradient fills, and he duplicated and rotated some feathers to follow the growth pattern of real feathers. He then Option-clicked/Alt-clicked on the New Symbol icon in the Symbols panel to add the selected object without open-

ing the Symbol Options dialog. Simonson drew the main body of the bird and began filling small areas with layers of feathers, using the Symbol Sprayer with short strokes to manage their placement. To get the look he wanted, he often added feathers one by one instead of in looser symbol sets. He also applied clipping masks to further shape areas of feather symbols (see the *Advanced Techniques* chapter for more on clipping masks). To create the glare and the shading, he used the Transparency panel to reduce opacity and add transparency masks (see the *Transparency* chapter). He used similar methods for adding the seeds.

Symbolism Basics

Creating and Working with Symbols

Overview: *Create a basic background; define symbols; use Symbolism tools to place and customize symbols; add finishing details.*

The artwork for the symbols that were used to complete the piece

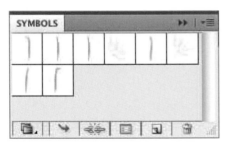

The Symbols panel containing the library of symbols

The Symbolism tools tear off panel; see "Tear off panels" in the Illustrator Basics *chapter*

One of several symbol sets of the raw grass after being sprayed with the Symbol Sprayer tool

JACKMORE

Lisa Jackmore created this illustration using a variety of effects possible with the Symbolism tools. Jackmore defined a library of symbols and then used the Symbolism tools to place and customize the symbols. Symbols can provide a "brush-like" painting experience, with easier (and more fun!) adjustments and editing.

1 Creating a background and symbols. Because she would be drawing many light-colored objects, Jackmore began by using the Rectangle tool to draw a blue background. Locking the layer with the background, Jackmore created a new layer on top, into which she drew the artwork for each of the symbols she would use to create the illustration. (See the *Layers & Appearances* chapter for more on layers.) To turn selected artwork into a symbol, either drag it onto the Symbols panel, or press F8; Illustrator automatically takes your artwork on the Artboard and swaps it for an instance of the symbol.

2 Applying symbols. Jackmore next selected the grass symbol in the Symbols panel and created the first row of grass with a single stroke of the Symbol Sprayer tool. You can experiment with the Symbol Sprayer by adjusting the Density and Intensity settings (double-click on any Symbolism tool to access the Symbolism Tools Options), and the speed of your spray strokes. Don't worry about getting an exact number or precise placement for each symbol as you spray; you'll fine-tune those and other symbol attributes next by applying Symbolism tools to a selected set.

3 Resizing symbols. To imply depth, Jackmore applied the Symbol Sizer tool to resize blades of grass in a selected set. By default, the Symbol Sizer tool increases the size of symbols within the tool's brush radius; to reduce the size of symbols within the radius, hold down Option/Alt.

To make the diameter of a Symbolism tool visible, double-click on any Symbolism tool and enable the Show Brush Size and Intensity checkbox. To enlarge and reduce the diameter of a Symbolism tool, use the same shortcuts as you do with brushes: the] key enlarges the diameter, and the [key reduces it.

4 Modifying symbol transparency and color. To modify the appearance of a symbol set, use the Symbol Screener, Stainer, and Styler tools. The Screener tool adjusts the transparency of symbols. The Stainer tool shifts the color of the symbol to be more similar to the current fill color, while preserving its luminosity. The Styler tool allows you to apply (in variable amounts) styles from the Graphic Styles panel. (For more details about the Styler and Screener tools, see *Illustrator Help*.) Jackmore used the Symbol Stainer tool, set to Random, to tint the dandelion symbols a lighter shade with just one stroke.

5 Rotating symbols. To make adjustments to the orientation of the dandelion symbol set, Jackmore used the Symbol Spinner tool set to User Defined, which set the spin based on the direction that the mouse was moved. (Search *Illustrator Help* for "Symbolism tool options" for an explanation of the User Defined and Average modes.)

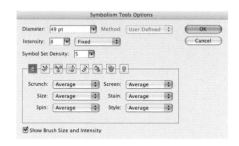

Symbolism Tools Options

Jackmore used the Symbol Sizer tool to make some of the blades of grass larger

Jackmore used the Symbol Stainer tool to make some of the dandelion symbols a brighter white

Jackmore used the Symbol Spinner tool to rotate the dandelion symbols

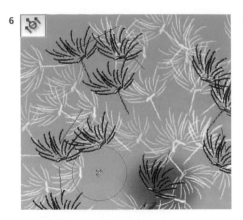

After using the Symbol Shifter tool with a smaller brush size to adjust the dandelion symbol positions

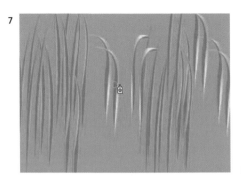

Thinning the grass by removing unwanted grass using the Symbol Sprayer tool while holding down the Option/Alt key

The background

6 Moving symbols. Jackmore used the Symbol Shifter tool with a smaller brush size to adjust the position of the dandelion symbol set.

The Symbol Shifter tool doesn't easily move symbols across large distances. To maximize symbol movement with the Symbol Shifter tool, first make the brush size as large as you can—at least as large as the symbol you wish to move. Then drag across the symbol, as though you were trying to push the symbol with a broom.

7 Deleting and adding symbols. At this point, Jackmore felt there were too many blades of grass. To remove unwanted grass, Jackmore used the Symbol Sprayer tool with the Option/Alt key held down. She chose a narrow brush size and clicked on the blade to be removed. She worked on the grass symbol set until she was satisfied with the amount of grass. If she needed to add more of that symbol (or even a different symbol) to a selected symbol set, she just applied the Symbol Sprayer tool without any modifier keys.

8 Adding finishing touches. To finish her illustration, Jackmore converted her blue rectangle to a gradient mesh. To create the luminous background, Jackmore applied different colors to individual mesh points. For more about gradient mesh, see the *Blends, Gradients, & Mesh* chapter.

Making symbols and keeping the art too

To keep your original artwork on the Artboard *and* use it to define a new symbol, hold down the Shift key as you drag the artwork onto the Symbols panel.

Symbol stacking order within a layer

You can change the symbol stacking order within a Symbol Set by adding these modifier keys to the Symbol Shifter tool:

- Shift-click the symbol instance to bring it forward.
- Option-Shift-click/Alt-Shift-click to push the symbol instance backward.

Gary Powell

Gary Powell created this illustration using his own set of custom symbols. He began with a template layer and hand-traced two pine cones and a simple branch. He combined the three into a new variation. Once he finished with the variations, he grouped and dragged them into the Symbols panel. With just five symbols,

Powell used the Symbol Sprayer tool and the Symbol Spinner tool to randomly spray branches into the scene and rotate them into position. As a finishing touch, he found the cloud symbol in the Nature Symbol Library, sprayed in a few clouds, and then used the Symbol Sizer tool to give them a sense of depth.

Symbol Libraries

Making Symbols and a Symbol Preset File

Overview: *Create artwork; add it to the Symbols panel; save the file as a Symbol Library that can be accessed from Illustrator's Symbols panel.*

SAXBY / NG

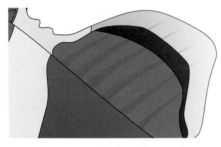

The original image (photo by Richard Ng for iStock Photo, www.istockphoto.com/richard_ng)

Enlargement of the dorsal fin showing the fin filled with a gradient at 75% opacity and fin rays filled with black at 12% opacity

To facilitate communication about environmental issues among scientists and environmentalists, the University of Maryland's Center for Environmental Science designed a library of symbols for use in reports, web sites, and multimedia. These symbols, numbering over 1500, are free of copyright and royalty restrictions. A sampling of the symbols are included on the *Wow! CD*. For the latest update to the symbol library files (as well as other non-symbol images), go to http://ian.umces.edu.

1 Importing and tracing an image and painting objects with gradient fills. Many sources exist for images that you can access and download from the Internet, providing a treasure-trove of visual inspiration for your symbols. Designer Tracey Saxby placed a clownfish photograph from iStockphoto (www.istockphoto.com/richard_ng) on a template layer and began tracing using the Pen and Pencil tools. If you plan to create a symbol library—a file that you access as an additional Symbols panel in Illustrator—consider keeping the artwork simple, using as few points, lines, and fills as necessary to create an expressive image. By keeping artwork simple, your symbols will be smaller in file size, making them load faster if you incorporate them in a Flash movie or in another kind of digital file.

Saxby completed the clownfish by painting the objects with linear and radial gradient fills. You can also experiment with reducing opacity and applying feathering

(Effect > Stylize > Feather) to some objects, like fins or feathers, to lend transparency to the artwork and to fade the artwork into the background behind the symbol.

2 Creating an Illustrator symbol from the artwork and organizing the Symbols panel. Once Saxby completed the artwork, she opened the Symbols panel. Saxby selected the clownfish artwork and dragged it into the Symbols panel, which automatically opened the Symbol Options dialog. She entered "Clownfish" in the Name field and clicked OK.

You can rearrange the order of symbols in the Symbols panel to make it easier for you or others to find a needed symbol. To reposition a symbol, drag the symbol to a new location in the panel. Also consider naming your symbols and having Illustrator arrange them alphabetically. To do this, select the Symbols panel menu and then select Sort by Name. (Illustrator is sensitive to initial caps in symbol names; Zebrafish will precede Angelfish in the Symbols panel when you select Sort by Name.)

3 Saving the symbol file as an Illustrator symbol library and opening the library. To quickly access your symbol file in the future, save it as a custom Symbol Library. To do this, choose Save Symbol Library from the Symbols panel's pop-up menu, and save it to the default "Symbols" location. To then access this library in the future, click on the Symbol Library Menu icon (in the bottom left of the Symbols panel) and choose your library from the User Defined menu at the bottom of the list.

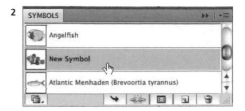
The Symbols panel after the artwork has been dragged to the panel to create a new symbol

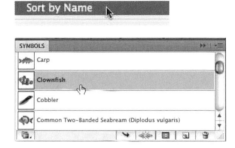
The Symbol Options dialog after the new symbol has been double-clicked in the Symbols panel

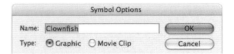
Top, the Sort by Name selection from the Symbols panel menu; bottom, the Symbols panel with the clownfish symbol among the symbols organized alphabetically using the panel menu's Sort by Name option

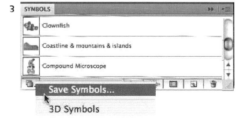
Choosing Save Symbols from the Symbols Library panel's Symbol Library Menu icon

Accessing symbols from the bottom of the Symbol Library Menu icon in the Symbols panel

---

Loading a Library from Bridge (CS3 or later)

Do you know that you can load document-specific libraries as you browse using Bridge (CS3 or later)? In Bridge, press the Control key (Mac) or right-click on a thumbnail of any native Illustrator document, and near the bottom of the contextual menu you'll see "Open as AI Library" with an option to load Brushes/Swatch/Symbol/Graphic from that file. —*Jean-Claude Tremblay*

Nature's Brushes

Illustrating Nature with Multiple Brushes

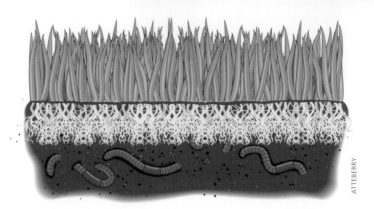

Overview: *Draw artwork and create an art brush; use the Paintbrush tool to make objects with the art brush; create a pattern brush from brushed objects; create and use a scatter brush.*

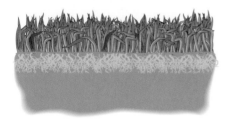
1

The three objects comprising a blade of grass

The Colorization options and Tips button from the Art Brush Options dialog

The completed art brush

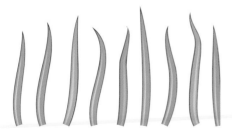

Brushed paths drawn with the Paintbrush tool

Faced with an assignment to contrast healthy and unhealthy grass and soil for a graphic to be placed on bags of organic fertilizer, Kevan Atteberry dug deep into Illustrator's Brushes panel to build his own grass, soil, and worm brushes. With the art and scatter brushes he made, Atteberry developed an easy way to create the visually complex elements of his illustration.

1 Drawing brush artwork, creating an art brush, and modifying copies of brushed paths. Creating a complex, natural-looking clump of grass was a challenge Atteberry solved by building art brushes. First, Atteberry drew a blade of grass using three objects that he overlapped. He selected the objects and dragged them into the Brushes panel. In the New Brush dialog, he selected New Art Brush and clicked OK. Then in the Art Brush Options dialog, Atteberry clicked on the Method menu in the dialog's Colorization section and chose Tints and Shades. (If you're unsure of how the Method options affect brushes, click the Tips button to display an informational dialog comparing different Methods applied to colored brush strokes.)

With the brush created, Atteberry drew several paths using the Paintbrush tool, choosing a different shade of green for each blade as he drew its path. To save time when making a large number of objects, consider duplicating paths and then editing them to make them appear different. To do this, copy and paste your paths and then apply the Scale, Reflect, Rotate tools to vary sizes and orientations of the copies. Repeat this process until you've built a complex set of brushed paths that fills up the space you've allocated in your illustration.

Brushed paths that have been scaled, reflected, and rotated

2 Creating a pattern brush from brushed paths. You can take your artwork a step further by building a pattern brush from your artwork. This provides extra flexibility in case your illustration calls for your objects to be set along a wavy path or stretched to fill a space in your composition. To create a pattern brush, select your set of objects and drag them into the Brushes panel. From the New Brush dialog, pick New Pattern Brush; in the Pattern Brush Options dialog, keep the default setting of Side Tile and adjust the Colorization and Fit settings as needed. (Atteberry chose "Stretch to fit" so that the grass would stretch automatically to fit the length of the path he would draw when continuing work on the illustration.)

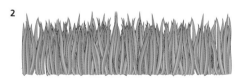

Brushed paths selected to make the pattern brush

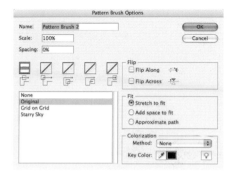

The Pattern Brush Options dialog

3 Making an art brush, drawing strokes, and covering with paths of solid and gradient fills. To show a healthy ecosystem, Atteberry drew the artwork for a worm, turned it into another art brush, and then used the Paintbrush tool to draw several paths with the worm brush. Behind the worms he drew a closed path filled with brown to make the background soil. To conceal parts of the worms, he drew brown-filled paths on a layer above the worms. For worm holes and tubes, he created dark-brown blends shaped like crescents and cylinders.

The worm artwork used to make an art brush

Path painted with the worm art brush and then partially covered by filled paths

4 Making and using a scatter brush. To add a natural complexity to the brown soil, Atteberry added random particles. He first drew small shapes that he filled with light and dark browns. Then he selected the shapes and dragged them into the Brushes panel, specifying New Scatter Brush in the New Brush dialog and adjusting the settings in the Scatter Brush Options dialog. Next, with the new brush still selected, he drew a curlicue path with the Paintbrush tool, which scattered the soil particles along the path.

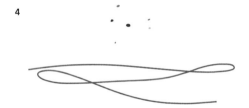

Above, particle shapes used to make the scatter brush; below, the path used to paint the brush

6 Layers & Appearances

Layers can dramatically improve your ability to organize complicated artwork and simplify your work. Think of layers as sheets of clear acetate stacked one on top of the other so that you can keep dozens of objects—even groups of them—separate. By default, new documents have one layer but you can create as many additional layers and sublayers as you wish. You can also rearrange the stacking order of the layers; lock, hide, or copy layers; and move or copy objects from one layer to another. You can use the Layers panel to select objects and groups, and you can even open up a layer so you can view, identify, and select individual paths or groups contained within a layer!

A few shortcuts will help when you're adding layers to the Layers panel (also see Tip at left). Click the Create New Layer icon to add a layer (labeled in numeric sequence) above the current layer. Hold Option/Alt when you click this icon to open Layer Options as you add the layer. To add a layer to the top of the Layers panel, hold ⌘/Ctrl when you click the Create New Layer icon. To make a new layer below the current layer and open the Layer Options, hold ⌘-Option/Ctrl-Alt when you click the Create New Layer icon (the Layer Options dialog will also open). Finally, you can easily duplicate a layer, sublayer, group, or path by dragging it to the Create New Layer icon at the bottom of the Layers panel. To delete selected layers, click on the Trash icon or drag the layers to the Trash.

You can also create sublayers to help stay organized. Sublayers, like layers and groups, can hold either objects, groups, or other sublayers. They are themselves contained within the layer listed above them, so if you delete the *container* layer holding sublayers, all of its sublayers will be deleted as well.

Another icon in the Layers panel is a target (the circle to the right of the layer name). See the "Selecting & Targeting with the Layers Panel" section later in this chapter for details about the target indicator, targeting objects

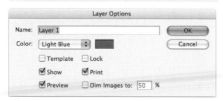

Layers panel navigation

- To hide a layer, click the Eye icon. Click again to show it.
- To lock a layer, click in the column to the right of the Eye icon (a lock displays). Click again to unlock.
- To Lock/Unlock or Show/Hide all *other* layers, Option-click/Alt-click on a Lock or Eye icon.
- To duplicate a layer, drag it to either the Create New Layer or Create New Sublayer icon.
- To select multiple contiguous layers, click one layer, then Shift-click the other. To select (or deselect) *any* multiple layers, ⌘-click/Ctrl-click layers in any order.
- Double-click any layer to open Layer Options for that layer (this works with multiple layers selected also).

Layer Options (double-click a layer name)

from the Layers panel, and to learn exactly what all this target stuff means.

USING LAYER OPTIONS

You can double-click on any layer, sublayer, or named object or group in the Layers panel to access Layer Options such as the Name, Show, and/or Lock status. If you want to know what type of object they are after you've renamed them, retain the name of the subcomponent. For example, you can rename a group to help organize your layer list, but keep the bracket description as part of the renaming of the layer (e.g., *floral <Group>*).

Double-click on a layer name, sublayer name, or on one of multiple selected layer/sublayer names to access the Layer Options discussed below:

- **Name the layer.** When creating complicated artwork, giving layers descriptive names keeps your job, and your brain, organized.

- **Change the layer's color.** A layer's color is visible next to its disclosure arrow, and it determines the selection color for paths, anchor points, bounding boxes, and Smart Guides. If necessary, adjust the layer color so selections stand out against artwork.

- **Template layer.** Illustrator's template layers are special layers that don't print or export. They're useful whenever you want to base new artwork on existing art or use the artwork as a guide for placing new objects. For example, place the existing art on a non-printing template layer, and then, on a regular layer, hand-trace the artwork or align new objects to the artwork in the template. There are three ways to create a template layer: You can select Template from the Layers pop-up menu, double-click a layer name and enable the Template option, or enable the Template option when you first place an image into Illustrator. By default, Template layers are locked. To unlock a Template in order to adjust or edit objects, click

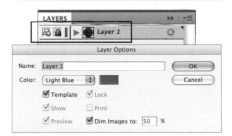

In the Layers panel, template layer names are slanted and template layers are locked by default; there is also a Template icon instead of an Eye icon. Placed raster images are dimmed on a template layer (can be adjusted in Layer Options).

To change the stacking order of several objects:

- Reorder the layers they are on.
- Cut the bottom objects, select the topmost object, and Paste in Front with Paste Remembers Layers *off*.
- Drag selection indicators (large square) from one layer to another.
- Shift to select multiple layers and choose Reverse Order from the Layers panel pop-up menu.
- Move objects within a layer using Object > Arrange: Bring to Front/Bring Forward/Send to Back/Send Backward.
- Select the objects you want to move; make a new layer (click the New Layer icon) or highlight a layer into which you want to move these objects, and choose Object > Arrange > Send to Current Layer.
- If the selection is a blend, choose Object > Blend > Reverse Front to Back.

When a layer name is slanted, it has been set *not* to print in the Layer Options dialog. To create a more obvious visual clue that a layer is set to non-printing, choose the Template layer option (see the "Template layer" section earlier in this chapter).

the Lock icon to the left of the layer name.

There is no restriction to how many of your layers can be template layers (sublayers can't be template layers); see Steven Gordon's Galleries following this chapter introduction for examples of using multiple template layers. **Note:** *Template layers shouldn't be confused with Illustrator's Templates feature.* Templates *are a special file format ending in .ait; whereas* template layers *are simply a special kind of layer. For more about* Templates, *see the* Illustrator Basics *chapter.*

- **Show/Hide layer.** This option functions the same way as the Show/Hide toggle, which you access by clicking the Eye icon (see the Tip "Layers panel navigation" at the beginning of this chapter introduction). By default, hiding a layer sets that layer *not* to print.

- **Preview/Outline mode.** If you have objects that are easier to edit in Outline mode, or objects that are slow to redraw (such as complicated patterns, live blends, or gradients), you may want to set only those layers (or objects) to Outline mode. Toggle this option on and off directly by ⌘-clicking/Ctrl-clicking the Eye icon in the view column. Alternatively, double-click selected layers and, in Layer Options, disable Preview to set those layers to Outline.

- **Lock/Unlock layer.** This option functions the same way as the Lock/Unlock toggle, which you access by clicking the lock column of the layer (see the Tip "Layers panel navigation" at the beginning of this chapter).

- **Print.** When you print from Illustrator you can use this feature to override the default, which sets visible layers to print. If you need a quick visual clue to ensure that a layer will not print, make it into a Template layer (see the Tip "*Slanted* layer names?" at left).

- **Dim images.** You can only dim raster images (not vector Illustrator objects) from 1% to 99% opacity.

The Layers pop-up menu

This section will look at functions unique to the Layers pop-up menu, not discussed in previous sections of this introduction.

With the ability to nest sublayers within other layers and create group objects comes the potential for confusion. It can become difficult to find objects when they're buried deep in the layer list. To find selected objects, use Locate Object (which becomes Locate Layer when Show Layers Only is checked in Panel Options). When you've selected two or more layers, Merge Selected is available and will place *visible* objects in the topmost layer. You can consolidate all visible items in your artwork into a single layer using the Flatten Artwork command (though be aware that you might lose effects and masks applied to the layers involved). To make a flat version in another file, unlock all layers and objects, Select > All, Copy, make a new document, and Paste (with Paste Remembers Layers disabled).

Paste Remembers Layers is a great feature: When it's enabled, pasted objects retain their layer order; when unchecked, pasted objects go into the selected layer. If the layers don't exist, Paste Remembers Layers will make them for you! This feature can be turned on and off even after the objects have been copied—so if you Paste, and wish that the toggle were reversed, you can Undo, toggle the Paste Remembers Layers option, then Paste again.

Collect in New Layer moves all of the selected layers into a new layer. Release to Layers (Build), or Release to Layers (Sequence), allows you to make individual object layers from a group of objects, such as a blend, a layer, or art created by using a brush. (See the *Web & Animation* chapter for applications of these options for animation.)

Sometimes easier than dragging, using Reverse Order will reverse the stacking order of selected layers or sublayers. Hide All Layers/Others, Outline All Layers/Others, and Lock All Layers/Others all perform actions on unselected layers or objects. Send to Current Layer sends selected objects to your currently highlighted layer.

Layers panel pop-up menu

Go Big... or Go None

Layers panel thumbnails can be very useful when you're trying to find and select objects, but they're sometimes difficult to see. For a closer look, set Row Size larger in Panel Options—up to 100 pixels! Or, if you have too many layers, eliminate the icons altogether.

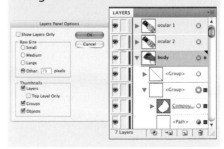

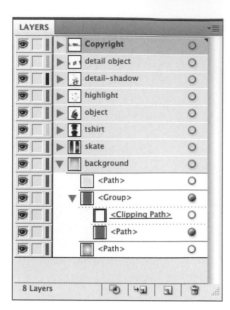

LAYERS

			Copyright	O
		▶	detail object	O
		▶	detail–shadow	O
		▶	highlight	O
		▶	object	O
		▶	tshirt	O
		▶	skate	O
		▼	background	O
			<Path>	O
		▼	<Group>	O
			<Clipping Path>	O
			<Path>	O
			<Path>	O

8 Layers

Layers panel demonstrating organizing content through layer hierarchy

Select to change layers

Instead of changing the active layer by selecting a new layer in the Layers panel, let Illustrator make the change for you. When you select an object from an unlocked layer, its layer automatically becomes active. By default, the next object you create will use the same Stroke and Fill as the last selected object and will be placed on that same active layer.

To select *all* objects

First, make sure Unlock All and Show All are unavailable in the Object menu. Then choose Select > All (⌘-A/Ctrl-A), or, with multiple artboards, Select > All In Artboard (Opt-⌘-A/Alt-Ctrl-A) to limit the selection to the active Artboard.

Panel Options customizes the layer display. This is a great help to artists who have complicated files with many layers. Show Layers Only hides the disclosure arrow so you only see the container layer thumbnail. Adding sublayers reveals the arrow, but you still can't target groups or individual paths in this mode. Row Size defines the size of the thumbnail for a layer. You can specify a thumbnail size from Small (no thumbnail) to Large, or use Other to customize a size up to 100 pixels. Thumbnail lets you individually set thumbnail visibility for the Layers, Top Level Only (when Layers is checked), Group, and Object.

CONTROLLING THE STACKING ORDER OF OBJECTS

Layers are crucial for organizing and building your illustration, but controlling the stacking order of objects *within* a layer is just as essential. The intuitive layers and sublayers disclose their hierarchical contents when you open the disclosure arrow. Following is a summary of the functions that will help you control the stacking order of objects within layers and sublayers.

Sublayers and the hierarchical layer structure

In addition to regular main, or "parent" layers, there are sublayers and groups, both of which can act as *containers* for objects or images.

Grouping objects together automatically creates a container "layer" named <Group>. Double-click the <Group> layer to open its options. Group layers are much like sublayers and can contain either objects or other groups. You can target them to apply appearances that affect all the objects within the group, and you can double-click on a group's Contents in the Appearance panel to alter any appearances that the group shares. In some cases, such as when Pathfinder effects are applied, objects have to be grouped and the group layer must be targeted in order to apply the effect.

Note: *If you rename your <Group>, you might get confused when you can't select individual objects with the* *same tools used on normal objects on regular layers. Instead, leave <Group> as a part of your new name.*

Paste in Front, Paste in Back (Edit menu)

If you choose Paste in Front or Paste in Back with nothing selected, Illustrator will paste the cut or copied object at the extreme front or back of the current layer. Whereas if you do have an object selected, Illustrator will paste the cut or copied object *directly* on top of or behind the selected object in the stacking order. Equally important is that both Paste in Front and Paste in Back paste objects that are cut or copied into the exact same location—in relation to the *ruler origin* (*x* and *y* coordinates). This capability transfers from one document to another, ensuring perfect registration and alignment when you use Edit > Paste in Front/Back. (See the Ch02-Zen folder on the *Wow! CD* for the zen_lessons, including one using paste commands: 2aZen-Layers-Moving_Pasting.ai.)

Lock/Unlock All (Object menu)

In the days before it was even possible to open layers in Illustrator and select the individual items they contain, the Lock/Unlock All commands were essential. They're a little less indispensable now, but can still be very useful if you can't locate your path from within the layer contents.

When you're trying to select an object and you accidentally select an object on top of it, try locking the selected object (⌘ 2/Ctrl-2 or Object > Lock) and clicking again. Repeat as necessary until you reach the correct object. When you've finished the task, choose Unlock All (⌘-Option-2/Ctrl-Alt-2) to release all the locked objects.

Hide/Show All (Object menu)

Alternatively, you can hide selected objects with Object > Hide > Selection (⌘-3/Ctrl-3). To view all hidden objects, choose Object > Show All (⌘-Option-3/Ctrl-Alt-3). **WARNING:** *Hidden objects may print if they're on visible layers. If you'll be sending your file elsewhere for printing, and if your workflow includes the Hide command, make*

There are now several ways to make a selection and several other ways to target an object. The main difference is that selections don't always target, but targeting always makes a selection. In this example, "Layer 1" contains the selected object but is not currently the target. The circled "<Path>" is the current target.

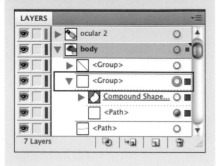

 Target indicator for any layer or sub-component

 Selection is also currently targeted

■ Selection indicator for a container layer

■ Selection indicator when all objects are selected

An object has a basic appearance as long as it does not contain multiple fills or strokes, transparency, effects, or brush strokes. A basic appearance is indicated by an open circle in the Layers panel. More complex appearances are indicated by a gradient-filled circle in the Layers panel.

sure to choose Object > Show All before saving your final file. And beware—Show All always unhides all objects and hidden layers!

Bring to Front/Forward, Send to Back/Backward

These commands work on objects within a layer. Bring Forward (Object > Arrange) stacks an object on top of the object directly above it; Bring to Front moves an object in front of all other objects on its layer. Similarly, Send to Back sends an object as far back as it can go in its stacking order, whereas Send Backward sends an object behind its closest neighbor.

Note: *Bring Forward/Send Backward work best with simple object groupings, and may not work as expected on complex images. If it doesn't suit your needs, expand the Layers panel and relocate your path or group.*

SELECTING & TARGETING WITH THE LAYERS PANEL

There are several ways to make selections. Click the layer's target indicator or Option-click/Alt-click the layer name to select all unlocked and visible objects on the layer, including objects on sublayers and in groups. Click a sublayer's target indicator to select everything on the sublayer, including other sublayers or groups. Clicking the *group's* target indicator will also select all objects within that group. Either Shift-click or ⌘-click/Ctrl-click each of the target indicators to select multiple objects on different layers, including sublayers and groups. When you intend to modify the appearance of a layer, sublayer, or group, you must click on the *target* indicator to make your selection first, then make your adjustments.

If you have only some (but not all) objects selected on a layer, you will see a small square to the right of the target indicator. Click on the small square to select all of the objects on the layer or in the group. A larger square means that all of the objects on that layer or group are already selected. Clicking in the small space to the right of the target indicator will also select all unlocked and visible objects on the layer, sublayer, or group.

IMPORTANT: *Be aware that if you target a top-level layer and apply strokes, fills, effects, or transparency and then copy/paste that layer into a new document, all appearance attributes that were* applied to that layer *will be lost in the new document, even when Paste Remembers Layers is enabled. Try this workaround by Jean-Claude Tremblay (which also works to maintain masks and effects applied to the layer): Since the attributes of a top-level layer are not retained and you get no warning when pasting into the new document, you need to nest the top layer into another layer and make it a sublayer. Then Copy/Paste this layer into the new document to retain the appearance attributes.*

THE APPEARANCE PANEL

The Appearance panel has been a part of Illustrator for a long time. Whenever you need to view a selected object's stroke, fill, or transparency, for instance, you can view those characteristics in the Appearance panel. The Appearance panel tells you about other properties as well, such as whether or not it is part of a Group or has an effect or named graphic style applied to it. Here you can also add additional strokes or fills to the object, choose whether or not the next object you draw will have the same appearance, or construct a new graphic style to save for future objects. The Appearance panel has always provided a wealth of information about an object, but now it does much more than that. Select an object and not only will you see how that object was constructed, but you can change most of its properties right there in the Appearance panel. It has now become the "go to" place to get your work done when you need to change any aspect of an appearance that has been applied to an object. Instead of opening and locating many panels, you now only need to have one panel open for most of your everyday creating and editing. The Appearance panel has become a hub of a productive and efficient workflow.

So just what constitutes an appearance? At a minimum, an object has a stroke and fill (even if one or both are set to None), and transparency (even if the blending

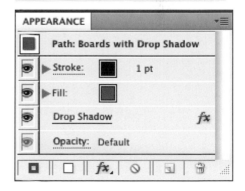

Appearance panel showing Stroke, Fill, effect, Transparency, and a named Graphic Style

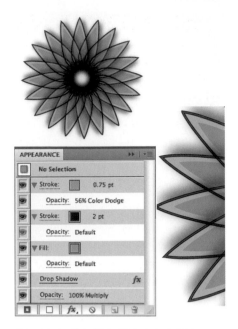

An example of multiple Strokes, including a .75-pt lavender stroke at 56% Opacity with a Color Dodge blending mode, a solid fill, a Drop Shadow effect (see the Live Effects & Graphic Styles chapter for more about live effects), and the layer set to a Multiply blending mode.

New Art Has Basic Appearance

The Appearance panel's New Art Has Basic Appearance option is *on* by default. So, unless you toggle this option off in the panel menu, Illustrator will not apply effects, brush strokes, transparency, blending modes, or multiple fills or strokes to new objects you create. —*Brenda Sutherland*

Target all elements

When a group or layer is targeted, you can double-click the Contents line in the Appearance panel to target any shared appearances, such as the Fills, Strokes, Effects, or Opacity, inside the group or layer.—*Pierre Louveaux*

mode is the default Normal and Opacity is the default 100%). This is defined as a *basic appearance.* Add to that effects, such as drop shadows and warps, transparency, and any additional strokes or fills, and you can create very complex appearances. Save and name an object's attributes as one item and you have constructed a *graphic style.* An appearance can be applied to any path, object (including text), group, sublayer, or layer. Attributes within the appearance are added to the panel in the order they are applied, so changing the order of the attributes will change the appearance. An object and its enclosing groups and layers can all have their own appearances.

To modify an appearance, make a selection or click on a target indicator (Layers panel). Then add transparency, effects, multiple fills, and/or multiple strokes (see the "Editing an object's appearance" and "Beyond the Basic Appearance" sections later in this introduction). When you've targeted a group, sublayer, or layer, strokes and fills will be applied to the individual objects within the selection, but any effects or transparency settings will be applied to the *target* (see the Tip "Selecting vs. targeting," later in this introduction). Drag the target indicator (in the Layers panel) from one layer to another to move an appearance, or Option-drag/Alt-drag the indicator to copy the appearance. To reuse an appearance, save it as a style in the Graphic Styles panel (for more about Graphic Styles see the *Live Effects & Graphic Styles* chapter).

Creating objects

When you've selected or targeted an item, the Appearance panel displays all the attributes associated with the current selection. If there isn't a selection, the panel will display the attributes for the next object to be drawn. When the current target is an object, the Appearance panel always lists, in order, at least one stroke, one fill, and the object-level transparency. When the target is a group or layer, no fill or stroke is shown unless one has been applied (see the "Beyond the Basic Appearance" section later in this chapter) and you double-click the Contents line in the Appearance panel. "Default Transparency" means 100% opacity, Normal blending mode, Isolate Blending off, and Knockout Group off or neutral. (See the *Transparency* chapter for more about these options.)

If the current selection has more than the *basic* attributes you can choose what attributes the next object will have. The Appearance panel menu holds the New Art Has Basic Appearance option. When a checkmark is beside the option (the default), your next object will only inherit the basic attributes of the object, such as the fill, stroke, and the default blend mode and opacity. If you want your object to maintain all of the attributes and effects of the current selection, choose New Art Has Basic Appearance to toggle it *off* (no checkmark beside it).

Also in the Appearance panel menu are the Clear Appearance and Reduce to Basic Appearance options. Clear Appearance reduces attributes to no fill, no stroke and 100% opacity, blending mode Normal. Reduce to Basic Appearance retains a single fill and stroke. To toggle these on or off, select the option in the panel menu. You can also click on the Clear Appearance indicator at the bottom of the panel instead of going through the menu. **Note:** *Keep in mind that Reduce to Basic Appearance removes all brush strokes and live effects!*

Editing an object's appearance

Once you've drawn an object and want to alter or add to any of its attributes, you'll appreciate how handy the Appearance panel has become. No longer do you need to select your object, and then separately locate and open an individual panel for each attribute. Now if you click on an <u>underlined</u> attribute, the relevant panel or dialog will open; click on <u>Stroke</u> to open the Strokes panel, on <u>Opacity</u> to open the Transparency panel, etc. If you click on the color swatch beside <u>Stroke</u> or <u>Fill</u>, it turns into a pop-up arrow that opens the Swatches panel. A stroke-weight list box with a pop-up arrow also appears beside the Stroke color swatch list box. If you Shift-click on a color swatch, the Color panel opens instead of the Swatches panel. Click

Move or copy appearances

In the Layers panel, drag the appearance indicator from one object, group, or layer to another to *move* the appearance. To *copy* the appearance, hold Option/Alt as you drag.

If you can't see an appearance

If you're trying to alter an appearance, but nothing is changing on the screen, check that:
- Your objects are selected.
- You're in Preview mode.

Add New Fill
Add New Stroke
Duplicate Item
Remove Item

Clear Appearance
Reduce to Basic Appearance

✓ New Art Has Basic Appearance

Appearance panel menu—ready to draw with Basic Appearance only

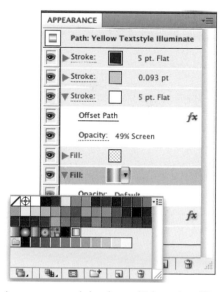

Appearance panel showing multiple strokes, fills and effects, as well as transparency, after clicking on a Fill's arrow to open the Swatches panel

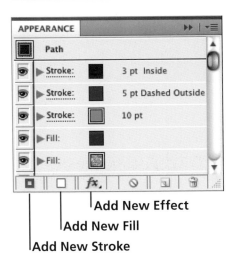

Add New Effect
Add New Fill
Add New Stroke

GORDON/CARTAGRAM

Creating an appearance using multiple strokes to construct a highway for a map

the underlined name of a live effect, and that effect's dialog will reopen for editing. Double-clicking on the *fx* icon will do the same thing.

The Appearance panel has a stacking order similar to that of the Layers panel. Items at the top of the panel are at the top of the stacking order. You can click on items in the panel list to select them, and you can rearrange them by dragging and dropping. Each attribute also has a visibility icon to the far left. Clicking on the Eye icon toggles the attribute on or off, allowing you to experiment easily with different looks for any object. If you target one or more layers, or select objects with hidden attributes, clicking on Show All Hidden Attributes will restore visibility to everything that is selected. If you select a group or multiple objects and double-click on Contents, any shared attributes will show up in the Appearance panel and are editable right there.

There are several ways to duplicate or delete a fill, stroke, or effect. If the attribute is a stroke or fill, you can select the object and then click on either the Add New Stroke or Add New Fill icon at the bottom of the panel to duplicate it. You can also drag an attribute to either the Duplicate Selected Item or the Delete Selected Item icon at the bottom of the panel. Finally, you can choose the appropriate item from the pop-up menu.

Beyond the Basic Appearance

Create a more complex appearance of multiple, overlapping, or layered strokes by adding additional strokes to the same path. Select a path, group, or layer, and either click on the Add New Stroke icon at the bottom of the panel, or choose Add New Stroke from the panel's pop-up menu. This adds a new stroke to the Appearance. In order to see the additional stroke on the path, you must give it different attributes from the initial stroke. First, target one of the strokes in the Appearance panel. Then, click on <u>Stroke</u> to open the Stroke panel, or on the color swatch to open the Swatches panel and pop up the Stroke Weight list box. Now, still in the Appearance panel, change any of these attributes. One way to layer strokes is to make the strokes successively smaller as they go up in the stack. Or you might want to make the upper stroke dashed using the pop-up Stroke panel. Change the color at the same time (using the pop-up Swatches panel) and the dashed line will show against the solid line. Align the strokes (using the Stroke panel pop-up) separately to the filled object to create yet another complex appearance.

To create multiple fills, target an object, group, or layer and click on the Add New Fill icon at the bottom of the panel, or choose Add New Fill from the panel's pop-up menu. As with multiple strokes, before you can see the effect of the added fill, it needs a different appearance. To vary the results of additional fills, apply an effect or different transparency settings; you can also use patterns or gradients with transparency.

Now when you're creating an appearance, you don't even have to leave the Appearance panel in order to add a live effect. Whenever you want to apply effects such as Distort & Transform or 3D, simply click on the *fx* icon at the bottom of the Appearance panel. A list pops up from which you can choose any of the effects available in the Effects menu. For "one stop shopping," use the convenience of the Appearance panel to access the different properties that make up the look of any object you create.

Whenever you are creating a complex appearance, try out different "looks" by toggling visibility for a stroke, fill, or effect on and off, and even add additional appearances to see if you prefer one look over another. Don't hesitate to reorder the fills and strokes to achieve a different result, especially when you have added blending modes or opacity to them, which will further change the way they interact. Comparing different effects and settings is now easy. Using the visibility icons in the Appearance panel gives you a wide range of options for creative experimentation.

For practice working with Appearances, see the "Basic Appearances" lesson in this chapter. Find additional examples of art with multiple strokes and fills, in the *Artboards & Type* and *Live Effects & Graphic Styles* chapters.

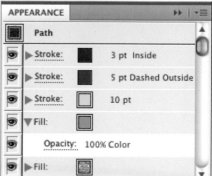

Creating a complex appearance with multiple strokes aligned separately to the object and multiple fills using blending modes.

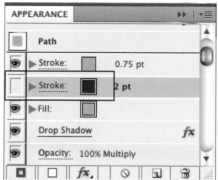

Turning off the Eye icon on a Stroke to experiment with a different appearance

Digitizing a Logo
Learning to Use a Template Layer

Overview: *Create a scan and place it on a template layer in Illustrator; hand-trace the template, modify the paths with the Direct Selection tool; refine lines with the Pencil tool; use basic objects for ease and speed.*

1

A clean, high-contrast scan of the sketch

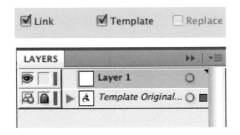

Creating the template and a drawing layer

2

Using the Direct Selection tool and dragging on the direction handles to adjust the path to better fit the sketch

Beginning with his scanned sketch imported as a template layer, Jack Tom used Illustrator's basic drawing tools to create this logo for the Bertz Design Group. Illustrator's Pen, Pencil and basic geometric tools, such as the Rectangle and Ellipse tools, can handle any object you need to make, creating a polished logo for any occasion.

1 Placing a scanned image as a template. Create a high-contrast copy of your sketch for the logo by scanning the image at a high resolution to provide the detail you need for hand-tracing. If you have an image-editing program such as Photoshop, you can increase contrast first, thus making your sketched lines more distinct, before placing the file in Illustrator. Save your scan as a PSD or TIFF and choose File > Open to select your scan. From the Layers panel pop-up menu, choose Template, and then create a new, empty layer for your tracing. Or create your Illustrator document first, choose File > Place, and enable Template in the Open dialog. A Template layer is placed beneath the original layer. Template layers are automatically set to be non-printing and dimmed layers.

2 Hand-tracing the template. With the template as an on-screen tracing guide, begin using the Pen tool on the empty layer for tracing the straight lines and smooth curves. Don't worry too much about the tracing being a bit off at first. You'll adjust the paths to fit the sketch more closely next. As you trace, remember to click for corners, click-drag for curves, and to hold down the Option/Alt key when dragging out a direction handle in order to create a hinged curve in the path. (See the *Zen lessons* on the *Wow! CD* for help with Bézier curves.) Once you've drawn a basic path, zoom in close and use the Direct Selection tool to adjust anchor points and direction handles. Use the Convert Anchor Point tool to switch between corners and curves, if necessary. You can simplify your view of an object by entering Outline mode. You can toggle between Outline and Preview modes for that object's layer by holding down the ⌘/Ctrl key and clicking on the visibility icon. Use ⌘-Y/Ctrl-Y to toggle the entire image between Outline and Preview modes.

Using Option/Alt with the Pen tool to "scallop" (make a hinged curve) while you draw

Toggling between Outline and Preview mode on a single layer by holding down ⌘-D/Ctrl-D as you click on the layer's visibility icon

3 Drawing, and redrawing, irregular lines with the Pencil tool. Using the mouse or a graphic tablet (such as a Wacom tablet), draw as you would with an actual pencil. Double-click the Pencil tool icon to customize settings. Create smoother lines by setting higher Fidelity and Smoothness numbers, or zoom in closer on the path while editing with the Pencil or Smooth tools. You can also select any path and start drawing close to or overlapping that path in order to redraw it (in Options specify the pixel distance from the selected path so that you can edit it instead of starting a new one). Use the Pencil tool with low settings to transform Pen tool paths into jagged lines. That will help you to express natural elements, such as the mountains in this logo.

3

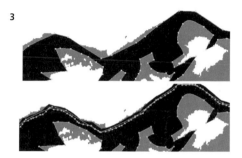

Using the Pen tool for a quick path (top), then using the Pencil tool to add a stroke expressing jagged, rough elements

4

Constructing elements quickly from geometric objects

4 Using basic objects to help build your logo. Illustrator includes ready-made objects to speed up drawing rectangles, ellipses, and even stars (or the sun, as in this logo). Layer these on top of each other, and add paths and filled objects drawn with the Pen or Pencil tools to finish converting your sketch to a clean illustration easy to color and/or modify to suit any purpose.

Vector logos adapt well to B&W or color printing

Organizing Layers
Managing Custom Layers and Sublayers

Overview: *Sketch and scan a composition; set up basic, named layers in Illustrator for the objects you will create; place art into sublayers; hand-trace the placed art; delete the temporary sublayers.*

1

The initial concept sketches for the illustration

The final composition for the illustration

Beginning your illustration with well-organized layers and sublayers can be a lifesaver when you're constructing complex illustrations. Using these layers to isolate or combine specific elements will save you an immense amount of production time by making it easy to hide, lock, or select related objects within layers. Artist Nancy Stahl saved time and frustration when she was commissioned to design this illustration for an article in the Condé Nast Traveler magazine. She created multiple layers and sublayers to facilitate the manual tracing and arrangement of various components in the illustration.

1 **Collecting and assembling source materials.** Prepare your own source materials to use as drawing references and templates in Illustrator. To prepare this illustration, Stahl hand-sketched several concepts then scanned the approved composition into Adobe Photoshop where she prepared it for hand-tracing.

2 Setting up illustration layers. Before you begin to import any photos or drawings, take a few moments to set up layers. Naming and assigning a color to each layer will help you isolate and manage the key elements in your illustration. Before Stahl actually started drawing in Illustrator, she set up separate layers for the water, the sky, the railing, the steward, and the tray and ship. You can quickly name a layer while creating it by Option-clicking/Alt-clicking on the Create New Layer icon in the Layers panel. You can also name or rename an existing layer or sublayer by double-clicking on it in the Layers panel.

3 Placing art to use as a drawing reference. Click on the layer in which you plan to hand-trace your first object, then click on the Create New Sublayer icon in the Layers panel to create a sublayer for your drawing reference (Option-click/Alt-click on the icon to name your sublayer as you create it). Stahl created a sublayer that she named "JPEG Images." Use File > Place to select the scan or artwork to be placed into this sublayer. If you wish, you can enable the template option before placing the file. The sublayer should now be directly below the object layer in which you will be hand-tracing. Lock the sublayer and draw in the layer above using the Pencil, Pen, or other Drawing tools of your choice.

Using the Layers panel, Stahl repurposed the "JPEG Images" sublayer by freely moving it below each of the key element layers as she drew. To move a layer, drag and drop it to another position in the Layers panel.

4 Hand-tracing and drawing into your layers. Now you can begin drawing and hand-tracing elements in your compositional layers. Activate the layer or sublayer in which you want to draw by clicking on the layer's name. Make sure the layer or sublayer is unlocked and visible (there should be an Eye in the Visibility column and an empty box in the Lock column). It also helps to turn off the visibility of all non-essential layers before you begin working. From the Layers panel, you can lock, unlock,

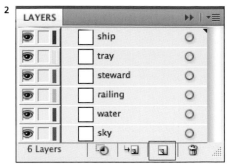
Setting up layers to isolate key elements

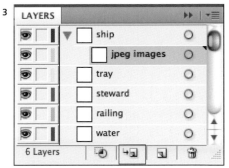
The sublayer before placing the scan

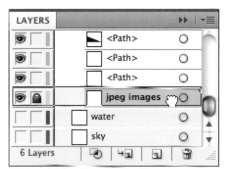
Moving the drawing reference layer

Setting up the Lock and Show options for hand-tracing an object

4

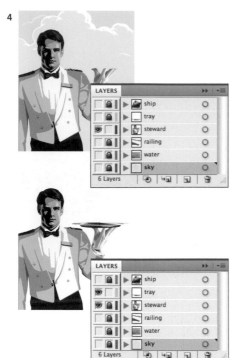

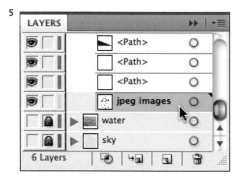

Viewing only the essential layers for each task

5

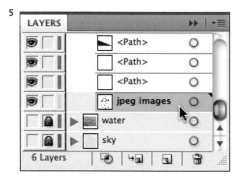

Clicking on a visible and unlocked sublayer to make it active for placing new art

6

Clicking on or dragging the sublayer to the Trash icon, or choosing Delete from the Layers panel pop-up menu

hide or show layers, as well as toggle between Preview and Outline modes, switch to your active layer, or add a new layer or sublayer (see the "Layers panel navigation" Tip on the first page of this chapter for helpful shortcuts in working with the Layers panel). By maneuvering in this way, Stahl could easily hand-trace a drawing reference or sketch in the layers above a locked layer.

5 **Adding new placed art to a layer or sublayer.** If you need to import art into an existing layer or sublayer, first make sure the layer is visible and unlocked, then make it the active layer by clicking on it. Use the Place command to bring the new scan or art into the selected layer. When Stahl needed additional drawing references she placed new art into the "JPEG Images" sublayer.

6 **Deleting layers or sublayers when you are finished using them.** Extra layers with placed art can take up extra disk space and increase the time it takes to save your document, so you'll want to delete them when you are done with them. When you finish using a drawing reference or template layer, first save the illustration. Then, in the Layers panel, click on the layer or sublayer you are ready to remove (Shift-click to select multiple layers) and either drag it to, or simply click on, the Trash icon in the Layers panel. Alternatively, you can choose the Delete option from the Layers panel pop-up menu. With these temporary layers deleted, use Save As to save this new version of the illustration with a meaningful new name and version number. Stahl eventually deleted all the sublayers she created as templates so that she could save her final cover illustration with all the illustration layers but without the excess template sublayers or placed pictures.

Easily changing placed art

Select the image you wish to replace and click on the name of the image that appears in the left side of the Control panel; choose Relink at the top of the resulting pop-up menu.

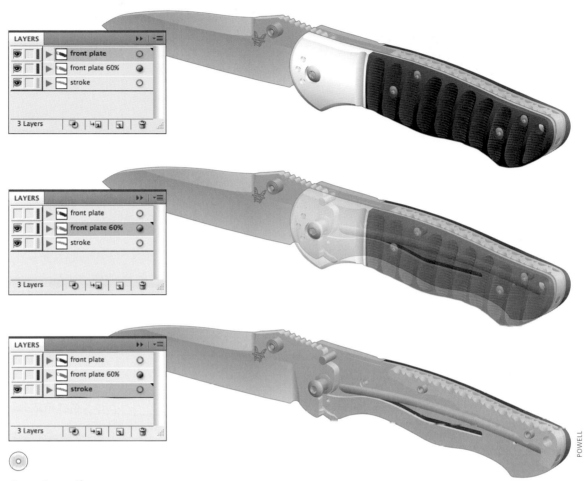

Gary Powell

Using the same techniques as in "Organizing Layers," Gary Powell created this image for Benchmade Knife Company's training manual for product resellers. He duplicated the top layer by dragging it to the Create New Layer icon in the Links panel. He applied an Opacity value to the duplicated layer to create the transparent handle effect. When finished, he could toggle the visibility of the layers to print or export them individually.

Moving and Copying an object from one layer to another

To move a selected object to any other unlocked layer (visible or not!) open the Layers panel, grab the colored square to the right of the object's layer, and drag it to another layer (near right). To move a copy of an object, hold down the Option/Alt key while you drag (far right).

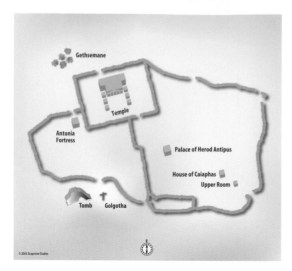

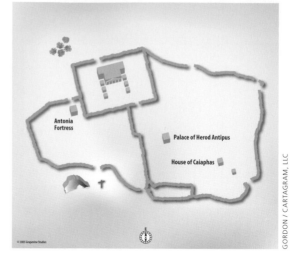

GORDON / CARTAGRAM, LLC

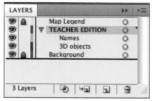

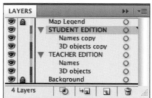

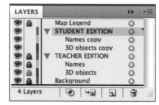

Steven Gordon / Cartagram, LLC

Steven Gordon created this map illustrating Jerusalem during New Testament times as one in a series of Bible workbook maps for Grapevine Studies. Gordon needed to design the maps for use in two versions—a detailed Teacher edition and a Student edition (in which the students would label selected map features). To simplify his work, Gordon combined both editions of each map in a single Illustrator file. He did this by first creating a layer for all of the paths and labels needed in the Teacher edition. Then, to create the Student edition, he duplicated the Teacher layer by dragging it onto the Create New Layer icon in the Layers panel. He renamed the layer and deleted the labels as required by the Student edition. Having both editions in the same file helped in

making changes and corrections. When Gordon added a building, he copied and pasted the shape on the Teacher layer and then moved the copy in the Layers panel to the Student layer. When he repositioned a building, he selected the shapes on both layers and moved them simultaneously. To output each edition, Gordon first double-clicked the Student layer and chose Template from the Layer Options dialog; choosing Template both disabled the Print option and italicized the layer name, making it easy to locate. After he output the file, he repeated the process, this time turning the Teacher layer into a template layer, and returning the Student layer to its non-template condition. (Illustrator ignores non-template sublayers within a template master layer during output.)

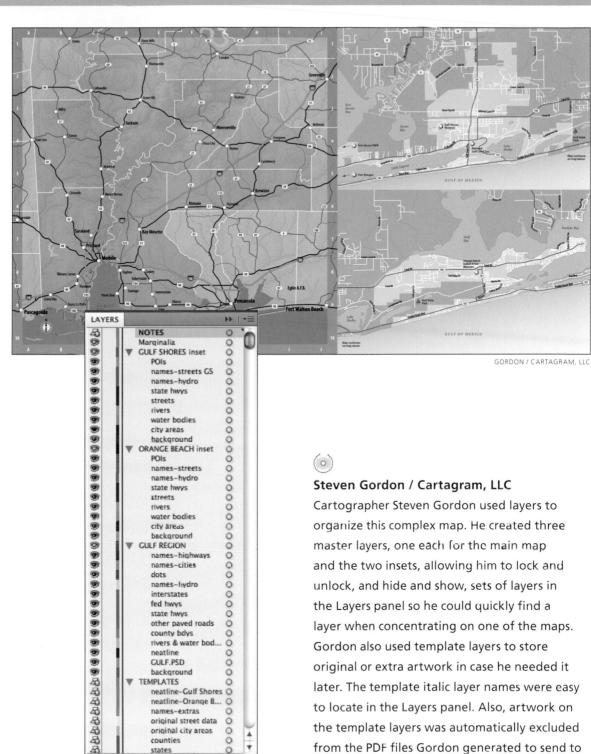

GORDON / CARTAGRAM, LLC

Steven Gordon / Cartagram, LLC

Cartographer Steven Gordon used layers to organize this complex map. He created three master layers, one each for the main map and the two insets, allowing him to lock and unlock, and hide and show, sets of layers in the Layers panel so he could quickly find a layer when concentrating on one of the maps. Gordon also used template layers to store original or extra artwork in case he needed it later. The template italic layer names were easy to locate in the Layers panel. Also, artwork on the template layers was automatically excluded from the PDF files Gordon generated to send to his client as intermediate proofs.

Nested Layers

Organizing with Layers and Sublayers

Overview: *Plan a layer structure; create layers and sublayers; refine the structure by rearranging layers and sublayers in the Layers panel's hierarchy; hide and lock layers; change the Layers panel display.*

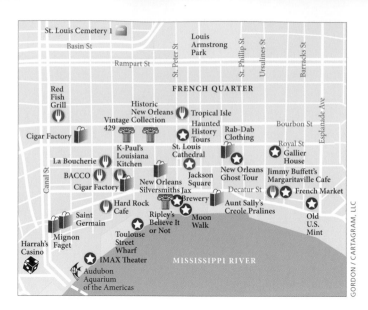

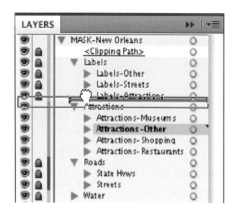

1

The completed layer structure for the map showing layers and two levels of sublayers (with Thumbnails disabled via Panel Options from the Layers panel's pop-up menu)

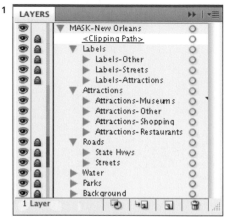

Selecting and dragging the Attractions-Other sublayer up and out of the Attractions sublayer, then, placing the Attractions-Other sublayer on the same level in the hierarchy as Attractions

Layers have always been a great way of organizing artwork. With Illustrator, you can organize your Layers panel as a nested hierarchy, making it easier to navigate and manipulate. For this map of New Orleans, created for the Metairie Hampton Inn, Steven Gordon relied on layers and sublayers to organize the map artwork.

1 Planning, then creating and moving layers and sublayers. Gordon began by planning a layer structure for the map in which layers with similar information would be nested within several "master" layers, so he could easily navigate the Layers panel and manipulate the layers and sublayers. After planning the organization of your layered artwork, open the Layers panel and begin creating layers and sublayers. (When you start a new document Illustrator automatically creates a Layer 1; it's a good habit to double-click Layer 1 to rename it.) To name a new layer or sublayer as you create it, hold Option/Alt and in the bottom of the Layers panel click on the Create New Layer icon or the Create New Sublayer icon (this creates a sublayer nested within a currently selected layer).

As you continue working, you may need to refine your organization by changing the nesting of a current layer or sublayer. To do this, drag the layer name in the Layers panel and release it over a boundary between layers. To convert a sublayer to a layer, drag its name and release it above its master layer or below the last sublayer of the master layer (watch the sublayer's bar icon to ensure that it aligns with the left side of the names field in the Layers panel before releasing it). Don't forget that if you move a layer in the Layers panel, any sublayer, group, or path it contains will move with it, affecting the hierarchy of artwork in your illustration.

2 Hiding and locking layers. As you draw, hide or lock sublayers of artwork by simply clicking on the visibility (Eye) icon or edit (Lock) icon of their master layer. Gordon organized his map so that related artwork, such as different kinds of labels, were placed on separate sublayers nested within the Names layer, and thus could be hidden or locked by hiding or locking the master Names layer.

If you click on the visibility or edit icon of a master layer, Illustrator remembers the visibility and edit status of each sublayer before locking or hiding the master layer. When Gordon clicked the visibility icon of the Names layer, sublayers that had been hidden before he hid the master layer remained hidden after he made the Names layer visible again. To make the contents of all layers and sublayers visible, Option-click/Alt-click on a visibility icon. To unlock the content of all layers and sublayers, Option-click/Alt-click on an edit icon. If you have layers hidden or locked you can also choose Show All Layers, or Unlock All Layers from the Layers panel's pop-up menu.

3 Changing the Layers panel display. You can change the Layers panel display to make the panel easier to navigate. In Layers Panel Options (from the panel pop-up) you can set custom rows and thumbnails sizes, or choose no icons at all. Double-click a layer name and change its layer color using the Color menu. Or do as Gordon did: Shift-click to select contiguous related layers (⌘-click/Ctrl-click for non-contiguous layers) to set the same layer color in order to help identify them in the Layers panel.

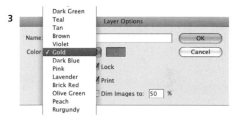

Top, the Labels "master" layer with three sublayers locked; bottom, after the master layer is locked, the three sublayers' edit icons are not dimmed, indicating that they will remain locked when the layer is unlocked

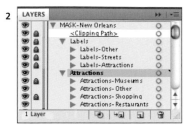

Changing the Color for the layer using the Layer Options dialog

Another way to unlock layers

A quick way to unlock all the contents of a layer: Make sure the layer itself is unlocked (the lock icon is gone) and then choose Unlock All from the Object menu.

Let Illustrator do the walking

Illustrator can automatically expand the Layers panel and scroll to a sublayer that's hidden within a collapsed layer. Just click on an object in your artwork and choose Locate Layer or Locate Object from the Layers panel's menu.

Basic Appearances

Making and Applying Appearances

Overview: *Create appearance attributes for an object; build a three-stroke appearance, save it as a style, and then draw paths and apply the style; target a layer with a drop shadow effect, create symbols in the layer, then edit layer appearance if needed.*

GORDON / CARTAGRAM, LLC

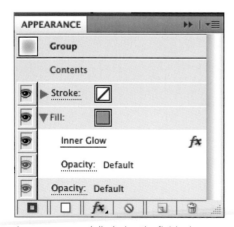

On the left, the ocean with blue fill; on the right, the water with the Inner Glow added to the appearance attribute set

Appearance panel displaying the finished set of attributes with an Inner Glow effect applied

Complexity and simplicity come together when you use Illustrator's Appearance panel to design intricate effects, develop reusable styles, and simplify production workflow. In this location map of the California coastline, cartographer Steven Gordon relied on the Appearance panel to easily build appearances and apply them to objects, groups and layers.

1 Building an appearance for a single object. Gordon developed a set of appearance attributes that applied a soft vignette and blue fill to a path symbolizing the Pacific Ocean. To begin building appearance attributes, make sure the Appearance panel is open. Gordon first drew the outline of the water with the Pen tool and then he gave the path a dark blue fill. To create the effect of water lightening as it approaches the shore, he applied an Inner Glow effect. To do this he opened the Appearance panel and clicked on the Fill attribute. Then he clicked the Add New Effect icon at the bottom of the Appearance panel and chose Stylize > Inner Glow from the pop-up menu. In the Inner Glow dialog, he set the Mode to Normal, Opacity to 100%, Blur to 0.25 inches (for the width of the vignette edge), and enabled the Edge option. To finish the glow, he clicked the dialog's color swatch and chose white for the glow color.

2 Creating a style for your highway paths. In the early days of Illustrator, the way you created a multi-stroked line like this "map symbol" for an interstate highway was by overlapping copies of a path and giving each copy a different stroke width. Now you can use the Appearance panel to craft a multi-stroked line that you apply to a single path. Deselect any objects still selected and reset the Appearance panel by clicking the Clear Appearance icon at the bottom of the panel (this eliminates any attributes from the last selected style or object). To make Gordon's interstate highway, click the Stroke attribute (it will have the None color icon) and give it a light color and a 0.5-pt width. Click the Add New Stroke icon to make a second stroke. Next, select the bottom of the two strokes and choose a dark color and a 3-pt width. Because you'll reuse this set of appearance attributes, open the Graphic Styles panel and Option/Alt-click the New Graphic Style icon at the bottom of the panel to bring up the Graphic Style Options dialog where you can name your new style.

3 Assigning a style to a group. Draw the paths you want to paint with the new style you created above. Next, select all the paths you just made and Group (⌘-G/Ctrl-G). To get the two levels of strokes to merge when paths on the map cross one another, make sure Group is highlighted in the Appearance panel and apply your new interstate style.

4 Assigning appearance attributes to an entire layer. By targeting a layer, you can create a uniform look for all the objects you draw or place on that layer. Create a layer for the iconic "map symbols" and click the layer's target indicator in the Layers panel. In the Appearance panel, click the *fx* icon and select Stylize > Drop Shadow. Now each "map symbol" you draw or paste on that layer will be painted automatically with the drop shadow. You can modify the drop shadow by clicking the layer's targeting icon and then clicking the Drop Shadow attribute in the Appearance panel and changing values in the pop-up Drop Shadow dialog.

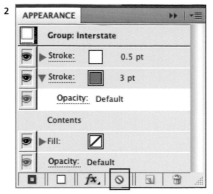

Appearance panel for Gordon's interstate highway symbol, with the Clear Appearance icon indicated

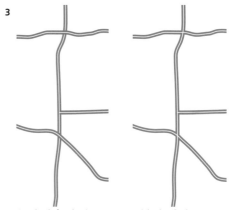

On the left, the interstates with the Style applied to the individual paths; on the right, the interstate paths were grouped before the Style was applied

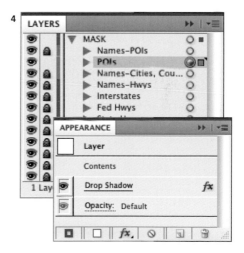

Top, targeting the layer in the Layers panel; bottom, the Appearance panel showing the Drop Shadow attribute (double-click the attribute to edit Drop Shadow values)

Establishing Perspective

Using Layers and a Perspective Grid

MARIC

Advanced Technique

Overview: *Scan a sketch; create working layers using your sketch as a template; in each "guides" layer, draw a series of lines to establish perspective; convert the perspective lines to guides; construct your image using the applicable perspective guides.*

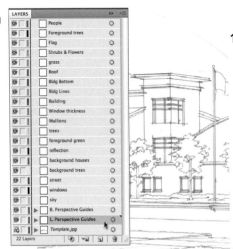

Portion of the original drawing placed on a template layer with a custom layer ready for creation of guides

Architectural renderings must be both attractive to the eye and faithful to the rules of perspective. Pete Maric was hired by the firm of ThenDesign Architecture of Willoughby, Ohio to create a realistic rendering of the proposed Charles A. Mooney PreK-8 School. Maric relied on a carefully constructed perspective grid to create a convincing scene and practiced careful layer management to keep the numerous elements of his complex illustration well organized as he worked.

1 Setting up layers. Begin by scanning a schematic drawing. After saving the scan as a JPG, TIF or PSD, place it in Illustrator and choose Template from the Layer panel's pop-up menu. Analyze your image to determine the number of vanishing points in your illustration (points along the scene's horizon where parallel lines seem to converge). Create new layers (click the Create New Layer icon in the Layers panel) for your compositional elements, and an additional layer for each of the vanishing points in your illustration.

2 Establishing the location of vanishing points. In the Layers panel, select the first layer you'll use for creating a set of perspective guides. Using your drawing as reference, find a feature that ought to be parallel with the horizon, such as a roofline and floor, or set of windows. With a high horizon, the features may actually be below the horizon line, but the vanishing point will always be directly on the line. With the Line tool, draw lines following the top and bottom of your chosen feature until the lines cross (figure A). You have now found one vanishing point. Vanishing points may need to extend beyond the borders of your artwork. Zoom out or scroll to view enough of your Artboard to see where your vanishing point lies. Now, with the Direct Selection tool, select the anchor point of a line that is opposite to its vanishing point, and swing it to the highest point (or lowest) that encompasses the objects on that plane, dragging the line out even longer if necessary (see figure B).

3 Creating multiple perspective lines. To create in-between lines through the same vanishing point, select both of the lines you created, then double-click the Blend tool to choose Specified Steps (for Spacing) and enter the number of lines you want. Then use Object > Blend > Make, or the keyboard shortcut, ⌘-Option-B/Ctrl-Alt-B, to create the blends (for help with the Blend tool, see the *Blends, Gradients & Mesh* chapter).

For each different vanishing point, repeat the above procedure. Remember to create each set of perspective lines on its own layer so you can work more easily with them as you proceed.

4 Making and using the guides. Because Illustrator can't create guides from blended objects, select them with the Selection tool and then choose Object > Expand. Next, transform the blends into guides by using View > Guides > Make Guides, or the keyboard shortcut, ⌘-5/Ctrl-5. Now begin drawing on a new layer. You may want to lock other layers containing vanishing point guides so you don't find your objects snapping to the wrong guides when you drag them into position.

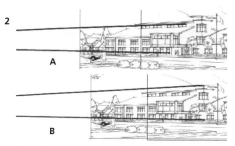

Dragging a perspective line to follow elements such as windows to a vanishing point, here beyond the edge of the art (top), then swinging the anchor points to the highest and lowest points, stretching the lines longer if necessary (bottom)

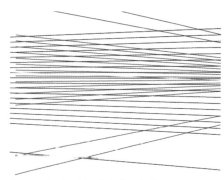

Using the Blend tool with Specified Steps to create multiple in-between lines from the two main bounding lines

Perspective line blends before being transformed into guides

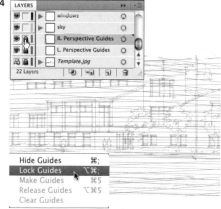

Turning off the "snap to" function for guides by locking the layer (left); locking guides in place by using the Lock/Unlock toggle in the View > Guides submenu

7

Artboards & Type

Adding bleed setting

You can define a bleed setting when creating a new document, or later using the Document Setup. All Print settings are the same for every artboard in a single document, so bleed values are equal for all the artboards.

Artboard Rulers

You can display Artboard Rulers for the active artboard with View > Show Artboard Rulers (⌘-Option-R/Ctrl-Alt-R), but they are only acting as a visual indicator. You cannot snap your guides to them, nor position your objects across the document according to their coordinates. There is still only one ruler for position (your X,Y coordinates), and that acts as if the multiple artboards were just one file.

The New Document dialog showing options for creating and arranging artboards at the outset. Settings such as Bleed, Color Mode, and Raster Effects are document-wide, while the artboards themselves can be altered later for size, spacing, and order.

Maintaining a consistent look throughout multi-page document projects, such as stationery, product campaigns, or video storyboards, is difficult when you have to create each document in a separate file. Now Illustrator has the capability of creating many documents in one file—up to 100 artboards in a single file, each one sharing assets—such as your type styles, graphic styles, symbols, swatches, and print and color settings. You can create new artboards at any size and at any time, making it easy to add a new business card to the file, for instance. Or you can duplicate an artboard, with or without its contents, to assure maximum consistency, making only those few changes that are absolutely necessary.

SETTING UP MULTIPLE ARTBOARDS

You can set up multiple artboards in the New Document dialog if you know your project's needs right from the start—perhaps four letter-sized pages for an ad campaign or standard-sized pieces for company stationery. You'll be able to decide in the dialog if you want your artboards placed in a row, a single column, or a grid of user-specified rows and columns. For a storyboard, for instance, you may want to place ten scenes in a row, reading left to right, and then have the next artboard start back at the left, one row down. Since Illustrator automatically numbers the artboards, a sequence like this helps you locate an artboard later on. Multiple artboards allow you several printing options, including printing some or all as separate pages, tiling, or saving as a multi-page PDF for file-sharing, so there is no loss of output flexibility when using multiple artboards. See the "Exporting and Printing Multiple Artboards" section later in this introduction.

Creating new artboards

You'll find the greatest flexibility of artboards, however, comes with the ability to create custom artboards on the fly in the Artboard Edit Mode, rather than in the New Document dialog, These can be based on existing artboards, or artwork, or can be sized independently. To create new artboards:

- Select the Artboard tool in the toolbox (Shift-O) and drag in the window to create a new artboard of your desired dimension. With Smart Guides turned on, you can see dimensions as you draw, or you can type position and size into the Control panel fields.

- With the Artboard tool selected, click on the "New Artboard" icon in the Control panel. By default, you'll see a ghosted outline of a new artboard that duplicates the dimensions and orientation of the currently selected artboard. Click to create the new artboard right there, or Option/Alt-click to create it and keep your cursor loaded to add yet another duplicate.

- If you find it easier to quickly draw rectangles the size and position you're going to want for your artboards, Illustrator allows you to draw a series of these objects, and then, after selecting them, choose Object >Convert to Artboard. If you select them all at once, they'll be numbered in the order in which they were drawn. If, however, you select them individually and then convert them to artboards, they'll be numbered in the order in which you select and convert them.

Positioning and adjusting artboards

After creating your new artboard, you can alter it precisely by using the Presets list pop-up menu, or by opening the Artboard Options dialog (double-click on the Artboard tool or click on the icon in the Control panel). The Presets list is a quick way to repurpose an artboard from, say, a print medium using traditional paper sizes, to appropriate sizes for video, film, web pages, or features such as banners and monitor sizes. But if you want to create the artboard's proportions for HD video, for instance, yet make the artboard larger or smaller, clicking on the Artboard Options icon to open the dialog allows for greater precision when adjusting your artboards to suit

Rasterizing Multiple Artboards

If you need a rasterized version of every artboard in your document, Illustrator allows you to export each artboard separately to a TIF, JPG, PSD, or PNG file.

Design to the edge

If your artwork extends beyond the edge of an artboard, make sure you add a bleed setting value; if it gets placed in InDesign or saved as EPS, anyone can still see it.

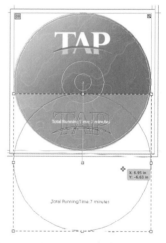

Moving an artboard with the Artboard tool, red outside lines indicate a Bleed setting (see Putnam's "Create an Identity" lesson for more Artboard basics)

Pattern warning

If your design contains a pattern, and you want to change your coordinates as you work among multiple artboards, turn the object containing the pattern into a symbol to freeze the pattern's position in the artwork. Don't break the link!—*Jean-Claude Tremblay*

Renumbering artboards

Future versions of Illustrator will probably make it easy to renumber your artboards. Today you can use this clever work-around developed by Jean-Claude Tremblay:

• First, use the Rectangle tool to draw a rectangle over each of your artboards, exactly to the size of each artboard, *except for the one you want as the first artboard. Using Smart Guides will force your rectangles to snap to the artboards.* **IMPORTANT:** *Draw the rectangles in the order you want your artboards to be renumbered.*

• Second, using the Artboard tool, delete all of the artboards *except* the one you chose as the first artboard.

• Finally, select all the rectangles from the first bullet above and choose Object > Convert to Artboards. The command will now renumber your new artboards according to the order in which you created them.

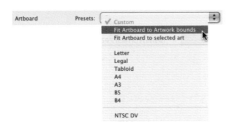

With artwork both on and off existing artboards, choosing "Fit Artboard to Artwork bounds" from the Artboard Presets menu turns the active artboard into the smallest possible artboard that encompasses all the art

a new purpose. The Artboard Options dialog is the only place where you can draw new artboards while constraining the proportions to an existing artboard.

For positioning the artboard relative to the rest of the document, you can simply move the artboard to a new location, allowing Smart Guides to help you line it up with other artboards, or you can type the X,Y coordinates into the Control panel fields. Note that artboards can overlap each other, just as artwork can overlap multiple artboards. When artboards overlap, the artwork that exists on each, even if only partially, becomes an "instance" on each.

Creating/adjusting artboards to fit existing art

There are quite a few ways for you to create and then adjust your artboards to fit existing art:

• If you've already created artwork in one artboard, and now want to place it on its own separate artboard that is sized exactly to the artwork, select the object and choose the Artboard tool from the toolbox. Then choose "Fit Artboard to selected art" from the Presets menu in the Control panel to resize the artboard. If you now have unselected art on the artboard that was left outside the new artboard boundaries, and still want to use it in your project, you'll need to create a new artboard for it. Use one of the methods for creating new artboards, or one of the following methods as appropriate for your project.

• Choose the Artboard tool and click once on an object or group, whether it is on an existing artboard or not. This draws a new artboard to fit the art, but doesn't work with multiple objects or groups. If you want to move the artboard and its art, you now can enable the "Move/Copy Artwork with Artboard" icon in the Control panel, then drag the new artboard to a new location. The artwork will stay with the new artboard.

• You can work in the opposite direction, creating a single artboard to encompass all artwork already on an artboard or not. With the Artboard tool active, choose "Fit Artboard to Artwork bounds" from the Preset list in the Control panel, which resizes that artboard precisely to fit all the artwork. Use this when you need to organize artboards with art on them into a single page as small as is possible, especially if you also need to scale that page for your printer.

- You can manually resize the artboard to fit the artwork by using the snapping properties of Smart Guides. Be sure you have Smart Guides enabled, then drag on the artboard edges with the Artboard tool until they snap to the edges of the artwork. Once you start dragging the artboard edges, you won't be able to see your regular bounding box boundaries, so drag slowly.

Targeting and Viewing Your Artboards

Once your artboards are laid out, you have options for viewing some, all, or only one selected artboard. You can select an artboard manually by clicking on it with any tool. To locate an artboard visually when another artboard fills your view, choose View > Fit All in Window (⌘-Option-0/Ctrl-Alt-0). Once you see the artboard you want, you can use the Zoom tool (Z) to click on or marquee that artboard and zoom in at the same time, or you can choose View > Fit Artboard in Window (⌘-0/Ctrl-0), which will center and fit the active artboard to your window as large as possible. You can also use View > Actual Size (⌘-1/Ctrl-1) to view your artboard at 100% magnification. This may be more or less magnification than Fit Artboard in Window, but regardless of the View command you choose, your active artboard will always be centered in the window.

With any artboard or tool active, you can choose to activate and view a different artboard, if you know its number, by using the Artboard Navigation list located in the status bar at the bottom-left region of your Document window. Selecting an artboard from this list is the same as activating an artboard and choosing View > Fit Artboard in Window, but you don't have to take any extra steps to locate and target it. You can also use the arrow keys beside the Navigation list to "page" between neighboring artboards or to jump to the first or last artboard.

Targeting an artboard from the Artboard Navigation pop-up list on the Status bar in the bottom-left region of the Document window

Print dialog showing just 2 of 5 artboards selected for printing, Skip Blank Artboards enabled, and the print preview showing bleed with overlapping artwork

Remember that whenever you want to work with the artboard itself, and not the artwork, you need to select the Artboard tool to target the artboard. Otherwise, using any tool on an artboard automatically activates that artboard for whatever comes next.

MOVING OR COPYING ART BETWEEN ARTBOARDS

Working productively and maintaining consistency within a project often means duplicating elements from one document to another, and with Multiple Artboards you have a variety of methods to accomplish this task, depending upon your needs:

- Turn artwork created on one artboard into a symbol, then drag that symbol from the shared Symbols panel to any other artboard. Now just update the symbol to update all instances of it used on any artboards.
- Using the measure tool, measure the distance between the artwork and where you want it on another artboard, and use Transform > Move to move or copy the artwork.
- With "Move/Copy Artwork with Artboard" enabled and the Artboard tool selected, hold down the Option/Alt key while dragging an active artboard to a new location in order to duplicate the artboard and all its contents.
- In some circumstances, you may want to use the Transform Effect to copy "instances" of artwork to another artboard (see the "Making Masters" lesson in this chapter for an example of this workflow).

EXPORTING AND PRINTING MULTIPLE ARTBOARDS

When you're ready to output your project, you have several options. If you need to hand off your project to someone using a version of Illustrator prior to CS4, you can choose to save each artboard as an individual file, along with a merged file with a Guides for Artboard layer showing the original artboard boundaries. All artboards in a file share the same print options, including color mode, bleed settings, and scale, and you can choose to print either to PDF or a local printer (see the Tip "Save As or Print to PDF?" on this page). In the Print dialog, choose whether or not you want to print artboards as separate pages (the default), or to ignore artboards and tile the artwork. If you have resized an artboard to fit all your artwork, choosing just that artboard in the Range section of the dialog may help if you plan to scale it all down to a single printed page. If your artwork overlaps artboards, the boundaries of each artboard are cropped when printing artboards as pages. When two or more artboards overlap the same artwork and you've chosen to print separate pages, each artboard will print with the portion of the artwork that's visible within that artboard. Further, in the Range section of the Print dialog, you can treat artboards exactly like pages in a layout program, choosing to print some artboards, but not others. Additional printing options allow you to Reverse Order and Skip Blank Artboards. When you choose the Ignore Artboards option, it is as if you have only one artboard, and the boundaries of your artwork determine what will print.

TYPE

When Adobe released the first Creative Suite (CS), they changed Illustrator's type engine, bringing the improvements in typesetting pioneered in InDesign to Illustrator and the rest of the Creative Suite. Today, not only can you depend upon greater compatibility moving text between Creative Suite programs, but Illustrator's enhanced typesetting abilities, coupled with its new Multiple Artboard feature for smaller multi-page projects, allow you to tackle many projects using Illustrator alone.

But because this type engine is fundamentally different, any text created prior to Illustrator CS is considered *legacy text*, and must be updated before it's editable in later versions of Illustrator (see the Tip "Legacy text" later in this intro). Further, continuing improvements can result in yet another break between a current and an earlier version. Any version prior to CS4 that uses the Type on a Path tool will prompt a legacy text warning when opened in CS4 (or later) before path type can be edited, (see later in this introduction for a full description), and

Opening Freehand files
Illustrator can open and convert Freehand multi-page documents into multiple artboards.

Selecting type by accident
If you keep selecting type when you're trying to select an object, enable Type Object Selection by Path Only in Preferences. With this option turned on, you can only select type objects if you click directly on the baseline or path of the type. (If you have trouble finding the path, you can select the text object in the Layers panel by clicking the space to the right of the <Type> target icon, or marquee at least one full letterform with a Selection tool or the Lasso tool.)

Typographic controls
Most of Illustrator's default settings for type are controlled in the Type section of Preferences. However, set the unit of measurement for type in Preferences > Units & Display Performance.

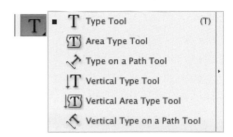

The Type tool, Area Type tool, Type on a Path tool, Vertical Type tool, Vertical Area Type tool, and Vertical Type on a Path tool. Press Shift to toggle the tool between orientations.

Multi-language font support

Illustrator supports Asian fonts, including Chinese, Japanese, and Korean. Check the Show Asian Options box in the Type area of Preferences to reveal Asian text options in the Character panel (if necessary, click on the double arrows on the Panel tab to fully expand it). To use Asian font capabilities you must have the proper fonts and language support activated on your system. Other languages are also supported, including Middle Eastern fonts. For more detailed information, see Thomas Phinney's blog about multi-language support at http://tinyurl.com/phinneyfonts.

Type tool juggling

To toggle a Type tool between its vertical and horizontal mode, first make sure nothing is selected. Hold the Shift key down to toggle the tool to the opposite mode.

The quick-changing Type tool

When using the regular Type tool, look at your cursor very carefully in these situations: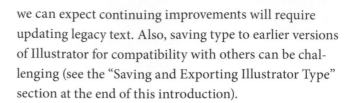

- If you move the regular Type tool over a closed path, the cursor changes to the Area type icon.
- If you move the Type tool over an open path, the cursor will change to the Type on a Path icon.

we can expect continuing improvements will require updating legacy text. Also, saving type to earlier versions of Illustrator for compatibility with others can be challenging (see the "Saving and Exporting Illustrator Type" section at the end of this introduction).

THE EIGHT TYPE PANELS

For creating and manipulating type, Illustrator offers no fewer than eight panels, all accessible from the Window > Type submenu. By default, nested in with the Paragraph and Character panels is the OpenType panel, which gives you convenient access to the options of OpenType fonts. The Tabs panel lets you add and manage tabs, and create customized tab leaders. The Character Styles and Paragraph Styles panels, by default nested together, are where you'll manage Illustrator's automatic text formatting capabilities by creating or importing your own styles to streamline your formatting process. The Glyphs panel lets you choose quickly from a wide range of special characters. The Flash Text panel allows you to set options for exporting text to your Flash projects.

The Character and Paragraph panels may first appear in a collapsed view; cycle through display options by clicking the double arrow on the Panel tab.

THE THREE TYPES OF TYPE

There are three kinds of type objects in Illustrator and all are accessible through the Type tool: *Point type*, *Area type*, and *Path type*. The Type tool lets you click to create a Point type object, click-drag to create an Area type object, click on a path to create Path type (discussed a bit further on), or click within any existing type object to enter or edit text. Use the File > Open, File > Place, and Copy and Paste commands to access type created in other applications.

Select letters, words, or an entire block of text by dragging across the letters with the Type tool. To edit text that's not selected, click on it with the Type tool, or double-click it with a selection tool. To select a text block as an *object*, either click on it once with a Selection tool, or select-marqee the text baseline (the non-printing line that the type sits on).

- **Point type:** Click with the Type tool or the Vertical Type tool anywhere on the page to create Point type. Once you click, a blinking text-insertion cursor called an "I-beam" indicates that you can now type text using your keyboard. To add another line of text, press the Return or Enter key. When you're finished typing into one text object, click on the Type tool in the Toolbox to simultaneously select the current text as an object (the I-beam will disappear), and be poised to begin another text object.

- **Area type:** Click and drag with the Type tool to create a rectangle, into which you can type. Once you've defined your rectangle, the I-beam awaits your typing, and the text automatically wraps to the next line when you type inside the confines of the rectangle.

Another way to create Area type or Vertical Area type is to construct a path (with any tools you wish) forming an object within which to place the type. Click and hold on the Type tool to access the Area Type tools or press the Shift key to toggle between horizontal and vertical orientations for area type (see the Tip "Type tool juggling" in this chapter intro). Choose the Area Type or Vertical Area Type tool and click on the path itself (not inside the object) to place text within the confines of the path. Distort the confining object by grabbing an anchor point with the Direct Selection tool and dragging it to a new location, or reshape the path by adjusting direction lines. The text within your Area Type object will reflow to fit the new shape of the confining object.

Illustrator's Area Type Options dialog (Type > Area Type Options) gives you precise control over a number of important aspects of Area type. You can set numerical values for the width and height of the selected Area type object. You can set precise values for Rows and Columns (i.e., you can divide a single Area type object into multiple columns or rows that will reflow as you type), and

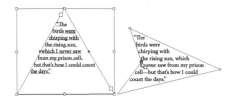

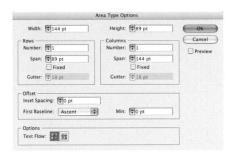

After hovering the cursor over the edge of the object to reveal the Area type cursor and entering the desired text, the object can be easily reshaped, causing the text to reflow

Area Type Options dialog

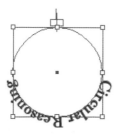

You may notice that if you try to set Path type on a circle, and the text is set to Align Center, the text will be forced to the bottom of the circle.

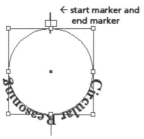

← start marker and end marker

That's because each Path type object has two handles (the start marker and the end marker) that the type is centered between. When you first draw the circle and apply the Path type to it, those two handles appear together at the top of the circle, due to the fact that the circle is a closed path.

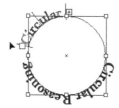

To position the text on top of the circle, all you have to do is grab the start marker handle and drag it to the 9 o'clock position, and then drag the end marker handle to the 3 o'clock position. Your text will now be centered between the two handles, on top of the circle.

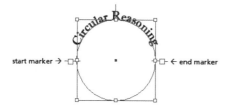

start marker →   ← end marker

Moral of the story: When you're working with center-aligned Path type, be sure to keep an eye on those start and end marker handles, and make sure they're where you need them to be.

choose whether or not those values remain fixed as you scale. You can also specify Offset options, including the amount of inset (defined as the margin between the text and the bounding path) and the alignment of the first baseline of text. And finally, you can determine how text flows between rows or columns by choosing one of the Text Flow options.

To set tabs for Area type, select the text object and choose Window > Type > Tabs. The Tabs panel will open aligned with the text box. As you pan or zoom, you'll notice the Tab ruler doesn't move with the text box. Don't sweat: If you lose your alignment, just click the little Magnet button on the Tabs panel, and the panel will snap back into alignment.

You can also use the Tabs panel to create a custom tab leader. A tab leader is a repeated pattern of characters (such as dots or dashes) between a Tab and the text that follows it. Select a tab stop on the ruler in the Tabs panel, type a pattern of up to eight characters in the panel's Leader box, then press Return or Enter. Your customized Leader pattern will repeat across the width of the tab.

- **Path type:** Path type is created with the Type on a Path tool, which allows you to click on a path to flow text along its perimeter. (The path will then become unstroked and unfilled.) With the release of CS4, Illustrator has refined the placement of type along a path, in particular, composing type along tight curves or corner paths (see Steven Gordon's galleries later in this chapter for a number of path-fitting tricks). For this reason, if you open files with Path type created before CS4, Adobe needs to update the type before you can edit it; just how it accomplishes this can become a bit tricky. If type needs updating, Illustrator will prompt you, possibly more than once, depending upon the version of the file being updated (first for Point or Area type, then for Type on a Path). Adobe has made this as painless as possible, though. Follow along and everything that needs to be updated with a particular version will be.

When you select a Path type object, you'll see three brackets appear: one at the beginning, one in the center, and one at the end of the Path type. The beginning and end brackets carry an in port and an out port, respectively, which can be used to thread text between objects (see the Tip "Ports defined" earlier in this section). The center bracket is used to control the positioning of the Path type. Hold your cursor over it until a small icon that looks like an upside-down **T** appears. You can now drag the center bracket to reposition the type. Dragging the bracket across the path will flip the type to the other side of the path. (For example, type along the outside of a circle would flip to the inside.) Dragging the bracket forward or backward along the direction of the path will move the type in that direction.

As with Area type, use the Direct Selection tool to reshape the confining path; the type on the path will automatically readjust to the new path shape.

The Type on a Path Options dialog (Type > Type on a Path > Type on a Path Options) lets you set a number of Path type attributes. You can choose from five different Path Type Effects (Rainbow, Skew, 3D Ribbon, Stair Step, and Gravity); a Flip checkbox that will automatically flip type to the other side of the path; a menu that lets you set the alignment of type relative to the path; and a Spacing control that lets you adjust the spacing of type as it moves along and around a curve. (All of the Type on a Path Effects are also available directly via the Type > Type on a Path submenu.)

WORKING WITH THREADED TEXT

If a text object contains more text than it has room to display, you'll see a plus sign in the small box along its lower-right side. (This box is called the *out port*; see the Tip "Ports defined," earlier in this chapter.) To enlarge the object to allow for more text, use the Selection tool to grab the object by a bounding side, and drag to resize it (hold down the Shift key if you want to constrain proportions as you resize).

To manually flip type on a path to the other side of the path, select the type and drag the center handle (the thin blue line perpendicular to the type) across the path, as indicated by the red arrow above. Note the tiny **T**-shaped icon that appears next to the cursor as you position it near the handle.

The same type, after dragging across the path, but before releasing the mouse. After release, the type will be in the position indicated by the blue type above the path; you can then drag the center handle from side to side to adjust the position of the text—just don't drag across the path again or you'll flip the type back. You can also flip type across a path automatically by choosing Type > Type on a Path > Type on a Path Options, enabling the Flip box (shown below), and clicking OK.

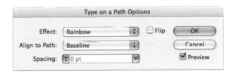

The Type on a Path Options dialog

Turning the corner—Path type

When type on a tightly curved path is squeezed together or spread apart, select Type > Type on a Path > Type on a Path Options and choose Center from the Align to Path menu. Set Baseline Shift to 0 in the Character panel and move the path until the type is where you want it on the page.
—*Steven H. Gordon*

Path type and closed paths

Even though the feedback you get from the Type tool cursor seems to indicate that you can only apply Path type to open paths, you actually *can* apply Path type to both open and closed paths (hold Option/ Alt and watch for the cursor to change from the Area type icon to the Type on a Path icon).

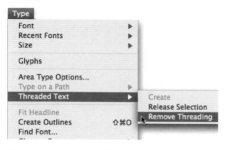

Cascading Type menu for threaded text frames

Loading the cursor with text from the overflow port, indicated by a red plus sign

The first text object is threaded (linked) to the next one. The blue line connects the out port of the left object to the in port of the right one, showing that the two objects are threaded together; text thus flows from the first object to the second. The red plus sign in the out port of the text object indicates that there is still more overflow text, which could flow into a third threaded object.

To add a new text object that can receive overflow text, use the Selection tool to select the first text object. Next, click on the red plus sign in the out port. The cursor will change to the "loaded text" cursor, which looks like a miniature text block. Then you can click on the Artboard to create a new text object the same size and shape as the original; or drag to create a text object of any size. Either way, the new text object will be *threaded* (linked) to the original, and the text that wouldn't fit in the first object will flow into the second.

Similarly, you can link existing text objects together by clicking the plus sign on the first object, and then clicking on the path of the object that will receive the overflow text. (Keep your eye on the cursor, which will change to indicate valid "drop" locations.) You can also link objects using a menu command: Select the first object with a Selection tool, then Shift-click to select the second object as well (or marquee both objects with the Lasso or a Selection tool). Choose Type > Threaded Text > Create, and the objects are linked.

Of course, the threads between objects can be broken as easily as they're created. If you want to disconnect one object from another, first select the object. Then double-click its in port to break the thread to a preceding object, or double-click its out port to break the thread to a subsequent object. Alternatively, you can select the object and click once on either the in port or the out port. Then click on the other end of the thread to break the link.

You can also release an object from a Text thread by selecting it, then choosing Type > Threaded Text > Release Selection. Or, if you want to remove the threading from an object while leaving text in place, select it and choose Type > Threaded Text > Remove Threading.

WRAPPING AREA TYPE AROUND OBJECTS

Text wrapping is controlled as an object attribute and is set specifically for each object (known as a *wrap object*) that will have Area type wrapped around it (this only works with Area type). First, in the Layers panel make sure the object you want as a wrap object is above Area type you want to wrap around it. Then select the wrap object and choose Object > Text Wrap > Make. To change options for the wrap object, keep it selected and choose Object > Text Wrap > Text Wrap Options. The Text Wrap Options dialog will appear. Here, you'll choose the amount of offset and also have the option to choose Invert Wrap (which reverses the side of the object that text wraps around). To wrap text around multiple objects, add new objects to the text wrapped group; in the Layers panel, expand the triangle to reveal the layer content, and drag the icon for your new object into the <Group>. To release the text wrap effect, select the wrap object and choose Object > Text Wrap > Release, or move the type above the wrap object in the stacking order.

CHARACTER AND PARAGRAPH STYLES

Illustrator's Character and Paragraph panels lets you format text by changing one attribute at a time. The more powerful Character Styles and Paragraph Styles panels take formatting to the next level by allowing you to apply multiple attributes to text simply by applying the appropriate style. (All four of these type-related panels are found under the Window > Type submenu.)

Illustrator always assumes that a paragraph style has been applied to an open document. Therefore, if you open a new document, select the Type tool, then modify its attributes in the Control panel, Illustrator will think you are modifying the default, [Normal Paragraph Style], on the fly. If you look at the Paragraph Styles panel with that new text selected, you'll see a + (plus) sign next to the style name, indicating you have applied extra formatting, or *overrides*. To avoid unnecessary overrides, see the Tip "Avoiding Formatting Overrides" on the next page.

New character and paragraph styles can be either created from scratch or based on existing styles. To create a new style, highlight the style and click the Create New Style button in either the Character Styles or the Paragraph Styles panel. This duplicates the highlighted style,

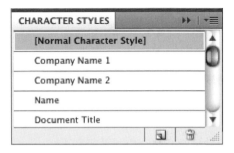

Text wrapping is controlled as an object attribute and is set specifically for each object that will have text wrapped around it (known as a *wrap object*). First, make sure that the object you want to be wrapped with text is above the text you want to wrap around it in the Layers panel. Then select the wrap object and

Wrapping text around an object by placing the object above the text and choosing Object > Text Wrap > Make

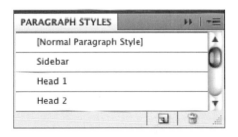

Character Styles panel

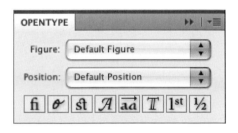

Paragraph Styles panel

OpenType panel

When your project calls for several text objects using the same font, you might want to consider using a custom paragraph style, rather than attempting to change the font in the Control panel. Created properly, this will prevent Illustrator from applying the default, [Normal Paragraph Style], to all your new text, and then adding formatting overrides to apply your specific font attributes. Overrides take more time to deal with when you want to change a font's attributes quickly.

- If you are going to use the same font attributes in several documents, you can create a New Document Profile that will always include your preferred font attributes as part of the [Normal Paragraph Style]. (See the Tip "Create Document Profiles" in *Illustrator Basics*.)
- If you only need to change the font for a single document, however, either double-click on the [Normal Paragraph Style] and modify the default for just this document, or create a new paragraph style. In either case, by not changing font attributes in the Control panel, you will avoid creating formatting overrides that must then be cleared in order to apply a different font with different attributes.

—Cristen Gillespie

and you can now double-click its name in the Character Styles or Paragraph Styles panel, or select it and choose Character Style Options or Paragraph Style Options from the panel menu. The Style Options dialog will let you set all your desired attributes for the style—everything from basic characteristics (such as font, size, and color), to OpenType features (see below for more about OpenType). If you want to name your new style as you create it, hold down the Option/Alt key while clicking the New Style button. This opens Style Options, where you can both name the style and change the attributes.

To create a style based on existing formatting, format the text as you want it to appear using the Control panel (or the Character or Paragraph panels), select it and click on the New Style button (Opt/Alt-click to name the style). The selected attributes are embedded into the new style.

To apply a paragraph style to text, just insert your cursor into the paragraph you want to format and click the name of the style in the Paragraph Styles panel. When you first apply a paragraph style, it won't remove overrides. To remove all overrides, click on the desired style name, select all the text you want to apply it to, and finally click again on the style name. To apply a character style, select all the letterforms you want to change, and then click on the name in the Character Styles panel.

TAKING ADVANTAGE OF OPENTYPE

A big reason why Adobe revamped the way Illustrator handles text is to allow users to take full advantage of the sophisticated features of OpenType fonts. (To underscore the point, Illustrator ships with free OpenType fonts, so you can put them to work immediately.) One great benefit of OpenType fonts is that they're platform-independent, so they can move easily between Mac and Windows.

When you use any OpenType font, Illustrator will automatically set standard ligatures as you type (see the example in this introduction using the words *taffy* and *scuffle*). You can set options for other OpenType features by using the OpenType panel, which is nested by default with the Character and Paragraph panels, and is accessible via the menu command Window > Type > OpenType.

The OpenType panel includes two pop-up menus that let you control the style and positioning of numerals. It also has a row of buttons that let you choose whether or not to use standard ligatures (for letter pairs such as fi, fl, ff, ffi, and ffl), optional ligatures (for letter pairs such as ct and st), swashes (characters with exaggerated flourishes), titling characters (for use in uppercase titles), stylistic alternates (alternative versions of a common character), superscripted ordinals, and fractions.

If you'd like more information on what the various commands in the OpenType panel do, we've included a helpful PDF guide by InDesign expert Sandee Cohen on the *Wow! CD* (look for the file named OpenType. pdf). These pages, which are excerpted from Cohen's *InDesign Visual QuickStart Guide* from Peachpit Press, give you a primer on how to work with OpenType fonts, in the form of a handy reference table.

THE GLYPHS PANEL

Illustrator's Glyphs panel provides you with quick access to a wide variety of special characters, including any ligatures, ornaments, swashes, and fractions included in any given OpenType font. Choose Window > Type > Glyphs to display the panel. With the Type tool, click to place the insertion point where you want the special character to appear, and then double-click the character you want in the Glyphs panel to insert it in the text. In the Glyphs panel you'll find many specialty characters (like ✳ or ❤), that once required separate fonts, sitting right there in your Glyphs panel.

THE EVERY-LINE COMPOSER

Illustrator offers two composition methods for determining where line breaks occur in a paragraph of text: the Single-line Composer and the Every-line Composer.

The Single-line Composer applies hyphenation and justification settings to one line of text at a time. But this

OpenType fonts automatically set standard ligatures as you type (unless you turn this feature off in the OpenType panel). In the example above, the type on the top row is set using the standard version of Adobe's Minion font. The bottom row is set using Minion Pro, one of the OpenType fonts likely installed with your Illustrator application. Minion Pro supplies the ligatures for "ff" and "ffl" (visible in the bottom row), which give the type a more sophisticated look.

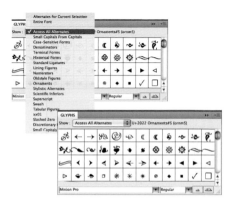

Selecting specific type features to display in the Glyphs panel—here alternate swashes

Lorem ipsum dolor sit amet, consectetuer adipiscing elit. Sed at nibh. Nam ultrices erat nec pede. Vivamus est ante, aliquet vel, fermentum et, nonummy eget, ante. Morbi metus nisl, placerat ut, accumsan id, aliquet vel, nulla. Aenean scelerisque dapibus nunc. Proin augue. Vestibulum dictum. Morbi eget

Text composed using Single-line Composer

Lorem ipsum dolor sit amet, consectetuer adipiscing elit. Sed at nibh. Nam ultrices erat nec pede. Vivamus est ante, aliquet vel, fermentum et, nonummy eget, ante. Morbi metus nisl, placerat ut, accumsan id, aliquet vel, nulla. Aenean scelerisque dapibus nunc. Proin augue. Vestibulum dictum. Morbi

The same text composed using Every-line Composer, automatically creating less ragged-looking text blocks with more uniform line lengths

No Faux Small Caps

You'll find Illustrator's Small Caps option in the

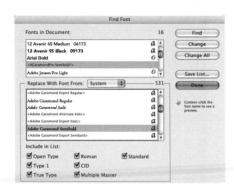

SMALL CAPS

SMALL CAPS

SMALL CAPS

pop-up menu of the Character panel. It converts all selected characters, both cap and lowercase, to small caps (top). However, if true-drawn small caps aren't available in a font, Illustrator creates the fake, scaled-down version (middle), which is a typographic taboo. To prevent Illustrator from creating fake small caps, go to File > Document Setup > Type > Options and change the Small Caps percentage from 70% to 100%. This option is *only* used when Illustrator is faking small caps, so when your small caps are the size of capital letters, you'll instantly recognize it (bottom). This option doesn't persist between documents, so you'll have to choose it each time. (See the *Wow! CD* for the full creativepro.com article.)
—*Ilene Strizver, The Type Studio*

The Find Font dialog

can result in uneven, ragged-looking blocks of text, so the Every-line Composer thinks ahead by automatically determining the best combination of line breaks across the entire paragraph of text. The result is even-looking text blocks with minimal hyphenation and consistent line lengths and spacing, without having to fine-tune line breaks by hand. However, if your design requires a more exacting control over line breaks, you need to use the Single-line Composer.

To change the composition methods for your current paragraph, choose Adobe Every-line Composer or Adobe Single-line Composer from the Paragraph panel menu. To change the composer for multiple paragraphs, select the text first, then choose the composition method from the Paragraph panel menu.

MORE TYPE FUNCTIONS (TYPE & WINDOW MENUS)

From the Type and Window menus, you'll find these additional type-related functions and options:

- **Find Font:** If you try to open a file and don't have the correct fonts loaded, Illustrator warns you, lists the missing fonts, and asks if you still want to open the file. You do need the correct fonts to print properly, so if you don't have the missing fonts, choose Find Font to locate and replace them with ones you do have.

  Find Font's dialog displays the fonts used in the document in the top list; an asterisk indicates a missing font. The font type is represented by a symbol to the right of the font name. You can choose replacement fonts from ones on your system or those used in the document. To display only the font types you want to use as replacements, uncheck those you don't want to include in the list. To replace a font used in the document, select it from the top list and choose a replacement font from the bottom list. You can individually replace each occurrence of the font by clicking Change and then Find. To change every occurrence at once, simply click the Change All button to replace all occurrences.

Note: *When you select a font in the top list, the first text object in the document using that font becomes selected. Click again on the font and the next type object using the font will be selected and centered on the monitor.*

- **Type Orientation** lets you change orientation from horizontal to vertical, or vice versa, by choosing Type > Type Orientation > Horizontal or Vertical.

- **Change the Case** of text selected with the Type tool via the Type > Change Case submenu, which offers four choices: UPPERCASE, lowercase, Title Case, and Sentence case.

- **Fit Headline** is a quick way to open up the letter spacing of a headline across a specific distance. First, create the headline within an area type object, not along a path. Select the headline by highlighting it, then choose Type > Fit Headline. This works with both the Horizontal and Vertical Type tools.

- **Show Hidden Characters** reveals soft and hard returns, word spaces, tabs, and an end-of-text flow symbol. Toggle it on and off with Type > Show Hidden Characters (⌘-Opt-I/Ctrl-Alt-I).

CONVERTING TYPE TO OUTLINES

You can use the Appearance panel to apply multiple strokes to editable type (see the *Layers & Appearances* chapter for details about working with multiple strokes or fills). You can also reliably mask with live, editable type! So although there are fewer and fewer reasons to convert your type to outlines, there are still some times when converting type to outlines is your best option (see "Why convert type to outlines?" following).

As long as you've created type with fonts you have installed on your system (and can print), and you've finished experimenting with your type elements (for example: adjusting size, leading, or kerning/tracking),

---

Legacy Type on a Path?

If you save a file from CS4 to CS, CS2, or CS3, and your document contains Type on a Path, your layout will revert to the CS3 Type on a Path engine. If you convert to Illustrator 10 or earlier, your type will be converted to outlines or Point type.

Vertical Area Type flows

If you use the Vertical Area Type tool, you'll see that your text flows automatically from the right edge of the area toward the left! Those of you who use Roman fonts and typographic standards won't have much use for this tool, because Roman type flows from left to right (see the Tip "Multi-language font support" earlier in this chapter introduction.).

Don't outline small type

If you're printing to a high-resolution imagesetter or using larger type sizes, you can successfully convert type objects to outlines. However, for several very technical reasons, type at text sizes and smaller, or type with delicate forms or details, when converted to outlines, won't look as good on the computer screen, or print as clearly at resolutions of 600 dots per inch or less, as it would have if it had remained a font.

The text engine that Adobe introduced in Illustrator CS, and is refining with each release, made a lot of new features possible. But that change also meant that text is handled very differently from older versions, so *legacy text* (text created in older editions of Illustrator) needs to be updated before it can be edited in CS4. When you open a file containing legacy text, a dialog warns you that it contains text that needs to be updated. You can choose to update the text then and there by clicking Update, or wait until later by clicking OK. Text that hasn't been updated can be viewed, moved, and printed, but it can't be edited. When you select legacy text, it is displayed with an **X** through its bounding box. When you then update the legacy text, you may see the following types of changes:

• Changes to leading, tracking, and kerning

• In Area type: words overflowing, shifting between lines or to the next linked object.

You can choose to update all legacy text at any time by choosing Type > Legacy Text > Update All Legacy Text. Specific legacy text can be updated by clicking it with the Type tool. You can also preserve legacy text on a layer below the updated text for comparison.

you have the option to convert your live type to outlines. Your type will no longer be editable as type, but instead will be constructed of standard Illustrator Bézier curves that may include compound paths to form the "holes" in the outlined letter forms (such as the see-through centers of an **O**, **B**, or **P**).

As with all Illustrator paths, you can use the Direct Selection tool to select and edit the objects. To convert type to outlines, select all blocks of type you wish to outline (it doesn't matter if non-type objects are selected as well) and choose Type > Create Outlines. To fill the "holes" in letters with color, select the compound path and choose Object > Compound Path > Release (see the *Beyond the Basics* chapter for more about working with compound paths).

IMPORTANT: *Outlining type is not recommended for small font sizes—see the Tip "Don't outline small type" earlier in this chapter introduction.*

Why convert type to outlines?

Below are several cases where converting type to outlines may be useful:

• **So you can graphically transform or distort the individual curves and anchor points of letters or words.** Everything from the minor stretching of a word to an extreme distortion is possible. See the Galleries later in this chapter for examples. (Warp Effects and Envelopes can sometimes be used on live type for these purposes, too; see the *Live Effects & Graphic Styles* chapter.)

• **So you can maintain your letter and word spacing when exporting your type to another application.** Many programs that allow you to import Illustrator type as "live" editable text don't support the translation of your custom kerning and word spacing. Convert text to outlines before exporting Illustrator type in these instances to maintain custom word and letter spacing.

• **So you don't have to supply the font to your client or service bureau.** Converting type can be especially useful when you need to use foreign language fonts, when your image will be printed while you're not around, or when you don't have permission to embed the fonts. If your service bureau doesn't have its own license for a font, your own license for the font may not permit you to give it to them. If this is the case, convert your fonts to outlines.

THE DOUBLE-DUTY EYEDROPPER

The Eyedropper tool allows you to copy appearance attributes from one type object to another, including stroke, fill, character, and paragraph attributes. The double-duty Eyedropper both picks up and applies text formatting. It has two modes: *sampling* and *applying*; a small **T** means it is in position to sample or apply text attributes. To copy text formatting from one object to another using the Eyedropper tool, first select the Eyedropper from the Toolbox, and position it over an unselected type object. When it angles downward to the left, it's correctly positioned over the type object. Click the type object to pick up its attributes.

Now position the Eyedropper tool over the unselected text object to which you want to apply the attributes, and hold down the Option/Alt key. In applying mode, it angles downward to the right, and looks full. To apply the attributes that you just sampled, move the cursor to the text you want to change and click. (A simple click will apply the sampled attributes to the whole paragraph; you can also drag the cursor to apply the attributes only to the specific text you dragged over.)

Alternatively, for a one-step method, you can first select the type object with appearance attributes you want to change, and then move the Eyedropper tool over the unselected type object that has the attributes you want and click on it.

If you think you've sampled and applied text attributes with the Eyedropper, but nothing actually happens, double-click on the Eyedropper tool and make sure that Character Style and Paragraph Style are checked under Eyedropper Options.

As you click on text with the sampling Eyedropper, "ink" appears in the Eyedropper to show that it has sampled the attributes of the text.

We are healthy only to the extent that our ideas are humane.
— *Kilgore Trout (via Kurt Vonnegut)*

The applying Eyedropper tool, which appears when you press the Option/Alt key, applies attributes to an object. Note that the applying Eyedropper angles downward to the right.

Making one text block of many

To join separate Area text boxes or Point type objects, select all the text objects with any Selection tool and Copy. Then draw a new Area text box and paste. Text will flow into the box, in the *stacking order* in which it had appeared on the page. (It doesn't matter if you select graphic elements with your text—these elements won't be pasted.) —*Sandee Cohen*

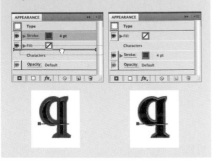

USING THE APPEARANCE PANEL WITH TYPE

When you work with type, you work with the letter characters or with the container that holds the characters—or both. Understanding the difference between characters and their container (the "type object") will help you access and edit the right one when you style type. To help understand the difference, you'll need to watch the Appearance panel as you work.

Type Characters

When you click with the Type tool and enter text, you are working directly with the letter characters. In the Appearance panel, you'll see a blank Stroke and a black Fill listed underneath the Characters line in the panel. You can apply a color or pattern to a character's fill and stroke. To edit a character's fill and stroke, drag across the text with the Type tool or double-click Characters in the Appearance panel.

These are some of the things you *can't* do when working with the characters (although you can with their containers): move the stroke under the fill or the fill above the stroke; apply a live effect to the fill or stroke; apply a gradient fill; add multiple fills or strokes; or change the opacity or blending mode.

The Type "Object"

All text is contained in a Point, Area, or Path type object. You are working with the type "object" when you select the text with the Selection tool and then move the object around on your page. You can think of the type object as a group whose members are the letter characters. There are things you can do to this group that you couldn't do when working directly with the letter characters.

For example, you can add another fill (click on the Add New Fill icon in the Appearance panel). Notice that the Appearance panel changes—now there is another listing of Fill and Stroke, but this time they are positioned above the Characters line in the panel.

The fill and stroke you worked with at the character level still exist. You can reveal them by double-clicking Characters in the panel. Doing so, however, brings you back to character editing; reselect the type object with the Selection tool to return to editing the type object rather than its characters.

When you add a new fill or stroke to the type object, its color or effects interact with the color of the characters. You can predict the visual results of changes to the type object and characters by knowing that all the fills and strokes applied to type are painted, with those listed at the top of the panel painted on top of those listed below (including the stroke and fill you see listed when you double-click Characters in the panel). So if you add a new fill and apply white to it, the type appears white (the white fill of the type object is stacked above the black fill of the characters).

To experiment with how this works, create two type objects in a large font size (72 pt, for example). Next, edit at the character level by dragging through the objects with the Type tool, and then changing the default black fill to green in the Appearance panel.

To edit at the type object level, select one of the type objects with the Selection tool. Add a new fill (choose Add New Fill from the Appearance panel menu); by default, the type object is filled with black, which will cover up the green fill you gave the character. With the type object still selected, click on the Swatch Libraries menu button in the lower-left corner of the panel (or from the Swatches panel menu choose Open Swatch Library > Other Library). In the pop-up menu click Swatches > Patterns > Decorative and then select Decorative_Ornament.ai. From the Decorative_Ornament panel, click on the Quilt 1 swatch. When the type object fills with the pattern, the pattern's black objects overlay the green of the character, while its empty areas let the green show through. Working through the lessons and Galleries that follow will help you master the difference between characters and their type object.

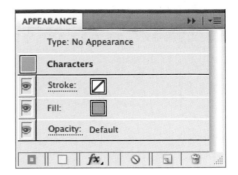

The Appearance panel showing the green fill applied to the type at the Character level

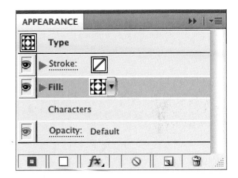

The Appearance panel showing the pattern Quilt 1 (from the Decorative_Ornaments pattern library) filling the type at the type object level

CAPITOL REEF
Hickman Natural Bridge
2.5 miles (4.0 km) round trip
400 ft (122 m) elevation change
Moderate Hike: 1 to 2 hours
Attractions: two natural bridges

GORDON/CARTAGRAM

See Gordon's "Floating Type" lesson in the Transparency chapter to learn how to create transparent backgrounds for your area type objects

Typography

Typography

Typography

The original Point type object at the top; in the middle, the same type object exported using Preserve Text Editability; at the bottom, the type object exported using Preserve Text Appearance

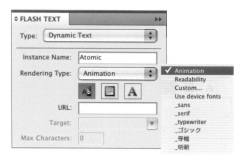

The Flash Text panel with render options

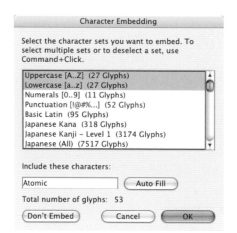

Clicking on the "Edit character options" button in the Flash Text panel brings up a dialog that lets you choose whether or not to embed type. Embedding increases file size, but ensures your page will look as designed.

SAVING AND EXPORTING ILLUSTRATOR TYPE

While Illustrator's modern text engine has opened the door to new levels of typographic control and flexibility, sending your typography out into the world can be a tricky process. Type objects in files that you save to legacy versions of Illustrator (Version 10 and before) or as EPS files will either be broken into groups of point or path type objects, or converted to outlines. Choose File > Document Setup, and from the Export menu at the bottom of the dialog, select Preserve Text Editability or Preserve Text Appearance.

As the example shows, choosing Preserve Text Editability breaks the word "Typography" into a group of eight separate point type objects. By contrast, choosing Preserve Text Appearance will convert all type to outlines. In either case, editing your type will be very difficult or impossible for others who need to use it in legacy versions of Illustrator.

The Flash Text panel offers several options for exporting text to Flash. Select the text object with the Selection tool, open the Flash Text panel and tag your text as Static, Dynamic, or Input. If tagged as Dynamic or Input text, you additionally can provide an Instance name for the object, as well as state the Rendering Intent (animation, readability, etc.) for the object. You can add other instructions for treating text in Flash, and specify a URL for collecting Input text. All text becomes regular area text in Flash, but it can start as point, area, or type on a path in Illustrator. See the Help in your Flash application for more about your options. To learn more about choosing and using text with your Illustrator and Flash project, see the *Web & Animation* chapter later in this book.

Remember to test importing Illustrator's type in other applications before proceeding during a critical project or deadline. While you may not need to edit the type in another program, you want to ensure that it imports as you expect, and preserves the appearance it had in Illustrator, if that's important to your project.

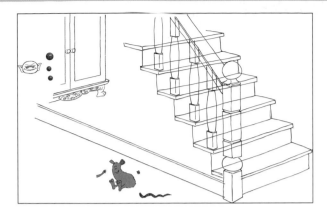

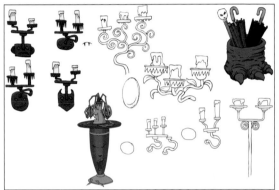

ATTEBERRY

Kevan Atteberry

When Kevan Atteberry starts work on a new book, such as his *Frankie Stein* series of children's books, he first gathers together characters and elements he might use. He works to create them (and parts of them) in various moods and poses; anything, even inanimate objects such as wall sconces and doorknobs, can become a character in Atteberry's world. Before Illustrator featured multiple artboards, Atteberry had to open several files and keep switching his focus from one file to another. Now he creates custom art brushes and swatches that every artboard has immediate access to, builds his characters and the parts he'll later use in a scene, and then begins drawing his final scene.

The artboard that is to become a final scene usually begins with a line drawing. As he sets the stage for his characters, he begins dragging them in from the outlying artboards, as he has done here with the mouse. The mouse looks a bit disjointed because it actually resides on separate layers, so that it can be sandwiched later with layers that will make up part of the scene. By keeping the mouse in pieces, Atteberry can build around it, and then size and rotate the mouse parts into place. With multiple artboards, it's easier for him to focus on these complex constructions, rather than having to concentrate on finding his characters in another file. To view one of the finished pieces for this project, see the *Illustrator & Other Programs* chapter.

Create an Identity

Working Efficiently with Multiple Elements

Overview: *Create artboards for each type of content, then resize the artboards to match contents; use symbols for logos; duplicate artboards with artwork for multiple variations.*

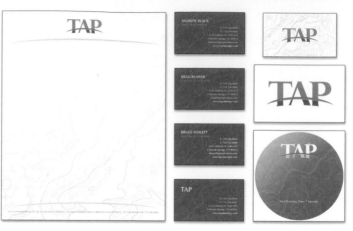

PUTNAM

Setting up multiple artboards

Using the resize fields in the Control panel with the Artboard tool active

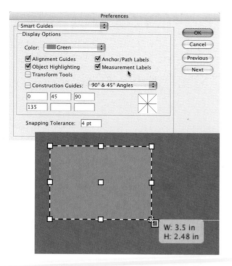

Dragging with the Artboard tool to manually size the artboard with Measurement Labels enabled in Preferences

A company's typical identity package may contain several types and sizes of materials, such as business cards, letterhead stationery, even CD labels. Illustrator used to make it necessary to create, and keep track of, several files in order to make up a complete identity package. Today Ryan Putnam can rely on multiple artboards and symbols to create the collateral materials in a single file, which makes adding to or updating the identity package much simpler and less prone to errors and omissions.

1 Setting up the artboards. Putnam began by setting up four artboards using the default settings in the New dialog. He then customized the sizes of each artboard to fit the needs of the project by clicking on each in turn with the Artboard tool (Shift-O) and then adjusting the Artboard size fields in the Control panel. He adjusted the artboards to fit the actual dimensions of letterhead stationery, a business card, and a CD label, with one artboard used for the design of the logo itself. If you need to make other changes to how the artboards are drawn or displayed, you can choose the Artboard Options icon in the Control panel to open a full dialog. You also can draw individual artboards using the Artboard tool with Smart Guides turned on (⌘-U/Ctrl-U). The Smart Guides Measurement Labels show the size while you draw, but you often have to fiddle to get the exact size while dragging out the rectangle. If you're only resizing, it's usually easiest to simply type measurements into the size fields.

2 Making symbols for replication and quick updates.

Putnam designed the logo first, dragged it into the Symbols panel to save it as a symbol, named it, and clicked OK. Using a symbol he could easily make changes, automatically updating all instances of it throughout the document. And breaking the link to the symbol in order to modify it makes it easy to create a new symbol, as Putnam did here when he needed the logo to have a different color (see the *Brushes & Symbols* chapter for more about creating and modifying symbols). Using multiple artboards with symbols appreciably adds to productivity. Artboards in one file share the same libraries, so if there were any changes in the future, Putnam wouldn't have to open separate files for each item in the identity package, and then open the library containing the modified symbol. One file would always contain all the libraries and correctly-sized artboards ready for modifications.

3 Copying and duplicating artwork with artboards.

Putnam created the design for each element of the identity package, placing the logo symbol on the artboard and adding text and artwork as needed. Although the letterhead and CD label only required a single version, he needed to personalize several business cards and to create the back side. To make this a speedy process, Putnam first activated the Artboard tool and enabled the Move/Copy Artwork with Artboard icon on the Control panel. Holding down the Option/Alt key, he clicked on the first business card he created and dragged to copy it to a new location. The artwork and formatted text was in place, ready for him to alter the text quickly and move on to creating the next card. Because he used separate artboards, each business card could be printed on demand, yet it would only take a minute to add a new employee's card to the file. The reverse side of the card replaced the text with the logo symbol, and Putnam recolored the artwork.

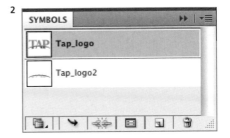

Using symbols for logos to maintain consistency, make updates a snap, and to place or modify where needed from a shared library onto different artboards

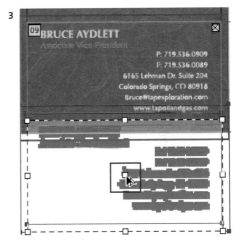

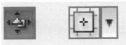

Duplicating the artboard with the artwork by enabling the Move/Copy Artwork with Artboard icon and holding down the Option/Alt key

For Client Review

Creating Presentations from Artboards

Overview: *Use a separate artboard for each variation of a logo; use Recolor Artwork to recolor each version; save the file as a PDF for a client's initial review; create multiple artboards, then place artboards for a new presentation; save the new presentation for the client's final review.*

SCOTT CITRON DESIGN

1

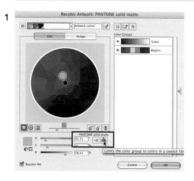

Using the Recolor Artwork dialog to limit to a Pantone Color Book in order to recolor variations for a logo (for more about Recolor Artwork, see the Live Color chapter)

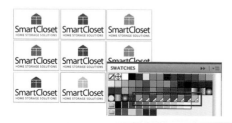

Multiple artboards duplicated with the Artboard tool, then using Recolor Artwork to automatically save Spot colors to the Swatches panel

When Scott Citron needed to create a new logo for a client, he decided to take advantage of multiple artboards, both to keep each task organized, and to use printing options for his client presentations. With Illustrator's ability to print separate pages for each artboard, and to print only selected artboards, making a PDF presentation becomes quick work using multiple artboards.

1 Creating multiple versions on multiple artboards, and preparing a multi-page PDF for review. Citron used a single artboard for the new logo. Once he was satisfied with the art, he selected the Artboard tool (Shift-O) and enabled the Move/Copy Artwork with Artboard icon. He held down the Option/Alt key and dragged to make several copies. Inspired by a workflow Sandee Cohen developed, he selected one of the duplicated logos and clicked on the Recolor Artwork icon in the Control panel. On the Edit tab, he clicked on the Limit to swatches library button, then he chose Color Books from the list and a Pantone Solid book from the sublist. Citron dragged in the Color Wheel to locate interactively a fresh Pantone Spot color. He clicked OK to exit the dialog and automatically save the new Spot color to the Swatches panel.

Citron then needed to make a single Acrobat (PDF) document so the client could see and comment on each colored logo separately. To create one multi-page PDF from the artboards, he chose File > Save As > Adobe PDF (also see "Exporting and Printing Multiple Artboards" in the introduction to this chapter).

2 Creating the identity and presentation. Once the client approved a color, Citron copied the chosen logo to a new document, added it to the Symbols panel, and created a new artboard sized for every requested printed piece. Adding the symbol and text, he completed making the collateral materials and saved the file with PDF compatibility enabled. To present the overall effect to the client, Citron wanted to create a pleasing arrangement of the materials. He created a new document at default settings. He didn't worry about the size; he would resize it to fit all the artwork later. He then chose File > Place, with Link enabled, selecting the first artboard in the file he just previously saved.

Because placed artwork can't display a stroke, fill, or drop shadow, Citron used a technique developed by Mordy Golding in order to delineate the boundaries of each visible piece. In the Appearance panel, he first added a new Stroke, and chose Convert to Shape > Rectangle (no added width or height) from the *fx* menu. He then added a new white Fill (temporarily concealing everything), chose Convert to Shape > Rectangle, and with the Fill still targeted, chose *fx* > Stylize > Drop Shadow. He dragged the Fill below "Contents" in the Appearance panel to reveal the artwork. In the Graphic Styles panel, he Option/Alt-clicked the New icon to save this style as "Boundary." For each additional artboard, he chose Place and clicked the "Boundary" style. He arranged the placed artwork and, to prepare the presentation as a PDF, selected the Artboard tool and chose Presets > Fit Artboard to Artwork bounds. Now if he updated the original file containing the collateral materials, he could choose to update his presentation instantly, while the original file was kept "printer-ready."

2

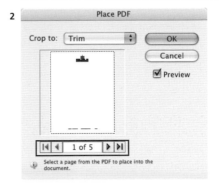

Placing artwork in a file one artboard at a time, cropped to Trim

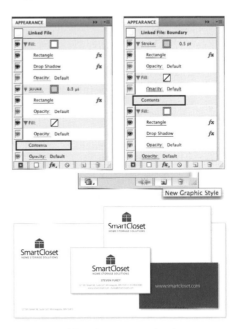

Using a graphic style to create a border as a visual aid—adding a Stroke will define the outline; adding a Fill creates an object that can have a Drop Shadow applied, but first conceals the artwork; after adding the Drop Shadow, the Fill is moved below "Contents," revealing the artwork and defining the boundaries

Making Masters

Transforming with Multiple Artboards

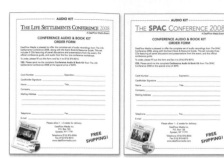

Overview: *Create multiple artboards; design a "master" page, separating mutable from fixed elements; use the Transform effect to duplicate the design across artboards; make changes to objects as needed; add pages based on the "master."*

Transform effect vs. symbols

When you create "master pages" using the Transform effect, you'll be able to duplicate objects in exactly the same position, across multiple artboards, and then easily modify or add elements, or change the number of duplicates. Using this method, however, you won't be able to "break the link" to modify an instance individually, as you can with symbols. The kinds of changes you anticipate making should dictate which method you use (see the other artboard lessons in this chapter for alternative solutions).

1

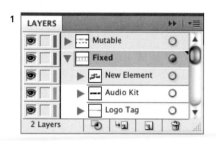

Setting up separate layers for fixed and mutable elements

When he needed to create a series of flyers for a company's year of conferences, Gary Newman decided to use multiple artboards to create a "master template" and all the location-specific flyers in one document. Pondering the need to duplicate all elements but alter some, Newman recognized that using the Live effect, Transform, would make it possible to duplicate design elements from the "master" to each of the individual artboards. By using one layer for elements that would change and another for elements that would stay the same, he simplified locating elements and making changes to them later on.

1 Setting up the document for multiple artboards. For this type of project, artboards all must be the same size. Newman chose 4 for the Number of Artboards (three are shown above), set the Spacing to 20 pt, and selected Arrange by Row, which placed all artboards in a single row. These settings would allow him to apply the Transform effect using Move and Copy, since Move with the Transform effect can only work in one direction at a time.

2 Designing the "master." As Newman designed the master page, he determined which elements were going to stay the same, such as logos or standard forms, and placed those on one layer. Objects that he planned to change, whether text, images, or graphic elements, he placed on a second layer. By separating fixed from mutable elements, he made it easier to select objects for the two different handling techniques (described in the following steps) simply by targeting their layers.

3 Duplicating objects to the other artboards. In order to create "instances" of the original art on each of the artboards, he selected all the objects on the non-changing layer by clicking on the layer's target icon, and chose Effects > Distort & Transform > Transform. Newman added the width of the artboard plus the space created between artboards and entered that number in the Move > Horizontal field of the dialog (he needed 612 pt for the paper size plus 20 pt for spacing, or 632 pt). In the "copies" field he entered the number of artboards. No new layers get created, and Outline mode only shows the original objects, but all the objects placed by the Transform effect are displayed on each of the artboards.

Next Newman selected everything on the mutable layer and repeated the same Transform process. He then immediately chose Object > Expand Appearance, followed by Object > Ungroup. These steps created several expanded objects. He created a sublayer for each original object (the text or graphic, etc.) and dragged the objects to their respective sublayers. He gave each layer a distinctive name to quickly locate them again. With Expand Appearance, he broke the link to the "master" page, and was now free to change any of the object's properties.

4 Making future changes. If later you wish to modify the fixed objects, change them on the "master" artboard and they'll instantly update on all artboards (much like with symbols). If your project later expands, you can easily use the Transform effect to duplicate the objects once again to the newly-added artboards. Because you applied a Live Effect, you can use the Appearance panel to change the Transform effect. Click the underlined "Transform" (or double-click the *fx* icon) to reopen the Transform dialog, change the number of copies to the number needed, and click OK to apply the change. To include the mutable objects, which are no longer part of a live effect, select those objects from the last previously existing artboard in the row, and choose Effect > Transform to duplicate, then Expand and Ungroup; you're now ready to modify them.

Need two or more rows?

What if you need to have two or more rows instead of one very long one? Make the same number of artboards in each row, copy the "master" over one row with the Transform effect, and target the layer for either fixed or mutable objects as before, which will target that entire row. Again use the Transform effect, this time making only one copy per each row you created, and moving Vertically. (Remember that if you place a row beneath another row, you will be moving a *negative* number of points.) Expand and ungroup the mutable objects as before. This, in effect, mimics the Step and Repeat function often used in layout programs such as InDesign.

3

Targeting the "fixed" objects layer and using the Transform effect with Move and Copy to duplicate "instances" of the selected objects to identical positions on different artboards

Expanding Objects

Note that when you choose Expand Appearance, your objects will be broken into the discrete elements that formed them. A rectangle with a fill and stroke becomes two objects, while a Raster effect ceases to be "live," but becomes a bitmap.

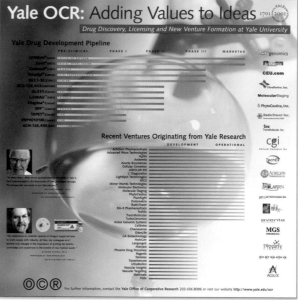

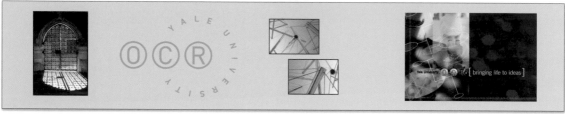

CRISCOLA

Jeanne Criscola

The usefulness of multiple artboards goes beyond storing elements for a single project. When Jeanne Criscola updates a logo or completes an entire project for a regular client, she can store related materials in a client file. Any project or part of a project that might get reused or presented in a different way from the original is a good candidate for storing on its own artboard. One of Criscola's clients, Yale's Office of Cooperative Research, has commissioned artwork at various times. They asked her to produce another project (a mural-sized exhibit illustrated here) into which they wanted her to incorporate some of the memorable projects they had commissioned earlier. Now, instead of tracking down files scattered in many places, Criscola only need open her Yale client file (Illustrator can store up to 100 artboards in a single file), and everything is at her fingertips, ready to be pulled together into her new project.

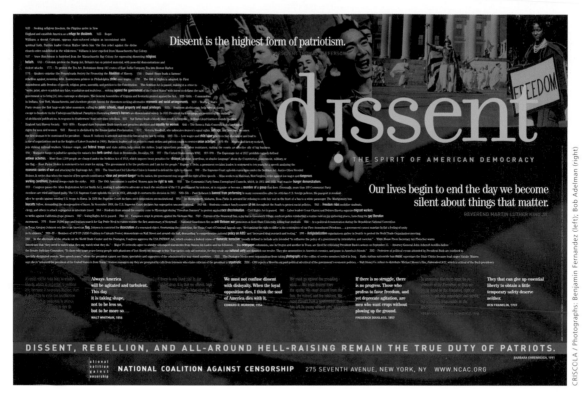

Jeanne Criscola

When the National Coalition Against Censorship (NCAC) commissioned Jeanne Criscola to create a poster that expressed the need for an engaged public in a democracy, they had in mind the many historic moments when dissent has given rise to momentous decisions, from the founding of our country through every crisis up to today. Criscola wanted to create a poster that would inform the public about the history of free political expression in America, that would be visually appealing, and would immediately convey the thrust of the message, even at a distance. In QuarkXPress she reworked a timeline of historic events and notable quotations and saved it as EPS. She then switched to Illustrator because it provided

greater graphical control over individual type elements, and better scaling options for the final poster. Opening the EPS, she next chose type size and color to create both a visual and communicative hierarchy. While her use of red, white, and blue obviously echoed the colors of American patriotism, she alternated the use of sans and serif fonts to echo the structure of free debate. She placed the type dynamically on the diagonal "wave," with "pillars" of paragraphs about dissent running along the bottom as support. Once the layout was approved, Criscola saved universal (EPS and PDF) versions of the poster that the NCAC could easily scale, distribute, and print through their website.

Book Cover Design

Illustrator as a Stand-Alone Layout Tool

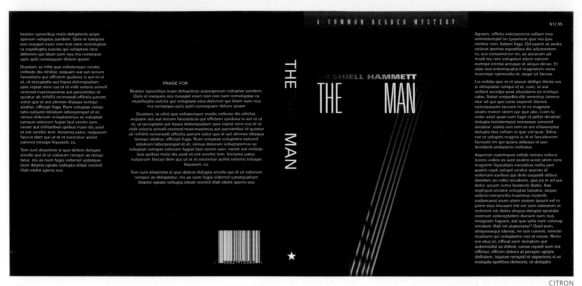

CITRON

Overview: *Set your document's dimensions and bleeds; make custom guides; make Area type for columns and thread text.*

Changing the name, setting the number of Artboards to 1, changing units to Picas, setting Orientation to landscape, entering dimensions, and entering bleed measurements

Even with multiple artboards in Illustrator, you'll still need a page-layout program (such as InDesign or QuarkXPress) for the production of complex multi-page documents. But for simpler projects, such a book cover design, Scott Citron often finds that Illustrator's bleeds, custom guides, and the Area Type tool are a better fit for the job.

1 Setting up the page. To create a new document, Scott Citron chose File > New. While in the New Document dialog, he changed the Name of the file and set the Number of Artboards to 1. For the document's dimensions, Citron chose Picas under Units, clicked the Landscape icon under Orientation, and entered the dimensions of his book cover in the Width and Height fields. He also needed a bleed for the book cover, so while still in the New Document dialog, he entered his bleed measurement in the Top Bleed input field and clicked the "Make all settings the same" icon to populate the other Bleed fields with the same measurement. Once he entered all his settings, he clicked OK to exit the New Document dialog.

2 Customizing your guides. To make it possible to set up guides for the inside jacket flaps, back cover, spine, and front cover, Citron first chose View >Show Rulers. To create the first guide, he clicked on the left-side ruler and dragged a guide to, roughly, his first position. He then chose View >Guides >Unlock Guides, so he could numerically adjust the positions of a selected guide by relocating the X (or Y) axis positions in the Transform panel precisely. To create a rectangular guide (rather than a linear one), he could convert a selected rectangle into a guide using ⌘-5/Ctrl-5. With his guides in place, Citron chose View >Guides >Lock Guides. To access lock, hide, and release guide functions quickly later, he could use the Context-sensitive menu (Control key for Mac, or right-click on a two-button mouse).

3 Placing and refining the elements. When the page was set with the correct dimensions, bleeds, and guides, Citron added artwork to the book cover. Although Citron's book cover contains all vector artwork, you can import a raster image into your document by choosing File >Place.

Citron then created rectangles with the Rectangle tool to define areas for columns of text. With the Area Type tool, he clicked on one of these rectangles, making it possible to type directly into the box or to paste text. He then double-clicked on the Type tool from the Tools panel to open the Area Type Options dialog. Within the dialog, Citron changed the Offset in the Inset Spacing field to inset the text from the edge of the text box. You can also use the Area Type Options dialog to change the Dimensions, Rows, Columns, and Text Flow Options. Citron then repeated these steps for the other rectangles he wanted as text boxes. To make the overset text of one text box flow to another, he used the Selection tool. He clicked on the red box in the overflowing text box and then on the new text box he wanted the text to flow into. As an alternative to using the Area Type tool, you can use the Type tool to create Point type for titles, headlines, and other individual type elements.

2

Choosing View >Show Rulers and dragging a guide into position

Selecting guide and numerically positioning from the Transform panel

3

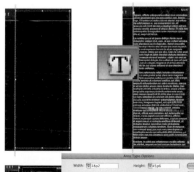

Placing artwork

Creating rectangles with the Rectangle tool, using the Area Type tool, and setting Inset Spacing

Flowing overset text to another text box

Curvaceous Type

Fitting Type to Curved Paths

HUERTA

Overview: *Create artwork objects; copy object paths, then cut the paths to workable length; add text to the paths and offset the text; convert type to outlines and edit character paths.*

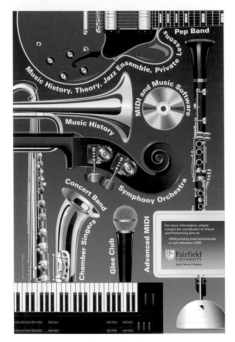

The finished poster for Fairfield University

1

The Outline view of the paths for the guitar

Using the flowing curves of musical instruments coupled with strings of text, designer Gerard Huerta captured the variety of musical studies offered by Fairfield University in this poster promoting its music program to campus and high school students. To give the type characters a more organic fit with the tight curves of some of the instruments, Huerta converted the type to outlines and then edited the shapes of the character paths.

1 Sketching and scanning the shapes, then redrawing them in Illustrator. Huerta started the poster by sketching the shapes of musical instruments by pencil. Then he scanned the drawing and placed the scan in Illustrator as a template layer. By using the Pen tool to draw the shapes, and using gradients and gradient meshes for color, Huerta built the musical instruments and then arranged them to leave space for the text he would create next.

2 Drawing paths for type and creating the type on the paths. You can draw the paths that will parallel your objects with the Pen or Pencil tool for setting type, or, like Huerta, use copies of the objects themselves. First, copy the path you want the type to parallel and paste in front (Edit > Paste in Front) so the copy directly overlays the original. Use the Scissors tool to cut the path so that it's an open-ended path instead of a closed path. Next, with the Type tool, click on the line and type the words you want on that path. Grab the type's I-beam and slide it along the path to position the text—flip it to the other side of the path if the text you typed ended up on the wrong side of the path. Make sure that the Character panel is open and your type is still selected. From the Character panel, enter a negative number in the Baseline Shift field or pick a negative number from the field's pop-up menu. Adjust the offset of the type from its path by increasing or decreasing the Baseline Shift value. Reshape the path by using the Direct Selection tool or by drawing over a section of the path with the Pencil tool.

3 Converting type to outlines, then editing character paths. Violins and guitars have sharply curved bodies that can make some letter characters look too angular and straight when positioned along the curve of the path. To correct this, Huerta changed the shapes of individual letter characters so that their strokes conformed more naturally to the curved shape of the path.

You can change character shapes by first converting the type to outlines. (Make copies of the type first in case you need to edit the type or its paths later.) To do this, select the Type on a Path object (don't select the text itself using the Type tool) and choose Type > Create Outlines. Look for characters with parallel strokes, like **m, n, h,** and **u.** Using the Direct Selection tool, move points and adjust control handles to reshape characters, or reshape selected paths with the Pencil tool. Huerta relied on the Direct Selection and Pencil tools to add curves to the straight edges of the original character shapes. He also changed the angle of some character strokes so that the characters appeared to bend with the tight curve of their paths.

2

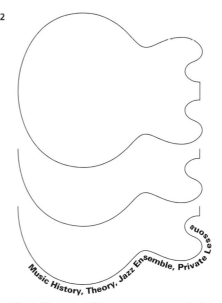

The Outline view of the original outer path for the guitar body (top); path cut from the guitar path (middle); text added to the path and then offset using a negative Baseline Shift

3

*On the left, the letter **T** character from the Univers font; on the right, the **T** character after Huerta edited the character's outline paths by curving the top stroke of the letter*

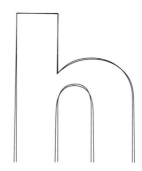

*The original letter **h** character shown here as a magenta outline; superimposed on the original letter **h** is the black outline of the **h** that Huerta edited by angling the bottoms of the vertical strokes*

Spacey characters

Although much improved, the Illustrator type engine may still create some kerning problems with Type on a Path characters. To minimize issues, double-click the Type tool to open Path Options and choose Align to Path: Center (instead of the default Baseline). Also, in the Character panel make sure the Baseline Shift is 0, and manually kern character pairs if necessary.

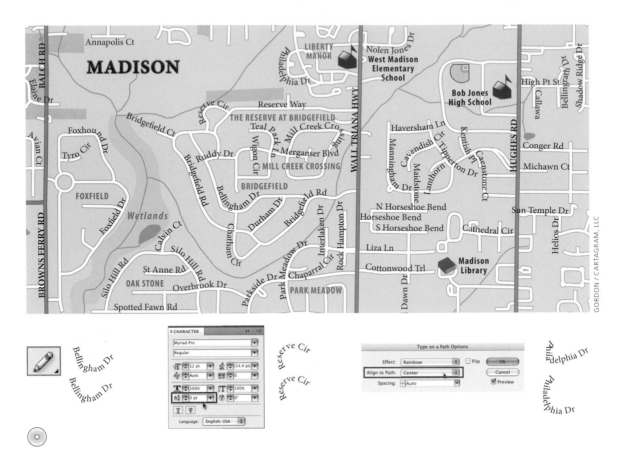

GORDON / CARTAGRAM, LLC

Steven Gordon / Cartagram, LLC

To label curving features like rivers and roads on his maps, cartographer Steve Gordon relies on type on a path. Gordon copies and pastes the river or road paths on a separate layer before applying type to them. He sets the Baseline Shift to 1 pt in the Character panel in order to move the type away from the underlying road or river path. In this map of Madison, Alabama, Gordon encountered paths with sharp turns and tight curves that pinched letters together or spread them apart with unsightly gaps. He smoothed the kinks from some paths by clicking to select a path with type, selecting the Pencil tool, and then drag-ging it over or near the path. For paths that couldn't be smoothed solely with the Pencil, Gordon reset the path's Baseline Shift to 0 and then dragged the path away from the street path so that its lettering was the same distance away from the street as the labels with the 1-pt Baseline Shift. Some of the type paths required another adjustment: Gordon chose Type > Type on a Path > Type on a Path Options, and in the dialog box changed Align to Path from the default value of Baseline to Center. Gordon employed these techniques, separately or in various combinations, as he worked with hundreds of type objects in the map.

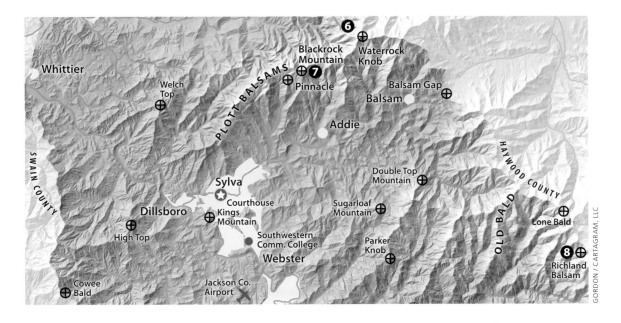

GORDON / CARTAGRAM, LLC

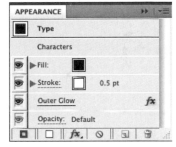

Steven Gordon / Cartagram, LLC

When cartographer Steven Gordon creates a map with a terrain image in the background, he has to ensure that type is not lost in the mountains of the image. For this map of North Carolina's Jackson County, Gordon received directions to create a bold, colorful terrain image by his client, *The Sylva Herald*. He began the map by creating the terrain image in Photoshop, placing it in the Illustrator file, and positioning it on the artboard. After creating the type labels, Gordon opened the Appearance panel, chose Add New Stroke from the panel menu, and dragged the Stroke attribute below Characters in the panel. Next, he set the width of the stroke to 0.5 pt using the Stroke Weight menu and then clicked the Stroke attribute's color icon to pop up the Swatches menu and selected the white swatch. Gordon wanted to soften the contrast between the white stroke and image behind it and decided to add a white glow around the type. To do this he clicked Characters in the Appearance panel and then clicked the Add New Effect icon and chose Stylize > Outer Glow. In the Outer Glow dialog, he clicked the Color Picker, selected white, and changed Opacity to 100% and Blur to 0.04 inches to complete the effect.

Arcing Type

Transforming Type with Warps & Envelopes

Overview: *Create and color a title using appearances; explore the three Envelope distortions for creating an arc effect; use an Arc Warp effect to arc the type; create a graphic style and apply arc effect to other title elements.*

Putnam's 50-point Cabaret font headline

Applying Object > Envelope Distort > Make with Warp and changing the bend to 20%

Applying Object > Envelope Distort > Make with Mesh, setting the number of Rows and Columns to 1, and editing the anchor points with the Direct Selection tool

Creating an arc-shaped object with the Pen tool over the type, selecting the arc-shaped object and type, and applying Object > Envelope Distort > Make with Top Object

PUTNAM

Adding an arc effect to a headline turns boring type into a dynamic engaging headline that grabs the viewers' attention. With Illustrator you can explore a number of ways to create arcing text; using effects and graphic styles, you can quickly create an arcing effect easily applicable to any other titles or sub-titles!

1 Creating your headline text. To create headline text, choose a font with distinct, bold characteristics. For his headline text, Ryan Putnam chose 50-point Cabaret font.

Amongst the many ways to create an arcing effect in Illustrator, there are three different Envelope distortions that you can apply to your text: Warp, Mesh, and Make with Top Object.

First, Putnam applied Object > Envelope Distort > Make with Warp. Next, he chose Arc from the Warp options, and changed the Bend to 20%. For a second option, he then applied Object > Envelope Distort > Make with Mesh, set the number of Rows and Columns to 1, and edited the anchor points with the Direct Selection tool. For the final option, he used the Pen tool to draw a separate arc-shaped object over the type, selected the type and arc-shaped object, and applied Object > Envelope Distort > Make with Top Object.

2 Applying an Arc Warp effect to arc the title. Even though using Envelope distortions created the effect Putnam was looking for, and provided significant control for customizing his warp, he ultimately decided that he wanted a quick way to add the same simple arc effect to other titles and subtitles on the cover. Putnam figured out that if he created the arc using Effect > Warp, he could save his effect as a graphic style that he could then apply to additional titles.

There are 15 standard Warp shapes you can choose from when creating a title. For the "Spiritual" title, Putnam applied Effect > Warp > Arc. With Preview enabled, he changed the Bend to 20%, then clicked OK.

3 Saving and applying a graphic style. With the title selected, Putnam clicked the New Graphic Style icon in the Graphic Styles panel. With the graphic style now saved, Putnam could easily apply that style to other titles and subtitles.

To create a variant of this style, he replaced the text with "Muscles:", changed the font to 28 points, the Rotation to 355°, and then clicked the New Graphic Style icon in the Graphic Styles panel. (For more on graphic styles, see the *Live Effects & Graphic Styles* chapter.)

4 Applying finishing touches. To custom color the individual characters in his headline, Putnam decided to outline the type (Type > Create Outlines). He then applied a custom gradient and adjusted it for each character. (For more on working with gradients, see the *Blends, Gradients & Mesh* chapter.)

2

In Effect > Warp > Arc, changing the bend to 20%

3

Selecting the title and clicking the New Graphic Style icon in the Graphic Style panel

Applying the graphic style

Using Add New Effect from the Appearance panel, apply Distort & Transform, change the Rotation to 355°, and click the New Graphic Style button in the Graphic Style panel

4

Applying Type > Create Outlines to the titles

Applying a linear gradient to the titles

Applying a custom gradient

Masking Words
Masking Images with Letter Forms

Overview: *Create text on top of a placed raster image; select all and make the text into a clipping mask for the placed image.*

1

(Top) text in the HooskerDoo typeface, which includes the splotches; (middle) placing scanned fabric, and moving it below the type using the Layers panel; (bottom) text above the fabric

2

After selecting the type and the image below, choosing Object>Clipping Mask>Make

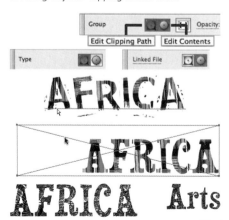

With the clipping mask and type kept live, it's easy to change the typeface, the linked art, the type size, and the text

This "Africa" type treatment (using the HooskerDoo font) was created by Johannesburg, South Africa-based artist Ellen Papciak-Rose. Working on shoestring budgets for non-profit organizations, Papciak-Rose often scans regional textiles and crafts to incorporate into her work.

1 Creating text and placing an image. Select a typeface with sufficient weight for an image to show through (HooskerDoo includes the splotches) and create text with the Type tool. Choose File > Place, select an image, enable Link, disable Template, and click OK. In a clipping mask, the topmost selected object becomes the mask. To use your type as a mask, in the Layers panel, expand your layer and move the <Linked File> below your type.

2 Creating the clipping mask. Select the text and the image to be masked and choose Object > Clipping Mask > Make; this will group the mask and the masked objects.

3 Making changes to image and text. Select the type or image to adjust its position. To select type click on it (or along its baseline) with the Direct Selection tool, or click the Edit Clipping Path button in the Control panel. To select the image within the text mask, click the Edit Contents button in the Control panel. With the image selected you can move it using the cursor keys, or apply any transformation to it using tools or the Control panel. With type selected you can change many attributes (such as size or typeface) in the Control panel, or in the Character panel (Window > Type > Character). To swap the background image, select it and click its name in the Control panel to access the Relink option, then locate the replacement file. To change the text, select it with the Type tool and retype!

Transforming Conflict, TRANSFORMiNG LIVES

The emergence of Partners in Conflict Transformation (PICOT)

SIERRA LEONE

Case study: A conflict transformation approach to peace and development work By: Richard Smith

PAPCIAK-ROSE (Photographer: Richard Smith)

Ellen Papciak-Rose

Using similar techniques as in the lesson opposite, Ellen Papciak-Rose created this cover for a 64-page book by Richard Smith (he is also the photographer). She used a cropped copy of the woman's skirt from the photo for the fabric in the words "SIERRA LEONE." Papciak-Rose chose the light blue and lime green color scheme to match the colors of the Sierra Leone flag.

Making a Typeface

Creating a Typeface from a Grid

GORSKA

Overview: *Create a grid and draw letter shapes; combine and cut shapes with pathfinders; use shapes to build other letters; use transparency to integrate the letters with other artwork.*

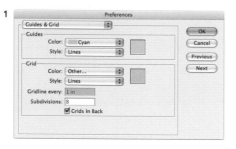

Illustrator's Preferences dialog

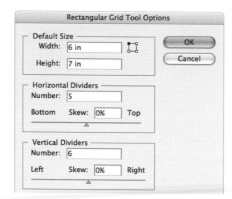

Using the Rectangular Grid Tool Options dialog to create a grid

Inspired by the Cyrillic type adorning the film posters of *avant garde* Russian Constructivists, and drawing on her own Eastern European heritage, Caryl Gorska designed a typeface in the course of creating this self-promotion poster. After crafting the type, Gorska developed the poster artwork and added words set in her typeface.

1 Defining the working grid for creating the alphabet.
Gorska began the poster by constructing the letter characters. She drew the letters directly on-screen instead of on paper because the geometric nature of the characters benefited from Illustrator's precise measuring, drawing, and editing tools (Pen, Pencil, and the Pathfinders).

You'll discover another benefit of using Illustrator when you create letter characters: grids. Why grids? A grid helps save production time and improve the character of your typeface by spreading visual consistency across varied letterforms. To make a grid, decide whether the guiding shape of your letterforms will be a square or a rectangle. If it's a square, use Illustrator's Guides & Grid tab, found within the Illustrator > Preferences dialog. Simply set the size and number of subdivisions that you want in order to create an Artboard-wide grid.

If the dominant letter shape is rectangular, then select the Rectangular Grid tool found within the Line Segment tool in the Tools panel. With the tool selected, click on the Artboard to display the Rectangular Grid Tool Options dialog. Specify the overall grid size using the Default Size fields and the proportions of the grid cells using the Horizontal and Vertical Dividers fields.

2 Drawing, and copying and pasting objects, to build the letterforms. Gorska made full use of Illustrator's tools in drawing and editing the letter characters: Pen and Pencil for drawing shapes, the Pathfinders for combining shapes or cutting letter counters (holes) from the shapes, and the Direct Selection tool for fine-tuning the control points of curves to vary letter proportions. Gorska started with basic characters like **o**, **e**, **b**, and **r** that visually define the general look of the other letter characters. Once you complete several basic characters, arrange them in pairs or words to test how well they look together. Feel free to access the artwork of these characters when building other letters that are similar in structure. You can recycle shapes like stems, serifs, punctuation marks, and counters throughout the alphabet to speed up your work and make the typeface more visually consistent.

Adding a twist to her typeface, Gorska designed a second set of letterforms based on an oval shape using the same grid, complementing the rectangular shapes of the first set she created. This gave her the freedom to mix shapes when arranging the letters as words for a more eclectic look.

3 Drawing background art, composing words, and changing type opacity. To complete the poster, Gorska filled facial and geometric background shapes she drew with blends and gradients. Then she composed the words "red scare" from the letter characters she'd drawn earlier and positioned them over the artwork. She grouped the characters and changed their opacity in the Control panel to 20% to blend them visually with the artwork in the background. Setting her name against the gradient at the top of the poster, Gorska gave each yellow letter a stroke using the same red as the color well in the gradient behind the letters. This unified the appearance of the letters with the background colors in the poster.

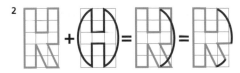

2

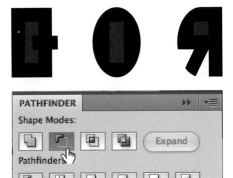

Using the parts of one letter (shown in red) in constructing another letter (shown in green)

Forming the letter counters, shown here as red shapes, by punching a hole using the Pathfinder panel's Minus Front from Shape Modes

3

Letters with 20% opacity applied from the Control panel

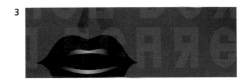

Red-stroked letters set against a gradient

Expand your repertoire

It's easy to re-create an out-of-print typeface using non-copyrighted type found in antique books, or from a royalty-free source like Dover Publications (www.doverpublications.com). Draw the fundamental shapes and copy and paste them to construct the rest of the typeface.

Brush Your Type

Applying Brushes to Letterforms

CRONAN

Overview: *Create, layer, and blur text objects; draw paths and apply brushes; modify paths and brushes; change path transparency.*

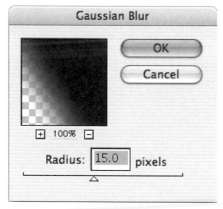

The finished illustration's Layers panel showing the separation of artwork on layers to produce the poster's visual hierarchy

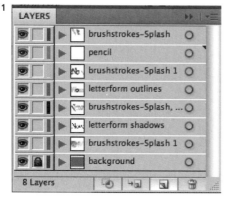

The Effect > Blur > Gaussian Blur dialog with the Radius set to a value appropriate for the smaller working size of the illustration

Designed for a corporate setting where a simple, bold poster could serve as a powerful communication, San Francisco artist Michael Cronan used Illustrator's Pencil and Brush tools to blend artistry with bold type, making the simple words eye-catching and provocative.

1 Converting type to outlines and adding a custom blurred shadow. Cronan began the poster by typing "Now" in the font Didot Regular. Because Illustrator limits the maximum font size to 1296 points, you may need to work at a smaller size and then enlarge the illustration later. (When you enlarge, you may need to convert the type to outlines using Type > Create Outlines if your type will be larger than 1296 points.) To layer artwork you'll create later between the type and a blurred shadow of the type, first duplicate the type layer (drag the type layer and drop it on the Create New Layer icon in the Layers panel). Then, select the type objects on the duplicate layer you just created and from the Effect menu select Blur > Gaussian Blur and choose a blur radius that blurs enough without obliterating the letterforms.

2 Drawing and painting paths with brushes and applying transparency to paths. Painting letterforms couldn't be easier. Using the type you created previously as a visual guide, start by simply drawing lines with the Pen or Pencil tool. Coupling the Pencil tool with a tablet (such as the Wacom tablet) makes drawing even easier and more spontaneous. For a smoother path (with fewer points and more gentle contours) use the Zoom tool to zoom out, *then* draw with the Pencil tool. Cronan mixed paths that followed the shapes of the letterforms with circles and curlicues (letter **o**) and scribbles (letter **w**).

With paths drawn, you're ready to apply brushes. Click the Brush Libraries button (in the lower left of the Brushes panel) and choose Artistic_Paintbrush. Then click on a path and select the Splash brush from the Artistic_Paintbrush panel. With the path still selected, you can refine the shape of the brushed path by selecting the Pencil tool and drawing over or near the selected path to smooth or reshape it. Use the Zoom tool to zoom in or out before you apply the Smooth or Pencil tools to give your reshaped path a smoother or more angular contour.

Because Illustrator's brushes use a path's stroke color, you can color the path before or after applying a Brush. To adjust the thickness of the brushed path, change the path's stroke weight. To change the look of all paths in the illustration painted with a brush, double-click the brush in the Brushes panel and change settings in Art Brush Options. Use the Colorization Method to control how the stroke color is applied to the brush, and adjust the Size > Width field to make the brush stroke wider or thinner.

3 Handwriting with the Pencil tool and setting transparency. Cronan completed the poster illustration by selecting the Pencil tool and drawing paths to mimic handwritten words. Be sure to experiment with the Stroke panel's Cap and Join settings to change the look of the paths. (As an alternative to the Pencil tool, consider using a Calligraphic brush with a small point size from the Brushes panel.) To blend the handwriting-like white-stroked paths with the artwork below, Cronan used the Control panel to reduce the Opacity to 65% for some paths and 31% for others.

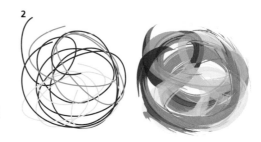

On the left, the colored strokes of paths drawn with the Pencil tool; on the right, Splash brush applied to the same paths

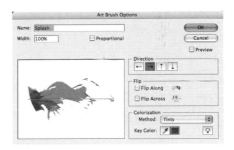

Original path on the left; the same path smoothed with the Pencil tool and zoomed out on the right

The Art Brush Options dialog showing the Splash brush

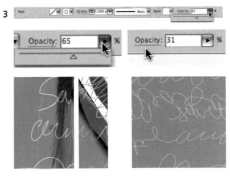

Reducing the opacity of the white-stroked paths in the Control panel

Antiquing Type
Applying Scribble in an Opacity Mask

Advanced Technique

Overview: *Create a type object; copy the object, then style the text with the Roughen effect; create an opacity mask and paste the type object; apply the Scribble effect to the opacity mask; return to Outline mode.*

1

Top, the original type object with letter characters filled with black; bottom, the type object filled with a custom gradient

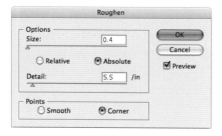

The Roughen dialog

Every type is unique

Your settings for one type object will look different applied to another typeface. Experiment!

When you want to re-create a hand-rendered or historical look, but don't want to stray from the fonts you're already using in a project, consider using Illustrator's live effects and an opacity mask. Ari Weinstein created this poster title for the African Art exhibit at the Bundy Museum in Binghamton, New York, by using an opacity mask and the Scribble effect to chip away the edges of lettering, turning contemporary type into antiqued letters.

1 Creating text, adding a new Fill, and applying the Roughen effect. Weinstein started the poster title by typing "African Art" using the font Marigold. Before taking his type any further, Weinstein clicked on the Selection tool and then chose Edit > Copy. (You'll need a copy of the type object for the opacity mask that you'll make later in the second step.)

Then Weinstein was ready to start styling his type. First, he made sure the type object was still selected. He then opened the Appearance panel and clicked the Add New Fill button from the bottom of the panel. Then clicking on the new Fill's pop-up, Weinstein chose a gradient he'd built from brown colors sampled from other artwork in the poster. (For information on creating or editing gradients, refer to the *Blends, Gradients & Mesh* chapter.)

You can simulate a hand-rendered look by applying the Roughen effect. This will change the smooth, precise edges of an object to jagged or bumpy edges. To roughen your type object, make sure the Fill attribute is not selected (deselect it by clicking in an empty area of the

Appearance panel) so that Roughen will be applied to the whole object. Then click the *fx* button from the Appearance panel and choose Distort & Transform > Roughen. In the Roughen dialog, adjust the Size, Detail, and Points controls. (Weinstein chose Size=0.5, Detail=6.5, and Points=Smooth for his type.)

2 Pasting the type object, creating an opacity mask, pasting the object, and applying Scribble. You can antique your type by making it look chipped or scratched. To do this, select your type object, open the Transparency panel and, from the panel menu, choose Make Opacity Mask from the panel menu. Next, click on the opacity mask thumbnail (the rightmost thumbnail) and make sure Clip and Invert Mask are checked. Lastly, paste the type you copied in the first step (use Paste in Front instead of Paste so this copy will overlay the original you copied).

Changes you make in the opacity mask will affect the transparency of the original type object—black artwork in the mask will punch holes in the original type. With the copy you just pasted still selected, choose Stylize > Scribble from the *fx* button in the Appearance panel. In Scribble Options, choose a pre-made setting from the Settings menu, or customize it using the controls. Weinstein started with the Sharp setting and then changed several values. With Preview enabled, he moved the Path Overlap slider to 0.04" to thin some of the chips in the edges. To make the chips align better with the angles in the type characters, he changed the default 30° Angle to 15°.

3 Editing the type. Once you've finished with the Scribble effect, click the artwork thumbnail (the leftmost thumbnail) in the Transparency panel. If you need to edit the type—to change the text or modify kerning, for example—you'll have to do it in *both* the original type object and in the copy in the opacity mask. For some edits you make to the type—like scaling or rotating—you only need to work with the type object, since the opacity mask will be changed simultaneously with the type object.

Choosing the opacity mask in the Transparency panel

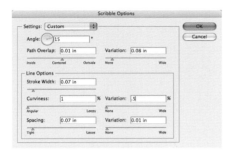

Customizing the options in the Scribble Options dialog

Selecting the artwork mode (instead of the opacity mask mode) in the Transparency panel

Getting your fill (to work)

If the type object you copied for creating an opacity mask already has a colored fill applied (for example, a gradient or another color besides black), don't worry. Continue to make the opacity mask by clicking the opacity mask thumbnail and choosing Edit > Paste in Front. With the pasted type selected, open the Appearance panel, select the Fill attribute and choose the Black swatch. This will prevent a non-black fill from reducing the opacity of the mask.

Type Subtraction

Applying Live Subtract from Shape on Type

Advanced Technique

Overview: *Create several interleaved groups of shapes; create type objects and a shape; subtract the shape from the type using the Pathfinder panel.*

NAGARA / DESIGN ACTION

For a conference on protecting the world's rivers, Innosanto Nagara of Design Action designed a logo that could appear in applications as diverse as posters, report covers, and t-shirts—and stand out against a variety of backgrounds, including a solid black square and a photograph. Illustrator's Pathfinder effect subtracted Nagara's wave shapes, leaving a gap between the logo type that would remain invisible against different backgrounds.

1

Left, the three groups of wave shapes made from one group (top); right, their combination in the final form used in the logo

Rotate by center

When you double-click the Rotate tool, Illustrator automatically sets the rotation centerpoint at the exact center of the selected artwork. This means your copy precisely overlays the original on the Artboard.

1 Creating a wave shape, rotating and copying it, and reflecting and copying it. Nagara designed the logo as two components: the conference title, "Rivers For Life," split into two lines, and the interleaving colored waves that separated them. To re-create Nagara's design, begin by drawing a set of curved blue shapes. Instead of drawing a second set of green waves, select the blue wave shapes you just drew with the Selection tool, and then double-click the Rotate tool. In the Rotate dialog, enter 180° in the Angle field and then click the Copy button. With the copy still selected, change its fill color from blue to green.

With the set of green waves still selected, complete the interleaving of blue and green waves by creating a third set of wave shapes. Use the Reflect tool this time (to access the Reflect tool, click and hold on the Rotate tool icon in the Tools panel, or press the **O** key). In the Reflect dialog, set the reflection axis to Horizontal and click the Copy button. Then change the fill of the wave shapes to blue, producing a blue-to-green-to-blue series of interleaving wave shapes.

2 Creating two type objects, drawing a subtracting shape, then applying the Pathfinder effect. Suggesting the action of waves, Nagara decided to use a flowing wave shape to cut into the top and bottom edges of the logo's lettering. To ensure that the wave shape allows the different backgrounds to appear, you'll need to cut into the lettering with your shapes and not simply paste the shape in front of the type to visually block it.

After typing the two lines of type as separate type objects, Nagara drew a new wave shape with the Pen tool and copied it so he could use it later with the second line of type. He moved the wave shape over the type until it blocked the lettering the way he wanted. Then he selected the type object and the wave shape and, from the Shape Modes section of the Pathfinder panel, held down Option/Alt and clicked the Minus Front icon.

To maintain the separate colors in "FOR" and "LIFE," Nagara selected the first word and used Paste in Front to overlay the wave form above that second line of lettering. Selecting that word and the wave, he held down Option/Alt and clicked Minus Front to cut the wave from the word. He then repeated the sequence for the other word.

3 Modifying the subtracting shape. If you hold Option/Alt when you apply one of the Pathfinder's Shape Modes to artwork, the result is a compound path in which the top object (in Nagara's case, the wave shape that subtracts from the type object below it) remains "live" and editable. You can select and modify the subtracting shape with the Direct Selection tool, or redraw with the Pencil tool if you'd like. This is especially useful when the uneven contours and counters (holes) of a line of lettering require you to tweak the subtracting shape. If you use the same object more than once, as Nagara did, you can tweak each one to make them appear a little different, giving greater spontaneity to the finished artwork.

2

Type with the wave shape that will subtract from the type

The wave placed above the top type object and the resulting cut in the type

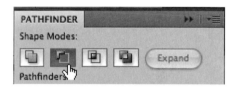

Top shows the wave pasted above word "FOR" and then after then applying Minus Front from the Pathfinder panel; bottom shows these steps repeated for the word "LIFE"

PATHFINDER

Shape Modes:

Expand

Pathfinders

The Pathfinder panel and the Minus Front icon (hold down Option/Alt when you apply a Shape Mode in order for the effect to remain "live" and not be permanently applied)

3

Using the Direct Selection tool to select the subtracting shape to modify its points

Avoiding strokes

When working with a compound shape, remember that selecting the subtracting shape and applying a stroke will not change how much that shape cuts into the object below it. Adding a stroke or increasing its width will affect the bottom object—when that object is type, a stroke will change how the letter characters look.

Jean-Claude Tremblay

When it came time to pair type for his company's name with his newly-designed logo, Jean-Claude Tremblay looked for a typeface that would match the letterforms he had created. He settled on ITC Avant Garde Gothic, Book style, for its echoing roundness, clean simplicity of letterform, and contrast in weight. Since this particular font's **fi** ligature carries a dot that visually closes up and clutters the **f** at display sizes—especially when properly kerned for the entire name—Tremblay chose to create his own ligature for the **fi** combination. First, he spelled out the entire name and converted the type to outlines (⌘-Shift-O/Ctrl-Shift-O). He then used the Group Selection tool (the Direct Selection tool with Option/Alt) to select the dot over each **i,** and clicked Delete. Next,

after setting the Keyboard Increment to .1 pt (in General Preferences), he Group Selected the two **i** objects that followed an **f**, zoomed in close, and used the left arrow key to nudge both **i** objects until each touched the adjacent **f**'s bar. Still using the Direct Selection tool, he carefully selected each letter following the first **p** and used the arrow keys to move the letters closer together until they looked equally "kerned." He filled the letterforms for each word in the company name with the color that corresponded to their initial. Shown above is the grayscale version as it developed, with the color version in the last example of the type. (To learn how Tremblay created the initials, see the "Interlock Objects" lesson in the *Beyond the Basics* chapter.)

Lance Jackson /
San Francisco Chronicle

For the wonderful type "LONG STRANGE TRiP" in this poster for the cross-country "Green Tortoise" bus, illustrator Lance Jackson used a combination of many effects. Starting with the typeface Akzident ExtraBold, Jackson created three text blocks (one for each word) and chose a bright red fill. Combining so many effects creates unique results because of variables such as type size, kerning, and the ordering of effects, so just experiment. You can keep your type live or outline it (⌘-Shift-O/Ctrl-Shift-O). If you outline your text, you must then select it and choose Object > Compound Path > Make so it operates as one unit (see the *Beyond the Basics* chapter for more on compound paths). To emulate Jackson's effects using live effects, keep your type live and select one word at a time; then from the bottom of the Appearance panel click the *fx* icon to choose Distort & Transform > Zig Zag (do this to each of the words separately so you can vary the amount of Zig Zag you're applying). Next, make a green Live Effects offset version of the type so that if you change your type, the offset changes as well. Select all three words and group (⌘-G/Ctrl-G). Click the Add New Fill icon in the Appearance panel and choose

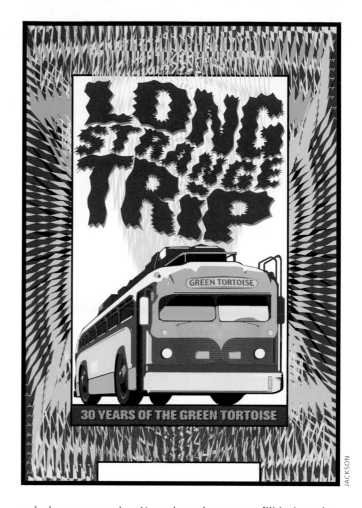

JACKSON

a darker green color. Now drag that green fill below the word "Contents" in the Appearance panel. Next, from *fx* choose Distort & Transform > Transform and enter a small Move for Horizontal and Vertical (enable Preview) to offset the green version. Now select Group in the Appearance panel and start experimenting. Try applying Distort & Transform > Twist. From here, add additional live effects, or remove Twist and start again. See how this differs from Warp > Twist (see the *Live Effects & Graphic Styles* chapter for more about multiple fills and live effects). For the psychedelic border effects, Jackson used techniques similar to those in his gallery in the *Blends, Gradients & Mesh* chapter.

8

Blends, Gradients & Mesh

"W" Blend tool   *"G" Gradient tool*   *"U" Mesh tool*

To create shading and modeling using fills and colors, it's important to learn how to work with blends, gradients and mesh. In the history of Adobe Illustrator, blends, came first, then gradients, then gradient mesh. Each can be both simple and very complex. So, we intermingle them in the lessons and galleries, even though we discuss these features, one at a time, based on the order in which they were added to Illustrator.

BLENDS

Think of blends as a way to "morph" one object's shape and/or color into another. You can create blends between multiple objects, and even gradients or compound paths such as letters. Blends are *live*, which means you can edit the key objects' shape, color, size, location, or rotation, and the resulting *in-between* objects will automatically update. You can also distribute a blend along a custom path (see details later in this chapter).

The simplest way to create a blend is to select the objects you wish to blend and choose Object > Blend > Make (⌘-Option-B/Ctrl-Alt-B). The number of steps you'll have in between each object is based on either the default options for the tool, or the last settings of the Blend Options (discussed in the following section). Adjust settings for a selected blend by selecting the blend, then double-clicking the Blend tool (or via Objects > Blend > Blend Options).

Another way to create blends between individual paths is to *point map* using the Blend tool. In the past, the Blend tool was used to achieve smooth transitions between blended objects. However, now that it's been modified, it's probably best to use it for special morphing or twirling effects. To use the *point map* technique, begin by clicking on an anchor point of one object, and then on an anchor point of another object. Continue clicking on anchor points of any object you want to include in

---

The speed of the blend

To control the speed of the blend, create the blend and set the number of blend steps. This creates the blend spine, which is editable just like any other Illustrator path. Using the Convert Anchor Point tool, pull out control handles from the anchor point at each end of the blend spine. By extending or shortening the control handles along the spine, the speed of the blend is controlled. —*Derek Mah*

Automatically updating colors

Changing a spot or global color definition (see the *Drawing & Coloring* chapter) automatically updates blends and gradients containing that color. Blends between tints of the same spot color (or a spot color and white) update when changes are made to that color, even if the blend isn't "live." (See David Cater's "Mini Cooper" Gallery in the *Advanced Techniques* chapter for a practical application of this technique.) —*ThoughtForm Design*

---

the blend. You can also click anywhere on the path of an object to achieve random blending effects.

When a blend first appears, it's selected and grouped. If you Undo immediately, the blend will be deleted, but your source objects remain selected so you can blend again. To modify a key object before or after making a blend, Direct-Select the key object first, then use any editing tool (including the Pencil, Smooth, and Path Eraser tools) to make your changes.

Blend Options

To specify Blend Options as you blend, use the Blend tool (see the *point map* directions in the previous section) and press the Option/Alt key as you click the second point. The Blend Options dialog will appear, allowing you to change any settings before making the blend. To adjust options on a completed blend, select it and double-click the Blend tool (or Object > Blend > Blend Options). Opening Blend Options without a blend selected sets the default for creating blends *in this work session*—these Options reset each time you restart the program.

- **Specified Steps** specifies the number of steps between each pair of key objects (the limit is 1000). Using fewer steps results in clearly distinguishable objects; a larger number of steps results in an almost airbrushed effect.
- **Specified Distance** places a specified distance between the objects of the blend.
- **Smooth Color** allows Illustrator to automatically calculate the ideal number of steps between key objects in a blend, in order to achieve the smoothest color transition. If objects are the same color, or are gradients or patterns, the calculation will equally distribute the objects within the area of the blend, based on their size.
- **Orientation** determines how the individual blend objects rotate as they follow the path's curves. Align to Page (the default, first icon) prevents objects from rotating as they're distributed along the path's curve (objects stay "upright" as they blend along the curve). Align to Path

The ripening tomatoes on a vine, above, was created using a variety of blends: the smooth color option for the vine, and groups of objects blended into each other with Specified Steps and a custom **S** curve "spine" (see Aaron McGarry's explanation on the Wow! CD).

MCGARRY

(the second icon) allows blend objects to rotate as they follow along the path.

Blends along a path

There are two ways to make blends follow a curved path. The first way is to use the Direct Selection tool to select the *spine* of a blend (the path automatically created by the blend) and then use the Add/Delete Anchor Point tools, or any of the following tools, to curve or edit the path: the Direct Selection, Lasso, Convert Anchor Point, Pencil, Smooth, or even the Path Eraser tool. As you edit the spine of the blend, Illustrator automatically redraws the blend objects to align to the edited spine.

Secondly, you can also replace the spine with a customized path: Select both the customized path and the blend, and choose Object > Blend > Replace Spine. This command moves the blend to its new spine.

You can also blend between pairs of grouped objects. If you're not getting the results you expect, try creating your first set of objects and grouping them (⌘-G/Ctrl-G). Now copy and paste a duplicate set (or Option/Alt and drag to create a copy of your group). Select the two sets of grouped objects and blend choosing Specified Steps as the blend option. Once the objects are blended, you can rotate and scale them, and use the Direct Selection tool to edit the objects or the spine. (To experiment with a pair of grouped blends in this way, find the figures at left on the *Wow! CD* as "AaronMcGarry-blends.ai.")

Reversing, releasing, and expanding blends

Once you've created and selected a blend, you can do any of the following:

- **Reverse** the order of objects on the spine by choosing Object > Blend > Reverse Spine.
- **Release** blends (Object > Blend > Release) removes blends, leaving key objects and spines. ***Hint:*** *Select > Select All releases multiple blends simultaneously.*
- **Expand** a blend to turn it into a group of separate, editable objects. Choose Object > Blend > Expand.

Reverse Front to Back

To reverse the order of a blend with only two key objects, Direct-Select one of the key objects and choose Object > Arrange, or for any blend choose Object > Blend > Reverse Front to Back. You can also reorder the objects by expanding the Blend in the Layers panel and dragging the <Path> to a new location within the Blend.

GRADIENTS

Gradients are color fills that seamlessly transition from one color into another. Adobe has made some great enhancements to gradients, allowing you to work faster and more efficiently. Before Illustrator CS4, all gradient adjustments had to be made within the Gradient panel. Now these adjustments can be made on the artboard, directly on the gradient itself. When you select an object with a gradient and select the Gradient tool, a white bar appears across the gradient on the artboard. This bar is called the Gradient Annotator (if this bar doesn't appear you may need to turn it on by choosing View > Show Gradient Annotator (⌘-Option-G/Ctrl-Alt-G).

To open the Gradient panel, double-click the Gradient tool icon on the Tools panel, or choose Window > Gradient. To apply a gradient to an object: select the object and click on a gradient swatch in the Swatches panel; click on the object with the Gradient tool to fill with the last-used (or default) gradient; or double-click the Gradient tool (to open the Gradient panel), and click on either the Gradient Slider or swatch. You can choose whether your current gradient is Linear or Radial from the Type pop-up.

If you intend to work a great deal with gradients, you may wish to either drag out the Gradient panel and allow it to be a floating panel, or dock it in a separate column from the Swatches panel. You can adjust the Gradient panel's size vertically or horizontally by grabbing and dragging the top, bottom, or side of the panel (your cursor becomes a two-way arrow when you hover on the edge); a special feature of the Gradient panel is that you can make it extra tall and wide and the Gradient Slider itself will increase in size, making it much easier to design complex gradients. (See the "Manipulating windows and panels" section in the *Illustrator Basics* chapter for help with panels and docking.) To start adjusting a gradient, first select the gradient object, then click on the Gradient tool in the Tools panel, which reveals a white Annotator bar across your gradient. As you move your cursor over the Annotator it changes to a Gradient Slider, complete

How long can a gradient be?

Click and drag with the Gradient tool anywhere in your image window; you don't need to stay within the objects themselves.

Adding color to your gradient

- Double-click the color stop on the Gradient Annotator bar, or slider bar in the Gradient panel, and select a color from the Swatches or Color panel.
- Drag a swatch from the Color or Swatches panel to the gradient slider until you see a vertical line indicating where the new color stop will be added.
- If the Fill is a solid color, you can drag color from the Fill icon at the bottom of the Toolbox.
- Hold down the Option/Alt key to drag a copy of a color stop.
- Option/Alt-drag one stop over another to *swap* their colors.
- Click just beneath the Gradient Annotator bar or slider of a gradient where the stops are to add a new stop (a small "+" sign appears next to your cursor when you are in the correct location for adding a new stop).

Making a new gradient

Start by selecting an existing gradient from the Swatches panel similar to the one you wish to create, and then proceed with the instructions shown in this chapter for adjusting and customizing it.

For the flame in his candle illustration, Aaron McGarry created a custom radial gradient

The Gradient panel for the candle flame above; the color stops with adjusted opacities are indicated by the additional rectangle below the stop. The opacity of the second color stop from the left is indicated in the field below the slider.

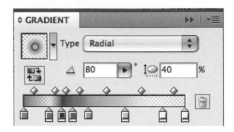

A detail of the candle flame above showing the gradient annotator on the flame with color stops; the flame has an aspect ratio of 40%, an angle of 80° and various opacity settings for each color stop so that the wick is partially visible through portions of the flame

Missing Gradient Annotator?

If you don't see the Gradient Annotator, then try using the toggle View > Show Gradient Annotator (⌘-Option-G/Ctrl-Alt-G). If you apply one gradient to multiple objects, however, the Annotator won't reliably appear.

with color stops (pointers representing colors). Customize gradients by adding and/or adjusting the stops along the lower edge of the Annotator; adjust the midpoint between the color stops by sliding the diamond shapes along the top of the Annotator (these same adjustments can also be made on the Gradient Slider within the Gradient panel).

Using the Gradient Annotator, you can make many precise adjustments on your actual illustration. To reposition the start of a gradient, grab and drag the circular endpoint. To resize a gradient, grab and drag the arrow endpoint. To rotate a gradient, move your cursor slightly beyond the arrow end of the Gradient Annotator, then grab and drag the Rotate icon. When you hover your Gradient tool cursor over a radial gradient, its circumference appears as a dashed line and four circles, and you can resize the circumference by dragging one of the circles. With a radial gradient you can also rotate from the circular endpoint, or from anywhere on the dotted circumference. To change the aspect ratio, grab and drag the solid black circle, or enter a value other than 100% into the Aspect Ration field in the Gradient panel.

When you double-click on a stop on the Gradient Annotator a special panel appears. The two icons on the left side of this panel determine whether this panel resembles the Swatches or Color panel. In addition, this special panel also includes an Opacity field and slider from the pop-up arrow. When you adjust opacity for a stop to be less than 100%, a small rectangle appears hanging from the stop (see stops on slider in the Gradient panel figure at left). The Location field and slider from the pop-up arrow numerically relocates the precise position of a selected stop in relation to the beginning of a gradient. Finally, when the panel is in Color mode, the icon in the upper right accesses a pop-up that allows you to switch between color modes (such as Grayscale, RGB, or CMYK).

You'll notice that the Gradient panel accommodates the features found on the Gradient Annotator plus some additional ones. The Gradient Fill pop-up menu (next to the sample swatch) in the top left corner of the panel allows you to choose from or save to a library of gradients. Below the swatch is the "Reverse Gradient" toggle, which allows you to reverse your gradient (and back again) with a single click. The fields below the Gradient Type pop-up are the numerical controls for angle and aspect ratio. As with the Gradient Annotator, you can double-click a stop to access the special version of the Swatches or Color panel. Or, simply click on a stop to adjust the opacity or location (by entering a number into field, or using the slider from the pop-up arrow). Because you can make the Gradient panel as tall or wide as you wish, using the panel can provide you greater control with for complex gradients than using the Gradient Annotator alone.

You can apply a gradient to multiple selected objects across a unified blend by clicking and dragging with the Gradient tool (see lessons in this chapter for detailed examples of how to use the Gradient tool). To create the illusion of a gradient within a stroke, convert the stroke to a filled object (Object > Path > Outline Stroke). You can use this method to create a "trap" for gradients.

To turn a gradient into a grouped, masked blend, use Object > Expand (see the *Advanced Techniques* chapter for more on masks and masked blends).

The Swatch Libraries menu button at the bottom left of the Swatches panel allows you to access additional pre-made gradients (or by choosing Window > Swatch Libraries > Gradients). Use the Show Swatch Kinds menu button to show only gradient swatches.

One of the simplest ways to save a selected gradient into the Swatches panel is to click the "new swatch" button at the bottom of the Swatches panel; this will prompt you to name your new gradient. You can also drag and drop the gradient preview from the Gradient panel to the Swatches panel. Or, if you've created a new gradient, while in the Gradient panel, you can choose the disk icon from the bottom of the Gradient Fill swatch pop-up menu. **Note:** *Aspect ratio and angle information are not saved with gradient swatches.*

Reset gradients to defaults

After you select an object that has an altered gradient angle (or highlight), new objects you draw will have the same settings. The simplest way to "re-zero" gradient settings such as angles is to have both the Swatches and Gradient panels open, and, with your selected gradient, select a solid color fill from the Swatches panel and then click on the slider in the Gradient panel. For linear gradients, you can type a zero in the Angle field. Or, you can use the Gradient panel to switch between the Radial type and Linear type and then back again to reset a custom angle without removing or relocating color stops.

Gradient or Blend?

Gradients and Blends are often confused due to the similar results both can produce, namely with color transitions. However, they are very different in nature.

- Gradients can only be applied as fills (not as strokes).
- Gradients are either linear (from one side to another), or radial (radiating in circles from a center point to the outside).
- Blends are morphed paths between two end paths and so, in addition to blending colors, can also morph shapes. Blends are not restricted to the directional confines of Gradients.

The amazing photorealistic work with mesh only starts in this chapter—don't miss the additional mesh artwork in the Advanced Techniques chapter (detail of an illustration by Ann Paidrick)

Adding rows and columns

To add new rows and columns to your mesh, click on the mesh object with the Mesh tool (U). To add a new mesh row, click on a column mesh line. To add a new mesh column, click on a row.

Adding color to the mesh

When adding a new mesh point, the color currently selected in the Swatches panel will be applied to the new point. If you want the new mesh point to remain the color currently applied to the mesh object, hold down the Shift key while adding a new point.

Moving rows and columns

When moving a mesh point, both the row and column mesh lines intersecting that point will move with it. To move a row or column mesh line independently, without moving the other, hold the Shift key while you drag a line. If you drag up or down, only the row line moves; if you drag left or right, only the column line moves.

GRADIENT MESH

In this book you'll find many amazing photorealistic images created using gradient mesh. A *mesh object* is an object on which multiple colors can flow in different directions, with smooth transitions between the *mesh points*. You can transform a solid or gradient-filled object into mesh (you can't transform compound paths into mesh). Once transformed, the object will always be a mesh object, so be certain that you work with a copy of the original if it's difficult to re-create.

Transform solid filled objects into gradient mesh objects either by choosing Object > Create Gradient Mesh (so you can specify details on the mesh construction) or by clicking on the object with the Mesh tool.

One way to get a head start in creating a mesh object, is to transform an object filled with a gradient, into a mesh object. To transform a gradient-filled object, select Object > Expand and enable the Gradient Mesh option.

Clicking with the Mesh tool within a mesh object, depending on where you click, allows you to add points, or lines and points, to the mesh. Select individual points, or groups of points, within the mesh using the Direct Selection tool, the Lasso tool, or the Mesh tool in order to move, color, or delete them. For details on working with gradient meshes (including the Warning Tip about printing mesh objects), see Galleries and lessons later in this chapter, as well as the *Advanced Techniques* chapter. **Hint:** *Instead of applying a mesh to a complex path, try to first create the mesh from a simpler path outline, then mask the mesh with the more complex path.*

Get back your (mesh) shape!

When you convert a path to a mesh, it's no longer a path, but a mesh object. To extract an editable path from a mesh, select the mesh object, choose Object > Path > Offset Path, enter 0, and press OK. If there are too many points in your new path, try using Object > Path > Simplify (for more on Simplify see the *Drawing & Coloring* intro). —*Pierre Louveaux*

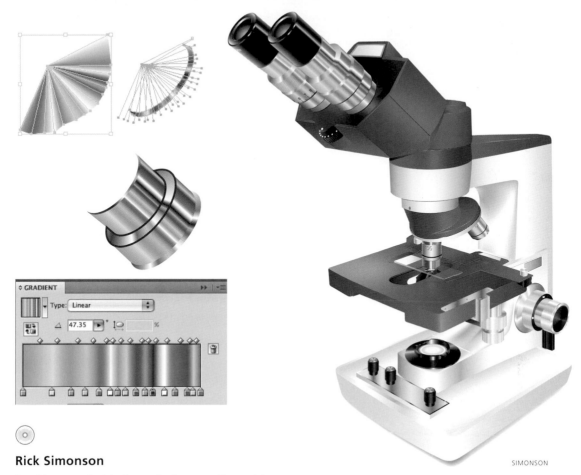

SIMONSON

Rick Simonson

For his remarkable feat of photorealism with this illustration of a microscope, Rick Simonson used blends and gradients to mimic reflections in metal. To make some of the metal sections that reflected multiple colors, he began by drawing with the Line tool. After drawing a line, he selected one end with the Direct Selection tool and left the other anchor point unselected. He dragged on the selected point, adding the Option/Alt key to duplicate the line in the start of a fan shape—the unselected anchor remaining in place. He repeated adding new lines at varying distances from each other, and coloring them, until he had enough lines to equal all the color changes in the reflection. He then selected all the lines and chose the Blend tool with Smooth Color selected in the tool's Options. With the keyboard shortcut ⌘-Option-B/Ctrl-Alt-B, he created a blend object from the lines. Next Simonson drew the object he required for a part of the microscope on top of his newly blended object. With both objects selected, he chose Object > Clipping Mask > Make (⌘-7/Ctrl-7). For other complex reflections, Simonson created gradients with multiple color stops that colored the objects to match up with those made from the blends.

Chapter 8 *Blends, Gradients & Mesh* **243**

Simplest of Mesh

Filling a Shape with a Gradient Mesh

Overview: *Draw paths; select paths and fill with colors; select a shape and click with the Mesh tool; choose a color for the mesh highlight point; copy and paste, and scale and rotate copies to compose the illustration.*

MIYAMOTO

1

Left, the paths drawn for the soybean pod; right, the paths filled with two shades of green

2

Left, the Preview View of a gradient mesh; right, the Outline View of the selected mesh

3

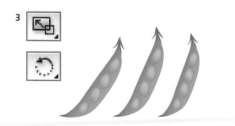

The three pods (original is on the left, and the two scaled and rotated copies are on the right)

For her book for the Japanese market, *Adobe Illustrator CS*, which she co-authored with Yukio Miyamoto, artist Nobuko Miyamoto found that creating a gradient mesh was easier and made a more shapely and editable gradient than creating a radial gradient with the Gradient tool.

1 Drawing and coloring the pod. Miyamoto began by drawing the vine and a soybean pod with its four beans. She filled the pod with a green gradient and then filled the bean shapes with a medium green. Use a color that contrasts with the colors around it for shapes that you'll paint later with a gradient mesh—this ensures that the mesh will not appear to fade into surrounding artwork.

2 Coloring the beans with gradient mesh. To create the gradient mesh for each bean, Miyamoto chose the Mesh tool, selected a light green for the highlight color, and then clicked on the unselected shape. When you click with the Mesh tool, Illustrator will automatically create a highlight point at the spot you clicked inside the shape. With the mesh still selected, you can change the highlight color by selecting another color from the Color or Swatches panel. If you want to move the highlight point, click on it with the Mesh tool and move it.

3 Copying, pasting, scaling, and rotating. Miyamoto completed the illustration by copying and pasting the pod twice, and then scaling and rotating each copy before arranging the three soybean pods and vine.

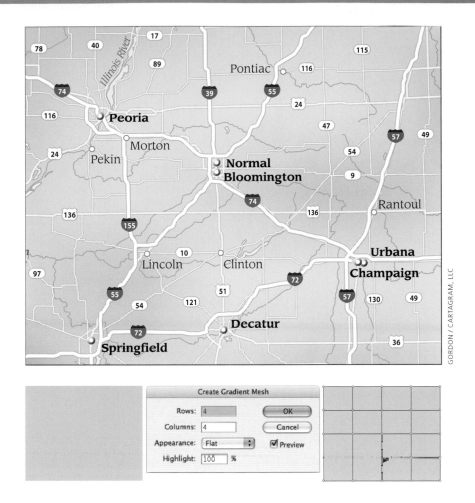

GORDON / CARTAGRAM, LLC

Steven Gordon / Cartagram, LLC

Large areas of solid color can be a necessary but boring fact of life for cartographers. With Illustrator's Mesh tool, however, they needn't stay boring for very long. In this location map, Gordon turned a solid green background into a natural-looking backdrop for his map. To create the background, Gordon first drew a rectangle and filled it with a solid green color. With the rectangle still selected, he chose Object > Create Gradient Mesh. In the Create Gradient Mesh dialog, he entered 4 in the Rows and Columns fields, and left the Appearance menu set on the default setting of Flat. This created a mesh with editable points along the edges and inside the rectangle. Next, Gordon chose the Mesh tool and clicked on several of the points in the selected mesh. For each point inside the rectangle he clicked on, Gordon changed the original green color to a lighter yellow-green using the Color panel. For the mesh points on the edges of the rectangle Gordon clicked on, he changed the color to a darker blue-green.

Contouring Mesh

Converting Gradients to Mesh and Editing

Overview: *Draw objects and fill with linear gradients; expand gradient-filled objects into gradient meshes; use various tools to edit mesh points and colors.*

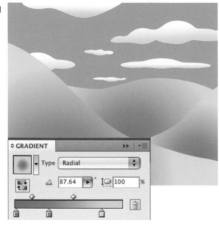

The hills shown filled with radial gradients—although there is some sense of light, it isn't possible to make the radial gradient follow the contours of the hills

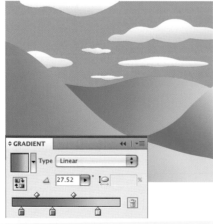

The hills shown filled with linear gradients, which when converted to gradient meshes are easier to edit than radial gradients

For many images, gradients can be useful for showing the gradual change of light to shadow (if you need to learn more about creating and applying gradient fills, first see "Unified Gradients" in this chapter). For these rolling hills, artist Lisa Jackmore expanded linear gradients into gradient mesh objects so she could better control the curves and contours of the color transitions.

1 Drawing objects and then filling them with linear gradients. Begin your illustration by creating closed objects with any of the drawing tools. After drawing each object, fill it with a linear gradient (although in some objects radial gradients might look better before you convert them to mesh objects, linear gradients create mesh objects that are much easier to edit). For each linear gradient, customize the colors, and adjust the angle and length of the gradient transition with the Gradient tool and Gradient Annotator until you can best approximate the desired lighting effect. Jackmore created three hill-shaped objects with the Pen tool, filled them with the same linear gradient, then customized each with the Gradient Annotator.

2 Expanding linear gradients into gradient meshes. To create a more natural lighting of the hills, Jackmore converted the linear gradients into mesh objects so the color transitions could follow the contours of the hills. To accomplish this, select all the gradient-filled objects that you wish to convert and choose Object >Expand. In the Expand dialog, make sure Fill is enabled and specify Expand Gradient to Gradient Mesh. Then click OK. Illustrator converts each linear gradient into a rectangle rotated to the angle matching the linear gradient's angle; each mesh rectangle is masked by the original object (see the *Advanced Techniques* chapter for help with masks).

3 Editing meshes. You can use several tools to edit gradient mesh objects (use the Object >Lock/Unlock All toggle to isolate objects as you work). The Mesh tool combines the functionality of the Direct Selection tool with the ability to add mesh lines. With the Mesh tool, click *exactly on* a mesh anchor point to select or move that point or its direction handles. Or, click *anywhere* within a mesh, except on an anchor point, to add a new mesh point and gridline. You can also use the Add Anchor Point tool (click and hold to choose it from the Pen tool pop-up) to add a point without a gridline. To delete a selected anchor point, press the Delete key; if that point is a mesh point, the gridlines will be deleted as well.

Select points within the mesh using either the Mesh tool or the Lasso tool, using the Direct Selection tool to move multiple selected points. Move individual anchor points and adjust direction handles with the Mesh tool in order to reshape your gradient mesh gridlines. In this way, the color and tonal transitions of the gradient will match the contour of the mesh object. Recolor selected areas of the mesh by selecting points, then choosing a new color.

If you click in the area *between* mesh points with the Eyedropper tool while holding down Option/Alt, you'll add the Fill color to the four nearest mesh points.

By using these tools and editing techniques, Jackmore was able to create hills with color and light variations that suggest the subtlety of natural light upon organic forms.

2

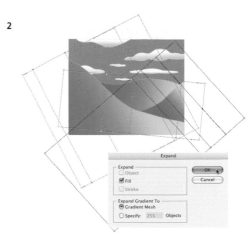

After Expanding the gradients into gradient mesh objects

3

Using the Mesh tool to add a mesh line, then moving the mesh point with the Direct Selection tool

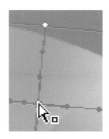

Using the Add Anchor Point tool, using the Lasso to select a point, moving selected point (or points) with the Direct Selection tool

The middle hill, shown after making mesh adjustments

Gleaming Gold

Simulating Shining Metal with Gradients

Overview: *Create the look of gold with gradients; create depth by offsetting paths and adding bevels; create custom-shaped gradients with blends.*

FERSTER (Client: Intuit, Inc., Product: Quickbooks 2005) (Creative Director: Riccardo Spina)

1

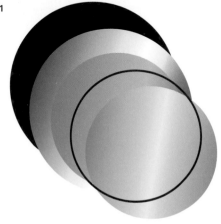

The coin paths pulled apart to show their fills

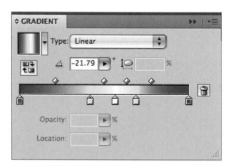

The Gradient panels for the coin edge (top) and the coin center (bottom)

This logo for the popular Intuit QuickBooks line of business accounting software is used for everything from packaging to marketing materials, in print and online. It was originally designed in Illustrator and Photoshop, but the original file size was so large that Gary Ferster was asked to re-create the logo as a smaller file. Ferster's efficiently rebuilt version of the logo, created exclusively in Illustrator, takes up 93% less disk space than the original. To suggest the gleam of gold, Ferster applied gradients or blends depending on which technique was most appropriate for various parts of the illustration.

1 Adding shiny highlights to the coin. Ferster built the coin as a set of concentric circles, each with a different fill. The outer golden band is a large circle filled with a customized linear gradient, and the center is another circle with a similar gradient. The outermost black outline is a circle filled with black, placed just behind and made slightly larger than the outer golden circle.

By default, gradients have one starting and one ending color stop. To create the metallic gleam, Ferster customized the gradients by clicking below the gradient bar to add a color stop, and then applied lighter colors to the middle sliders. The outer circle uses five color stops.

2 Creating the dollar sign. Just as he did for the coin circles, Ferster created depth for the dollar sign by stacking filled paths. He started from the smaller path (the raised surface of the dollar sign). He selected the path, chose Object > Path > Offset Path, entered a positive value to create a larger duplicate (Ferster entered 5 pt), and clicked OK. The new offset path became the base of the dollar sign. With the new outer path selected, he chose the Offset Path command again, but this time entered 2 pt to create the outer border of the dollar sign.

3 Making the gleaming bevels. Ferster created bevels by cutting up copies of the inner and outer paths. He drew lines to bisect the paths at their corners, selected the lines and both dollar sign paths, and then clicked the Divide button in the Pathfinder panel. The Divide button converts all enclosed areas into separate closed paths. Ferster used the Direct Selection tool to delete line remnants but kept all closed bevel paths. He applied no stroke and linear gradients to the bevel paths. Ferster refined the gradient angles and colors with the Gradient panel because he prefers its precision compared to the Gradient tool.

Ferster also applied a radial gradient fill to the clock hub and linear gradient fills to the clock hands. He built the bar chart by applying linear gradient fills to rectangles edited for perspective by dragging points and segments with the Direct Selection tool. The sides of the bars are filled with linear gradients. For the bar tops, Ferster applied linear gradients that used three gradient sliders.

4 Adding shadows and highlight blends to the man. Ferster wanted to add airbrush-like shadows and highlights to the human figure. The shape of this shading was too organic for linear or radial gradients, so Ferster created custom-shaped blends. For each blend, he drew a base path filled with the color of the man's body, and a smaller path filled with either a highlight or shadow color. Ferster selected both paths and then chose Object > Blend > Make to blend the fills.

2

Using Offset Path to create a larger duplicate

3

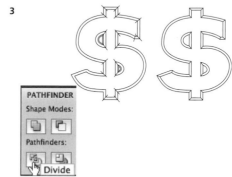

Lines drawn over path intersections (left), then using the Divide button to slice along paths to create closed paths (right) for the bevels

The completed dollar sign and its gradient-filled components (left to right): The original path, offset base path, and filled bevels (pulled apart)

4

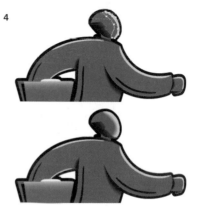

Before (top) and after (bottom) applying a blend to paths forming the highlight on his head

ROSTOMIAN

Zosia Rostomian / The Sharper Image®

Zosia Rostomian made complex combinations of stacked gradient and solid filled objects to render this Sharper Image® product illustration. Some of the many objects she stacked to make the phone are shown in the detail to the right (the bottom-most object is on the left). To apply a gradient to a selected object, she double-clicked on the Gradient tool, opened the Gradient panel (left detail), then selected either Linear or Radial for the Type. She expanded the height and width of the panel to get a better view of the gradient. Rostomian clicked under the Gradient bar to add more stops and moved them to make adjustments.

To change the midpoint between the stops, she moved the diamond-shaped stops on top. With the gradient-filled object still selected, she opened the Swatches panel and clicked the New Swatch icon, named the gradient, and clicked OK. Before she continued drawing, she Deselected All (Select > Deselect, or ⌘-Option-A/Ctrl-Alt-A) and changed the fill to None so the next object she drew would not have the same fill attribute as the previous one. She repeated this process for each object that required a different gradient. She adjusted the length and angle of the gradient fill for some objects by clicking and dragging across them with the Gradient tool.

ROSTOMIAN

Zosia Rostomian / The Sharper Image®

Blending between grouped objects was an ideal technique to use for this Sharper Image® product illustration of a laptop desk. Zosia Rostomian placed a product photo on a layer below her drawing to use as a template. To make the ridged area, she drew the initial ridged line with two 1-pt strokes in a light and dark gray (shown above). She grouped the two strokes (⌘-G/Ctrl-G), selected that group, and Option-clicked/Alt-clicked as she dragged to make a copy. Rostomian selected the first set of grouped strokes, chose the Blend tool, held down the Option/Alt key and clicked on one of the objects in the first group of strokes to open the Blend Options dialog. She set the Spacing to Specified Steps, entered 12, clicked OK, then clicked on one of the objects in the second set

of strokes to make the blend and complete the ridged lines. To draw the dotted pattern, Rostomian first created one dot with layered circles and then grouped them. The first row is made of two separate dot objects. She copied and pasted other dots into two columns (high-lighted in blue, above). To make one row of dots she Direct-selected one dot, then selected the Blend tool. She clicked on another dot, pressed the Option/Alt key, entered the num-ber of Specified Steps needed to fill in the row, clicked OK, then clicked on the other dot. Since Rostomian was working directly over a tem-plate, she knew how many dots were needed in the row and entered that amount in Specified Steps. Each row of dots was blended separately with a different number of Specified Steps.

BEAUREGARD

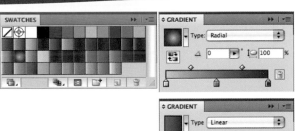

Christiane Beauregard

Christiane Beauregard created subtle color transitions throughout this illustration with linear and radial gradients. Beauregard drew each shape with the Pen tool, and as she progressed, created the gradient to fill the object. She clicked on the Gradient Fill square in the Gradient panel, selected the type of gradient (linear or radial), and added custom colors to the color stops and adjusted the midpoints.

(Two gradients Beauregard used are shown above.) She adjusted the length and direction of the gradient fills within the objects by using the Gradient tool and the Gradient Annotator.

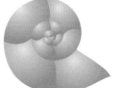

Christiane Beauregard

Using the same coloring technique as in the Fall illustration (opposite page), Christiane Beauregard created the shell (detail right) with separate shapes filled with the same radial gradient. With the shape selected, she clicked and dragged with the Gradient tool from the beginning to the end point of the area and changed the angle of the gradient to give each shape its specific highlight. She created a luminosity in the depths of the sea by varying the opacities in the gradient-filled shapes. Beauregard clicked on the word Opacity in the Control panel and reduced the opacity of the objects. She overlapped some of these shapes to enhance the sea's depth.

Shaping Blends
Controlling Shaped-Blend Transitions

Overview: *Prepare your base objects; create modified copies of the base objects to create simple blends; further modify top objects in blends to create special blending effects; add finishing details.*

1

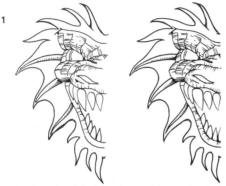

Atteberry's original drawing and the version he made using Live Trace

After drawing base objects, reflecting copies of the base objects that don't cross the center line

A manufacturer of theme park prizes commissioned illustrator Kevan Atteberry to create this logo to be printed on basketballs. After digitizing his initial line drawing, Atteberry colors his images with shape-to-shape blends, which he prefers over the less precise gradients, and more laborious gradient mesh. Creating shaped blends is a necessary skill to master before you can go on to the more complex techniques of masking shaped blends in the *Advanced Techniques* chapter.

1 Creating your base objects and setting options. Since his dragon is symmetrical, Atteberry drew half the face in ink on paper, scanned it in black and white at 600 dpi, and opened it in Illustrator. After applying Object > Live Trace, he chose Object > Expand, then selected and deleted the white objects (see the *Beyond the Basics* chapter for more details about working with Live Trace). Then he dragged out a vertical guide from the ruler to the face's center. Using the Reflect tool he clicked on the guide, then Option-Shift/Alt-Shift-clicked on another point of the guide to reflect a copy on the other side of the guide. With the line drawing complete, he locked the layer containing the line work, and created layers underneath to create his base, solid-colored objects with the Pen and Pencil tools. For objects that didn't cross the center line, Atteberry made one version and reflected a copy to the other side. To prepare for blending, double-click the Blend tool to set Smooth Color for Blend Options.

2 Making simple, smooth blends. For each of his blends, Atteberry begins by selecting the base object and copying. Then using Edit > Paste in Front (⌘-F/Ctrl-F), he modifies the top object and blends between the two. The modifications often include scaling the top copy of the object smaller, shifting the location of the object, or sometimes modifying the outline itself. In the example shown (the dragon's right cheek), Atteberry redrew the top object's path using the Pencil tool. Selecting both objects he chose Object > Blends > Make. Even though the top object contains many more points, the blend is still smooth.

3 Shaping blends for special effects. Sometimes smooth blending isn't the effect that you want. Atteberry achieves many different effects by altering the top object in the blend. Sometimes he wants to create an irregular shape (the dragon's eyebrow shown); other times he wants to create feathering or shaped effects. He uses the Direct Selection and Pencil tools, as well as the Free Transform tool and other transformation tools, to substantially modify the top shape. Although he generally just distorts the object and moves around the positioning of points, he does sometimes add new ones (using the Add Anchor Point Tool or redrawing with the Pencil). After applying the blend, because it's live, Atteberry continues to adjust the positioning and shape of the top object with all the tools at his disposal until he achieves the desired effect.

4 Adding finishing details. After adding the blends to his images, Atteberry adds finishing details with solid-filled, gradient-filled, and stroked small accents. For this image, Atteberry even filled the line work with a gradient. The menacing teeth arc on a layer above the line work.

2

Modifying a copy of the bottom object to create smooth blend transitions

3

Modifying the top object in blends to achieve special blending effects

4

The dragon with copied and modified versions in place, and after creating all of the blends

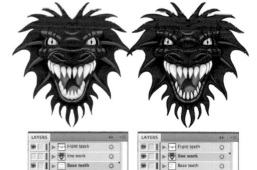

The final dragon with blends and details and then with the line work (still just in black) on a layer above (the front teeth are on the top layer)

Warping Blends

Creating and Warping 3D Blends

Advanced Technique

Overview: *Draw lines with the Pen or Pencil tools; create a blend from the lines then expand the blend; modify with the Warp and Eraser tools; extrude as a 3D object.*

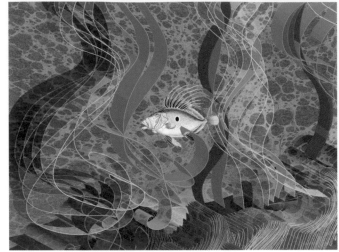

DREES

Drawing the eight lines that will become key objects in the blend

Blend produced by selecting the Object > Blend > Make command

Blend Options dialog with the Spacing menu set to 30 steps

Blend produced after increasing the Spacing menu steps to 30

Transparency & blends

To make part of your blend transparent, select one of the blend's key objects, open the Transparency panel and set its opacity to 0%.

Inspiring her students at the Community College of Baltimore County, artist and instructor Dedree Drees likes to bend the rules of graphic design and Illustrator techniques. In her undersea vignette "The Dory," Drees creates intricate blends that she warps and twirls and then extrudes as 3D coral and seaweed.

1 Creating, then expanding blends. Drees began her complex 3D blend by drawing eight lines using the Pencil tool. Each line served as a key object in the blend, marking a transition of shape, position, and color. When you're drawing the key object lines, be sure to experiment with the shape and color of each line and the distance between the lines. You can draw as many lines as you like, but the resulting blend may be complex and slow your computer when you later apply 3D effects later.

To create the blend, Drees selected the lines and chose Object > Blend > Make. With the blend selected, double-click the Blend tool (or use Object > Blend > Blend Options) to open the Blend Options dialog. From the dialog's Spacing menu, select Specified Steps and key in a value to control the speed or smoothness of the blend. Drees used 30 steps for her blend. When you're satisfied with the look of the blend, select Object > Blend > Expand to expand the blend to a group of lines.

2 Using the Warp, Twirl, and Eraser tools. With the blend expanded, Drees turned to the Warp tool to reshape the expanded blend. Double-click the tool to display the Warp Tool Options and then set the Width and Height to 100 pt and Intensity to 20%. Now click inside or outside the blend and drag with your mouse or stylus. Where you click inside or outside of the blend will govern how much of the object will morph as you drag the Warp tool.

Like Drees, you can sculpt your blend further by using the Twirl tool (click and hold down the Warp tool icon in the Tools panel to display its companion tools) to create wave crests and tight curves. To begin, double-click the Twirl tool to access the Twirl Tool Options dialog. Make sure you set a low number for Intensity (Drees used 20%) and for the Twirl Rate (a positive number twirls counterclockwise while the a negative number twirls clockwise). Try the companion tools to Warp and Twirl to see what effect they have on your blend; the Wrinkle tool, for example, creases and crinkles a blend's smooth lines.

Drees finished fine-tuning her blend by using the Eraser tool on the edges. You can modulate the shape and size of the Eraser tool by double-clicking the Eraser tool icon and resetting some of the default values.

3 Extruding the blend. Before applying the 3D effect, you'll need to simplify your blend by reducing the number of points your computer has to process. To do this, select Object > Path > Simplify. Now extrude the blend by opening the Appearance panel and clicking on the *fx* icon at the bottom of the panel. From the pop-up menu, select 3D > Extrude & Bevel. Enable the Preview checkbox in the 3D Extrude & Bevel Options dialog so you can see how the default settings, and any changes you make to them, affect the look of your blend.

To finish the illustration, Drees saved the blend as a Photoshop file (File > Export > Photoshop), which she opened in Photoshop and layered with other elements. (See the gallery in the *Live 3D Effects* chapter for more about Drees' techniques with blends.)

2

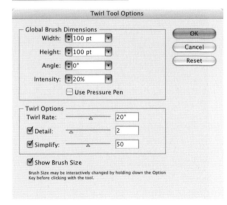

The Warp tool palette above and the Twirl Tool Options dialog below

The blend after being expanded and then modified with the Twirl and Eraser tools

3
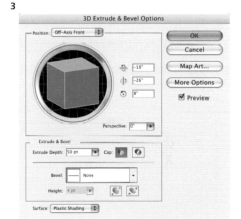

The 3D Extrude & Bevel Options dialog above and the finished 3D object below

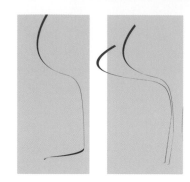

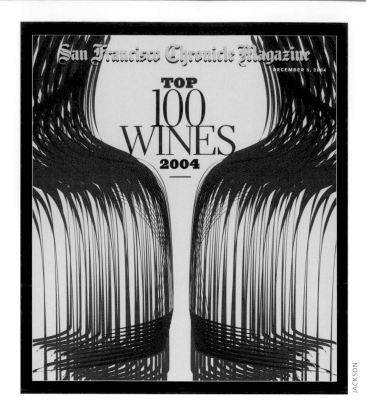

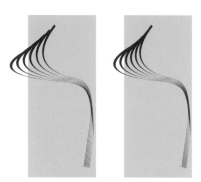

JACKSON

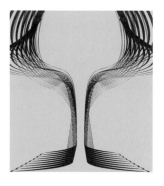

Lance Jackson / *San Francisco Chronicle Magazine*

For this *San Francisco Chronicle Magazine* cover, staff illustrator Lance Jackson made artistic use of blended brush strokes. Jackson customized a calligraphic brush and chose the Brush tool. Then with a pressure-sensitive tablet, he drew a simple, elegant, gestural silhouette evoking a wine goblet. Using a variety of tools, Jackson modified a copy of this silhouette. Selecting the original and modified strokes, he chose Object > Blend > Make (although you can blend live brush strokes, Jackson prefers to expand them first by using Object > Expand). While still selecting the blend he double-clicked the Blend tool to access Blend Options, where he adjusted the number of Specified Steps. Next Jackson expanded the blend using Object > Blend > Expand (the expanded blend is automatically grouped). He then adjusted the position and shape of each blend object, and recolored the grouping. By copying these expanded groups, Jackson created new silhouettes, modifying colors and strokes. He created one side of the glass and used the Reflect tool to create the other silhouette by reflecting along the Vertical axis.

GORSKA

Caryl Gorska

Gradient fills with transparencies colorize this pencil sketch based on Les Usines by Fernand Léger. Caryl Gorska placed the black and white pencil sketch on a bottom layer and selected Filter > Colors > Adjust Colors to give the sketch an overall ocher hue (shown above). On a layer above the sketch, Gorska drew the geometric shapes with the Pen tool. She filled the shapes with a variety of linear and radial gradients that shared the same five colors Gorska designated in the Swatches panel. With the Gradient panel open, Gorska dragged the colors from the Swatches panel to the gradient sliders and adjusted the stops. She applied the individual gradients to the shapes with the Gradient tool. Gorska adjusted the opacity ranging from 30% to 70% in the Transparency panel where she wanted the texture to show through the gradient. To further darken some areas, she applied the blending mode of Multiply. The detailed image in the upper left shows the variety of gradients in the drawing without the texture of the pencil sketch underneath. For more about Transparency and Blending modes see the *Transparency* chapter.

Unified Gradients

Controlling Fills with the Gradient Annotator

Overview: *Fill objects with gradients; use the Gradient tool with the Gradient Annotator to adjust fill length and angle; unify fills across multiple objects with the Gradient tool and Gradient panel.*

JOLY

Working with the Gradient panel, Gradient tool, and Gradient Annotator

2

A single click with the Gradient tool on a selected object fills the object with either the default or last-used gradient swatch, and displays the Gradient Annotator, if selected in the View menu (be sure you don't click and drag when applying for the first time—you can click-drag to adjust the gradient later)

Using the Gradient Annotator to shorten the length of the gradient and to rotate the angle when the Rotate icon appeared

With the advent of the Gradient Annotator in conjunction with the Gradient tool, you can apply and customize gradients in most instances without needing to keep the Gradient panel open. In this illustration, Dave Joly only needed the Gradient panel to switch between Linear and Radial gradients, and to work with creating unified gradients. To control the colors, length, and angle of gradients for individual objects, Joly adjusted each gradient with the Gradient Annotator. He unified gradients across multiple objects using the Gradient tool and Gradient Panel.

1 Applying gradients. To apply a gradient to a single object, such as the fish's body, Joly first made sure that the Gradient Annotator toggle was visible (if View > Show Gradient Annotator is available, choose it). Next he selected an object and the Gradient tool, and then clicked once on the object to fill it with either the document's default gradient (for the first object) or with the last gradient used in the document.

2 Editing single objects with the Gradient Annotator. Joly was able to edit a gradient almost exclusively using the Gradient Annotator. With the Annotator, he could modify the gradient length, angle, and colors on the object itself. He only needed to turn to the Gradient panel to choose a different existing gradient swatch, switch the current gradient between linear and radial gradient in Type, or reverse the gradient. Joly began his edits by moving his cursor just beyond the arrow endpoint of the Gradient Annotator. When his cursor turned into the Rotate icon, he dragged to interactively set the angle he wanted the gradient to take. With his cursor directly on top of the arrow end, he click-dragged to lengthen or shorten the gradient, and he dragged on the large circle at the other end to move the whole gradient to another position over the object. To adjust the colors, Joly double-clicked on a color stop along the Annotator, which gave him immediate access to proxies for both the Swatches and the Color panels, and a subset of the Gradient panel, as well. After choosing a suitable color, he dragged the stops on the Annotator to position the color blends more precisely, and on the gradient sliders to adjust their blend.

3 **Unifying gradients across multiple objects.** Unifying gradients across multiple objects is a bit trickier with the Gradient Annotator involved. Joly first created the gradient swatch he would need—for the tail fins, for example. Next he selected all the objects and clicked on the swatch in the Swatches panel to apply it. This automatically created a new Gradient Annotator for every object, but Joly wanted to unify the gradients under just *one* Annotator. Still using the Gradient tool with the Gradient Annotator visible, Joly dragged across all the objects. This now appeared to unify the multiple gradients under one Annotator, but it's then only possible to change the length or position of the unifying gradient. Instead, while adjusting one gradient that had been unified across multiple objects, Joly discovered the Gradient Annotator wasn't providing reliable feedback or controls. Therefore, when working with one unified gradient applied to multiple objects, instead of relying on the Gradient Annotator, it was easiest to ignore or hide the Annotator (Window > Hide Gradient Annotator). Joly simply used a combination of the Gradient tool (to make length and angle adjustments to the unified gradient interactively) and the Gradient panel itself (for numeric precision, adjustments to color stops, and opacity).

Changing the gradient colors by double-clicking on the Gradient Annotator Color Stops to pop up both the Color and Swatch panel proxies

3

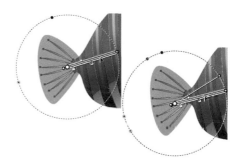

After first selecting all objects and applying a gradient tool to them, but before unifying them

Unified gradients sometimes appear to retain the function of the Gradient Annotator, but if you attempt to edit angles or colors with the Gradient Annotator, you'll discover you aren't actually editing a single gradient

By using only the Gradient panel and/or the Gradient tool to edit unified gradients, you ensure that all changes will be made in unison

Moonlighting

Using Transparency for Glows & Highlights

Advanced Technique

Overview: *Create a Radial gradient with transparency for a circular object; use the Blend tool with a duplicate object to create a circular or oval blend with transparency; create a glow or highlight for a non-circular object.*

1

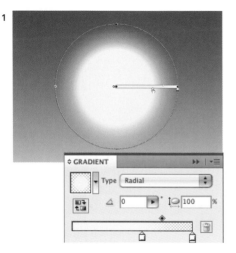

Using the Gradient tool with either the Gradient Annotator (top) or Gradient panel (bottom) to create a gradient with transparency

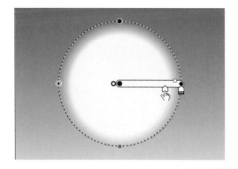

Drag the color stop for the inner object toward the transparent stop to make the object larger; drag the diamond to alter the size of the glow

Because the glowing moon is circular in Annie Gusman Joly's "Solo-Flight" illustration about growing up an identical twin, it could be created by using either a radial gradient or a shaped blend. The key to making a gradient or blend work against any background is to use transparency for the edge of the object that touches the background.

1 **Creating a glow from a Radial gradient.** With the object selected, click on it once with the Gradient tool to fill with the last-used or default gradient, and, if necessary, change the type in the Gradient panel to Radial. Either in the Gradient panel or with the aid of the Gradient Annotator, double-click on each color stop and choose the same color for them. Reduce the Opacity for the stop that represents the outer edge to 0%; drag the opposite color stop inward to make the solid part of the object bigger and more solid, and adjust the Gradient slider between them (the diamond shape on the top of the gradient bar) to create a larger or smaller amount of feather (or "glow").

2 Creating a glow for a circular object from an object blend. With a pale yellow Fill color, choose a stroke of None, and draw a circle (Shift-drag with the Ellipse tool). With Smart Guides on (View menu), move your cursor over the circle until you see the word "center," hold down Option/Alt, and Shift-drag out a new, smaller circle. Set the Opacity of the larger circle to 0%. Select both circles and choose Object > Blend > Make (⌘-Option-B/Ctrl-Alt-B); then double-click the Blend tool in the toolbox to adjust the steps. For this example, somewhere between 20 and 30 steps makes a very glowing moon.

3 Shaping a glow with a blend made from non-circular objects. When you don't have a circle or oval path, only a blend can "shape" the glow evenly around the object. So that the glowing object can be placed over any background, we'll continue to create the glow with transparency. Create your first object—here, a crescent moon filled with pale yellow and no stroke. Many asymmetrical shapes don't scale easily relative to the original's boundaries, so with your object selected, choose Object > Path > Offset Path. Enable Preview and use a negative number for a smaller object. Select the larger object and, in the Transparency panel, set the Opacity to 0%. Now select both paths and choose Object > Blend > Make. If you haven't already created a blend with the Specified Steps or Specified Distance Spacing option in your current working session, Illustrator might use Smooth Color. Smooth Color doesn't create a glow, but rings the inner crescent moon with a lighter color. To get the glow, double-click on the Blend tool to open the dialog and choose Specified Steps for the Spacing option. Around 25 steps should create a decent glow. If necessary, adjust the offset, miter, and path edges until the blend is smooth and glowing.

This shaped-blend method can also be used for making any shape or size of highlight for any object. By creating the highlight as a separate object, you gain the advantage of being able to change the object's color later without having to reconstruct the object and the blend.

2

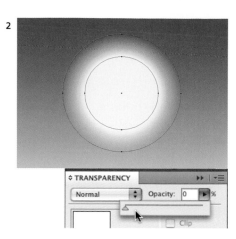

Creating a blend between two circles with one set to 0% Opacity.

3

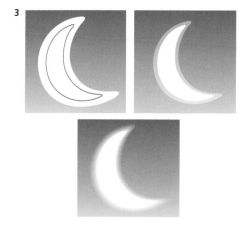

Creating the second object with Offset Path (top left) and using Object > Blend > Make; the default Smooth Color doesn't blend (top right), but switching to Specified Steps creates the glow

Creating a highlight using a shaped blend with one opaque and one transparent object

Creating Depth
Gradients Add Dimension in Space

Advanced Technique

Overview: *Create paths with solid colors for basic shaping; substitute shaped and transparent gradients for solid fills to add realism; add live effects to further blend gradients for added depth.*

1

Paths ready to be filled with solid color

Paths filled with solid color, using a range of values for each hue that a gradient would later express

2

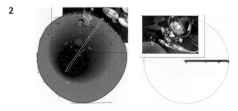

Creating objects that extend beyond the picture frame to hold a radial gradient, or even moving the gradient itself beyond the boundaries for subtle realism

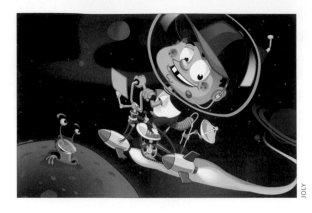

Dave Joly creates illustrations for both printed pieces and animation. When he created "Biker Kid in Space," he made extensive use of Illustrator's gradient capabilities, such as elliptical gradients (with an aspect ratio of less than 100%), or full circle; and transparency, for greater realism and more depth than a flat illustration can convey. He also added Gaussian Blur and Outer Glow effects to some of his gradient-filled objects to further enhance the illusion of deep space.

1 Establishing color for all the objects. After sketching on paper, Joly began his artwork in Illustrator with a line drawing of his main subject. He organized the elements by placing all the paths for the boy's hat, for instance, on one layer, and then filled the paths with solid colors. He prepared for the gradient fills in advance by filling the paths with several closely-related colors, the better to see if the overall lighting and illusion of depth was working, and to establish the range of values that the gradients would need to encompass for the different objects.

2 Creating gradients for light and depth. Once Joly had drawn the background and subject paths, and established general color and tonal values, he began to construct the gradients that would blend the colors smoothly. When creating the gradients, Joly found it helpful to see the "big" picture—the planets and space itself that extended beyond the picture frame. He mocked up the entire planet, seen in the foreground, before applying a radial gradient to shape the sphere. For deep space, one radial gradient was centered completely off the page. In this way, subtle gradations created a believably smooth transition between light and shadow, modeling his objects realistically.

For the nebula swirling in the background, Joly used Illustrator's ability to alter the aspect ratio of a radial gradient to make it elliptical. This helped color the swirling gases, bending their appearance without creating another planet-like shape. With the Gradient tool selected (G), he applied the Radial gradient to the nebula, grabbed the solid black circle at the top of the Radial gradient, and pulled it down to form an oval. He dragged on the circle with a black dot in the center to size the gradient, and used the arrow endpoint of the Gradient Annotator to rotate the angle of the gradient. He also used the Gradient Annotator to interactively position the color stops.

Joly made extensive use of transparency in his gradients, notably to blend the rocket flares and create the illusion of their trails disappearing into space, and for the shadows and highlights in the space kid's shirt and helmet. He used the same color for each stop, but reduced the opacity for one stop to nothing (0). He then moved the gradient slider (the diamond above the gradient bar) to control how abruptly the gradient switched from fully opaque to fully transparent.

3 **Using live effects for the final touches.** Although the gradients themselves provided most of the form and depth in his objects, Joly clicked the *fx* icon in the Appearance panel to add live effects to some of them in order to further enhance lighting and a sense of the objects receding into space (see the *Live Effects & Graphic Styles* chapter for details about live effects). Joly added a Gaussian Blur effect to several background elements, as well as to the highlights on the helmet, to add depth and to blend the helmet highlight more completely. Joly added a Glow effect around the planet, increasing the light in the radial gradient, bringing it further into the foreground.

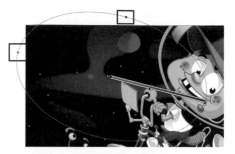

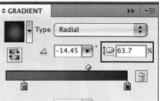

Transforming the aspect ratio of the gradient from circular to elliptical, and using another anchor to size the gradient

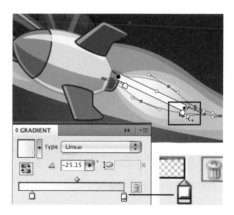

Adding transparency to gradients, indicated on the Gradient Annotator or panel by a hollow rectangle added to the bottom of the color stop

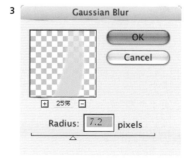

Adding a Gaussian Blur effect to a gradient that uses transparency for shaping, thus increasing the illusion of an object receding into space

Rich Floyd

To symbolize a paintball in a logo, illustrator Rich Floyd coupled a color and grayscale gradient. Floyd began by drawing a paintball with the Ellipse tool. To accentuate the roundness of the paintball, he opened the Gradient panel and selected the Radial Gradient from the Gradient Fill menu. Next, he double-clicked on the gradient slider's default black gradient stop and chose a green swatch from the pop-up Swatches menu. To change the position and intensity of the white highlight in the gradient, Floyd clicked the Gradient tool icon to show the Gradient Annotator. He grabbed the circular end of the Annotator and dragged it up and slightly to the right. He then repositioned the white and green color stops, and adjusted the rate of gradation between the two colors, using the Gradient Slider diamond. To add a darker shadow to the paintball, Floyd opened the Appearance panel and chose Add New Fill from the panel menu. Next, he chose a black-to-white radial gradient from the Fill's pop up Swatches menu. After adjusting the gradient with the Gradient Annotator, Floyd returned to the Appearance panel, opened the Fill attribute and clicked on Opacity. From the pop-up Transparency menu, he changed the object's Blending Mode from the default Normal to Multiply so that the black and grays of the gradient darkened the green gradient of the fill below.

LIVINGSTON

Randy Livingston

When a new promotional T-shirt was needed for the Fellowship of Christian Athletes' Motocross team, Randy Livingston wanted to develop a design that would work when printed on any color fabric. A transparent gradient, allowing "tire tread marks" to fade in and out, as if blurred by speed, proved to be the solution. He first created the pattern of dots by duplicating half a row, and then reflecting the group to the opposite side. He chose neutral white,

and then, with the entire pattern selected, dragged the Gradient tool (G) at a slight angle across the pattern to create a unified gradient (see the "Unified Gradients" lesson earlier in this chapter for help with this technique). He created three color stops, each filled with the same White, but set the first and last stop to 0% Opacity. He set the middle stop to 11% Opacity. Now, no matter what color fabric the design was printed on, the pattern would appear to have been printed in the same color.

Molding Mesh

Forming Bottles Using Gradient Mesh

Advanced Technique

Overview: *Create a basic rectangle; add mesh lines; use the Scale tool to move points in tandem; use the Direct Selection tool to edit paths; color the mesh; add finishing details.*

MIYAMOTO

Making a basic rectangle, adding mesh points where the shape will be contoured, and using the Scale tool to move groups of points inward

Using the Direct Selection tool to round curves, and adding new grid lines by clicking with the Gradient Mesh tool

Yukio Miyamoto is one of the world's experts in creating objects using the Gradient Mesh tool. This wonderful collection of bottles was created for the book and CD that he and his wife Nobuko Miyamoto write and produce; published in Japan, the *Adobe Illustrator CS* book is an amazing compendium of Illustrator techniques.

1 **Creating mesh from rectangles.** To create his complex mesh objects, Miyamoto begins with a colored rectangle. Then using the Gradient Mesh tool, he clicks on the rectangle to create basic horizontal mesh lines where he intends to modify the exterior shape of the object.

To narrow the bottle neck, Miyamoto then used the Direct Selection tool to select the anchor points at the top of the bottle. With these points selected he switched to the Scale tool. By default the Scale tool is centered on the object, so he grabbed one of the selected points and holding the Shift key, dragged toward the center of the bottle, narrowing the neck symmetrically. He also selected the bottom two points and dragged the points inward. (For another variation of this bottle illustration, see Miyamoto's gallery in the *Advanced Techniques* chapter.)

2 **Shaping mesh objects.** To continue to transform your rectangle into a rounded bottle, you'll next modify the corner points along the edge into curves. Using the Convert Anchor Point tool (hidden under the Pen tool) and the Direct Selection tool, select anchor points, smooth

anchor points, and modify the corners to rounded curves. Miyamoto smoothed curves at the bottom of the bottle, holding Shift to constrain the path curves.

With the new shape contour established, Miyamoto used the Gradient Mesh tool to click within the bottle to establish vertical mesh lines, aligned with the new curve at the bottom of the bottle.

3 Modifying the mesh lines to create distortion, shadows, and highlights. Light reflects and refracts on glass bottles. Once the basic inner and outer topography of the bottle is in place, Miyamoto uses the Direct Selection tool to modify the mesh lines within the bottle to mimic the affects of light. Using the Direct Selection tool, select points and groups of points to adjust their position. Click on anchor points to activate their direction handles so you can modify the length and angle of the curves.

Once your mesh lines are in place, you can select individual or groups of points, or click in areas between points and adjust colors using the Color panel sliders. You can also click on a color swatch in the Swatches panel, or pick up colors from another object by clicking in on the color you want with the Eyedropper tool. Miyamoto used a photographic reference to help him decide where to place lights and darks.

4 Creating finishing details. Although Gradient Mesh objects are an astoundingly flexible and powerful drawing tool, sometimes it's necessary to create details in layers above the mesh object. To make selections and isolated viewings of the various objects easier, create new layers for your detail objects above your mesh objects. For the blue bottle (in a layer above the mesh), Miyamoto created a few punctuations of color and light using objects drawn with the Pen tool, and filled with solid colors or custom gradients. For his beer bottle, Miyamoto created type shapes, for the small milk bottle he added additional rim colors, and for the green wine bottle he added more reflections and a raised inner bottom.

3

Coloring the bottle

The finished blue bottle mesh in Outline, hidden, and Preview, with details on a layer above

4

The final bottles shown with the mesh layer in Outline mode, and the finishing details (mostly gradient-filled objects) in Preview mode

Yukio Miyamoto

Yukio Miyamoto created the numerous complex linear and radial gradients throughout this illustration with ease using the Gradient tool and the Gradient Annotator. Miyamoto drew each path with the Pen tool and filled it either with the default linear or radial gradient from the Swatches panel. He selected the Gradient tool to reveal the Gradient Annotator, which appeared on top of the object. Miyamoto double-clicked on the color stop of the Gradient Annotator to show the options. He clicked on the Swatches icon and chose a custom color from the Swatches panel that he had previously created to color the stop. Miyamoto clicked along the Gradient Annotator to add more color stops. He continued to add color stops and color them until he was satisfied with the results. Miyamoto click-dragged the color stops and moved them into the exact locations to achieve the desired gradient effect. He grabbed the arrow endpoint and stretched the Gradient Annotator to change the length of the gradient. Miyamoto moved the endpoint side to side and adjusted the angle of the gradient. He made additional angular adjustments with the circular endpoint and clicked the center point, then moved it to various positions within the gradient-filled object. The entire illustration is made of gradient-filled objects with two very small exceptions; there is one blended object (the pen tip) and one mesh object

Caran d'Ache 1010 I LIMITED EDITION

MIYAMOTO

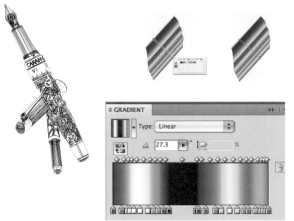

(grip area, just beneath the tip). The Gradient Annotator enabled Miyamoto to have exceptional control of the gradient fills to achieve exacting realism.

MIYAMOTO

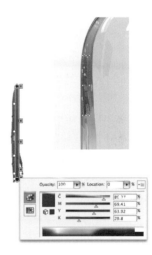

Yukio Miyamoto

Using similar techniques as in the Fountain Pen illustration (opposite page), Yukio Miyamoto made additional adjustments to his radial and linear gradients using the Gradient Annotator. Miyamoto double-clicked a color stop on the Gradient Annotator and selected the color palette icon to create colors not originally in his custom Swatches panel. He adjusted the CMYK sliders until he was satisfied with the new color. In some of the gradient filled objects, Miyamoto applied transparency effects. He double clicked on a color stop, then clicked on

the Opacity slider in the Annotator options panel and moved the slider to the desired position. He also applied a Feather effect to some of the gradient filled objects (Effect > Feather). Miyamoto does not save the gradient fills to the Swatches panel, and each gradient is specific to its individual shape and location in the drawing. The Gradient Annotator is essential to his method of drawing. With the Gradient Annotator, Miyamoto easily made numerous dynamic changes within the countless gradients that make up this illustration.

9

Transparency

You're introducing transparency whenever you apply an opacity percentage, a blending mode, an opacity mask from the Transparency or Control panel; and whenever you apply certain kinds of effects (such as shadows, feathers, and glows) or styles that include those features. It's easy to apply transparent effects to your artwork without actually understanding what takes place "under the hood." However, some knowledge about how transparency works will help you later when you print or export art that uses transparency.

If the concepts of *Appearances* or *Targeting* are new to you, it's very important that you start first with the "Appearances" section of the *Layers & Appearances* chapter. By the time you've arrived here at the *Transparency* chapter, the assumption is that you have a basic knowledge of fills, strokes, and layers in particular. If you find you become confused while reading this chapter, it may help to first revisit the *Drawing & Coloring* and *Layers & Appearances* chapters.

BASIC TRANSPARENCY

Although the Artboard may look white, Illustrator treats it as transparent. To visually distinguish the transparent areas from the non-transparent ones, choose View > Show Transparency Grid. Change the size and colors of the transparency grid in the File > Document Setup dialog. You can enable Simulate Colored Paper if you'll be printing on a colored stock (click on the top swatch next to Grid Size to open the color picker and select a "paper" color). Both Transparency Grid and paper color are non-printing attributes that are only visible in on-screen preview once you click OK to exit the dialog.

The term *transparency* refers to any Blending Mode other than Normal and to any opacity setting that is less than 100%. Opacity masks or effects, such as Feather or Drop Shadow, use these settings as well. As a result, when you apply opacity masks or effects, you're using Illustrator's transparency features.

It can be tricky to print or export correctly when working with transparency. To make this easier, Illustrator has a few tools to help you control how transparency will translate when you print or export.

Opacity and Blending modes

To apply transparency, select or target an object, layer, or group in the Layers panel, then choose a Blending Mode or reduce the Opacity slider in the Transparency panel. You can also reveal Transparency panel controls for a selected object by clicking Opacity in the Appearance or Control panels. An object or group is completely opaque when its opacity is set to 100%. It is completely seethrough, or invisible, when its opacity is 0%.

Blending modes control how the colors of objects, groups, or layers interact with one another. Blending modes will yield different results in RGB and CMYK. As in Photoshop, the blending modes show no effect when they're over the *transparent* Artboard. To see the effect of blending modes, you need to add a color-filled or white-filled element behind your transparent object or group.

OPACITY MASKS

With an opacity mask, you can use the dark and light areas of one object (the mask) to mark transparent areas of other objects. Black areas of the mask will create transparent areas in the artwork it masks, white areas of the mask leave corresponding areas of the artwork opaque and visible, and gray values create a range of transparency. (This works exactly like Photoshop *layer masks*.)

To create an opacity mask, position one object or group you want to use as the mask in front of the artwork you want to mask. Select both the artwork and the masking object. (To mask a layer, first target the layer in the Layers panel.) Finally, choose Make Opacity Mask from the Transparency panel menu. The topmost object or group automatically becomes the opacity mask.

An opacity mask partially hides circles and a pattern grouped in front of a red rectangle; the group's opacity mask uses a rectangle filled with a white-to-black radial gradient

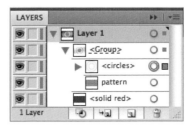

Objects being masked by an opacity mask are indicated by a dashed line in the Layers panel

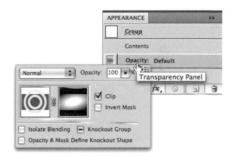

While you can open the Transparency panel by choosing Window > Transparency, you can also display the Transparency panel by clicking the underlined word Opacity for a selected object in the Appearance or Control panel

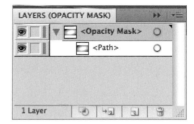

When you click the opacity mask thumbnail in the Transparency panel, the Layers panel displays only the objects within the opacity mask; this is indicated by the Layers panel tab name. It's a good idea to keep the Layers, Transparency, and Appearance panels open when editing opacity masks

- **Disable**: Shift-click the mask thumbnail to turn it off. A red **X** will appear over the preview.
- **Enable**: Shift-click to reapply the mask.
- **Mask View**: Option-click/Alt-click the mask thumbnail to toggle between viewing and editing the masking objects on the Artboard, or the mask grayscale values.
- **Release Opacity Mask (panel menu**: releases the masking effect.
- **Toggle between working on artwork or opacity mask**: click the appropriate icon to control what you are editing.
- **Link or unlink the opacity mask to artwork**: click between the mask and artwork to toggle the link/unlink option.

Why can't I draw now?

You may be in mask-editing (isolation) mode and not know it if:

- You draw an object, deselect it, and it seems to disappear;
- You fill an object with a color, but the color doesn't display.

When in mask-editing mode, the file title and Layers panel tab will show <Opacity Mask>. To exit mask-editing mode, click on the artwork thumbnail in the Transparency panel.

You may want to start with an empty mask and draw into it—in effect, painting your objects into visibility. To create an empty mask, start by targeting a single object, group, or layer. Since the default behavior of new opacity masks is clipping (with a black background), you'll need to turn off the "New Opacity Masks Are Clipping" option in the Transparency panel menu. If you don't do this, and your targeted artwork disappears when you first create the empty mask, simply enable the Clip checkbox in the Transparency panel. This creates an empty mask and puts you in mask-editing mode; the Layers panel changes to show the <Opacity Mask>. Next, click in the right thumbnail area. Use your drawing and editing tools to create your mask. (For instance, if you create an object filled with a gradient, you'll see your artwork through the dark areas of the gradient.) While the <Opacity Mask> thumbnail is selected, you won't be able to select or edit anything else in your document because Illustrator puts you into an isolated mask-editing mode. To exit this mask-editing mode, you must click the artwork thumbnail in the Transparency panel (the artwork thumbnail is on the left; the opacity mask is on the right).

A few hints can help you with opacity masks. First, opacity masks are converted to grayscale, behind the scenes, when a mask is created (even though the opacity mask thumbnail still appears in color). The gray values between white and black simply determine how opaque or transparent the masked object is—light areas of the mask will be more opaque and dark areas will be more transparent. In addition, if you select Invert Mask, you'll reverse the effect of dark and light values on the opacity—dark areas of the mask will be more opaque and light areas will be more transparent. To identify which elements have been masked by an opacity mask, look for the dashed underline in the Layers panel.

The link icon in the Transparency panel indicates that the position of the opacity mask stays associated with the position of the object, group, or layer it is masking. Unlinking allows you to move the artwork without moving the mask. The content of the mask can be selected and edited just like any other object. You can transform or apply a blending mode and/or an opacity percentage to each individual object within the mask.

Option-click/Alt-click on an opacity mask thumbnail in the Transparency panel to hide the document's contents and display only the masking element in its grayscale values. Shift-click the opacity mask thumbnail to disable the opacity mask.

For more on opacity masks, see the "Opacity Masks 101" and "Opacity Collage" lessons in this chapter, and lessons and galleries in the *Advanced Techniques* chapter.

Knockout controls

Choose Show Options from the Transparency panel pop-up menu to display the checkboxes that control how transparency is applied to groups and multiple objects.

If you enable Isolate Blending for a selected group, then the transparency settings of the objects inside the group only affect how those objects interact with each other, and transparency isn't applied to objects underneath the group.

With a group or layer targeted, check the Knockout Group option to keep individual objects of the group or layer from applying their transparency settings to each other where they overlap. This is particularly useful for blends containing one or more transparent objects. For this reason, Illustrator automatically enables the Knockout Group option for all newly created blends.

The Opacity & Mask Define Knockout Shape (OMDKS) checkbox gives you more control over the knockout shape for an object within a knockout group. When enabled, this option defines the knockout shape using the transparency levels of the object you apply it to, instead of using the object's path shape or bounding box. This can be useful when important areas of an object are semitransparent or feathered, such as when you apply the Drop Shadow and Feather effects, or apply Photoshop effects such as Blur. To see the effects of OMDKS, the

Each of five grouped circles is filled with a different color, and the Hard Light blending mode is applied to each circle individually. By default, an object's blending mode affects overlapping objects in the group as well as objects behind the group

With Isolate Blending applied to the group, each object's blending mode and other transparency settings interact with other objects in the group, but not objects behind the group

With Knockout Group applied to the group, each object's transparency settings don't interact with other objects in the group, but do interact with objects behind the group

Knockout Group checkbox

In addition to being enabled or disabled, the Knockout Group checkbox has a third or neutral state indicated by a dash (in the Mac version) or grayed checkmark (in the Windows version). Illustrator automatically sets all new groups and layers to this neutral state so that simply grouping objects will not affect transparency.

Saving can flatten

Because transparency was not introduced until Illustrator 9, saving in any earlier version will permanently flatten your objects.

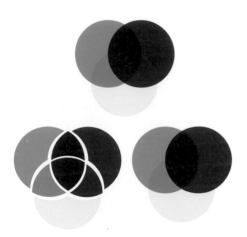

Top (live transparency): A multiply blending mode applied to each individual circle; Bottom left (flattened transparency, exploded view): Flattening the three circles results in seven separate regions; Bottom right (flattened transparency, non-exploded view): The final printed circles appear the same as the original non-flattened version

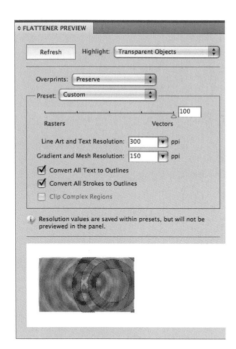

The Flattener Preview panel with all options showing (choose Show Options from the panel menu), including the Flattening Preset settings in the center of the panel. Click the Refresh button at the top of the panel, and the current document will be displayed in the preview area at the bottom of the panel. The circles marked in red are the only objects with transparency applied. The section "Using the Flattener Preview panel" explains how to use this preview to highlight areas of your art that flattening will affect

object you select must be within a knockout group (don't select the group), have less than 100% Opacity, and use a Blending Mode other than Normal.

Precisely targeting and editing transparency

You can apply transparency to so many levels of a document that it can be a challenge to keep track of where you've applied it. For example, you can apply a blending mode to a path, then group it with several other objects and apply an opacity level to that group or to the layer that contains the group. To quickly and precisely locate and edit any transparent object, use the Layers, Appearance, and Transparency panels together. This is especially useful when you want to identify and edit the transparency of specific objects after using the Flattener Preview panel (covered in the next section) to see how current transparency settings will affect flattened output.

Remember that a gradient-filled circle in the Layers panel indicates that transparency is applied to an object, group, or layer, and an underlined name indicates that an opacity mask is applied. If the Appearance panel is open, it gives you access to the appearance details for the targeted object. Clicking the word Opacity in the Appearance panel (or the Control panel) displays detailed transparency settings for the targeted object. If you targeted an opacity mask, clicking the opacity mask thumbnail in the Transparency panel makes the Layers and Appearance panels provide information about the opacity mask.

Working with transparency is much faster and easier once you're used to the rhythm of targeting with the Layers panel and inspecting with the Appearance and Transparency panels. Consider creating an arrangement of these three panels so you can see them all at once, then save this panel arrangement as a new workspace (see the "Workspaces" section in the *Illustrator Basics* chapter).

THE ART OF FLATTENING

PostScript output devices and file formats such as EPS can only reproduce transparent artwork in "flattened" form. Illustrator's flattening process is applied temporarily if you print, and permanently if you save in a format that doesn't support transparency natively (transparency was first introduced in Illustrator 9). Flattening occurs when areas of transparent overlap are converted into opaque pieces that look the same. Some of your objects may be split into many separate objects, while others may be rasterized.

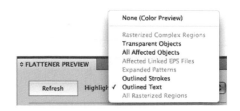

The Flattener Preview panel's Highlight pop-up

Using the Flattener Preview panel

The Flattener Preview panel (Window > Flattener Preview) highlights objects that will be affected by specific flattening settings. Use the preview to gauge the effects of different flattening settings so that you can determine the most appropriate settings to apply to a document.

To begin, choose a preview mode from the panel menu: either Quick Preview (which gives you the fastest preview, but excludes the All Rasterized Regions option in the Highlight menu) or Detailed Preview (which enables All Rasterized Regions). Then choose an option from the Overprint menu: Preserve, to retain overprinting; Simulate, to imitate the appearance of printing to separations; or Discard, to prevent any Overprint Fill or Overprint Stroke settings that have been set in the Attributes panel from appearing on the composite.

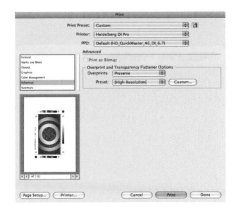

The Advanced section of the Print dialog (choose File > Print, then select Advanced in the menu just above the preview)

Now you're ready to choose a flattening preset from the Preset menu (or create a new one), as described later in the "Working with Flattener Presets" section. When you've done that, click the Refresh button at the top of the panel, which will update the display in the panel's preview area according to the settings you've chosen. At this point, you can use the panel's Highlight menu to highlight areas that will be affected by the flattening process. You can choose from a variety of options—from All Affected Objects to specifics such as Outlined Strokes or Outlined Text. You'll see the areas in question flagged in red in the preview area of the dialog. See *Illustrator Help* for more details about the various Highlight Options, and other aspects of using the Flattener Preview panel.

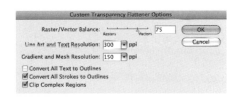

Click the Custom button in the Advanced section of the Print dialog to display the Custom Transparency Flattener Options dialog, where you can create a new custom preset; you can access essentially the same dialog (without going through File > Print) via Edit > Transparency Flattener Preset > Options > New

The Flatten Transparency dialog (Object > Flatten Transparency)

The Flatten Transparency dialog (Object > Flatten Transparency) and the Advanced section of the Print dialog both let you change transparency and flattening settings for a document. The Transparency Flattener Presets dialog (Edit > Transparency Flattener Presets) lets you create and edit flattener presets (this is discussed further in the following section, "Working with Flattener Presets").

Here are the flattening options you can adjust:

- **Name** lets you name settings to be saved as a preset.
- **Raster/Vector Balance** lets you control the degree to which your artwork is rasterized (discussed in greater detail in the "Setting Raster/Vector Balance" section a little further on in this chapter).
- **Line Art and Text Resolution** sets the resolution for vector objects that will be rasterized when flattening.
- **Gradient and Mesh Resolution** lets you set the resolution for gradient and mesh objects that will be rasterized in the course of flattening.
- **Convert All Text to Outlines** keeps the width of text consistent during flattening by converting all type objects to outlines and discarding glyph information.
- **Convert All Strokes to Outlines** ensures that the width of objects stays consistent during flattening by converting all strokes to simple filled paths.
- **Clip Complex Regions** reduces stitching artifacts by making sure that the boundaries between vector artwork and rasterized artwork fall along object paths.
- **Preserve Alpha Transparency** (Flatten Transparency dialog only) preserves the alpha transparency of flattened objects, which can be useful if you are exporting to SWF.
- **Preserve Overprints and Spot Colors** (Flatten Transparency dialog only) preserves spot colors and overprinting for objects that aren't involved in transparency.

To access these settings in the Flattener Preview panel, open the panel and choose Show Options from the panel menu. In the Flatten Transparency dialog, you can select any existing preset as a starting point and then make changes in the dialog. In the Advanced section of the Print dialog, choose any existing Preset from the Presets menu and click the Custom button to change the settings. See *Illustrator Help* for more flattening options.

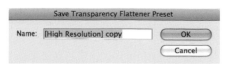

Object > Flatten Transparency > Save Preset

Working with Flattener Presets

Once you've adjusted any of the settings in the Flattener Preview panel, you can save the results as a preset, so you won't have to create them from scratch the next time you want to apply the same (or similar) flattening settings.

Illustrator comes with three default presets to get you started: High Resolution (for final press output and high-quality proofs such as color separations), Medium Resolution (for desktop proofs and print-demand-documents to be printed on PostScript color printers), and Low Resolution (for quick proofs to be printed on black-and-white desktop printers). You can't edit these default presets, but you can use them as a starting point, making changes and saving them as your own custom presets.

You can create and save your own custom flattening presets in any of the four following ways:

- **Using the Flattener Preview panel:** Select an existing preset from the Preset menu. Make your changes to its settings in the panel (choose Show Options from the panel pop-up menu if they aren't visible), and then choose Save Transparency Flattener Preset from the panel menu. Give your new preset a name and click OK. (If the existing preset you chose isn't one of the predefined default presets, you can also choose to apply your changes as an edit to that preset by choosing Redefine Preset.)

- **Using the Object > Flatten Transparency dialog:** Choose an existing preset from the Presets drop-down menu, adjust the settings in the box, and click Save Preset to name and save your new settings.

- **Using the Edit > Transparency Flattener Presets dialog:** Click the New button to create and name a new preset; click the Edit button to make changes to an existing (non-default) preset.

- **Using the Advanced section of the Print dialog:** Under the Overprint and Transparency Flattener Options heading, click the Custom button next to the Preset

The Transparency Flattener Presets dialog *(Edit > Transparency Flattener Presets)*

Transparency in PDF

Not all versions of PDF support transparency, so it's important to pay attention to the version of PDF you're using as you save (the default for Illustrator CS3 is PDF 1.5, which is compatible with Acrobat 6). Also be aware that the Mac application Preview will open PDF but doesn't always display transparency correctly.

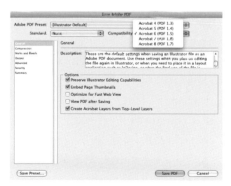

The Illustrator Save Adobe PDF dialog, showing the different PDF versions you can choose (File > Save/Save As, then choose Adobe PDF from the Format menu and click Save)

Exporting to Photoshop

When exporting Illustrator artwork in Photoshop (PSD) format, many sublayers may result if the artwork uses objects such as brushes, symbols, and blends. To simplify the exported document, target the sublayer that contains the problematic objects, enable the Knockout Group checkbox in the Transparency panel, and then export again.

Resolution of live effects

The Flattener Preview panel doesn't alter the resolution of live effects. For instance, if you've applied a Photoshop live effect with a specific resolution, to increase its resolution you'll need to reapply your effect at the resolution you want (see the *Live Effects & Graphic Styles* chapter for more on applying live effects).

A last note on opacity masks...

You can use any artwork to make an opacity mask; don't feel limited to using a single vector object. Experiment with placed images, gradient meshes, and even objects that contain opacity masks of their own. Remember that it's the grayscale luminosity of the masking artwork that determines the opacity of the masked artwork, not its color or vector structure.

dropdown menu to create a custom preset. Click the Save Preset button at the bottom of the Print dialog to name and save your settings into a new print preset. Note that saving a print preset with flattening settings doesn't affect the Transparency Flattener Presets list.

To apply flattening presets when you print or Save As to a format that doesn't support transparency, choose an existing preset (or create a new custom preset) in the Advanced section of the Print or format options dialog.

Setting Raster/Vector Balance

The Raster/Vector Balance setting (one of the flattening settings mentioned in "The Art of Flattening" earlier in this chapter) determines how much art is rasterized and how much remains vector. In case you're unfamiliar with the terms, raster art is made up of pixels, while vectors are discrete objects. These days, most programs contain aspects of both vectors and rasters, but Photoshop is primarily raster and Illustrator primarily vector.

By default, Illustrator's Raster/Vector Balance setting is 100—which results in the greatest possible amount of art remaining in vector form. At the highest setting, the file contains the most vector objects and may produce longer print times. As you move the slider to the left, toward zero, Illustrator tries to convert vectors (like pure Illustrator files) to rasters (like Photoshop files). At a setting of zero, Illustrator converts *all* art to raster. Usually, you get the best results using the all-vector setting of 100, but if this takes too long to print, try the all-raster setting of 0. In some cases, when transparent effects are very complex, this might be the best choice. Generally, the in-between settings create awful results.

Because objects are always flattened to a white background, you might see color shifts after you flatten your artwork. To preview the way your artwork would look if flattened, you can turn on Simulate Paper (Document Setup > Transparency) or Overprint Preview (in the View menu), and you can use the Flattener Preview panel to highlight the areas that would be affected.

HUBIG

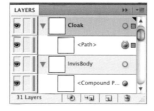

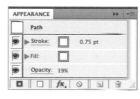

Dan Hubig

In this Illustration for *California Magazine*, Dan Hubig first combined blends, gradients, and transparency in Illustrator, and then enhanced his image in Photoshop with Blurs, Brushes, and Adjustment layers. Hubig used Transparency to render the cloak and torso only partially opaque, which kept his options open for expressing invisibility in Photoshop. He created his "cloak of invisibility" in Illustrator with a white Fill and Stroke and an opacity of only 19%, then duplicated it with a Stroke and no Fill to a new layer on top. By planning ahead, he would be able to reduce the cloak's visibility to zero, if he chose, but maintain that important outline. For one version, Hubig also made the man's torso completely invisible, but for the final version, he retained a hint of opacity. To learn more about how Hubig creates his illustrations, see the "Planning Ahead" lesson in the *Illustrator & Other Programs* chapter.

Transparent Color

Customizing Transparent Brushes & Layers

Overview: *Create customized Cal-*
ligraphic brushes; set Paintbrush
Tool preferences; assign basic
Transparency to individual strokes
and layers; use selections to easily
choose brush styles; use layers to
organize different types of strokes.

Customize the settings for each new Calligraphic
brush using the Brush Options window

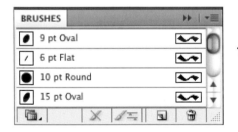

Four custom Calligraphic brushes in List view
(from the Brushes panel pop-up menu)

Adjusting the Opacity slider to preset the default
opacity for the next brush; use the Opacity slider
in the Control panel or Appearance panel

Illustrator provides an extremely forgiving way to create
transparent "watercolor-like" marks. Unlike traditional
media, or even digital tools such as Adobe Photoshop or
Corel Painter, individual marks can be easily altered after
the fact. In painting "Cyclamen in winter," artist Sharon
Steuer used a few custom Calligraphic brushes, Transparency settings to adjust the appearance of overlapping
marks, and Layers to control whether marks would be
made above or below previous ones.

1 Creating custom Calligraphic brushes and setting the
Opacity. You'll first customize a few brushes so you can
better control the size of the marks you make. If you have
a pressure-sensitive tablet, you can customize brushes
so they respond to your touch. To make the first brush,
start a new file, then open the Brushes panel and click the
New Brush icon at the bottom of the panel. Select New
Calligraphic Brush, and click OK. In the resulting Calligraphic Brush Options window, experiment with various settings, then click OK and make a stroke to test the
brush. For her first custom brush, Steuer chose a Pressure
setting for Diameter (9 pt with a 9-pt Random Variation),
set the Angle to 60° and the Roundness to 60% with both
Fixed, and clicked OK. For greater stroke variation, try
choosing Pressure or Random options (pressure settings

are unavailable and don't work unless you have a pressure-sensitive graphics tablet installed). To create additional brush variations, drag a custom brush over the New Brush icon in the Brushes panel and double-click the desired brush to adjust the settings.

To set the defaults for your next brush stroke and to paint in transparent color, first choose a Calligraphic brush and stroke color, then set the Opacity setting in the Control panel. To set opacity, click and hold the triangle to the right of the Opacity field to reveal the Opacity slider, which you can adjust. Alternatively, you can click on the word "Opacity" in the Control panel, which temporarily reveals the Transparency panel, or you can adjust the opacity and other transparency settings in the floating Transparency panel.

2 **Setting Paintbrush Tool Preferences.** In addition to creating your initial custom brushes, you'll need to set the Paintbrush Tool Preferences so you can freely make overlapping brush strokes. Double-click on the Paintbrush tool, then disable the Options "Fill new brush strokes" (so your brush strokes will be stroked and not filled) and "Keep Selected" (so new strokes won't redraw the last drawn stroke). With the "Keep Selected" option disabled, you can still repaint a stroke by selecting it first with a selection tool, then drawing a corrected mark within the distance specified in the Within field of the Paintbrush Tool Preferences dialog. To create accurate marks, Steuer set the Fidelity to .5 pixels and the Smoothness to 0%. If you want Illustrator to smooth your marks, experiment with higher settings.

3 **Painting and using the last selected object to determine the next brush style.** For this step to work, you must turn off New Art Has Basic Appearance (the checkmark is *on* by default); toggle it on/off from the Appearance panel pop-up menu. One of the wonderful aspects of working with Illustrator is that your last selected object determines the appearance for the next object you paint.

2
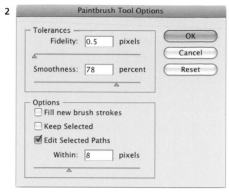

Setting the Paintbrush Tool Options to prevent new brush strokes from filling and to prevent redraw of marks already made

3

To make sure that any settings are maintained after each completed stroke, turn off the New Art Has Basic Appearance feature

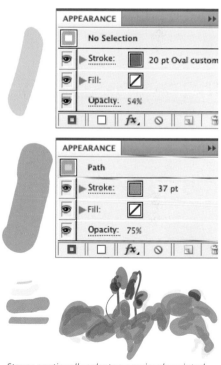

Steuer continually selects a previously painted stroke so the appearance settings from that selection are remembered for the next stroke. Working this way allows her to quickly change brushes and colors as she paints

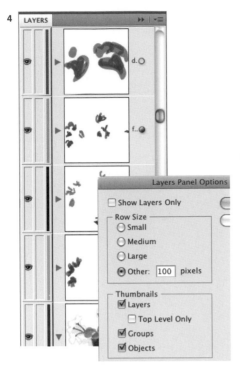

By changing the size of the thumbnails in the Layers panel (from the Layers panel pop-up menu), it's easier for Steuer to identify each kind of stroke and what layer it's on

Steuer selected the layer containing a batch of flowers and experimented with different Blending Modes and Opacity settings until she was satisfied with their appearance

To see how this works, select one of your brushes and start to paint. Notice that the brush, stroke color, and opacity you choose will continue to apply after you complete each stroke. By selecting a specific stroke that's similar to the one you want to create next, you can minimize the time it takes to customize your next brush stroke.

4 Using layers to organize different types of strokes. To organize your artwork, keep sets of similar brush strokes in their own layers. When you are ready to make more strokes, create a new layer for them (click the New Layer icon). If you want the new set of strokes to be underneath a previous set, drag that layer below the layer containing the previous strokes. By keeping your layers organized in this way, you can use layer thumbnails to easily identify different strokes and manage the placement of new strokes. You can use layers to hide, lock, delete, and select groups of similar strokes efficiently.

Since Illustrator remembers the layer of the last selected object, your brush strokes will remain conveniently organized into separate layers. For instance, say you select a petal, then deselect it by clicking outside of the object itself (or ⌘-Shift-A/Ctrl-Shift-A): The next stroke you make will be placed at the top of the same layer. If you want the new stroke to be placed on a different layer, first select the desired layer, then begin painting.

5 Assigning Opacity and Blending Modes to selected layers. Once you have organized different types of brush strokes into separate layers, you have the opportunity to globally adjust the Opacity and Blending Mode on entire layers. For example, after creating a batch of flowers on one layer, Steuer wanted them to appear brighter, so she changed the Blending Mode and Opacity for the entire layer by first clicking that layer's targeting circle (this selects and targets all objects within a layer, allowing any transparency settings to be applied to the entire layer). After changing the Blending Mode from Normal to Color Burn, she reduced the opacity to 55%.

GUSMAN JOLY

Annie Gusman Joly

Transparency can be created with Blending Modes that interact with the layers beneath, forming new colors based on the type of Blending Mode used. Artist Annie Gusman Joly uses them here to create a complex pattern of shadows. In this tropical forest, light filters through the leaves and flowers to fall on the ground beneath the white bird's feet. To create the random and overlapping patterns, Joly first fills a large object on one layer with a solid blue. After drawing the path for the shadows on

the layer above, she fills it with blue and sets the Blending Mode to Multiply. If the shadow color is too dark, she reduces the Layer Opacity to increase the shadow layer's transparency. She uses the same technique for the shadow beneath her three-toed sloth.

Adding Highlights

Using Transparency to Create Highlights

Overview: *Create highlights in objects for the interior of the cell using the Blend tool; stack them and lower Opacity; create highlights with gradients for other objects and reduce opacity; create a bright lens flare.*

1

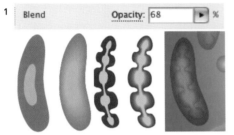

After creating an object by blending a light object with a darker, same-shaped object to represent a highlight, transparency further blends the "lit" object (mitochondrion) into its surroundings

Adjusting the radial gradient adjusts the size and edge of the highlight, while transparency settings adjust the final blend into another object

2

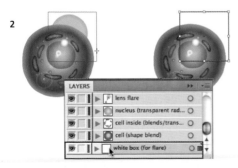

The Lens Flare tool needs a non-transparent background to reach maximum brightness

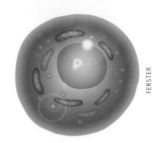

Adding transparency to blended or gradient-filled objects, or conversely, eliminating transparency beneath a lens flare, gives you a great deal of versatility when constructing believable highlights.

1 Using multiple techniques for blending colors in order to simulate natural highlighting. When Gary Ferster wanted to illustrate a living cell, he chose various methods for constructing blended highlights. For the mitochondrion (pinkish objects), he used the Blend tool to create two initial shapes, one very light, and one the "local" color. When blended smoothly, this method created soft highlights. He then stacked one blended object over the other and reduced the opacity in each, in order to make them appear to be part of the cell. For the small bubbles (lysosomes) and nucleus in the cell, however, Ferster used simple radial gradients with a very light center gradating to the local color of the object. By adjusting the gradient stops, he could make highlights bigger or smaller, with sharper or more feathered edges, and then adjust Opacity to blend these objects into the cell.

2 Using the Lens Flare tool for maximum highlighting. Nothing suggests a powerful light source quite like a lens flare, but Ferster had observed that using the Lens Flare tool over a transparent background creates a dulled, gray flare. A simple solution was to draw a solid white rectangle, at least as big as the flare, behind all the objects. The part of the lens flare that extended beyond the cell became white, disappearing into the background entirely.

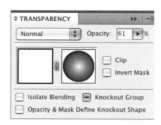

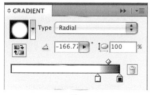

BEAUREGARD

Christiane Beauregard

Christiane Beauregard created this illustration as a "prequel" version to a commissioned piece she would later submit to her client. To create the glows around some of her stars and flowers, she used opacity masks, a technique that gives her the control she needs over each object, and also scales readily when she copies the object. For the stars, she drew a circle filled with solid white to blend with the background, and placed it behind a star. She used the White, Black Radial gradient in the opacity mask to

make the "glow" partially transparent over most of its range, and reduced Layer Opacity to soften the glow even more. She used the same technique for the glowing flower centers, but adjusted the Radial gradient in the opacity mask to ensure that most of the flower retained full Opacity, and the glow was restricted to just the outer edge. For more about making and using opacity masks, see her "Opacity Masks 101" lesson following this gallery.

Opacity Masks 101

Transparency Masks for Blending Objects

Overview: *Create a simple mask and apply it to an object; refine transparency by adding controlled masking with a precise opacity mask; choose opacity mask options.*

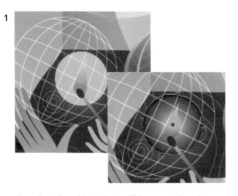

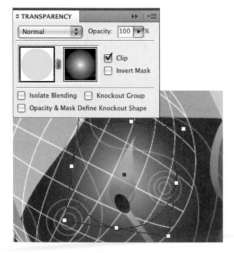

Drawing the object that will become the glow around the match, and the gradient-filled object that will become the object's opacity mask

The semitransparent object after adding a gradient-filled opacity mask

BEAUREGARD

Christiane Beauregard's illustrations often depend upon the intertwining and overlapping of objects to convey connections between ideas and elements. She frequently uses transparency to express those connections in a direct, visual manner, and depends upon opacity masks to control more precisely the extent of the transparency than the Opacity setting allows. In "Global Warming," Beauregard used opacity masks to immerse her objects in their surroundings.

1 Creating and applying an opacity mask. Beauregard expressed one aspect of global warming by showing her subject holding a match to the globe. To create the glow, she first drew a circle filled with a yellow-orange. Next she drew a circle directly on top and fully covering the first circle so that transparency would carry to the very edges of the glow. She filled it with the White, Black Radial gradient. She selected both circles, opened the Transparency panel's pop-up menu, and chose Make Opacity Mask. This automatically placed the top object (the gradient-filled circle) in the right thumbnail pane to make the mask. The glow is fully visible where the mask is white, transparent where it's gray, and invisible where it's black. You can use colored artwork for the masking object, but the mask only uses the luminosity values of the hues.

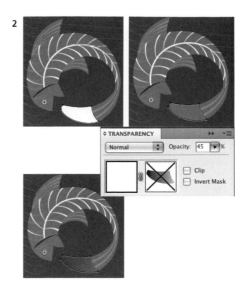

2 **Combining transparency with a precisely constructed opacity mask.** For several objects, Beauregard used both transparency (to blend objects with the objects below), and an opacity mask for localized, typically gradated transparency. She created the effect of the fish's tail fading into the water by drawing a separate object filled with white for the tip of the tail. So that the mask would align precisely with its path, she copied the tail path and used Paste in Front (⌘-F/Ctrl-F) to create the mask object. This time she filled the mask with the first (default) Linear Gradient, using the Gradient tool to adjust it so that it faded to black at the tip. With both objects selected, she chose Make Opacity Mask to place the gradient-filled path into the Transparency panel's mask pane. She could further adjust the opacity of the masked object using the Opacity slider in the Transparency panel, or even toggle the mask on and off by Shift-clicking the mask pane.

Original object, copied and pasted into mask; mask disabled (above right); and enabled (below), with object's Opacity lowered

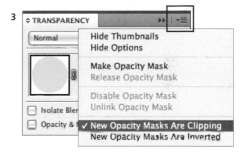

Choosing default settings for creating opacity masks through the Transparency panel pop-up menu

3 **Clipping and non-clipping masks.** Because Beauregard's masks typically are either contoured to the objects they mask, or are larger than the object, she doesn't normally bother to alter the default setting of New Opacity Masks Are Clipping, since clipping will not clip off any portion of the masked object. If the masking object is the exact same size or larger, and in the same position, a clipping mask affects transparency only. If the mask is smaller than the object being masked, enabling the option will clip the object. At any time, she can change a mask's clipping behavior with the Clip checkbox, and choose to invert the mask then as well, if an object is inadvertently being clipped or the transparency needs to be reversed.

Objects that make masks

Opacity masks can be made from any artwork, whether comprised of a single object or several. These objects can be distorted, filtered, stroked, or otherwise manipulated like any normal object. They can even have their own opacity masks. However, only the luminosity values of the masking object will determine the masked object's transparency.

Floating Type

Type Objects with Transparency & Effects

Overview: *Create an area type object, key in text; add a new fill attribute in the Appearance panel; convert the fill to a shape; change transparency and add an Effect.*

Top, the Selection tool (at right selected); bottom, the Type tool in the Toolbox (right selected)

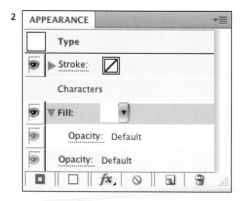

The type object after clicking with the Selection tool (the background photograph has been hidden in this view)

APPEARANCE

The Appearance panel after selecting the fill attribute and applying white to it

Using the Convert to Shape effect, you can create an area type object with transparency and effects that will save you from making and manipulating two objects (a type object and a rectangle with transparency and effects below it). For a virtual guide to Capitol Reef National Park, Steven Gordon created a transparent area type object with a hard-edged drop shadow that provided information for each of the park's most popular hiking trails.

1 Making the area type object. Start by selecting the Type tool, dragging it to create an area type object, and then typing your text. When you have finished typing, click on the Selection tool (the solid arrow icon) in the Tools panel. This deselects the text characters while selecting the type object, preparing the object (rather than the characters) for editing in the next step.

2 Creating a new fill and converting to a shape. Open the Appearance panel and select the Add New Fill icon at the bottom of the panel menu. Drag the new Fill attribute below Characters in the panel. The Fill attribute will be automatically deselected when you move it in the panel so you'll need to click on it again to select it. Next, apply a light color to it (Gordon chose white from the Swatches panel). Now click the panel's Add New Effect and choose Convert to Shape > Rectangle from the pop-up menu. In the Shape Options dialog, control the size of the rectangle around your type object by modifying the two Relative options (Extra Width and Extra Height).

3 Adjusting transparency and adding a drop shadow effect. Gordon designed each trail information box to incorporate transparency and a drop shadow, so its text would float above, but not obscure, the background photograph. To adjust the transparency of the object you converted in the previous step, first ensure that the type object's Fill or Rectangle attribute is selected in the Appearance panel. (If either attribute is not selected, then the transparency changes you're about to make will also affect the text characters.) Click on the Opacity attribute and in the Transparency panel adjust the transparency slider, or enter a value.

Instead of creating a soft drop shadow, Gordon opted to make a hard-edged shadow. To create this shadow, make sure the Fill attribute is still selected in the Appearance panel. Click the Add New Effect icon and choose Stylize > Drop Shadow. In the Drop Shadow dialog set Color to black, Blur to 0, and then adjust the X Offset and Y Offset sliders so the shadow is positioned as far down and to the right as you wish.

4 Editing the area type object. As you continue working, you may decide to resize the type object you originally created when you dragged with the Type tool. (This is different from editing the Shape Options dialog values to change the size of the transparent rectangle around the type object, as you did previously.) To resize the object, choose the Direct Selection tool and click on the edge of the type object you want to resize, then drag the side of the object inward to make it smaller, or outward to enlarge it. Because the transparent drop shadow shape was formed using the Convert to Shape effect, it is "live" and will automatically resize as you resize the type object.

Similarly, if you edit the text by adding or deleting words, the type object will resize, causing your transparent drop shadow shape to resize automatically.

The Shape Options dialog with the Relative options edited

Left, the Appearance panel with the transparency attribute selected; right, the Transparency panel

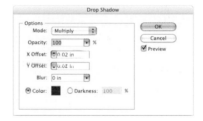

The Drop Shadow dialog

The Direct Selection cursor when it nears the edge of an area type object

Getting an edge

To help click on the edge of a type object rather than on the type itself, make sure Smart Guides are enabled in the View menu and Object Highlighting is enabled in the Illustrator > Preferences > Smart Guides dialog.

Glass and Chrome

Highlights and Shadows with Transparency

Advanced Technique

Overview: *Apply transparency to white to simulate a glass highlight, and reinforce overall lighting by combining the Multiply blending mode with an underlying gradient.*

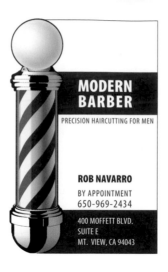

1

Kelley's hand-tracing without the reflected highlights and shadows, shown in Outline mode (left) and Preview mode (right)

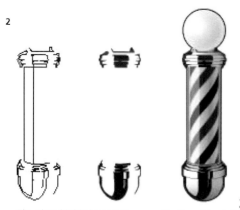

2

The glass highlight and chrome reflection shapes shown in Outline mode (left), Preview mode (center), and in position over the finished barber pole (right)

The transparency and blending modes in Illustrator can greatly enhance the look of glass and chrome reflections. Andrea Kelley created this barber pole illustration for a business card designed by Jodie Stowe. To heighten the realism of the barber pole, Kelley used Illustrator's transparency features to reproduce the long, clean highlights that appear when glass and chrome reflect ambient lighting and surrounding objects. The finished business card was die-cut along the barber pole edge to set it apart from other business cards. You can use this technique by Kelley to create convincing glass and chrome highlights.

1 Placing the template image and tracing the pole. Kelley was given a JPEG image of the original barber pole art, which was a useful reference for getting the alternating blue and red stripes just right as they wrapped around the pole. She placed the JPEG image as a template and then used the Pen tool and other drawing tools to hand-trace the objects making up the barber pole. To draw the perfectly round, white light globe on top of the pole, Kelley Shift-dragged the Ellipse tool. At this point, the chrome and glass reflections hadn't been traced yet.

2 Tracing the reflections. Next, Kelley traced the reflections—the highlight in the glass cylinder, and the dark reflections in the chrome at the bottom of the barber pole. Kelley recognized that the highlight was vertically continuous throughout the glass and chrome, so she made sure to position and align her highlight and reflection paths accordingly. She filled the glass highlight with white, and filled the dark chrome reflections with black.

To model the lighting on the frosted light globe, Kelley applied a radial gradient between white and warm gray (Kelley used 12.8% C, 16% M, 12.8% Y, 18% K), and also added a slight Inner Glow effect. To add a shine to the chrome base, Kelley applied a linear gradient between the same light gray as above, and a medium gray (16% C, 20% M, 16% Y, 16% K).

3 Applying transparency to the highlight shape.
To reveal the objects under the glass highlight, Kelley selected the highlight and used the Transparency panel to apply an Opacity value of 50%.

4 Unifying the lighting. Kelley reinforced the overall lighting by combining the Multiply blending mode with a gradient to create a soft, vertical shadow along the entire right side of the pole. Kelley first needed to create a separate path for the entire perimeter of the barber pole. She duplicated the pole and, with the paths still selected, she clicked the Unite button in the Pathfinder panel to make the shapes behave as a single object. She applied a light, linear gradient to the new object.

Kelley wanted to reproduce how various pole and reflection paths would be affected to different degrees by the shadow. To control this, Kelley first positioned the gradient behind the other paths by choosing Object > Arrange > Send to Back. Kelley then applied the Multiply blending mode to pole and reflection paths so that their fills and strokes were darkened by the shadow. She created the variations she wanted by varying the Opacity values of different paths. To emphasize the overall barber pole outline, Kelley applied a 7.5-pt black stroke to a duplicate of the perimeter path, and positioned the duplicate path behind the rest of the drawing.

3
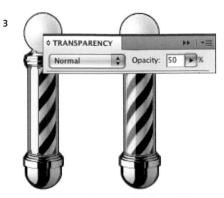

The glass highlight selected (left), and the same highlight deselected after applying 50% opacity with the Transparency panel (right)

4
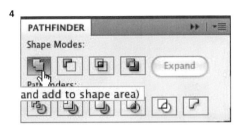

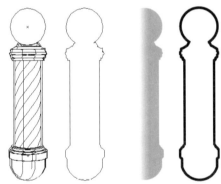

Kelley unified the lighting by uniting the pole's paths (left) with the Pathfinder panel, and filling the new path (second from left) with a linear gradient (third from left); a duplicate with a heavy stroke (right) strengthens the outline

The Multiply blending mode was applied to the barber pole objects so that the unifying background gradient could show through

Tinting a Scan

Adding a Color to a Grayscale Image

Advanced Technique

Overview: *Prepare a grayscale image; import the image into Illustrator; colorize the image; trim the artwork to the required shape; add a vignette.*

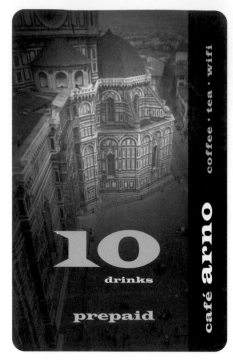

1

The original scanned image

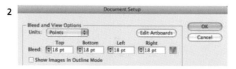

2

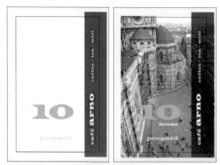

The layout (left) and the image placed in the layout (right)

Conrad Chavez created this concept for a prepaid coffee card that can feature different background photographs. To preserve design flexibility, Chavez imported a grayscale version of the image and added color in Illustrator so that he could change the image color at any time.

1 Scanning and preparing the image. Chavez started by scanning a photograph and saving it as a grayscale image. Save the image in a format Illustrator can place, such as a TIFF or PSD (Photoshop) file. If your original image is in color, you must first convert the image to grayscale in a program like Photoshop. Color images can't be tinted in Illustrator.

2 Importing the image. Before importing the image, Chavez clicked the Document Setup button in the Control panel and entered 18 pt for the Bleed amount. On the artboard, a nonprinting red line now indicated the bleed amount beyond the artboard edge. Chavez then dragged the image directly from Adobe Bridge, dropped it into the Illustrator document window, and positioned it.

3 Colorizing the image. Chavez selected the image, clicked the Fill box in the Toolbox, and then clicked a solid color swatch in the Swatches panel to tint the image. He had already applied the dark brown swatch to other elements in the design, unifying the composition.

If applying a color doesn't change the image, make sure the Fill box is active and that the image was saved as a true grayscale image, not as an RGB or CMYK image.

4 Visualizing a trim. To preview the composition as it would appear after trimming, Chavez drew a rounded-corner rectangle at the trim size. With the rectangle in front of both the background image and the dark vertical rectangle, he selected all three objects and chose Object > Clipping Mask > Make, which created a clipping group.

5 Adding a vignette. Chavez created a vignette to better distinguish the foreground and background. He drew a rectangle the same size as the bleed, and used the Gradient panel to apply a radial gradient. He changed the gradient's default black slider to the same dark color swatch applied to the image. In the Control panel, he clicked Opacity and then chose Multiply from the pop-up menu to blend the gradient with the image under it.

The vignette needed to be behind all objects except the scan. In the Layers panel, Chavez not only dragged the vignette further back in the stack but also into the clipping group, so that the vignette could be visualized within the temporary clipping group.

6 Editing the vignette. To refine the vignette, Chavez selected the vignette in the Layers panel and clicked the Gradient tool, causing the Gradient Annotator to appear over the vignette. He repositioned the gradient center and dragged the Annotator sliders to widen both the light center and the dark edge of the gradient. To restore the bleed required for the press, Chavez selected the clipping group and chose Object > Clipping Mask > Release, and then deleted his temporary clipping path.

3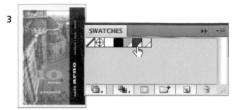

Colorizing the image (left) by selecting it and then clicking the dark brown solid color swatch on the Swatches panel (right)

4

Rounded-corner rectangle indicating final trim (left) and after clipping artwork to it (right)

5

Applying a radial gradient to the new rectangle (left), applying the Multiply blending mode to the rectangle (middle), and after dragging the vignette path into the clipping group (right)

Layers panel before (left) and after (right) dragging the vignette into the clipping group

6

Using the Gradient tool's Gradient Annotator to edit the Gradient slider positions (left); ready for prepress with mask deleted (top right)

Blending Elements

Using Transparency to Blend and Unify

Advanced Technique

Overview: *Prepare images in Photoshop to integrate in Illustrator; use Multiply and opacity masks to blend; make Backgrounds transparent.*

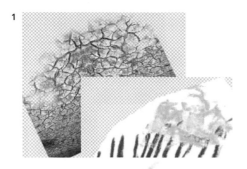

Using a photo or hand drawing for texture, prepared in Photoshop for use in Illustrator—here two are shown with Photoshop's Transparency grid, while the fire is completely opaque

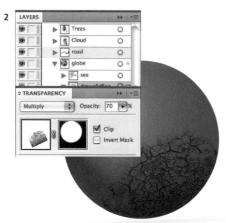

A gradient-filled globe with a grayscale photo, and using the Blending Mode to Multiply, and an opacity mask to add texture

When David Jennings was hired to make an illustration about environmental issues for Climate Concern UK, he wanted to use contrasting textures to highlight negative influences on the global climate. He used Photoshop for some of the textural elements, but because most of the details would be vector, he used Illustrator for blending all the objects, raster and vector, into one coherent whole.

1 Preparing images to place in Illustrator. Jennings began the project by using pastels on paper to hand-draw smoke, clouds, trees, and fire. He scanned these into Photoshop and adjusted color. He also adjusted a grayscale image of cracked earth that, once blended with a globe in Illustrator, would depict drought. With these files ready and saved as PSD images, he turned to Illustrator.

2 Using Multiply, Opacity Mask, and reduced opacity to blend textures and add shading. Now in Illustrator, Jennings drew a circle for the planet, filled it with a brown radial gradient, and copied the circle to the clipboard. He then chose File > Place to bring in the earth texture, then scaled and rotated it. He then used the Transparency panel to fit the texture into the circle. First he changed the Normal blending mode to Multiply, allowing only the values of the texture darker than the gradient to appear. He then created a transparency mask by double-clicking the blank "mask" spot to the right of the texture icon, used ⌘-F/Ctrl-F (Paste in Front) to paste the copied circle in place, changed the fill to white, and reduced the opacity (Clip should be enabled, Invert mask disabled). To exit mask mode, he double-clicked the texture icon.

Using mainly the Pen tool, Jennings then began drawing manmade and solid natural elements—the cars and planes, the factory and housing, the human and polar bear. To create shading he added darker objects on top of the originals, switching the Blending Mode to Multiply and/or changing Opacity in the Transparency panel to alter the appearance of the objects below. If he needed the shading to be even darker than the color he had already chosen, he used Multiply to deepen the colors. If the color was a bit too dark, he lowered the opacity. To create the shadow for the factory, he not only used Multiply to deepen the colors below his shadow shape, but he also chose Gaussian Blur as a Live Effect to add even more transparency and softness to the shadow's edges.

3 Making transparent backgrounds for Photoshop images. Jennings now needed to add the textured, natural elements he had prepared in Photoshop. He knew that Multiply mode drops out the white backgrounds often imported with raster images, so he placed the cloud, trees, and smoke images, scaled and transformed them to fit, and then selected Multiply to merge them seamlessly with the objects below. For the fire, however, Jennings needed both transparency within the fire image itself and opacity when he placed it over the tree layer. If he used Multiply, then the fire, being lighter than the trees, would seem to disappear. In this instance, Jennings painted a transparency mask for the fire in Photoshop, which Illustrator recognized and preserved upon import. (See the *Illustrator & Other Programs* chapter for more about Photoshop.)

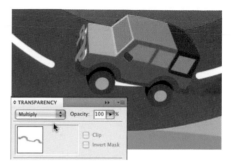
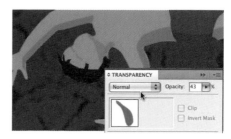

Adding shading with an object in Multiply mode

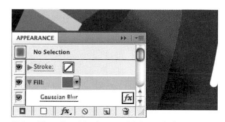

Adjusting Opacity to precisely determine degree of shading and depth

Using Blending Mode > Multiply and also applying Effect > Blur > Gaussian Blur, creates transparent shadows

3

Trees and tree trunks set to Multiply drop their white background against the globe, but the lighter-colored fire requires transparency painted into a mask in Photoshop

Opacity Collage

Combining Objects using Transparency

Advanced Technique

Overview: *Apply an opacity mask; experiment with blending modes; shade with a gradient mesh.*

The heart path, doily image, and currency image

Before and after using a gradient as an opacity mask for the currency image; the Transparency panel when the masked result is selected

money can't buy me love...

Sharon Steuer created this Valentine's Day card using type, vector graphics with applied effects, and imported bitmap images. Steuer created this project for a Valentine's Day feature article on creativepro.com. She started from a hand-drawn heart and images of currency and a lace doily. Illustrator lends itself to Steuer's process of continuous experimentation by making it easy to copy objects or layers, vary their appearance, and hide or show different combinations of objects or layers.

1 Setting up the main elements. Steuer chose File > Place to import the image of scanned currency. Steuer also placed a scan of a doily with a blue background, and chose Object > Arrange > Send to Back to position the doily behind the currency. Next, Steuer used the Pen tool to draw a heart shape, and gave it a red outline stroke.

2 Masking an image with opacity. Steuer used an opacity mask to fade the currency image vertically. In an opacity mask, black areas are transparent, white areas are opaque, and gray areas are semitransparent. To create the mask, she drew a rectangle and filled it with a black-to-white gradient. She positioned the rectangle over the currency image, selected both objects, and chose Make Opacity Mask from the Transparency panel menu.

3 Varying the heart outline. To add texture and visual interest, Steuer created playful variations on the heart outline. She first chose Edit >Copy, then Edit >Paste in Front to duplicate the heart outline. Her experiments led her to enlarge the heart outline and choose Effect > Stylize >Scribble. She also applied a thicker stroke weight and a shade of red. Steuer also used the Ellipse tool to draw a circle that echoed the doily shape. She stylized the circle using the same technique she used for the heart outline, but with a bluish gray color instead of red.

4 Experimenting with blending modes. With the main elements in place, Steuer experimented with integrating the design elements. She tried different opacity values and blending modes to adjust the color and tone relationships among objects and layers.

While opacity applies an overall level of transparency, blending modes change the tone and color relationships between areas that overlap. For example, the Overlay mode increases the contrast between light and dark over-lapping areas, and the Color mode applies an object's hue and saturation to underlying areas. Steuer used the Transparency panel to change the blending mode and opacity for the layer or objects she selected. If a blend-ing mode created a stronger effect than she wanted, she adjusted the opacity of the layer or object.

When you apply appearance attributes, the object or layer's target circle in the Layers panel becomes shaded. This makes it easy to identify objects and layers for which attributes like Opacity and Blending Mode have changed. Simply click an object's target indicator in the Layers panel, and then look at the Appearance panel to see the appearance settings for the object.

3

The red heart and blue circle over the composed elements, before and after applying the Scribble effect first to the heart and then to the circle

4

The blending mode pop-up menu and Opacity value in the Transparency panel

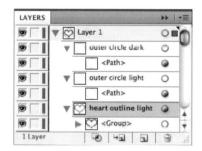

Shaded circles indicate objects or layers with appearance changes such as blending modes, opacity, and effects

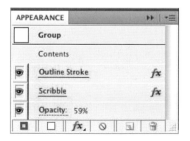

The Appearance panel for a selected heart out-line displays effects and transparency settings

5

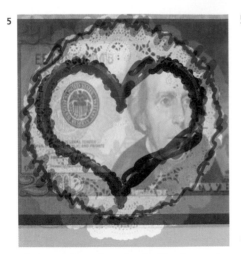

The composition after adjusting blending modes and opacity values

6

The heart with a custom gradient fill, and after expanding the gradient fill into a masked gradient mesh and adding a mesh point

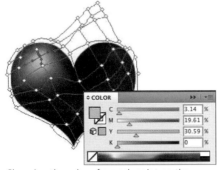

Changing the color of a mesh point on the edited gradient mesh

7

Detail of the type and the underlying hand-drawn shadow

5 Creating variations. Steuer felt the illustration needed a bit more depth and impact. She duplicated the heart outline, changed the Scribble effect settings (by double-clicking the Scribble effect in the Appearance panel when the heart outline was selected), and changed the blending mode. In the completed piece, one heart outline uses the Multiply blend mode at 59% opacity, the other heart outline uses the Color Burn blend mode at 100%, and their Scribble settings are different. Steuer created similar variations of the currency and the doily.

6 Shading with a gradient mesh. To achieve the surface modeling she wanted, Steuer decided to use a gradient mesh to shade a duplicate of the heart. Using the Gradient panel, Steuer created a custom linear gradient. She applied it as a fill to the duplicate heart outline, and used the Gradient tool to adjust the gradient's endpoints and angle. She then chose Object > Expand to convert the gradient fill into a gradient mesh. The heart outline became a clipping mask with the rectangular gradient mesh inside it. The expanded mesh rectangle is rotated because the original gradient fill was at an angle. Steuer shaped the mesh by adding mesh points with the Mesh tool, adjusting mesh point colors using the Color panel, and using the Direct Selection tool to move the mesh points and edit their direction lines.

7 Finishing up with type. Steuer used the Type tool to add the line of text "Money can't buy me love…" below the heart. She added a scribbled type shadow by hand with a graphics tablet, and tried different blending modes and opacity settings for the shadow before settling on the Saturation blending mode at 25% opacity.

Faster access to a clipping mask and its contents
When a clipping mask is selected, two buttons appear at the left end of the Control panel: Edit Clipping Path and Edit Contents. Click them for direct access to a clipping mask's path or contents.

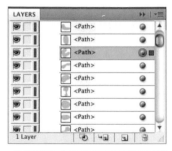

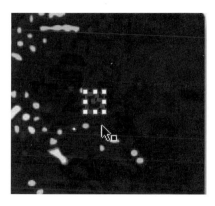

HESS (Parker photo by Milton H. Greene, ©2007 Joshua Greene, www.archiveimages.com)

Kurt Hess

As an exercise to refine his technique, Kurt Hess created this portrait of Suzy Parker, based on a 1952 photo. Hess located the owner of the copyright of the original image, who generously granted permission for the illustration to be published here with the photo credit by Milton H. Greene (©2007 Joshua Greene, www.archiveimages.com). He used the Watercolor filter in Photoshop to add important contrast to the image, and then, layer by layer, he built a convincing portrait in Illustrator. Hess began by creating a palette of global colors that he would use as he traced areas in the photograph onto separate layers, using both Pen and Pencil tools. He created the illusion of depth by overlapping individual objects depicting tonal values. He then adjusted their settings in the Transparency panel—using Multiply, Overlay, or Screen for contrast control, while fine-tuning Opacity as well. This method permitted Hess to return to each object and readjust the settings as often as needed until the shading was exactly what he wanted. Further, using a global palette made it easy to refine the colors later to create a glowing rendition of "Suzy."

10

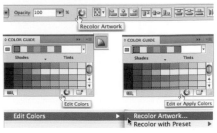

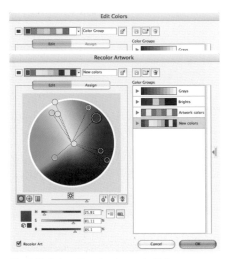

Different ways to enter the Recolor Artwork/Edit Colors dialog: from the Control panel (top); from the Color Guide panel (center), via the menu Edit >Edit Colors >Recolor Artwork

The Edit Colors/Recolor Artwork dialog

Live Color swatches & brushes

If you use Live Color to edit objects styled with symbols, brushes, patterns, or gradients, once you click OK, Live Color will automatically save new styles using the adjusted colors into the appropriate brushes, patterns, or gradients panel. (The lesson "Night Into Day," later in this chapter, creates new brushes and gradients.)

Live Color

Hue, or color, is relative. Individual hues are perceived differently when juxtaposed. Live Color lets you examine color relationships in a way that is not possible with other software applications. You can quickly explore new color combinations, find an exact color faster, and determine which hues work well together based on scientific color theory and predefined color harmony rules. Live Color provides a tool set you can use to mix and adjust color in new ways, as well as the capability to extract color from artwork and create color groups. (See the *Drawing & Coloring* chapter introduction for a discussion of the Color, Swatches, and Color Guide panels, as well as a lesson that includes a basic Live Color workflow.)

Live Color is not just a single panel or feature. Instead, it's an interactive color exploration environment comprised of various interfaces and tools that work together. So despite the fact that there isn't anything actually labeled "Live Color," we will continue to use the term in the way Adobe does: to discuss the feature set that lets you interactively work with color in Illustrator (see "Setting up a Live Color workspace" below for details).

While Live Color can be intimidating, this chapter and its lessons should help you add at least a few Live Color features and functions to your artistic arsenal.

SETTING UP A LIVE COLOR WORKSPACE

Included in the components that make up the feature set Adobe calls Live Color: the Color panel, Color Guide panel, Swatches panel, kuler panel (see the Tip "Where's kuler?" opposite), and last but not least, what people probably consider the heart of Live Color: a dialog that is alternately, and somewhat confusingly, labeled either Edit Colors or Recolor Artwork. The key to how this "heart of Live Color" dialog changes title (and functions you can access from within the dialog) is that the title is different depending on how you enter it.

So, if you have nothing selected, you can enter a mode called Edit Colors. You can access this mode by clicking the Edit Colors button at the bottom of the Color Guide panel. Once you're in the Edit Colors dialog, you'll be in Edit mode, which means that you can mix and store colors (see below for specific instructions on how to do this). You'll see a tab next to the word "Edit" titled "Assign," but it will be grayed out; since you don't have any objects selected, you can't access this tab. You can only assign colors to selected objects.

If, however, you have artwork selected, this multifaceted dialog will now be titled "Recolor Artwork." There are a number of ways to access this mode. As long as your selection contains at least two colors, you'll be able to simply click the Recolor Artwork button that will have magically appeared in the Control panel. Another option is the button at the bottom of the Color Guide panel mentioned above; note, though, that when artwork is selected this button will now be called "Edit or Apply Colors." In the Swatches panel, with a color group selected, you can click the Edit or Apply Color Group button. A final way into this dialog is Edit > Edit Colors > Recolor Artwork. Which of these routes you choose into the dialog will affect what is going on when you get there (more about the details of this follows). The first thing you'll notice when you enter the dialog with objects selected is that you're in Recolor Artwork mode, which means that you'll have access to the Assign tab of the dialog as well as all of the features in the Edit mode.

As to the other panels involved in Live Color, think of the Color panel as your color mixing tool, the Swatches panel as a kind of color filing cabinet to store and organize the hues you've mixed, and the Color Guide panel as a color laboratory—a place to seek inspiration. The kuler panel is an internet-based environment for creating and sharing color ideas.

To work with Live Color most effectively, you'll often want to have the Color, Color Guide, Swatches, and perhaps the kuler panel, visible simultaneously; you'll need

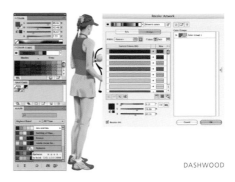

DASHWOOD

To work with Live Color effectively, you'll often want to see all your color-related panels and the artwork you're recoloring simultaneously; selection edges are automatically hidden when you enter the Recolor Artwork dialog

Powerful Recolor Artwork

One of the many powerful capabilities of the Live Color toolset is the ability to globally change the colors of almost any kind of colored object in your Illustrator artwork. Colors in envelopes, meshes, symbols, brushes, patterns, raster effects (but not RGB/CMYK raster images), and in multiple fill and stroke objects can all be easily recolored with the Recolor Artwork dialog!
—*Jean-Claude Tremblay*

Recolor Artwork button

If you have a selection containing at least two distinct colors, just click the Recolor Artwork button in the Control panel to enter Recolor Artwork.

Where's kuler?

See the kuler Appendix (adapted from Mordy Golding's *Real World Adobe Illustrator CS4* book) for details on kuler.

Active Colors appear in the upper-left field of the Edit Colors/Recolor Artwork dialog; you can rename and create new Color Groups here; left button is "Set current color as base color," right button is "Get colors from selected art"

The center-right section of the Edit Colors/ Recolor Artwork dialog has more powerful mini buttons; left button is "New Color Group," center button is "Save changes to color group," and right button is "Delete Color Group"

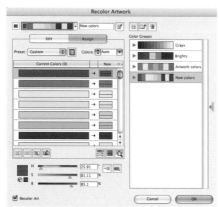

The Recolor Artwork dialog viewed in Assign mode; each color bar represents a color in your selected art objects

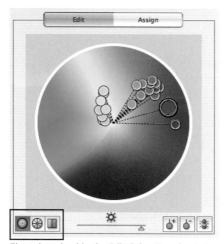

The color wheel in the Edit Colors/Recolor Artwork dialog can be viewed as smooth, segmented, or as bars (by using the buttons highlighted in red); each circle or "marker" represents a color in your selected artwork; the large marker is the current base color

the artwork you are recoloring available as well. With all color-related panels visible, you can generate and save color groups, drag and drop color between panels, and see how each panel changes contextually. For help with arranging panels and customizing your workspace, see the "Workspaces" section in the *Illustrator Basics* chapter.

RECOLORING ARTWORK (AND EDITING COLORS)

Live Color can be used to recolor artwork methodically or completely at random. Click the Recolor Artwork button in the Control panel (available as long as your selection contains at least two colors) to open the Recolor Artwork dialog; the colors from your selected art should still be all in order, and the selection edges will automatically be hidden. If you enter the Recolor Artwork dialog via another path (such as from the Color Guide's Edit or Apply Colors button), your image might initially appear with reassigned colors. If that's not what you intended, click the "Get colors from selected art" button to reload the original colors into your artwork.

Recolor Artwork dialog highlights

At the very top left of the Recolor Artwork dialog is the Active Colors field. Clicking the arrow to the right will drop down a menu showing several of Adobe's "Harmony Rules." Color harmonies are hues that work well together or appear harmonious. The leftmost color among the Active Colors field is the "base color"; all of the harmonies are based on this color. You can drag and drop colors within the Active Colors field. To change the base color, select a different color and click the "Set current color as the base color" button in the upper left of the dialog.

The Recolor Artwork dialog can use the specific color combination you choose as a "rule" to recolor artwork. When you select one of these rules, you change the Active Colors to a new, unlabeled "Color Group." You can enter a new name in the field and then save this group by clicking the New Color Group button. This will add your new color group to the Color Groups section of the dialog.

Clicking on any of your saved color groups will load those colors into the Active Colors field.

The Color Groups section lists any color groups you saved in your Swatches panel before you entered the Recolor Artwork/Edit Colors dialog, and also any color groups you created during this work session. Be aware that deleting and creating new color groups in the Recolor Artwork dialog will delete and add color groups in your Swatches panel, so don't click the trash icon unless you're positive you want to delete that color group from your document entirely. If you create color groups you want to save during a work session, but don't want to apply the changes to your artwork, disable the "Recolor Art" checkbox and click OK. If you click Cancel instead, all the work you did creating (or deleting) new color groups will be deleted.

In Recolor Artwork mode, just below the Active Colors are two main tabs—Edit and Assign. If the Assign tab is inactive when you enter the dialog, it means that you don't have any artwork selected and you're in the Edit Colors mode, instead of the Recolor Artwork mode. If Assign isn't available, click Cancel, select artwork, then re-enter the dialog in Recolor Artwork mode.

The Assign tab displays a row of long horizontal color bars, with each long bar representing one of the colors in the artwork currently selected. To the right of each long color bar is a right-pointing arrow indicating a smaller color swatch that's initially the same color as the larger bar. This small swatch, under the column heading "New," is where you can load or mix a replacement color. Clicking on the right-pointing arrow transforms it into a straight line and protects that color from change. You can also drag and drop colors within this area, and access Context-sensitive menus by holding the Control key (Mac) or right-clicking with a two-button mouse.

With the Edit tab active, you'll see a color wheel with lines (in default view). Attached to the lines are small circles called markers. Each marker represents one of the colors in the objects currently selected. Depending

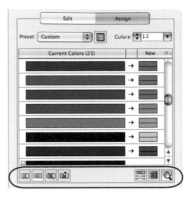

In Assign mode, these buttons (circled) allow for merging, separating, excluding, and adding new color rows; you can also randomly change color order, saturation, and brightness, and find a particular color in your artwork

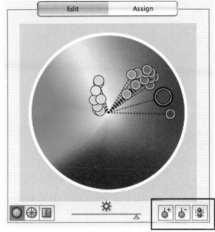

The buttons on the lower right will add markers, delete markers, and link/unlink markers

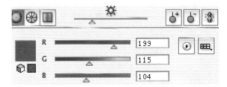

In Edit mode, these color adjustment tools appear just below the color wheel. Hue, saturation, and value (brightness) can be tweaked here.

The color modes menu button (the left button) specifies the mode of the color adjustment sliders; the swatch libraries button (the right button) lets you limit your color group to a particular swatch library

The Color Reduction Options button (under the Assign tab in Recolor Artwork)

The Color Reduction Options button opens this dialog

In Edit or Assign mode, clicking the miniature grid-like button will present a pop-up menu of swatch libraries and "Limits the color group to colors in a swatch library"

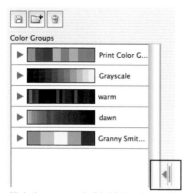

Click the arrow tab (highlighted in red) to hide and show the Color Group storage area of the Recolor Artwork/Edit Colors dialog; all Color Groups that exist in your Swatches panel will show here; directly above the storage area are buttons for Save changes, New, and Delete Color Groups (see previous page for details)

on whether the Lock icon is enabled or disabled, you can move the markers around on the color wheel individually (unlocked) or in unison (locked) to adjust the color in your art. In addition to the default "smooth" Color Wheel, you can also click the icons to display a segmented color wheel, or color bars (see the "Night Into Day" lesson later in this chapter for a practical example of using the color bars view). From this area of the dialog you can also access limited Context-sensitive menus via the Control key (Mac) or right-clicking with a two-button mouse.

In addition to dragging markers around on the color wheel, you can use the sliders and controls just below the color wheel to adjust the various aspects of color (hue, saturation, and value). You can work in the standard color modes (RGB, CMYK, and so on) to adjust individual colors of your artwork, or you can Global Adjust all colors at once. As you adjust individual colors with the sliders, notice that the color marker you selected moves on the color wheel as you move a slider. (For examples of Edit and Assign mode functions, see lessons in this chapter.)

Limiting and reducing colors

Perhaps the most significant benefit of Live Color is the ability to reduce and limit colors to a predefined set of colors in order to recolor your artwork. You can limit color usage to a swatch library, such as one of the Pantone Color Books; you can use a Harmony Rule; or you can choose a recoloring Preset. You can even use your own custom Color Groups as the limiting color set.

When you select one of the 23 color "rules" from the Harmony Rules menu, Live Color chooses hues in "harmony" with your base color, i.e., harmonious in terms of color theory. (For more about working with Adobe's Color Rules and Color Guide, see the *Drawing & Coloring* chapter: the "Color Guide" section in the introduction and lessons "Color Guidance" and "Custom Coloring.")

In Assign mode, click the Color Reduction Options button (to the right of Presets) in order to bring up the Recolor Options dialog. Limit to Library in this dialog allows you to choose a specific swatch library to limit your color choices. In Edit or Assign mode, you can click the small grid-like icon to the right of the sliders named "Limits the color group to colors in a swatch library." The color wheel will be noticeably different when limited to a swatch library. In Assign mode, New colors will be populated exclusively with hues from the chosen swatch library, replacing all original colors with what it determines to be the closest match.

Occasionally, designers and illustrators are asked to produce artwork that will print in only one, two, or three colors. That's what Recolor Artwork's Presets are all about. You can map your artwork's multiple original colors to one or two hues you've specifically defined. Live Color can be a huge timesaver for reducing colors. In Assign mode, choose Preset > 1 Color Job (or 2 Color Job, and so on) and then select a swatch library (most likely Pantone if you're going to press) from which you'll specify the replacement color(s). Recolor Artwork will use tints and shades of the replacement color to transpose colors from your original art. (See the "Recoloring Black" lesson later in this chapter for a practical example of using Presets to replace colors.)

LIVE COLOR, NOT MAGIC COLOR

Think of Live Color as a way to automate and enhance color experimentation, and not as a failsafe scientific process. Using a Harmony Rule will not automatically deliver spectacularly colored artwork, but Harmony Rules can help you quickly find colors considered "harmonious" with your base color. You may or may not find these suggestions harmonious for each of your projects. The bottom line is: Live Color allows you to explore coloring possibilities quickly and easily and perhaps find some inspiration along the way.

Studying and applying (rather than just reading) the lessons that follow in this chapter is the best way to internalize working with Live Color, and to discover how Live Color might enhance your Illustrator workflow.

Special color sets

If your work requires that you use a very specific set of colors, such as team colors or specific "designer" hues for a season, you'll want to first create and save a Color Group (or groups) in the Swatches panel. Then, when you open Live Color, your Color Groups will be in the storage area, ready to recolor your artwork.

What to do with NO Undo?

One of the biggest problems with the Recolor Artwork/Edit Colors dialog is that there is no Undo! To be super safe, use Save a Copy to store a copy of your artwork before entering the Recolor Artwork dialog. Then, if you make a mistake that you can't recover from, either click Cancel to toss out all your work so far, or, if you want to save color groups that you've created, disable the Recolor Artwork checkbox and click OK. If the mistake seems unfixable, start again from your saved copy.
—*Randy Livingston*

More help with Live Color?

If you're looking for more help working with Live Color, see www.adobe.com/designcenter/video_workshop and also *Real World Adobe Illustrator CS4* by Mordy Golding.

Recolor Artwork

Creating Color Schemes with Live Color

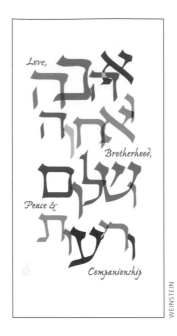

Overview: *Use the Color Guide panel to create color groups based on rules; add groups of swatches to Live Color while launching the dialog; manipulate several colors at once and allow for serendipity in Live Color.*

1

The original fine art piece called "Ahava," meaning "Love"

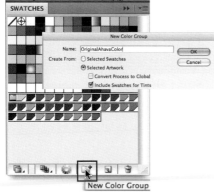

Saving the colors in the original artwork by creating a New Color Group from the selection

When you need to change colors in your artwork, you will want to look at the newest color features in Illustrator. The Color Guide panel can jumpstart your ideas for new color schemes as well as help you create color groups, while features in Live Color can help you inject spontaneity into a makeover. Ari Weinstein found this to be true when he changed the colors of his original fine art print to those that would reflect the warmth of a greeting card and work well on a new background.

1 Using the Color Guide panel and creating new color groups in the Swatches panel. Weinstein began altering his original file by deleting the background watercolor wash and substituting a layer filled with a cream color. He selected all the lettering for placement on a new layer, so the background wouldn't be affected. With the lettering still selected, Weinstein opened the Swatches panel and clicked on the New Color Group icon to name and save the original artwork swatches. He deselected the artwork and selected the red swatch he had used for the English lettering and opened the Color Guide panel. This way the red was set as the base color for the Color Guide panel to use. Clicking on the Harmony Rules arrow, Weinstein looked at the several color schemes that could be based on the swatch color he had just selected, and applied as a harmony "rule." He decided he liked Analogous 2, and clicked on the "Save color group to Swatches panel" icon, which automatically named the group "Color Group 1." After reselecting the artwork, Weinstein selected Color Group 1 and clicked on the Edit or Apply Color Groups icon on the Swatches panel. When Recolor Artwork opens, all the color groups should be listed in the Color Group storage, but the selected group (or groups) is at the top of the list with the topmost group previewed in the artwork. (If you enter Recolor Artwork from the button in the Control panel instead, no color group will be automatically previewed in the artwork, which you might prefer before choosing a color group.)

2 **Editing the colors and allowing a measure of randomness to keep color edits lively.** From the Assign tab, Weinstein noted that the colors in the artwork were combined (reduced) to the number of colors in Color Group 1. Weinstein then clicked on one color bar at a time in the "New" column, adjusting the HSB sliders to taste. Mainly he chose to increase saturation, making the artwork brighter and warmer. When using the sliders made it difficult to adjust a color, he double-clicked on the Color Picker swatch beside the sliders to open the Color Picker. These controls are much bigger and allow more room in which to make very fine changes. Finally, Weinstein inserted some randomness in the color assignments by dragging the small color bars from one row to another in the Current Colors column. (Alternatively, you can click on the "Randomly change color order" button.) The artwork updated in real time, showing the changes as he dragged. When he saw what he liked, he clicked OK to exit the dialog and apply his color edits.

With the major changes complete, Weinstein made a few final changes to color by the time-honored method of painstakingly selecting individual sections and manually adjusting the colors in the Color panel.

2

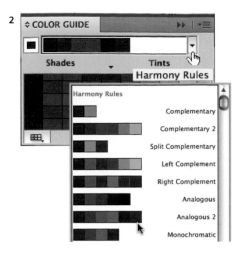

Selecting the Harmony Rules drop-down list and choosing a color rule based on a selected color

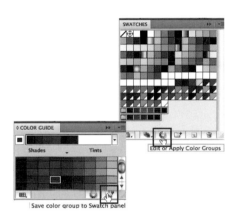

Saving a color group created in the Color Guide panel to the Swatches panel, then selecting a group or groups for use in Recolor Artwork

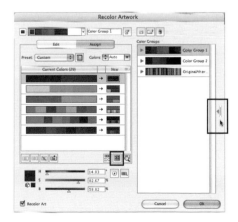

Reducing and grouping colors by assigning a saved color group from the Color Groups panel

Fashionable Colors

Applying Spot Colors with Live Color

Overview: *Apply colors with Live Paint; duplicate images; use Live Color to create Spot colors; Merge colors in Live Color.*

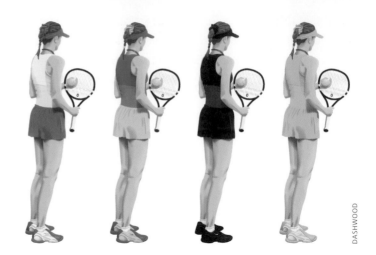

DASHWOOD

1

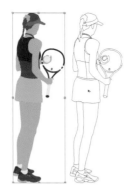

Option-drag/Alt-drag to create duplicates of your artwork on the Artboard

Enter the Recolor Artwork dialog by clicking on the Recolor Artwork button in the Control panel

2

Access color books inside of Recolor Artwork using the flyout menu

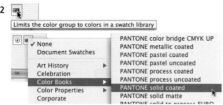

Choose Exact from the New Color pop-up menu to avoid creating tints of Spot Colors

To create these seasonal apparel color changes for an interactive series of instructional materials, Andrew Dashwood used the Recolor Artwork dialog of Live Color to Preview and Assign multiple color variations.

1 Preparing for Live Color. Dashwood began by drawing the tennis player's outline, using the Pen tool to make closed paths. To prepare paths for future recoloring, first block out a basic color scheme by clicking on paths and choosing colors, or use the Live Paint Bucket to convert your figure to a Live Paint object and fill colors with it. Choose the colors first for the parts of the drawing that will not change, in this case, the hair, skin, and tennis racket. Then, choose a random color for each piece of apparel and footwear. You'll find it easier to experiment with color combinations if you begin with a wider variety of colors than you anticipate using in your final image. It's not possible to divide colors inside of the Recolor Artwork dialog, but it is very easy to merge them together.

Create duplicates of your artwork so you'll be able to apply different color changes to each of the versions. Select your artwork, hold Option-Shift/Alt-Shift, and drag it sideways. Then let go of your mouse to create a duplicate of your art. Use ⌘/Ctrl-D to create additional duplicates. Select objects and click the Recolor Artwork button in the Control panel to enter the Recolor Artwork dialog.

2 Working with Live Color and Spot Colors. Once you enter the Recolor Artwork dialog, make sure the Assign tab is active; once it is, you'll be able to change the colors in your image. Since most clients want you to use a specific palette of colors, you can load a color book or custom library of spot, process, or global colors by clicking on the rightmost bottom button called "Limits the color group to colors in a swatch library." To avoid creating tints of a spot color, choose Exact from the pop-up next to the New Color swatch. Once you return to the Artboard, if you select objects containing a Global or Spot swatch, its name will be displayed in the Color panel.

Using Recolor Artwork you can choose to protect colors you don't want to change (such as the skin tone, hair, and tennis racket colors). To protect a color from change, click the arrow to the right of its Current Color icon. The arrow toggles to a straight line, protecting that Current Color from changing to a New Color (click again to toggle protection off). To begin changing the colors, click on the Edit tab. If you chose a custom color book, the color wheel will be divided to display only those colors. Make sure the Link Color Harmony button is unlocked on the color wheel, so that moving one of the color values on the color won't affect the others. Once you find a tonal range that suites your image well, click on the Link Color Harmony button to enable the lock option. Once the lock is enabled, you can then drag the linked colors around the wheel to experiment with different color combinations.

3 Reducing Colors. To merge two or more Current Colors into a single New Color, click on the Assign tab, select one Current Color, and then drag onto another one. The color bar in the Current Colors will be divided in two, and an arrow to the right of it will show you the changed effect. Alternatively, you can select colors in a row and use the buttons at the bottom-left of the section, or Control-click (Mac)/right-click to choose Context-sensitive options. Once you've created a color scheme you like, click OK to exit the Recolor Artwork dialog and apply your changes.

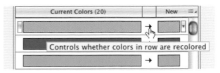
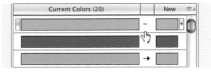

Click on the arrow between a Current Color and New Color to prevent the original color from being modified

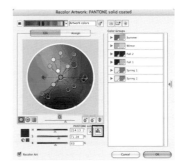

The color wheel when limited to a color book; Link Harmony Color button highlighted in red

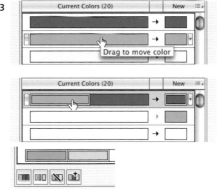

Merging Current Colors by dragging them into one another, or using the buttons

Recoloring Black

Using Live Color to Replace Blacks

Overview: *Work with the Recolor Artwork dialog; limit color choices to a Swatch library; choose the right settings to ensure the appropriate colors change; protect specific colors from change.*

The original artwork

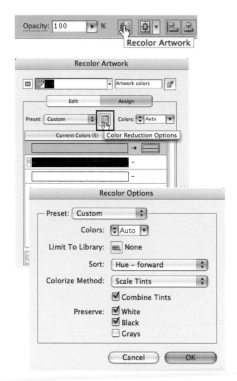

Default settings for Recolor Options and how they affect the assignment of color in Recolor Artwork's main dialog

Live Color provides exciting ways to experiment with color changes, but there are times when you'll get unexpected results if you don't know how to control it. After Laurent Pinabel gave Jean-Claude Tremblay this poster and flyer artwork for printing, a last-minute client request required changing the process black to a Pantone metallic silver spot color. Knowing the ins and outs of the Recolor Artwork dialog made it possible for Tremblay to edit only the black objects without having to select them manually, while protecting the gold and white colors.

1 Opening the Recolor Artwork dialog and changing default settings in the Recolor Options dialog. Tremblay began by selecting the entire graphic. This ensured that he quickly captured all tints and shades of any color, should there be more than one for each. He clicked the Recolor Artwork button in the Control panel to enter the dialog. With default settings, Black and White are protected colors in Recolor Artwork (meaning new colors will not be assigned to them), so there will not be a color bar for Black in the New column of the dialog. Tremblay clicked the Color Reduction Options button to open the Recolor Options dialog. This dialog helps set up colors to suit the type of document being worked on before they are edited in the main Recolor Artwork dialog. While Tremblay worked in the Recolor Options dialog, the main Live Color dialog updated to reflect his current settings in the Recolor Options dialog.

If the Recolor Options settings are changed out of sequence, Recolor Artwork will not update properly.

Therefore, Tremblay began adjusting the settings at the top and worked his way down. With only two spot colors used for printing, he first chose Preset: 2 color job. This opens the Limit To Library dialog where he selected Color Book > Pantone metallic coated. In the Live Color dialog, swatch colors were updated, with Black still below the gold. For Recolor Artwork to work properly in a 2-color job when you're only changing one of the protected colors (Black, White, or Grays), you must move that color to the top of the Current Colors column. Tremblay clicked the Color Reduction Options button and chose Sort: Lightness - dark to light, and disabled Preserve: Black. The Recolor Artwork dialog updated, placing Black at the top.

Tremblay also wanted to make certain that if the artwork had any tints of the Black in it, these would be replaced by a single metallic color. He chose Exact for the Colorize Method and unchecked Combine Tints since he only wanted one color to replace any black found in the artwork. If he had wanted to keep tints of a process color while exchanging it for another process color (a CMYK black to a CMYK purple, for instance), he would have kept the default setting of Scale Tints for the Colorize Method, and kept Combine Tints checked. (For a more complete explanation, search for *Colorize Method* in Adobe Illustrator Help.) Tremblay clicked OK to close the Recolor Options dialog. When settings have been changed, some settings in Recolor Options will be remembered, while others will return to their default. It's a good idea to look in the Recolor Options dialog when you first enter Recolor Artwork to see that the settings are appropriate for the current job.

2 Protecting a color from change and assigning a new color. Back on the Assign tab, Tremblay clicked on the arrow connecting the gold color bars to eliminate gold from any further change. He double-clicked on the color bar in the New column to the right of the Black's arrow, and chose 877 C from the Color Picker. Clicking on the color swatch also would bring up the same Color Picker.

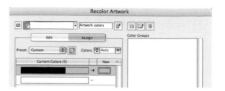

Settings made in random sequence, or not made at all, causing the Recolor Artwork dialog to fail to update properly

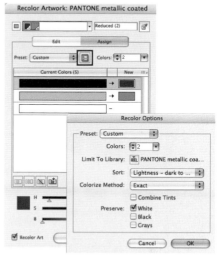

Correct settings for a 2 color job (set via the Color Reduction Options button) changing a protected color (Black), with Recolor Artwork updating to reflect the new assignment and Swatch Library colors replacing original colors

The Recolor Artwork dialog with all Recolor Options settings in place, gold protected from change and a metallic silver being exchanged for Black

Night Into Day

Recoloring a Complex Composition

Advanced Technique

Overview: *Simplify selections for color edits; switch views in Recolor Artwork for greater manageability; isolate values within a hue in Recolor Artwork to control color changes.*

1

The original nighttime Palms image

Select All makes it difficult to isolate color for editing, but selecting just a few layers simplifies viewing and editing in the Recolor Artwork dialog, which hides selection edges

Complex illustrations often contain many colors inside a large variety of objects, including colors in gradients and gradient mesh. Using the Recolor Artwork dialog, you can edit all of these at once, but in order to make it practical for handling large numbers of color, Sharon Steuer found methods for selecting and viewing colors in "bite-size" chunks. There are myriad ways to approach editing in Recolor Artwork, but she chose to focus on restricting selections. She then used different ways of viewing selections to isolate the colors she wanted to change.

1 Making targeted selections to reduce complexity in Live Color. When Steuer decided to produce a daytime version of her Palms art, instead of having to rework the many gradients and mesh objects in her illustration individually, she decided to use the Recolor Artwork dialog so that she could make compositional color changes quickly. At first she selected the entire image, but this resulted in selecting so many colors that finding any individual color was impractical. Instead she decided to hide the foreground layers containing the main subject (the palms and grasses), working on just the background layers of sky, sand, and water. She clicked on the Recolor Artwork button in the Control panel to enter the dialog.

2 Using the Color Bars and Color Wheel views to target and edit colors. In the Recolor Artwork dialog,

Steuer clicked on the Edit tab. The default smooth color wheel view showed far too many markers to distinguish just the values she wanted, so she clicked on the "Display color bars" button for the linear view. Now the values among the blues were much easier to select. Steuer clicked on the darkest value she could find in order to change the shadow of night into a shaft of sunlight. By clicking on the color bar she highlighted the color easily, but now Steuer had to decide which color mode to use. If she clicked on the arrow to the right of the sliders, Steuer could choose to work in any standard color mode, select Tint for working with Spot colors, or check Global Adjust to ignore hue selections and globally change all the colors by the same amount. Steuer decided to use the default HSB mode, since changing just the Saturation and Brightness sliders would create a very pale blue "shaft of light."

After creating color for the shaft of light, Steuer wanted to change the hue of all the blues, including those in the shaft of light. To shift the hues without changing the overall range of brightness or saturation, she clicked back on the "Display smooth color wheel" button and then enabled the "Link harmony colors" button. The icon now displayed an unbroken link so that any marker Steuer moved on the color wheel would move all others in tandem, thus preserving the relationship between separate hues. She slid the "chain" of markers to a slightly more turquoise blue. Since the "moon" was almost completely neutral, it wasn't noticeably affected. She disabled the link to allow for individual hue changes later on.

3 Using the magnifier on the Assign tab to target very specific colors. Steuer now wanted to lighten those blues that were still too dark, but she found they were difficult to distinguish with certainty on either the color wheel or on the color bars. Steuer returned to the Assign tab and clicked on the "magnifier" button (labeled "Click on colors above to find them in the artwork"). Clicking with the "magnifier" on a color bar isolates that color in the image. The rest of the image is dimmed, or "screened back."

Choosing "Display color bars" to make it easier to find, select, and edit values within a gradient

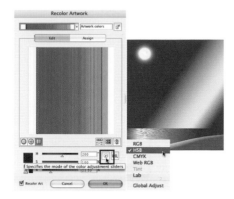

Choosing a color mode for the color adjustment sliders

Linking colors and sliding linked markers on the smooth color wheel to adjust hue

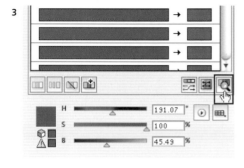

Getting ready to isolate a color by clicking on the "magnifier" button ("Click on colors above to find them in the artwork" button)

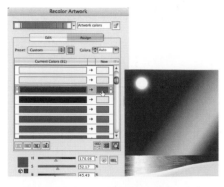

Finding the dark blue that fills the sky and water, isolating it from all other colors in the image by using the magnifier button on the Assign tab

Lightening the sky and water and restoring visibility to all the layers except the stars

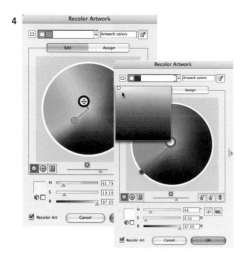

Click-dragging on a smooth color wheel's marker makes it easy to change hue along with saturation and brightness, whereas Control-clicking/right-clicking on the marker opens the Context-sensitive menu to access Select Shade to adjust a color by saturation and brightness only

Steuer scrolled through the list of colors, looking for the darkest of blues to lighten up. Clicking on any dark blue permitted her to see where that particular color was used in the image. When the image displayed the original dark blue of the sky and water and nothing else, she knew she had the right color bar selected. With the main area that needed to be lightened now targeted for change, Steuer switched back to the Edit tab and used the Saturation and Brightness sliders once again to lighten and brighten the sky and water for a daytime appearance. She made certain that the Recolor Art option was enabled (so her edits would be applied to the image), then she clicked OK to exit the Recolor Artwork dialog.

4 **Live Color controls editing color for restricted changes in the newly created sun.** Steuer restored the visibility to all the layers except those containing the stars. Looking at the new sun, she decided the glow was too cool for a bright sunny day. She selected just the "moon" layer (not the "moon mesh") and reentered the dialog. With so few colors, it would be easy to select just the yellow marker on the smooth color wheel. However, sliding the marker manually by clicking and dragging on it can change the hue itself, even with very small movements. Steuer decided to Control-click/right-click the yellow marker instead to open the Context-sensitive menu. Choosing Select Shade brought up a restricted color picker for that particular hue, which allowed more precision than dragging on the sliders would have, while also preserving the hue. The color representation of the swatch also made it easy for Steuer to pick out a slightly more saturated, but not much darker, yellow. The moon now looked like a sun with a gentle, warm glow around it, completing the night-into-day transformation.

Recolor Artwork saves new brushes and gradients

If the artwork that you recolor includes brushes and gradients, newly recolored versions of the brushes and gradients will automatically be saved to your panels!

SUTHERLAND

Brenda Sutherland

Brenda Sutherland created the original logo for
a micro-brewery. With the advent of Live Color,
she realized she could easily create color variations to accompany the different micro-brews.
Because the original coloring is very complex,
she divided the logo into three sections—the
text portion, the center of the logo, and the
outer circle. The inner circle alone has two
gradient fills and multiple strokes, which only
Live Color can handle easily. She selected the
Text layer and saved the artwork colors to the
Swatches panel. She repeated this for both
the center and outer circles. Sutherland placed
copies of the logo on their own layers. She
selected just the outer circle on one layer and
opened the Recolor Artwork dialog. There
she chose the Edit tab and moved the markers
on the smooth color wheel until she found a
scheme she liked. She saved the colors as a new

color group, then clicked OK to apply the color
scheme and return to the main image. Sutherland repeated this process for the other two
areas in the logo, and again to create two more
color schemes.

Reducing Color

Going Monochromatic with Live Color

Advanced Technique

Overview: *Place color groups in the Swatches panel; reduce colors in a grayscale conversion; make a modified color version using the grayscale values and Global Adjust sliders.*

Why Live Color for Grayscale?

With automatic grayscale conversions such as Edit > Edit Colors > Convert to Grayscale, you can't make many decisions about how your image is converted. However, using a grayscale color group and Live Color you can control replacing color with grayscale values to achieve optimal contrast.

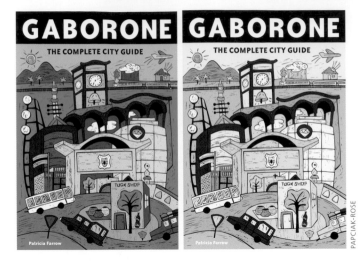

PAPCIAK-ROSE

Designers and artists frequently need to reduce the number of colors they used in original artwork in order to feature the same piece in another venue. In this book cover for *Gaborone: The Complete City Guide* by Patricia Farrow, South African illustrator Ellen Papciak-Rose used a full range of bright colors. Using Live Color's remarkable ability to combine and replace colors, you can control the way colors are reduced in number to make subtle or exaggerated changes. Live Color allows you to experiment or to make specific color changes, such as converting color to grayscale, protecting accent colors if desired, and even to create color-tinted versions of your newly converted grayscale image.

Finding the Grayscale color group in the Default Swatches library

1 Placing Color Groups in the Swatches panel for a monochromatic scheme. Before you can convert colors in your image, you need to make sure that your file contains the color groups that you'll be applying to your image. In this case, your file should contain a grayscale color group, and at least one hue-based monochromatic color group. New documents contain a grayscale color group in the Swatches panel. If your image hasn't been saved with the grayscale color group, open the Swatches Libraries icon and select Default CMYK (or RGB) from the menu. For the monochromatic color group, select a swatch or use the Color panel to create a color that will become the base in the Color Guide for your color group.

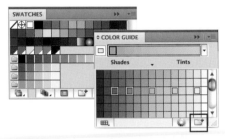

Saving color groups to the Swatches panel; using the Color Guide panel to generate monochromatic palettes

Select a series of tints and shades and click on the "Save color group to Swatch panel" icon. Four or five swatches for the tints and shades (the same number that the Harmony Rules include in a group) are normally enough for a grayscale conversion. Once you've created the color groups you like and saved them to the Swatches panel, select your artwork and click on the Recolor Artwork button in the Control panel.

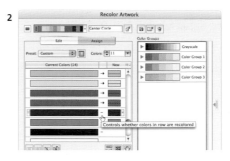

Protecting colors from change in Live Color

2 Reducing colors in Live Color for a monochromatic scheme. When Live Color opens, scroll through the list on the Assign tab until you come to any colors you want to protect from change, such as the red, black, and white of the "Gaborone" image. If any of these colors has an arrow between its color bars, click on it to toggle protection on. To create a satisfactory grayscale conversion, click on the Grayscale color group in the color group storage area, then begin dragging color bars in the Current Colors column from one row to another, combining and changing the value of the gray that has been assigned to each color. Watch the live update in the image as you experiment with combining colors in order to arrive at good contrast. If you now want to "tint" this grayscale, make sure the grays don't exceed the number of swatches in your color group and proceed with Step 3; otherwise, if you want to keep the grayscale conversion, stop here and, with Recolor Art enabled, click OK to apply the change.

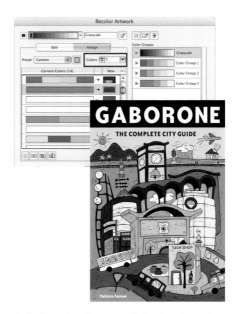

Reducing colors for grayscale by dragging color bars together in combinations that get assigned to the same values and/or hues

3 Using your grayscale conversion to generate "tints." While your grayscale color conversion is still in Live Color, you can now tint your image using the monochromatic color groups you created. Click on a color group to preview the color scheme in the image. If you wish to make adjustments to the selected color scheme, click on the Edit tab, and use the color adjustment sliders (such as Global Adjust, used here) or drag linked color markers. If you find a scheme you want, click the New Color Group icon to add it to your list. Once you like the results, with Recolor Art enabled, click OK to apply the change.

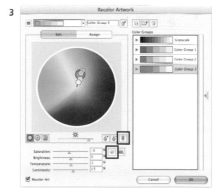

Choosing a monochromatic color scheme to "tint" the grayscale conversion, and modifying the colors on the Edit tab using color adjustment sliders or dragging markers on the color wheel

A Live Workflow

Moving From Photograph to Illustration

Advanced Technique

Overview: *Use default settings in Live Trace on a photograph; duplicate the tracing and adjust Live Trace settings for each object; change the values for the Global swatches; use Live Paint to adjust outlines; edit tones with the Recolor Artwork dialog.*

Running Live Trace from the Control panel with default settings

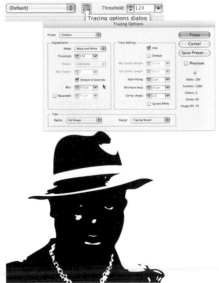

Increasing Thresholds using the Tracing Options dialog results in silhouette with saved swatches

To create Chris Daddy, Brenda Sutherland developed a method for using Live Trace with Live Paint that allowed her to maximize control over the process. By duplicating and adjusting tracing objects, she was able to build dark to light variations, creating a custom posterization effect, rather than depending upon the values in the photograph to create the tones. She edited the tones in Live Color to complete the transition from photograph to illustration.

1 **Starting the Live Trace portrait.** Sutherland began her illustration with the portrait of Chris Daddy isolated on a transparent background. On the Control panel, she clicked on the Live Trace button, which traced the portrait with the default Black and White settings. She then selected the traced object and clicked on the Tracing options dialog button. Sutherland turned on Preview and increased the Threshold setting until the image was almost a silhouette. To prevent the paths from becoming overly complex, she added a small amount of Blur and increased the Corner Angle to a fairly large amount. In

order to create global swatches, she checked Output to Swatches and clicked on Trace to apply the new settings. Next Sutherland copied the tracing three times by dragging the sublayer to the Create New Layer icon in the Layers panel. She renamed the sublayers for ease of use.

2 Creating the posterized effect with four tracing layers. In order to see the change in Threshold as she adjusted it, Sutherland locked "Tracing" and turned off the visibility icon on "Tracing 3" and "Tracing 4." She selected "Tracing 2," the first copy she had made, and again clicked on the Tracing options dialog button. She enabled Preview and Ignore White. Because new swatches aren't generated when Live Trace settings are adjusted, and Illustrator still sees "Tracing 2" as a copy of "Tracing" instead of a new tracing, she temporarily disabled Output to Swatches. She then immediately enabled it again to force Live Trace to create a new Global swatch that would be associated with this tracing. (Illustrator automatically names the swatch it outputs as "Tracing 2" in the Swatches panel, and Live Trace treats "Tracing 2" as an independent object.) Then, in order to see the Threshold adjustment she was about to make to "Tracing 2," she changed the Vector setting to Outlines with Tracing and adjusted the Threshold to a smaller amount than the first. Until she saw new tonal values applied to the tracings, she had to rely on the outlines to show the separation of tones. However, by keeping the objects live, she could later adjust the Threshold settings while viewing the separate tones once she had edited the values of the Global swatches. Sutherland clicked Trace to apply the new settings and repeated these steps for the last two tracings, each time decreasing the Threshold amount.

3 Using Global Swatches to color the tracings and adjusting the outlines. With Global swatches now assigned to each of the tracings, Sutherland doubleclicked on the first Black Global swatch that had been added to the Swatches panel (called "Tracing" or

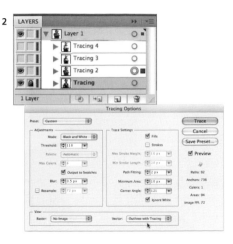

Duplicating the original tracing, setting up visibility for adjusting Threshold settings and creating new swatches for every tracing object

Four tracings made with different Threshold settings, Vector set to Outlines with Tracing, and a Black swatch output for each object

After changing the tones for three of the four Black swatches

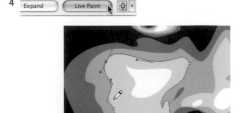

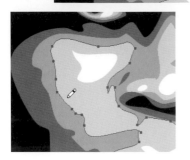

Selecting and smoothing paths on a Live Paint object with the Pencil tool

After choosing the Monochromatic Harmony Rule

Disabling Preserve: Black, permitting it to be colorized with the other shades of gray

"Tracing 1"), and changed the Black to a pale gray. She then changed the second and third Black swatches in the panel to successively darker grays and left the last Black ("Tracing 4") alone. Now she could see the four-color shading of the portrait, and further adjust the Threshold for the tracing objects to achieve a better balance.

4 Creating a Live Paint object to gain control over Live Trace outlines. Sutherland wanted to be able to adjust some of the outlines without worrying about creating gaps between filled objects, which could happen if she expanded the Live Trace objects and then altered some of the paths. Live Paint adjusts fills as the paths are adjusted. She selected all the tracing objects and clicked the Live Paint button in the Control panel. She didn't merge the new Live Paint objects at first because Live Paint's performance is better with less complex objects. She selected paths with the Direct Selection tool that weren't pleasing and used the Pencil tool to redraw and smooth some areas. When done, she selected Merge Live Paint from the Control panel. This reduced her objects to a single Live Paint object, but still kept the object "live" enough that she could easily edit the paths later on.

5 Editing Global Swatches using Live Color. With her Live Paint object still selected, Sutherland clicked on the Recolor Artwork button in the Control panel. When the dialog opened, she clicked on the Harmony Rules arrow next to the swatches and selected Monochromatic from the drop-down list. (The Monochromatic Harmony Rule locks the Harmony link on the Edit tab automatically, holding the markers in a single "line" to restrict changes as you drag to the same Hue setting for all the markers.) The assigned colors didn't match the tones she had established in the portrait, but she could change that easily. She clicked on the Color Reduction Options button to open the Recolor Options dialog and disabled Preserve: Black in order to permit Black to be colorized. She clicked OK and returned to the Assign tab. The tonal values were still misassigned, with lighter values being assigned to the original dark values. To correct this, Sutherland dragged the color bars in the New column from one row to another until the darkest values were in one row, the next darkest in another, and so on. She used the HSB sliders to change the Brightness levels to the range of values she wanted, making sure both Hue and Saturation were identical for each tone. These preliminary adjustments made it easier to visualize the relationship between the values when she switched to the Edit tab.

When she had the Brightness variances approximately correct, she clicked on the Edit button and carefully dragged the color markers on the smooth color wheel until she found a monochromatic color scheme that she liked. She could still change Saturation by dragging a marker closer to or further away from the center of the wheel, or by double-clicking on the marker to open the Color Picker. She could use the Brightness slider to change overall brightness, or use the B slider for individual markers. Each time she found a harmony she liked, she saved it as a Color Group in the color group storage. (See the "Night Into Day" lesson in this chapter for more on the editing features in the Recolor Artwork dialog.) After experimenting, Sutherland chose a harmony of blues for Chris Daddy. She looked to see that Recolor Art was enabled and clicked OK to apply the colors.

To create the background, Sutherland repeated this entire process on another layer—again using Live Trace, converting to Live Paint, and using the Recolor Artwork dialog—to turn the city scene from photograph to illustration, harmonizing color and style with the portrait.

When to use Expand before Live Paint

When you create several tracings of the same subject and then convert them to Live Paint, occasionally a color will flood the image because the objects bleed off the edge. Undo, and this time, first click Expand on the Control panel. This turns the tracing into paths Live Paint can then identify and fill individually.

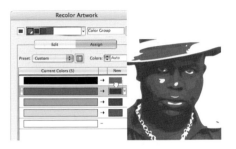

Dragging color bars in the New column up or down to reorder the assignment of values

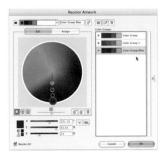

Choosing a monochromatic color scheme and creating and saving several color groups

Too many black colors?

Too many blacks, as in the figures below, is caused in this case by Preserve: Black already disabled when you enter Recolor Artwork and try to select a Harmony Rule. To fix it, open the Recolor Options dialog, enable Preserve: Black, close the dialog and select your Harmony Rule. Now you can open Recolor Options again and disable Preserve: Black if you want Black to be an editable color.

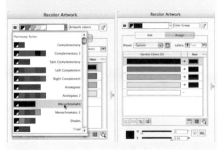

Live Effects & Graphic Styles

The Effect Menu

```
Effect
Apply Transform                    ⇧⌘E
Transform...                      ⌥⇧⌘E

Document Raster Effects Settings...

Illustrator Effects
    3D                              ▶
    Convert to Shape                ▶
    Crop Marks
    Distort & Transform             ▶
    Path                            ▶
    Pathfinder                      ▶
    Rasterize...
    Stylize                         ▶
    SVG Filters                     ▶
    Warp                            ▶

Photoshop Effects
    Effect Gallery...
    Artistic                        ▶
    Blur                            ▶
    Brush Strokes                   ▶
    Distort                         ▶
    Pixelate                        ▶
    Sharpen                         ▶
    Sketch                          ▶
    Stylize                         ▶
    Texture                         ▶
    Video                           ▶
```

The Effect menu

The fx icon in the Appearance panel

Photoshop effects don't scale

Keep in mind that Photoshop effects won't scale along with an object—not even if you have the Scale Strokes & Effects option enabled in your Preferences.

—Jean-Claude Tremblay

Illustrator boasts a formidable array of live effects—from the warps and envelopes to 3D, Gaussian Blur, and Scribble. A few of the more robust live effects reside in their own chapters: Live Trace and Live Paint are in *Beyond the Basics*, and 3D is in the *Live 3D Effects* chapter. This chapter will focus on bringing you up to speed on working with all of Illustrator's other live effects, and creating and working with graphic styles.

THE EFFECT MENU

The Effect menu is divided into two sections. The effects in the upper section (labeled Illustrator Effects) are mostly for use with vector images. Those in the lower section (labeled Photoshop Effects) were originally developed for use with raster images, but their use was eventually expanded to apply to vector images as well. Although none of the effects let you save or export presets of settings that you like from within their dialogs, you *can* save any set of effect attributes that you like as a graphic style. To save your set of effects as a graphic style, just drag the thumbnail in the Appearance panel to the Graphic Styles panel, or use the New Graphic Style icon in the Graphic Styles panel. (For more about graphic styles, see the final section of this chapter intro, as well as the Lessons and Galleries that follow it.)

EFFECTS IN THE APPEARANCE PANEL

One convenient new feature in Illustrator CS4 is the ability to add and edit effects directly from the Appearance panel. You can add an effect to a selected object by clicking the Add New Effect (*fx*) icon and choosing an effect from the pop-up menu, which contains all the same commands as the Effect menu in the main menu bar.

To edit an existing effect, simply select the object that has the effect, and click the effect name in the Appearance panel. (Or double-click the *fx* icon next to the name.)

Note: *Although in many cases using the Appearance panel will be the most convenient way for you to add effects, to simplify this chapter's instructions we'll use the convention "choose Effect >" followed by the name of the effect.*

RASTER EFFECTS

In the New Document dialog, when you choose a profile from the New Document Profile drop-down menu, Illustrator automatically selects a default resolution for your raster effects based on the profile you've chosen. For instance, if you choose the Print profile, Illustrator will set a document raster effects setting of 300 ppi, and for a Web profile it sets it to 72 ppi. Once your document has been created, you can always view or change the document raster effects resolution by choosing Effect > Document Raster Effects Setting.

There's an important distinction between the raster effects that originated in Photoshop (and were then added in the bottom part of Illustrator's Effect menu, such as Gaussian Blur) and the raster effects developed specifically for Illustrator, such as Feather, Glow, and Drop Shadow. The Photoshop effects specify their options in pixels, whereas the native Illustrator effects specify their distances in ruler units. So if you apply a Gaussian Blur at 3 pixels, it looks much more blurry when the resolution is 72 ppi compared to 288 ppi. On the other hand, if you have a drop shadow with a 3-pt blur, it automatically adjusts to the resolution, and just covers more pixels at a higher resolution. For this reason, if you have Photoshop effects applied and you change the Document Raster Effects resolution, you may need to adjust the specific effect options, like Blur Distance, as well. (This process should be familiar to anyone who has changed the resolution of a Photoshop document containing Layer Effects.)

Our output expert Jean-Claude Tremblay advises that you should never send a file to be printed without setting the desired high resolution yourself and proofing it. Illustrator files created with raster effects might need adjustments, and you cannot trust that those who haven't seen

Transform effects!

Any transformation can be applied as an *effect* (Effect > Distort & Transform > Transform). You can Rotate, Shear, Scale, or even make multiple copies, as Vicki Loader did, from a single seahorse.

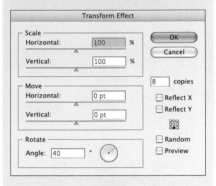

LOADER

Keep spot colors with effects!

You can use and preserve spot colors as spot colors, even with live effects such as Drop Shadow, Gaussian Blur, and Feather applied! To take advantage of this, make certain that the "Preserve spot colors" option is enabled in Effect > Document Raster Effects Settings.—*Jean-Claude Tremblay*

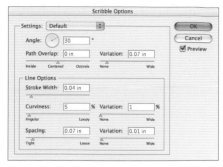
The Scribble Options dialog

The Scribble effect can be applied to an object's stroke, fill, or both

WEINSTEIN

For more lessons with Scribble, see Ari Weinstein's "Antiquing Type" lesson in the Artboards & Type chapter

Crosshatching using Scribble

You don't have to duplicate an object to create a crosshatch effect using Scribble. Instead, after applying Scribble to the object's fill (and selecting your object), choose Add New Fill from the Appearance panel menu. Then choose Effect > Stylize > Scribble, and for the Angle setting, add 90° to the angle. —*Mike Schwabauer*

Isolation mode for envelopes

Another convenient way to edit an envelope: double-click it to enter isolation mode.
—*Jean-Claude Tremblay*

your art will know how it should look, or that they know how to make adjustments to the file.

SCRIBBLE EFFECT

The Scribble Effect (Effect > Stylize > Scribble) lets you quickly create a variety of scribble effects—from loose and *scribbly* to a tight crosshatch. Scribble effects can be applied to the fill and/or stroke of an object depending on what you have targeted in the Appearance panel when you apply the effect.

The Scribble Options dialog is divided into three sections. The Settings menu contains a fixed number of Scribble presets. Use the Angle dial to control the overall direction of the Scribble lines. A setting of 0° causes the Scribble lines to run left to right; 90° makes them run up and down. Use the Path Overlap slider to control how much the scribble stays inside or extends outside of a path boundary. In the Line Options section of the Scribble dialog, use the Stroke Width control to specify how fat or thin you want the scribble line to be. Use the Curviness slider to set how Angular or Loopy the ends of each scribble stroke should be. Use the Spacing slider to specify how tight or loose you want your strokes to be. Use the Variation sliders to further control how each attribute is applied: For a very regular, machine-made look, set the slider to None, and for a more freehand and natural look, move the slider toward Wide.

By combining other effects, or applying brushstrokes to your scribbles, you can create an almost infinite variety of looks. Use them as fills or masks to transform type, or save them as graphic styles to apply to other artwork.

WARPS AND ENVELOPING

Illustrator's Warp Effects and Envelope tool are robust and very powerful, offering much more than just simple transformations. Warps and envelopes may look similar at first, but there's an important difference between them. Warps are applied as live *effects*—meaning they can be applied to objects, groups, or layers. Create them by choosing from the predefined options in the Warp dialogs; you can save them within a graphic style. Envelopes, on the other hand, are also live, but rather than effects, they're actual *objects* that contain artwork. You can edit or customize the envelope shape, and Illustrator will conform the contents of the envelope to the contour (see "Arcing Type" in the *Artboards & Type* chapter).

Warps

Applying a warp is actually quite simple. Target an object, group, or layer and choose Effect > Warp > Arc. (It doesn't matter which warp effect you choose, because you'll be presented with the Warp Options dialog, where you can choose from any of the 15 different warps.) While the warp effects are "canned" in the sense that you can't make adjustments to the effects directly, you can control how a warp appears by changing the Bend value, as well as the Horizontal and Vertical Distortion values.

Once you've applied a warp, you can edit it by opening the Appearance panel and clicking on the warp effect. Like all effects, a warp can be applied to just the fill, or just the stroke—and if you edit the artwork, the warp updates as well. Since warps are effects, you can include them in a graphic style (discussed later in this chapter), which can then be applied to other artwork.

Envelopes

While warp effects do a nice job of distorting artwork (and allow you to save the effect as a graphic style), Illustrator envelopes provide a higher level of control.

There are three ways to apply envelopes. The simplest way is to create a shape you want to use as your envelope. Make sure it's at the top of the stacking order—above the art you want to place inside the envelope. Then, with the artwork and your created shape both selected, choose Object > Envelope Distort > Make with Top Object. Illustrator will create a special kind of object: an envelope. This object you created becomes an envelope container, which appears in the Layers panel as <Envelope>. You can

Add a bounding rectangle

Since warps start at the bounding box of objects, when using inside a group or layer, it is often useful to draw a large square/rectangle with no stroke or fill as the definer of the bounding box. This allows the possibility to add to a group/layer with a warp without seeing too much rewarping. This is also true for envelopes.
—*Jean-Claude Tremblay*

Envelope distort options

If your artwork contains pattern fills or linear gradients, you can employ envelopes to distort them by choosing Object > Envelope Distort > Envelope Options and enabling the appropriate items in the dialog. —*Mordy Golding*

Smart people use Smart Guides

Smart Guides can be quite helpful when you work with warps or envelopes, as it may become difficult to edit artwork that has an appearance applied to it. With Smart Guides turned on, Illustrator will highlight the art for you, making it easier to identify where the actual artwork is (and not the appearance). Make use of the ⌘-U/Ctrl-U keyboard shortcut to turn Smart Guides on and off.
—*Mordy Golding*

The three Envelope buttons in the Control panel, from left to right: Edit Envelope, Edit Contents, and Envelope Options

The tools that appear in the Control panel when an envelope warp is selected; you can change the shape of the warp using the pop-up menu

The controls that appear in the Control panel when an envelope mesh is selected; you can easily change the number of rows and columns, and restore the object to its original shape using the Reset Envelope Shape button

Deleting a mesh point

To delete a mesh point from a warp or mesh envelope in one easy step, simply choose the Mesh tool and then Option-click/Alt-click the point you'd like to delete. —*Jean-Claude Tremblay*

Flare—tool or effect?

The Flare tool turns up in Ted Alspach's Gallery later in this chapter. That's because although the Flare tool isn't technically an effect, it behaves like one—you can select and re-edit your Flare tool work using the Flare Tool Options dialog (double-click the Flare tool to open it).

edit the path of the envelope with any transformation or editing tools; the artwork inside will update to conform to the shape. To edit the contents of the envelope, click the Edit Contents button in the Control panel or choose Object > Envelope Distort > Edit Contents. If you then look at the Layers panel, you'll notice that the <Envelope> now has a disclosure triangle that reveals the contents of the envelope—the artwork you placed. You can edit the artwork directly or even drag other paths into the <Envelope> in the Layers panel. To again edit the envelope itself, choose Object > Envelope Distort > Edit Envelope.

There are two other types of envelopes, and they're closely related. Both types use meshes to provide even more distortion control. When using the first type, *envelope warp*, you choose the overall envelope form from a pop-up list of options. When you use the *envelope mesh*, instead of starting from presets, you begin by choosing how many rows and columns your mesh will contain.

To create an envelope warp, select an object and choose the Make with Warp command found in the Object > Envelope Distort submenu. This will open the Warp dialog. Once you choose a warp and click OK, Illustrator converts that warp to an envelope mesh. The Control panel will display the Envelope Warp controls, including a pop-up menu that lets you choose a different shape for the warp if you want to. You can edit the envelope warp's individual mesh points with the Direct Selection tool to distort not only the outer edges of the envelope shape, but also the way art is distorted within the envelope itself. To provide even more control, use the Mesh tool to add more mesh points as desired.

To create an envelope mesh, select your artwork and choose Object > Envelope Distort > Make with Mesh. After you've chosen how many mesh points you want, Illustrator will create the envelope mesh. The Envelope Mesh tools in the Control panel will appear, allowing you to easily change the number of rows and columns, and restore the envelope mesh to its original shape if necessary. You can also use the Direct Selection tool to edit the points and use the Mesh tool to add mesh points. (But if you use other tools, you'll need to switch back to the Selection tool if you want the Envelope Mesh controls to reappear in the Control panel.)

EFFECT PATHFINDERS

The effects listed in the Effect > Pathfinder menu (or via *fx*) are effect versions of the Pathfinders described in the *Beyond the Basics* chapter. To apply a Pathfinder effect, you should either group the objects, making sure that the group is also targeted, or target the layer with the objects (which applies the effect to *all* objects in that layer). Then, select Effect > Pathfinder and choose an effect. If you don't do one of those two things before applying the effect to a non-group, you might not see a visible result.

Pathfinder Effects vs. Compound Shapes

With live Pathfinder effects, you create a container (group or layer) and then apply one effect (Add, Subtract, Intersect, or Exclude) to the container. But in a compound shape, *each component* independently specifies whether it adds to, subtracts from, intersects with, or excludes from the components below it.

When you're using more than one or two shape modes, you'll find it simpler to work with compound shapes. One of the great benefits compound shapes have over Pathfinder effects is that they behave much more reliably when the objects being combined aren't simple. Compound shapes can be exported live in Photoshop files, or copied in Illustrator and pasted into Photoshop as shape layers. See the *Beyond the Basics* chapter for more about Pathfinders and compound shapes.

GRAPHIC STYLES IN ILLUSTRATOR

If you think that you'll want to apply an appearance more than once, whether it's a simple stroke and fill, or a complex combination of effects, save it as a graphic style in the Graphic Styles panel. A *graphic style* is simply a combination of one or more appearance attributes that can

Pathfinder Group Alert

Even if you already grouped your objects, you may still get a warning when you apply a Pathfinder from the Effect menu (or via *fx*):

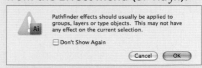

This happens if you Direct-Select the objects and miss some of their points, causing the objects to get targeted. To fix this, target the <Group> the objects are in, then apply the Pathfinder effect.

Load graphic styles easily

The quickest way to load graphic styles installed by Illustrator, or custom saved styles, is by using the handy Graphic Styles Libraries Menu icon in the lower-left corner of the Graphic Styles panel.
—*Jean-Claude Tremblay*

Replacing graphic styles

To replace a saved appearance in the Graphic Styles panel with a new set of attributes, Option-drag/Alt-drag the thumbnail from the Appearance panel (or an object from the Artboard), to the Graphic Styles panel and drop it onto the highlighted graphic style. To replace the currently selected graphic style, make adjustments and choose Redefine Graphic Style from the Appearance panel menu. The applied styles will update.

By default, the Graphic Styles panel shows you what each style would look like when applied to a square object

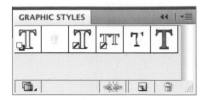

Choosing the Use Text for Preview command from the panel menu changes the thumbnails to show a preview of each style applied to the letter T; choose the Use Square for Preview command to switch the thumbnails back

Control-clicking (Mac) or right-clicking (Windows only) a thumbnail in the panel shows you a preview of the graphic style applied to your selected object

No-fill, no-stroke styles

Some graphic styles don't apply any fill or stroke attributes—for example, a graphic style might apply only an effect, such as a drop shadow. In that case, the style appears in the panel with a black outline and a white fill.

Preserving type color

To prevent type from changing color when you apply a graphic style to it, disable Override Character Color in the Graphic Styles panel pop-up menu.

be applied to objects (including text objects), groups, and layers. See the *Layers & Appearances* chapter to learn the basics of working with appearances.

To save a set of appearance attributes as a graphic style, in the Appearance panel (with or without an object selected) select the desired appearance attributes, and then either click the New Graphic Style icon in the Graphic Styles panel or drag the appearance thumbnail from the Appearance panel to the Graphic Styles panel. You can also drag an object into the panel to create a graphic style with that object's style attributes.

To apply a graphic style, simply select an object, or target a group or layer, and click on a style in the Graphic Styles panel. You can also sample a style from another object using the Eyedropper. You can also drag a style from the Graphic Styles panel directly onto an object.

You can see how a graphic style will look before you apply it to an object by selecting the object and then Control-clicking (Mac) or right-clicking (Windows only) on the style in the panel for a pop-up preview.

Illustrator also gives you the option to add a graphic style to an object that already has style attributes applied—without replacing or losing those existing attributes. (This means you can apply multiple graphic styles to the same object.) Just select the object and then Option-click/Alt-click the style in the Graphic Styles panel, and the new attributes will be added on top of the existing ones. (You can also Option-drag/Alt-drag the style from the panel onto the object for the same results.)

To separate a graphic style from the object to which it's applied, click on the Break Link to Graphic Style icon at the bottom of the panel, or select the command from the Graphic Styles panel menu. You might want to do this when you are replacing a graphic style and don't want to change all the objects using the current graphic style to the updated or replaced version. Select two or more styles in the Graphic Styles panel, and choose Merge Graphic Styles from the panel menu to combine appearance attributes into a new style.

Ted Alspach

Ted Alspach initially experimented with Effects and the Flare tool to create an interesting desktop background, but ultimately ended up with a striking image he then made into a large wall hanging. He created this effect with multiple fills applied to a single textured rectangle. Working in RGB mode, Alspach filled a rectangle with a multicolored gradient (center figure, left). He applied Effect > Pixelate > Color Halftone, and entered a Pixel Max. Radius of 8 (center). Alspach then applied Effect > Pixelate > Crystallize, and adjusted the cell size slider to 40 (center figure, right). He made two copies of this rectangle by selecting Duplicate Item in the Appearance panel pop-up menu. He made adjustments to the duplicated rectangles by selecting the Fill appearance attribute in the Appearance panel. Using the Gradient tool, Alspach applied gradients of varying colors and angles. He double-clicked on the effects (Crystallize and Color Halftone) and changed the values for the Max. Radius and Screen Angles. Alspach also adjusted the Opacity (between 20% and 80%) and applied Soft Light, Multiply, and Color Burn blending modes. To make the flare, he selected the Flare tool, clicked and dragged to set the halo, and click-dragged again to set the distance and direction of the rings while using the arrow keys to adjust the number of rings (bottom figure). Alspach made another copy of the rectangle and applied a blue gradient fill. He positioned this copy as the topmost fill and masked the flare to fit the image.

ALSPACH

Scratchboard Art

Combining Strokes, Fills, Effects, & Styles

Overview: *Apply multiple strokes and fills to simple objects; offset strokes; apply effects to strokes and fills; create and apply graphic styles.*

POWELL

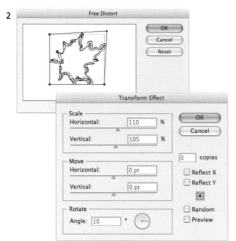

The original scratchboard art consists of simple primitive shapes

To offset a path's Stroke from its Fill, select the Stroke in the Appearance panel and apply Free Distort and Transform from Effect > Distort & Transform (from fx in the Appearance panel)

Artist Gary Powell created a variation of a technique developed by author and consultant Sandee Cohen that uses an assortment of Art Brushes, multiple strokes and fills, and effects, which are then combined and saved as a Graphic Style. Once a series of effects is saved as a graphic style, you can easily apply that graphic style to multiple objects to create or quickly modify a design theme. Art directors may find this method helpful for unifying and stylizing art created by different artists.

1 **Applying Art Brushes and Fills.** To create a natural-looking stroke, Powell applied an assortment of Art Brushes to simple primitive objects. He used Waves, Weave, Dry Brush, and Fire Ash Brushes (on the *Wow! CD*), then he applied solid fills to each object. Select a simple object, then click on your choice of Art Brush in the Brushes panel or in a Brush Library. (For more on Art Brushes, see the *Brushes & Symbols* chapter.)

2 **Offsetting a stroke.** To develop a loose, sketchlike look, Powell offset some of the strokes from their fills. To do this, select a stroke in the Appearance panel and choose either Effect > Distort & Transform > Free Distort, or

Effect > Distort & Transform > Transform to manually or numerically adjust the position of the stroke so that it separates from the fill. This gives the stroke the appearance of a different shape without permanently changing the path. (You can further reshape the stroke by clicking the Transform attribute in the Appearance panel and adjusting the offset of the Stroke attribute.)

3 Adding more strokes and fills to a path. To add to the sketchlike look of the square background, Powell applied additional strokes to the path. First, he chose the Stroke attribute in the Appearance panel and clicked the Duplicate Selected Item icon at the bottom of the panel. With the new Stroke copy selected, he changed the choice of Art brush. He also clicked the stroke's Distort & Transform effect in the Appearance panel and changed the settings to move the Stroke copy's position. Powell repeated this until he had as many strokes as he liked.

To create the scratchboard look in the leaves, Powell applied additional fills and effects to each of them. First, he chose the Fill attribute in the Appearance panel and duplicated it. With the new Fill copy selected, he changed the color and applied Effect > Stylize > Scribble. (You can apply as many fills and effects to a path as you like, then drag and drop to change their stacking order.)

4 Working with graphic styles. To automate the styling of future illustrations, Powell used the Appearance and Graphic Styles panels to create a library of graphic styles. Whenever you create a set of strokes and fills you like, click the New Graphic Style icon in the Graphic Styles panel to create a new graphic style (hold down Option/Alt when you click to name your style as you create it).

Once Powell assembled a palette of graphic style swatches, he altered the look and feel of the artwork by applying a variety of graphic styles to selected paths. The use of graphic styles allows an artist or designer to create a variety of themes in a graphic style library and then apply them selectively to illustrations or design elements.

The individual strokes that Powell combined to create multiple strokes for the background

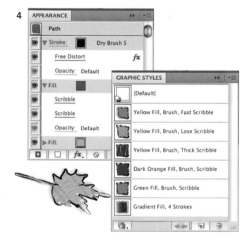

Multiple Strokes, Fills and Effects applied to an object shown in the Appearance panel; appearance attributes saved in the Graphic Styles panel by clicking the New Graphic Style icon

Applying different graphic styles to objects can give the same artwork several different looks and create a cohesive look throughout a project or series

Scribble Basics

Applying Scribble Effects to Artwork

Overview: *Apply default Scribble effect settings; choose from preset Scribble styles; make custom adjustments to Scribble settings.*

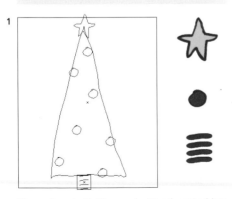

Shown here in Outline mode, Stead created her first tree by drawing with the Brush tool

Judy Stead's evergreen tree began simply, but with the help of Illustrator's Scribble effect, it evolved into an eye-catching Christmas card. Here, you will learn how to apply the Scribble effect to your artwork, how to make use of the preset Scribble styles, and how to make custom adjustments to the effect in order to add excitement and energy to your art.

1 Creating the base art and the variations. Stead began by using the Brush tool to create a simple, filled shape for the tree. She used a 5-pt round Calligraphic brush to create the star, and applied a red stroke and a yellow fill to the path. She drew the ornament using the same brush and stroke with a magenta fill. Stead copied and pasted this shape several times to decorate her tree. She created the base of the tree using a 12-pt oval Calligraphic brush to draw a single horizontal stroke. She then made three copies and grouped them against a white rectangle.

Stead decided that her card would contain three variations of the first tree, so she copied and pasted them into position and gave each one a different color scheme. Beginning with the first variation, she selected the red background rectangle. She chose Effects > Stylize > Scribble, after first hiding the selection edges of her art (⌘-H/Ctrl-H) in order to observe the results more clearly. When the Scribble Options menu appeared, Stead clicked Preview. Satisfied with the Default settings, she clicked OK. These settings applied the appearance of a loose, continuous stroke to her solid red rectangle.

2 Using the Scribble presets. For her next variation, Stead first selected the light green tree and chose the Scribble style set entitled Sketch. She decided to leave the Sketch settings as they were and clicked OK. Then she selected the magenta background. After applying the Scribble style set entitled Sharp, she opened up the denseness of the effect's strokes by using the slider to change the Spacing value from 3 pt to 5 pt. The Scribble Options dialog also contains sliders to control the Stroke Width, the general Curviness of the strokes, and the degree of Variation or evenness of the effect.

3 Further Scribble settings. For the final variation, Stead selected the green background and chose Swash from Settings in the Scribble Options. Using the circular Angle slider, she changed the preset angle of the strokes from 0 to –30 degrees. Stead then selected all the tree ornaments and applied a final Scribble effect using Dense from the Settings pop-up in Scribble Options. Stead was able to go back and readjust all her settings, as needed, by clicking the instance of the effect in each object's Appearance panel. As a final touch, Stead selected the solid red tree and sent it backward (Object > Arrange > Send Backward) so that the green Swash Scribble effect would overlay the tree and provide an interesting texture.

2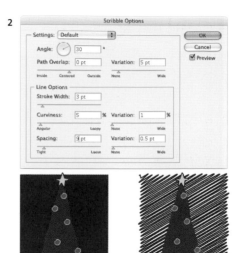

After switching the color scheme, Stead selected the red background, hid the edges, and applied a Custom Scribble (Effects menu)

For the light green Christmas tree, Stead chose the Sketch Settings from the Scribble Options

In Scribble Options, Stead applied the Sharp settings to the background, changing spacing setting from 3 pt to 5 pt for a looser appearance

3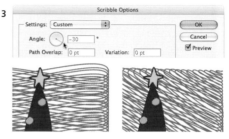

In Scribble Options, Stead applied Swash (from Settings) to the green background of the final tree art, and changed the Angle slider (which then automatically changed Settings to Custom)

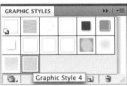

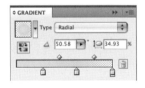

GLITSCHKA

Von R. Glitschka

For "Beautiful," Von R. Glitschka placed his model and Japanese text against one of his intricate patterns (see the *Advanced Techniques* chapter for more on the pattern). He then used Live Effects throughout to create the interaction between his objects and their environment. To lift the Kanji characters from the background, he used Outer Glow in Multiply mode, creating an even shadow around the calligraphy. But to separate his model from the background pattern, he maintained directional lighting. He filled an object that matched her shape with the same blue as the background, and moved it a bit to the right, added a 20 pixel Gaussian Blur, and set the layer to Mul-

tiply mode with a slightly reduced Opacity. He used the Gaussian Blur effect frequently to create the shadows cast on her skin by her hair and to soften transitions when modeling the skin tones. He used the Inner Glow effect in Multiply mode to add a soft shadow within an object. Because he modeled her in a very detailed fashion, Glitschka streamlined some of his work by creating a few graphic styles to use when creating the fine shading and blending in her skin tones. Gradients—often using transparency—added to the Live effects to create a soft, romantically styled illustration.

MACADANGDANG

   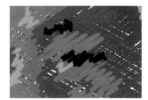

Todd Macadangdang

Todd Macadangdang used the Scribble effect to turn this photo into an artistic crosshatch sketch. He started by adjusting the colors and posterizing the photograph in Photoshop, using adjustment layers. Macadangdang then placed the image in Illustrator and drew filled objects based on the posterized areas. Starting with the smallest, front-most area, he clicked on the area with the Eyedropper tool to set the Fill color (with Stroke of None) then hand-traced over it using the Pencil tool. He repeated this process, working his way toward the largest, rearmost areas, using Object > Arrange > Send Backward as he went along to keep the shapes in the correct visual stacking order. He then applied the Scribble effect to each traced area. To give his image a greater depth, he used fatter, looser Scribble strokes (with Settings such as Childlike, Loose, or Snarl) for the front-most areas, and smaller, denser strokes (with the Angle setting rotated 90°) for the larger, rearmost crosshatched areas.

SCHWABAUER

Mike Schwabauer

To create this banner for a benefit performance, Mike Schwabauer made extensive
use of Live Effects, and the Transparency and
Appearance panels. He started by drawing a
rectangle and filling it with a gradient. For the
main text, he chose a bold font (Impact) that
could stand up to the effects he planned to
apply. He set the Stroke to 1.5 pt with white as
the color, and the Fill to either red or green.
He typed the text for each color on a separate
layer, and manually kerned and adjusted the
leading in the Character panel. To give the
stroke dimension, he targeted it in the Appearance panel and added a small Drop Shadow
by choosing Effect > Stylize. He then targeted
Fill and set the Transparency Blending Mode

to Multiply, and reduced the opacity slightly.
Schwabauer clicked the Add New Fill icon, and
then dragged it below the original Fill. He set
white as the color and set the Blending Mode
in the Transparency panel to Screen. He set
the Opacity to 50%. He chose Effect > Stylize >
Scribble and adjusted the settings to taste. To
soften the scribbles, he used a small amount
of Gaussian Blur (Effect > Blur > Gaussian Blur).
Schwabauer chose Duplicate Item from the
Appearance panel's menu. On the duplicate,
he double-clicked on the *fx* icon beside Scribble to open the dialog, and adjusted the angle
setting to form the crosshatch. For the type at
the bottom, he used Helvetica Black and added
a drop shadow to give it an embossed look.

Yukio Miyamoto

Illustrator Yukio Miyamoto, well-known for his photorealistic illustrations with gradient mesh and author of several books on Illustrator in Japanese, has recently produced the *Illustrator Appearance Book* (with DVD), currently available only in Japanese. He used Live Effects and multiple Fills, among other features. He has kindly given us some examples for the *Wow! CD*. He has saved these as graphic styles that can be applied to type with a click of the mouse. They can be modified through the Appearance panel, and the type is live (see the inset for examples of changing Appearance attributes and text for the "Gold" button).

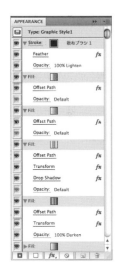

You can see several more of his graphic styles at http://venus.oracchi.com/Illustrator/appearance/appearance.html.

12

3D 3D

Extruding an object using the Effect >3D > Extrude & Bevel dialog—the two-dimensional object on the left was extruded to create the three-dimensional version

2D or not 2D...?

Although Illustrator's 3D effect does a terrific job of rendering objects that look fully three-dimensional, bear in mind that Illustrator's 3D objects are only *truly* three-dimensional while you're working with them in a 3D effect dialog. As soon as you're done tweaking your object and you click OK to close the dialog, the object's three-dimensional qualities are "frozen"—almost as if Illustrator had taken a snapshot of the object—until the next time you edit it in a 3D dialog. On the page, it's technically an impressive 2D rendering of a 3D object that can only be worked with in two-dimensional ways. But because the effect is live, you can work with the object in 3D again any time you want, by selecting the object and then double-clicking the 3D effect listed in the Appearance panel.

Live 3D Effects

3D effects are much like the other live effects, except... they're 3D. If "live effects" or graphic styles are new concepts to you, please first see the *Live Effects & Graphics Styles* and *Layers & Appearances* chapters.

Illustrator offers you the power to transform any two-dimensional (2D) shape, including type, into a shape that looks three-dimensional (3D). As you're working in Illustrator's 3D effect dialogs, you can change your 3D shape's perspective, rotate it, and add lighting and surface attributes. And because you're working with a live effect, you can edit the source object at any time and observe the resultant change in the 3D shape immediately. You can also rotate a 2D shape in 3D space and change its perspective. Finally, Illustrator lets you map artwork previously saved as a symbol onto any of your 3D object's surfaces. Remember that Illustrator is primarily a 2D program—its 3D capabilities are very limited when compared to the plethora of available 3D programs.

To begin, think of Illustrator's horizontal ruler as the X axis and the vertical ruler as the Y axis. Now imagine a third dimension that extends back into space, perpendicular to the flat surface of your monitor. This is the Z axis. There are two ways to create a 3D shape using 3D effects. The first method is by extruding a 2D object back into space along the Z axis, and the second is by revolving a 2D object around its Y axis, up to 360°.

To apply a 3D effect to a selected object, you can either choose one of the 3D effects from the *fx* button in the Appearance panel, or choose one from the Effect menu. To simplify the instructions throughout this chapter, we'll be using the convention choose Effect >3D. Once you apply a 3D effect to an object, it will show up in the Appearance panel. As with other appearance attributes, you can edit the effect, change the position of the effect in the panel's stacking order, and duplicate or delete the effect. You can also save 3D effects as reusable graphic styles so that you can apply the same effect to a batch of objects. Once the style has been applied, you can modify any of the style parameters by clicking the underlined effect name in the Appearance panel, or double-clicking the *fx* icon to the right of the effect name.

EXTRUDING AN OBJECT

To extrude a 2D object, begin by creating an open or closed path. Your path can contain a stroke, a fill, or both. If your shape contains a fill, it's best to begin with a solid color. (See the Tip "Solid advice on 3D colors" later in this in chapter.) With your path selected, choose Extrude & Bevel from the Effect > 3D submenu. The top half of the 3D Extrude & Bevel Options dialog contains rotation and perspective options that we'll examine a bit later, but for the moment we'll concentrate on the lower portion of the dialog. Choose the depth to which you'd like your 2D object extruded by entering a point size in the Extrude Depth field or by dragging the pop-up slider. Choosing to add a cap to your object will give it a solid appearance (the end will be "capped off"), while choosing to turn the cap option off will result in a hollowed-out-looking object (see the figures at right).

You also have the option to add a beveled edge to your extruded object. Illustrator offers you ten different styles of bevels to choose from, and a dialog in which to enter the height of the bevel. You can choose between a bevel that will be added to the original object (Bevel Extent Out) or a bevel that will be carved out from the original shape (Bevel Extent In). These options result in objects that appear radically different from each other (see the second pair of figures at right).

Note: *When you apply bevels to some objects (like stars), you might generate the error, "Bevel self-intersection may have occurred" when you click "Preview"—this may or may not actually mean that there is a problem.*

Any changes you make to the original 2D source shape will immediately update the 3D object. The original shapes of the vector paths will be highlighted when

Left to right: Turn cap on for solid, Turn cap off for hollow, Bevel Extent In, Bevel Extent Out

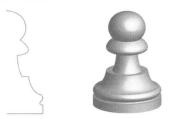

Revolving an object using the Effect > 3D > Revolve dialog—the open path on the left was revolved to create the 3D chess pawn on the right

You can rotate objects in three dimensions by using the Effect >3D >Rotate dialog (or the upper halves of the Revolve and the Extrude & Bevel dialogs). The symbol on the left was rotated in 3D space, resulting in its new position on the right. This function is useful when a 2D object only needs to be rotated in 3D space without making the object itself 3D.

Another example of rotating an object in three dimensions

3D effect—pass it on

Although in this book we generally recommend working with the New Art Has Basic Appearance setting disabled, you might want enable it when working with 3D effects. Otherwise, any new paths that you create subsequent to applying 3D effects to an object will also have the same appearance set, unless you first clear the appearance set from the panel, or click on the default fill and stroke icon in the Tools panel. On the other hand, if you *want* your next object to have the same 3D effects as the one you just created, leave New Art Has Basic Appearance disabled.

you select the 3D shape—you can easily edit them just as you would any other path. You can always edit the settings you've entered for a particular 3D effect by clicking the underlined effect name in the Appearance panel, or double-clicking the *fx* icon to the right of the effect name.

REVOLVING AN OBJECT

You can also create a 3D object from a 2D path (either open or closed) by revolving it around its Y (vertical) axis. Solid strokes work just as well as filled objects. Once you've selected your path, choose Effect >3D >Revolve. In the 3D Revolve Options dialog you can set the number of degrees you wish to revolve the object by entering a value from 1 to 360 in the Angle text field, or by dragging the slider. An object that is revolved 360° will appear solid. An object revolved less than 360° will appear to have a wedge carved out of it. You can also choose to offset the rotation from the object's edge. This will result in a 3D shape that appears to be carved out in the center. And finally, as with extruded shapes, because the 3D options you've chosen are live effects, any changes you make to your original source object will immediately change the look of the 3D shape you've revolved.

ROTATING AN OBJECT IN 3D SPACE

You can rotate both 2D and 3D objects by choosing Effects >3D >Rotate. The 3D Rotate Options dialog contains a cube representing the planes that your shape can be rotated through. You can choose a preset angle of rotation from the Position menu, or enter values between –180 and 180 in the X, Y, and Z text fields. (The Rotate controls also appear in the upper half of both the Extrude & Bevel and the Revolve Options boxes.)

If you'd like to manually rotate your object around one of its three axes, simply click on the edge of one of the faces of the white cube and drag. The edges of each plane are highlighted in a corresponding color that tells you through which of the object's three planes you're rotating it. Red represents the object's X axis, a green highlight represents the object's Y axis, and blue edges represent the object's Z axis. The object's rotation is constrained within the plane of that particular axis. Remember, to constrain the rotation you must be dragging an edge of the cube. Notice the numbers changing in the corresponding text field as you drag. If you wish to rotate your object relative to all three axes at once, click directly on a surface of the cube and drag, or click in the black area behind the cube and drag. Values in all three text fields will change. And if you simply want to rotate your object, click and drag inside the circle, but outside the cube itself.

Changing the perspective of an object

You can change the visible perspective of your object by entering a number between 0 and 160 in the Perspective text field, or by dragging the slider. A smaller value simulates the look of a telephoto camera lens, while a larger value will simulate a wide-angle camera lens, with more of an "exploded" perspective.

APPLYING SURFACE SHADING TO 3D OBJECTS

Illustrator allows you a variety of choices in the kind of shading you apply to your 3D object. These range from dull and unshaded matte surfaces to glossy and highlighted surfaces that look like plastic. And because you can also choose how you light your object, the possible variations open to you are then limitless.

The Surface shading option appears as part of both the 3D Extrude & Bevel and the 3D Revolve Options dialogs. Choosing Wireframe as your shading option will result in a transparent object, the contours of which are overlaid with a set of outlines describing the object's geometry. The next choice is No Shading, which will result in a flat-looking shape with no discernible surfaces. Choosing the Diffused Shading option results in your object having a soft light cast on its surfaces, while choosing the Plastic Shading option will make your object look as if it's molded out of shiny, reflective plastic. For mapped surfaces, enable "Shade Artwork" in the Map Art dialog.

Solid advice on 3D colors

You'll get best results using solid fill colors for 3D objects. Gradients and pattern fills don't produce reliable results.

For the smoothest 3D

When creating profile objects for 3D, your goal should be to draw the objects with as few anchor points as possible, since each anchor point will produce an additional surface. Also, extra surfaces might create potential problems you'll encounter when mapping artwork onto the surfaces later.
—*Jean-Claude Tremblay*

Hiding the 3D…

To speed up your screen redraw, you can temporarily hide a 3D effect without losing the settings. To do so, click on the Eye for that 3D effect in the Appearance panel (click again to make it visible).

Not enough steps…

If you click on the More Options button, you'll get the opportunity to adjust Surface and Shading Color options. The default setting for Blend Steps is 25—not nearly enough steps to create smooth color transitions from light to shaded areas. Since the maximum setting of 256 is smooth but slows you down, experiment to find the best resolution-to-speed setting for each image.

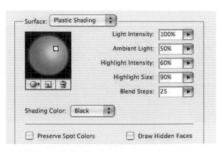

The sphere located in the expanded More Options dialog shows the position of your light source within the sphere; the three icons located below this sphere from left to right are: "Move selected light to back of object," "New Light," and "Delete Light."

Mapping—don't get lost!

Here are some tips to help you avoid confusion about the surface to which you're mapping symbols:

• Remember to choose a surface. Select by clicking the Arrow keys to view each surface.

• When clicking through the various surfaces, it's sometimes easier to identify the surface you want by the red highlight on the object itself, rather than by the flattened proxy in the Map Art dialog.

• Even the red highlight can fool you. If the symbol isn't mapping to a selected surface, it may be because it's being mapped to the *inside* of the surface.

• A stroke will add more surfaces to an object than a fill because a stroke creates a hollow inside the object, which is also treated as a surface.

• A stroke can obscure mapped art on a side or inside of a sur-face that can't be seen.

—*Brenda Sutherland*

If you choose either the Diffused Shading or Plastic Shading option, you can further refine the look of your object by adjusting the direction and intensity of the light source illuminating your object. By clicking the More Options button, the dialog will enlarge and you'll be able to make changes to the Light Intensity, Ambient Light level, Highlight Intensity, Highlight Size, and number of Blend Steps. The default for Blend Steps is quite low (25 out of a maximum of 256)—see the Tip "Not enough steps…" on the previous page. You can also choose a custom Shading Color to add a color cast to the shaded surfaces. If you want to maintain a spot color assigned to your Extruded object during output, then enable the Preserve Spot Colors checkbox. However, be aware that Preserve Spot Colors removes custom shading and resets your Shading Color to Black. If you choose Preserve Spot Colors, you should enable Overprint Preview (View menu) so you can see your shading and color accurately.

With the More Options dialog expanded, you'll also see a sphere to the left of the lighting controls (shown at left). The small white dot within this sphere indicates the position of the light source, while the black box around it highlights this light source as currently selected. There is always one light source by default. Simply click and drag this dot within the sphere to reposition your light. If the Preview option is enabled (located below the "Fewer Options/More Options" button), you'll see the lighting automatically updated on your 3D object.

You can add more light sources by clicking on the "New Light" icon (middle icon below the sphere). The new light source will now be selected (indicated by the black "highlight" box around it). You can add as many light sources as you wish and adjust each source independently using the lighting controls (to the right of the sphere). Use the first icon below the sphere, the "Move selected light to back of object" feature, to create back lighting for an object. When your light source is behind an object, the source indicator inverts to a black dot within a white square. When using multiple light sources, this difference helps you see which light sources are behind or in front of an object. At any time, you can select a light source and click this icon to toggle the light to the front or back of your object. To delete a light source, first select it, then click on the trash icon beneath the sphere (you can delete all but one default light source).

MAPPING ART ONTO AN OBJECT

One of the most exciting aspects of the 3D effect is the ability to map artwork onto the surfaces of your 2D or 3D shape (as with the design on the ring to the right). The key is to first define the art that you wish to map onto a surface as a symbol; select the artwork you want to map, and drag it to the Symbols panel. For some images, you'll want to define a number of symbols. For instance, the design on the ring above right is from one symbol. To add engraving inside the ring, you'd create a second symbol and add it in the Map Art dialog.

Once you've made your artwork into symbols, you can map the symbols onto your 3D objects from the Extrude & Bevel or Revolve Options dialogs. In either of these 3D options boxes, you simply click on the Map Art button, then choose one of the available symbols from the menu. You can specify which of your object's surfaces the artwork will map onto by clicking on the left and right Arrow keys. The selected surface will appear in the window; then you can either scale the art by dragging the handles on the bounding box, or make the art expand to cover the entire surface by clicking the Scale to Fit button. Note that as you click through the different surfaces, the selected surface will be highlighted with a red outline in your document window. Your currently visible surfaces will appear in light gray in the Map Art dialog, and surfaces that are currently hidden will appear dark. (See the "Quick Box Art" lesson later in this chapter for an example of mapping 3D surfaces with custom symbols.)

Note: *To see artwork mapped onto the side surfaces of your object, make sure the object has a stroke of None.*

The above design was mapped onto the ring below it using the Map Art feature (result shown above right). The ring was created using the 3D Revolve effect with an "offset" value added.

To map or wrap...?

Although maps can be used in a variety of ways to add designs or texture effects to an object, such as a label on a bottle, they can also be used to cover an entire object (see pawn above mapped with a wood grain image). However, complex objects produce a greater number of surfaces, which can make the rendering process very slow and perhaps generate errors. Enable "Shade Artwork" in the Map Art dialog if you intend to use lighting and shading options on a mapped surface.

Mapping with gradients

Gradients can be saved as symbols, but they are rasterized when mapped. The rasterized resolution of the resulting image is determined from the resolution setting in the "Document Raster Effects Settings." You can adjust this resolution by going to Effects > Document Raster Effects Settings.

Quick & Easy 3D

Simple 3D Techniques

Overview: *Draw or modify 2D artwork; prepare artwork for 3D; apply 3D Effect; expand artwork and edit objects to complete visual effects.*

Steven Gordon was hired to design a set of contemporary map symbols for Digital Wisdom, Inc. that would be sold as a clip-art set of map symbol artwork and Illustrator symbols (www.map-symbol.com). To make this set stand out from other map symbol sets and fonts, Gordon explored Illustrator's new 3D Effect and found that it made it easy to turn the ordinary into the unusual.

1

Some of the standard map symbols that Gordon modified for the map symbol set

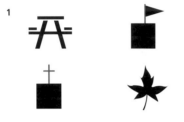

Left, the original tent artwork objects; center, the white triangle selected; right, the tent after subtracting the white triangle from the black triangle and changing the fill color to green

1 Drawing artwork, visualizing 3D appearance, and using editing tools to prepare for 3D. Gordon started with some standard map symbol clip-art. For the camping symbol, he modified the tent artwork by removing the bottom horizontal object and applying a light green fill to the remaining triangle. When visualizing how the object would look in 3D, Gordon realized that the white and green triangles would both be rendered as 3D objects; instead, he needed the white triangle to form a hole in the green triangle that would become the tent. He selected the white and green triangles and clicked the Subtract from Shape Area icon in the Pathfinder panel to punch a hole in the green triangle.

As you prepare artwork for the 3D Effect, refer to the *Beyond the Basics* chapter to review techniques for making compound shapes by combining or cutting objects (as Gordon did to make the tent opening), and for making compound paths (which may yield different results than applying a 3D Effect to separate artwork objects). You can also experiment with changing stroke attributes for caps, joins, and miter limits to round off path intersections for the 3D rendering.

Single-axis movements in 3D

In the 3D Extrude & Bevel Options dialog, you click on a *side* of the cube and drag to rotate artwork using the X, Y, or Z axis. If you want to move the artwork by just one axis, click instead on a white *edge* of the cube and then drag.

2 Applying 3D Effect, modifying Position controls to extrude and rotate objects, and creating a Style.
When you finish creating your artwork, make sure it is selected, and then choose Effect > 3D > Extrude & Bevel. In the 3D Extrude & Bevel Options dialog, enable the Preview checkbox to see what your artwork will look like using the dialog's default settings.

You can change the artwork's rotation by clicking on the three-dimensional cube in the Position pane of the dialog and dragging until the artwork moves to an orientation you like. You can also fine-tune the position by keying in values in the X, Y, and Z axes rotation fields.

To change the amount or depth of the extrusion, use the Extrude Depth slider in the Extrude & Bevel pane of the dialog. To give the tent less depth than the default setting (50 pt), Gordon dragged the slider to extrude by 40 pt. To simulate perspective, drag the Perspective slider to adjust the amount of perspective from none/isometric (0°) to very steep (160°). Gordon used 135° for his artwork. When you are satisfied with your artwork's appearance, click OK to render the object.

Gordon converted the 3D appearance he had created for the tent into a reusable style. Refer to the *Live Effects & Graphic Styles* chapter for instructions on creating and modifying graphic styles. You can use a style for other artwork, as a way of providing a uniform 3D appearance for several objects, or as a starting point for creating a new 3D appearance for an object.

3 Editing the artwork after using the 3D Effect. After applying the 3D Effect to the tent artwork, Gordon decided to make color and shape changes to the artwork. Although you can use the Direct selection and path editing tools to make simple path and color changes, to fully edit objects or change colors of a particular surface in the 3D artwork, you must first expand the appearance by choosing Object > Expand Appearance. (**Hint:** *As this will remove the "live" editability of the artwork, it's safer to work with a copy of the artwork instead of the original.*)

2

Artwork in Preview mode for several adjustments of the Position cube in the 3D Extrude & Bevel Options dialog

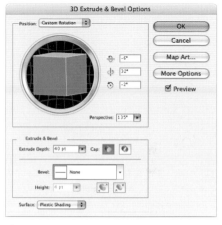

The 3D Extrude & Bevel Options dialog with the settings Gordon used for the final version of the tent symbol

3

Left, the tent artwork after expanding the 3D artwork (Object > Expand Appearance); right, after filling surfaces with different colors

Selecting and modifying one of the surfaces to create the interior floor of the tent

3D with a 2D Twist

Using 3D Effects to Achieve 2D Results

Overview: *Start with a sketch; create the 3D objects using the 3D Extrude & Bevel features; rotate and position the objects; use the 3D version as a reference for a 2D version.*

ATTEBERRY

1

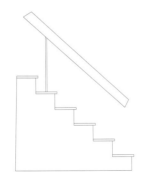

The scanned sketch used for reference and the Illustrator profile of the staircase

2

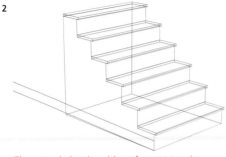

The extruded stairs with surface set to wireframe

Illustrator Kevan Atteberry creatively uses 3D as a guide to produce a 2D painting of a staircase in this portion of an illustration for his book *Frankie Stein* (see the *Illustrator & Other Programs* chapter for the full illustration).

1 Creating the 2D line art. Atteberry began by drawing a traditional pencil sketch for the stairs, which he then scanned, and saved. Atteberry next placed his sketch on a template layer in Illustrator so he could create and position his 3D correctly in relation to his sketch. To do this, Atteberry chose File > Place, located his file, enabled the Link and Template checkboxes, and clicked the Place button (see the *Layers & Appearances* chapter for more information on template layers). Using the Pen and Rectangle tools, he constructed a profile of his stairs. He then grouped the objects making up the stairs (since they would be extruded as a single unit). Next he created the rail and post as separate objects, since he would be extruding each separately (only one post was needed because he later duplicated it to make the rest).

2 Extruding the line art. Atteberry selected his 2D staircase and chose Effect > 3D > Extrude & Bevel. In the Extrude & Bevel Options dialog, he set the Surface field to Wireframe, so that he could still see the sketch through his 3D stairs. He set an estimated depth for the Extrude Depth field (until the stairs were rotated and positioned at the proper angle). After enabling Preview so he could see the 3D image as he worked, he grabbed a side of the 3D cube in the dialog and rotated the stairs until they matched the position of the stairs in the sketch. Atteberry clicked OK to apply the effect and exit the dialog. He then used the Selection tool to move his 3D object into position so that it aligned to the sketch. Once in position, he needed to make adjustments to the dimensions and angle of the stairs; to do this he clicked the underlined 3D Extrude & Bevel effect in the Appearance panel to reopen the dialog, and then he adjusted both the Extrude Depth field and the angle in the Perspective field until the object depth and angle of the stairs matched the sketch.

3 **Finishing the 3D.** Once Atteberry positioned the extruded 3D stairs, he repeated the Extrude process for the post and rail. This time, however, it was easier. The dialog remembered the exact X, Y, and Z axes angles from the position of the stairs (it remembers the last applied 3D 3D Extrude & Bevel Options in a working session). The only value he needed to adjust separately for the post and rail was the Extrude Depth. Whereas, while working with the stairs, Atteberry wanted to see through a wireframe to the sketch below for positioning, he wanted the post and rails to appear more solid, so he set the Surface field in the dialog to Plastic Shading for the post and rail. Atteberry returned to the artboard to move and position all the 3D objects in place. To create duplicates of the one rail, he used Option-drag/Alt-drag to move the first post to the second position and then used the Duplicate command (⌘-D/Ctrl-D) to create the others. He made finishing adjustments by clicking on the 3D effect in the Appearance panel for a selected object and adjusted them live.

4 **Returning to 2D.** Atteberry hid the original sketch (in the Layers panel), printed his new 3D art, and used this print as a guide for a traditional ink drawing. Scanning and placing the new drawing back into Illustrator, he re-vectorized the stairs using Live Trace (see the *Beyond the Basics* chapter for more on Live Trace).

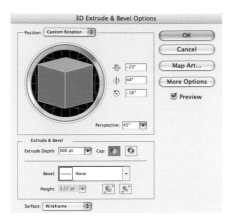

The 3D Extrude & Bevel Options dialog for the staircase

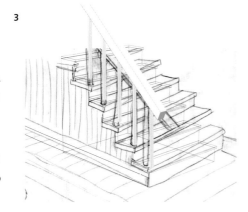

Atteberry's 3D stairs positioned over his scanned hand sketch

Using two windows

When positioning 3D objects in relationship to a template, try working with two windows at once. To create a second window, choose Window > Arrange > New Window. Leaving the first window in Preview mode, set the new window to Outline mode (View > Outline). This way, the outlined objects can be moved in relation to the sketch, and also seen live in the Preview window.

—*Kevan Atteberry*

3D Logo Object

Revolving a Simple Path into a 3D Object

Overview: *Draw a cross-section; use the 3D Revolve feature to build a 3D object from the cross-section.*

GILBERT

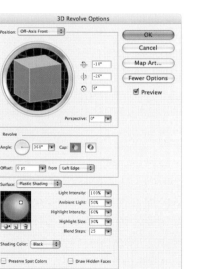

1

The cross-section path for the mortar, shown here with a black stroke for clarity; the actual path has a very light black fill and no stroke

2

3D Revolve Options dialog with settings for the final mortar bowl

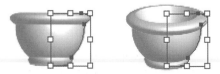

The mortar with all rotation angles set to 0° (left), and at the default angles (right)

When Reggie Gilbert redesigned this logo for an herbal extract company, he decided to draw the mortar and pestle as 3D objects. Gilbert used the 2D basic shape tools and gradient fills to easily draw the pestle, but for the more complex mortar, he used the 3D Revolve feature.

1 Drawing the cross-section of the mortar. Gilbert drew a path for the cross-section of the mortar and applied a white fill to it. He didn't need to draw more than that, because in the next step he formed the whole mortar by revolving the path in 3D. Because 3D is a live effect, you can edit the path later and the 3D result will update, so you don't need to be concerned about drawing the cross-section path perfectly the first time.

2 Applying the 3D Revolve Effect. With the cross-section selected, Gilbert chose Effect > 3D > Revolve. In the Revolve section of the 3D Revolve Options dialog, he entered 360° for Angle, which swept the cross-section around in a full circle. The Offset option showed that by default, the center of the revolution was the path's left edge. The Surface settings shaded the mortar, using the fill color Gilbert applied to the original path (clicking the More Options button reveals Surface settings). You can rotate a 3D object by dragging the proxy cube in the 3D Revolve Options dialog or by entering rotation angles next to the cube. Gilbert used the default values for the rotation angles and the Surface settings.

Joseph Shoulak

This tower of Tupperware (left) accompanied a *San Francisco Chronicle* story about the history of the Tupperware container. Shoulak created each container by using the 3D features in Illustrator (see his lesson later in this chapter). The round containers were made by drawing a 2D path of a container's profile, then applying the Effect > 3D > Revolve command to revolve the path 360° (above). He created the square containers by applying the Effect > 3D > Extrude & Bevel command to 2D paths. When a container used complex surfaces or multiple colors, Shoulak assembled it from multiple components. As he arranged the tower on the Artboard, he drew shadows and used the Control panel to adjust opacity.

Assembling in 3D

Building 3D Objects from Multiple Paths

Overview: *Draw 2D paths with rounded corners; use 3D Extrude & Bevel effects to create 3D objects from 2D paths; arrange 3D objects to build a more complex 3D object.*

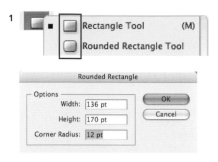

The Rectangle and Rounded Rectangle tools in the toolbox, and Rounded Rectangle dialog

The Effect > Stylize > Round Corners dialog for adding rounded corners to rectangles that don't already have them

These four paths will eventually form the entire container

SHOULAK

Joseph Shoulak drew this plastic container as part of a larger illustration for a *San Francisco Chronicle* story about a Tupperware documentary film. Shoulak cleverly rendered complex plastic forms in Illustrator by stacking and aligning paths that were extruded and rotated using the 3D features in Illustrator.

1 Drawing the 2D paths. The container is like a beveled box with non-beveled lips that extend where the white base and blue lid meet. These attributes led Shoulak to draw four paths for extrusion: the white container body, the white lip, the blue lip, and the blue body. The need for four shapes will become evident when they are later extruded in 3D.

Seen from the top, the container consists of rectangles with rounded corners. To create them precisely, draw with the Rectangle tool; the rectangle for the blue top is 136 pt by 170 pt. Then choose Effect > Stylize > Round Corners (or via *fx* in the Appearance panel) and enter 12 pt for Radius. Alternatively, you can use the Rounded Rectangle tool, adjusting the corner radius by pressing the up or down arrow keys before releasing the mouse button.

The 3D Effects in Illustrator pick up the fill and stroke colors applied to paths. Shoulak filled the rectangles with the blue and white colors of the container body and lid. He set the stroke color to None, because a stroke color would have colored the sides of the objects.

2 Extruding the 2D paths into 3D. Shoulak selected the blue container lid and chose Effect > 3D > Extrude & Bevel. He entered an Extrude Depth of 40 points. Shoulak also applied a bevel by choosing the Classic style and entering a Height of 4 points. He also adjusted the 3D rotation angles (X axis: 77, Y axis: 35, Z axis: –10). When he was satisfied, he clicked OK.

For the other three paths, Shoulak used the same rotation angles, but slightly different extrusion and bevel settings. For the thin blue lip path, he entered an Extrude Depth of 10 points with no bevel. For the thin white lip, Shoulak entered an Extrude Depth of 5 pt with no bevel. For the white container base, he used an Extrude Depth of 45 pt with a 4-pt Classic bevel.

Enable the Preview checkbox to see your changes interactively, but be aware that previewing 3D Effects can take time. Because a 3D Effect is live, you can edit it by selecting the object using the effect, then clicking the effect name in the Appearance panel. If selecting 3D objects becomes a challenge, you can select objects using the Layers panel, or working in Outline view. (3D objects in Outline view appear without the 3D Effects.)

3 Assembling the objects. To complete the illustration, Shoulak repositioned the four 3D objects into their final arrangement. He used the Control panel to center all four objects horizontally. Then he moved each path up or down until they fit together perfectly.

There are several ways to keep objects along a vertical axis as you move them. You can Shift-drag an object, drag an object vertically with View > Smart Guides enabled, press the up or down arrow keys to nudge the object, or enter a value into just the Y field in the Control panel or Transform panel.

While you can rotate individual 3D objects by using the 3D Extrude & Bevel Options dialog, you can't position 3D objects relative to each other in 3D space. 3D objects on the Artboard behave like 2D page objects—you can position them only on the Artboard's 2D space.

2

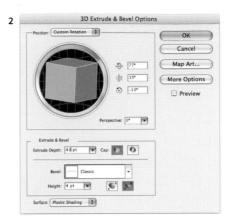

The 3D Extrude & Bevel dialog settings for the larger blue lid piece

The four paths after applying extrusion settings

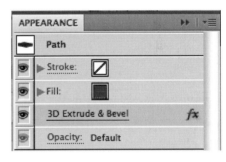

Appearance panel showing the 3D Effect

3

The Control panel with the Horizontal Align Center button highlighted; Align buttons appear when multiple objects are selected

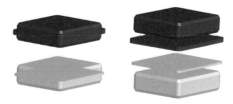

The four extruded paths after horizontal centering (left) and after repositioning them vertically (right), closing in on their final positions

3D Effects

Extruding, Revolving, and Rotating Paths

Overview: *Create basic paths working with a custom template layer; extrude, revolve, and rotate paths; map artwork onto shapes.*

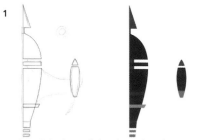

The original pencil drawing, placed as a template, and the vector shapes drawn over them

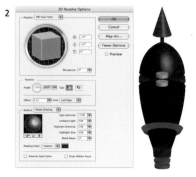

The original group of paths, selected and revolved as a group with the same settings

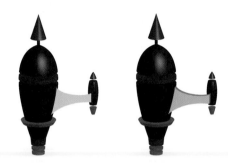

The wing shape drawn to follow the contour of the hull and then extruded and rotated slightly

HAMANN

To complete this illustration, Brad Hamann created a set of basic paths and applied a series of live 3D Effects to them. He then added lighting and mapped artwork to the components.

1 Planning ahead. Because he would be rotating his shapes, Hamann needed to draw only one side of the symmetrical space cruiser. Working over a pencil drawing he had scanned in Photoshop and placed on a designated template layer, he drew one closed shape for the hull. He divided it into sections using the Pathfinder tool so he could color each part differently. He filled the paths with solid color and no stroke. When revolved, a filled path with no stroke will present the fill color as its surface color. A stroked shape that is revolved uses the stroke color as its surface color, regardless of fill color.

2 Applying the 3D Revolve Effect to a group of shapes and extruding the wings. Hamann chose to revolve the group of objects that make up the ship's hull all at the same time, because they shared the same left-side vertical rotation line. He also revolved the three shapes making up the rocket-shaped wing end as a group, using the same settings. Once the shapes were revolved, Hamann selected and moved each shape into its proper position within the group, using the Bring to Front command. He deleted the two inner green circles, because they would be invisible within the 3D model anyway.

For the wings Hamann then drew a flat shape for the right wing that followed the contour of the 3D hull and chose Effect > 3D > Extrude & Bevel. He selected an extrusion depth and rotational angle for the wing that would be visually consistent with the hull.

3 Mapping artwork. Hamann decided to map a star pattern, which he had previously saved as a symbol, onto the wing to liven up the look of the spaceship. He was able to return to the 3D Effects settings window by selecting the wing and clicking the Effect setting from the Appearance panel. He then clicked the Map Art button to access the Map Art window, which presented an outline of the first of the six surfaces available on the wing for mapping. Hamann chose his star pattern from the menu of available symbols. He scaled the pattern using the handles on the bounding box and then clicked OK. At this time, he also changed the wing color from green to red. Finally, Hamann selected the wing and the rocket at its end, and reflected and copied the wing to the opposite side of the spacecraft. He made a slight adjustment to the rotational angle of the new wing's Y-axis to account for its new position.

4 Ready for takeoff. Hamann completed his rocket ship by creating a porthole from a circular path to which he applied a 5.5-pt ochre-colored stroke. He then extruded the path and applied a rounded bevel. Using the Appearance panel, he applied a blue gradient fill to the path, and a Gaussian Blur, which completed the porthole.

3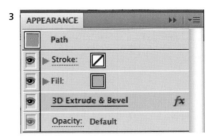
Clicking in the wing's Appearance panel to return to the 3D Effects settings window

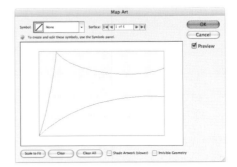
The Map Art window showing the first of the wing's surfaces available for art mapping

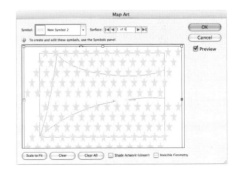
After selecting the star pattern from the Symbol menu, the pattern was scaled and positioned onto the wing outline

4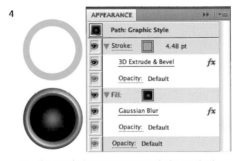
For the porthole Hamann extruded a stroked circular path with a rounded bevel; for the fill he used a radial gradient with Gaussian Blur

Quick Box Art
Converting 2D Artwork to 3D Packages

Overview: *Start with a 2D package drawing; create symbols from package sides, use 3D Extrude & Bevel to rotate a box in perspective; map side art to each surface.*

The prepress-ready flat box drawing

The three required sides separated from the main drawing

Gary Moss designed this easy-to-carry box for assorted beer bottles. The client requested a rendering of the finished box for a catalog. Moss used the 3D Extrude & Bevel effect to simulate the final three-dimensional box and to quickly map the box sides to their surfaces.

1 Drawing the flat box. Moss created a design sketch in Illustrator. Then using an Illustrator file provided by the box manufacturer, he applied precise dimensions to his sketch to meet the printing specifications, including all necessary sides, folds, bleeds, and die cuts.

2 Separating the sides. Moss created a copy of the flat box drawing, then used the Selection and Direct Selection tools to delete everything except the three sides that would be visible in the simulated box. For the 3D box, he wouldn't need the bleeds that extended beyond the actual edge of a side, so Moss trimmed them back, resizing the bleed paths to meet the actual box edge.

3 Creating symbols from the sides. Moss planned to use the 3D Extrude & Bevel feature to map the art to the sides of the box; this feature requires each side to be made into an Illustrator symbol first. If you're not using other symbols, you can delete them to reduce panel clutter: In the Symbols panel, choose Select All Unused, and click the Delete Symbol button. To create a symbol, select the objects making up one side and click the New Symbol icon in the Symbols panel. Repeat for each side.

In Illustrator, a symbol is normally used to creatively reuse an object many times. Mapping art in the 3D Extrude & Bevel feature is a special use of symbols.

4 Creating the 3D form. Moss drew a rectangle the size of the box front. With the rectangle selected, he chose Effect > 3D > Extrude & Bevel. He set the Extrude Depth to 120 pt (the side panel width). He adjusted the rotation angles (X axis: –20, Y axis: 30, Z axis: –10), and to add slight linear perspective, he set Perspective to 19°.

5 Mapping the art. To apply art to each box surface, Moss used the Map Art feature in the 3D Extrude & Bevel Options dialog. Click the Map Art button, click the arrows to select next and previous surfaces (the current surface highlights in red on the Artboard), and select the desired symbol. Click the Scale to Fit button to size the art to the surface, or use the handles to position, rotate, or size the art manually. It may be simpler to create the symbols at the proper orientation and size, as shown in step 3.

If mapped art doesn't preview, it may be mapped to the non-visible surface of a side. When viewing non-mapped surfaces in the Map Art dialog, a light gray surface faces you, while a dark gray surface faces away.

6 Finishing the illustration. Although you can add lighting in 3D Extrude & Bevel (click More Options), Moss chose to manually add creative lighting and shading effects (and insert photos of the labels) with Photoshop. In Photoshop, choose File > Open to open an Illustrator file.

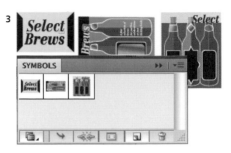

Symbols created from each side of the bottle box, after deleting all unused symbols

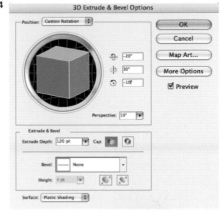

3D Extrude & Bevel dialog (top), the 2D front side before (bottom left) and after (bottom right) applying 3D extrusion

Map Art dialog (top) and the art on the Artboard (bottom) as each side is mapped

DREES

Dedree Drees

As part of her undersea illustration, "The Dory," artist and instructor Dedree Drees mimicked blades of seagrass by building an intricate blend that she then extruded as a 3D object. Drees started by drawing four overlapping, wavy lines using the Pencil tool and then giving each stroke a unique color. To begin blending, Drees selected all four lines and then double-clicked the Blend tool. In the Blend Options dialog she set Spacing > Specified Steps to 2, and then chose Object > Blend > Make. To make the lines of the blend look like flat seagrass blades, Drees extruded the blend by opening the Appearance panel, and from the *fx* button choosing 3D > Extrude & Bevel. She experimented with different Extrude Depth values to make sure that the seagrass blades would not appear thick and dense. To finish, Drees brought this object into Photoshop where she positioned it among other elements and then selected individual seagrass blades that she masked for transparency.

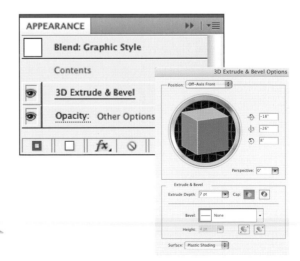

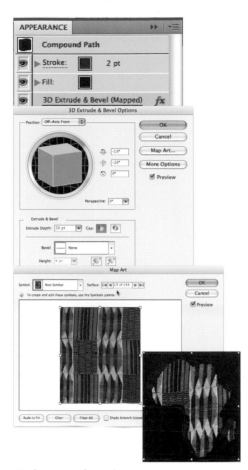

JOGIE

Mohammed Jogie

Mohammed Jogie created this bookcover for the African Peer Review Mechanism, an arm of NEPAD, for an annual progress report on Ghana. He purchased and photographed some of the objects and created the pattern for the map of Africa based on fabrics he bought. The fabric is Kente cloth, entirely hand-woven by Ghanaian weavers, which he obtained from the African art market in Johannesburg. He saved the fabric pattern as a symbol, a step necessary to map art to a 3D object. Jogie next created the flat, 2D object to represent Africa and Madagascar. He used a red Fill and a 2-pt Stroke to give the extruded edge the color

and detail he wanted. He selected his "Africa" object and chose Effect > 3D > Extrude & Bevel. He set an amount for the extrusion, set the Cap to produce a solid edge, and rotated the object to the position he wanted, using the Preview to judge the effect. Jogie then chose Map Art and selected the surfaces he wanted to display the fabric. After mapping the fabric pattern, he clicked OK to exit the Map Art dialog, and OK again to exit and apply the 3D Effect. He used other illusions of depth, such as gradients within Opacity Masks and drop shadows, to complement the 3D structure of the map and used a copy of the 3D map for the reflection.

GOLDING / ADOBE SYSTEMS, INC.

Mordy Golding

To demonstrate the 3D Effect of Illustrator for Adobe Systems, Inc., Mordy Golding created a wine label and then dragged the label to the Symbols panel (so he could use it next to create the 3D rendering). He drew a half-bottle shape and selected Effect > 3D > Revolve. In the 3D Revolve Options dialog, Golding enabled the Preview checkbox and then clicked on the Map Art button. From the Map Art dialog's Symbol menu, he selected the wine label symbol he had created previously. Back in the 3D Revolve Options dialog, Golding adjusted the preview cube, changing the rotation angles until he was satisfied with the look of the bottle. He finished the effect by adding lights, using the New Light icon in the Surface panel of the dialog; this created the cascading highlights on the bottle. After creating the cork, using the same technique as he used for the bottle, Golding selected the bottle, moved it above the cork, and changed its opacity to 94% in the Transparency panel.

Ted Alspach

Ted Alspach creates a new version of his comic strip "Board2Pieces" twice a week (plus a large-format bimonthly strip). When creating the whole concept for the strip, he understood he would need to create his characters and their positions and expressions consistently and quickly. To have time to concentrate on the written content instead of repetitive drawing, Alspach chose to use 3D objects for their live, editable effects, and a full Symbols panel of facial expressions to control his characters' appearance frame to frame. Early in the process he determined an extrusion amount for each character, using 3D's ability to rotate the character without the need to redraw the basic figure. Next he created a variety of facial expressions that would allow his characters to respond to each other. Alspach saved even more time by creating some characters that could share facial expressions. He saved all these expressions as symbols in order to be able to use 3D's ability to map symbols as art to a selected surface on the 3D object. (For more on creating symbols, see the *Brushes & Symbols* chapter.) Now, instead of laboriously drawing

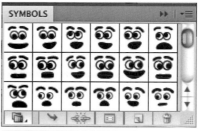

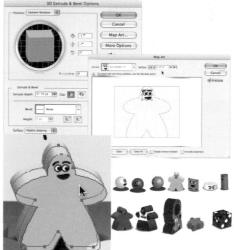

every frame, Alspach can select the desired character and place it where he needs it in the frame. He can then click on the effect name in the Appearance panel to modify the figure's position, and remap its facial expression using a library of symbols, which leaves him a lot more time for writing.

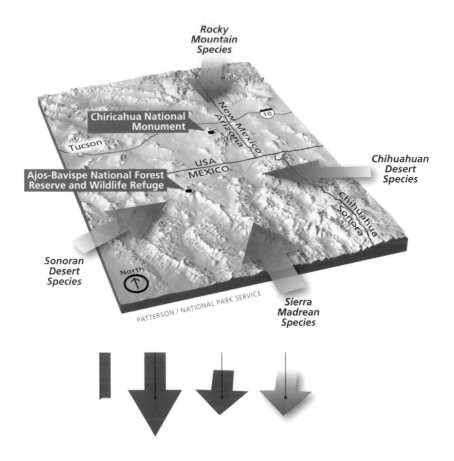

Tom Patterson / National Park Service

Cartographer Tom Patterson used Illustrator's 3D Effect to show species movement across the Sonoran Desert. Patterson drew a straight path with the Pen tool and chose a 20-pt stroke. To turn the path into an arrow, he chose Effect > Stylize > Add Arrowheads (or you can choose it from *fx* in the Appearance panel). In the Add Arrowheads dialog, he selected an arrowhead design (11) and specified 25% for Scale. Next, Patterson chose Effect > 3D > Rotate, and in the 3D Rotate Options dialog, he enabled the Preview and dragged the three-dimensional cube

in the Position pane to adjust the spatial orientation of the arrow. When the arrow looked right, he clicked OK. To fill the arrow, Patterson first chose Object > Group to change the arrow from an object to a group. Then he selected Add New Fill from the Appearance panel menu and applied a custom gradient to the new fill. He repeated these steps to create the other three arrows. To finish, Patterson targeted the layer containing the arrows and changed opacity to 80% in the Transparency panel; he also added a drop shadow (Effect > Stylize > Drop Shadow) to the layer.

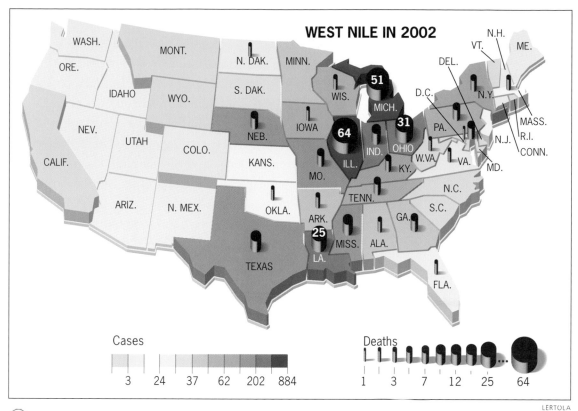

WEST NILE IN 2002

Cases

3 24 37 62 202 884

Deaths

1 3 7 12 25 64

LERTOLA

Joe Lertola / *TIME Magazine*

Joe Lertola of *TIME Magazine* relied on the 3D Effect (Effect > 3D > Extrude & Bevel) to turn an otherwise flat map into an eye-catching 3D thematic map. After drawing all the artwork, Lertola created groups for the gray states and the colored states. To give each group a different height, he applied the 3D Effect to each group, but specified a different Extrude Depth value in the 3D Extrude & Bevel Options dialog for each group (6 pt for the gray states and 24 pt for the colored states). Lertola completed the effect by adding a second light (he clicked on the New Light icon in the Surface panel) to change the position of the highlight and shadow of each group.

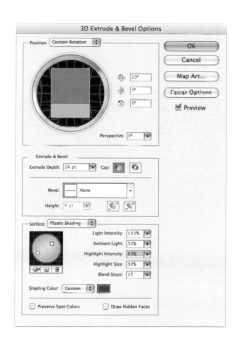

13

Advanced Techniques

Choose Clipping Mask >Make from the Object menu or use the Make/Release Clipping Mask button on the Layers panel (right)

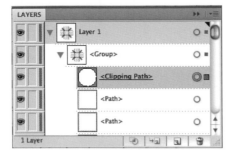

Choosing Object >Clipping Mask >Make puts all of the masked objects into a group with the clipping path at the top of the group

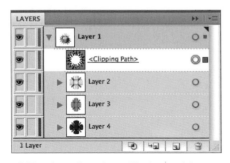

Clicking the Make/Release Clipping Mask button at the bottom of the panel turns the first item within the highlighted group or layer into a clipping path, without creating a new group

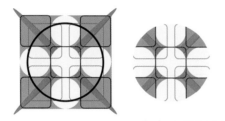

Before masking (left), the black-stroked circle is positioned as the topmost object in the stacking order, so it will become the clipping path when the clipping mask is created (right)

The organized whole is more than the sum of its parts. Combining tools and techniques in Illustrator can yield *Wow!* results. In this chapter we'll look at such synergy.

Please keep in mind that this chapter will be quite daunting if not overwhelming unless you're comfortable with what has been covered in previous chapters. If you're having trouble following the lessons in this chapter, then please revisit layers and stacking order (see the *Layers & Appearances* chapter), blends and gradients (the *Blends, Gradients & Mesh* chapter), and compound paths, compound shapes and Pathfinder panel (the *Beyond the Basics* chapter).

Although this chapter contains a variety of techniques, this introduction focuses on creating and working with clipping masks. Masks control what portion of an object or image is visible, and what portion is hidden. Illustrator features two kinds of masks: *clipping masks* and *opacity masks*. Since Opacity Masks are made using the Transparency panel, see the *Transparency* chapter for details on creating and working with opacity masks.

CLIPPING MASKS

All of the objects involved in a mask are organized in one of two ways depending on how you choose to make your mask. One method collects all selected objects into a group. The other method allows you to keep your layer structure and uses the master "container" layer (see the Layers panel illustrations at left). With any kind of clipping mask, the topmost object of that group is the *clipping path*; this clips (hides) portions of the other objects in the group that extend beyond the clipping mask boundaries leaving only the parts within these boundaries visible. Regardless of the attributes assigned to this top object, once you create the mask, it will become an unfilled and unstroked clipping path (but, keep reading to see how you can apply a stroke and fill to the new clipping path).

In the Layers panel, there are two indicators of an active clipping mask. First, your <u><Clipping Path></u> will be underlined and will remain underlined even if you rename it. Second, with an active clipping mask, you'll see dotted lines, instead of the standard solid lines, between the clipped items in the Layers panel.

To make a clipping mask from an object, you must first create that object. Only a single path can be used as a clipping mask, which means that complex shapes or multiple paths must be combined into a single "compound path" before being used as a mask (using Object > Compound Path > Make). Make sure your path or compound path is above the objects to be clipped, then create the clipping mask using one of two options. Use either the Make/Release Clipping Mask button on the Layers panel, or the Object > Clipping Mask > Make command. Each has its inherent advantages and disadvantages. The Object menu command gathers all the objects into a new group as it masks, allowing you to have multiple masked objects within a layer. It also gives you the ability to freely move masked objects within a layer structure without breaking the mask. However, if you have a carefully planned layer structure, it will be lost when everything is grouped. In contrast, the Layers panel command maintains your layer structure as it masks, but you can't have separately masked objects within a layer without building sublayers or grouping them first. This makes it difficult to move masked objects as a unit.

After you've created a clipping mask, you can edit the masking object, as well as the objects within the mask, using the Lasso, Direct Selection, or any path-editing tools. When you're using the Selection tools on masks created using the Object menu, a CS4 enhancement to object clipping masks prevents you from inadvertently selecting hidden parts of the masked objects.

To move your clipped object (path and contents) simply select it with the Selection tool and move it. If you wish to select, move, or edit the clipping path or the contents independently, then you have a few options. If

Clipping Mask icon disabled

In the Layers panel, you must select the *container* (layer, sublayer, or group) that holds your intended clipping object before you can apply a clipping mask. Also, in order for the button to be enabled, the top item inside the highlighted container must be something that can be turned into a clipping path.

The Edit Clipping Path (left) and the Edit Contents (right) buttons appear in the Control panel when an object using a mask is selected

Compound Path & Shape mask

When creating masking objects, use Compound Paths to combine simple objects. Use Compound Shapes for more control over the "holes" in overlapping objects or to combine more complex objects (see the *Beyond the Basics* chapter for more about Compound Paths and Compound Shapes).

Clipping Mask Release warning

In a layer that contains more than one clipping mask, clicking the Make/Release Clipping Mask button will release all clipping masks within that layer (not just the one you may wish to release). The safest way to release a single clipping mask is to select it and choose Object > Clipping Mask > Release.—*Jean-Claude Tremblay*

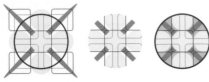

You can add a stroke and fill to a mask; the middle figure shows an unstroked mask, the right figure shows a dark blue stroke added to the clipping mask.

Alignment

When aligning or distributing content that is masked, Illustrator now considers the shape of the mask as the basis for alignment or distribution.

Pasting objects into a mask

To paste objects into a Clipping Mask, turn off Paste Remembers Layers (in the Layers panel menu), then Cut or Copy the objects you wish to insert. Next, select an object within the mask and use Paste in Front or Back to place the copied object into the mask. Or create or paste objects while in Isolation Mode to insert more objects into the group.

Mask error message

If you get the message, "Selection cannot contain objects within different groups unless the entire group is selected," the objects you've chosen to mask are a subset of a group. To create a mask with these objects, Cut or Copy your selected objects, then Paste in Front (⌘-F/Ctrl-F). Now you'll be able to apply Object > Clipping Mask > Make.

neither is selected, you can simply click on the clipping path or contents with the Direct Selection or Group Selection tool to edit or move that path or selection. If any portion of the mask or contents is already selected you can click the Edit Clipping Path or Edit Contents buttons in the Control panel to focus on which portion will be selected and can be edited.

You also can now edit your clipping group in Isolation mode. To isolate the entire clipping <Group>, double-click on any portion of it with the Selection tool; this dims all other objects on your artboard. You can now use the Control panel buttons to edit the path or contents, or use the Direct Selection and Group Selection tools.

You can also enter isolation Mode via the Layers panel. Highlight the <Clipping Path> or any of the paths within the <Group> and choose Enter Isolation Mode from the Layers panel pop-up menu. Once in Mode you can freely edit or move the paths without affecting any other objects. If you are in isolation mode with one of the objects within the mask, you can even add additional objects within that grouping. To exit isolation mode, double-click on the artboard (outside of the clipping group), or choose Exit Isolation Mode from the Layers panel pop-up menu.

Yet another way that you can determine which portion of your clipping group you wish to edit is by choosing Object > Clipping Mask > Edit Mask (or Object > Clipping Mask > Edit Content).

Once you have a clipping group, and the mask has been created, you can then add a stroke (it will appear as if it's in front of all masked objects) and/or fill (it appears as if it's behind all masked objects). In addition, once the mask has been made, in the Layers panel you can even move the clipping path lower in the stacking order of the group or container and still keep its masking effect.

Masking technique #1: The Object menu command

The simplest way to create masks for objects is using the Object menu command. Use this method when you want to confine the clipping mask to a specific object or group of objects that need to be easily duplicated or relocated. Since this method modifies your layer structure, don't use it if you need to maintain objects on specific layers.

As before, start by creating an object or compound object that will become your clipping mask. Make sure that it's the topmost object, then select it and *all* the objects you want to be masked (this topmost object will become the mask). Now, choose Object > Clipping Mask > Make. When you use this method, all the objects, including the new clipping path, will move to the layer that contains your topmost object and will be collected into a new <Group>. This will restrict the masking effect to only those objects within the group; you can easily use the Selection tool to select the entire clipping group. If you expand the <Group> in the Layers panel (by clicking the expansion triangle), you'll be able to move objects into or out of the clipping group, or move objects up or down within the group to change the stacking order. (Don't miss the Tip "Magical Clipping Path" following.)

When working with masks created using the Object menu, clipped objects are now truly hidden when clipped by a mask; as of CS4 you can no longer accidentally select the clipped portion of an object outside of the masked perimeter.

Masking technique #2: The Layers panel options
To mask unwanted areas of art within a *container* (meaning any group, sublayer, or layer), first create an object to use as your mask—make sure it's the topmost object in your container. Next, highlight that object's *container* and click the Make/Release Clipping Mask button on the Layers panel. The result: The topmost object, *within* the highlighted container, becomes the clipping path, and all elements within that container extending beyond the clipping path are hidden (for details on using complex objects as a mask, see the section: "Using type, compound paths or shapes as a mask" later in the chapter).

Once you've created a clipping mask, you can move

Figuring out if it's a mask
- <Clipping Path> in the Layers panel will be underlined if it's a mask (even if you've renamed it), and the background color for the icon will be gray.
- Object > Clipping Mask > Release being enabled means a mask is affecting your selection.
- An *opacity mask* has a dotted underline in the Layers panel.
- Select > Object > Clipping Masks can help you find masks within a document as long as they aren't inside linked files (such as EPS or PDF).

Multiple Artboard masks
Since layers are common to multiple artboards, if you make a mask the Layer panel way, that mask will apply across multiple artboards. In order for artwork on other artboards to be seen, it must be above or below the layers being masked.

Collect in New Layer
To collect selected layers into one "master layer" Shift-click to select contiguous layers, or ⌘-click/Ctrl-click to select noncontiguous layers and choose Collect in New Layer from the Layers menu.

Better Object mask selecting
CS4 enhancements to selecting masks only affect masks created using Object > Mask > Make.

The clipping mask (outlined in blue) above the floral illustration (left) was created as 7 separate objects (6 petals and 1 center circle) and then united into a single compound path (using Object > Compound Path command); positioned on top of other objects, it was then used as a clipping mask (right).

When a placed image is selected, the Mask button appears in the Control panel

Masking the mask

Clipping masks can also be used to clip other masks. First create your initial masked object and then just treat it like another object to be masked beneath another clipping mask.

(See later in this chapter, and the *Artboards & Type* chapter, for lessons in masking using live type.)

Magical clipping path

Once an object is a clipping path, you can move it anywhere *within* its layer or group in the Layers panel—it will still maintain its masking effect!

objects up or down within the container (layer, sublayer, or group) to change the stacking order. However, if you move items outside of the clipping mask container, they will no longer be masked. Moving the clipping path itself outside of its container releases the mask completely.

Mask button

If you use File > Place to place an image, when the placed image is selected, you can instantly create a clipping path for the image by clicking the Mask button in the Control panel. However, masking is not immediately apparent because the clipping path has the same dimensions as the placed image's bounding box. Make sure the Edit Clipping Path button (in the Control panel) is enabled and then adjust the clipping path to shape the mask that is "cropping" your image.

Using type, Compound Paths or Shapes as a mask

You can use editable type as a mask to give the appearance that the type is filled with any image or group of objects. Select the type and the image or objects with which you want to fill the text. Make sure the type is on top, then choose Object > Clipping Mask > Make.

To use separate type characters as a single clipping mask, you have to first make them into a Compound Shape or Compound Path. You can make a Compound Shape from either outlined or live (i.e., non-outlined) text. You can make a Compound Path only from outlined text (not live text). Once you've made a Compound Path or Shape of your separate type elements, you can use it as a mask. (See the Tip "Compound Paths or Shapes?" in the *Beyond the Basics* chapter. And see the *Artboards & Type* chapter, and later in this chapter, for examples of masking with type.)

Selecting all your clipping masks

You can easily select all your clipping masks at once by choosing Select > Object > Clipping Masks.

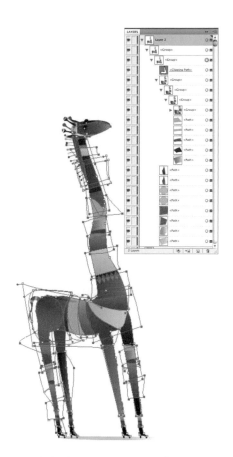

BEAUREGARD

Christiane Beauregard

Christiane Beauregard relies on Illustrator's clipping masks to provide her with the maximum flexibility when creating the intricate patterns in the giraffes, palms, and snake. In order to easily edit the individual objects that fit precisely into these curvilinear shapes, Beauregard first created her objects by very loosely and roughly following the intended outline. She allowed the objects to overlap, using their stacking order in the Layers panel to help delineate the interior edges. Throughout the development of the illustration, she could adjust where each object met another, because the objects weren't "cut to fit." The clipping masks then hid all the extraneous, outside portions of her layered objects, giving her palms, snake, and giraffes their final form. By clicking the Edit Clipping Path or Edit Contents icon in the Control panel, she could hide the clipped objects to edit just the clipping path, or reveal the objects to edit them Using clipping masks, she retained both the vector edge of her objects, and the ability to edit again at any time in the future. Her use of gradients with several objects provided additional complexity and dimension, and she used Opacity Masks to soften the edges of the clouds and shadows (see the *Transparency* chapter for more).

Simple Masking

Applying the Basics of Clipping Masks

Advanced Technique

Overview: *Create a clipping mask; gather and order objects to clip; use the mask to clip multiple objects; use a mask to clip another mask.*

This custom surfboard design was created by San Diego based illustrator Aaron McGarry, who finds much of his work inspired by a life tailored to the beach communities and industries of southern California.

Above are the three objects to be used, first the image, next the text, and topmost is the board

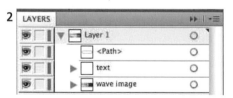

The Layers panel showing the correct stacking order of the objects before masking

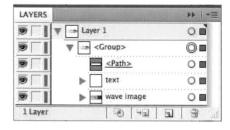

The Layers panel showing the objects <Group> after applying the clipping mask

The surfboard uses two clipping masks: the text is used to clip the image and then the board clips the text.

1 Preparing the elements for masking. Create the objects that you'll use as a clipping path, and collect the objects that you'll be masking within the clipping path. McGarry created a surfboard outline using the Pen tool. He next painted a wave in Photoshop, then in Illustrator he chose File > Place, selected the image, disabled Template, and clicked OK. With the Type tool, McGarry created text on top of his placed image, with white fill and no stroke. He chose the Earth (normal) font because he felt it was a modern, fresh typeface with enough weight to show an image through the characters if he later wanted to use the text as a clipping mask. To create a slightly "edgier" feel, he rotated the text using the bounding box.

2 Positioning the objects and applying the mask. Position the object you'll be using as a clipping path within the Layers panel, as the topmost object above the objects it will mask. With the surfboard above his image and text McGarry selected them all and chose Object > Clipping Mask > Make (⌘-7/Ctrl-7); this placed all the objects in a clipping group (on one layer), with the type and image being masked by the surfboard <Clipping Path>.

For a variation of the surfboard, McGarry masked the image with the text first; selecting text and image he applied ⌘-7/Ctrl-7. Next selecting this new clipping group, the surfboard path, and the yellow background he applied ⌘-7/ Ctrl-7. He created finishing details (edges) for both surfboards using blends with transparency (see *Blends, Gradients & Mesh,* and *Transparency* chapters).

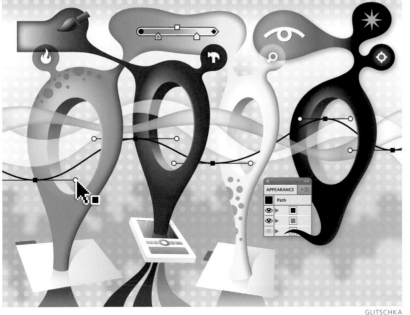

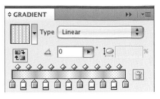

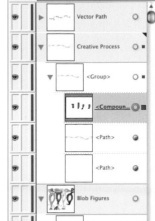

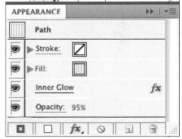

GLITSCHKA

Von R. Glitschka

When Von R. Glitschka created this illustration for Mordy Golding's *Real World Adobe Illustrator CS4* book (designed by Charlene Charles-Will), he demonstrated virtually every method for seeing through an object with the creation of just one object—the green ribbon that flows across the design. The ribbon itself is on a layer above all other objects except the black "vector path" object. He used a Compound Clipping Mask to allow other objects to appear to overlap the green ribbon, letting it seem to weave in and out. He created the gauzy appearance of the ribbon itself with a gradient that uses transparency, and reduced Layer Opacity. Live Effects, with their Blending modes and Blurs, are another means to generating transparency, as well as adding dimension; the Inner Glow effect does this by means of a darker green and the "glow" set to Multiply. Thus it darkens

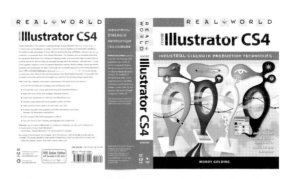

and creates a modeling inner shadow. Creating transparency is so vital to illustration that the chapters *Transparency, Layers & Appearances*, *Live Effects*, and *Blends, Gradients & Mesh* discuss methods for creating it in great detail.

Masking Details
Using Masks to Contour & Hide Elements

Advanced Technique

Overview: *Create basic elements; make basic masks; mask compound path objects with Live Effects; make compound paths to act as masks; create an overall cropping mask.*

1

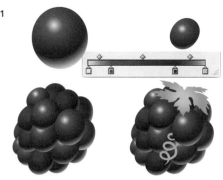

Making radial gradients for a grape shapes, drawing and combining basic objects

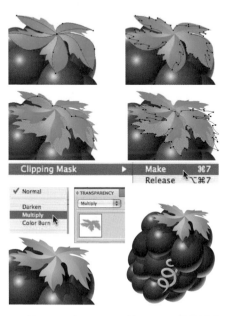

Masking to make two-toned leaves; making shadows by masking and setting the fills to Multiply mode; the final grapes with masking and shadows throughout

To be a true Illustrator expert, you must master a range of masking techniques. Russell Benfanti's lush and masterful illustrations are filled with masks. This lesson looks at four applications of masking in Illustrator.

1 Contouring masks for detail and shadows. First create your basic objects using any tools, including blends and gradient mesh. Benfanti used ovals filled with radial gradients customized using the Gradient tool, so that the blue would appear as a reflection on the bottom edge.

In a layer above his grapes, Benfanti drew a two-toned leaf. He began by drawing the outline shape, filled it with a radial gradient, and copied it. Then he quickly drew teardrop shaped wedges extending beyond the leaf-shapes, filled with a darker green gradient. With the leaf shape still on the Clipboard, he used Paste In Front (⌘-F/Ctrl-F). Next, selecting *all* the leaf objects, he chose Object>Clipping Mask>Make (⌘-7/Ctrl-7).

To create the shadow for the leaf, he used Paste In Back (⌘-B/Ctrl-B) to paste another copy of the leaf underneath. He then shifted the position of this "shadow" down and to the right, and gave it a medium blue solid fill. To fit that object within the silhouette of the grapes (not extend beyond it), he needed to make a contouring object that matched the silhouette of the grapes. Selecting the grapes, he copied and used Paste In Front. In the Pathfinder panel he clicked the Unite icon to permanently unite the grapes into one simple contouring-outline object.

Masking objects must be above the objects they mask, so move your grape-contour object above the "shadow" using the Layers panel. With the grapes contour above the blue leaf, Benfanti selected both and made a new clipping mask (⌘-7/Ctrl-7). To make the shadow more realistic, he selected only the blue leaf object and from the Control panel Opacity pop-up, he changed the blending mode from Normal to Multiply (you can change the blending mode before applying the mask). Benfanti also created shadows for individual grapes and the stem curl.

2 Masking roughened compound paths. To make the watermelon stripes, Benfanti drew arcs over the oval using the same gradient as the oval, and chose Object > Compound Path > Make, unifying the color. He then used the Gradient and Color panels to make the colors of the arc gradient warmer and lighter. To ripple the selected arcs he chose Effect > Distort & Transform > Roughen, and used Preview to decide on Size: 2%, Relative, Detail: 5.53/in, and Corner. He used a copy of the melon oval as a mask so the arcs stay within the contour.

3 Using compound paths to mask. You can use multiple objects to act as one masking object by first making the selected objects into a compound path. For Benfanti's orange sections, he created the overall shapes and the inner textures. Next he drew section wedges, selected them all, and chose Object > Compound Path > Make. Selecting the textures of the orange with this compound path, he used ⌘-7 (Ctrl-7) to section the orange. Before adding the finishing details, he selected the compound path mask object, and applied a darker orange gradient that shows through as a background.

4 Cropping the image with a layer mask. Benfanti placed all layers within one enclosing layer. Loose in that enclosing layer he created a rectangle that would define the cropping area. Finally, he clicked the master layer to highlight it, and then the Make Clipping Mask icon.

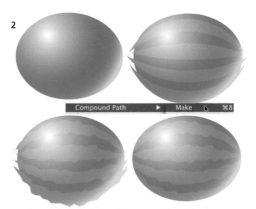

The original oval, making arcs and combining them into a compound path, applying Roughen, and masking with a copy of the original oval

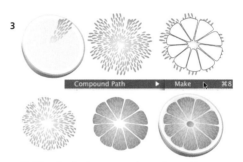

Making the basic orange elements; making wedge objects into one compound path; using the compound path as a mask; finishing details

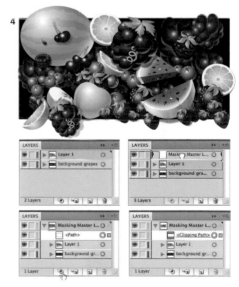

The final illustration before cropping the margins and the original layers panel; after making a new layer, dragging the two original layers into it, clicking the Create Layer Mask icon and the final panel showing the clipping mask

Glowing Starshine

Drawing Stars with Gradients and Strokes

Advanced Technique

Overview: *Create a star shape on top of a circle and adjust the shape using the Direct Selection tool; add a glow by applying a radial gradient to the star and circle shapes.*

1

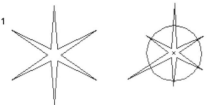

The original star, and the modified star positioned over a circle

2

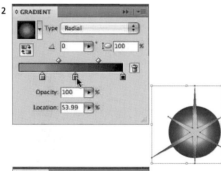

Color panel displaying color for selected slider on the Gradient panel with star shape selected

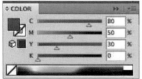

Gradient-filled shapes on the sky background

Illumination is the key to creating a realistic nighttime sky. This technique by Kenneth Batelman will help you create glowing lights of all sizes, simply and directly.

1 Drawing a big star. Batelman used the Ellipse tool to create a circle, and then the Star tool to draw a star on top of the circle. To make the star shape more interesting, he repositioned some of the star points using the Direct Selection tool.

2 Applying a radial gradient. To make the star glow, Batelman applied a radial gradient to the star. The gradient slider at the edge matches the sky color (he used 100% C, 80% M, 60% Y, and 20% K), and the slider at the center is the star glow at its brightest (he used 30% C, 5% M, 0% Y, and 0% K). Batelman added a third gradient slider between the original two, set to an intermediate color (he used 80% C, 50% M, 30% Y, 0% K). Applying the same radial gradient to the circle adds a halo effect to the star (for more on creating and storing gradients see the *Blends, Gradients & Mesh* chapter). To keep the star and glow together, he selected the star and circle and chose Object > Group (⌘-G/Ctrl-G).

Batelman created the small stars by overlapping specialized dashed strokes; see the Gallery opposite for details on this technique.

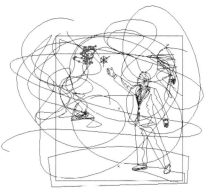

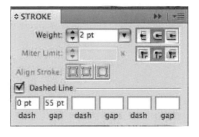

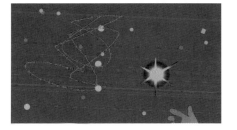

Kenneth Batelman

Batelman blanketed his sky with small stars by using dashed-line paths drawn with the Pencil tool. He created dots along the path by entering a Dash value of 0. For the Gap value, Batelman entered a value between 20 and 90 points. He chose the rounded options for both the cap and join so that the dots would be circular instead of square, and then set Weight values ranging from .85 to 2.5 points. By overlapping multiple paths with varying weights and dash gap values, Batelman's "dashes" appear to be points of light that vary in size and spacing. The Stroke panel settings shown above left are for the path of small stars selected above right.

AUBÉ

Jean Aubé

For his "Nuit de Terreur" poster, Jean Aubé began by using the Pen tool to trace the outline of a photograph he took of a friend. He added a gradient fill and applied Effect > Stylize > Outer Glow. For the overall lighting, he created a background with a radial gradient, position-ing the center between the hands. He then drew a circle for the moon. He made a tiny blue circle to represent a star and saved it as a sym-bol. Using the Symbol Sprayer, he sprayed the "stars" on two layers for depth. He expanded the symbols in order to delete unwanted extras. He set "Nuit de Terreur" as a block of

type, then converted the type to outlines. Aubé chose Object > Envelope Distort > Make with Mesh to distort the type. He set the other blocks of type separately. On a layer behind the stars and type he created spooky swirls by drawing many ovals, and then used Pathfinder operations on the ovals until he had broken them down to strands. He selected and deleted portions of the strands that remained. Finally he arranged, grouped, and filled them with a single linear gradient. He made the ovals appear ghostly by placing them in Overlay Mode and applying Outer Glow to them.

GILBERT

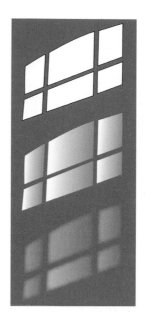

Reggie Gilbert

To create his photorealistic fire station, illustrator Reggie Gilbert laid his bricks like a master. He began by creating five different rectangles and customizing a gradient for each using the Gradient panel. Then creating one solid-colored brick on an angle, he duplicated that brick and moved the duplicate along that angle, a distance away. Selecting the two angled bricks he double-clicked the Blend tool to set Blend Options to Specified Steps for Spacing, and entered 8. Gilbert then chose Object > Blend > Make to create the blend, then Object > Expand to break the blend into 10 separate objects. He next used the Direct Selection tool to select individual bricks to move them slightly out of alignment, giving the line of bricks a more organic look. Then he again selected each of the angled bricks and this time use the Eyedropper tool to click on one of the pre-made gradients to fill it with that gradient. With this

line of bricks complete, he grouped them (⌘-G/Ctrl-G) and starting with the blended line of bricks, he'd customize a new line. By creating each line of bricks with deliberate randomness Gilbert avoids the appearance of repeating patterns in the bricks. To create the windows (shown against blue at top), he drew the objects, grouped them, then filled them with a custom light-to-slightly-darker gradient in the hue of the objects that behind the glass. In the Layers panel he targeted the <Group>, and in the Control panel he reduced the opacity and applied Effect > Stylize > Feather (for the windows shown above he used 40% Opacity and 9 pt Feather).

Von R. Glitschka

Von Glitschka begins his pattern-making process by creating a very precise pencil sketch to place as a Template layer (see the *Layers & Appearance* chapter for help). On a layer above the placed sketch, he used the Rectangle tool to draw a square to define the pattern repeat area. From the View menu, Glitschka enabled Snap to Point and Smart Guides. Using both the Pen and Ellipse tools, Glitschka drew the main pattern. Although he followed his template very closely, Smart Guides ensured exact placement of his paths. Glitschka refined the curve of the paths with the aid of an Illustrator Plug-in, Xtream Path (CValley Software, demo on the *Wow! CD*). And to complete the main pattern elements he applied Pathfinder commands to the closed paths (Unite, Minus Front, and Intersect). To place repeating elements in perfect registration (such as the large flower at the top) Glitschka relied on Option-dragging/Alt-dragging a copy of the element along with the square, using Snap to Point to guide in the alignment. At this point

GLITSCHKA

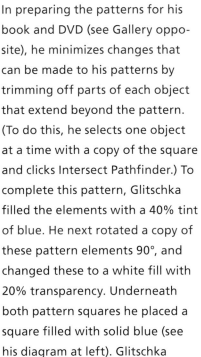

Glitschka could have defined his pattern by simply placing an unstroked, unfilled, unrotated copy of the tile bounding square behind the other elements (see the "Intricate Patterns" lesson in the *Drawing & Coloring* chapter for help with alignment and this method of pattern definition).

In preparing the patterns for his book and DVD (see Gallery opposite), he minimizes changes that can be made to his patterns by trimming off parts of each object that extend beyond the pattern. (To do this, he selects one object at a time with a copy of the square and clicks Intersect Pathfinder.) To complete this pattern, Glitschka filled the elements with a 40% tint of blue. He next rotated a copy of these pattern elements 90°, and changed these to a white fill with 20% transparency. Underneath both pattern squares he placed a square filled with solid blue (see his diagram at left). Glitschka grouped the completed pattern and dragged it to the Swatches panel to define it as a pattern. See an illustration using this pattern in the *Live Effects & Graphics Style* chapter.

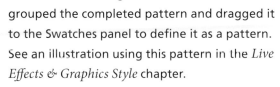

Psychotronic

Graphic Bloom

Single Cell

Grate Expectations

Funkus

Scorn Thistle

Alien Cells

Frillicious

Greener

Von R. Glitschka

Shown above is just a small sample of unique patterns from Von R. Glitschka's latest book and DVD entitled, *Drip.Dot.Swirl. 94 incredible patterns for design and illustration* (How Publishing). Using similar techniques described on the opposite page (with some variation such as applying blending modes or effects to a layer), Glitschka created editable patterns in a wide range of styles. See www.vonsterbooks.com for details about the book.

FLESEY

Erick Flesey

Erick Flesey captures the essence of underwater life in his imaginative illustrations filled with subtle gradients (creating this very large illustration for the San Diego Oceans Foundation). He begins his drawings by roughly shaping the animal or plant he wants to illustrate, then creates a highly detailed image using the Pencil tool, which preserves the natural, hand-drawn appearance that compliments his subjects. After creating some basic gradients, Flesey begins to apply them to his objects using the updated Gradient tool with the Gradient Annotator toggled on (⌘-Option-G/Ctrl-Alt-G). Now he can quickly edit a gradient without taking his eyes off his artwork, and at the same time easily select several gradients that must work together and see that their angles correspond to the direction of the objects and the lighting. For example, the curved structure of the fin, while delineated in separate objects, is now easy to visualize and maintain by interactively

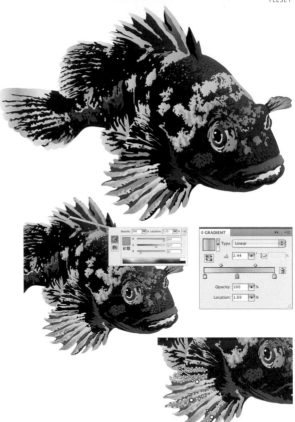

dragging with his cursor when the Rotate icon appears at the arrow end of the Gradient Annotator. Reducing layer Opacity with the gradient-filled objects increases the appearance of depth and consistent lighting across the image. (See a larger version of this at www.erickflesey.com.)

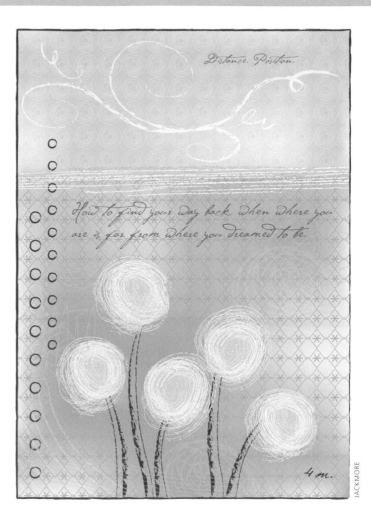

Lisa Jackmore

Lisa Jackmore combined layers of patterns, brushes, and gradient mesh, to create texture in this interpretation of a page in her sketchbook. For each gradient mesh background, she filled a rectangle with a solid fill and added mesh points with the Mesh tool. Jackmore kept most of the mesh points near the edges of the rectangle, and filled them with a light color to achieve a faded appearance. She created two patterns to layer above the mesh. For the circle pattern, she drew several concentric circles with the Ellipse tool, grouped them, and applied the Pencil Art brush. She selected the Twirl tool, and while holding Option-Shift/Alt-Shift, she click-dragged on the Artboard, and sized the diameter of the Twirl to fit over the circles. Then she clicked on the circles with the Twirl tool until she was happy with the amount of twirl. She grouped the objects and dragged them to the Swatches panel. To make the diamond pattern, Jackmore used a combination of Rectangle, Ellipse, and Rotate tools. She then grouped the objects and

dragged them to the Swatches panel. Jackmore colored the pattern the same base color as the gradient mesh background so the pattern disappears in the dark areas. She then added more details to the background, and made the flowers with custom brushes she created. (For details about how she made some of these brushes, refer to her galleries in the *Brushes & Symbols* chapter). Jackmore also used several default brushes from the Artistic_ChalkCharcoalPencil library. Finally, she created a clipping mask to contain the brush marks that extended beyond the rectangle.

Scott Crouse

Scott Crouse required the flexibility of a vector drawing and the realism of a photograph for use in a variety of mediums (various sizes of signs and banners). He created this fishing lure with a combination of blends and solid filled paths. Crouse made the realistic head, beads of water, and the shadows with blended shapes. He layered vibrant solid filled shapes to construct the tail. Crouse used the contrast of the filled shapes next to the blended objects to emphasize the fine detail in this vivid illustration.

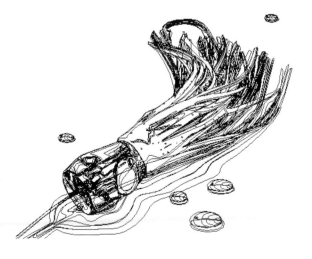

CROUSE

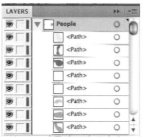

Scott Crouse

Scott Crouse created this photorealistic scene using layers of meticulously drawn and colored shapes (panel shown above). After drawing paths with the Pen tool to define an area, he colored the shapes with similar values (detail above right). In select areas such as the blue car trunk, he created a gradient. Crouse worked in a scale larger than what the final output required, so that after he reduced the image, the viewer would see smooth color transitions, not separate shapes. His technique created an illustration as lifelike as the photo from which Crouse drew inspiration (shown above the Layers panel at left).

"Red Indian"   Copyright © 2005 Chris Nielsen

NIELSEN

Chris Nielsen

When Chris Nielsen spotted a classic *Indian* motorcycle, fully restored, he wanted to illustrate it with his signature photorealistic technique. He knew his basic 8 MP digital point-and-shoot camera would capture enough detail, but with other bikes parked right next to the *Indian*, getting the reference shot at all was a major undertaking. Once he brought it into Illustrator, he used the same methods described on the opposite page, relying on the Pen tool to draw progressively smaller details, and the Pathfinder panel with the Divide command to create the areas representing every nuance of the bike and its reflections. He worked on a section at a time, starting with less detailed areas, and bringing each to near completion before moving to the next area. Nielsen would often zoom to a comfortable 300% or so to work on fine details, but rarely more than that. In this manner, he always managed to keep an eye on the way the area he was working on was affecting the image as a whole. Color started with the photo itself, but Nielsen didn't rely upon the photo to produce the most accurate and pleasing tones. He used his artist's eye to adjust those colors until the right hues and values were represented. When completed, Nielsen's *Indian* brought to life a rare, vintage motorcycle for everyone to enjoy.

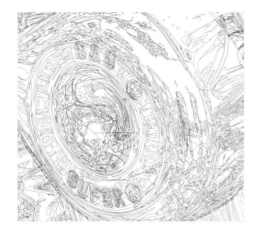

"Super Stock"

Copyright © 2005 Chris Nielsen

NIELSEN

Chris Nielsen

Chris Nielsen created another stunning image using the same drawing technique described on the opposite page. Nielsen likes to begin drawing an area of the photograph that contains a large object, such as a gas tank, or big pipe. Working over a template layer that contained his original photograph, he first drew the outline of a large object with the Pen tool. Then he drew paths for each area where the color value changed within that object. He selected the paths and clicked the Divide Pathfinder icon. He continued in this manner until there were enough shapes to define the object. This was a particularly challenging motorcycle to draw because there are only slight variations in one overall color. Nielsen filled each individual object with a custom color chosen from the Swatches panel. In all of his motorcycle illustrations, the reflection of Nielsen taking the photograph is visible—here it's shown in the magnified detail on the left.

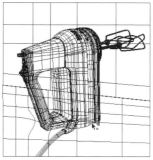

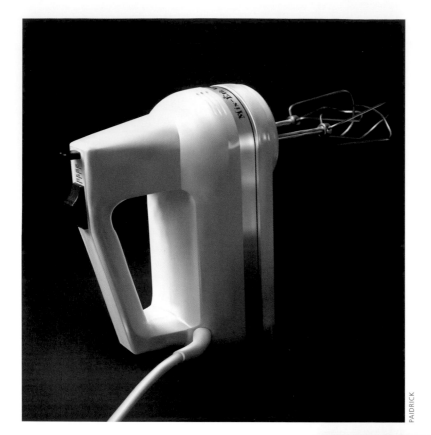

PAIDRICK

Ann Paidrick

Using an original photograph as a template, Ann Paidrick made gradient mesh objects to re-create this mixer with incredible precision. Focusing on one section at a time (such as the beaters, handle, or the cord), she drew rectangular paths with the Pen tool based on the relative size and shape of each object. She filled the rectangles with a base color sampled from the photograph, then changed the object into a mesh (Object > Create Gradient Mesh). In the Create Gradient Mesh dialog, she specified one row, one column, and a flat appearance. She added more rows and columns with the Mesh

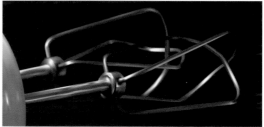

tool and adjusted the points to form the contour she desired. She continued to sample color from the photograph to color the mesh points. To further define the mesh, she also added individual points with the Add Anchor Point tool, then adjusted those points with the Direct Selection tool. See "Molding Mesh" in the *Blends, Gradients & Mesh* chapter for a lesson on contouring mesh.

PAIDRICK

Ann Paidrick

In addition to the technique used in the drawing opposite, Ann Paidrick used symbols to enhance the realistic appearance of this glass of iced tea (panel detail at right). To make the tiny bubbles at the top of the tea, she created blended circles of various sizes and colors to make a symbol set. (See the *Brushes & Symbols* chapter for more about symbols.) Paidrick created numerous complex gradient mesh shapes to complete the amazing level of detail

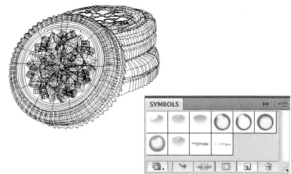

in the objects. Some of these gradient mesh objects are shown in the cookie detail above (shown in outline view).

CATER (©INMOTION 2003)

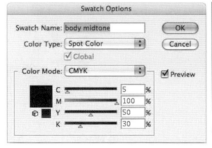

David Cater

David Cater created this Mini Cooper image for reproduction on T-shirts, posters, and note cards. Knowing that different clients would want the car in a variety of colors, he started by creating two spot color swatches for the mid and shadow tones of the car. He then used those two spot colors (global process colors would also work) to create the handful of gradients he used to fill each of the approximately 1,500 shapes he used to create the car. Because he was careful to color only the body panels using gradients created from those two colors, he was later able to easily change the color of the car by simply double-clicking on each of the two color swatches and using the CMYK sliders to redefine the colors. Although he could have used blends more extensively (he only used a few for the cowlings along the front and side of the car), Cater found it faster and easier to use simple, gradient-filled shapes.

MIYAMOTO

Yukio Miyamoto

The "Molding Mesh" lesson in the *Blends, Gradients & Mesh* chapter shows how Yukio Miyamoto created these amazing mesh bottles. To create the reflections in this version, Miyamoto used the Reflect tool to reflect a copy of the bottles along the base of the bottles. He next pulled a horizontal guide from the ruler to align with the end of the table top. For each of the reflections, he targeted the mesh and in the Transparency panel he reduced the opacity to 80%. To make the reflections fade, he used Path > Offset Path and entered 0 as the Offset. He filled this outline with a white-to-gray gradient, and then used the Gradient tool to run from white at the guideline to gray at the bottle bottom. To make certain that the reflection stopped abruptly at the table edge,

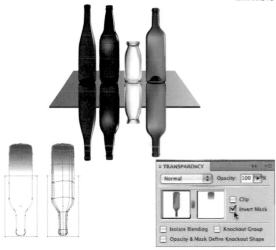

he grouped each gradient bottle with a white rectangle covering the neck half of the bottle, and ending at the guideline. He then selected each pair of gray and mesh bottle objects, chose Make Opacity Mask from the Transparency panel pop-up, and enabled the Invert Mask option.

Marc LaMantia

Marc LaMantia scanned one of his photographs to create this illustration of a subway exit, in which he used the techniques described on the opposite page. In this piece, LaMantia depicts the beauty of a single moment of an ordinary day in New York City. Transparency effects were used throughout the entire illustration (see the *Transparency* chapter). Many of the shadow areas (such as within the steps) are actually made of transparent pink, red, and magenta shapes, layered above black. Rarely is a color used at full opacity. The layering of numerous transparent layers (all in Normal mode) brings enormous depth and interest to the posterized style. When viewing the image in Outline mode (above right), the level of detail becomes apparent.

Chris Nielsen

Chris Nielsen has trained his artistic eye to recognize subtle shifts of color within a photograph and translate them into a striking image using layers of filled paths. Nielsen first placed an original photograph in a bottom layer to trace upon. He worked on one small section at a time, such as the eye in the detail to the right. With the Pen tool he made paths (no fill, with a black stroke) and traced the areas of primary color he saw in the photograph. He chose the darkest value first (dark blue or black), then on another layer, he drew the objects with progressively lighter values (a lighter blue, red, gray, etc.). He continued building layers of paths until the area was completely covered. He moved throughout the image this way until the portrait was finished. When all of the paths were drawn he began to fill them with color. Nielsen chose the Eyedropper tool, pressed and held the ⌘/Ctrl key to switch to the Direct Selection tool, and selected an object to color. Then he toggled back to the Eyedropper tool by releasing the ⌘/Ctrl key and sampled a color from the photograph. He toggled between the Direct Selection tool and the Eyedropper tool until the paths were filled. Most of the time, Nielsen liked the sampled colors, but if not, he would tweak the color using the sliders in the Color panel. Once

▶ NIELSEN

NIELSEN

all of the paths were filled with color, Nielsen hid the template layer. He saw gaps of white in his drawing where the paths didn't quite meet or overlap. To fill these gaps, he made a large object that covered the area, filled it with a dark color, and placed it on the bottom-most layer.

14

Use .ai for Flash

The best way to bring artwork into Adobe Flash Professional is to save a native Illustrator (AI) file, which you can then import to your stage. Saving in AI will preserve groups, layers, symbols, instance names, and even certain live effects, such as drop shadows.—*Andrew Dashwood*

Pixel Preview

While Illustrator's default preview is optimized for print, choosing View > Pixel Preview will allow you to see your art as it would appear when displayed on the web or on a digital screen. Pixel Preview will show the effects of antialiasing, which often will affect the visual appearance of your art.
—*Mordy Golding*

Pixel Preview off

Pixel Preview on

Web & Animation

Not long ago, designing for the web meant designing for small desktop or laptop monitors. Today, display sizes range from a 30" widescreen monitor with a typical pixel resolution of 2560 x 1600, to a cell phone with a pixel display area of less than 240 x 400 pixels. Web pages ceased to be static long ago, requiring more programming than basic HTML, and even web browsers are becoming less important as small applications and widgets allow the user to access the web directly. Few designers these days would attempt to create a website in a single program like Illustrator, but Illustrator is compatible with other applications, and can still bring to the table some very relevant features that make designing elements of websites—such as ad banners, icons, small animations, and interface elements for Rich Internet Applications (RIAs)—both efficient and versatile.

This chapter is designed to introduce illustrators and designers to some of the complexities of creating for modern displays. Today, Illustrator users need to understand both what scales well to a variety of devices, and what plays well with web-oriented programs. Adobe has worked to eliminate obstacles between Illustrator and web programs such as Flash, but some features will produce large files that result in long load times, or features that don't scale to large and small displays. For instance, symbols created in Illustrator are compatible with Flash, making both animation and file-size reduction much easier. But if you modify your symbols using the nifty Symbol Stainer or Symbol Styler tools, your Flash file becomes much larger. Flash then generates a copy for each symbol instance in order to preserve appearance, negating the file-reduction properties of using symbols in the first place. Many effects also add significantly to file size. This introduction focuses on Illustrator's web-related and animation features, with an eye to helping you to keep file sizes as small as possible.

WORKING WITH WEB DESIGN BASICS

Illustrator can help you set up a document that's destined for the screen. If you choose the "Web" or "Mobile and Devices" document profiles when creating a new document, most of the settings are geared for screen display including setting resolution to 72 ppi, RGB color mode, and pixels for ruler units. You may want to work with a custom artboard size, or click on Templates to find templates for items such as ad banners or Flex skins.

You can change the size of the artboard at any time and, with multiple artboards, even adapt your design for the different sizes within a single document—a great aid for sharing the resources when you need to maintain a look, but on vastly different scales. You can export only the *active* artboard from Save for Web, but your file will have all your assets in one place. (For more on working with artboards, see the *Artboards & Type* chapter.)

If your project is destined for both print and screen display, most experts advise you work in CMYK (since CMYK is the more limited color space), and then convert a copy of your artwork to RGB in a new document. Try not to jump back and forth between color modes, since rich colors can easily degrade with each conversion.

To save static images for the web, you'll probably want to choose either the GIF or JPEG format. Use File > Save for Web & Devices (⌘-Option-Shift-S/Ctrl-Alt-Shift-S) to convert your vector objects to optimized images for the web in the format best suited to both the art itself, and its destination. GIF is the smallest format for converting solid vector art into rasterized art, but it is less suitable if your vector artwork contains smooth blends, gradients, transparency, and raster effects involving transparency (such as glows and drop shadows). GIF uses an indexed color table of up to 256 colors, and has the ability to assign one of those colors to represent transparency; specify a subject's solid background color as transparent to blend it into a site's background. Many cell phones and computers still don't connect at broadband speeds, so the fewer colors you can use, the faster the download.

However, if your artwork contains photographs, gradients, or transparent effects that need to be rasterized
smoothly, you probably want to export your file as a
JPEG. (These types of effects are elements that require
many more colors than GIF's 256 limit to prevent band-
ing, dithering or other blocky artifacts.) The file size may
be much larger, but JPEG can display millions of colors.

PNG is similar to JPEG in the number of colors it can
display, and can also display up to 256 levels of transparency. For a very long time, however, browsers didn't support PNG, so the format is still less common than JPEG.
But if you know your artwork is destined to pass through
Fireworks, Dreamweaver, or Flex Builder, PNG is an
excellent format to consider selecting in Save for Web &
Devices. For a description of the features in the Save for
Web & Devices dialog, see the Tip at left.

CREATE AN ANIMATION WITH LAYERS

Illustrator can help you develop animations. Target a
blend, layer, or group, and choose either Release to Layers
(Sequence), or Release to Layers (Build) from the Layers panel menu. Choose the Sequence option if you want
each layer to become one frame in a future animation, or
you want to separately manipulate each object in every
frame. If instead you choose the Build option, the bottom layer's object gets placed on every layer, with the next
object placed on every layer except the first layer, and so
on, until the last object is placed on the top layer with all
the other objects.

You can export simple animations directly to the
SWF format, or save your AI file and import it in applications with more sophisticated tool sets, such as Flash and
After Effects. When saving art to import later in After
Effects, be sure the active artboard contains only what
you want to export, and that Create PDF Compatible File
is selected. After Effects supports transparency, and can
bring in all the layers created by the Release to Layers
command (see the "Animating Pieces" lesson later in this
chapter for more about working with After Effects).

FROM ILLUSTRATOR TO FLASH

Because Flash and Illustrator objects are both vector, you can create just about any artwork intended for a Flash project inside Illustrator. Now that both programs are part of the Adobe Creative Suite, you have many ways to get your work from Illustrator into Flash. If you own both programs, you can copy and paste or drag and drop between Illustrator and Flash. If you're producing an animation completely in Illustrator, or are working with a legacy version of Macromedia Flash, then you can choose File > Export > Flash (SWF). Be aware that exporting as SWF may break your artwork into many simple objects, even if you have created Flash Movie Clips of them. Saving your artwork as Illustrator (AI) format and choosing to import to the Stage or Library in Adobe Flash will usually give you the best results. The Flash import dialog provides several options for converting Illustrator Layers and Symbols to Flash layers, frames or a single image, and to deal with any incompatibility that might exist with an Illustrator object. Note that if you save an AI file and import it to Flash, you will need to have top-level layers, and not the sublayers that are automatically created by Illustrator's Release to Layers ability. Manually select all of the sublayers in Illustrator and drag them up to become top-level layers.

Here are some strategies for maximizing the quality and usefulness of your Illustrator files in Flash:

• **Use Illustrator symbols for repeating objects.** Illustrator lets you convert both raster and vector artwork into *symbols* that you can *place* multiple times, instead of using multiple copies of the original art (see the *Brushes & Symbols* chapter for more about symbols). Each time you place an instance of a symbol, you are creating a *link* to the symbol stored in the panel, rather than duplicating the artwork. This reduces the size of your Illustrator file, and can also reduce the size of any SWF files you export from Illustrator. Remember though, don't use the Symbol Stainer, Screener, or Styler on your symbols; using these tools will result in a larger SWF file with many unique

Adjusting slices

If you use the Slice tool to manually slice up your artwork into html-based tables, Illustrator creates other slices to fill any area of the page not manually sliced, but if you adjust the size of artwork or text within those slices, you'll need to manually resize the slices using the Slice Select tool. To make automatically adjusting slices, select an object instead, and choose Object > Slice > Make; these slices *will* update as you adjust your artwork.

Creative slicing

Instead of creating four artboards for four different banner sizes, you could create one artboard and define four slices—one for each banner. In File > Save for Web & Devices, you can only export one artboard at a time—but you can export all four slices at once, and name those slices so each file has a name. You can specify that Illustrator only export the slices you create (user slices), and you can choose to export just the images and not the HTML table.
—*Mordy Golding*

Some of the Flash Import dialog options when importing an Illustrator file

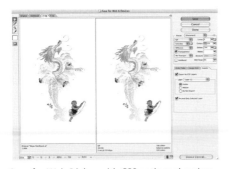

Save for Web Dialog with CSS options showing

symbols. Instead, use a selection tool to select symbol objects and apply Effects from the *fx* menu of the Appearance panel. Even if you've applied different effects to different occurrences of the same symbol, Flash will only import one symbol, and the altered appearances will be preserved (although some effects won't be live anymore).

- **Exporting as an SWF file and choosing Export Layers to SWF frames.** If you have all of the basic elements on your layers to create a Flash animation from within Illustrator, then use this method. Each Illustrator layer becomes a Flash frame in the animation.

- **When creating a SWF file, paths that are only partly contained within the work area will be exported in their entirety**. To reduce file size as much as possible, you can permanently remove the excess paths. To do this, try holding Option/Alt as you drag with the Eraser tool to define rectangular sections to remove.

- **When exporting SWF files,** switch between Preserve Appearance and Preserve Editability and check the Optimized view to discover if anything has changed.

- **Dashed strokes will be rasterized when exported to SWF.** Select dashed strokes and choose Object > Expand, so the strokes remain vectors in your SWF files.

- **Gradients with more than 8 stops, and all mesh objects, are rasterized.** Use gradients with fewer than 8 stops if you want them to remain gradients in Flash. Flash retains transparency in gradients (called Alpha).

DESIGNING FOR EXPANDED WEB ACCESS

These days more people around the world are connecting to the Internet using cell phones and other small, handheld devices. Illustrator's vector features make it well-suited to designing websites that scale easily and adapt to different screen sizes. If your target market includes Flash Lite enabled devices, the Adobe Device Central application can help you work to those device specifications. Inside Illustrator, to create a new document that Device Central will size to fit for selected devices, click "Mobile and Devices Document" on the Welcome Screen (Help

menu) to enter Adobe Device Central, or choose File >
Device Central and click on the New Document tab. Each
device listed includes the display dimensions and other
features the model offers, such as navigation controls and
the version of Flash Lite. When connected to the Internet,
you can install selected device emulators from the Adobe
site to your own hard drive and create sets for a project,
making it easier to use automated testing with scripts
when you want to check your design on multiple mobile
devices. Select a device in the left column and click Create; Illustrator will open with an artboard set to that size.
If you want your project to fit several different devices,
some with portrait and some with landscape orientation,
you can add artboards in other dimensions (which are
listed in the New Document tab in Device Central when
you select them), or you can create a custom-sized artboard in Device Central with enough pixels to encompass
different screen sizes and orientations. Note that what
you'll see in Device Central is the entire active and visible artboard. To preview your active artboard in Device
Central, choose Save for Web and Devices and click the
Device Central button in the bottom-right corner.

Designing for a variety of devices and display sizes is
difficult, but with Device Central, you can preview artwork on a representative sampling of Flash Lite enabled
devices. To review how the device responds under a variety of conditions—including how your art appears under
different lighting conditions, and how it works if the
device orientation switches from portrait to horizontal—
you can change various emulator settings and operate a
mock-up of the selected phone's interface. You can also
record or write test scripts to automate testing when you
need your project to work on several different devices.
You can work on something else while the script runs and
saves the results to a log for later review.

The Internet and the way we access it is constantly
evolving. Good sources for the latest innovations include
videos on Adobe's website (http://tv.adobe.com/), and
Smashing Magazine (www.smashingmagazine.com/).

Illustrator for RIAs

Illustrator can play an increasing role in the development of
Rich Internet Applications (RIAs)
by creating interface elements
and exporting to Flex. Use the
"Flex Skins" script (which has two
parts: create and export) to create a file with the SWF format
that Flex Builder can import. Flex
Builder won't recognize a SWF
file created in the Save or Save
As dialogs, and the FXG format
doesn't work with the current Flex
Builder 3 version—though it will
with version 4. Or, save your file
as a PNG, which Flex Builder can
also import. Flash Catalyst is able
to open native AI files, automatically converting graphic elements
to functional interface elements
used by Flex in building RIAs.

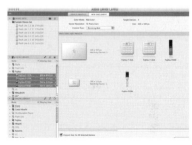

*In Device Central, creating a new document (top)
and previewing a file in the Emulator (bottom)*

Garden Slicing

Designing a Web Page in Illustrator

GORDON / CARTAGRAM, LLC

Overview: *Set up a document for web page design; use layers to structure artwork for pages; create guides for artwork positioning; save an image of a page; slice artwork to save an HTML file or sliced image files.*

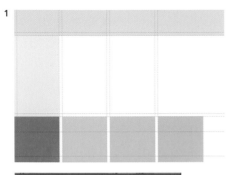

Gordon started the website by creating a 700 by 500 pixel file; he then created color-filled rectangles to represent areas of the home page and subsequent pages that would be filled with images and text, using layers to help organize

Limiting objects to Artboard...

To limit the objects that will be exported to those within the current Artboard, when using Save for Web & Device make sure the Clip to Artboard is enabled in the Image Size tab, or use the Object > Slice > Clip to Artboard—*Jean-Claude Tremblay*

If you're comfortable designing and drawing in Illustrator, why go elsewhere to design your web pages? Steven Gordon used Illustrator to design and preview web pages, create comps for client approval, and slice and optimize artwork for use in his web software.

1 Setting up your document. To start designing your website, create a new document using File > New. From the New Document Profile menu select Web, and then choose one of the default sizes from the Size menu or enter your own custom size. Because your artwork will be exported in a bitmap format like GIF or JPEG, consider turning on pixel preview (View > Pixel Preview). With pixel preview you can see the anti-aliasing of your artwork as if it were rasterized, and can therefore make any adjustments if necessary. Set up the various regions of your website using colored rectangles on separate layers (for layers help see the *Layers & Appearances* chapter).

2 Structuring pages with layers and adding artwork. Continue to let the Layers panel help you design and organize the content of the pages in your website. Gordon set up the full layer structure for his website, creating a master layer for each of the website's five pages; then within each layer were separate sublayers for the type, artwork, and images that would be on that particular page.

Next, to help you align and constrain artwork, create a grid (Preferences > Guides & Grid) or create a set of guides using View > Show Rulers (⌘-R/Ctrl-R), dragging guides into the Artboard from the rulers, and positioning them precisely using the Control or Transform panels (be sure View > Guides > Lock Guides is not enabled). Now you're ready to create the content of each web page.

3 **Saving an image and slices.** You can now save an image of each page to serve as a template for your web software. Simply hide all layers except the master layer, and its sublayers represent a web page. Then select File > Export and choose a file format compatible with your web software. Another option is to export the text, artwork, and images as image slices so that you can use them in your web software to build the finished pages. Use artwork selections, guides, or the Slice tool to divide a layer's artwork into slices. You can use non-contiguous objects for slicing: Illustrator will add empty slices to fill in any gaps between objects. To begin, select an object (if the slice will be a masked image, click on the clipping mask, not the image, with the Group Selection tool). Then choose Object > Slice > Create from Selection. Repeat these steps until you've created all of the slices you need. If you want to remove a slice, select and Delete; or in the Layers panel, drag its name (<Slice>) to the panel's trash icon.

When you've finished slicing your artwork, you can save the slices as text and images. Choose File > Save for Web and Devices; in the dialog, click on the Slice Select tool and click one of the slices. Pick the settings that you want to use for saving that selected slice. For the flower images, Gordon chose JPEG as the file format and enabled Optimized to make the file sizes smaller. After clicking on Save, he then entered a file name for the HTML file (which automatically became the root name of each of the sliced image files) and made sure that HTML and Images were selected in the Format pop-up menu. Gordon continued the website development by opening the HTML file in his web software.

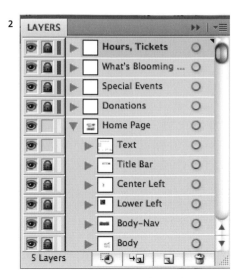

The layer structure for the webpage design, showing the various pages as master layers and the sublayers as elements within the Home Page

The numbered slices created after using the Object > Slice > Create from Selection command

216 colors, or millions?

The palette of 216 non-dithered, web-safe colors was designed for text and graphics displaying on 8-bit monitors. But how many people are restricted to 8-bit color anymore? Not many. Most computers are now equipped with 24- or 32-bit video boards, rendering web-safe colors unnecessary, so you can choose from millions of colors, not just 216.

Layering Frames

Turning Layered Artwork into Key Frames

Overview: *Draw artwork for print; design animation sequences using artwork; create layers and lay out art and text in positions for animation key frames; export layers as Shockwave Flash frames.*

Artwork originally created for The Red Grape's printed restaurant menu

Planning an animation sequence by positioning objects and text at the beginning and end of the sequence

After designing the brand identity, menu artwork, and a wall mural in Illustrator for The Red Grape, a Sonoma, California, restaurant, Hugh Whyte of Lehner & Whyte faced one more task. He needed to turn his artwork into Flash animations for the restaurant's website (www.theredgrape.com). The key to recycling the artwork was to develop a productive workflow between Illustrator and Adobe Flash that would allow Whyte and Mark Murphy of DigitalKick to work within the software each designer knew best.

1 Drawing artwork and planning objects and type for key frames. While his drawings of people and food were originally designed for the printed menus, Whyte returned to the artwork and prepared it for the web as a Flash animation.

Starting in Illustrator you can use artwork that you've already created. It will help if you think ahead in terms of how your artwork will move in the animation sequences. Identify the starting and ending locations of each object in an animation sequence. Also note where objects will change direction as they move during the sequence.

2 Arranging artwork on layers. To facilitate their collaboration, Whyte and Murphy devised a workflow in which Whyte created in Illustrator what Murphy would use as keyframes in Flash. You can do the same, and even produce the final animation yourself in Flash, using Illustrator to build the foundation of your animation.

Begin with File > New and select Web as your New Document Profile. Copy and paste a vector image or vector logo into your new file and then turn this into a symbol. To do this, select all your paths and click on the New Symbol icon at the bottom of the Symbols panel (F8), then choose Movie Clip in Symbol Options. You'll now have a new symbol in the Symbols panel and the paths on your Artboard will have been converted to an instance of it. Flash will be able to convert Illustrator's layers to keyframes for animation. If you're using symbols that have been rotated, scaled, or have transparency changes from one layer to the next, Flash can automatically create all of the frames in between the keyframes.

If you're only animating one symbol at time, you can arrange your content in a single Illustrator layer and then release your symbols to layers before importing to Flash. Keep the number of keyframes that you create in Illustrator to a minimum, as Flash's Motion Tween ability creates evenly distributed, in-between frames that are easier to control and are more easily synchronized to music.

To create an animation in which a symbol enters from beyond the "stage" (of the viewable screen), passes through in the center of stage, and then moves off stage, start by positioning the first instance of your symbol outside of your Artboard frame. Now Option-drag/Alt-drag the first instance of the symbol onto the Artboard, which will later become the second keyframe. Rotate, scale, or change the transparency of the symbol, then repeat this process for however many changes are required until the symbol leaves the Artboard again. To convert your artwork to keyframes that Flash will recognize, create a new blank layer for each symbol on the Artboard, then select each symbol individually and drag the selection highlight indicator in the layers panel up to the next layer. Repeat this until all of the symbols are on their own layers. Save as a native AI file, then import directly to the Stage of Adobe Flash choosing Convert Layers to Keyframes.

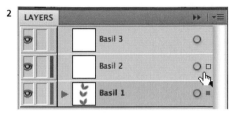

2

Selecting symbols on the Artboard, then dragging the selection highlight indicator to move your symbols to different layers

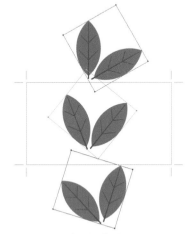

Symbol instances for the final animation sequence arranged on three layers which will become frames when brought into Flash

The Illustrator symbols viewed on a Flash stage after a Shape Tween has been applied with Onion Skin preview on the Timeline

Symbols to Flash

Turning Objects into Flash-ready Symbols

Overview: *Draw characters using discrete objects for each part which the animation will be constructed from; save objects as Symbols; import the saved AI file to a Flash library.*

1

The assembled snowbunny and carrot that would be animated in Flash

The working parts on the artboard that are later assembled in Flash as an animation

When designing a Flash animation, Kevan Atteberry uses Illustrator's advanced vector capabilities for preparing a "morgue" of parts, and converts those parts to symbols for easy import into Flash. There Atteberry assembles his scene and his characters, creating the final animation for SWF output. He created an animation to send to friends as his Christmas greeting e-card using a snowbunny who finds a Christmas carrot.

1 Creating characters and splitting artwork into parts for animating. In order for his snowbunny and candy carrot to have "moving" parts, Atteberry drew each part that might be animated with custom artbrushes. By starting off with parts even before planning the animation, he ensured that he would have the maximum "play" to all their features when it came time to create with motion. The snowbunny and carrot were designed with unarticulated separate parts. He planned to use Flash's transforming tools to generate motion "tweens." However, had he needed a leg to bend in the middle, for instance, he could have drawn a path stroked with his artbrush in a start and ending position, and used an object blend in steps to generate in-between positions. (See the *Blends, Gradients & Mesh* chapter for creating object blends.)

2 Converting the separate parts to Symbols. Having placed his objects on named layers, the next step to an animation was for Atteberry to select each part that he planned to animate in Flash, or parts of the scene he simply felt more comfortable drawing in Illustrator, and turn it into a Flash-compatible symbol. Since the panels are now "spring-loaded," he was able to simply hover over the icon with the object he was dragging until the panel popped open to receive it, which automatically opened the Symbols Options dialog. There he could give each symbol a descriptive name and designate it as either a Movie Clip or a Graphic. (He could also have used the keyboard shortcut F8, or, if he'd wanted to keep that panel open during this process, he could click on the New Symbol icon in the Symbols panel (Option-click/Alt-click to skip the dialog.). He kept the Movie Clip designation because Atteberry planned to animate most, if not all, of the symbols he imported. If he only wanted a symbol that would remain static in the scene, he could have chosen Graphic instead, but it wasn't really necessary to change the default for one or two symbols, since Flash lets you change the designation for a symbol at any time. Enable Guides for 9-slice scaling is used when Movie Clip is chosen and you want to create an interface element, such as a button, later on. Atteberry left that disabled. And finally, he could choose to save his symbols with a Flash registration point. This is the "transform" point that anchors an object being rotated or scaled, for instance, in the animation. This registration point, too, can be modified in Flash later on.

3 Importing Illustrator symbols to a Flash library. Once Atteberry had saved the Illustrator file, he opened Flash, began a new document, and chose File > Import > Import to Library. He browsed to his Illustrator file, and when the Import (file) to Library dialog opened, he checked that all the layers for the objects were enabled, he enabled Import unused symbols (just in case an object was left off the artboard), and accepted Flash's suggestion for handling an object that was not compatible with Flash. From this point on Atteberry was set to construct his scene and animate his characters using his Illustrator symbols.

2

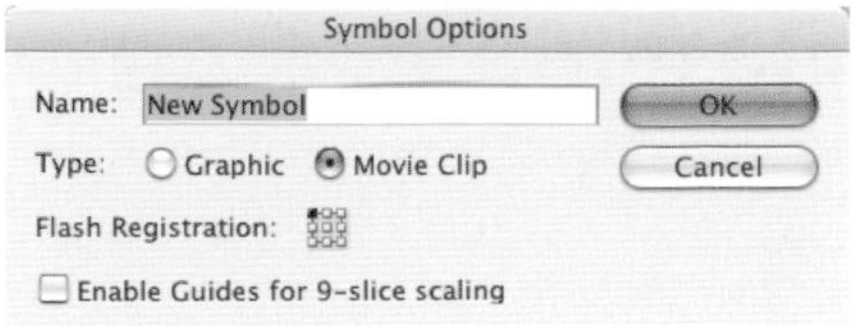

Checking out all the options for exporting symbols that are ready to go inside Flash

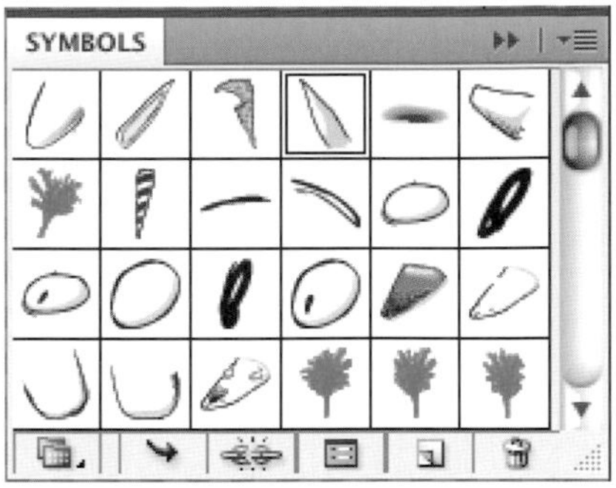

Everything that needs to be animated in Flash becomes a symbol

3

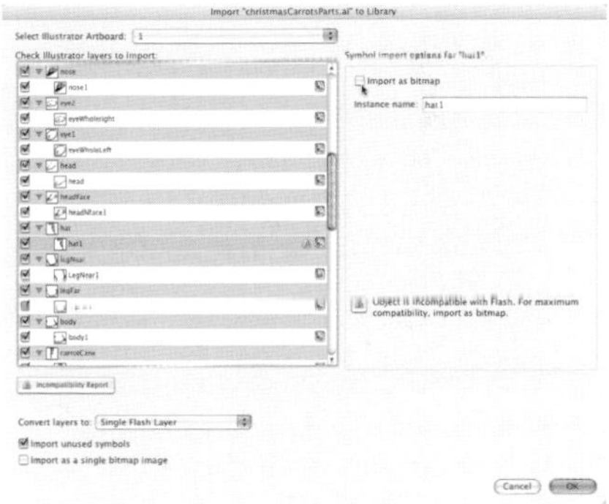

The Import to Library dialog in Flash

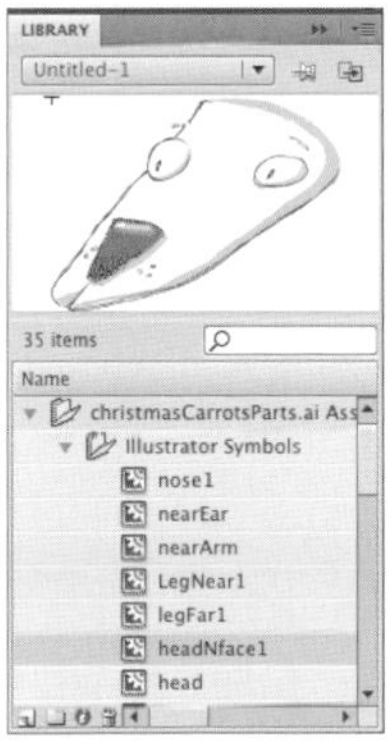

The Flash Library containing all the file's assets; here, previewing a symbol

Flash Animation

Creating Flash Character Animations

DASHWOOD

Illustrator with Flash

Overview: *Prepare your workspace; draw animated cels; optimize file size; import in Flash; animate in Flash.*

Andrew Dashwood created this eight cel animated figure as a background element to a larger interactive page. He used techniques requiring minimal programming in Flash so that the animation was web-ready.

1

The final screen from Dashwood's website

1 Setting the stage. The Illustrator artboard is the Flash stage, so it's worth spending time planning the animation carefully before you draw anything. As none of the default web presets compensate for the space taken up by a web browser user interface, Dashwood created a custom web document size by choosing File > New, selecting Web from the New Document Profile pop-up menu, and then setting the width to 1255 pixels and height to 600 pixels.

2

Select the inside of the screen with the Live Paint Selection tool and delete to reveal the artboard beneath.

2 Building your basic animation objects. To create the framing for his animation, Dashwood began by drawing two rectangular objects on the artboard in the shape of a TV screen. He then selected both of the closed paths, and used the Live Paint Bucket to fill the outer frame shape with a color. Next he highlighted the fill of the inner rectangle with the Live Paint Selection tool and then deleted it so that the artboard could be seen through the screen. Once your frame is created, open the Layers panel and double click the title of the layer you have been working on. When you are in the Layer Options dialog, change the name from the default title of "Layer 1" to "Foreground." Now create a new layer in the Layers panel, by

⌘-Option-clicking/Ctrl-Alt-clicking the New Layer icon, which will bring up the Layer Options dialog. Name this "Cel 1," click OK, and your layer will automatically be placed below the previous layer. Using any of the basic tools, draw the first cel of your animation so that it fills the screen of the television. As the anchor points in the paths on this layer will be moved in each of the subsequent cels, try to keep your paths simple, with a minimum number of anchor points.

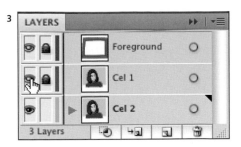

⌘-Click/Ctrl-Click the Eye icon to toggle a single layer between Outline and Preview viewing modes

3 Developing your animation. You can begin the process of animating by creating the second version of your character. Select "Cel 1" in the Layers panel and then drag and drop it onto the New Layer icon to duplicate it. Double-click the layer that you have just created ("Cel 1 copy") and rename it to "Cel 2". Then drag that layer below "Cel 1" in the Layers panel and lock the layer by clicking the Lock toggle icon next to its name. To use "Cel 1" as a guide for animating "Cel 2," ⌘-click/Ctrl-click the Eye icon next to the "Cel 1" name so that only this layer appears in Outline mode while everything else remains in Preview mode. Use the Direct Selection or Reshape tool to move the paths and anchor points of "Cel 2" to create the illusion of movement between the cels. Repeat these steps for the subsequent frames in your animation.

Move the anchor points and Bézier handles on the second layer to create movement

4 Preparing your file for importing to Flash. To reduce the file size and download time of the final animation, you can use the Symbols panel to create Flash Movie Clips of each animation cel. Instances of symbols can be used repeatedly in Flash without significantly increasing file size. Create Movie Clips of each layer in your animation by selecting all the paths on the "Cel 1" layer, then click the New Symbol icon in the Symbols panel or use the F8 key, and name it "Cel 1." Next, enable the Movie Clip checkbox and repeat this for all of the subsequent cels. When you have finished creating your animation, save the document as a native .AI file so it can be imported directly into the Adobe Flash library.

When creating symbols, you can choose between a Flash Graphic or Movie Clip

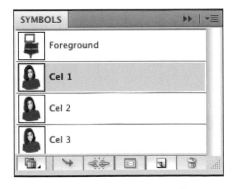

The Symbols panel containing Movie Clips

Animating Pieces

Preparing Files for Creating Animations

Illustrator with After Effects

Overview: *Make basic elements; cut elements using the Knife tool; order the <Path> elements and separate them into layers; export the file to create the actual animation.*

After drawing the huge letter forms using the Pen tool, Lush created "records" and ™ with the Text tool, then converted the text to outlines so he could modify the forms with the Direct Selection tool (final objects shown above in Outline and below in Preview modes)

The art shown after Lush cut the objects, in Outline mode above, and Preview mode below (the preview pieces have been moved so that you can see the cuts)

Terry Lush created the Illustrator portion of this animation for an ongoing "latest record release banner" on the hugerecords.com website.

1 Creating the basic elements. Use any tools to create your basic elements. For his animation, Lush drew the "huge" outlines with the Pen tool, based on the typeface Bauhaus. He then created the "records" and ™ text with the Type tool, and converted the text to outlines (Type > Create Outlines, or ⌘-Shift-O/Ctrl-Shift-O) so he could slightly modify the letterform paths with the Direct Selection tool. Lush saved his files in stages as he worked.

2 Cutting lines. To visualize where to cut elements, draw lines to use as guides (⌘-5/Ctrl-5 turns objects into guides). Lush used the Knife tool (under the Eraser tool) to cut the letters into pieces. To make straight cuts, he held Option/Alt while click-dragging with the Knife tool (adding Shift for straight lines). Objects are shown at left first in Outline then Preview mode (the Preview mode pieces have been moved apart so you can see the cuts).

3 Ordering the animation and distributing elements into layers. To figure out the order in which the pieces should appear in the animation, Lush expanded the layer containing the separate (cut) <Path> elements. First, while hiding all the paths, he experimented with showing paths one at a time until he determined the order in which he wanted the paths to appear. He then reordered the <Path> elements to match that viewing sequence.

Once you've rearranged the paths in the correct order within a layer, you'll need to distribute each <Path> onto its own layer. To do this, click the name of the enclosing layer and choose Release to Layers (Build) from the Layers panel pop-up menu. Now select these sublayers (click the top one and Shift-click the bottom one) and drag them above the enclosing layer so they are no longer sublayers.

4 Making the animation and creating variations. Lush imported the layered Illustrator file into After Effects (download a trial version of the latest version of After Effects from www.adobe.com). In After Effects, he selected all layers and trimmed the length of the layers to 7 frames. Choosing Animation > Keyframe Assistant > Sequence Layers, he set the parameters for the sequence so that each layer would be held for seven frames and then Cross Dissolve for two frames to the next layer. Keyframe Assistant automatically sequenced the layers (in order) and created the cross dissolves by generating keyframes with the correct opacity for each transition. With the file saved, Lush exported the After Effects movie in QuickTime format. Bringing this animation into his 3D program, Cinema 4D, he mapped the animation to the front surface of a 3D-rendered Times Square–like billboard. To create variations (such as the 30° rotation at right), Lush worked once more in Illustrator with a copy of the file. He selected all elements (without grouping them), double-clicked the Rotate tool, entered a 30° angle, and clicked OK. He then saved this version and imported it into After Effects, where he created a variation of the animation using the same procedures described above.

3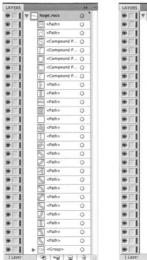

After cutting the objects, then after rearranging the pieces in the order of the desired animation

With the containing layer selected, choosing Release to Layers (Build), then moving the sublayers out of the containing layer

4

Selecting all of the objects in Illustrator to rotate the entire cut group of objects 30° for a variant of the animation

VAN DOOREN

Corné van Dooren

For one of his local clients, Dutch multimedia designer Corné van Dooren drew the basic elements of this Christmas card in Illustrator and then imported the frames into Flash where he added interactivity. Van Dooren began by taking a still photograph of a box with ribbon tied in a bow on top of it. He hand-traced his photograph with the Pen tool, creating separate elements for each of the sides of the box and bow. He moved the paths incrementally using a combination of the Free Transform, Direct Selection, and Convert Anchor Point tools to create the illusion of the bow untying itself and the box opening. After he drew each frame, van Dooren saved the file with a new version number. He was then able to preview the animation without needing to launch Flash by cycling through open documents using ⌘-~ (tilde)/Ctrl-Tab. (View multiple documents in a grid by choosing Window > Arrange > Tile.) To speed up production time of the artwork, van Dooren imported the sequence of images into Flash and colored the frames there, using Shape Tweens between the frames for the shading on the box, which he would otherwise have had to create manually in Illustrator.

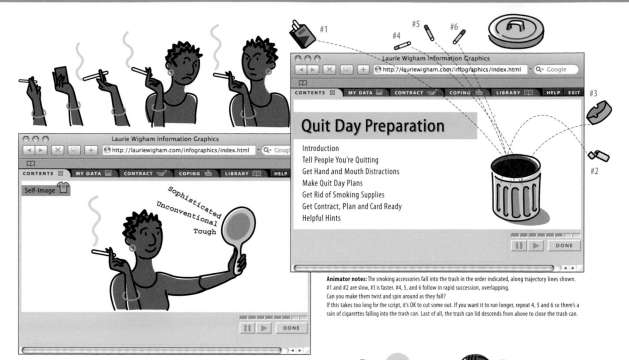

Animator notes: The smoking accessories fall into the trash in the order indicated, along trajectory lines shown.
#1 and #2 are slow, #3 is faster. #4, 5, and 6 follow in rapid succession, overlapping.
Can you make them twist and spin around as they fall?
If this takes too long for the script, it's OK to cut some out. If you want it to run longer, repeat 4, 5 and 6 so there's a
rain of cigarettes falling into the trash can. Last of all, the trash can lid descends from above to close the trash can.

Laurie Wigham

Using Illustrator, Laurie Wigham created the
art for the Flash animation, "The Last Draw,"
a web-based application designed to help
people stop smoking, (produced by Health Promotion Services, Inc., funded by the National
Heart, Lung and Blood Institute). To make the
lines simple and expressive, Wigham drew the
characters and other objects with the Pen tool.
To create a relaxed and casual look, she drew
open-ended unfilled paths, using a thick black
stroke with a rounded end cap and corners
(Window > Stroke). Beneath the outlines she
created unstroked solid-colored objects, deliberately misaligned with the strokes to produce
a loose, cut-paper look. Wigham created a collection of drawings that would provide a library
of symbols for the animator to later assemble
in Flash. She drew each character with different
positions and facial expressions, and included

a collection of separate body parts and props
that could move independently. She assembled
all the drawings needed for each tutorial unit
in a single file, positioned on a "stage," framed
by the navigation and play controls of the
website and browser. Each master layer in the
file contained all the elements for a key frame
within the animation, as well as motion paths
and detailed instructions for the animator.

15

Illustrator & Other Programs

This chapter showcases some of the ways you can use Illustrator together with other programs. Although the range of work you can create using Illustrator is virtually limitless, combining other programs with Illustrator increases your creative opportunities, and in many instances can save you significant time in creating your final work.

Following is a discussion about how you can place artwork in Illustrator, and then we'll provide a general look at how Illustrator works with other programs. Next we'll examine how Illustrator works with specific programs, including Photoshop, InDesign, Acrobat, and 3D programs. (For details about working with web and animation programs, see the *Web & Animation* chapter.)

PLACING ARTWORK IN ILLUSTRATOR

Illustrator can place more than two dozen different file formats. The major choice you'll need to make is whether to link or embed the placed file. When you link a file, you don't actually include the artwork in the Illustrator file; instead a copy of the artwork acts as a placeholder, while the actual image remains separate from the Illustrator file. This can help reduce file size, but keep in mind that linking is supported only for certain formats (see Tip at right). On the other hand, when you embed artwork, you're actually including it in the file. The Links panel keeps track of all the raster images used in your document, regardless of whether they were created within Illustrator, opened, or introduced via the Place command.

In general, you should embed artwork only when:
- The image is small in file size and you won't want to edit the original later so that the new edit updates the file.
- You want more than just a placeholder with a preview (e.g., you want editable objects and transparency).
- Your printer/service bureau requires embedded links.

Where are the *other* programs?

See the *Web & Animation* chapter for information about working with animation and Web programs, as well as detailed information about the Save for Web & Devices export options.

When EPS is *not* recommended

If the application you're working in can place or open native AI, native PSD, or PDF 1.4 or later formats, it's better to use those than EPS, which cannot preserve layers, transparency, and other features.

Resolution of placed images

Ensure optimal image reproduction by properly setting the pixels per inch (ppi) resolution of raster images before placing them into Illustrator. The ppi of images should be 1.5 to 2 times the size of the line screen at which the final image will print. For example, if your illustration will be printed in a 150 dpi (dots per inch) line screen, then the resolution of your raster images would typically be 300 ppi. Get print resolution specifications and recommendations from your printer *before* you begin your project!

And you should link (rather than embed) when:

- Your illustration uses several copies of the same image.
- The image is large in file size.
- You want to be able to edit the placed image using its original application.
- You can make changes to a linked file and resend only the linked file to your service bureau or client. As long as it has exactly the same name, it will auto-update without further editing of the Illustrator document itself.

ILLUSTRATOR & OTHER PROGRAMS

The first consideration when moving artwork between Illustrator and other programs is to decide which objects in your artwork you want to remain as vectors, if possible, and which you can allow to become rasterized. Next is whether you want to move the artwork between two open programs on your desktop (e.g., by using Copy and Paste or Drag and Drop), or if you will be moving your artwork via a file format. Finally, consider whether you want to move only a few objects or the whole file. Techniques for the above vary depending on the program, and are described in the corresponding program sections below.

Depending on the application, when you drag or paste objects between Illustrator and another open program, your objects will either drag or paste as vectors or as raster objects. In general, any program that supports PostScript drag and drop behavior will accept Illustrator objects via drag-and-drop, or Copy and Paste. In order for this to work, before drag-and-drop or copy and paste, make certain that the AICB (Adobe Illustrator Clipboard) is enabled in Preferences > File Handling & Clipboard.

When you copy and paste, or drag-and-drop Illustrator art into a raster-based program (other than Photoshop), it's likely that your art will be automatically rasterized at the same physical size, or pixels-per-inch ratio, that you have specified in that raster-based program. (See the following section "Illustrator & Adobe Photoshop," for details about Illustrator's special working relationship with Photoshop.)

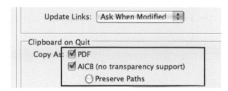

Illustrator File Handling and Clipboard Preferences dialog; to copy and paste vectors set the Clipboard preferences as shown here

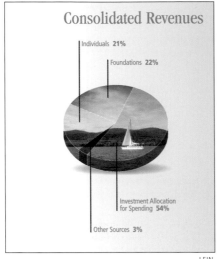

LEIN

For an annual report of the environmental organization Scenic Hudson, Adam Z Lein used Microsoft Excel and Excel's Chart Wizard to turn data into a pie chart, and then tilt in a perspective view. Lein used the Acrobat PDF maker to create a PDF of the graph. When he opened the PDF in Illustrator, the graph retained the vector objects as vectors. He completed the styling of the chart in Illustrator, incorporating images of New York's Hudson Valley using clipping masks and gradients (see the Advanced Techniques *and* Blends, Gradients & Mesh *chapters for more about masks and gradients).*

CS Formats
✓ **Illustrator CS4**
  Illustrator CS3
  Illustrator CS2
  Illustrator CS

Legacy Formats
  Illustrator 10
  Illustrator 9
  Illustrator 8
  Illustrator 3
  Japanese Illustrator 3

After choosing Adobe Illustrator Document, the Version pop-up choices give you access to Illustrator CS and later, and Legacy Formats

You can Save, or Export, your Illustrator artwork to many formats. From the File menu you can Save, Save for Web & Devices, Save for Microsoft Office, and Save As Template. From Save As you can choose vector formats and PDF. In order to save in legacy Illustrator AI formats when you need compatibility, choose Adobe Illustrator Document from the Save As > Format pop-up. From the Version pop-up menu, you can choose Illustrator Creative Suite Formats or earlier Legacy Formats.

From Export, you can access additional formats including raster and Flash. Know which file formats your other application supports (e.g., Flash prefers you save in .ai format!) and the type of information (vector, raster, layers, paths) you want to bring from Illustrator into the other program to determine which format to choose.

ILLUSTRATOR & ADOBE PHOTOSHOP

Moving artwork between Illustrator and Photoshop via a file format is fairly straightforward, since Photoshop can open or place Illustrator files, and Illustrator can open, place, and export Photoshop PSD files.

Illustrator to Photoshop

Using Illustrator files no longer means one-way rasterization, thanks to a marvelous feature called *Smart Objects*, which greatly improves the process of bringing Illustrator art into Photoshop. Smart Objects in Photoshop can be scaled, rotated, or warped without loss of data, and when you edit one instance of a Smart Object, Photoshop will automatically update all instances of that Smart Object.

You can create Photoshop Smart Objects from Illustrator data just by using the Clipboard (copying and pasting, dragging and dropping), or by inserting an Illustrator file using File > Place. You'll then have your choice of editing the placed Illustrator data either within Photoshop as rasters, or externally in Illustrator as vectors. When you double-click an Illustrator Smart Object in Photoshop's Layers panel, Photoshop will automatically launch Illustrator and open a working copy of your artwork. You can then edit the artwork in Illustrator and save the file, at which point Photoshop will re-rasterize it in place of the original Smart Object. With Adjustment layers and new Smart Filters, you can modify an Illustrator Smart Object in Photoshop with "live" raster effects, or rasterize the Smart Object for other raster techniques if you no longer need editable objects. For more info about Photoshop Smart Objects, see *Adobe Photoshop CS4 Help*.

To update the Smart Object from an Illustrator file on disk, choose Layer > Smart Objects > Replace Content to select the new file. This means you can use Smart Objects as placeholders for content you place in Photoshop later.

The rules governing how Illustrator layers get translated into Photoshop layers are complex. Following this introduction are lessons and galleries focusing on the basic issues of moving Illustrator objects into Photoshop.

Photoshop to Illustrator

Choose File > Place to import a Photoshop or TIFF file into an Illustrator document. If the file contains layers and you disable the Link checkbox in the Place dialog (to embed it), the Photoshop Import Options or TIFF Import Options dialog appears containing the Convert Layers to Objects option, which makes it possible to edit Photoshop text layers and import hidden layers. The import options also appear if you open a Photoshop file as a new Illustrator document by choosing File > Open.

Although Illustrator can't control the visibility of Photoshop layers directly, if you save an 8 Bits/Channel Photoshop file containing layer comps, the Layer Comp pop-up menu will be enabled at the top of the Import Options dialog. Choose a layer comp (or Last Document State) from the Layer Comp pop-up menu before you click OK. The Comments field displays comments that were entered in Photoshop for a selected layer comp. For more information about Photoshop layer comps, see the LayerComps.pdf excerpt from the Adobe Press book *Real World Adobe Photoshop CS4 for Photographers*, by Conrad Chavez and David Blatner.

Recovering missing linked files

If you don't have the original linked files for an .ai file, there is a way to get the images from the PDF side of the file—if the file was saved with Create PDF Compatible File enabled. Drag and drop the .ai file onto your Photoshop application icon, and choose Images in Photoshop's Import PDF dialog. You can then open any images from the PDF portion of the Illustrator file, save the images locally, and relink them in Illustrator.

Options
☑ Create PDF Compatible File

Placing Photoshop web slices

When you place a Photoshop or TIFF file that contains web slices, the Import Slices checkbox is available in Illustrator's Import Options dialog only if you disable the Link checkbox.

Why is it a "smart" object?

When you place an Illustrator file as a Smart Object in Photoshop, the original is embedded in the file and only an "instance" is transformed or duplicated, much like using a symbol in Illustrator. When you want to edit the Smart Object, and not the instance of it, the Smart Object "knows" to launch the originating program—in this case, Illustrator.

In this example of placing a layered TIFF file saved from Photoshop, conversion options are enabled and the When Updating Link options are disabled, either because the Link checkbox was disabled in the Place dialog, or because File > Open was chosen

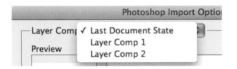

When a selected TIFF or Photoshop file contains layer comps, you can choose which layer comp controls layer visibility for the imported file

Illustrator layers in InDesign

In InDesign, you can control the layer visibility of an Illustrator file after you place the file. Select the Illustrator file in InDesign and choose Object > Object Layer Options. In the Object Layer Options dialog, click an Eye icon to hide or show any layer. At the bottom of the dialog you can choose whether to update layer visibility settings for a linked Illustrator file when the link is updated (similar to the "When Updating Link" pop-up menu in the "TIFF Import Options" dialog, shown above).

In the Place dialog, the Link checkbox controls how Illustrator will handle link updates to a Photoshop file that contains layer comps. If you enable Link and the Photoshop file contains layer comps, choosing Use Photoshop's Layer Visibility from the When Updating Link pop-up menu makes the placed file's layer visibility match the linked file's current layer visibility settings in Photoshop, every time you update the link. Choosing Keep Layer Visibility Overrides maintains the layer visibility settings of the file in Illustrator no matter how they change in Photoshop, which may be what you want if you place multiple instances of a file in Illustrator and set them to different layer visibility settings. After you place the document, there's no control over the visibility of imported Photoshop layers other than updating the link. Importing layers separately isn't possible if you link, while updating the link and updating layer visibility changes from Photoshop aren't possible if you embed.

ILLUSTRATOR & ADOBE INDESIGN

Before you copy and paste artwork from Illustrator into InDesign, decide whether you want transparent objects to remain transparent when placed over other elements in InDesign, or if you instead need to be able to edit the objects in InDesign. To preserve transparency, in Illustrator's File Handling and Clipboard preferences, you can leave both PDF and AICB enabled, and in InDesign's Clipboard Handling preferences enable "Prefer PDF When Pasting." This creates a non-editable file that preserves transparency from the PDF portion of the Illustrator file. Disabling the Prefer PDF preference in InDesign will paste an editable, but flattened, vector file that you can edit in InDesign but won't have transparency. If you want to paste paths without appearance, also select Preserve Paths in the Illustrator clipboard preferences.

To Place artwork, save your Illustrator file with the Create PDF Compatible File option enabled. InDesign, as well as other programs, recognizes and previews only the PDF portion of the file.

To control how an Illustrator file imports, after you choose File > Place, enable the Show Import Options checkbox. This displays the Place PDF dialog. If you're placing an Illustrator file containing multiple artboards, InDesign lets you select which artboard to import. Clicking the Layers tab in the Place PDF dialog lets you control visibility of the top-level Illustrator layers.

ILLUSTRATOR, PDF, & ADOBE ACROBAT

Acrobat's Portable Document Format (PDF) lets you transfer files between different operating systems and applications. And when newer versions of Illustrator open files created with older versions of Illustrator, they open the PDF portion of an .ai file. By default, the Adobe Illustrator Document format includes the "Create PDF Compatible File" option that allows Acrobat to open an .ai file. You'll see this option in the File > Save As dialog when you choose the Adobe Illustrator Document format.

For full control over PDF options, from Save As choose Adobe PDF (pdf) from the pop-up and click Save. In the Adobe PDF Options dialog you can enable the "Create Acrobat Layers From Top-Level Layers" option to save your layered Illustrator files as layered Acrobat 6, 7, or 8 files. Illustrator PDF files can also preserve Illustrator editability and native transparency support, as well as conform to one of the PDF/X standards.

Illustrator can open many kinds of PDF files, but you can only open and save one page at a time. Also, text in the PDF may be broken up into multiple text lines when opened in Illustrator.

ILLUSTRATOR & 3D PROGRAMS

In addition to Illustrator's 3D effects (see the *Live 3D Effects* chapter) you can also import Illustrator paths into 3D programs to use as outlines and extrusion paths. Once you import a path, you can transform it into a 3D object. Autodesk Maya, Strata's 3D StudioPro, SketchUp!, and LightWave 3D are just a few of the many 3D programs that you can use in combination with Illustrator.

Pasting text into InDesign

If you want to paste editable text from Illustrator into InDesign, choose Preferences > Clipboard Handling in InDesign and select Text Only. If you'd rather preserve the appearance of Illustrator text, such as transparency or a pattern fill, select All Information. This treats pasted text as an object so that you can apply effects and transform it, but you won't be able to edit the text.

InDesign preferences for pasting text

About PDF standards

The set of PDF standards known collectively as PDF/X have helped simplify file handoffs in prepress and advertising. PDF/X-1a and PDF/X-3 are based on PDF version 1.3 (Acrobat 4); the difference is that PDF/X-1a is used in legacy CMYK workflows, while PDF/X-3 supports color management. PDF/X-4 goes a step further by supporting live transparency as well. PDF/X-1a and PDF/X-3 require that transparency be flattened, for compatibility with older prepress systems. PDF version 1.7, which is based on Acrobat 8, is now an ISO standard.

Ready to Export

Exporting Options for Layers to Photoshop

Illustrator with Photoshop

Overview: *Organize objects on layers that Photoshop can understand; use Export to Photoshop (psd) or Copy/Paste as Smart Object for editing layers in Photoshop; add texture or run other filters as Smart Filters.*

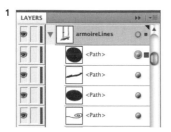

Brush objects are each listed in the Layers panel as a <Path> with a filled target icon --see the Layers & Appearances chapter for more

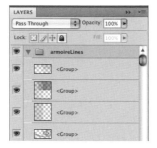

Upon Export to Photoshop, each object stroked with a brush in Illustrator becomes a layer within a Layer Group in Photoshop

With Knockout Group enabled in Illustrator's Transparency panel (see the Transparency chapter introduction for more about knockout groups), sublayers become one layer in Photoshop

ATTEBERRY

When Kevan Atteberry wants to add finishing touches to his illustrations in Photoshop, he has several options for preparing and exporting his artwork from Illustrator. Shown above is a detail from his "Frankie Stein" series, where Atteberry uses Illustrator's ability to write Photoshop layers when exporting to the PSD format, as well as Photoshop's ability to paste selected and copied objects directly as Smart Objects. Exporting layers as PSD layers is the quickest method for adding texture or other raster effects in Photoshop. To use Transform on the object (scale, rotate, etc.), Atteberry copies and pastes it from Illustrator as a Smart Object, which preserves the underlying vector for Photoshop to work with. (For the full illustration, see the "Frankie Stein" gallery following this.)

1 Organizing and rasterizing the layers in Illustrator for export as Photoshop PSD. When Illustrator writes layers for a Photoshop file, it attempts to maintain the layer structure, including all the sublayers. But some types of objects, such as those created with brushes, blends, symbols, or envelopes, generate an unmanageable number of extra sublayers. Two important steps in Illustrator can prevent this from becoming a nuisance in Photoshop. First, Atteberry collects all paths that make up a given object into a named layer. This might be a sublayer of a layer that contains more of a subject, such as the "MUM-layers" containing a "mumsDress" layer. This is just like organizing your hard drive in miniature, making it easy to quickly identify what objects the layers contain. Next, he targets the sublayers, opens the Transparency panel and enables Knockout Group (you may need to expand panel options). To extend our example, "mumsDress" now becomes a single, rasterized layer in Photoshop, but is still separate from "mumsHair," and both are contained in a Layer Group called "MUMlayers." Photoshop now can preserve Illustrator's file structure and layer names, without creating too many nested groups.

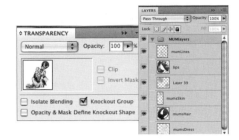

Well-named layers and enabling Knockout Group keeps layers manageable in Photoshop

2 **Using Smart Objects and Smart Filters.** Although any layer or Layer Group can be converted to a Smart Object inside Photoshop, Atteberry copies and pastes Smart Objects directly from Illustrator when he wants to Transform or Warp them. After importing and merging layers as described above, he goes back to Illustrator, selects and copies an object—such as Mum's hand—that he wants to fine-tune in the final version in Photoshop. With the object copied to the Clipboard, he returns to Photoshop and chooses Paste. A dialog pops up with options, and he chooses Smart Object. Once the Smart Object is in the right position both in the image and in the stack of layers, he hits Return/Enter to accept it. He then can delete the rasterized layer he had exported earlier, if it doesn't contain other paths. The new layer will always link to the vector file for transforming (so the art won't become degraded the way pixels would) and for editing in Illustrator.

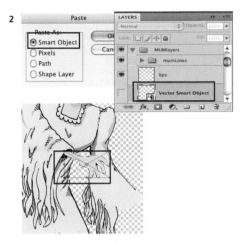

2

Pasting an object into Photoshop as a Smart Object in order to Transform the object without pixel degradation (blurring)

The dress before adding texture in Photoshop—and after, running Texturizer as a Smart Filter

If he doesn't need to transform an object, but wants to add texture inside Photoshop using a filter, instead of copying and pasting from Illustrator again, Atteberry converts the layer to a Smart Object from within Photoshop. Now he can run a Smart Filter on the Smart Object layer (in our example, mumsDress). This allows him to reopen the filter dialog at any time, change settings, delete or add filters, etc., all without altering the original object.

After choosing Filter > Convert for Smart Filters a Smart Object layer protects the original pixels and any filter becomes editable

ATTEBERRY

Kevan Atteberry
(Photoshop)

For his "Frankie Stein" series of illustrated children's books, Atteberry uses Illustrator to create the basic illustration, and then moves into Photoshop to add textures and special effects. He carefully constructs his layers in Illustrator to make sure that he can work freely and easily in Photoshop, taking advantage of Photoshop's unique way of creating original artwork. In this illustration (spread over two pages), he prepared his Illustrator layers to use filters, Layer Styles and Photoshop's soft, feathered brushes. He did this by ensuring the elements that would receive the same treatment in Photoshop were kept on different layers from other elements. See the "Ready to Export" lesson earlier in this chapter for more about layer organization.

ATTEBERRY

Kevan Atteberry
(Photoshop)

Once Atteberry has imported his descriptively-named Illustrator layers to become rasterized Photoshop layers, he depends upon Photoshop's ability to add texture with filters and images, blending it seamlessly into the objects he drew in Illustrator. He makes extensive use of Photoshop's natural soft, feathery brushes to add shadows and highlights to his characters and their environment. He even paints entirely new characters, such as the ghost, using soft brushes and building it up gradually with multiple layers set to varying opacities, giving it its ethereal, ghostly quality. Adjustment layers are added to tweak color. The final results of his multi-layered approach achieve his unique blend of the real and the imaginary.

Planning Ahead

Working Between Illustrator & Photoshop

Illustrator with Photoshop
Advanced Technique

Overview: *Plan ahead for export to Photoshop with layer organization; group or separate some objects on layers based on the Photoshop technique you will use; make a registration rectangle for precise placement.*

HUBIG

1

The Illustrator file before export to Photoshop

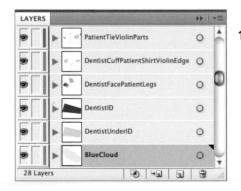

Keeping overlapping objects on separate layers, making it easier in Photoshop to add texture and effects to objects without making selections

When Dan Hubig creates an illustration like "Soothing Nervous Patients," above, he relies upon both Illustrator and Photoshop to get the job done efficiently and quickly. Consequently, he constructs his files in Illustrator with Photoshop's strengths and weaknesses in mind. Because the two programs have very different features, even when those features share the same name (such as brushes), Hubig organizes his objects so their Photoshop layers will allow him complete flexibility and ease in creating the finishing touches. And by setting his layers to flatten sublayers on export, he reduces the RAM requirements of his large files and shortens the time it takes Illustrator to create the Photoshop file.

1 Planning ahead. The main rule Hubig has when organizing his layers is that overlapping objects he will work on in Photoshop *do not* reside on the same layer. As long as they are on separate layers when exported to Photoshop, he'll be able to lock transparency (which acts like a mask limiting a tool to actual pixels), clip an Adjustment layer so it affects only that object, etc.—all without having to make tedious selections inside Photoshop. By constructing his layer organization this way, rather than grouping by subject (such as the Dentist on one main layer, with its parts as sublayers), he can rasterize all the sublayers, so Photoshop doesn't import them as nested Groups when he uses Knockout Group to export the blends he likes to use (see the lesson "Ready to Export" for a full description of this method). The trade-off, however, is that if Hubig doesn't pay careful attention to naming the layers, once they're in Photoshop, his layer organization may not always be as "intuitive" as it would be if grouped according to subject matter.

2 **Preparing artwork for finishing in Photoshop.** Aware of the Photoshop techniques he plans to use, Hubig is also able to save time by putting objects that will receive the same treatment in Photoshop on the same layer. If you look at the two floor shadows in the illustration, you can see they both have Gaussian Blurs and reduced Opacity. By creating them on a single Illustrator layer, Hubig is able to apply the blur and change the layer Opacity in Photoshop just once for both objects. On the other hand, by keeping the blue cloud on a separate layer, Hubig is able to make changes even though it overlaps other objects visually. He can adjust the cloud's Opacity, and by locking the layer's transparency he can loosely apply a brush with a broad "Scattering" (set in the Brushes panel), knowing his paint won't spill onto other objects.

3 **Bringing new objects into Photoshop with a registration rectangle.** Although Hubig typically eyeballs the placement of objects in Photoshop, you might have a need for precision when moving objects into Photoshop. Make sure your artboard and image sizes in Photoshop are the same. Then, to achieve precise registration, create an unstroked, unfilled rectangle on the top layer (to select easily) that is the same size as the artboard. Select both the object(s) and the registration rectangle, copy and paste them as pixels in Photoshop. This positions your new art precisely where it belongs with respect to earlier artwork, and on its own layer. Finally, drag the artwork layer into position among the other layers, if necessary.

2

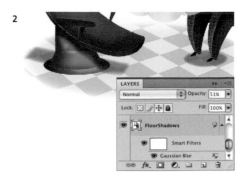

In Photoshop, creating a Smart Object to apply a Smart Filter on two Illustrator objects placed on one layer, and reducing Opacity for both at the same time

Locking just the transparency in a layer to limit the effect of a tool or command to just the pixels—essentially, "auto-masking" the object

3

Creating a registration rectangle with no stroke, no fill, and selecting both it and an object to paste as pixels in Photoshop for precise alignment with existing artwork

YIP

Filip Yip
(Photoshop)

Filip Yip began by drawing Illustrator objects and organizing them on many separate layers (so each object would remain on its own layer when he later exported them to Photoshop). He decided on the overall color scheme, colored the shapes, and added blends. Yip then exported his Illustrator objects into Photoshop in order to add transparency, feathering, and lighting effects. The artwork (shown above right) was exported as a Photoshop PSD file. In Photoshop, Yip was able to easily manipulate the Illustrator objects, since they were on separate layers. He enhanced the blends

with the Airbrush tool, adjusted the transparency, and applied the Add Noise filter. Blurring effects (such as Gaussian Blur) were used to highlight details of the image. To further soften the blends, Yip also applied the Fade Brush Tool (Edit > Fade Brush Tool > Fade > Dissolve) in the Dissolve mode.

Ron Chan
(Photoshop)

Ron Chan, illustrator and co-author of *How to Wow with Illustrator*, used Illustrator's drawing tools and Pathfinder commands (Effect > Pathfinder) to draw over a scanned template to create his initial composition. Illustrator is his primary drawing tool because it allows him to make color and compositional changes easily (middle detail). With the composition finalized (bottom detail), he chose File > Export and selected PSD. In the Photoshop Export Options dialog, he selected the Color Model CMYK, chose Write Layers, and specified a high resolution. In Photoshop he assembled his image in layers within his CMYK document. To give a more organic and less hard-edged feel to some of the objects (now rasterized as layers) Chan applied the Glass filter (Filter > Distort Glass). The Glass filter can only be applied to an RGB image, and Chan wanted to keep the layered file in CMYK; in order to selectively apply the effects to individual layers, he used a complex procedure that included dragging each layer he wanted filtered back and forth to an identically-sized RGB file, where he applied the filter. Then he dragged the filtered version back to the CMYK layered file (in registration).

Chapter 15 *Illustrator & Other Programs* **423**

SHOGLOW

Lisa Shoglow
(Photoshop)

When Lisa Shoglow created this CD cover for a spiritual singer and Jewish educator, she was mindful that the artwork should have an ethereal quality that evoked a strong spiritual sense, yet also reflected the singer's passion for education. Knowing that the words were of equal import as the feeling the image would express, Shoglow first created the words in Illustrator, to be sure the text maintained legibility after adding them to her Photoshop image. In Photoshop, Shoglow made adjustments to her original photograph with Hue and Saturation and also applied several filters in varying degrees (Filter > Distort). In Illustrator, she embellished the word T'Fillah with calligraphic flourishes drawn with the Brush tool using a pressure sensitive tablet. In the Brushes panel she clicked on a default 10-pt Round Calligraphy Brush and double-clicked to open the options dialog. Shoglow changed the diameter to 3 pt, then set the roundness and diameter to pressure and clicked OK. She selected the word and its calligraphic flourish, chose the Shear tool and stretched it to the desired angle. She placed (File > Place) the Illustrator text into Photoshop on separate layers above the image. She applied one or more filters to the words (such as Shear and Twirl) and she applied Gaussian Blur to the Hebrew text until they all mimicked the movement in the Photoshop image.

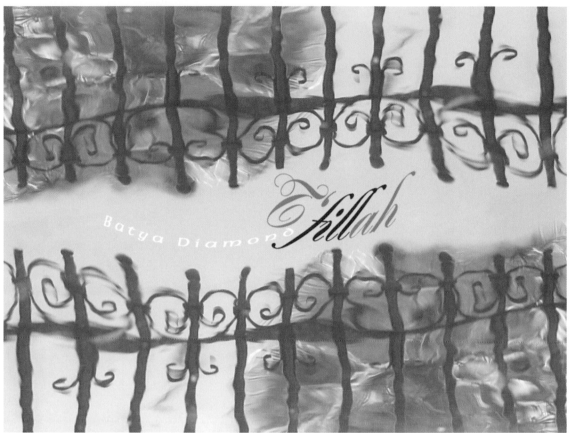

SHOGLOW

Lisa Shoglow
(Photoshop)

To make another version of the CD image shown on the opposite page, Lisa Shoglow applied many of the same techniques described in the previous page. In Photoshop, she duplicated the single gate image in her source photograph and airbrushed color in between to make the transition of the duplicated images seamless. She applied several filters (found in the Filter > Distort menu) to the image and created the reflective water-like appearance. In Photoshop Shoglow placed the Illustrator text into layers above the background and applied the same filters she used on the image on the opposite page (Shear and Twirl).

STEAD

Judy Stead
(Photoshop)

Judy Stead often begins her illustrations by making traditionally painted backgrounds that are manipulated in Photoshop. With one painted background, (shown above right) Stead can create several others varying in color by using the Image menu. Stead scanned the background into Photoshop and chose Image > Adjustments > Hue/Saturation. To enhance a specific color, she chose Image > Adjustments > Selective Color. Further adjustments were made on a duplicated layer where Stead applied Blending Modes such as Multiply and Hue. The background image was saved in TIFF format. To import the background into Illustrator,

Stead chose File > Place. She then drew with the Charcoal brush imported from the Artistic_ ChalkCharcoalPencil Brush Library. In the Transparency panel, Stead applied various Blending Modes to enhance specific areas. After drawing a shape, such as a leaf, she opened the Transparency panel and selected the Blending Mode, Overlay. The colored circles underneath the word "think" have the Blending Modes of Overlay, Hue and Multiply (top to bottom). The colored circles also have either a Gaussian Blur (Effect > Blur > Gaussian Blur) or a brush applied to the stroke.

POUNDS

**David Pounds
(Photoshop)**

David Pounds' highly detailed artwork began with photographing models, combining them into a single composition as needed, and paying careful attention to the lighting as he worked. He used Photoshop to bring out detail and then, with Convert Photoshop layers to objects enabled, he opened the image in Illustrator. Next Pounds began to draw each item on its own layer to keep all the detail organized. He found very complex subjects, such as the goggles, easier to handle by breaking them down into smaller sections, so he placed each one on a layer of its own. To achieve a high level of realism, he created blends for modeling smooth shadows and highlights. Blend modes added depth and sparkle, while he simulated metallics with gradients. For the propellers, he

duplicated and transformed a simple propeller blade numerous times, altering the Opacity for a motion blur. Finally, using Live Trace on a photograph of clouds added contrasting texture to the smoothness of the main image.

HULSEY

Kevin Hulsey
(Photoshop)

Kevin Hulsey uses the Pen tool to draw his complex technical illustrations in Illustrator. He creates all the perspective grids he requires on separate layers (see the "Establishing Perspective" lesson in the *Layers & Appearances* chapter). He then draws all the line art for the elements, again using Illustrator's layers to keep elements organized.Hulsey's illustrations tend to be so large (often 45 inches at 300 ppi), that in recent versions of Illustrator he has been unable to export his Illustrator layers to Photoshop without saving to the legacy Illustrator 9 format. He then exports from AI 9 as a grayscale PSD file with a resolution of 350 ppi and his layers preserved. Next he opens the layered file in Photoshop and converts it to a custom CMYK with Black Generation set to Maximum in order to force the lines into just the Black (K) channel. Hulsey sets each line art layer to Multiply as the blending mode, and creates new layers below the line art layers to hold his painting. He uses the Magic Wand to select the area of the object

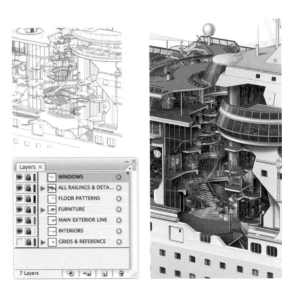

he intends to paint; then, with the selection still active, he uses a very soft, low-opacity brush to paint within the selection on the new layer. He builds up color gradually and smoothly in the same manner as he would with a traditional airbrush. For a detailed tutorial of Hulsey's digital airbrush technique using Photoshop, visit his website: http://www.khulsey.com/photoshop_tutorial_basic.html.

MONROY

Bert Monroy
(Photoshop)

Famous for his urban landscapes, author and master digital artist Bert Monroy relies upon Illustrator tools to deal with constructing the man-made, repeating elements that so often fill his urban environment. A case in point is the trash can at the Damon station. Monroy was able to quickly construct this complex-looking object by taking advantage of the Blend tool's ability to morph from one object to another. He drew a straight rectangle to represent the face-on view of the center slat. He then drew the curved slat of the trash can's edge and selected both objects. He double-clicked on the Blend tool, chose Specified Steps, and then typed in the number needed to complete half the trash can. To ensure the objects morphed correctly, Monroy used the Blend tool (rather than the Blend >Make command) to select an anchor point on one object, then clicked on the same relative anchor point on the other object. This told Illustrator exactly what the relationship was between the objects so it knew how to create the in-between objects. Next he expanded the blend (Object > Expand, or Object > Blend > Expand) in order to create

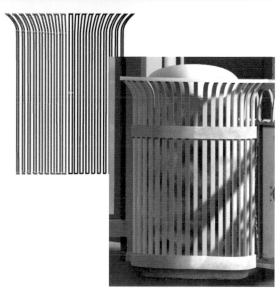

individual objects that he could manipulate separately. He selected all of the slats except the center slat and choose the Reflect tool. Monroy set the anchor point in the middle of the center slat, chose Vertical as the axis, and Copy to create the other half of the trash can. He finished drawing the rest of the trash can in Illustrator, then exported it to Photoshop where he added the colors, textures, shadows, and highlights that would complete his amazingly realistic painting of the trash can. (Go to www.bertmonroy.com to zoom in on this image and see many other amazing images.)

MCGARRY

Aaron McGarry
(Photoshop)

To create this urban portrait, Aaron McGarry used the combined strengths of Illustrator and Photoshop. He began in Illustrator by placing original photos as templates, and hand-tracing over them into another layer using the Pen, Rectangle, Ellipse, and Type tools (see the *Layers & Appearances* chapter for more on templates and the *Drawing & Coloring* chapter for more about drawing tools). To simulate metal on the various components, he filled the objects with gradients from the Metals library (Window > Swatch Libraries > Gradients > Metals). Since each of the main objects represented a different depth, he next selected each main grouping of objects and applied separate drop shadows (Effect > Stylize > Drop Shadow). With the objects complete and assembled on various layers, he hid

the template layer (see inset). Placing a photograph of a wall as a background layer (below the objects), McGarry then exported the file to Photoshop, preserving the layers. In Photoshop he created the illusion of a glass cover on the meter by placing a photo of the sky. Then, using the Warp command (Edit > Transform > Warp), he warped the photo to the roundness of the meter face. He next added a layer mask to the photo layer and used a gradient (Black, White) to fade the lower part of the photo, blending it in with the background image and adjusting the opacity to simulate the reflective, transparent quality of curved glass. For the finishing touches he used a variety of Photoshop's Brush tools, as well as the Eraser and Smudge tool (all with varying opacity), to paint the rust, stains, and grime, thereby creating a grittier look.

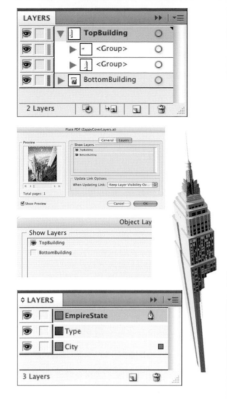

ZAPPY, HEFT

Michel Zappy (illustration), Mimi Heft (design)

When Mimi Heft from Peachpit Press saw Michel Zappy's New York illustration, she thought it would be perfect for the cover of the *Adobe Illustrator CS4 WOW! Book*—if only the Empire State Building could enhance the illusion of depth by being placed in front of the first **W**. In order to keep most of the image beneath the type, Zappy duplicated a portion of the Empire State Building to a second layer. He then fit his artboard precisely to the size needed for the book cover, saved it as an AI file with PDF compatibility enabled, and handed it over to Heft. She placed the artwork in InDesign's Place PDF dialog (enable Show Import Options in the Place dialog), setting the Crop option to Media to ensure the crop would be

the exact size of the artboard (important in the next steps for registration of the artwork layers). Still in the Place PDF dialog, she made sure that both layers would be placed and visible, and clicked OK. Back in InDesign, she duplicated the image by dragging its icon on top of the Create New Layer icon in the Layers panel. She now had two layers and two complete images in perfect registration. Selecting the second layer image, she chose Object > Object Layer Options. Here she turned off the background layer, leaving only the Empire State Building visible on that layer. Finally, Heft added a text layer between the other two and inserted the text for the cover.

BERGMAN

Eliot Bergman
(Autodesk Maya & Photoshop)

When the Japanese camping outfitter, A & F Country, asked Eliot Bergman to design a line of T-shirts with a camping theme, he turned to Illustrator, Maya and Photoshop to produce the graphic realism he desired. Using Illustrator for its precision and ease in drawing, Bergman drew the paths that would shape his 3D models in Maya. For "Fresh," he drew a profile for the coffee pot he would later revolve in Maya, and he drew paths for the handle and spout. Bergman imported these paths into Maya using the "Create Adobe Illustrator object" command, where he assembled the coffeepot and generated the materials that gave it its speckled, metallic appearance. He created the type in Illustrator using Type Warp, and then assembled all the elements in Photoshop for the final touches, including the soft shadows.

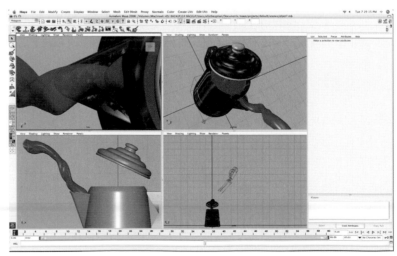

Eliot Bergman
(Autodesk Maya & Photoshop)

Continuing with his assignment for camping goods outfitter A & F Country, Eliot Bergman chose another icon of camping: the kerosene lantern. Again he began the process in Illustrator by drawing a profile for the lantern he would revolve using the 3D program, Maya. He also drew the lantern's handle, but the rest of the fittings he added in Maya with basic primitives. After rendering the lantern and creating the same appearance for the type in Illustrator he had used with "Fresh," he brought the various elements into Photoshop for the final assembly. Bergman created soft glows with brushes and blending modes, and created a soft shadow from a duplicate of the lantern filled with black, set to Multiply and a very low opacity. This ensured that the shadow, as with "Fresh," would show against light fabrics, while the glow would shine brightly against dark.

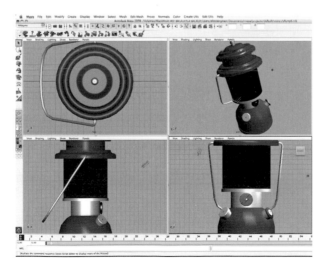

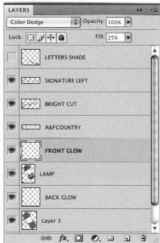

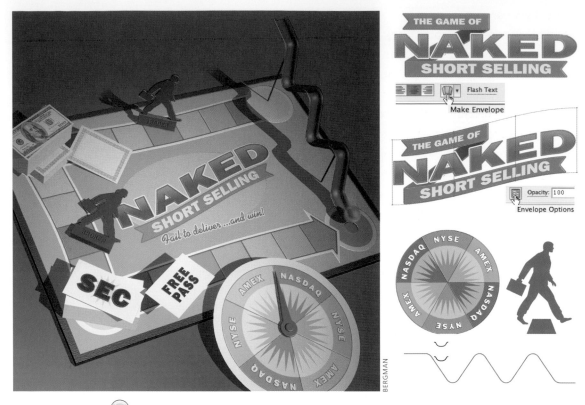

BERGMAN

Eliot Bergman
(Photoshop and Maya)

Bergman began the creation of this convincingly three-dimensional gameboard, done for *Bloomberg Markets* magazine, by drawing all of the basic elements—the cards, the game pieces, the path for the slide and most of the bump and image maps in Illustrator. Bergman appreciates the ease and accuracy with which he can control color and create typography in Illustrator. In this example, he first laid out the logo using Franklin Gothic Heavy. He then clicked the Add New Fill button from the bottom of the Appearance panel and added a gradient fill to the characters making up the word "Naked." He also clicked the Add New Stroke button to add white and blue strokes behind

the characters. Bergman then clicked on the Make Envelope button on the Control panel and chose Rise for Style. He set it to a 25% horizontal bend (use Envelope Options on the Control panel if you want to change it later). He then imported the vector objects into Autodesk Maya, a 3D modeling program within which the objects can be extruded, viewed from any angle, and then have precise custom lighting effects applied to them. After the 3D image is rendered, Bergman does additional retouching of the file in Photoshop as needed, such as adding motion blur to the pinball and additional texture to the blue edges of the gameboard. The result is a realistic gameboard that a reader might be tempted to reach out and touch.

Marcel Morin
(ArcScene and Photoshop)

Marcel Morin likes to use ArcScene, an ArcGIS plug-in for viewing and exporting 3D GIS data as images. He also uses Photoshop to composite those images. But he uses Illustrator's superb vector object handling to construct projects that rely on resolution-independent elements for high-quality output. For this two-sided waterproof map, he generated a large base image of the mountain range in ArcScene, over which he "draped" an image of the glaciers. He placed the image in Illustrator. There he traced the glaciers in order to create a clipping mask for later use in Photoshop. Back in ArcScene, he generated a grayscale version for the glaciers and exported an image of just the 3D wireframe model. In Photoshop, Morin layered the images, duplicating the base image in order to select areas representing the far distance, middle ground and foreground. He deleted portions of the images that he wouldn't need. He created the illusion of depth by applying Gaussian Blur to the far distant mountains, and again a lesser amount of Gaussian Blur to the middle ground, after which he sharpened the foreground. Morin added the grayscale layer with the clipping mask to reveal the glaciers on the mountains, and added the wireframe model in Multiply mode, masking it to show only in the foreground. Finally, Morin cropped the assembled image and placed it in an Illustrator document that would hold the entire map. There he added vector design elements used with the Summit Series maps and logos sized to suit this particular project. He set the text and got the complete map ready for the printer.

JOLY & RIDDLE

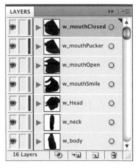

Dave Joly & Mic Riddle
(Flash & Cinema 4D)

When Dave Joly and Mic Riddle collaborated on the "Trick or Treat" movie, they produced a unique mix of 2D and 3D artwork, using everything from Flash to Maxon's Cinema 4D, to After Effects, to Apple's Final Cut Pro, and it all started with Illustrator. To begin the 2D animation, they drew all the parts in an Illustrator file that they would use for a segment. Every part was placed on its own layer. So, for example, the man and woman seen here were created with separate heads, bodies, and expressions—each change in position on its own layer. They only needed B&W in Illustrator; the color would come from other programs. Once all the parts were finished, they could choose either to create and name symbols in Illustrator for later importing into a Flash library, or they could save the file and import it to the Flash stage (which is what they did for

this scene). They chose to have Flash convert all the layers as Flash layers, which preserved Illustrator's layer names and organization. After animating the husband and wife talking, they were ready to export their 2D Illustrator art as a QuickTime file with an alpha channel (to create transparency around the animated characters), and from there take it into Cinema 4D to become a "texture" for a 3D type of "material" that controls how the 3D models appear. Eventually, with the aid of other programs, such as After Effects and Final Cut Pro, this 2D segment became incorporated into the rest of the movie.

436   **Chapter 15** *Illustrator & Other Programs*

RIDDLE & JOLY

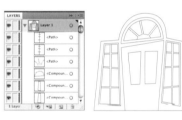

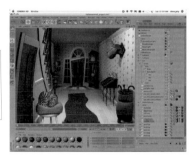

Mic Riddle & Dave Joly
(Cinema 4D & After Effects)

Still working on their "Trick or Treat" movie, Mic Riddle and Dave Joly created the 3D scenes for the animation. Again, they often began inside Illustrator. Most 3D programs are able to import Illustrator paths and use them as the start for creating an extruded or lathed object, such as the doorway and clock shown here, both of which have dimension. It's these surfaces that, once lit in Cinema 4D or another 3D application, cast and receive shadows that convince us the objects are no longer flat illustrations. And just as they created a layer for each 2D part they intended to animate in Flash, they drew each "object" on its own layer that would be extruded in Cinema 4D, making extensive use of compound paths to represent both a solid dimensional surface and a hole for windows, or the cavity for a clock's pendulum. They added more animation and camera movements, color, texture, and pattern, then rendered their movie "scenes" to be imported into After Effects. They used After Effects both for features that were easier to produce there, and to save some time tweaking a scene by not jumping back and forth between programs. Finally, files were collected in Final Cut Pro, where they added sound and performed final edits, and saved as a .mov file (find a low-res version of the animation on the *Wow! CD*).

Using the Kuler Website

To access the Kuler website, visit *http://kuler.adobe.com* (**Figure 1**). Adobe actually refers to Kuler as a *rich Internet application* (RIA), and you need to have Flash Player 9 or newer to use it (the site will redirect you if you need to download a newer version of Flash Player). Although you can use parts of Kuler without logging in, you'll get the full functionality by entering your Adobe ID. If you don't already have one, an Adobe ID is free and allows you to post to the Adobe user-to-user forums, access free content from the Adobe Design Center, and purchase items through the online Adobe Store. If you've recently registered any Adobe software, you probably already have an Adobe ID. If not, you can click the Register link at the top right of the Kuler website.

Figure 1 Free to all, Adobe Kuler can also generate themes of colors from photographs that you can upload or import directly from Flickr.

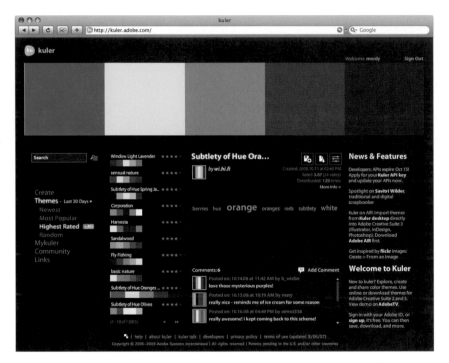

What's cool about Kuler is that, as part of the online community, you can view color themes that others have created, and you can even rate them. Themes are tagged with metadata, allowing you to easily search for colors (such as *winter* or *chocolate*). In fact, color themes are actually published as RSS feeds, allowing designers to search based on things like the most popular or the highest rated themes.

Using the Kuler Panel in Illustrator

Although the Kuler website is nice and all, you still have to leave your design environment and use your web browser to find your colors. That's why Adobe took the next step and brought Kuler directly into Illustrator (it also exists in other Adobe Creative Suite CS4 components). Choose Window > Extensions > Kuler to open the Kuler panel (**Figure 2**), which gives you access to the themes within the online Kuler community.

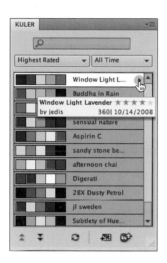

Figure 2 With the Kuler panel, you can browse color themes directly from within Illustrator for instant color inspiration.

Click the pop-up menus at the top of the Kuler panel to display specific RSS feeds, such as highest rated, most popular, and so on. You can also specify a time constraint (such as list all newest themes within the past 7 days). Enter any keyword in the Search field to find Kuler themes that fit your exact needs. If you find a theme you like, then select it, and click the Add Selected Theme to Swatches icon at the bottom of the panel. Illustrator automatically adds the selected theme to your Swatches panel as a color group. Alternatively, you can click the triangle to the far right of any theme to open it in Kuler directly (Illustrator launches your default web browser to do so).

The Kuler panel is also a two-way street, meaning that if you develop some colors you like while using Illustrator, create a group in your Swatches panel (of five colors or less), and then click the Upload from Swatch Panel to Kuler Community button in the Kuler panel. Illustrator transfers your colors to the Kuler website, where you can then add metadata tags and publish your theme.

DesignTools ^{Monthly}
The Executive Summary of Graphic Design News

Get 3 Free Issues:
www.design-tools.com/ilcs4wow/

Wow! technical editor Jean-Claude Tremblay and *Design Tools Monthly's* Jay Nelson teamed up to collect and summarize for you their favorite Illustrator-related plug-ins and utilities. We encourage you to explore them on the *Wow! CD.*

Artlandia's **LivePresets** ($125) lets you create live pattern swatches and symbols that are editable on the fly with Illustrator's tools. Artlandia **SymmetryWorks 4** ($229) lets you easily create seamless patterns. You draw a simple shape, and SymmetryWorks rotates, reflects and spaces it to create a seamless pattern. As you edit the shape, the pattern updates in real time. (Mac/Win) www.artlandia.com

Zevrix's **ArtOptimizer** ($130) reduces the size of linked images that were resized in Illustrator. If the effective resolution is higher than a target resolution you define, it backs up the image, opens the copy in Photoshop, changes its dimensions and reimports it into Illustrator at 100% size. It can optionally also convert the image's color mode to CMYK, RGB or Grayscale, apply sharpening filters and flatten the image. (Mac) www.zevrix.com

Hot Door's **CADTools** ($279) adds tools for computer-aided drafting to Illustrator, which already has filters for importing and exporting in DXF/DWG formats. It can add interactive dimensional text and arrows to any line or angle; measure and change angles, the areas of shapes, and radius of circles and curves. The Trim tool automatically trims excess from overlapping segments. The Fill and Chamfer tools let you automatically round or bevel a shape's corners. The Wall tool creates two-sided wall shapes, and the amazing Wall Healer tool cleans up the intersection of Wall shapes. (Mac/Win) www.hotdoor.com

CValley's **FILTERiT4.3** ($129), is a plug-in that provides a wide variety of options from simple distortion to 3D Transform on outlined objects. Its "killer feature" is that you work directly on your document page, seeing your results immediately as you change things, and that you can work on "live" type, while the objects and effects remain instantly editable—no more dialog boxes to open and close. We hesitate to use the term "must-have" with any product, but if you spend lots of time in Illustrator, it could change your world. (Mac/Win) www.cvalley.com

GraphicXtras has many creative plug-ins for Illustrator, affordably priced at just $15 each. www.graphicxtras.com

Jean-Louis Garrivet's **JLG•Dimension** ($25 euro) adds four new dimensioning tools. To use it, select a segment, angle, circle, or other path, and the dimensions of that selection are added to the outside edge of the selection. (Mac/Win)
http://perso.orange.fr/jlg.outils/Pages/ManuelCotationsUS.html

Stephen Vincent's **Kimbo** ($40) adds 11 new tools to Illustrator's tool panel including a rhombus, wave, rose, grid, golden rectangle, cut, rectangle cut, mirror, polar mesh, Archidedean spiral, and tile tool. The Golden Rectangle tool lets you draw a rectangle with proportions as defined by the ancient Greeks to be the most aesthetically pleasing. The cut, mirror, and tile tools help create interesting shapes by quickly cutting or duplicating portions of a path. (Mac/Win) http://members.shaw.ca/spvincent/plugins/default.html

Avenza Software's **MAPublisher 8** ($1,249) lets you import CAD drawings and maps in geographic information systems (GIS) format, including shapes, boundaries, routes and elevations. MAPublisher also lets you automatically create legends and keys. It can import database tables, which can be linked to existing map layers, and can export to ArcView Shape files and SVG and dBASE formats. It even supports Google's KML file format for use with Google Maps. Their website shows examples of the beautiful, detailed maps made by customers. (Mac/Win) www.avenza.com

Illustrator's Bevel feature can be too smooth; that's why Shinycore's **Path Styler Pro** is valuable. This plug-in for Photoshop or Illustrator ($99 each or $129 for both) creates sharp, clean bevels, accurate reflections, with multiple lighting options. You can apply multiple bevels, and each bevel can have its own material, contour, texture, and procedural map such as wood, metal, plastic, glass and others. Lights can be directional, omni, or tube. More than 100 presets are included. (Mac/Win) www.shinycore.com

Hot Door's **Perspective** ($179) saves lots of time when doing geometric perspective drawing. It adds isometric, oblique, and perspective drawing tools to draw lines, planes, cubes and cylinders over an adjustable background grid. Your flat artwork can project instantly to front, side or top faces. (Mac/Win) www.hotdoor.com

Astute Graphics' **Phantasm CS** (three versions, starting at $38) adds color controls similar to Photoshop's: brightness, contrast, hue, saturation, levels and curves—but you can use them on native Illustrator shapes and imported images. All controls are available as both a Filter and a Live Effect, so you can later edit or remove your changes. (Mac/Win) www.astutegraphics.com

Gluon's **SluggerAI** ($149) records who printed an Illustrator document and when, where it was saved and which

WOW! Appendix: Illustrator Plug-ins

version it was. This handy information is created and updated in a floating palette each time a document is printed. It can be hidden or deleted, as well as placed at any location on the page. (Mac)

www.gluon.com/product-sluggerai.html

Code-Line's **SneakPeek Pro** ($20) lets you preview Illustrator, InDesign, EPS, and FreeHand documents in the Finder, without actually launching the application. (Mac)

www.code-line.com

Stephen Vincent's **Tessela** ($40) lets you create patterns that are rectangular, rhombic, hexagonal, and triangular in shape. This plug-in also lets you curve the edges of tiles using the Escher Edit mode. (Mac/Win)

http://members.shaw.ca/spvincent/plugins/default.html

CValley's **Xtream Path 1.3** ($139) lets you click anywhere on a path and drag it to into a new shape, instead of dragging anchor points around. A new palette shows the numerical values of the position of anchor points and handles, as well as the length of segments. The palette also lets you copy and paste the position values from one anchor point onto another. You can symmetrically change a shape — pull on one side and the other side mirrors the change. A Smart Rounding effect changes sharp corners into rounded ones, even on editable type. A Multi-Line tool makes it easier to draw isometric shapes such as 3D boxes. You can even copy paths and insert them into other paths, bevel corners, round corners, and easily create arcs. (Mac/Win)

www.cvalley.com

Collect for Output: two options

Adobe Illustrator—even version CS4—doesn't have a "collect for output" feature. (Its Collect for Output script only collects linked images, not fonts.) Here are two options to collect everything:

Worker72a's **Scoop** ($47) collects placed graphics and fonts and can also extract embedded raster images. (Mac)

www.worker72a.com

Code Line's **Art Files** ($50) is a utility that collects and packages placed graphics and fonts. Several Illustrator documents can be packaged at the same time, and any images or fonts that are shared among the documents are collected only once, saving disk space. (Mac)

www.code-line.com

Rick Johnson: these and many more

www.rj-graffix.com

Concatenate ($20) lets you connect two or more paths into one continuous path. You tell it how close the endpoints should be to combine the paths, and whether to average the endpoints together. It's especially useful for cleaning up CAD drawings or connecting and filling borders in maps. (Mac/Win)

Cutting Tools ($5) adds new ways to cut paths: Hatchet cuts through all paths, not just the top path; Saber Saw cuts

through all paths as you drag over them; Table Saw cuts a straight line through all paths; Vector Vac deletes all paths you drag it across. (Mac/Win)

Nudge Palette ($15) lets you adjust the position of a patterned fill within an object or a dash pattern along a path. It also features an "Untransform" button to reset a dash or pattern to its previous position, removing transformations like scaling, rotating, etc. (Mac/Win)

Select (free) adds a "Select" item to Illustrator's Filter menu to select 15 additional things: guides, paths, open paths, closed paths, filled paths, unfilled paths, stroked paths, unstroked paths, dashed paths, undashed paths, compound paths, groups, live object groups, gradient meshes, envelopes, symbols, embedded raster art, and placed art. (Mac/Win)

Worker72a: focus on production

www.worker72a.com

Point Control ($10) puts Illustrator's most useful commands for manipulating anchor points and paths into one handy palette. (Mac)

Select Effects ($25) highlights any paths that use Transparency, Effects and Blend modes, which may cause problems when printing or flattening. (Mac)

SepPreview ($47) lets you view color separations, in color. Spot and process colors can be viewed and printed individually or in any combination. (Mac)

Tag72a ($25) automatically creates and updates special text objects such as User Name, Document Name, File Path, Print Date/Time and Save Date/Time. (Mac)

QuickCarton ($47) helps you build a complete corrugated carton layout in less than a minute. It supports different thicknesses, panels, inside or outside glue, and other details. It also adds registration marks and graphics safe area guides. (Mac)

Scoop ($47) collects placed graphics and fonts and can also extract embedded raster images. (Mac)

White Overprint Detector (free) scans each file as you open it, and tells you whether there are any paths or text that have been filled or stroked with a white overprint. The free version only shows an alert when white overprints are found while the $25 **WhiteOP2KO** version resets all white text and path object overprints to knockout. (Mac)

Zoom to Selection ($7) adds commands to the view menu to zoom into a selection or fit the selection in the window. (Mac)

Free Catalog of Plug-ins

PowerXChange has a free downloadable catalog/database of plug-ins for Illustrator, InDesign, Photoshop, Acrobat, QuarkXPress, and more. You can download it at:

http://www.thepowerxchange.com/catalogue_download.html

The Executive Summary of Graphic Design News

Get 3 Free Issues:
www.design-tools.com/ilcs4wow/

Design Tools Monthly brings you this selection of Illustrator tips from recent issues. Read these tips and dozens more in the printable PDF of Tips on the *Wow! CD*.

Quick-Select Fields

In most Adobe applications, you can quickly select the entire content of a text-entry field in a dialog box or panel, including the Control panel, by clicking on the label (name) of the field. So, instead of clicking and dragging across the current content of a field to select it, just click the text label next to the field to select its entire contents.

Select Similar Objects

You can use the Magic Wand tool to select objects that have similar attributes to the one you clicked, though you can also choose Select> Same> [attribute] or Select> Object> [attribute] to do the same thing.

However, these two approaches have different options: the Magic Wand has a Tolerance setting, letting it select objects with slightly different attributes; and the Select> Same... or Select> Object... menus contain attributes not available to the Magic Wand.

Surprises in Illustrator's Dock Icon

If you Control-click or right-click on the Mac OS X Dock icon of Illustrator while it's running, some surprising items appear:

- Recent Files lists the files most recently opened by that application.
- Scripts provides a list of automated actions you can apply to the open document, such as export to Flash, SVG or PDF, or use Live Trace. (If you don't see any scripts in the list, choose Other Script, navigate to the Adobe Illustrator CS4 folder, and choose Scripting> Sample Scripts.)
- Quick Links lets you launch or switch to any Creative Suite application.

Quickly Reset Adobe Preferences

One standard technique for troubleshooting the source of a problem in an application is to move or delete the application's preferences files. The application then rebuilds those files on its next launch. However, the location of those files isn't always obvious.

Adobe makes it easy to reset its applications' preferences to their defaults: just hold down all the modifier keys when launching an Adobe application (Mac: Control-Command-Option-Shift or Win: Ctrl-Alt-Shift).

This will reset any preferences you may have customized, so be sure you know which ones to change back.

Easier Circles

In Illustrator, if you know where a circle should begin, you can press the Command/Ctrl key while using the Ellipse tool. This lets you begin the circle's arc exactly where you click, instead of at a virtual "corner" of an imaginary enclosing box. Use this tip when tracing a template that has rounded corners.

Reset the Star Tool

The Star tool maintains your most recent settings, so you can easily draw more stars of the same shape. Unfortunately, to reset the Star tool to its default settings, you must quit and then relaunch Illustrator. (To reset it manually, the defaults are: Radius 1=25, Radius 2=50, Points=5.)

Disable Anti-aliasing for One Object

If you need to keep text from looking blurry on-screen or when rasterized, you can disable its anti-aliasing. First, select the text object, then choose Effect> Rasterize and set anti-aliasing to None in the Rasterize dialog. Because this is a live effect, the text remains fully editable, but is no longer anti-aliased.

The Hidden Flip Command

The two places that Illustrator hides the Flip command (to flip an object either horizontally vertically) are: in the side menu of the Transform panel; and in the side menu of the little palette that appears when you click on the blue X, Y, W or H in the Control panel.

If you can remember that Flip means the same thing as Reflect in Adobe-speak, you can also use the Reflect tool, which is hidden under the Rotate tool. You can also choose Object> Transform> Reflect, or invoke the Contextual menu (Control-click or rigwht-click) and then choose Reflect from the Contextual menu.

Use Illustrator Layers & Text in Photoshop

To copy the layers and text from an Illustrator file into Photoshop, choose File> Export in Illustrator and select Photoshop format. In the resulting dialog box, be sure to enable

Write Layers and Preserve Text Editability. Then, when you open the exported file in Photoshop, the text objects from Illustrator will appear as Type layers in Photoshop.

Smaller PDFs from Illustrator

By default, Illustrator embeds a copy of the native Illustrator document inside the PDFs you save from it, making the file size of the PDF much larger than it needs to be. To reduce file size when saving the document in PDF format from Illustrator, disable the checkbox named Preserve Illustrator Editing Capabilities. Be sure to keep a copy of the original Illustrator document, though, for future editing.

Live Trace & Live Paint at Once

Often, after you use the Live Trace feature to convert a bitmapped image into a vector object, you'll want to use the Live Paint feature to color it in. You can save a step by choosing Object> Live Trace> Make and Convert to Live Paint. Illustrator will use your current settings for Live Trace and then convert the tracing to a Live Paint group.

Choose a Complementary Color

In Illustrator, you can choose the complementary color of the current fill or stroke of a selected object by Command-Shift-clicking (Mac) or Ctrl-Shift-clicking (Win) in the color ramp at the bottom of the Color panel. You can also choose Complement from the side menu in the Color panel.

Match or Swap Stroke & Fill Colors

In Adobe's applications, it's easy to make an object's stroke and fill colors the same. In the Tool or Color panels, just drag the icon for one directly on top of the icon for the other. To swap the Fill color and the Stroke color of a selected object, press Shift-X.

Illustrator Smart Objects in Photoshop

When you paste artwork from Illustrator into Photoshop, you have the option of bringing it in as a Smart Object. Doing this will maintain the Illustrator artwork's infinite resolution, which means that if you resize it in Photoshop, or resize the entire Photoshop file, the Illustrator Smart Object will output at the full resolution of the Photoshop file.

An additional benefit is that the Illustrator artwork becomes embedded in the Photoshop file. You can edit the embedded file by selecting its layer in the Layers panel and either double-clicking the layer thumbnail or Control-clicking on the layer and choosing Edit Contents. The embedded Illustrator artwork will open in Illustrator, but you won't be changing the original Illustrator file on your hard drive.

Don't Convert Text to Outlines

Strangely, confusion about this crops up on a regular basis: you don't need to convert your text to outlines in any application just to be sure that the font will print. Instead, export in PDF format, and by default the fonts will be included in the file. The fonts don't need to be installed on the recipient's computer to print it. They'll be accessed directly from within the file.

Smooth Vector Graphics for Websites

Because Illustrator can export directly to Flash (SWF) format, and 99% of Web browsers can display Flash content, you can export your crisp vector artwork to Flash format and your website visitors will see nice, sharp artwork. Choose File> Export, then in the Format dropdown menu of the Export dialog, choose Flash (SWF).

Round Corners Your Way

Instead of using the Rounded Rectangle tool, create a standard rectangle with the Rectangle tool and choose Effect> Stylize> Round Corners. You can then change the roundness at any time in the Appearance panel. As a bonus, you can use this effect on any shape.

Save Gradients as a Style

One feature that has been a long-term headache for a lot of Illustrator users is gradients. The new Gradient tool (G) in CS4 makes a world of difference with really fun, on-the-artwork controls, but that's not all—when you're satisfied with the look of your gradient, save it as a graphic style. This will preserve the angle, aspect ratio, and other elements of the gradient that aren't saved in gradient swatches.

The Key to Aligning Objects

You can easily align a set of objects to a guide in Illustrator. Using the Selection tool (V), select both the guide and all of the objects, and click on the guide again. The guide is now the "key object" with which everything will line up when you use the Align functions on either the Control panel or Align panel (Window> Align). You can do the same thing with any object—the key doesn't have to be a guide.

Take Advantage of Document Tabs

Springs-loaded document tabs in CS4 let you copy artwork from one file to another, or create symbols, brushes, swatches, and graphic styles from artwork without interrupting your flow. Drag the artwork from the current file and hover over the tab of the document you want to copy it to. The document will pop to the top so you can drop your artwork in place.

Artists

Susan E. Alderman

Ted Alspach
ted@bezier.com
www.bezier.com

Kevan Atteberry
P.O. Box 40188
Bellevue, WA 98015-4188
206-550-6353
kevan@oddisgood.com
http://oddisgood.com

Jean Aubé
785 Versailles #302
Montréal Québec Canada
H3C 1Z5
jeanaube01@videotron.ca

Kenneth Batelman
128 Birch Leaf Drive
Milford, PA 18337
888-532-0612
Kenneth@batelman.com
www.batelman.com

Christiane Beauregard
514-935-6794
c.beauregard@videotron.ca
www.christianebeauregard.
com

Russell Benfanti
www.benfanti.com
represented by
www.mendolaart.com
212.986.5680

Eliot Bergman
12-1 Nishi-Gokencho, Shin-
juku-ku, Tokyo, 162-0812
Japan
212-693-2300
eliot@ebergman.com
www.ebergman.com

Dan Brown
79 Center Lane
Kensington, CT 06037
860-335-0480
drgn5ly@msn.com

Cinthia A. Burnett
cinabur@yahoo.com

David Cater
510-232-9420
adcater@aol.com

Ron Chan
24 Nelson Ave.
Mill Valley, CA 94941
415-389-6549
ronchan@ronchan.com

Conrad Chavez
design@conradchavez.com
www.conradchavez.com

Kazimiera Cichowlaz
136 Texas Dr.
New Britain, CT 06052
860-224-9053

Scott Citron
112 W. 27th St., #700
scott@scottcitrondesign.com
http://scottcitrondesign.com

Sandee Cohen
33 Fifth Avenue, #10B
New York, NY 10003
212-677-7763
sandee@vectorbabe.com
www.vectorbabe.com

Jeanne Criscola
1477 Ridge Rd.
North Haven, CT 06473
203-248-4285
info@criscoladesign.com
www.criscoladesign.com
www.jeannecriscola.net

Michael Cronan
mpc@cronan.com
www.michaelcronan.com

Scott B. Crouse
Lake Alfred, FL
scott@scottcrouse.com
scottcrouse.com

Andrew Dashwood
info@adashwood.com
www.adashwood.com

Design Action Collective
369 15th Street
Oakland, CA 94612
510-452-1912
info@designaction.org
www.designaction.org

Dedree Drees
5307 Wayne Ave.
Baltimore, MD 21207
410-448-3317; 443-840-4423
dedreedrees@cavtel.net
http://ddreesart.wordpress.
com/

Gary Ferster
10 Karen Drive
Tinton Falls, NJ 07753
732-922-8903
Fax: 732-922-8970
gferster@comcast.net
www.garyferster.com/

Erick Flesey
1405 Calle Goya
Oceanside CA 92056
619-654-0090
fleseyman@yahoo.com
www.EricFlesey.com

Rich Floyd
760-803-5773
portfolio@richfloyddesigns.
com
www.richfloyddesigns.com

Ian Giblin
408-448-2614
n.giblin@comcast.net

Reggie Gilbert
Tech Vector
1454 Ashland St PMB#141
Ashland, OR 97520
www.techvector.com

Nicole Gilbertie
ngilbertie@gmail.com

Von R. Glitschka
971-223-6143
von@glitschka.com
www.glitschka.com

Mordy Golding
Design Responsibly LLC
320 Leroy Avenue
Cedarhurst, NY 11516
info@designresponsibly.com
www.designresponsibly.com
www.mordy.com

Steven H. Gordon
Cartagram, LLC
136 Mill Creek Crossing
Madison, AL 35758
wow@cartagram.com
www.cartagram.com

Caryl Gorska
1277 8th Avenue 105
San francisco, CA 94122
415-664-7721
408-910-6545
gorska@gorska.com
www.gorska.com

Laurie Grace
info@lauriegrace.com
lauriegrace.com
http://lgraceworks.blogspot.
com/

Cheryl Graham
cherylgraham@earthlink.net
www.cherylgraham.net

Gusman, *see* Joly

Brad Hamann
Brad Hamann Illustration &
Design
41 West Market Street
Red Hook, NY 12571
845-758-6186 studio
bhamann@hvc.rr.com
www.darkdesign.com

Scott Hansen
scott@iso50.com
www.iso50.com

Pattie Belle Hastings
Ice House Press & Design
Pattie Belle Hastings
266 West Rock Ave.
New Haven, CT 06515
203-389-7334

Rick Henkel,
rhenkel@thoughtformdesign
see also ThoughtForm Design

Kurt Hess,
dashesshaus@comcast.net
see also ThoughtForm Design

Dan Hubig
209 Mississippi St.
San Francisco, CA 94107
415-824-0838
dan@danhubig.com
www.danhubig.com

Gerard Huerta
Gerard Huerta Design, Inc.
54 Old Post Road
Southport, CT 06890
203-256-1625
gerard.huerta@sbcglobal.net
www.gerardhuerta.com

Kevin Hulsey
www.khulsey.com

IAN Symbols (Integration and
Application Network)
University of Maryland Center
for Environmental Science
2020 Horns Point Rd
(PO Box 775)
Cambridge, MD 21613
410-228-9250 ext 254
ian@ca.umes.edu
http://ian.umces.edu/symbols

Lisa Jackmore
13603 Bluestone Court
Clifton, VA 20124
703-830-0985
ljackmore@cox.net

Lance Jackson
www.lancejackson.net

David Jennings
7 Castleton Avenue
Romanby
Northallerton
North Yorkshire
DL78SU
UK
+44(0)1609 770795
+44(0)7754 796831
david@davidjennings.co.uk
www.davidjennings.co.uk

Mohammed Jogie
PO Box 44007, Linden
Gauteng Province 2104
South Africa
+27 (0) 82 655 2999

Annie Gusman Joly
860-928-1042
annie@picturedance.com
www.anniejoly.com

Dave Joly
860-928-1042
dave@picturedance.com
www.picturedance.com

Andrea Kelley
Andrea Kelley Design
530 Menlo Oaks Drive
Menlo Park, CA 94025
650-326-1083
andrea@jevans.com

Stephen Klema
69 Walnut St.
Winsted, CT 06098
stephen@stephenklema.com
sklema@txcc.comnet.edu
www.stephenklema.com

Marc LaMantia
64 Macdougal Street Apt 5
New York, NY 10012
212-677-6907
lamantia2003@yahoo.com

Adam Z Lein
40 Morrow Ave., Apt 3HS
Scarsdale, NY 10583
914-437-9115
adamz@adamlein.com
www.adamlein.com

Joe Lertola
TIME / Editorial Art Dept
1271 Sixth Avenue / Rm 2442
New York, NY 10020
212-522-3721
www.joelertola.com

Randy Livingston
3403 Meadowwood Dr.
Murfreesboro, TN 37132
615-653-8718
randy3403@me.com

Vicki Loader
Sandhurst, Berkshire
Gu47 8Ja, United Kingdom
+447834783218
+441252874190
vickiloader@btinternet.com
www.purepixels.co.uk
www.vickiloader.com

Emily Looper
56 Wickham's Fancy
Canton, CT 06019
lady_krile@yahoo.com

Terrance (Terry) Lush
PO Box 185143
Hamden, CT 06518
t.lush@tlush.net
www.tlush.net

Todd Macadangdang
348 Arco St.
San Jose, CA 95123
408-536-6373
toddm@adobe.com
toddm@illustratorworld.com

Pete Maric
520 Terrace Plaza
Willowick, OH 44095
440-487-4205
contact@petemaric.com
www.petemaric.com

Greg Maxson
116 W. Florida Ave
Urbana, IL 61801
217-898-6560
gmaxti@sbcglobal.net
www.gregmaxson.com

Laura McCloskey

Aaron McGarry
aron@mcgarry.com
www.amcgarry.com

Nobuko Miyamoto
3-8 Matuba-cho
Tokorozawa-shi
Saitama-ken Japan/359-0044
04-2998-6631
venus@gol.com
http://venus.oracchi.com/

Yukio Miyamoto
Matubacho 3-8
Tokorozawasi
Saitama Prefecture/359-0044
+81-42-998-6631
yukio-m@ppp.bekkoame.ne.jp
http://www.bekkoame.
ne.jp/~yukio-m/intro/

Bert Monroy
www.bertmonroy.com

Marcel Morin
Lost Art Cartography
Box 66, Grand Pré
Nova Scotia
B0P 1MO
902-542-2934
cybermapper@gmail.com

Gary J. Moss
Moss Martin Graphic Design
319 Peck Street Box I-5
New Haven, CT 06513
203-785-8464
gm@mossmartin.net
mossmartin.net

Laura Mottai
860-307-3084
Lauramottai@hotmail.com
www.lauramottai.com

Innosanto Nagara
see Design Action Collective

Brad Neal
Thomas • Bradley Illustration
& Design
411 Center St. / P.O. Box 249
Gridley, IL 61744
309-747-3266
bradneal@thomas-bradley.com
www.thomasbradley.com

David Nelson
Mapping Services
721 Grape St.
Denver, CO 80220
303-333-1060

Gary Newman Design
2447 Burnside Rd
Sebastapol, CA 95472
gary@newmango.com
www.newmango.com

Chris D. Nielsen
6662 Timaru Circle
Cypress, CA 90630
714-323-1602
carartwork@ca.rr.com
chris@pentoolart.com
www.pentoolart.com

Richard Ng
www.istockphoto/richard_ng

Ann Paidrick
314-762-1431
annpaid@attglobal.net
www.ebypaidrick.com

Ellen Papciak-Rose
Johannesburg, South Africa
info@ellenpapciakrose.com
www.ellenpapciakrose.com

Theresa Palmer
Meltdw@hotmail.com
http://meltdw.deviantart.com

Tom Patterson
National Park Service
Media Development
Harpers Ferry Center
Harpers Ferry, WV 25425
304-535-6020
t.patterson@nps.gov
www.nacis.org

Daniel Pelavin
212-941-7418
daniel@pelavin.com
www.pelavin.com

Laurent Pinabel
laurent@pinabel.com
pinabel.com

Federico Platon
Jose Mtnez. Velasco 8
Madrid 28007
91-573 2467
grafintek@gmail.com
www.grafintek.com

Shana Popyk
860-302-5716

David S. Pounds
1810 Staimford Circle
Wellington, FL 33414
561-803-2414
david_pounds@pba.edu

Gary Powell
2417 SW Olson
Pendleton, OR 97801
541-276-6330
oil_artist@comcast.net

Ryan Putnam
719-229-6563
ryan@rypearts.com
http://rypearts.com

Michael (Mic) Riddle
micrid3d@mac.com

Jolynne Roorda
jroorda@folktheory.com
www.folktheory.com

Jessica Rosario
162 M Homestead St.
Manchester, CT 06042
860-713-8419
studio@jessicarosario.com
www.jessicarosario.com

Zosia Rostomian
zosia_rostomian@yahoo.com
www.ztrdesign.com

Tracey Saxby, *see* IAN Symbols

Mike Schwabauer
5808 W. 86th Terrace
Overland Park, KS 66207-1616
913-710-1345
kcmikey@mac.com

Rick Simonson
RLSimonson Studios
4010 Ave. R #G8
Kearney, NE 68847
rlsimonson@mac.com
www.RickLSimonson.com

Lisa Shoglow
64 Old Hyde Rd.
Weston, CT 06883
203-454-7977
LRShoglow@optonline.net

Joe Shoulak
joe@joeshoulak.com
joeshoulak.com

Nancy Stahl
nancy@nancystahl.com
www.nancystahl.com

Judy Stead
407-310-0051
judy@judystead.com
judystead.com

Sharon Steuer
c/o Peachpit Press
1249 Eighth St.
Berkeley, CA 94710
www.ssteuer.com

Ilene Strizver
The Type Studio
Westport, CT
ilene@thetypestudio.com
www.thetypestudio.com
203-227-5929

Barbara Sudick
California State University
Dept. of Communication
Design
Chico, CA 95929
530-898-5028

Brenda Sutherland
345 Park Avenue
San Jose, CA 95124

ThoughtForm
3700 South Water Street
Suite 300
Pittsburgh, PA 15203-2366
412-488-8600
www.thoughtformdesign.com

Kathleen Tinkel
MacPrePress
12 Burr Road
Westport, CT 06880
203-227-2357

Jack Tom
www.jacktom.com

Jean-Claude Tremblay
Proficiografik
135 Boul. Champlain
Candiac, Québec J5R 3T
Canada
514-629-0949
info@proficiografik.com
www.proficiografik.com

Matthew Triompo
29 Hawthorne Dr.
Southington, CT 06489
860-426-0473
MattTri88@hotmail.com

David Turton
thegraphiclibrary.com

Judy Valenzuela
judy valenzuela14@mac.com
www.judyvalenzuela.com

Alan James Weimer
67 Bliss Street
Rehoboth, MA 0276-1932
508-252-9236
illustrator51@comcast.net

Ari M. Weinstein
ari@ariw.com
ariw.com

Hugh Whyte
Lehner & Whyte
8-10 South Fullerton Ave.
Montclair, NJ 07402
201-746-1335

Filip Yip
877-463-4547
filip@yippe.com
www.yippe.com

Michel Zappy
6606 Drolet St.
Montreal, Quebec H2S 2S8
Canada
514-948-0477
michel.zappy@videotron.ca
www.michelzappy.com

General Index

~ (tilde) key, 16, 28, 408
[ ] (square brackets), 136, 153
+ key, 15, 30, 69
+ sign, 197, 239

2D effects, *see* effects
2D objects, *see also* objects
  extruding, 340, 341–342
  using 3D to create, 348–349
"3D with a 2D Twist" lesson,
    348–349
"3D Effects" lesson, 354–355
3D Extrude & Bevel Options dialog
  creating thematic 3D maps, 363
  modifying extrusion settings, 347,
    348–349, 353
  moving object on one axis, 346
  simplifying blend before
    extruding, 257
  Surface shading option in, 343
"3D Logo Object" lesson, 350
3D objects
  assembling and positioning, 353
  building plastic container, 352
  color selection for, 343
  designing tower of Tupperware,
    351
  disabling New Art Has Basic
    Appearance option, 342
  light sources for, 344–345
  map arrowheads, 362
  mapping art onto, 345, 357, 359
  plastic container, 352
  rotating in three dimensions, 342
  simplifying points for, 343
  surface shading for, 343–345
  using multiple windows to create,
    349
  using as symbols in repetitive
    drawings, 361
  warping, 256–257
  wine bottle and label, 360
3D programs with Illustrator art,
    415, 436, 437
3D Revolve Options dialog
  applying to rocket art, 354–355
  building objects from cross
    section, 350
  Surface shading option in, 343

A

A & F Country, 432–433
Acrobat, 415
actions, 35–36
activating artboard, 190
active, 60
Active Colors field (Recolor Artwork
    dialog), 304
Add Anchor Points tool
  about, 15
  adding anchor points, 41, 43, 45
  moving points, 41
Add New Effect button, 171, 324
"Adding Highlights" lesson, 286
Adobe Acrobat, 415
Adobe After Effects, 406–407, 436,
    437
Adobe Bridge, *see* Bridge
Adobe Device Central, 396–397
Adobe Fireworks, 396
Adobe Flash, *see* Flash
Adobe Illustrator, *see* Illustrator
*Adobe Illustrator CS4 Wow! Book
    cover,* 431
Adobe InDesign, 414–415, 431
Adobe kuler, 438–439
Advanced section (Print dialog),
    277, 279–280
advanced techniques, *see* combining
    tools and techniques
advertising banner, 338
African Peer Review Mechanism,
    359
After Effects, 406–407, 436, 437
"Ahava," 308
.ai files
  saving file as, 35, 395
  using with Flash, 392
Alderman, Susan E., 144, 444
Align panel, 20–22
Align Stroke buttons, 60
aligning
  controlling from Control panel, 20
  house peak, 46
  masked content, 366
alpha transparency, 278
Alspach, Ted
  Board2Pieces comic strip, 361
  contact information, 444

experiments with Effects and Flare
    tool, 328, 331
anchor points, *see also* mesh points
  adding, 41, 43, 45, 69
  adjusting size of, 13
  defined, 11–12
  interpreting cursor close to, 13
  joining and averaging, 22–23
  minimizing for 3D objects, 343
  moving, 41
  removing, 69
  simplifying paths, 69, 156
"Animating Pieces" lesson, 406–407
animation
  animating Scatter Brush layers,
    132
  character, 404–405
  combining multiple applications
    for, 406–407, 436–437
  creating, 394
  creating objects as Flash-ready
    symbols, 402–403
  exporting to Flash, 394
  hand tracing converted to, 408
  "Last Draw, The," 409
  layers converted to key frames,
    400–401
  Live Trace sketch for, 116–118
  symbols for Flash, 134
*Annual Progress Report National
    Programme of Action,* 359
antialiasing
  effect on type, 393
  previewing, 392
"Antiquing Type" lesson, 230–231
appearance attributes
  adding effects, fill, and stroke to,
    170–171
  clearing, 278
  copying, 67, 203
  defined, 20, 167–168
  editing object's, 169–170
  moving and copying, 169
  object, group, and layer, 182–183
  saving as graphic style, 320
  selecting, 60
  targeting shared, 168
  unable to view, 169
  using last object's, 283–284

attributes, *see* appearance attributes
Attributes panel, 36
Aubé, Jean, 376, 444
Auto Add/Delete function (Pen
    too), 14
Autodesk Maya, 432–434
Average feature, 22–23, 45
Awl, Dave, xv

B

backgrounds
    adding depth to, 336
    adjusting transparency of, 297
    coloring gradient mesh with
        mapped, 245
    de-emphasizing, 124–126
    editing painted, 426
    importing, 426
    linking with text, 224, 225
    removing, 97
    simulating colored, 32
    transparent, 297
backing up files, 27
bananas, 103, 104
barber pole image, 292
baseline
    defined, 193
    shifting type, 195, 219, 220
Basic Appearances, *see also*
        Appearance panel
    adding effects, fill, and stroke to,
        170–171
    defined, 167–168
    lesson on, 182–183
    New Art Has Basic Appearance
        option, xix, 168, 169, 342
Batelman, Kenneth, 374, 375, 444
Beauregard, Christiane
    contact information, 444
    creating color transitions, 252, 253
    giraffes, palms, and snakes, 369
    using transparent glows, 287
    working with opacity masks,
        288–289
"Beautiful," 336
Benchmade Knife Company, 177
Benfanti, Russell, 372–373, 444
Bergman, Eliot, 432–434, 444
Bertz Design Group, 172
Bevel join, 68
bevels, 249, 341

Bézier curves
    tools for editing, 14–16
    using, 11–13
    working with from Control panel,
        14
Bible workbook map, 178
"Biker Kid in Space," 264–265
bleeds, 186, 187, 216
Blend tool, 236
"Blending Elements" lesson, 296–297
blending modes
    adjusting by layer, 284
    applying transparency with, 273
    experimenting with, 299
    working with light and shadows,
        285
blends
    about, 236–237
    adding transparency with,
        262–263
    blending objects with opacity
        masks, 288–289
    controlling speed of, 236
    following curved path, 238
    gradients vs., 241
    reversing order of, 238
    setting options for, 237–238
    shaping, 254–255
    specifying blend steps, 237, 343
    warping 3D, 256–257
    when to use, 237
    working with blended brush
        strokes, 258
Blob Brush tool
    about, 15
    characteristics of, 133
    painting with, 93–95
    sketching with, 112
    tracing with, 110–111
    using with Eraser, 96
    viewing paths for, 93
Blob Brush Tool Options dialog, 95
Bloomberg Markets magazine, 434
Board2Pieces comic strip, 361
"Book Cover Design" lesson,
    216–217
book covers, 216–217, 371
bounding boxes
    drawing for warp effect, 327
    hiding edges with visible, 32
    using, 24
box art, 356–357

Break Link button (Control panel),
    134
Bridge
    adding metadata in, 27
    loading symbol library from, 157
    using, 37
Bring to Front/Forward commands,
    166
Brown, Dan, 144, 444
browser image previews, 394
Brush Libraries Menu button, 130
Brush tool
    closing paths with, 12
    Fidelity and Smoothness options
        for, 14
"Brush Your Type" lesson, 228–229
brushes, *see also* Blob Brush tool;
        custom brushes; and specific
        brushes
    applying to letterforms, 228–229
    changing diameter of, 136
    closing paths and reversing stroke
        for, 131
    developing textured, 142
    drawing transparent stroke, 140
    editing, 132
    expressive styles for, 144–145
    illustrating grass and soil with,
        158–159
    mimicking traditional media with,
        147
    naming, 130
    New Brush dialog to create,
        139–140
    organizing strokes on layers, 284
    saving, 302, 316
    scaling, 131
    scratchboard art, 332
    selecting from Control panel, 130
    types of, 130–131
    using previously painted stroke,
        283–284
    working with, 131–133
"Brushes & Washes" lesson, 138–140
Brushes panel
    editing brushes, 132
    illustrated, 131
    loading brush libraries, 130
"Building Houses" lesson, 40–47
Bundy Museum, 230–231
Burnett, Cinthia A., 145, 444
Butt cap, 67–68

G

grass and soil graphic, 158–159

grayscale
    colorizing art in, 294–295
    generating tints from, 319
    opacity mask conversion to, 274,
        280
    reducing colors to, 318–319

Green Tortoise poster, 235

Greene, Milton H., 301

grids
    customizing, 31
    designing typeface within, 226
    drawing, 17
    methods for constructing, 48–49
    transparency, 32, 272
    viewing, 31

group layers, 164–165

Group Selection tool, grouping and
    selecting objects, 19

grouping and selecting objects,
    18–19

groups, *see also* color groups
    appearance attributes for, 20,
        182–183
    applying Pathfinder effects to, 329
    applying transparency to, 272
    creating color, 64, 307
    editing clipping, 366
    Live Paint, 103–106
    setting appearances and styles
        for, 183
    targeting all elements in, 165
    using Bring Forward/Send Back
        for layers, 166

guides, *see also* Smart Guides
    configuring for book cover layout,
        217
    creating for arcs, 76–77
    customizing, 42
    developing perspective with, 185
    locking/unlocking, 217
    pulling out from ruler, 40
    using, 31

"Guides for Arcs" lesson, 76–77

H

Hamann, Brad, 354–355, 445

hand-drawn art, *see also* painterly
    techniques
    replicating hand-painted stroke,
        129

hand tracing
    adjusting template paths for,
        172–173
    converting to animation, 408
    rasterizing image of, 126

handheld devices, 396–397

handles
    about, 11
    adjusting size of, 13
    modifying Bézier curves with, 12

handwritten text
    opacity of, 229
    simulating, 300

Hansen, Scott, 128, 129, 445

Harmony Rules, 307, 308–309

Hastings, Patti Belle, xvii, 445

headlines
    arcing, 222–223
    letter spacing of, 202

Health Promotion Services, Inc., 409

Heft, Mimi, 431

help resources
    Community Support Web site,
        36–37
    innovative Web sites, 397
    Live Color, 307
    online training resources, 37
    printing resource guides, 36

Henkel, Rick, 79, 87, 445

Hess, Kurt, 78, 301, 445

hiding/showing
    appearances, 169
    characters, 201
    edges, 19, 32
    Gradient Annotator, 240
    grids, 31
    hidden object absent from moved
        artboard, 190
    layers, 160, 162, 177, 181
    objects, 165–166
    panels, 7, 9–10

hierarchy of layer structure, 164–165

high contrast drawing style, 107

Highlight Substituted Fonts option
    (Document Setup), 190

highlights
    creating with transparency, 286
    red mapping, 344
    simulating with transparency,
        292–293

hinging
    Bézier curves, 12
    corners, 13–14

holes
    controlling overlapping object, 365
    creating with Live Paint, 102
    cutting in type characters, 227
    making with Pathfinder panel
        shapes, 122–123
    using in spaces, 90–91

Hubig, Dan, 281, 420–421, 445

Huerta, Gerard, 218–219, 445

Hulsey, Kevin, 428, 445

I

I-beam cursor, 193

IAN Symbols, 445, 447

icons, *see also* indicators
    creating, 72
    dockable panel, 8–9
    Eye, 162, 175, 181
    Out of Web Color Warning, 62
    Selection indicators, 166
    Spot Color, 62, 64
    Target, 166
    Template, 161
    Wow! CD, xix

Illustrator, *see also* combining
        applications; legacy files
    aligning masked content, 366
    animating art from, 400–401,
        406–407, 436, 437
    Bridge used with, 37
    changes to type engine, 191–192,
        219
    combining with other
        applications, 410
    Community Support Web site,
        36–37
    compatibility of transparencies
        with, 275, 277
    creating text for Photoshop image,
        424–425
    editing images in Maya and
        Photoshop, 432–434
    effects for, 324

digitizing, 172–173
dragon, 254–255
geometric, 122–123
Intuit QuickBooks, 248–249
micro-brewery, 317
Paintball Superpark, 266
preparing versions for
    presentations, 210–211
saving as symbol, 209
3D design for, 350
"Long Strange Trip" poster, 235
Looper, Emily, 145, 445
Louveaux, Pierre
about transparency, 272
editing path from mesh, 242
expanding compound shapes, 89
targeting shared appearances, 168
luminosity, 298
Lurd pieces, 120–121
Lush, Terry, 406–407, 445

M

Macadangdang, Rodd, 337, 446
Macintosh computers
managing Workspaces for, 10
minimum system requirements
    for, 2
shortcuts for, xviii
using Application Frame with, 7
magnification of art, 29
magnifier (Assign tab), 315
Mah, Derek, 236
"Making Masters" lesson, 212–213
"Making a Typeface" lesson, 90,
    226–227
mapping
art onto 3D objects, 345, 357, 359
star pattern, 355
symbols, 344, 360
maps
adding appearances to, 182–183
adding background color to mesh,
    245
clip-art symbols for, 346–347
converting 3D GIS data to images,
    435
designing terrain for, 221
labeling features on, 220
multiple versions of, 178
organizing layers for complex, 179

thematic 3D, 363
3D arrowheads for, 362
Maric, Pete, 184–185, 446
Marina Green poster, 147
Mask button (Control panel), 368
mask-editing mode, 274
"Masking Details" lesson, 372–373
"Masking Words" lesson, 224
masks, see clipping masks; opacity
    masks
master artboards, 212–213
master layers, 180–181, 367
mastering Illustrator, 38–59
about, 38–39
constructing grids, 48–49
creating simple object with basic
    tools, 53
exploring basic construction tools,
    40–47
Finger Dances for, 54–58
object rotation exercises, 52
Pen tool, 59
scaling exercises, 50–51
Maximized Screen mode, 29
Maxson, Greg, 148–149, 446
Maya, 432–434
McCloskey, Laura, 144, 446
McGarry, Aaron
about, xiv, 446
blending along path, 238
electrical meter, 430
flame illustration, 240
Wave Warp illustration, 368, 370
menus
Artboard Presets, 188
context-sensitive, 10, 30
Control panel, 7
Effect, 324
Gradient Fill pop-up, 240–241
Layers pop-up menu, 163–164
Object, 366–367
Raster/Vector View options, 98
Type, 196
Vector View, 98
View, 278
Window, xvii
Merge shape mode (Pathfinder
    panel), 92
merging colors, 306–307, 311
mesh
applying gradient, 381
background color for gradient, 245
contouring gradient, 246–247

developing mixer image with, 386
envelope, 328–329
filling shape with gradient, 244
molded mesh bottles, 268–269
using gradient, 242, 300
mesh objects
defined, 242
editing, 247
molding, 268–269
mesh points
changing color of, 300, 386
defined, 242
deleting, 328
Mesh tool, 236
metadata, 27
metallic finish
adding gold's gleam, 248–249
adding to microscope image, 243
simulating chrome, 292–293
Metarie Hampton Inn, 180
micro-brewery logos, 317
microscope, 243
Microsoft Excel charts, 412
Microsoft Office files, 412
Mini Cooper image, 236, 388
Minus Back shape mode (Pathfinder
    panel), 92, 109
Minus Front shape mode
    (Pathfinder panel), 91, 233
Miter join, 68
Miyamoto, Nobuko
beaded necklace, 150
contact information, 446
gradient mesh lesson by, 244
Miyamoto, Yukio
beaded necklace, 150
contact information, 446
Fountain Pen illustration, 270
gradient adjustments by, 271
graphic styles and Live Effects
    used, 339
molded mesh bottles by, 268–269
reflections for bottles, 389
Mobile and Devices document
    profiles, 392, 393
modes, see also blending modes;
    Isolation Mode; and specific
    shape modes
Outline, 28, 55, 93, 162
Preview, 28, 162
screen, 29
text editing, 6
modifier keys, 40

R

radial gradients
  adjusting, 240
  applying, 266, 374
  creating glow from, 262–263
  opacity mask adjustments for, 287
random recoloring, 309
raster images
  adjusting Illustrator layers in
    Photoshop, 419
  antialiasing, 393
  controlling rasterization for, 278,
    280
  converting art to, 114, 126, 187,
    411–412
  dimming, 162
  effects for, 324
  expanding, 213
  Illustrator vs. Photoshop effects
    for, 325–326
  text on top of, 224
Raster/Vector Balance settings
  (Flatten Transparency
  dialog), 278, 280
"Ready to Export" lesson, 416–417
Real World Illustrator CS4, *see also*
  Wow! CD
  cover, 371
  excerpts from, 438, 439
Recolor Artwork dialog, *see also* Edit
  Colors dialog
  buttons of, 304, 305
  disabling Preserve: Black, 322–323
  editing colors, 314–315
  illustrated, 302
  magnifier on Assign tab, 315–316
  opening, 304, 310
  presets for, 306–307
  protecting color from changes, 313
  recoloring swatch groups, 311
  recovering from mistakes in, 307
  replacing blacks with, 312–313
  tabs of, 304, 305–306
  using, 303
"Recolor Artwork" lesson, 308–309
Recolor Options dialog, 306, 312
recoloring artwork
  allowing randomness when, 309
  editing recolored art, 304, 314–315
  isolating and recoloring, 314–316
  protecting color when, 313
  recoloring swatch groups, 311

replacing blacks with, 312–313
styles saved when, 302, 316
varying original by, 210–211
"Recoloring Black" lesson, 312–313
Rectangle dialog, 48
rectangles
  controlling size of, 290–291
  making, 42
  using to renumber artboards, 188
Rectangular Grid tool, 17, 49
Rectangular Grid Tool Options
  dialog, 226
Red Grape, The, 401
red mapping highlight, 344
red text, xix
redocking panels, 7
redrawing 3D effects, 343
reducing colors, 306–307, 311
Reflect tool, 45, 77, 389
registration rectangles, 421
releasing
  blends, 238
  Live Paint groups, 105–106
  selections to layer, 394
  single clipping masks, 365
  tracing objects, 99
renumbering artboards, 188
repeating Free Transform tool
  effects, 25
Replace control (Control panel), 134
replacing graphic styles, 329
Reshape tool, 26
resistor tube, 271
resizing
  art to artboards, 187, 188–189
  artboards, 187, 208
  symbols, 153
resolution
  live effect, 280
  placed image, 410
reversing
  blend order, 238
  brush stroke, 131
revolving 3D objects, 341, 342
RGB color
  advantages of, 393
  choosing, 33
  working and converting to, 32
RIAs (Rich Internet Applications),
  397, 438
Riddle, Michael (Mic), 436–437, 447
robots
  Jackmore's toy, 70–71

Joly's Live Trace, 116–118
rocket illustration, 354–355
Rogalin, Elizabeth, xv
Roorda, Jolynne, 114, 447
Rosario, Jessica, 145, 447
Rostomian, Zosia, 75, 250, 251, 447
rotating
  centerpoint when, 232
  exercises for, 52
  objects in three dimensions,
    342–343
  rectangles and squares, 42
  rocket art shape, 354–355
  symbols, 153
  wine bottle and label, 360
Roughen dialog, 230, 373
Round cap and join, 68
Round Corners dialog, 352
rounded rectangles
  dialog for, 352
  tool for, 16–17
  uniting and filling, 108–109
rulers
  displaying on artboards, 186
  hiding/showing, 30–31
  pulling out guides from, 40
  using Artboard, 186

S

San Diego Oceans Foundation, 380
San Francisco Chronicle Magazine
  cover, 258
San Francisco poster series, 146–147
Save Adobe PDF dialog, 34, 279
Save As dialog, 33–34
Save Swatches for Exchange feature,
  33
Save Transparency Flattener Preset
  dialog, 279
Save for Web dialog, 393, 394, 396
saving
  and backing up work, 27
  brushes, 302, 316
  color groups, 85, 307
  custom workspaces, 10
  graphic style, 334
  image for Web, 393, 394, 396
  logo as symbol, 209
  PDF files, 33–34, 190
  PNG files, 394, 397
  scanned images as grayscale, 294

spot colors
  about, 63–64
  applying with Live Paint, 310–311
  automatically updating, 236
  converting to process color, 66
  creating swatches for, 388
  preserving overprints and, 278
  replacing process color with, 312–313
  swatch thumbnail indicator for, 62, 63
  using effects with, 325
square brackets ([ ]), 136
stacking order
  adjusting, 162
  Appearance panel, 170
  bring to front/send to back, 166
  changing object, 162
  changing symbol, 154
  Live Paint, 102
  preparing objects before masking, 370
  reversing layer, 163
  stacking filled paths, 249
  sublayers and hierarchical layer structure, 164–165
Stahl, Nancy, 174–176, 447
Standard Screen mode, 29
star, mapping star pattern, 355
Star tool, 16–17
stars
  Batelman's techniques for, 375
  drawing with gradients and strokes, 374
  spraying symbols for, 376
Stead, Judy, 334–335, 426, 447
Steuer, Sharon
  about, xiv 447
  collaging objects using Transparency, 298–300
  "Cyclamen in winter," 282–284
  Illustrator CS4 Wow! Course Outline, xvii
  painterly pen and ink lesson, 138–141
  recoloring complex artwork, 314–316
  Zen of the Pen lessons, xvii
Stowe, Jodie, 292
Strizver, Ilene, 200, 447
stroke
  about, 60
  adding to appearance, 170–171

Blob Brush color for, 94
cap styles for lines with, 67–68
checking line overlap in, 67–68
clipping masks with, 366
controlling from Live Paint Bucket, 118
copying attributes for, 67
copying for objects, 19
corner, 68
Dash value for, 375
designing map terrain with, 221
drawing stars with, 374
graphic styles without, 330
modifying brush, 132
options for adding, 19–20
organizing on separate layers, 284
painting with Live Paint, 102
replicating hand-painted, 129
reversing brush, 131
selecting previously painted, 283–284
setting appearance attributes for, 183
swapping fill and, 60
text distortion with, 204
transparency with, 272
used for scratchboard art, 332–333
using transparent brush, 140
styles, see also graphic styles
  automatically saved when recoloring, 302, 316
  character and paragraph, 197–198
sublayers
  deleting unneeded, 176
  moving, 180–181
  nesting, 163, 180–181
  organizing layers in, 164–165
  placing scanned art in, 175
subtracting shapes, 233
subway exit, 390
Sudick, Barbara, 447
Sutherland, Brenda
  Chris Daddy portrait, 320–323
  contact information, 447
  dialogs for 3D objects, 341
  keeping track of surface being mapped, 344
  micro-brewery logos, 317
  New Art Has Basic Appearance option, 168
Swash scribble effect, 335
swatch libraries
  creating custom, 64, 73

experimenting with, 75
sharing, 64–65
Swatch Options dialog, 388
swatches, see also swatch libraries
  cautions deleting, 65
  icons on Swatches panel, 62, 64
  saving gradient, 241
  saving Live Color, 302
  thumbnail indicators for, 62, 63
  using with Live Trace, 99–100
  using spot color, 388
Swatches panel
  about, 62–63
  cautions deleting swatches, 65
  making new gradient from, 239
  saving color groups in, 85, 318–319
  shortcuts from, 63
  swatch icons, 62, 64
  working with Pattern Brushes in, 148
SWF files, 394, 395, 396, 397
Sylva Herald, The, 221
symbol instance sets, 135
Symbol Options dialog, 133, 136, 151, 157, 403
Symbol Sizer tool, 153
Symbol Spinner tool, 153, 155
Symbol Sprayer tool, 135, 155, 376
Symbol Stainer tool, 153, 210
"Symbolism Basics" lesson, 152–154
Symbolism tools, 135, 136, 152–154
symbols
  animating, 401
  applying, resizing, and editing, 152–153
  changing color of, 210
  converting box sides to, 356–357
  creating, 133
  defined, 133
  enhancing photorealism with, 387
  illustrating with custom, 155
  libraries of, 156–157
  mapping, 344
  modifying intensity and density of, 136
  optimizing Flash art with, 395–396, 402–403
  patterns converted into, 187
  Scatter Brushes vs., 136
  selecting from Control panel, 134
  selecting in Map Art dialog, 360
  sorting in Symbols panel, 157

stacking order within layers, 154
switching tools for, 153
tools for, 135
used in Chipping Sparrow art, 151
"Symbols to Flash" lesson, 402–403
Symbols panel
applying symbols from, 152–153
buttons of, 133–134
organizing and sorting symbols
on, 157
saving logo as symbol, 209
selecting repetitive drawings from,
361
system requirements, 2

T

T-shirt designs, 267, 432–433
tabbed documents, 6–7
Target icon, 166
targeting
all elements in group, 165
artboards, 189–190
selections with color, 314–315
selections vs., 166
shared appearances, 168
transparency and, 272, 276, 284
using opacity with, 272
tear-off panels, 10
Template icon, 161
template layers
about, 161–162
customizing, 139
developing photorealistic images
from, 385
templates
construction, 77
creating for map editions, 178
importing sketch as, 138–139
photos providing, 251, 386
saving web page as, 399
scanning image to create, 172
sketches used as, 110–111
template layers vs., 161–162
using, 3–4
Templates folder, 4
testing
patterns, 83
tracing, 98
text
about legacy, 191–192, 202
arcing headline, 222–223

choosing small caps for, 200
composition methods for, 199–200
copying attributes for, 203
creating for Photoshop image,
424–425
creating on top of raster image,
224
expandable text buttons, 170
finding missing fonts, 200–201
formatting, 197–198
indicator for overflow, 193
legacy, 191–192, 202
making new text objects, 204
offsetting, 194, 219
orientation, case, and letter
spacing of, 201–202
outline type, 201–203, 219, 228
overflow text indicator, 193
pasting in InDesign, 415
previewing graphic styles as, 330
red, xix
selecting special characters, 199
stroking without distorting, 204
threaded text arrow indicators,
193
transparency with, 272
working with threaded, 195–196
wrapping, 196–197
text buttons, 170
text editing mode, 6
Text Wrap Options dialog, 197
textured sketchbook page, 381
ThenDesign Architecture, 184
Thomas Bradley, Ltd., 74
ThoughtForm, 78, 79, 87, 447
threaded text, 193, 195–196
"3D with a 2D Twist" lesson,
348–349
"3D Effects" lesson, 354–355
3D Extrude & Bevel Options dialog
creating thematic 3D maps, 363
modifying extrusion settings, 347,
348–349, 353
moving object on one axis, 346
simplifying blend before
extruding, 257
Surface shading option in, 343
"3D Logo Object" lesson, 350
3D objects
assembling and positioning, 353
building plastic container, 352
color selection for, 343

designing tower of Tupperware,
351
disabling New Art Has Basic
Appearance option, 342
light sources for, 344–345
map arrowheads, 362
mapping art onto, 345, 357, 359
plastic container, 352
rotating in three dimensions, 342
simplifying points for, 343
surface shading for, 343–345
using multiple windows to create,
349
using as symbols in repetitive
drawings, 361
warping, 256–257
wine bottle and label, 360
3D programs with Illustrator art,
415, 436, 437
3D Revolve Options dialog
applying to rocket art, 354–355
building objects from cross
section, 350
Surface shading option in, 343
thumbnails
identifying brush stroke with, 284
on Layers panel, 163
Opacity Mask, 273
selecting opacity mask, 275
TIFF files, 413–414
tiger's head, 113
TIME magazine, 363
Tinkel, Kathleen, 12, 447
"Tinting a Scan" lesson, 294–295
tints
adding to scanned art, 294–295
creating with Global color
swatches, 71
generating from grayscale color,
319
tip boxes, xix
Tom, Jack, 48, 49, 172–173, 447
tools, see also combining tools and
techniques; and specific tools
activating artboard with, 190
assigning keyboard shortcuts for, 6
creating geometric objects, 16–17
creating simple objects with basic,
53
editing diameter of, 136
Fidelity and Smoothness options
for, 14
Flattener Preview panel, 278

unable to draw in mask-editing mode, 274
True Love tattoo, 110–111
Turton, David, 113, 447
tweening symbols in Flash, 401, 402–403
Twirl tool, 257, 381
2D effects, *see* effects
2D objects, *see also* objects
    extruding, 340, 341–342
    using 3D to create, 348–349
type, *see also* text
    antialiasing effect on, 393
    antiquing, 230–231
    applying brushes to letterforms, 228–229
    arcing headline, 222–223
    baseline shift of, 195, 219, 220
    changing orientation and case of, 201
    clipping mask from, 368
    converting to outline, 201–203, 219, 228
    copying attributes with Eyedropper, 203
    creative uses of, 215
    customizing ligature for, 234
    designing poster, 235
    designing typeface, 226–227
    distorting, 376
    finding missing fonts, 200–201
    flow for vertical, 192, 201
    kinds of, 192–195
    Live Subtract shape mode on, 232–233
    OpenType advantages, 198–199
    panels for, 192
    on path, 194–195, 196, 218–219
    Point,, 192–193
    preserving color when styling, 330
    saving and exporting, 206
    selecting, 191
    setting unit of measurement, 191
    small caps for, 200
    special characters, 199
    stroking without distorting, 204
    working with, 204–205
    wrapping Area, 196–197
Type menu, 196
Type on a Path Options dialog, 195
Type on a Path tool, 194–195, 219
"Type Subtraction" lesson, 232–233

Type tool
    changing vertical/horizontal modes in, 192
    cursor indications for, 192
    fitting type to paths, 196
    kinds of type objects, 192–195
    other varieties of, 191
    tips for modifying and creating text, 204

U

underwater illustrations, 380
Undo command
    unavailable in Recover Artwork/ Edit Colors, 307
    undoing work, 27–28
    using in Finger Dance, 54, 55
ungrouping objects, 18
"Unified Gradients" lesson, 260–261
unit of measurement
    entering in panels, 24
    setting preferences for, 9
    type, 191
Unite Pathfinder command, 108–109, 122, 123
University of Maryland Center for Environmental Science, 156
unlinking
    objects from graphic style, 330
    opacity masks, 274–275
unlocking, *see* locking/unlocking
updating Smart Objects, 412–413
Use Preview Bounds, 21

V

Valentine's Day card, 298–300
Valenzuela, Judy, 115, 447
van Dooren, Corné, 408
vanishing points, 184–185
Variation Options dialog, 65
vector images
    copying and converting to symbol, 401
    effects for, 324
    moving to other programs, 411–412
    rasterizing, 278, 280
Vector View menu, 98

vertical type, 192, 201
View menu, 278
viewing
    art in multiple windows, 29
    artboards, 189–190
    source images for tracings, 97
vignettes, 295
visibility (Eye) icon, 162, 175, 181

W

Wacom tablet, *see* pressure-sensitive tablets
Warp Options dialog, 222, 223
warping
    3D blends, 256–257
    about, 326–327
"Warping Blends" lesson, 256–257
watercolor techniques
    adding color washes, 140
    using transparency for, 282–284, 301
    watercolor filter for photo images, 301
web graphics
    about, 392
    creating animated, 394
    document profiles and files for, 393–394
    expanding compatibility of, 396–397
    previewing, 392
    using web safe color, 399
Web pages
    document profiles for, 392, 393
    document setup for, 398
websafe color, 399
Web sites
    innovative, 397
    Kuler, 438, 439
    training videos on Adobe, xvii
Weimer, Alan James, 82–83, 447
Weinstein, Ari
    antiquing type, 230–231, 326
    color schemes with Live Color, 308–309
    contact information, 447
Welcome screen
    bypassing, 4
    New Features option, xvii
    starting documents from, 2–3

WOW! BOOK PRODUCTION NOTES:

Interior Book Design and Production

This book was produced in InDesign CS3 using primarily Adobe's Minion Pro and Frutiger OpenType fonts. Barbara Sudick is the artist behind the original *Illustrator Wow!* design and typography, using Jill Davis's QuarkXPress layout of *The Photoshop Wow! Book* as a starting point. Cary Norsworthy and Mimi Heft contributed to new page-design specs. Victor Von Salza oversaw the porting of our templates from QuarkXPress to InDesign. Jean-Claude Tremblay is our technical editor; his company Proficiografik produces (and troubleshoots) the press-ready PDFs for the book and cover. Computer Documentation Services (CDS) printed this book.

Additional Hardware and Software

Most of the *Wow!* team uses Macintosh computers, though we now have a few testers and writers who do Windows (or both Mac and Win). In addition to InDesign CS3 we used Adobe Illlustrator CS4 (of course!), Photoshop CS3, and Ambrosia Software's Snapz Pro X for the screenshots. We used Adobe Acrobat 7 and 8 for distribution of the book pages to testers, the indexer, Peachpit, and the proofreaders. Many of us use Wacom tablets. Adam Z Lein created an online *Wow!* database for us so the team could track the details of the book production.

How to contact the author

If you've created artwork using the newer features of Illustrator that you'd like to submit for consideration in future *Wow!* books, please send printed samples to: Sharon Steuer, c/o Peachpit Press, 1249 Eighth Street, Berkeley, CA 94710. Or email a web address that contains samples of your work (no files please!): **wowartist@ssteuer.com**

Windows Wow! Glossary of Terms

Ctrl **Alt**	**Ctrl** will always refer to the Ctrl (Control) key. **Alt** will always refer to the Alt key, and is used to modify many of the tools.
←↑→↓	The keyboard Arrow keys: Left, Up, Right, Down.
Toggle	Menu selection acts as a switch: choosing once turns on, again turns it off.
Marquee	With any Selection tool, click-drag from your page over object(s) to select.
Hinged curve	A Bézier curve that meets a line or another curve at a corner.
Direct Selection tool **Group Selection tool** **Selection tool**	Direct Selection tool selects points and paths. Group Selection tool. The first click always selects the entire object, subsequent clicks select "next group-up" in the grouping order. Selection tool (selects the biggest grouping which includes that object— if an object is ungrouped, then only that object is selected). **Note:** *See the* Basics *chapter for more on selection tools.*
Select object(s)	Click on or marquee with Group Selection tool to select entire object. Click on or marquee with the regular Selection tool to select grouped objects.
Deselect object(s)	To Deselect *one* object, Shift-click (or Shift-marquee) with Group Selection tool. To Deselect *all* selected objects, with any selection tool, click outside of all objects (but within your document), or press Shift-Ctrl-A.
Select a path	Click on a path with the Direct Selection tool to select it. **Note:** *If objects are selected, Deselect first,* then *click with Direct Selection tool.*
Select anchor points	Click on path with Direct Selection tool to see anchor points. Then, Direct-select marquee around the points you want selected. Or, with Direct Selection tool, Shift-click on points you want selected. **Note**: *Clicking on a selected point with Shift key down deselects that point.*
Grab an object or point	After selecting objects or points, use Direct Selection tool to click and hold down mouse button and drag to transform entire selection. **Note:** *If you click by mistake (instead of click-and-hold), Undo and try again.*
Delete an object	Group-Select the object and press the Delete (or Backspace) key. To delete grouped objects, use the Selection tool, then Delete.
Delete a path	Direct-Select a path and press the Delete (or Backspace) key. If you delete an anchor point, both paths attached to that anchor point will be deleted. **Note:** *After deleting part of an object the entire remaining object will become selected; therefore, deleting twice will always delete the entire object!*
Copy or Cut a path	Click on a path with Direct Selection tool, then Copy (Ctrl-C) or Cut (Ctrl-X). **Note:** *See the "Windows Finger Dance Summary" for more ways to copy paths.*
Copy or Cut an object	Click on an object with Group Selection tool, then Copy (Ctrl-C) or Cut (Ctrl-X). For grouped objects, Click on one of the objects with the Selection tool, then Copy (Ctrl-C) or Cut (Ctrl-X).

Mac Wow! Glossary of Terms

⌘ **Option (Opt)**	The Command key (this key may have a ⌘ or a 🍎 on it). The Option key can be used to modify many of the tools.
←↑→↓	The keyboard Arrow keys: Left, Up, Right, Down.
Toggle	Menu selection acts as a switch: choosing once turns on, again turns it off.
Marquee	With any Selection tool, click-drag from your page over object(s) to select.
Hinged curve	A Bézier curve that meets a line or another curve at a corner.
➤ **Direct Selection tool** ➤₊ **Group Selection tool** ➤ **Selection tool**	Direct Selection tool selects points and paths. Group Selection tool. The first click always selects the entire object, subsequent clicks select "next group-up" in the grouping order. Selection tool (selects the biggest grouping which includes that object— if an object is ungrouped, then only that object is selected). **Note:** *See the* Basics *chapter for more on selection tools.*
Select object(s) ➤₊ ➤	Click on or marquee with Group Selection tool to select entire object. Click on or marquee with the regular Selection tool to select grouped objects.
Deselect object(s) ➤ ➤₊ ➤	To Deselect *one* object, Shift-click (or Shift-marquee) with Group Selection tool. To Deselect *all* selected objects, with any selection tool, click outside of all objects (but within your document), or press Shift-⌘-A.
Select a path ➤	Click on a path with the Direct Selection tool to select it. **Note:** *If objects are selected, Deselect first, then click with Direct Selection tool.*
Select anchor points ➤	Click on path with Direct Selection tool to see anchor points. Then, Direct-select marquee around the points you want selected. Or, with Direct Selection tool, Shift-click on points you want selected. **Note**: *Clicking on a selected point with Shift key down deselects that point.*
Grab an object or point ➤	After selecting objects or points, use Direct Selection tool to click and hold down mouse button and drag to transform entire selection. **Note:** *If you click by mistake (instead of click-and-hold), Undo and try again.*
Delete an object ➤₊ ➤	Group-Select the object and press the Delete (or Backspace) key. To delete grouped objects, use the Selection tool, then Delete.
Delete a path ➤	Direct-Select a path and press the Delete (or Backspace) key. If you delete an anchor point, both paths attached to that anchor point will be deleted. **Note:** *After deleting part of an object the entire remaining object will become selected; therefore, deleting twice will always delete the entire object!*
Copy or Cut a path ➤	Click on a path with Direct Selection tool, then Copy (⌘-C) or Cut (⌘-X). **Note:** *See the "Macintosh Finger Dance Summary" for more ways to copy paths.*
Copy or Cut an object ➤₊ ➤	Click on an object with Group Selection tool, then Copy (⌘-C) or Cut (⌘-X). For grouped objects, Click on one of the objects with the Selection tool, then Copy(⌘-C) or Cut (⌘-X).

Mac Finger Dance Summary *from "The Zen of Illustrator"*

Object Creation	*Hold down keys until AFTER mouse button is released.*
⇧ **Shift**	Constrains objects horizontally, vertically or proportionally.
Option	Objects will be drawn from centers.
Option click	Opens dialog boxes with transformation tools.
[ ]	Spacebar turns into the grabber Hand.
⌘ [ ]	Turns cursor into the Zoom-in tool. Click or marquee around an area to Zoom in.
Option ⌘ [ ]	Turns cursor into the Zoom-out tool. Click to Zoom out.
Caps lock	Turns your cursor into a cross-hair.

Object Selection	*Watch your cursor to see that you've pressed the correct keys.*
⌘	The current tool becomes the last chosen Selection tool.
Option ⌘	Current tool becomes Group Selection tool to select entire object. Click again to select next level of grouping. To move selection release Option key, then Grab.
⌘ **Tab**	Toggles whether Direct Selection or regular Selection tool is accessed by the ⌘ key.
⇧ **Shift** click	Toggles whether an object, path or point is selected or deselected.
⇧ **Shift** click ▶	With Direct Selection tool, click on or marquee around an object, path or point to toggle selection/deselection. **Note:** *Clicking inside a filled object may select the entire object.*
⇧ **Shift** click ▶ ▶+	Clicking on, or marqueeing over objects with Selection tool or Group Selection tool, toggles selection/deselection (Group Selection tool chooses objects within a group).

Object Transformation	*Hold down keys until AFTER mouse button is released.*
⇧ **Shift**	Constrains transformation proportionally, vertically and horizontally.
Option	Leaves the original object and transforms a copy.
⌘ **Z**	Undo. Use Shift-⌘-Z for Redo.
(angle diagram: 90°, 30°, −30°, −90°, 30°, −30°)	To move or transform a selection predictably from within dialog boxes, use this diagram to determine if you need a positive or negative number and which angle is required. (*Diagram from Kurt Hess / Agnew Moyer Smith*)

Windows Finger Dance Summary *from "The Zen of Illustrator"*

Object Creation	Hold down keys until AFTER mouse button is released.
⇧ Shift	Constrains objects horizontally, vertically or proportionally.
Alt	Objects will be drawn from centers.
Alt click	Opens dialog boxes with transformation tools.
[spacebar]	Spacebar turns into the grabber Hand.
Ctrl [spacebar]	Turns cursor into the Zoom-in tool. Click or marquee around an area to Zoom in.
Ctrl Alt [spacebar]	Turns cursor into the Zoom-out tool. Click to Zoom out.
Caps lock	Turns your cursor into a cross-hair.

Object Selection	Watch your cursor to see that you've pressed the correct keys.
Ctrl	The current tool becomes the last chosen Selection tool.
Ctrl Alt	Current tool becomes Group Selection to select entire object. Click again to select next level of grouping. To move selection release Alt key, then Grab.
Ctrl Tab	Toggles whether Direct Selection or regular Selection tool is accessed by the Ctrl key.
⇧ Shift click	Toggles whether an object, path or point is selected or deselected.
⇧ Shift click ↖	With Direct Selection tool, click on or marquee around an object, path or point to toggle selection/deselection. **Note:** *Clicking inside a filled object may select the entire object.*
⇧ Shift click ↖ ↖+	Clicking on, or marqueeing over objects with Selection tool or Group Selection tool, toggles selection/deselection (Group Selection tool chooses objects within a group).

Object Transformation	Hold down keys until AFTER mouse button is released.
⇧ Shift	Constrains transformation proportionally, vertically and horizontally.
Alt	Leaves the original object and transforms a copy.
Ctrl Z	Undo. Use Shift-Ctrl-Z for Redo.
	To move or transform a selection predictably from within dialog boxes, use this diagram to determine if you need a positive or negative number and which angle is required. (*Diagram from Kurt Hess / Agnew Moyer Smith*)